Macmillan Encyclopedia of Physics

MACMILLAN
ENCYCLOPEDIA OF
PHYSICS

John S. Rigden

Editor in Chief

Volume 4

MACMILLAN REFERENCE USA
Simon & Schuster Macmillan
NEW YORK

Simon & Schuster and Prentice Hall International
LONDON   MEXICO CITY   NEW DELHI   SINGAPORE   SYDNEY   TORONTO

Simon & Schuster Macmillan
1633 Broadway
New York, NY 10019

Library of Congress Catalog Card Number: 96-30977

PRINTED IN THE UNITED STATES OF AMERICA

Printing Number
1   2   3   4   5   6   7   8   9   10

LIBRARY OF CONGRESS CATALOGING-IN-PUBLICATION DATA

Macmillan Encyclopedia of Physics / John S. Rigden, editor in chief.
    p.   cm.
    Includes bibliographical references and index.
    ISBN 0-02-897359-3 (set).
    1. Physics—Encyclopedias.   I. Rigden, John S.
QC5.M15   1996
530′.03—dc20   96-30977
                                                         CIP

This paper meets the requirements of ANSI-NISO Z39.48-1992
(Permanence of Paper).

COMMON ABBREVIATIONS AND MATHEMATICAL SYMBOLS

$=$	equals; double bond
$\neq$	not equal to
$\equiv$	identically equal to; equivalent to; triple bond
$\sim$	asymptotically equal to; of the order of magnitude of; approximately
$\approx, \simeq$	approximately equal to
$\cong$	congruent to; approximately equal to
$\propto$	proportional to
$<$	less than
$>$	greater than
$\nless$	not less than
$\ngtr$	not greater than
$\ll$	much less than
$\gg$	much greater than
$\leq$	less than or equal to
$\geq$	greater than or equal to
$\nleq$	not less than or equal to
$\ngeq$	not greater than or equal to
$\cup$	union of
$\cap$	intersection of
$\subset$	subset of; included in
$\supset$	contains as a subset
$\in$	an element of
$\ni$	contains as an element
$\rightarrow$	approaches, tends to; yeilds; is replaced by
$\Rightarrow$	implies; is replaced by
$\Leftarrow$	is implied by
$\downarrow$	mutually implies
$\Leftrightarrow$	if and only if
$\perp$	perpendicular to
$\parallel$	parallel to

$\vert\ \vert$	absolute value of
$+$	plus
$-$	minus
$/$	divided by
$\times$	multiplied by
$\oplus$	direct sum
$\otimes$	direct product
$\pm$	plus or minus
$\mp$	minus or plus
$\sqrt{\ }$	radical
$\int$	integral
$\oint$	contour integral
Σ	summation
Π	product
∂	partial derivative
$^\circ$	degree
$^\circ B$	degrees Baumé
$^\circ C$	degrees Celsius (centigrade)
$^\circ F$	degrees Fahrenheit
$!$	factorial
$'$	minute
$''$	second
∇	curl
ϵ_0	electric constant
μ	micro-
μ_0	magnetic constant
μA	microampere
$\mu A\ h$	microampere hour
μC	microcoulomb
μF	microfarad
μg	microgram
μK	microkelvin
μm	micrometer
μm	micron

μm Hg	microns of mercury
μmol	micromole
μs, μsec	microsecond
μu	microunit
$\mu\Omega$	microhm
σ	Stefan–Boltzmann constant
Ω	ohm
Ω cm	ohm centimeter
Ω cm/(cm/cm³)	ohm centimeter per centimeter per cubic centimeter
A	ampere
Å	angstrom
a	atto-
A_s	atmosphere, standard
abbr.	abbreviate; abbreviation
abr.	abridged; abridgment
Ac	Actinium
ac	alternating-current
aF	attofarad
af	audio-frequency
Ag	silver
A h	ampere hour
AIP	American Institute of Physics
Al	aluminum
alt	altitude
Am	americium
AM	amplitude-modulation
A.M.	ante meridiem
amend.	amended; amendment
annot.	annotated; annotation
antilog	antilogarithm
app.	appendix
approx	approximate (in subscript)
Ar	argon
arccos	arccosine
arccot	arccotangent
arccsc	arccosecant
arc min	arc minute
arcsec	arcsecant
arcsin	arcsine
arg	argument
As	arsenic
At	astatine
At/m	ampere turns per meter
atm	atmosphere
at. ppm	atomic parts per million
at. %	atomic percent
atu	atomic time unit
AU	astronomical unit
a.u.	atomic unit
Au	gold

av	average (in subscript)
b	barn
b.	born
B	boron
Ba	barium
bcc	body-centered-cubic
B.C.E.	before the common era
Be	beryllium
Bi	biot
Bi	bismuth
Bk	berkelium
bp	boiling point
Bq	becquerel
Br	bromine
Btu, BTU	British thermal unit
C	carbon
c	centi-
c.	circa, about, approximately
C	coulomb
c	speed of light
Ca	calcium
cal	calorie
calc	calculated (in subscript)
c.c.	complex conjugate
CCD	charge-coupled device
Cd	cadmium
cd	candela
CD	compact disc
Ce	cerium
C.E.	common era
CERN	European Center for Nuclear Research
Cf	californium
cf.	confer, compare
cgs, CGS	centimeter-gram-second (system)
Ci	curie
Cl	chlorine
C.L.	confidence limits
c.m.	center of mass
cm	centimeter
Cm	curium
cm³	cubic centimeter
Co	cobalt
Co.	Company
coeff	coefficient (in subscript)
colog	cologarithm
const	constant
Corp.	Corporation
cos	cosine
cosh	hyperbolic cosine
cot	cotangent
coth	hyperbolic cotangent

cp	candlepower	e.u.	electron unit
cP	centipoise	eu	entropy unit
cp	chemically pure	Eu	europium
cpd	contact potential difference	eV	electron volt
cpm	counts per minute	expt	experimental (in subscript)
cps	cycles per second	F	farad
Cr	chromium	F	Faraday constant
cS	centistoke	f	femto-
Cs	cesium	F	fermi
csc	cosecant	F	fluorine
csch	hyperbolic cosecant	fc	foot-candle
Cu	copper	fcc	face-centered-cubic
cu	cubic	Fe	iron
cw	continuous-wave	fF	femtofarad
D	Debye	Fig. (pl., Figs.)	figure
d	deci-	fL	foot-lambert
d.	died	fm	femtometer
da	deka-	Fm	fermium
dB, dBm	decibel	FM	frequency-modulation
dc	direct-current	f. (pl., ff.)	following
deg	degree	fpm	fissions per minute
det	determinant	Fr	francium
dev	deviation	Fr	franklin
diam	diameter	fs	femtosecond
dis/min	disintegrations per minute	ft	foot
dis/s	disintegrations per second	ft lb	foot-pound
div	divergence	ft lbf	foot-pound-force
DNA	deoxyribose nucleic acid	f.u.	formula units
Dy	dysprosium	g	acceleration of free fall
dyn	dyne	G	gauss
E	east	G	giga-
e	electronic charge	g	gram
E	exa-	G	gravitational constant
e, exp	exponential	Ga	gallium
e/at.	electrons per atom	Gal	gal (unit of gravitational force)
e b	electron barn	gal	gallon
e/cm3	electrons per cubic centimeter	g-at.	gram-atom
ed. (pl., eds.)	editor	g.at. wt	gram-atomic-weight
e.g.	exempli gratia, for example	Gc/s	gigacycles per second
el	elastic (in subscript)	Gd	gadolinium
emf, EMF	electromotive force	Ge	germanium
emu	electromagnetic unit	GeV	giga-electron-volt
Eng.	England	GHz	gigahertz
Eq. (pl., Eqs.)	equation	Gi	gilbert
Er	erbium	grad	gradient
erf	error function	GV	gigavolt
erfc	error function (complement of)	Gy	gray
Es	einsteinium	h	hecto-
e.s.d.	estimated standard deviation	H	henry
esu	electrostatic unit	h	hour
et al.	et alii, and others	H	hydrogen
etc.	et cetera, and so forth	h	Planck constant

H.c.	Hermitian conjugate		ks, ksec	kilosecond
hcp	hexagonal-close-packed		kt	kiloton
He	helium		kV	kilovolt
Hf	hafnium		kV A	kilovolt ampere
hf	high-frequency		kW	kilowatt
hfs	hyperfine structure		kW h	kilowatt hour
hg	hectogram		$k\Omega$	kilohm
Hg	mercury		L	lambert
Ho	holmium		L	langmuir
hp	horsepower		l, L	liter
Hz	hertz		La	lanthanum
I	iodine		LA	longitudinal-acoustic
ICT	International Critical Tables		lab	laboratory (in subscript)
i.d.	inside diameter		lat	latitude
i.e.	id est, that is		lb	pound
IEEE	Institute of Electrical and		lbf	pound-force
	Electronics Engineers		lbm	pound-mass
if	intermediate frequency		LED	light emitting diode
Im	imaginary part		Li	lithium
in.	inch		lim	limit
In	indium		lm	lumen
Inc.	Incorporated		lm/W	lumens per watt
inel	inelastic (in subscript)		ln	natural logarithm (base e)
ir, IR	infrared		LO	longitudinal-optic
Ir	iridium		log	logarithm
J	joule		Lr	lawrencium
Jy	jansky		LU	Lorentz unit
k, k_B	Boltzmann's constant		Lu	lutetium
K	degrees Kelvin		lx	lux
K	kayser		ly, lyr	light-year
k	kilo-		M	Mach
K	potassium		M	mega-
kA	kiloamperes		m	meter
kbar	kilobar		m	milli-
kbyte	kilobyte		m	molal (concentration)
kcal	kilocalorie		M	molar (concentration)
kc/s	kilocycles per second		m_e	electronic rest mass
kdyn	kilodyne		m_n	neutron rest mass
keV	kilo-electron-volt		m_p	proton rest mass
kG	kilogauss		$M_\odot$	solar mass (2×10^{33} g)
kg	kilogram		MA	megaamperes
kgf	kilogram force		mA	milliampere
kg m	kilogram meter		ma	maximum
kHz	kilohertz		mb	millibarn
kJ	kilojoule		mCi	millicurie
kK	kilodegrees Kelvin		Mc/s	megacycles per second
km	kilometer		Md	mendlelvium
kMc/s	kilomegacycles per second		MeV	mega-electron-volt; million
kn	knot			electron volt
kOe	kilo-oersted		Mg	magnesium
kpc	kiloparsec		mg	milligram
Kr	krypton		mH	millihenry

mho	reciprocal ohm	No.	number
MHz	megahertz	Np	neper
min	minimum	Np	neptunium
min	minute	ns, nsec	nanosecond
mK	millidegrees Kelvin; millikelvin	n/s	neutrons per second
mks, MKS	meter-kilogram-second (system)	$n/s\ cm^2$	neutrons per second per square centimeter
mksa	meter-kilogram-second ampere	ns/m	nanoseconds per meter
mksc	meter-kilogram-second coulomb	O	oxygen
ml	milliliter	$o()$	of order less than
mm	millimeter	$O()$	of the order of
mmf	magnetomotive force	obs	observed (in subscript)
mm Hg	millimeters of mercury	o.d.	outside diameter
Mn	manganese	Oe	oersted
MO	molecular orbital	ohm^{-1}	mho
Mo	molybdenum	Os	osmium
MOE	magneto-optic effect	oz	ounce
mol	mole	P	peta-
mol %, mole %	mole percent	P	phosphorus
mp	melting point	p	pico-
Mpc	megaparsec	P	poise
mph	miles per hour	Pa	pascal
MPM	mole percent metal	Pa	protactinium
Mrad	megarad	Pb	lead
ms, msec	millisecond	pc	parsec
mu	milliunit	Pd	palladium
MV	megavolt; million volt	PD	potential difference
mV	millivolt	pe	probable error
MW	megawatt	pF	picofarad
mwe, m (w.e.)	meter of water equivalent	pl.	plural
Mx	maxwell	P.M.	post meridiem
$m\mu m$	millimicron	Pm	promethium
$M\Omega$	megaohm	Po	polonium
n	nano-	ppb	parts per billion
N	newton	p. (pl., pp.)	page
N	nitrogen	ppm	parts per million
N	normal (concentration)	Pr	praseodymium
N	north	psi	pounds per square inch
N, N_A	Avogadro constant	psi (absolute)	pounds per square inch absolute
Na	sodium	psi (gauge)	pounds per square inch gauge
NASA	National Aeronautics and Space Administration	Pt	platinum
nb	nanobarn	Pu	plutonium
Nb	niobium	R (ital)	gas constant
Nd	neodymium	R	roentgen
N.D.	not determined	Ra	radium
NDT	nondestructive testing	rad	radian
Ne	neon	Rb	rubidium
n/f	neutrons per fission	Re	real part
Ni	nickel	Re	rhenium
N_L	Loschmidt's constant	rev.	revised
nm	nanometer	rf	radio frequency
No	nobelium	Rh	rhodium

r.l.	radiation length
rms	root-mean-square
Rn	radon
RNA	ribonucleic acid
RPA	random-phase approximation
rpm	revolutions per minute
rps, rev/s	revolutions per second
Ru	ruthenium
Ry	rydberg
s, sec	second
S	siemens
S	south
S	stoke
S	sulfur
Sb	antimony
Sc	scandium
sccm	standard cubic centimeter per minute
Se	selenium
sec	secant
sech	hyperbolic secant
sgn	signum function
Si	silicon
SI	*Système International* (International System of Measurement)
sin	sine
sinh	hyperbolic sine
SLAC	Stanford Linear Accelerator Center
Sm	samarium
Sn	tin
sq	square
sr	steradian
Sr	strontium
STP	standard temperature and pressure
Suppl.	Supplement
Sv	sievert
T	tera-
T	tesla
t	tonne
Ta	tantalum
TA	transverse-acoustic
tan	tangent

tanh	hyperbolic tangent
Tb	terbium
Tc	technetium
Td	townsend
Te	tellurium
TE	transverse-electric
TEM	transverse-electromagnetic
TeV	tera-electron-volt
Th	thorium
theor	theory, theoretical (in subscript)
THz	tetrahertz
Ti	titanium
Tl	thallium
Tm	thulium
TM	transverse-magnetic
TO	transverse-optic
tot	total (in subscript)
TP	temperature-pressure
tr, Tr	trace
trans.	translator, translators; translated by; translation
u	atomic mass unit
U	uranium
uhf	ultrahigh-frequency
uv, UV	ultraviolet
V	vanadium
V	volt
VB	valence band
vol. (pl., vols.)	volume
vol %	volume percent
vs.	versus
W	tungsten
W	watt
W	West
Wb	weber
Wb/m^2	webers per square meter
wt %	weight percent
W.u.	Weisskopf unit
Xe	xenon
Y	yttrium
Yb	ytterbium
yr	year
Zn	zinc
Zr	zirconium

JOURNAL ABBREVIATIONS

Acc. Chem. Res.
Accounts of Chemical Research
Acta Chem. Scand.
Acta Chemica Scandinavica
Acta Crystallogr.
Acta Crystallographica
Acta Crystallogr. Sec. A
Acta Crystallographica, Section A: Crystal
Physics, Diffraction, Theoretical, and General Crystallography
Acta Crystallogr. Sec. B
Acta Crystallographica, Section B: Structural
Crystallography and Crystal Chemistry
Acta Math. Acad. Sci. Hung.
Acta Mathematica Academiae Scientiarum
Hungaricae
Acta Metall.
Acta Metallurgica
Acta Oto-Laryngol.
Acta Oto-Laryngologica
Acta Phys.
Acta Physica
Acta Phys. Austriaca
Acta Physica Austriaca
Acta Phys. Pol.
Acta Physica Polonica
Adv. Appl. Mech.
Advances in Applied Mechanics
Adv. At. Mol. Opt. Phys.
Advances in Atomic, Molecular, and Optical
Physics
Adv. Chem. Phys.
Advances in Chemical Physics
Adv. Magn. Reson.
Advances in Magnetic Resonance
Adv. Phys.
Advances in Physics

Adv. Quantum Chem.
Advances in Quantum Chemistry
AIAA J.
AIAA Journal
AIChE J.
AIChE Journal
AIP Conf. Pro.
AIP Conference Proceedings
Am. J. Phys.
American Journal of Physics
Am. J. Sci.
American Journal of Science
Am. Sci.
American Scientist
Anal. Chem.
Analytical Chemistry
Ann. Chim. Phys.
Annales de Chimie et de Physique
Ann. Fluid Dyn.
Annals of Fluid Dynamics
Ann. Geophys.
Annales de Geophysique
Ann. Inst. Henri Poincaré
Annales de l'Institut Henri Poincaré
Ann. Inst. Henri Poincaré, A
Annales de l'Institut Henri Poincaré,
Section A: Physique Theorique
Ann. Inst. Henri Poincaré, B
Annales de l'Institut Henri Poincaré,
Section B: Calcul des Probabilites et
Statistique
Ann. Math.
Annals of Mathematics
Ann. Otol. Rhinol. Laryngol.
Annals of Otology, Rhinology, & Laryngology
Ann. Phys. (Leipzig)
Annalen der Physik (Leipzig)

Ann. Phys. (N.Y.)
Annals of Physics (New York)
Ann. Phys. (Paris)
Annales de Physique (Paris)
Ann. Rev. Mat. Sci.
Annual Reviews of Materials Science
Ann. Rev. Nucl. Part. Sci.
Annual Review of Nuclear and Particle
Science
Ann. Sci.
Annals of Science
Annu. Rev. Astron. Astrophys.
Annual Reviews of Astronomy and Astrophysics
Annu. Rev. Nucl. Part. Sci.
Annual Reviews of Nuclear and Particle
Science
Annu. Rev. Nucl. Sci.
Annual Review of Nuclear Science
Appl. Opt.
Applied Optics
Appl. Phys. Lett.
Applied Physics Letters
Appl. Spectrosc.
Applied Spectroscopy
Ark. Fys.
Arkiv foer Fysik
Astron. Astrophys.
Astronomy and Astrophysics
Astron. J.
Astronomical Journal
Astron. Nachr.
Astronomische Nachrichten
Astrophys. J.
Astrophysical Journal
Astrophys. J. Lett.
Astrophysical Journal, Letters to the Editor
Astrophys. J. Suppl. Ser.
Astrophysical Journal, Supplement Series
Astrophys. Lett.
Astrophysical Letters
Aust. J. Phys.
Australian Journal of Physics
Bell Syst. Tech. J.
Bell System Technical Journal
Ber. Bunsenges. Phys. Chem.
Berichte der Bunsengesellschaft für
Physikalische Chemie
Br. J. Appl. Phys.
British Journal of Applied Physics
Bull. Acad. Sci. USSR, Phys. Ser.
Bulletin of the Academy of Sciences of the
USSR, Physical Series

Bull. Am. Astron. Soc.
Bulletin of the American Astronomical Society
Bull. Am. Phys. Soc.
Bulletin of the American Physical Society
Bull. Astron. Instit. Neth.
Bulletin of the Astronomical Institutes of the
Netherlands
Bull. Chem. Soc. Jpn.
Bulletin of the Chemical Society of Japan
Bull. Seismol. Soc. Am.
Bulletin of the Seismological Society of
America
C. R. Acad. Sci.
Comptes Rendus Hebdomadaires des Seances
de l'Academie des Sciences
C. R. Acad. Ser. A
Comptes Rendus Hebdomadaires des Seances
de l'Academie des Sciences, Serie A:
Sciences Mathematiques
C. R. Acad. Ser. B
Comptes Rendus Hebdomadaires des Seances
de l'Academie des Sciences, Serie B: Sciences
Physiques
Can. J. Chem.
Canadian Journal of Chemistry
Can. J. Phys.
Canadian Journal of Physics
Can. J. Res.
Canadian Journal of Research
Chem. Phys.
Chemical Physics
Chem. Phys. Lett.
Chemical Physics Letters
Chem. Rev.
Chemical Reviews
Chin. J. Phys.
Chinese Journal of Physics
Class. Quantum Grav.
Classical and Quantum Gravity
Comments Nucl. Part. Phys.
Comments on Nuclear and Particle Physics
Commun. Math. Phys.
Communications in Mathematical Physics
Commun. Pure Appl. Math.
Communications on Pure and Applied
Mathematics
Comput. Phys.
Computers in Physics
Czech. J. Phys.
Czechoslovak Journal of Physics
Discuss. Faraday Soc.
Discussions of the Faraday Society

Earth Planet. Sci. Lett.
    Earth and Planetary Science Letters
Electron. Lett.
    Electronics Letters
Fields Quanta
    Fields and Quanta
Fortschr. Phys.
    Fortschritte der Physik
Found. Phys.
    Foundations of Physics
Gen. Relativ. Gravit.
    General Relativity and Gravitation
Geochim. Cosmochim. Acta
    Geochimica et Cosmochimica Acta
Geophys. Res. Lett.
    Geophysical Research Letters
Handb. Phys.
    Handbuch der Physik
Helv. Chim. Acta
    Helvetica Chimica Acta
Helv. Phys. Acta
    Helvetica Physica Acta
High Temp. (USSR)
    High Temperature (USSR)
IBM J. Res. Dev.
    IBM Journal of Research and Development
Icarus.
    Icarus. International Journal of the Solar System
IEEE J. Quantum Electron.
    IEEE Journal of Quantum Electronics
IEEE Trans. Antennas Propag.
    IEEE Transactions on Antennas and
        Propagation
IEEE Trans. Electron Devices
    IEEE Transactions on Electron Devices
IEEE Trans. Inf. Meas.
    IEEE Transactions on Instrumentation and
        Measurement
IEEE Trans. Inf. Theory
    IEEE Transactions on Information Theory
IEEE Trans. Magn.
    IEEE Transactions on Magnetics
IEEE Trans. Microwave Theory Tech.
    IEEE Transactions on Microwave Theory and
        Techniques
IEEE Trans. Nucl. Sci.
    IEEE Transactions on Nuclear Science
IEEE Trans. Sonics Ultrason. Ind. Eng. Chem.
    IEEE Transactions on Sonics Ultrasonics
        Industrial and Engineering Chemistry
Infrared Phys.
    Infrared Physics

Inorg. Chem.
    Inorganic Chemistry
Inorg. Mater. (USSR)
    Inorganic Materials (USSR)
Instrum. Exp. Tech. (USSR)
    Instruments and Experimental Techniques
        (USSR)
Int. J. Magn.
    International Journal of Magnetism
Int. J. Mod. Phys. A
    International Journal of Modern Physics A
Int. J. Quantum Chem.
    International Journal of Quantum Chemistry
Int. J. Quantum Chem. 1
    International Journal of Quantum Chemistry,
        Part 1
Int. J. Quantum Chem. 2
    International Journal of Quantum Chemistry,
        Part 2
Int. J. Theor. Phys.
    International Journal of Theoretical Physics
Izv. Acad. Sci. USSR, Atmos. Oceanic Phys.
    Izvestiya, Academy of Sciences, USSR,
        Atmospheric and Oceanic Physics
Izv. Acad. Sci. USSR, Phys. Solid Earth
    Izvestiya, Academy of Sciences, USSR, Physics
        of the Solid Earth
J. Acoust. Soc. Am.
    Journal of the Acoustical Society of America
J. Am. Ceram. Soc.
    Journal of the American Ceramic Society
J. Am. Chem. Soc.
    Journal of the American Chemical Society
J. Am. Inst. Electr. Eng.
    Journal of the American Institute of Electrical
        Engineers
J. Appl. Crystallogr.
    Journal of Applied Crystallography
J. Appl. Phys.
    Journal of Applied Physics
J. Appl. Spectrosc. (USSR)
    Journal of Applied Spectroscopy (USSR)
J. Atmos. Sci.
    Journal of Atmospheric Sciences
J. Atmos. Terr. Phys.
    Journal of Atmospheric and Terrestrial Physics
J. Audio Engin. Soc.
    Journal of the Audio Engineering Society
J. Chem. Phys.
    Journal of Chemical Physics
J. Chem. Soc.
    Journal of the Chemical Society

J. Chim. Phys.
Journal de Chemie Physique

J. Comput. Phys.
Journal of Computational Physics

J. Cryst. Growth
Journal of Crystal Growth

J. Electrochem. Soc.
Journal of Electrochemical Society

J. Fluid Mech.
Journal of Fluid Mechanics

J. Gen. Rel. Grav.
Journal of General Relativity and Gravitation

J. Geophys. Res.
Journal of Geophysical Research

J. Inorg. Nucl. Chem.
Journal of Inorganic and Nuclear Chemistry

J. Lightwave Technol.
Journal of Lightwave Technology

J. Low Temp. Phys.
Journal of Low-Temperature Physics

J. Lumin.
Journal of Luminescence

J. Macromol. Sci. Phys.
Journal of Macromolecular Science, [Part B] Physics

J. Mater. Res.
Journal of Materials Research

J. Math. Phys. (Cambridge, Mass.)
Journal of Mathematics and Physics (Cambridge, Mass.)

J. Math. Phys. (N.Y.)
Journal of Mathematical Physics (New York)

J. Mech. Phys. Solids
Journal of the Mechanics and Physics of Solids

J. Mol. Spectrosc.
Journal of Molecular Spectroscopy

J. Non-Cryst. Solids
Journal of Non-Crystalline Solids

J. Nucl. Energy
Journal of Nuclear Energy

J. Nucl. Energy, Part C.
Journal of Nuclear Energy, Part C: Plasma Physics, Accelerators, Themonuclear Research

J. Nucl. Mater.
Journal of Nuclear Materials

J. Opt. Soc. Am.
Journal of the Optical Society of America

J. Opt. Soc. Am. A
Journal of the Optical Society of America A

J. Opt. Soc. Am. B
Journal of the Optical Society of America B

J. Phys. (Moscow)
Journal of Physics (Moscow)

J. Phys. (Paris)
Journal de Physique (Paris)

J. Phys. A
Journal of Physics A: Mathematical and General

J. Phys. B
Journal of Physics B: Atomic, Molecular, and Optical Physics

J. Phys. C
Journal of Physics C: Solid State Physics

J. Phys. D
Journal of Physics D: Applied Physics

J. Phys. E
Journal of Physics E: Scientific Instruments

J. Phys. F
Journal of Physics F: Metal Physics

J. Phys. G
Journal of Physics G: Nuclear and Particle Physics

J. Phys. Chem.
Journal of Physical Chemistry

J. Phys. Chem. Ref. Data
Journal of Physical and Chemical Reference Data

J. Phys. Chem. Solids
Journal of Physics and Chemistry of Solids

J. Phys. Radium
Journal de Physique et le Radium

J. Phys. Soc. Jpn.
Journal of the Physical Society of Japan

J. Plasma Phys.
Journal of Plasma Physics

J. Polym. Sci.
Journal of Polymer Science

J. Polym. Sci., Polym. Lett. Ed.
Journal of Polymer Science, Polymer Letters Edition

J. Polym. Sci., Polym. Phys. Ed.
Journal of Polymer Science, Polymer Physics Edition

J. Quant. Spectros. Radiat. Transfer
Journal of Quantitative Spectroscopy & Radiative Transfer

J. Res. Natl. Bur. Stand.
Journal of Research of the National Bureau of Standards

J. Res. Natl. Bur. Stand. Sec. A
Journal of Research of the National Bureau of Standards, Section A: Physics and Chemistry

J. Res. Natl. Bur. Stand. Sec. B
Journal of Research of the National Bureau of Standards, Section B: Mathematical Sciences

J. Res. Natl. Bur. Stand. Sec. C
Journal of Research of the National Bureau of Standards, Section C: Engineering and Instrumentation

J. Rheol.
Journal of Rheology

J. Sound Vib.
Journal of Sound and Vibration

J. Speech Hear. Disord.
Journal of Speech and Hearing Disorders

J. Speech Hear. Res.
Journal of Speech and Hearing Research

J. Stat. Phys.
Journal of Statistical Physics

J. Vac. Sci. Technol.
Journal of Vacuum Science and Technology

J. Vac. Sci. Technol. A
Journal of Vacuum Science and Technology A

J. Vac. Sci. Technol. B
Journal of Vacuum Science and Technology B

JETP Lett.
JETP Letters

Jpn. J. Appl. Phys.
Japanese Journal of Applied Physics

Jpn. J. Phys.
Japanese Journal of Physics

K. Dan. Vidensk. Selsk. Mat. Fys. Medd.
Kongelig Danske Videnskabernes Selskab, Matematsik-Fysiske Meddelelser

Kolloid Z. Z. Polym.
Kolloid Zeitschrift & Zeitschrift für Polymere

Lett. Nuovo Cimento
Lettere al Nuovo Cimento

Lick Obs. Bull.
Lick Observatory Bulletin

Mater. Res. Bull.
Materials Research Bulletin

Med. Phys.
Medical Physics

Mem. R. Astron. Soc.
Memoirs of the Royal Astronomical Society

Mol. Cryst. Liq. Cryst.
Molecular Crystals and Liquid Crystals

Mol. Phys.
Molecular Physics

Mon. Not. R. Astron. Soc.
Monthly Notices of the Royal Astronomical Society

Natl. Bur. Stand. (U.S.), Circ.
National Bureau of Standards (U.S.), Circular

Natl. Bur. Stand. (U.S.), Misc. Publ.
National Bureau of Standards (U.S.), Miscellaneous Publications

Natl. Bur. Stand. (U.S.), Spec. Publ.
National Bureau of Standards (U.S.), Special Publications

Nucl. Data, Sect. A
Nuclear Data, Section A

Nucl. Fusion
Nuclear Fusion

Nucl. Instrum.
Nuclear Instruments

Nucl. Instrum. Methods
Nuclear Instruments & Methods

Nucl. Phys.
Nuclear Physics

Nucl. Phys. A
Nuclear Physics A

Nucl. Phys. B
Nuclear Physics B

Nucl. Sci. Eng.
Nuclear Science and Engineering

Opt. Acta
Optica Acta

Opt. Commun.
Optics Communications

Opt. Lett.
Optics Letters

Opt. News
Optics News

Opt. Photon. News
Optics and Photonics News

Opt. Spectrosc. (USSR)
Optics and Spectroscopy (USSR)

Percept. Psychophys.
Perception and Psychophysics

Philips Res. Rep.
Philips Research Reports

Philos. Mag.
Philosophical Magazine

Philos. Trans. R. Soc. London
Philosophical Transactions of the Royal Society of London

Philos. Trans. R. Soc. London, Ser. A
Philosophical Transactions of the Royal Society of London, Series A: Mathematical and Physical Sciences

Phys. (N.Y.)
Physics (New York)

Phys. Fluids
Physics of Fluids
Phys. Fluids A
Physics of Fluids A
Phys. Fluids B
Physics of Fluids B
Phys. Konden. Mater.
Physik der Kondensierten Materie
Phys. Lett.
Physics Letters
Phys. Lett. A
Physics Letters A
Phys. Lett. B
Physics Letters B
Phys. Med. Bio.
Physics in Medicine and Biology
Phys. Met. Metallogr. (USSR)
Physics of Metals and Metallography
(USSR)
Phys. Rev.
Physical Review
Phys. Rev. A
Physical Review A
Phys. Rev. B
Physical Review B: Condensed Matter
Phys. Rev. C
Physical Review C: Nuclear Physics
Phys. Rev. D
Physical Review D: Particles and Fields
Phys. Rev. Lett.
Physical Review Letters
Phys. Status Solidi
Physica Status Solidi
Phys. Status Solidi A
Physica Status Solidi A: Applied Research
Phys. Status Solidi B
Physica Status Solidi B: Basic Research
Phys. Teach.
Physics Teacher
Phys. Today
Physics Today
Phys. Z.
Physikalische Zeitschrift
Phys. Z. Sowjetunion
Physikalische Zeitschrift der Sowjetunion
Planet. Space Sci.
Planetary and Space Science
Plasma Phys.
Plasma Physics
Proc. Cambridge Philos. Soc.
Proceedings of the Cambridge Philosophical
Society

Proc. IEEE
Proceedings of the IEEE
Proc. IRE
Proceedings of the IRE
Proc. Natl. Acad. Sci. U.S.A.
Proceedings of the National Academy of
Sciences of the United States of America
Proc. Phys. Soc. London
Proceedings of the Physical Society, London
Proc. Phys. Soc. London, Sect. A
Proceedings of the Physical Society, London,
Section A
Proc. Phys. Soc. London, Sect. B
Proceedings of the Physical Society, London,
Section B
Proc. R. Soc. London
Proceedings of the Royal Society of London
Proc. R. Soc. London, Ser. A
Proceedings of the Royal Society of London,
Series A: Mathematical and Physical Sciences
Prog. Theor. Phys.
Progress of Theoretical Physics
Publ. Astron. Soc. Pac.
Publications of the Astronomical Society of the
Pacific
Radiat. Eff.
Radiation Effects
Radio Eng. Electron. (USSR)
Radio Engineering and Electronics (USSR)
Radio Eng. Electron. Phys. (USSR)
Radio Engineering and Electronic Physics
(USSR)
Radio Sci.
Radio Science
RCA Rev.
RCA Review
Rep. Prog. Phys.
Reports on Progress in Physics
Rev. Geophys.
Reviews of Geophysics
Rev. Mod. Phys.
Reviews of Modern Physics
Rev. Opt. Theor. Instrum.
Revue d'Optique, Theorique et Instrumentale
Rev. Sci. Instrum.
Review of the Scientific Instruments
Russ. J. Phys. Chem.
Russian Journal of Physical Chemistry
Sci. Am.
Scientific American
Sol. Phys.
Solar Physics

Solid State Commun.
Solid State Communications
Solid State Electron.
Solid State Electronics
Solid State Phys.
Solid State Physics
Sov. Astron.
Soviet Astronomy
Sov. Astron. Lett.
Soviet Astronomy Letters
Sov. J. At. Energy
Soviet Journal of Atomic Energy
Sov. J. Low-Temp. Phys.
Soviet Journal of Low-Temperature
Physics
Sov. J. Nucl. Phys.
Soviet Journal of Nuclear Physics
Sov. J. Opt. Technol.
Soviet Journal of Optical Technology
Sov. J. Part. Nucl.
Soviet Journal of Particles and Nuclei
Sov. J. Plasma Phys.
Soviet Journal of Plasma Physics
Sov. J. Quantum Electron.
Soviet Journal of Quantum Electronics
Sov. Phys. Acoust.
Soviet Physics: Acoustics
Sov. Phys. Crystallogr.
Soviet Physics: Crystallography
Sov. Phys. Dokl.
Soviet Physics: Doklady
Sov. Phys. J.
Soviet Physics Journal
Sov. Phys. JETP
Soviet Physics: JETP
Sov. Phys. Semicond.
Soviet Physics: Semiconductors
Sov. Phys. Solid State
Soviet Physics: Solid State
Sov. Phys. Tech. Phys.
Soviet Physics: Technical Physics
Sov. Phys. Usp.
Soviet Physics: Uspekhi
Sov. Radiophys.
Soviet Radiophysics
Sov. Tech. Phys. Lett.
Soviet Technical Physics Letters
Spectrochim. Acta
Spectrochimica Acta
Spectrochim. Acta, Part A
Spectrochimica Acta, Part A: Molecular
Spectroscopy

Spectrochim. Acta, Part B
Spectrochimica Acta, Part B: Atomic
Spectroscopy
Supercon. Sci. Technol.
Superconductor Science and Technology
Surf. Sci.
Surface Science
Theor. Chim. Acta
Theoretica Chimica Acta
Trans. Am. Cryst. Soc.
Transactions of the American Crystallographic
Society
Trans. Am. Geophys. Union
Transactions of the American Geophysical
Union
Trans. Am. Inst. Min. Metall. Pet. Eng.
Transactions of the Amercian Institute of
Mining, Metallurgical and Petroleum
Engineers
Trans. Am. Nucl. Soc.
Transactions of the American Nuclear Society
Trans. Am. Soc. Mech. Eng.
Transactions of the American Society of
Mechanical Engineers
Trans. Am. Soc. Met.
Transactions of the American Society for
Metals
Trans. Br. Ceramic Society
Transactions of the British Ceramic Society
Trans. Faraday Society
Transactions of the Faraday Society
Trans. Metall. Soc. AIME
Transactions of the Metallurgical Society of
AIME
Trans. Soc. Rheol.
Transactions of the Society of Rheology
Ukr. Phys. J.
Ukrainian Physics Journal
Z. Anal. Chem.
Zeitschrift für Analytische Chemie
Z. Angew. Phys.
Zeitschrift für Angewandte Physik
Z. Anorg. Allg. Chem.
Zeitschrift für Anorganische und Allgemeine
Chemie
Z. Astrophys.
Zeitschrift für Astrophysik
Z. Elektrochem.
Zeitschrift für Elektrochemie
Z. Kristallogr. Kristallgeom. Krystallphys. Kristallchem.
Zeitschrift für Kristallographis, Kristallgeome-
trie, Krystallphysik, Kristallchemie

Z. Metallk.
Zeitschrift für Metallkunde
Z. Naturforsch.
Zeitschrift für Naturforschung
Z. Naturforsch. Teil A
Zeitschrift für Naturforschung, Teil A Physik,
Physikalische Chemie, Kosmophysik

Z. Phys.
Zeitschrift für Physik
Z. Phys. Chem. (Frankfurt am Main)
Zeitschrift für Physikalische Chemie (Frankfurt
am Main)
Z. Phys. Chem. (Leipzig)
Zeitschrift für Physikalische Chemie (Leipzig)

S

SAKHAROV, ANDREI DMITRIEVICH

b. Moscow, Russia, May 21, 1921; *d.* Moscow, Russia, December 14, 1989; *nuclear physics, particle physics, plasma physics, cosmology.*

Sakharov was born into a family of intellectuals; his father was a well-known physics teacher and the author of textbooks and popular articles. Sakharov graduated with honors from Moscow University in 1942, perhaps the best physics major they had ever had. He spent the years of World War II in a munitions factory, where his creativity was already evident. After the war, he did his graduate work at the Physics Institute of the Academy of Sciences (FIAN). Immediately after that, Sakharov joined The Installation, which was the Soviet atomic bomb laboratory. He worked closely with four great theoretical physicists: Yakov Zeldovich, Nikolai Bogolubov, Igor Tamm, and Isaak Pomeranchuk. Sakharov is often credited with being the "father" of the Soviet hydrogen bomb.

Besides his military work (which involved a deep knowledge of nuclear and plasma physics), Sakharov made major contributions to basic science in three areas. In plasma physics he was the first in the Soviet Union to suggest the use of lasers to initiate a controlled thermonuclear burn. He also proposed the tokamak (a device using a large current induced directly in the plasma) which is, even to this day, a major line of fusion energy research. In particle physics he put forward the first rational explanation of the baryon asymmetry of the universe; that is, why there are more particles than antiparticles; in short, why we exist. His explanation is based on the elementary violation of CP invariance: Under simultaneous charge conjugation (C) and parity inversion (P) the universe is not invariant. In cosmology Sakharov proposed an alternative gravitational theory to that of Albert Einstein. In sum, his work was recognized early, and at age thirty-two he was elected to the Soviet Academy of Sciences, an honor that has no precedent in Soviet science.

Sakharov devoted himself to the societal aspects of science. He was one of the first to realize the health consequences of atmospheric nuclear explosions, and he was instrumental in convincing Nikita Krushchev to sign an agreement with John Kennedy that ended such tests. He was also very concerned about the uses of nuclear weapons. His 1968 publication on "Coexistence" galvanized the world's attention onto this subject, while causing him, within the Soviet system, much personal distress.

It is on human rights that Sakharov is best known. In fact, his work in the defense of human rights resulted in his being awarded the Nobel Peace Prize in 1975. He was active in the defense of many dissidents, including Sergei Kovalev and Yuri Orlov. For this activity, he was tried and sentenced, in January 1980, to house arrest in the (closed city) of Gorky. He was released by Mikhail Gorbachev in December 1986. In his last years, Sakharov was elected to the Congress of People's Deputies. Many feel he would have played, if it had not been for his early death, a significant role in the transition from the Soviet Union to Russia.

See also: BARYON NUMBER; *CPT* THEOREM; PLASMA PHYSICS; TOKAMAK

Bibliography

BABYONYSHEV, A. *On Sakharov* (Knopf, New York, 1982).

BONNER, E. *Alone Together* (Knopf, New York, 1986).

SAKHAROV, A. *Memoirs* (Knopf, New York, 1990).

SALISBURY, E. *Progress, Coexistance, and Intellectual Freedom* (W. W. Norton, New York, 1968).

SESSLER, A. M., and HOWELL, Y. "Andrei Sakharov: A Man of Our Times." *Am. J. Phys.* **52,** 397–402 (1984).

TER HAAR, D., ed. *Collected Scientific Works of Andrei Sakharov* (Dekker, New York, 1982).

ANDREW M. SESSLER

SCALAR

Scalars are physical quantities that are not related to orientation. Examples are mass, electric charge, kinetic energy, potential energy, density, pressure, and temperature. Unlike vectors, where the components change with a rotation of the coordinate system, scalars have a single value that does not vary when the coordinates are rotated. Hence scalars are sometimes referred to as invariants.

While some scalars are quite simple, such as mass and charge, others are combinations of vectors and tensors. An obvious example is the kinetic energy of a particle that involves the scalar product of the velocity (a vector) with itself. More generally, both the magnitude of a vector and the angle between two vectors are scalar quantities.

Analysis methods based on scalars, such as energy conservation, are simpler than those based on vectors, such as Newton's second law, so finding useful scalar products is desirable. Indeed, the advanced methods in mechanics, Lagrangian and Hamiltonian dynamics, start from scalar quantities: the kinetic and potential energies.

See also: TENSOR; VECTOR; VECTOR, UNIT

IAN R. GATLAND

SCALE AND STRUCTURE

In any physical problem, only a certain range of size and time scales are relevant for a particular process. If we want to study plate tectonics, we need to think in terms of hundreds of kilometers and thousands of years, whereas if we want to understand the spectral lines emitted by hot atoms of a particular element, we must concentrate on the size scale of (10^{-8} m) and time scales of a fraction of a second (10^{-19} s). By isolating the size and time scales that we are interested in, we can separate the problem we wish to study from many other problems. This simplifies the task of understanding what is going on. Ultimately, all of the scales affect the others (processes in atoms deep in the earth provide the heat energy that drives the motion of the crustal plates), but it is useful to divide up problems by size and time scale. This is one of many idealizations that we make in science. It helps reduce the complexity of the world around us into a series of separated problems, each one simple enough for us to have a chance of solving it.

What we observe depends very much on the tools we use to observe, since each gives us sensitivity to a different size or time scale. A piece of matter that looks solid and smooth to the eye has a very complicated surface when viewed with an electron microscope, and it appears to be mostly space with a pattern of isolated massive points when viewed via x-ray diffraction scattering. The differences can readily be explained by the size sensitivity of the viewing instrument. The same is true with time sensitivity; a camera with a very fast film and shutter speed can record details of a process that are quite invisible to the eye.

When we ask what is the substructure of a system—what are its components—the answer depends very much on the size and time scales that we wish to study. The physics of smaller scales can be summarized by some parameters that appear in the equations describing larger-scale behavior. At the scale detected by our senses, a table top can be described by bulk properties of the materials from which it is built (mass density, tensile strength, coefficient of friction between it and any other given surface, etc.). These parameters are enough to determine how objects behave when sliding across its surface, how much it will sag if a heavy weight is placed on it, and so on. You do not need to know anything about its atomic structure by what you can observe directly with your own senses.

However, if we want to explain the observations made by diffraction scattering, using x rays with a wavelength of about 10^{-10} m, then we need to think in terms of structure at that scale—which indeed means we need to think in terms of atoms. The wavelength of the probe determines the size of the structure it can resolve. To probe subatomic structure, we need to produce probes with even smaller wavelengths. Since wavelength λ is inversely proportional to the energy per quantum in the wave: $E = h/\lambda$, this means that one needs high-energy accelerators to study physics at subatomic scales.

There is a relationship between size scale and time scale in the basic laws of physics. Typically, small length scales mean processes that occur on short time scales, whereas objects with large length scales generally change only over longer time scales. This is not a precise relationship; there are, for example, nuclear transition processes that have a half-life of thousands of years. However, the fastest processes that can occur for objects of a certain size scale are inversely proportional to the size, because the time it takes for a signal to propagate across the system cannot be shorter than the time for light to travel that distance. The system cannot act as a coherent whole without such a signal. The speed of light thus determines a relationship between the distance scale and minimum time scale of a physical process.

Physicists talk not only about distance and time scales, but also energy scale, mass scale, temperature scale, and so on. For each of these quantities, only certain ranges will be relevant in a particular problem. The accuracy with which one needs to measure these quantities will depend on the question being studied.

Scaling Laws

One very interesting application of the concept of scale is the question of how objects change when the scale is changed. Let us consider the following question: Why does an elephant look so different from a giant ant? Would it be possible to have an ant the size of an elephant? The answer to the second question is no. Why not? Let us define a length scale r as the typical size scale of an ant. To be definite, pick r as the length of the ant's body; all other parts of the ant can be defined in terms of r. Notice that

the cross-sectional area of the ant's leg is some number times r^2, while the weight of its body is another number times r^3. Now what will happen if we try to make an ant that has length $1,000r$ and maintains all the same proportions to its body? Everywhere we had an expression with r we now have $1,000r$. Clearly the cross-sectional area of its legs, and thus the strength of them for supporting weight, grows by a factor of $1,000 \times 1,000 = 1,000,000$. However, unfortunately for the poor ant, its weight has grown by $1,000 \times 1,000 \times 1,000 = 1,000,000,000$. If we assume the skeleton has the same strength of material as the original ant, the legs cannot support the weight of the body and the giant ant cannot stand. Thus, we immediately understand why the legs of an elephant are much thicker in proportion to its body than those of an ant.

This type of exercise, calculating how an object changes when all its dimensions are changed by an overall factor, is known as a scaling calculation. It is surprising how much we can understand about the sizes and shapes of objects around us just by making such simple calculations.

Fractal Behavior

Recently a lot of attention has been given to systems that look the same no matter at what scale you view them—at least over a very large range of scales. These systems are called self-similar or fractal. Mathematically, one can imagine systems for which it is exactly true that the behavior is the same at every scale. Physically, the natural scale of atomic structure in all materials places a limit on the small-scale structure of any matter, and large-scale limits are imposed by the strength of materials. However, over a limited range, the mathematics of scaling in self-similar systems has a number of interesting applications to real systems, such as the structure of a fern frond.

See also: APPROXIMATION AND IDEALIZATION; FRACTAL; PARAMETERS; SYSTEMS

Bibliography

MORRISON, P., et al. *Powers of Ten: A Book About the Relative Size of Things in the Universe and the Effect of Adding Another Zero* (Scientific American Library, San Francisco, 1982).

HELEN R. QUINN

SCANNING PROBE MICROSCOPIES

Scanning probe microscopes are high resolution imaging instruments that probe various characteristics of a material surface. The most common types are: scanning tunneling microscopes, force microscopes, and near-field optical microscopes. This family of microscopes has in common a scanning mechanism that moves a probe along the surface of a sample making measurements as it proceeds. These measurements are used to construct digital images that allow researchers to "see" the surface. The types of microscopes differ in what characteristics they measure and therefore in what properties of the surface are represented in the image. For example, a magnetic sample will have both a surface topography as well as a magnetic landscape. Figure 1a shows the topography of a magnetic thin film while Fig. 1b shows the magnetic bit pattern over the same region. Historically, these versatile microscopes developed out of the merging of two areas: near-field microscopy and stylus profilometry.

Near-field microscopy requires studying the sample at close range. The combination of the probe-sample distance and the probe size determines the image resolution. The smaller the probe and the closer it is to the sample, the finer the detail which

can be observed. This is very different from light microscopy where the resolution is instead determined by the wavelength (color) of light used to image the sample. In normal light, microscopy images become blurred when the feature size becomes comparable to the wavelength of light. This is called the diffraction limit and is approximately 0.25 μm for yellow light. By working closer to the sample one can get around this diffraction limit and try to see features smaller than a wavelength of light. In this type of near-field instrument the lens which is used to focus the light in typical light microscopy, is replaced by a very small probe which acts like an extremely tiny flashlight.

What distinguishes light microscopy from near-field microscopy is the relative size of the probing radiation (light) to the probe size and to the tip-sample spacing. In light microscopy the wavelength of the probing radiation (color of light) is small compared to either the probe or the tip-sample distance whereas in near-field microscopy it is the other way around. To test the near-field imaging concept, experimentalists first used relatively long wavelength radiation, microwaves with wavelengths of 30 mm. This meant that they could use a probe diameter of 1.5 mm, which was smaller than the wavelength of radiation but still large enough to make easily. In 1972, Eric Ash and coworkers successfully imaged with a resolution of one-fifteenth of the wavelength of radiation, well below the diffraction limit. Even after this demonstration of the near-field scanning technique, the construction of a super-resolution optical microscope appeared problematic due to the submicron positioning and control necessary for use with visible light.

Development of near-field microscopy proceeded in parallel with the development of stylus profilometry. Scanning profilometers typically employ a diamond stylus which contacts the sample and when scanned over the surface produces a three-dimensional map. A major problem of the technique is that the contact between the stylus and sample can lead to contamination and damage of the sample surface. In 1972, a group at the National Bureau of Standards, led by Russell Young, developed a noncontacting profilometer. By injecting a constant current of electrons into the sample and monitoring the voltage between the tip and the sample, the distance between probe and sample could be determined. Young named this instrument the "topografiner" from the Greek "to describe a place."

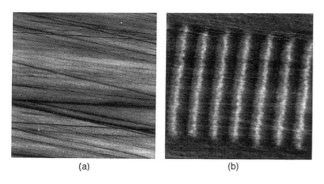

(a) (b)

Figure 1 Magnetic force microscope (MFM) image of a magnetic bit pattern: (a) shows a 20 μm $\times$ 20 μm region of the surface topography and (b) shows the magnetic field gradient above the sample in the same region. The magnetization is in the plane of the sample and where the direction of magnetization changes, there is a large change in the magnetic field above the sample—it is this magnetic field gradient which is being imaged. (Thin film disk courtesy Dean Palmer)

A major advance toward present day scanning probe microscopies involved combining near-field techniques with that of the topografiner. If instead of using field-emitted electrons from a probe one used the decaying wave associated with quantum mechanical electron tunneling, the resolution of the technique could be increased substantially. The result of this combination was the scanning tunneling microscope. In 1986 Gert Binnig and Heinrich Rohrer received the Nobel Prize in physics for this invention.

With the profound success of the scanning tunneling microscope, researchers were quick to generalize to other tip-sample interactions. Although the scanning tunneling microscope (STM) and the near-field scanning optical microscope (NSOM) use the decaying waves of tunneling electrons and photons, respectively, the near-field probe is now generally taken to include interactions such as surface forces (repulsive hard-core, attractive van der Waals, magnetic, and electrostatic), and thermal convec-tion. In this broader sense, scanning probe micros-copies are characterized by tip-sample interactions that have a lateral extent determined by the local ge-ometry at the point of closest approach.

To produce an image, this interaction strength is determined—it may be a measurement of the tun-neling current in the case of an STM, the intensity of light in the case of an NSOM, or the deflection of a cantilever due to surface forces in the case of the force microscope—but in all cases this is then put into a feedback loop which maintains this value. As the probe is scanned across the surface the tip is moved up or down by the feedback loop so that the interaction is kept constant. The image produced by recording the motion of the tip then gives a contour map of constant interaction strength. Typically these images are grey-scale where each pixel is given a color that corresponds to its height, for example, light tones are used for bumps and dark tones are used to indicate valleys. Figure 2 shows an STM image of a semiconductor surface in this format.

One of the virtues of scanning probe microscopes is the ability to image in a variety of environments. It is possible to operate in vacuum, liquid, and gas at-mospheres as well as at different extremes of tem-perature. The neuron in Fig. 3 is imaged in the

Figure 2 Scanning tunneling microscope image of a 500 Å × 500 Å area of gallium arsenide surface grown at a relatively low temperature (350 °C). This image shows three main heights (colors) indicating three atomic steps. Additionally the surface shows two different types of surface reconstructions; the 2 × 4 reconstruction resembles rows while the 4 × 4 reconstruction has a crosshatch pattern. (Image courtesy Mark Johnson)

Figure 3 Force microscope (contact mode) image of a neuron imaged live in a droplet of ionic medium. The scan area is 50 μm × 50 μm. (Neuron culture courtesy Karen Hall)

liquid environment necessary to keep it alive, clearly an advantage for biological samples.

Since the mid-1980s scanning probe microscopes have proven themselves to be valuable in a diverse set of problems and many of these microscopes are now commercially available. One of the exciting aspects of scanning probe microscopy is the continuing development of new probes that expand our means to study and visualize surfaces.

See also: SCANNING TUNNELING MICROSCOPE

Bibliography

ASH, E. A., and NICHOLLS, G. "Super-Resolution Aperture Scanning Microscope." *Nature* **237,** 510–512 (1972).

BINNIG, G.; QUATE, C. F.; and GERBER, Ch. "Atomic Force Microscope." *Phys. Rev. Lett.* **56,** 930–933 (1986).

BINNIG, G., and ROHRER, H. "The Scanning Tunneling Microscope." *Sci. Am.* **253,** 50–56 (1985).

BINNIG, G.; ROHRER, H.; GERBER, Ch.; and WEIBEL, E. "Surface Studies by Scanning Tunneling Microscopy." *Phys. Rev. Lett.* **49,** 57–61 (1982).

POHL, D. W.; DENK, W.; and LANZ, M. "Optical Stethoscopy: Image Recording with Resolution $\lambda/20$." *Appl. Phys Lett.* **44,** 651–653 (1984).

QUATE, C. F. "Vacuum Tunneling: A New Technique for Microscopy." *Phys. Today* August, 26–33 (1986).

WICKRAMASINGHE, H. K. "Scanned-Probe Microscopes." *Sci. Am.* **261,** 98–105 (1989).

WILLIAMS, C. C., and WICKRAMASINGHE, H. K. "Scanning Thermal Profiler." *Appl. Phys Lett.* **49,** 1587–1589 (1986).

YOUNG, R. D.; WARD, J.; and SCIRE, F. "The Topografiner: An Instrument for Measuring Surface Microtopography." *Rev. Sci. Instrum.* **43,** 999–1011 (1972).

CHRISTINE ORME

BRADFORD G. ORR

SCANNING TUNNELING MICROSCOPE

The Scanning Tunneling Microscope (STM) is a remarkable instrument that allows one to generate detailed images of the surface of a material. Sufficient resolution can be achieved to "see" individual atoms, groups of atoms, and atomic-height steps on the outermost atomic layers of the surface. While the idea that atoms are the building blocks of matter dates back to the ancient Greeks, only a few experimental techniques allow a person to observe *directly* how atoms are arranged at the surface of a material. Thus, Gerd Binnig and Heinrich Rohrer, working at the IBM Research lab in Zurich, Switzerland, created a sensation in the scientific community with their first reports in the early 1980s that they had developed an STM capable of spatially resolving atoms on surfaces. Binnig and Rohrer received the 1986 Nobel Prize in physics for this work, along with Ernst Ruska for his pioneering work on the electron microscope. The technique developed rapidly as scientists built more sensitive and specialized scanning tunneling microscopes that could image surfaces in ultrahigh vacuum, in air, under liquids, and at temperatures ranging from within a few degrees of absolute zero to hundreds of degrees above room temperature. The STM, which relies on detecting electrical currents, can be used to study the surfaces of metals, semiconductors, superconductors, and other materials with sufficiently high electrical conductivity. Many variations of the STM have been developed (which rely on detecting electrical signals at high frequencies, contact forces, magnetic and electrostatic forces, etc.), some of which can image non-conducting surfaces. Because of their versatility, the STM and related instruments are now widely used in scientific and engineering applications. For example, one can study the subtle atomic rearrangements that occur at many surfaces, watch how atoms deposited in a thin film growth process have assembled on a surface, image biological molecules such as DNA, and take high-resolution pictures of the small features that are formed on a surface when a computer chip is manufactured. The STM can also be used as an atomic-scale spectroscopic tool for probing the properties of electrons near surfaces, leading to a better understanding of surface properties and surface chemical reactions. New fields are emerging as scientists and engineers succeed in using the STM to move individual atoms around on surfaces and work toward developing it as a tool for building tiny features of known composition and structure.

The STM works by exploiting the phenomenon of quantum mechanical tunneling of electrons. A very sharp metal tip is brought close to the surface of the sample one is interested in studying (see Fig. 1). At very small separations S, electrons can tunnel between the tip and sample. Under appropriate conditions, a net current I of tunneling electrons flows. Monitoring this current, and thus monitoring the separation S, provides the basis for using the STM to image surfaces.

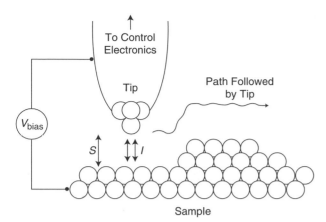

Figure 1 Schematic of the tip of an STM located a distance s from the sample surface. When a potential difference V_{bias} is applied between the tip and sample, a net tunneling current I can flow. The sign of V_{bias} determines the direction of I. (Courtesy of D. R. Peale and J. G. McLean)

Tunneling is a quantum mechanical process involving the electrons in the sample and tip, described here for the specific case of a metal sample. (The tunneling is similar for other types of materials.) In atoms, the electrons are spatially confined, or bound, around the atomic nuclei by attractive electrostatic forces; the most weakly bound ones are called the valence electrons. In a metal, the most weakly bound electrons, called the conduction electrons, can move about freely from atom to atom (which is why metals conduct electricity) but are bound inside the surface of the metal by the electrostatic forces from all the atomic nuclei. Classically, the conduction electrons are never found outside the surface. Quantum mechanically, however, electrons have wave-like properties, and there is a probability of finding the conduction electrons outside the surface of the metal, in our case the sample or tip. This probability decreases exponentially as the distance from the surface increases. As a result, when the sample and tip are brought sufficiently close together, electrons can tunnel through the gap separating the two with a probability that decreases exponentially with increasing tip-surface separation S. When an electrical potential difference V_{bias} is applied between the tip and sample, a net current I of electrons can tunnel in one direction; I also depends exponentially on S.

Because of its exponential dependence on distance S, the magnitude of the tunneling current, $I \propto$

$e^{-\alpha S}$, is extremely sensitive to changes in S, which is what gives the STM sufficient sensitivity to resolve individual atoms on a surface. The quantity α (which depends on properties of the tip and sample) has units of inverse length and a typical value of approximately 2 inverse angstroms. (1 Å $= 10^{-10}$ m; spacings between surface atoms are a few angstroms and typical tip-sample separations s of several angstroms are used when imaging surfaces.) Thus, if we change the separation of the tip and sample by 0.1 Å, the tunneling current will change by approximately 20 percent, which is easily measured. This sensitivity is sufficient to resolve atoms on a surface. The challenge for the experimentalist is to control the tip position down to distances that are smaller than the diameter of an atom.

To obtain an image showing surface atom positions, the STM can be used in the "constant current" mode in which the tip is scanned laterally across the surface while an electrical feedback circuit monitors the tunneling current I. As the tip moves laterally, I will change in response to height variations, or "bumps," in the sample surface. A feedback mechanism senses any changes in the tunneling current and moves the tip closer to or further from the sample surface in order to hold I constant. (Typical tunneling currents are on the order of 1 nA.) The path of the tip is recorded (see Fig. 1) for several

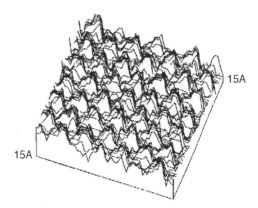

Figure 2 Topographic map of a gold surface taken in "constant current" mode. The individual line scans are shown for a region of the surface 15 Å by 15 Å. On a given line scan the maximum height variation corresponding to scanning across an atom is on the order of 0.6 Å. This image was taken with $V_{bias} = 30$ mV (tip negative) and $I = 1$ nA. (Courtesy of D. R. Peale)

closely spaced scans, giving a topographic map of the sample surface like the one shown in Fig. 2 for tunneling on gold. Often these maps are computer processed so that the images are easier to interpret visually. Figure 3 shows the corresponding greyscale

image in which height variations are shown with different shades of grey. The regular pattern of bumps corresponds to the ordered array of individual atoms on the gold surface.

Figures 4 and 5 show examples of images taken on different surfaces and illustrate the type of information that can be obtained with the STM. Figure 4 is an image of a Si(111) surface; the notation (111) means that a single crystal of Si has been cut in such a way as to expose particular planes of atoms. When such a surface has been made, the atoms in the top layers of the crystal experience different forces than when they are embedded in the bulk and, in response, may move to new positions. Such a rearrangement is called a surface reconstruction. Figure 4 is an example of a 7×7 reconstruction of Si(111). Since silicon is technologically such an important material, an enormous amount of effort has gone into studying its surface properties. STM images like the one shown in Fig. 4 have contributed to a better understanding of the forces that bind the atoms on the Si surface. The STM is also useful for studying a wide range of phenomena at surfaces. For example, it can be used to characterize larger scale features, such as steps (as shown in Fig. 4) and surface roughness, which result from incompleted planes of atoms on an otherwise ordered crystalline surface. Steps, which are present on all

Figure 3 Greyscale image corresponding to the topographic map in Fig. 2. Height variations are shown with different shades of grey. The regular pattern of bumps corresponds to the positions of individual atoms on the surface of the gold crystal.

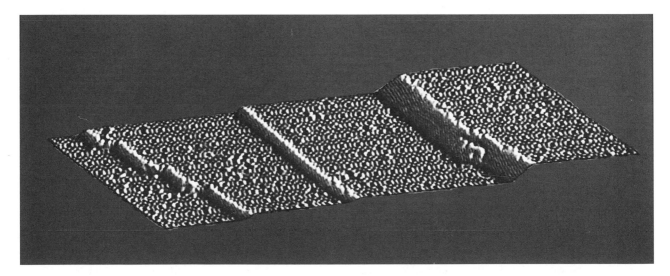

Figure 4 Image of a Si(111) surface showing the 7×7 reconstruction. The image corresponds to a region of the surface 200 Å by 800 Å. The intricate pattern shown results from the positions of the atoms at the surface, which are different from those they would occupy in the bulk material. Also visible are two single and one triple atomic layer height steps. This image was taken with $V_{bias} = 2$ V and $I = 1.2$ nA. (Courtesy of E. D. Williams and N. C. Bartelt)

surfaces, are important in understanding surface properties since they interact with atoms and molecules that bind and react with the surface. The STM can also be used to detect whether atoms and molecules deposited on a surface sit on top of or are embedded in the crystal surface, whether they bind at steps or on flat portions of the surface, and whether they form ordered patterns. From such information, scientists can develop a better understanding of the electronic interactions that occur between atoms and surfaces, how deposited atoms move around on surfaces, and how chemical reactions and binding occur. These, in turn, help scientists to understand technologically important processes like surface catalytic reactions and thin film growth.

Figure 5 illustrates the remarkable and unique capability of the STM to manipulate the positions of individual atoms. Scientists are learning to use in a controlled way the interactions between the tip and an atom adsorbed on the sample surface so that they can "build" structures atom by atom. The stick figure shown in Fig. 5 is made of carbon monoxide molecules separated by a few atomic diameters on a platinum surface.

There are several technical challenges the scientist must overcome to achieve atomic-scale resolution with the STM. One is to control the position of the tip; one must be able to place it several angstroms from the sample surface and, once there, control its position and scan it across the surface with subatomic precision. Such control is accomplished by mounting the tip on piezoelectric materials, which are ceramics that change size in response to a change in an electric potential difference applied across them. Numerous configurations of tip mounts have been devised to achieve a high level of tip control. A second challenge is to isolate the microscope and sample from any mechanical, electrical, or acoustical noise in the environment. Even the slightest mechanical disturbance, for example, can amount to vibrations of the tip with amplitudes large enough to preclude atomic-scale resolution or to crash the tip into the sample. Also, very small temperature gradients can cause minute length changes in the microscope, the sample mount, or the sample itself so that the tip drifts out of position. Finally, the quality of the tunneling tip itself is crucial. The tip is made of a metal that is prepared to have a sharp point on the end. However, to achieve atomic-scale lateral resolution, the tip must end with one or few atoms.

The actual tunneling tip is often a "whisker" that forms while the tip is being prepared and processed. Much effort is expended in preparing and maintaining good and stable tunneling tips. The basic components of an STM are shown in Fig. 6.

As noted in the introduction, the STM has capabilities other than determining the positions of atoms. One is the capability to probe the properties of electrons at a sample surface with atomic-scale resolution. This is possible because of the way in which the STM works. To say that we "see" an atom really means that we detect differences in tunneling due to perturbations or modulations of the electrons by the atoms. A topographic map like that shown in Fig. 2 reflects the corrugations in the electron distribution associated with the atomic positions in the sample surface. We can also get information about how these electrons are distributed in

Figure 5 CO molecules on a platinum surface. The individual CO molecules are located a few atomic diameters from one another. (Courtesy of D. Eigler and P. Zeppenfeld)

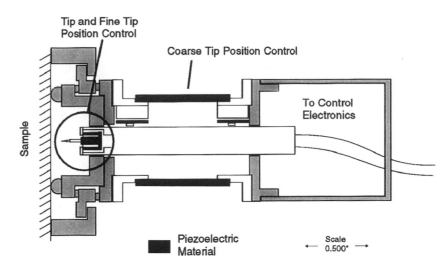

Tip and Fine Tip
Position Control

Coarse Tip Position Control

To Control
Electronics

Sample

Piezoelectric
Material

Scale
0.500"

Figure 6 Schematic of the basic components of an STM. The tip is mounted on piezoelectric tubes that can control the position of the tip with subatomic precision and scan it laterally across the surface, i.e., they provide fine-control of the tip position. The tip is brought into tunneling range of the surface using a device called an inchworm, which also contains piezoelectric materials. This design is particularly stable to vibrations because it makes use of tubular piezoelectrics and is a compact instrument. The whole sample and STM are mounted on a vibration isolation stage. (Courtesy of D. R. Peale and J. G. McLean)

energy by varying the potential difference V_{bias} applied between the tip and sample. To see why this happens, we need to understand about the energies of electrons in a material.

Electrons in a solid, like those in an atom, can exist in any of a set of allowed energy levels, which are determined by the forces that bind the electrons. These can be depicted on an energy-level diagram, like that shown in Fig. 7 for the conduction electrons in a metal; recall that these are the ones that participate in the tunneling. Due to the Pauli exclusion principle, each level can contain only two electrons (one spin up and one spin down). For the conduction electrons, there are so many allowed energy levels that they form a nearly continuous distribution like that shown schematically in Fig. 7. At low temperatures, the levels are filled approximately up to the Fermi energy E_F and empty above that. The minimum energy required to pull an electron out of the metal (i.e., from the Fermi level) is known as the work function Φ. Now we can visualize the tunneling process. Let us assume that the tip and surface are both metals with equal work functions and sepa-

rated by a distance s. When we apply a potential difference V_{bias} between the tip and sample, we are shifting the Fermi energies of the two metals by an energy of eV_{bias}, where e is the charge on the electron. If the separation s is sufficiently small, for the bias shown in Fig. 7, this shift causes electrons to tunnel from filled levels in the tip to empty levels in the sample. When we change V_{bias} we are changing the electron energy levels that participate in the tunneling. Thus, images taken at different values of V_{bias} may look quite different. The sign of V_{bias} determines which way the current will flow. In real metals, the energy levels for the conduction electrons are not distributed uniformly in energy. Futhermore, atomic-scale variations on the surface, such as atoms, vacancies, or steps, can locally alter these distributions. By varying V_{bias} and monitoring the tunneling current, we can get information about these energy distributions. Such measurements help scientists to understand very fundamental questions about surfaces—why they reconstruct, why atoms bind at certain sites, and why certain surface chemical reactions occur.

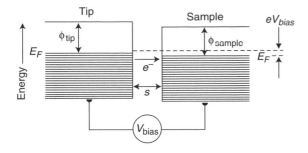

Figure 7 Schematic of the conduction electron energy levels involved in tunneling. The schematic assumes the tip and sample are metals with equal work functions Φ. Applying a potential difference V_{bias} between the tip and sample shifts the Fermi level (denoted by E_F) of the tip relative to that of the sample by an energy of eV_{bias}. For the bias voltage shown, electrons tunnel through the gap of width s from occupied levels in the tip to unoccupied ones in the sample. (Courtesy of J. G. McLean)

See also: ELECTRON, CONDUCTION; ELECTRON MICROSCOPE; ENERGY LEVELS; FERMI SURFACE; SCANNING PROBE MICROSCOPIES; WORK FUNCTION

Bibliography

BINNIG, G., and HEINRICH, R. "The Scanning Tunneling Microscope." *Sci. Am.* **253** (Aug.), 50–56 (1985).

CHEN, C. J. *Introduction to Scanning Tunneling Microscopy* (Oxford University Press, New York, 1993).

GOLOVCHENKO, J. A. "The Tunneling Microscope: A New Look at the Atomic World." *Science* **232** (4746), 48–53 (1986).

HANSMA, P. K., and TERSOFF, J. "Scanning Tunneling Microscopy." *J. Appl. Phys.* **61** (2), R1–R23, (1987).

LAGALLY, M. G. "Atom Motion on Surfaces." *Phys. Today* **46** (Nov.), 24–31 (1993).

QUATE, C. F. "Vacuum Tunneling: A New Technique for Microscopy." *Phys. Today* **39** (Aug.), 26–33 (1986).

STROSCIO, J. A., and EIGLER, D. M. "Atomic and Molecular Manipulation with the Scanning Tunneling Microscope." *Science* **254** (5036), 1319–1326 (1991).

WICKRAMASINGHE, H. K. "Scanned-Probe Microscopes." *Sci. Am.* **261** (Oct.), 98–105 (1989).

WIESENDANGER, R. *Scanning Probe Microscopy and Spectroscopy: Methods and Applications* (Cambridge University Press, Cambridge, Eng., 1994).

BARBARA H. COOPER

SCATTERING

Scattering is the phenomena whereby a directed incident beam of energy is deflected by its interaction with some localized target object in its path. The scattered energy emanates from the target area usually in all directions, hence the word scatter. The target itself may be changed as the result of the scattering, as may the constituent nature of the beam itself. Scattering is a singularly important method by which we interactively explore nature.

For example, we see an object when some of the light (photons), used to illuminate it, is scattered into our eyes. The moon and planets are visible because light from the sun, which was passing into outer space, is deflected back to us; our brain interprets the phenomena as sight.

To perform a controlled scattering experiment the following is needed: a source of energy, a target, a detector to catch the scattered energy and very importantly an interpretation. Scattering theory attempts to relate the nature of the target object to the deflection, the change, or the by-products produced in the reaction. To be useful in this regard the incident beam must usually have a wavelength smaller, or be made of particles which have a size smaller, than the details of the object to be investigated. Further the energy of the particles in the beam must be sufficient to produce the desired reactions in the target. Beams of particles other than photons are often used for this purpose.

For such beams the detection of photons by the retina of our eyes can be mimicked by specially designed instruments (e.g., microphones for acoustic beams; photographic plates for x-ray beams; Geiger counters, cloud chambers, bubble chambers, wire chambers, or scintillators for particle beams and their by-products). In their range and sensitivity these detectors easily outstrip the human senses. But the interpretation of the received scattered signal, literally speaking the sensing, is still an essential element of any observation. The dots produced on a photographic plate when DNA was illuminated with x rays had to be interpreted before Francis Crick and James Watson could conjecture the double helicity of its structure.

Modern scattering theory began in 1899, when Lord Rayleigh formulated an explanation of why the sky appears blue when viewed by light scattered through a large (about 90°) deflection angle. White sunlight is a mixture of light of different wavelengths, or colors. Different wavelengths are scattered differently by the air; the smaller wavelengths are favored, and blue light has a smaller wavelength than red. Hence the sky viewed along the line toward the sun appears red as the blue light has been scattered away out of the forward beam; the deflected blue light can be observed as the beam passes overhead.

The scattering mechanism in the earth's atmosphere is complicated by the various target objects that are responsible. Local density fluctuations scatter some 50 percent of the light, known as Brillouin scattering. The light is also scattered by individual molecules, Rayleigh scattering. Scattering by small aggregates like dust, or droplets of water, is not thought to be an important component of this particular phenomena.

Raman scattering occurs when a photon excites or de-excites a molecule causing transitions between quantum states. The scattered photon is not just deflected; it is changed in frequency and wavelength. The discovery of quantum states followed directly from another scattering experiment using a beam of alpha rays (the nuclei of helium atoms).

Ernest Rutherford had demonstrated the nature of alpha rays as an energetic beam of heavy (relative to an electron) charged particles. The beams could be deflected by magnetic and electric fields. In 1911, Rutherford, with Hans Geiger, noticed that the beam could also be scattered if passed through a mica screen. The angle of deflection was very small but he calculated that the local electric field gradient inside the mica would have to be very strong. Ernest Marsden, Geiger's student, found that alpha rays could be deflected even through 90 degrees, or more, by a gold foil! This Rutherford scattering could be explained if all the positive charge of the atom, and perforce most of its mass, was concentrated at the center of the atom in a nucleus. The less massive, negatively charged electrons would have to be distributed around this nucleus to balance the total charge. Some seven years earlier, Hantaro Nagaoka had suggested such a planetary model of the atom; his idea had been dismissed because electrons accelerating in orbitals would emit light continuously, lose energy and hence eventually fall in to the nucleus. Niels Bohr overcame this difficulty by postulating stability (no radiation) for certain electron orbits with quantized energies.

Scattering experiments played a decisive role in the development of the new quantum or wave mechanics that grew from the Bohr model. In 1914, James Franck and Gustav Hertz bombarded mercury vapor with electrons and showed the by-product radiation was emitted in quanta corresponding to differences in atomic energy levels. In 1923 Louis de Broglie conjectured the wave–particle duality of matter. The same year, x-ray beams, which Max von Laue, William Henry Bragg, and Peter Debye had scattered from solids to determine the nature of crystal structure were used by Arthur Compton to establish that photons behave like particles. In 1927, Clinton Davisson used beams of electrons to demonstrate, through diffraction, that electrons behave like waves.

The illuminating ion beams were produced from radioactive sources until, in 1932, John Cockcroft and Ernest Walton, in England, used a linear accelerator, a voltage multiplier generator, to produce a beam of protons so they could bombard lithium atoms. Two alpha particles per lithium nucleus were produced. This was heralded as the first splitting of the atom. In fact though, Rutherford had demonstrated, in 1917, that beams of alpha particles striking nitrogen can knock out protons; the truly first example of nuclear fission.

A year earlier than Cockcroft and Walton, working in the United States, Ernest Lawrence had built the first workable ring accelerator: a cyclotron. Charged particles were trapped in circulating orbits and energized each time they passed around through a potential gradient. This ring design proved very effective. Linear Van de Graaff generators, and ring cyclotrons and synchrotrons proliferated at research laboratories throughout the world. The result has been the discovery of numerous, evermore elementary, particles.

As noted above, circulating charged particles radiate light. So accelerators can generate an intense numbers of photons. Synchrotron radiation is used to determine the structure of surfaces, atoms, molecules, and biological cells.

The use of electron microscopes, tunneling microscopes, radar installations, subsurface sonic detectors, seismic measurements, x-ray photos, and cathode-ray tubes to explore our world is based on the principles of scattering.

See also: ACCELERATOR, HISTORY OF; BOHR, NIELS HENRIK DAVID; BRILLOUIN ZONE; BUBBLE CHAMBER; CLOUD CHAMBER; CYCLOTRON; DAVISSON–GERMER EXPERIMENT; ELECTRON MICROSCOPE; ELEMENTARY PARTICLES; RUTHERFORD, ERNEST; SCANNING TUNNELING MICROSCOPE;

SCATTERING, LIGHT; SCATTERING, RAMAN; SCATTERING, RAYLEIGH; SCATTERING, RUTHERFORD; VAN DE GRAAFF ACCELERATOR; VISION

Bibliography

ANDRADE, E. N. DA C. *Rutherford and the Nature of the Atom* (Doubleday, Garden City, NY, 1964).

EWALD, P. P. *Fifty Years of X-Ray Diffraction* (International Union of Crystallography, Utrecht, 1962).

LINDSAY, R. B. *Lord Rayleigh: The Man and His Work* (Pergamon, Oxford, Eng., 1970).

JOHN READING

SCATTERING, LIGHT

The scattering of light is a natural phenomenon with omnipresent effects. It causes the sky to appear blue, sunrise and sunset to seem red, and clouds to look white.

The optical properties of a transparent medium are characterized by its refractive index. As long as this index is uniform, light will pass through the medium undeflected. Whenever there are variations in the refractive index, due for example, to the presence of particles or random fluctuations in density, part of the radiation will be redirected, or scattered. A typical light-scattering geometry is shown in Fig. 1. The beam of light is incident on a scattering medium (dots), most of the radiation is transmitted (I_{trans}) and some of the light is redirected at various angles to the incident direction (I_s).

Although discussed qualitatively by Leonardo da Vinci in the early sixteenth century, the quantitative study of light scattering began in 1869 with the experiments of John Tyndall. Tyndall, like da Vinci, demonstrated in his laboratory that the blue of the sky could be produced by the scattering of light by small particles. Tyndall sent a beam of white light through a tube of glass containing fine particles of dust suspended in the air. He found that the scattered light, observed at right angles to the beam, was highly polarized. In a subsequent theoretical treatment, Lord Rayleigh (1871) calculated the scattering from a random collection of small (compared to the wavelength) but widely separated spheres. For this regime, which is well known as Rayleigh scattering, he predicted the observed polarization

by scattering, as well as the inverse fourth-power dependence of scattered intensity on wavelength. It is this latter property that gives the sky its blue color, since blue light of wavelength 450 nm is scattered over four times as strongly as red light of wavelength 650 nm [$(650/450)^4 \cong 4$], and gives sunrise and sunset their red color, since white light, with blue light scattered out of it, appears red.

When particles are not so small compared to the wavelength, the scattering depends in a more complicated way on wavelength and particle shape. For this regime the polarization at right angles is also less pronounced. Rayleigh and Peter Debye made significant contributions to the theory of these large particles and extended the calculation to particles of nonspherical shape, although only for the case of spheres does there exist a closed form solution. In 1908 Gustav Mie determined the exact solution for the scattering from an isolated sphere. His work also includes a qualitative understanding of scattering by nonspherical particles, and it reduces to Rayleigh's theory when the spheres are very small. When these spheres are large, the scattering, termed Mie scattering, is largely independent of wavelength (as compared to the very strong dependence in Rayleigh scattering). This scattering causes clouds to appear

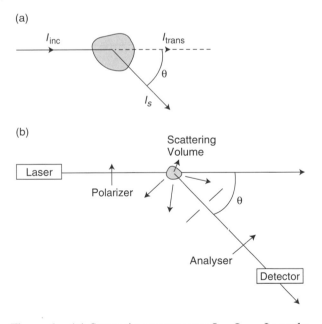

Figure 1 (a) Scattering geometry: I_{inc}, I_{trans}, I_s are the incident, transmitted, and scattered intensity, respectively, and θ is the scattering angle. (b) A schematic representation of the light-scattering experiment.

1403

white due to the white sunlight that is scattered uniformly from small droplets of water in the cloud.

Rayleigh's and Mie's scattering applies only where it is proper to add the intensities of light scattered by individual molecules, and thus applies only when the scatterers are separated by distances that are large compared to the wavelength. When the scatterers are close to one another, as in a liquid or solid, it is the scattering fields that must be added, and details of the arrangement of particles begins to have an impact on the scattering. Therefore, intermolecular interactions have to be taken into account and a detailed computation of the induced electromagnetic field surrounding a particle becomes very complex. In calculating the scattering from gases and liquids in 1910, Einstein bypassed this difficulty. He used a model suggested by Marian Smoluchowski and assumed that local density fluctuations in neighboring volume elements could be independent of one another. Einstein was thus able to explain the scattering from pure liquids and to predict the enormous increase in the scattering as the critical point was approached (the so-called critical opalescence). Leonard Ornstein and Frits Zernike included the effects of correlations in the fluctuations of neighboring volume elements. Later, in the 1940s, Debye and B. H. Zimm developed light scattering as a method for studying the molecular weights, sizes, shapes, and interactions of macromolecules in solutions.

In a typical light-scattering experiment, shown in Fig. 1, collimated light is directed into the scattering medium. The scattered light then enters a detector. The position of the detector, relative to the incident beam, defines the scattering angle θ. In addition, the intersection of the incident beam and the beam intercepted by the detector defines the scattering volume. The molecules in this region are perpetually translating, rotating, and vibrating by thermal fluctuations. Because of this motion, the total scattered electric field at the detector will fluctuate in time. Dynamic light scattering permits one to extract from these fluctuations important structural and dynamical information about the individual position, orientation, and motion of the molecules, and Brillioun and Raman scattering provide information about the collective motions (i.e., sound waves).

As with a great many optical techniques, the invention of the laser in 1960 eliminated many of the difficulties associated with light-scattering experiments, providing a spectrally narrow, strongly polarized source of intense light. Recent advances in laser techniques have made possible measurement of very small frequency shifts in the light scattered in gases, liquids, and solids. Moreover, because of the high intensities of laser sources, it is possible to measure even weakly scattered light. With the considerable advantages of a laser light source, light scattering offers several advantages as an analytical tool. It is a nondestructive technique; the amount of solution required is small; the experiments can be performed under a variety of conditions (different temperatures, various solvents, etc.); and the measurement is quick. This explains the remarkable proliferation of laser light-scattering techniques in both fundamental and applied research. Currently, physicists, chemists, biochemists, biophysicists, and engineers use light-scattering techniques to study the structure and dynamics of such diverse systems as solids, liquid crystals, gels, biological molecules, simple molecular fluids, electrolyte solutions, macromolecules, colloids, and micelles.

See also: BRILLOUIN ZONE; LASER; LIGHT; REFLECTION; REFRACTION; SCATTERING, RAMAN; SCATTERING, RAYLEIGH; SKY, COLOR OF

Bibliography

BERNE, B. J., and PECORA, R. *Dynamic Light Scattering*, 2nd ed. (Wiley, New York, 1976).

CHU, B. *Light Scattering*, 2nd ed. (Academic Press, New York, 1974).

KERKER, M. *The Scattering of Light* (Academic Press, New York, 1969).

RICHTER, J. P. *The Notebooks of Leonardo da Vinci*, Vol. 1 (Dover, New York, 1970).

VAN DE HULST, H. C. *Light Scattering by Small Particles* (Wiley, New York, 1957).

CORINNE VINCHES

SCATTERING, RAMAN

In 1928 C. V. Raman and K. S. Krishnan of India first observed and explained a new type of light scattering occurring in liquids. This light scattering is inelastic in the sense that the scattered light is changed in frequency, or equivalently, in wavelength. This inelastic light scattering has become known as Raman scattering, and for his discovery, Raman received the Nobel prize in 1930. Also in 1928, Leonid Mandelstam and Grigory Landsberg in the Soviet Union observed and reported similar inelastic light scattering in crystals of quartz (SiO_2).

The physical process of Raman scattering is best described with quantum theory. When a light quantum (photon) with an energy $E = hf$ (h = Planck's constant and f is the light frequency) passes through a solid, liquid, or gas it may be scattered elastically with no change in frequency or energy. This is called Rayleigh scattering. (Elastic scattering from dust particles is called Mie scattering.) Light may also scatter inelastically with a small change in photon energy if the medium has a natural oscillation mode which can absorb or emit quanta of energy hf_0. These modes are typically quantized rotations and vibrations in molecules, hindered rotations (librations) in liquids, and traveling vibrational waves in liquids and solids (phonons).

The frequency unit used in Raman scattering is the wave number or kayser (K) which is f/c where the speed of light c is written in cm/s. Thus the units are cm^{-1}. In these units, green light has a frequency of ~20,000 cm^{-1}. The frequency of the quantized oscillations that are seen in Raman scattering may range from a few cm^{-1} for rotational modes of molecules and floppy bending modes of long chain molecules such as DNA, 50 to 1,000 wave numbers for phonons in crystals, and up to 4,395 wave numbers for the vibrational stretch mode in the lightest molecule H_2.

One of the most powerful properties of Raman scattering is that such a wide range of oscillation frequencies may be observed with a single instrument, and the spectroscopy can be done entirely in the visible range. Thus, if the standard argon ion laser wavelength of $\lambda = 5,145$ Å $= 5.145 \times 10^{-5}$ cm is used, the laser frequency in wave numbers is $f = 1/\lambda = 19,434$ cm^{-1}. The first rotational Raman transition in N_2 at 12 cm^{-1} would appear at 19,422 cm^{-1} ($\lambda = 5,148.8$ Å) and the H_2 vibrational mode would appear at 15,434 cm^{-1} ($\lambda = 6,649.3$ Å), still in the visible spectral range.

Although Raman's original observations used sunlight as the light source for this inelastic scattering, most Raman work was done using high intensity mercury lamps until the laser was invented in 1960. The monochromatic (single wavelength) light from a laser was the ideal source for Raman scattering studies. In the mid-1960s argon and krypton lasers

with continuous power of 0.1 to 5 W became available and Raman scattering exploded in popularity. Furthermore, the intensity of the scattered Raman light or the Raman scattering cross section is often a strong function of the laser photon energy or wavelength. This occurs in media such as semiconductors with band gaps in the visible and near absorbing bands in molecules. Thus the development of wavelength tunable lasers based on organic dye molecules (dye lasers), on sapphire crystals doped with titanium (Ti:sapphire laser), and on tunable diode lasers has led to another leap forward in Raman studies. This is called resonant Raman scattering when the laser is tuned near an electronic transition.

In addition to the laser, the equipment needed for Raman studies includes a good diffraction grating spectrometer and a sensitive detector, usually a photomultiplier or a semiconductor detector array such as a charge-coupled device (CCD). Because the Raman scattering is a very weak process, typically only one photon of scattered light is detected for every 10^{14} incident photons of laser light, it is necessary for the spectrometer to have very good discrimination against Rayleigh-scattered laser light, which may be from 10^6 to 10^{10} times more intense. The typical solution for this is the use of a double or triple (grating) spectrometer, which is essentially two or three spectrometers in series.

These vibrational and rotational modes are often observed in the infrared (IR) as well. A mode with a frequency shift of 4 cm^{-1} would absorb or emit electromagnetic waves of $\lambda = 0.25$ cm. This is the wavelength of microwaves of frequency 120 GHz. At 4,000 cm^{-1} the corresponding IR emission wavelength would be 2.5 μm. In highly symmetric molecules and solids, vibrational and rotational motions may be silent in IR absorption but active in Raman scattering, and vice versa. Thus Raman and IR spectroscopies are often regarded as complementary techniques.

Not surprisingly Raman scattering has become a powerful and flexible tool in the modern laboratory for the chemical identification of gases, liquids, and solids. It is also used widely for fundamental studies of the way in which these modes of oscillation relax or decay into other oscillatory modes and other degrees of excitation involving, for example, electrons, spin waves, and sound waves.

See also: CRYSTAL; CRYSTAL STRUCTURE; ELECTROMAGNETIC WAVE; GAS; INFRARED; LIQUID; MOLECULAR

PHYSICS; PHOTON; SCATTERING; SCATTERING, LIGHT; SCATTERING, RAYLEIGH; SOLID; SPECTROSCOPY; WAVELENGTH

Bibliography

ANDERSON, A. *The Raman Effect,* 2 vols. (M. Dekker, New York, 1971, 1973).

COLTHRUP, N. B.; DALY, L. H.; and WIBERLEY, S. E. *Introduction to Infrared and Raman Spectroscopy,* 3rd ed. (Academic Press, Boston, 1990).

GANS, P. *Vibrating Molecules: An Introduction to the Interpretation of Infrared and Raman Spectra* (Chapman and Hall, London, 1971).

ALVIN D. COMPAAN

SCATTERING, RAYLEIGH

The scattering or dispersion of light by particles whose dimensions are much smaller than the wavelength of the light rays is called Rayleigh scattering. This was first studied in detail in the late nineteenth century by John W. Strutt, an Englishman, who was also the third Baron Rayleigh. Lord Rayleigh's theoretical calculations provide quantitative and qualitative explanations for both the wavelength dependence for the scattering of light and the polarization of the scattered light by small particles.

Molecules or small aggregates of molecules which are too small to serve as reflectors behave as secondary light sources and scatter light in all directions. The oscillating electric and magnetic fields of visible light have frequencies, f, between 4.3×10^{14} Hz and 6.7×10^{14} Hz corresponding to wavelengths, λ, between 7,000 and 4,000 Å ($f = c/\lambda$ where c is the speed of light). The electric field from the light wave acts as a driving force to cause the electrons in the molecules to oscillate at the same frequency as the light wave. As the applied frequency of the light approaches the natural (resonant) frequency of the molecules, the amplitude of the forced oscillation increases very rapidly. The natural frequencies for electronic excitation of the atmospheric molecules, O_2 and N_2, lie beyond the violet end of the visible spectrum. The amplitude for the excitation by short wavelength light (blue) is much larger than the amplitude of excitation by longer wavelength light (red) because the frequency of the blue light is closer to the natural resonant frequency of the O_2 and N_2 molecules than is the frequency of red light. The wavelength dependence of the scattered light is thus the result of the electrons within the scattering atmospheric molecules, whose natural resonant frequencies lie outside the visible spectrum, being forced to vibrate at the driving frequency of the incident light.

The calculated intensity of the scattered radiation is proportional to $1/\lambda^4$, where λ is the wavelength of the light. For blue light of 4,500 Å and red light of 6,800 Å, the intensity ratio would be $I_B/I_R = [6,800/4,500]^4$ which is greater than a factor of five. Rayleigh scattering thus explains why the sky is blue. Since the intensity of the scattered light is inversely proportional to the fourth power of the wavelength, significantly more blue light is scattered than red light. Violet light is scattered even more strongly than blue light; however, the observed sky light is the result of multiple scattering by the earth's atmosphere. The sky appears blue rather than violet because the violet has been largely removed by absorption of the violet light by N_2. The degree of polarization of sky light is also reduced by multiple scattering; but, as predicted by Rayleigh scattering, sky light is polarized most strongly in the direction perpendicular to the rays of the sun.

The light rays from the rising and setting sun have taken a long path through the earth's atmosphere. The light from the rising and setting sun appears to be red because a greater fraction of the shorter wavelengths (toward the blue) have been scattered out of the light rays which reach the observer's eye.

Scattering from larger particles is not explained by Rayleigh scattering and is relatively independent of wavelength. As a result, clouds, haze, and smog caused by larger particles appear to be gray or white.

Rayleigh scattering has been used to explain a wide range of phenomena. The Rayleigh scattering of starlight by interstellar dust grains has an important influence on the extinction and polarization of starlight. The extinction of starlight is a result of both absorption and scattering of the light by the dust particles. Since the Rayleigh scattering process is more effective for shorter wavelengths than for longer wavelengths, the distant star appears redder in color than the light originally emitted by the star. Ultraviolet telescopes are unable to study distant stars because the extinction of starlight is so severe at the very short wavelengths of ultraviolet light.

See also: CLOUD, GRAY; CLOUD, WHITE; LIGHT; SCATTER-ING, LIGHT; SKY, COLOR OF

Bibliography

STRUTT, J. W. (LORD RAYLEIGH). "On the Transmission of Light Through an Atmosphere Containing Small Particles in Suspension and on the Origin of the Blue Sky." *Philos. Mag.* **47** (5), 375 (1899); *Sci. Papers* **IV**, 397 (1903).

JOHN T. PARK

SCATTERING, RUTHERFORD

"Rutherford scattering" is the term used to describe the scattering of heavy charged particles, such as α particles, by the electric field of the nucleus. It acquired its name from the pioneering work of the English physicist Ernest Rutherford in the early 1900s. Rutherford scattered α particles, emitted by radioactive substances, from heavy atoms such as gold and silver. These experiments resulted in the discovery of the atomic nucleus.

The electron had been discovered only a few years earlier in 1897, and there was much conjecture as to the structure of the atom. One of the popular models was called the "plum pudding" model because it assumed that the positive charge of the atom was arranged uniformly as a fluid in a spherical volume with electrons distributed throughout (like raisins in a plum pudding), making the atom electrically neutral.

To learn more about atomic structure, Rutherford devised an experiment in which rapidly moving α particles were scattered from a thin gold foil. Since the α particle is more than 7,000 times heavier than the electron, it was expected that all of the α particles would be transmitted with perhaps very slight deflections as the result of scattering from the electrons. Rutherford was astounded to find that a few of them were scattered at angles greater than 90°. To him this was rather like shooting cannon balls into a region populated by ping pong balls and having the cannon ball bounce backward as the result of the collision. From this result he concluded there had to be very heavy and, probably, positively charged objects in the foil, which he surmised must be the nuclei of the atoms.

With these results in mind, Rutherford proposed a new atomic model. According to this model the atom would consist of a small, massive, positively charged nucleus with charge Ze, where Z is the atomic number and e is the charge on the electron. Almost all of the mass of the atom would be concentrated in this nucleus. The electrons must circulate in some manner about this nucleus. The observed scattering of α particles could be explained by a single encounter of the α particle with a nucleus. Assuming that the force experienced by the α particle was given by Coulomb's law, Rutherford was able both to predict that the α particles would be deflected in a hyperbolic path, and to derive an expression for the number of particles scattered into a detector placed at some angle relative to the direction of the incident α particles (see Fig. 1). He predicted that this number would be proportional to the square of the atomic number of the scattering nucleus, proportional to the thickness of the foil (if not too thick), inversely proportional to the square of the kinetic energy of the α particle, and inversely proportional to the fourth power of the sine of half the scattering angle. These predictions were all verified by very careful experiments performed by Hans Geiger and Ernest Marsden in 1913.

Using this model, Rutherford also was able to make a rough estimate of the size of the nucleus. By assuming a head-on collision between the α particle and the nucleus, one can estimate the distance of closest approach for the α particle and nucleus. This turns out to be something like 4×10^{-14} m for the gold nucleus. This is much larger than the radius of

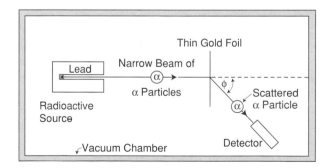

Figure 1 Schematic diagram of a Rutherford scattering experiment. Since the range of α particles in air is only a few centimeters, the experiment must be carried out in a vacuum chamber from which most of the air has been removed.

the gold nucleus (which we now know to be about 6 $\times 10^{-15}$ m), but still small enough to show that the nucleus is very small compared with the size of the atom as a whole, which even at that time was known to be roughly 10^{-10} m.

See also: ATOM; NUCLEUS; PARTICLE PHYSICS; RUTHERFORD, ERNEST

Bibliography

ANDRADE, E. N. DA C. *Rutherford and the Nature of the Atom* (Doubleday, Garden City, NY, 1964).

EVE, A. S. *Rutherford* (Macmillan, New York, 1939).

RICHTMEYER, F. K.; KENNARD, E. H., and COOPER, J. N. *Introduction to Modern Physics*, 6th ed. (McGraw-Hill, New York, 1969).

WILSON, D. *Rutherford: Simple Genius* (MIT Press, Cambridge, MA, 1983).

ROBERT L. STEARNS

SCHRÖDINGER, ERWIN

b. Vienna, Austria, August 12, 1887; *d.* Vienna, Austria, January 4, 1961; *quantum theory.*

Schrödinger's mother, Georgine, was the daughter of a famous Austrian inorganic chemist, Alexander Bauer, and his English wife, Emily Russell. His father, Rudolf Schrödinger, had been a student of Bauer's. Erwin, an only child, grew up in a prosperous Viennese household, bilingual in German and English. After attending the Akademisches Gymnasium (high school), where he was first in his class each year, Schrödinger entered Vienna University in 1906 and studied experimental physics under Franz Exner and theoretical physics under Friedrich Hasenöhrl, the successor to Ludwig Boltzmann. Schrödinger graduated with a Ph.D. in 1910. After a year of military training, he returned to Vienna University to take charge of the large first-year physics laboratory. His research in theoretical physics earned him in early 1914 a position as *Privatdozent*, the first rank on the academic ladder.

At the outbreak of World War I, Schrödinger was called to service as an officer in the Fortress Artillery. He received a citation for valor in the Battle of Isonozo on the Italian front (1915). When the war ended, he returned to his university post.

Hasenöhrl had been killed in the war, and the postwar economic chaos had reduced university physics in Vienna to a miserable situation. Nevertheless, Schrödinger managed to publish a fair amount of competent, but hardly outstanding, theoretical work. He became recognized as an expert in color theory. At this time (1920), he married Annemarie [Anny] Bertel, an unsophisticated young lady from Salzburg. Despite many perturbations, due mainly to Erwin's extramarital love affairs, their marriage endured until they were separated by his death. The Schrödingers had no children of their own, but Erwin fathered three daughters by three different lovers. To secure a salary adequate to support a wife, Schrödinger was forced to leave Austria. After brief stays at Jena, Stuttgart, and Breslau, he was appointed professor of theoretical physics at the University of Zürich.

Schrödinger's work now moved into the mainstream of European physics, the study of the theory of subatomic particles and the interaction of radiation with matter. He maintained contacts with Albert Einstein, Niels Bohr, Max Planck, and Hendrik Lorentz. The immediate inspiration for his discovery of wave mechanics was his work on the quantum statistics of ideal gases, which led him to study the 1924 Paris doctoral thesis of Louis de Broglie on the wave nature of particles. In an explosion of creative activity unsurpassed in the history of science, Schrödinger published in 1926 six papers that changed forever the foundations of physics. He provided a fundamental equation that governed the development of physical systems in space and in time. (Matrix mechanics, discovered by Werner Heisenberg in 1925, was shown to be a mathematical alternative of the Schrödinger equation, but it does not provide a conceptual model of the system under study nor lend itself to philosophical interpretation.)

The Schrödinger equation can be written as it appears with his portrait on the Austrian 500-schilling banknote:

$$(h/2\pi i)\, \partial\Psi/\partial t = H\Psi.$$

Here Ψ is the wave function, which is the fundamental entity that determines the probability that the system will be found in a specified state, $\partial\Psi/\partial t$ is the rate of change of Ψ with time, H is the operator for the total energy of the system, h is Planck's constant, and i is $\sqrt{-1}$.

In 1927 Schrödinger was called to succeed Max Planck as professor of theoretical physics at the University of Berlin. He was now forty years old, and he never again published any work nearly as important as his wave mechanics. When Adolf Hitler assumed power in 1933, Schrödinger left for a fellowship at Magdalen College, Oxford. (He was the only outstanding physical scientist, without any Jewish family, who left Germany in opposition to Nazi policies.) Just as he reached England, it was announced that he and P. A. M. Dirac had been awarded the 1933 Nobel Prize in physics for "the discovery of new forms of atomic theory and applications of them."

In 1936 Schrödinger accepted joint professorships at the Universities of Graz and Vienna and, thus, was trapped in Austria when Hitler seized the country in the *Anschluss* of 1938. After failing in an attempt to appease the Nazis, he escaped with Anny to Dublin, where Eamon de Valera had established an Institute for Advanced Studies with a division of theoretical physics designed especially for him. Schrödinger stayed in Dublin for seventeen years. His principal work there was an ultimately unsuccessful search for a unified field theory of gravitation and electromagnetism, carried out in parallel with similar unsuccessful research by Einstein in Princeton. In 1944 he published *What Is Life?*, based on a series of Dublin lectures. This small book heralded the beginnings of a new science, molecular biology. It clearly stated the concept of the genetic code and inspired many creative scientists, such as James Watson and Francis Crick, to turn to biological problems. A later book, *Mind and Matter* (1958), contains highly original insights into psychobiology and the possible future of science.

In 1956 Schrödinger returned to Vienna, where he was received with great acclaim and a special professorship at the university. He died in 1961 of complications due to a weakened heart and respiratory system and was buried in a corner of the churchyard in the village of Alpbach in the Tirol, the place in the world that he loved the best.

Schrödinger was the most philosophical of the creators of modern physics. Amid the cold and starvation of postwar Vienna, he read every word of the writings of Arthur Schopenhauer and through him was led to study in depth the Indian philosophers. He came to believe in the ideas of Vedanta, an orthodox system of Hindu philosophy that teaches the coherent unity of all individual minds in a universal mind, which is the cause and essence of our being and our world. His book *My World View* (1961) contains an eloquent presentation of this philosophy.

See also: SCHRÖDINGER EQUATION; WAVE FUNCTION; WAVE MECHANICS; WAVE–PARTICLE DUALITY, HISTORY OF

Bibliography

MEHRA, J., and RECHENBERG, H. *The Historical Development of Quantum Theory* (Springer-Verlag, New York, 1987).

MOORE, W. *Schrödinger: Life and Thought* (Cambridge University Press, Cambridge, Eng., 1989).

SCHRÖDINGER, E. *What Is Life?, with Mind and Matter, and Autobiographical Sketches* (Cambridge University Press, Cambridge, Eng., 1992).

WALTER MOORE

SCHRÖDINGER EQUATION

The Schrödinger equation is a partial differential equation of quantum mechanics used to calculate wave functions and energies of atomic and molecular systems. It is a phenomenological equation that applies to nonrelativistic physical situations and is solved to gain insight into the properties of a physical system. For the general case, an infinite set of coupled integro-differential equations have to be calculated.

The discovery of the electron in 1897 by Joseph John Thomson led to a model of the atom as a structure made up of positively charged protons and negatively charged electrons. Ernest Rutherford and his colleagues, in a series of experiments in 1911, discovered that the positive charge in an atom was concentrated in a region of space much smaller than the size of the atom. This led to a picture of the atom as a miniature solar system consisting of a heavy positively charged nucleus about which a group of electrons move.

In 1900 Max Planck explained the distribution of electromagnetic radiation emitted by a blackbody by postulating that the radiation was emitted in discrete quanta; that is, electromagnetic radiation can be particle-like. If the frequency of the radiation is ν, then the energy E is related to ν through the equation

$$E = h\nu, \qquad (1)$$

where h is Planck's constant. Albert Einstein used the Planck hypothesis to explain how light caused metals such as sodium to emit electrons. He predicted that the kinetic energy of the emitted electrons is directly proportional to the frequency of the radiation and that variation of the intensity of the incident light only changed the number of electrons emitted, not their kinetic energy. Thus, Einstein hypothesized that the energy of light is not spread out through the wave, as classical electrodynamics would have it, but is concentrated into photons of energy $h\nu$. The emission of an electron from the surface only takes place when the electron is struck by a photon whose energy exceeds the energy binding the electron to the metal.

Niels Bohr subsequently combined the insight provided by the Rutherford experiment with the quantum hypotheses of Planck and Einstein to make the first quantitative model of the atom. Bohr postulated that only circular orbits for the electron were possible and, more specifically, only those orbits for which the angular momentum of the electron was an integral multiple of the Planck constant divided by 2π. (Classically, the angular momentum of an electron moving in a circular orbit is equal to the product of its momentum p and the radius of the orbit.) Contrary to classical electromagnetic theory, Bohr postulated that the total energy of the electron was constant while it moved around the proton in one of its allowed orbits and that it radiated energy only when it passed from one allowed orbit to a second allowed orbit of lower energy. With these postulates, Bohr calculated that a spectral transition in hydrogen from the state with a quantum number m to that with a quantum number n could take place with emission of light of frequency

$$\nu = \frac{E_m E_n}{ch}, \qquad (2)$$

where c is the velocity of light. When the values for the allowed energy levels are substituted into this expression, the allowed frequencies are

$$\nu = R_H \left(\frac{1}{n^2} - \frac{1}{m^2} \right), \qquad (3)$$

where R_H is the Rydberg constant. This expression agrees with an empirical formula that describes the hydrogen spectrum lines, where n has the values 1, 2, 3, 4, 5 for the Lyman, Balmer, Paschen, Brackett, and Pfund series of lines, respectively.

Louis de Broglie hypothesized that the electron behaved like a wave, with wavelength λ, that depended for its momentum on the relationship

$$\lambda = \frac{h}{p}; \qquad (4)$$

that is, electromagnetic radiation is wavelike, and electrons obey the laws of wave motion in the same way that photons do. This hypothesis was confirmed by a series of experiments by Clinton J. Davisson and Lester H. Germer, who demonstrated that diffraction experiments very similar to those on light may be performed with a beam of electrons. De Broglie explained the Bohr orbits as circles of circumference given by an integral number of wavelengths.

Erwin Schrödinger described the wave behavior of the electron in 1926 by a partial differential equation, now known as the Schrödinger equation. Solutions of this equation are called the wave functions Φ of the electron. Schrödinger found that those solutions for which the amplitude of the wave function remained large around the nucleus predicted for the electron a discrete set of possible energies, which were the same as those predicted by the Bohr theory. Max Born showed that the absolute value squared of the wave function gives the relative probability of the electron at a given point in space and time if a measurement is made.

Consider the motion of photons in an electromagnetic field. According to Maxwell's equations, the photons move in the form of waves that obey the equation of wave motion

$$\frac{d^2 A}{dx^2} + \frac{d^2 A}{dy^2} + \frac{d^2 A}{dz^2} = \frac{1}{c^2}\frac{d^2 A}{dt^2}, \qquad (5)$$

where A is the amplitude of the wave. The photon is not definitely located in any part of the wave, but the probability of finding a photon at any point is given by the square of the amplitude at that point.

The energy E of the photon is connected with the frequency ν of the wave motion by the Einstein relation, Eq. (1), and the momentum of the photon p is given by Eq. (4).

If the Einstein relation is also valid for electron waves, the velocity of the waves is

$$v = \lambda \nu = \frac{E}{p}. \tag{6}$$

The differential equation of the wave motion is then

$$\frac{d^2\Phi}{dx^2} + \frac{d^2\Phi}{dy^2} + \frac{d^2\Phi}{dz^2} = \frac{1}{v^2}\frac{d^2\Phi}{dt^2} = \frac{p^2}{E^2}\frac{d^2\Phi}{dt^2}, \tag{7}$$

where Φ is the amplitude of the electron wave. For a solution that represents standing waves, Φ may be written in the form

$$\Phi = \phi \exp(-2\pi i \nu t), \tag{8}$$

where ϕ is a function of the Cartesian coordinates x, y, and z, but not of time t. For the probability of finding the electron at a point to be real and positive, the square of the absolute value of Φ must be taken. Substituting Eq. (8) into Eq. (7) gives

$$\frac{d^2\phi}{dx^2} + \frac{d^2\phi}{dy^2} + \frac{d^2\phi}{dz^2} = \frac{-4\pi^2 p^2}{h^2}\phi \tag{9}$$

as the differential equation for ϕ. The kinetic energy of the electron is $T = E - V$, where V, the potential energy, is connected with the momentum by the relation $T = p^2/(2m)$, where m is the mass of the electron. Thus, Eq. (9) may be written

$$\frac{d^2\phi}{dx^2} + \frac{d^2\phi}{dy^2} + \frac{d^2\phi}{dz^2} + \frac{8\pi^2 m}{h^2}(E - V)\phi = 0. \tag{10}$$

This is the first of Schrödinger's equations, the time-independent equation, by means of which most applications of nonrelativistic quantum mechanics are made. Each function $\phi(x,y,z)$ satisfying Eq. (10) corresponds to a state of the particle for which the energy is precisely known and does not change with time. From the form of Eq. (8), it may be noted that Eq. (10) may also be written as

$$\frac{d^2\phi}{dx^2} + \frac{d^2\phi}{dy^2} + \frac{d^2\phi}{dz^2}$$
$$+ \frac{8\pi^2 m}{h^2}\left(\frac{h}{2\pi i}\frac{d}{dt} - V\right)\Phi = 0, \tag{11}$$

which is the second of Schrödinger's equations, the time-dependent equation. The full wave function $\Phi(x,y,z,t)$ for the state is given by Eq. (8). Such a state is called a stationary state in which the energy of the state is sharp or well defined. For a given system, there are, in general, many stationary states with negative energy ($E < 0$), which are necessarily bound states, and an infinity of stationary states with positive energy ($E > 0$), which are usually referred to as continuum states. In general, a system whose potential energy is independent of time will be in a mixture of stationary states, and its energy will not be sharp.

In 1925 Werner Heisenberg developed the first version of quantum theory, which led to a formulation in which the observables are represented by matrices. This matrix-mechanics approach is completely equivalent to the Schrödinger time-dependent wave-function formulation. The approaches have a common abstract-vector-theory skeleton. The simple one-electron hydrogenic-atom system—that is, an electron of charge $-e$ moving around a nucleus of charge $+Ze$—can be solved exactly. The Schrödinger equation for the problem can be reduced to that of a central-force problem and then solved. The energy eigenvalues are

$$E_n - \frac{hcR_H Z^2}{n^2}, \tag{13}$$

where n is an integer. The energy levels of the hydrogen-like atom are degenerate because more than one state corresponds to a specific value of n, the principal quantum number. These degenerate states are characterized by additional quantum numbers l and m, which are related to the spherical harmonics of the wave function.

While it is possible to describe the Hamiltonian for a system more complicated than hydrogen, it is not possible to solve exactly the resulting Schrödinger equation to obtain the wave functions that contain all that is known about the properties of the system. There are three conflicting goals in the solution of Schrödinger's equation that have to be balanced:

accuracy; ability to interpret the results; and ability to treat as large a system as possible. Most progress has been made through some form of an orbital approximation in which the electronic states of a system are constructed from one-electron orbitals.

To understand more complex atoms containing many electrons, the many-electron Schrödinger equation must be solved, which is complicated because the motion of any electron is coupled to the motion of the other electrons with which it interacts. One approach to a solution is to treat the electron-electron interaction as a perturbation. An entire electronic sequence may be handled in a single calculation by using nonrelativistic Z^{-1} expansions of atomic energies.

Another simplifying approximation for the many-electron case is to use an independent-particle model in which the electron moves in the average central field of the other electrons. Douglas R. Hartree used an iterative method of self-consistent fields to make significant advances in the determination of energy levels for complex atoms. Hartree and Vladimir Fock refined this method by explicitly allowing for spin pairing.

The Schrödinger equation for molecules is more difficult to solve than that for atoms. However, Born and J. Robert Oppenheimer introduced an approximation that permits the motion of the molecular electrons to be treated independently of that of the nuclei. This approximation is valid in a wide variety of cases and is applicable to solids as well as molecules. Wave functions are obtained that describe the motion of the electrons, keeping the nuclei fixed in space, since the electrons traverse their orbits in a much shorter time than that required for nuclear motion. Then the motion of the nuclei is considered in a smeared-out negative-charge density for a particular electronic state throughout the region of space immediately surrounding the nuclei.

In 1928 P. A. M. Dirac discovered a generalization of the Schrödinger equation that takes proper account of special relativity. Dirac found that this equation required that the electron have intrinsic spin $\frac{1}{2}$. One of the assumptions in the nonrelativistic Schrödinger theory is that all material particles move with small velocities. This assumption is relaxed in the Dirac equation.

See also: BOHR'S ATOMIC THEORY; BROGLIE WAVELENGTH, DE; DAVISSON–GERMER EXPERIMENT; DIFFRACTION, ELECTRON; ELECTRON, DISCOVERY OF; MAXWELL'S EQUATIONS; QUANTUM MECHANICS, CREATION OF; QUANTUM THEORY, ORIGINS OF; SCHRÖDINGER, ERWIN; WAVE FUNCTION

Bibliography

EISBERG, R.; and RESNICK, R. *Quantum Physics: Of Atoms, Molecules, Solids, Nuclei, and Particles,* 2nd ed. (Wiley, New York, 1985).

MORRISON, M. A. *Understanding Quantum Physics* (Prentice Hall, Englewood Cliffs, NJ, 1990).

SCHIFF, L. I. *Quantum Mechanics,* 3rd ed. (McGraw-Hill, New York, 1968).

RONALD J. W. HENRY

SCHWARZSCHILD BLACK HOLE

See BLACK HOLE, SCHWARZSCHILD

SCIENTIFIC METHOD

Richard Feynman, one of the leading theoretical physicists of the twentieth century, wrote, "The principle of science, the definition, almost, is the following: *The test of all knowledge is experiment.* Experiment is the *sole judge* of scientific 'truth'" (Feynman, Leighton, and Sands, 1963, p. 1). Although an activity as varied and successful as science cannot be summed up in any simple method, Feynman has gotten at its essence. The scientific method given in introductory physics texts (i.e., gather data, form a hypothesis, work out the implications of the hypothesis, test it by experiment, and then formulate a theory) is also far too simple.

The interaction between theory and experiment is quite complex. One cannot really answer the question, "Which comes first, experiment or theory?" Experiment plays many roles in science. One of its important roles is to test theories, but it can also call for a new theory, either by showing that the accepted theory is incorrect or by exhibiting a new phenomenon that needs explanation. Experiment can also provide hints toward the structure or mathematical form of a theory. It can also have a life of its own, independent of theory. Scientists may investigate a phenomenon just because it looks interesting, and this will also provide evidence for a future theory to explain. Theory also does more than provide predictions for experiments to test, although this is certainly one of its important roles. Theory can suggest fruitful directions for experimental research and can help in the design of an experiment by providing an estimate of the size of the effects expected, which can determine whether or not the experiment is feasible. Theory may also be crucial in the analysis of experimental data.

In all of this activity, however, we must remember that science is fallible. Theoretical calculations, experimental results, or the comparison between experiment and theory may all be wrong. Science is more complex than "The scientist proposes, nature disposes." It may not always be clear what the scientist is proposing. Theories often need to be articulated and clarified. It also may not be clear how nature is disposing. Experiments may not always give clearcut results, and they may even disagree for a time.

We can learn about the methodology of science not by a priori thought, but rather by looking at illustrative episodes from the history of physics. It is in the practice of science that we can see its methods. Let us consider first an episode in which science worked clearly and simply. This was a crucial experiment, one that decided unequivocally between two competing theories. The episode was that of the discovery that parity, mirror-reflection symmetry or left-right symmetry, is not conserved in the weak interactions. Parity conservation was a well-established and strongly believed principle of physics. As every student of introductory physics learns, if we wish to determine the magnetic force between two currents, we first determine the direction of the magnetic field due to the first current and then determine the force exerted on the second current by that field. We use two right-hand rules. We get exactly the same answer, however, if we use two left-hand rules. This is left-right symmetry, or parity conservation, in electromagnetism.

In the early 1950s physicists were faced with a problem known as the "$\tau - \theta$" puzzle. Based on one set of criteria, that of mass and lifetime, two particles (the τ and the θ) appeared to be the same, whereas on another set of criteria, spin and intrinsic parity, they appeared to be different. Tsung-Dao Lee and Chen-Ning Yang realized that the problem

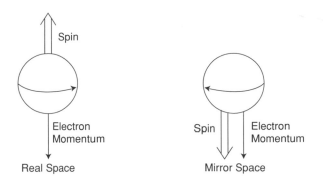

Figure 1 Spin and momentum in beta decay in both real space and in mirror space.

would be solved and that the two particles would be different decay modes of the same particle if parity were not conserved in the decay of the particles, a weak interaction. They examined the evidence for parity conservation and found, to their surprise, that although there was strong evidence that parity was conserved in the strong (nuclear) and electromagnetic interactions, there was, in fact, no supporting evidence that it was conserved in the weak interaction. It had never been tested.

Lee and Yang suggested several experiments that would test their hypothesis that parity was not conserved in the weak interactions. One was the beta decay of oriented nuclei (see Fig. 1). Suppose the decay electron is emitted in a direction opposite to the spin of the nucleus. In the mirror the electron is emitted in the same direction as the spin. The mirror image of the decay is different from the real decay. This would violate parity conservation, or

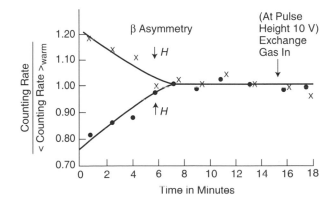

Figure 2 Relative counting rates for beta particles from the decay of oriented Co^{60} nuclei for different orientations of the nuclear spin (field directions).

mirror symmetry. Parity would be conserved only if, in the decay of a collection of nuclei, equal numbers of electrons were emitted in both directions. This was the experimental test performed by Chien-Shiung Wu and her collaborators. They aligned Co^{60} nuclei and counted the number of decay electrons in the two directions, along the nuclear spin and opposite to the spin. Their results are shown in Fig. 2 and indicate clearly that more electrons are emitted opposite to the spin than along the spin. Parity is not conserved.

The development and acceptance of the theory of beta decay during the 1930s and early 1940s illustrates a more complex interaction between theory and experiment, as well as their varied roles in science. Although radioactivity had been discovered by Henri Becquerel in 1896 and experimental work on the energy spectrum of electrons emitted in beta decay began in the early twentieth century, there was no successful theory of the phenomenon until Enrico Fermi's theory in 1934.

Part of the reason for this delay was that the constituents of the atomic nucleus were not known. It was only after the discovery of the neutron by James Chadwick in 1932 that it was realized that the nucleus was composed of protons and neutrons. The continuous energy spectrum of beta-decay electrons also posed a problem (see Fig. 3). If beta decay were a two-body decay (neutron → proton + electron), then applying the laws of conservation of energy and of conservation of momentum requires that the energy of the electron have a definite value, not a continuous spectrum. Thus, the observed continuous energy spectrum cast doubt on both of these

conservation laws. Wolfgang Pauli suggested that a neutral particle of small or perhaps zero mass, the neutrino, was also emitted in beta decay. This solved the problem of the continuous energy spectrum (a three-body decay, neutron → proton + electron + neutrino, will have such a spectrum) and also saved the conservation laws. This was a case in which experimental results, the continuous energy spectrum, called for a new theory and suggested the existence of a new particle. (The neutrino was not directly observed until 1956, although the empirical success of Fermi's theory of beta decay, as well as its role in the preservation of conservation of energy and momentum had already persuaded physicists that it existed). Fermi incorporated a nucleus consisting of protons and neutrons as well as the proposed neutrino in his theory.

Fermi's theory fit the general features of the experimental results, but it was quickly pointed out by Emil Konopinski and George Uhlenbeck that Fermi's theory predicted fewer low-energy electrons than were observed (see Fig. 4). They proposed a modification of Fermi's theory that fit the experimental results better. Throughout the 1930s the experimental evidence favored the Konopinski–Uhlenbeck (KU) theory over Fermi's theory (see Fig. 5), although it was not conclusive. It was found that if the radioactive sources used in the experiments were made thinner, Fermi's theory fit better than the KU theory. The excess of low-energy elec-

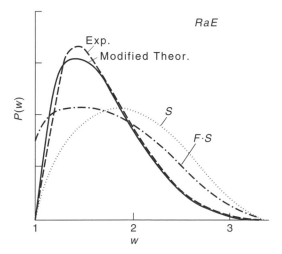

Figure 4 Energy spectrum of the beta decay of RaE. S is the statistical factor, $F \cdot S$ is the Fermi theory, and Modified Theory is the KU prediction. Exp. is the experimental result.

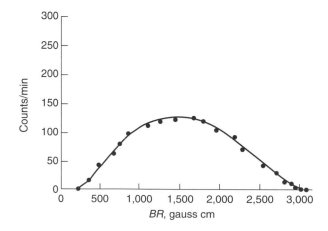

Figure 3 Continuous energy spectrum from the beta decay of Cs^{137}.

trons was caused by electron energy loss in the source.

It was also found that the comparison between theory and experiment was incorrect. Fermi's theory applied only to what were called "allowed" decays, whereas some of the observed decays were "forbidden" decays. The energy spectra predicted for allowed and forbidden decays were different. When the experimental data were compared with the appropriate theoretical predictions, the evidence supported Fermi's theory (see Fig. 6). This combination of improved experimental apparatus and proper theory-experiment comparison led to the acceptance of Fermi's theory. As Konopinski himself remarked, "Thus, the evidence of the spectra, which has previously comprised the sole support of the KU theory, now definitely fails to support it" (Konopinski, 1943, p. 218).

Thus, experimental evidence decided between two competing theories, those of Fermi and of Konopinski and Uhlenbeck, but it was not a simple process. Not only were experimental results incor-

rect, but so was the comparison between theory and experiment. Scientists had to find these errors and correct them before a proper decision could be made. Even before Fermi proposed his theory, experimenters had already acquired many results that could be used to test it. In order for Fermi to propose his theory, other physicists had to determine the structure of the nucleus. We have also seen how experimental results led Pauli to suggest the existence of a new particle that would explain those results, which was then used by Fermi in his theory. This is the complexity of real science and its methods.

If experiment is to play all of these important roles in science, then we must have good reasons for believing in the correctness of experimental results. Physicists use many strategies to argue for the correctness of their results. Perhaps the most important and widely used strategy is that of experimental checks. The experimenter checks that the apparatus can reproduce known results. For example, if we wished to argue that the spectrum of a substance obtained with a new type of spectrometer is correct, we might check that this new spectrometer could reproduce the known Balmer series in hydrogen. If we correctly observe the Balmer series, then we strengthen our belief that the spectrometer is working properly. This also strengthens our belief in the results obtained with that spectrometer.

Another widely used strategy is that of independent confirmation, observing the same result with two different experimental apparatuses. If we observe the same astronomical object with both an

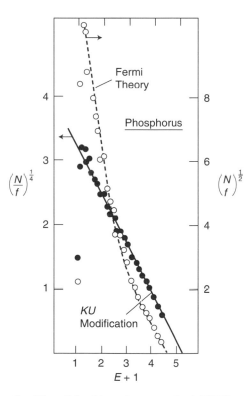

Figure 5 The (black) points marked "KU" modification should fall as they do on a straight line. If the Fermi theory is followed the (white) points should follow a straight line as they clearly do not.

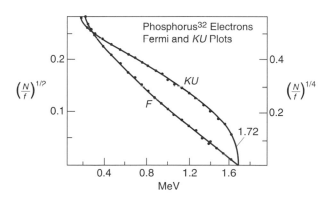

Figure 6 Fermi and KU plots for electrons from the decay of phosphorus. The better theory is that which gives the better fit to a straight line.

ordinary telescope and with a radiotelescope, then we have good reason to believe the observation. It would be extremely unlikely that two such different experimental apparatuses would produce the same incorrect result. If we can eliminate all plausible sources of experimental error and all alternative explanations of the result, then we also have good reason to believe the result. When scientists claimed to have observed electric discharges in the rings of Saturn, they argued for their result by showing that it could not have been caused by defects in the telemetry, by interaction with the environment of Saturn, by lightning, or by dust. The only explanation left of their result was that it was due to electric discharges in the rings. In addition, the same result was observed by both Voyager 1 and Voyager 2. This provided independent confirmation.

Sometimes scientists may argue for a result by intervening in their experiment. One reason we might believe that the image of a cell observed with a microscope is correct is because we have injected fluid or stain into the cell. We expect to observe that the cell changes size or color. When we do, we believe our microscope is working properly, and we trust the images we see.

These strategies provide us with good reasons to believe experimental results. The results are then legitimately used in the various ways we have already discussed.

The two episodes we have discussed, that of the discovery of parity nonconservation and that of the development of a theory of beta decay, have shown us that science does not always work simply, although they have shown us that it works well. There is, in fact, no one scientific method. There are, rather, many scientific methods. Which one is used depends on the circumstances. It is this flexibility that makes the practice of science so interesting.

See also: CPT THEOREM; DECAY, BETA; EXPERIMENTAL PHYSICS; INTERACTION, WEAK; NEUTRINO, HISTORY OF; NEUTRON, DISCOVERY OF; PARITY; RADIOACTIVITY, DISCOVERY OF; THEORETICAL PHYSICS

Bibliography

ACKERMANN, R. *Data, Instruments, and Theory* (Princeton University Press, Princeton, NJ, 1985).

FERMI, E. "Attempt at a Theory of β-Rays." *Il Nuovo Cimento* **11**, 1–21 (1934).

FEYERABEND, P. *Against Method* (Humanities Press, London, 1975).

FEYNMAN, R. P.; LEIGHTON, R. B.; and SANDS, M. *The Feynman Lectures on Physics*, Vol. 1 (Addison-Wesley, Reading, MA, 1963).

FRANKLIN, A. *The Neglect of Experiment* (Cambridge University Press, Cambridge, Eng., 1986).

FRANKLIN, A. *Experiment, Right or Wrong* (Cambridge University Press, Cambridge, Eng., 1990).

GALISON, P. *How Experiments End* (University of Chicago Press, Chicago, 1987).

HALLIDAY, D. *Introductory Nuclear Physics* (Wiley, New York, 1950).

KONOPINSKI, E. "Beta-Decay." *Rev. Mod. Phys.* **15**, 209–245 (1943).

KONOPINSKI, E., and UHLENBECK, G., "On the Fermi Theory of Radioactivity." *Phys. Rev.* **48**, 7–12 (1935).

KUHN, T. S. *The Structure of Scientific Revolutions*, 2nd ed. (University of Chicago Press, Chicago, 1970).

KURIE, F. N. D.; RICHARDSON, J. R.; and PAXTON, H. C. "The Radiation from Artificially Produced Radioactive Substances." *Phys. Rev.* **49**, 368–381 (1936).

LAWSON, J. L. "The Beta-Ray Spectra of Phosphorus, Sodium, and Cobalt." *Phys. Rev.* **56**, 131–136 (1939).

POPPER, K. *The Logic of Scientific Discovery* (Basic Books, New York, 1959).

WU, C. S.; AMBLER, E.; HAYWARD, R. W.; HOPPES, D. D.; and HUDSON, R. P. "Experimental Test of Parity Nonconservation in Beat Decay." *Phys. Rev.* **105**, 1413–1415 (1957).

ALLAN FRANKLIN

SCIENTIFIC NOTATION

Scientists must deal with numbers ranging from the extremely small to the extremely large. For example, physicists explore distances from the size of a proton (about 10^{-15} m) to the size of the known universe (about 10^{26} m) and masses that range from the mass of an electron (about 10^{-30} kg) to the mass of the Sun (about 2×10^{30} kg). To accommodate these wide ranges of numbers in a compact form, scientists make use of scientific notation, also known as exponential notation, to express numbers like those in the examples. In addition to providing a simplified way of writing large and small numbers, scientific notation provides a handy way of easily representing the precision one may want to claim for such numbers.

As indicated in the previous examples, scientific notation makes use of powers of ten to avoid writing

Table 1 Common Prefixes and Abbreviations

Abbreviation	Prefix	Power of Ten	Example	Numerical Equivalent
a	atto	10^{-18}	attojoule	10^{-18} J
f	femto	10^{-15}	femtosecond	10^{-15} s
p	pico	10^{-12}	picosecond	10^{-12} s
n	nano	10^{-9}	nanometer	10^{-9} m
μ	micro	10^{-6}	microwatt	10^{-6} W
m	milli	10^{-3}	milligauss	.001 G
c	centi	10^{-2}	centimeter	.01 m
d	deci	10^{-1}	decibel	.1 bel
d	adeka	10^{1}	dekagram	10 g
h	hecto	10^{2}	hectometer	100 m
k	kilo	10^{3}	kilogram	1000 g
M	mega	10^{6}	megabyte	10^{6} byte
G	giga	10^{9}	giga-electron volt	10^{9} eV
T	tera	10^{12}	terawatt	10^{12} W
P	peta	10^{15}	petajoule	10^{15} J
E	exa	10^{18}	exajoule	10^{18} J

an excessive number of zeros. For instance, Earth has a radius of about 6,370,000 m = 6.37 × 1,000,000 m = $6.37 \times 10 \times 10 \times 10 \times 10 \times 10 \times 10$ m = 6.37×10^{6} m. As a second example, the radius of the core of a typical optical fiber used in communications is about 0.000001 m = 1/1,000,000 m $1/(10 \times 10 \times 10 \times 10 \times 10 \times 10)$ m = 1×10^{-6} m. Therefore, the general rule is that to obtain the appropriate power of ten starting from a number in standard decimal format (e.g., 5,280 or 0.004), the decimal point must be moved a certain number of digits to the right or left. If it is moved to the left, the power of ten is increased by one unit for each place moved, so 5,280 is represented by 5.28×10^{3}. If the decimal point is moved to the right, the power of ten is decreased by one unit for each place moved, so 0.004 is the same as 4×10^{-3}. Thus the following representations are all equivalent (i.e., they all express the same number): $0.637 \times 10^{2} = 6.37 \times 10^{1} = 63.7 \times 10^{0} = 63.7 \times 10^{-1}$, and so on.

In addition to using powers of ten, scientists often use single-letter abbreviations or prefixes based on Greek roots to express numbers. Table 1 lists the most common of these abbreviations along with some examples. The mostly commonly used prefixes and abbreviations are those, such as milli, micro, kilo, and mega, that increase or decrease in multiples of 1,000. Centi appears most commonly with centimeter, and deci almost exclusively with decibel (a unit of power). Hecto and deka are rarely used in physics.

Scientific notation also permits one to express easily the precision with which one knows a number. The precision is most commonly expressed in terms of the number of significant figures. For example, suppose the electrical resistance of a piece of material has been measured to be 10,300,000 Ω. When the number is expressed in this form, it is not clear whether the resistance has been determined to a precision of eight decimal digits (which would require extremely careful measurements and well-calibrated instruments) or if the last five zeros are simply place markers. If the latter situation holds, then the resistance should be written using scientific notation, as 1.03×10^{7} Ω or equivalently as 10.3×10^{6} Ω or 0.103×10^{8} Ω. The standard abbreviations could also be used to write the result as 10.3 MΩ (mega-ohms) or 0.0103 GΩ (giga-ohms). By convention, only the significant figures in the number (those known with confidence) are multiplied by ten raised to the appropriate power. Also, by convention, any leading zeros are ignored in determining the significant figures. For example, 0.0103 has only three significant figures.

See also: SIGNIFICANT FIGURES; SI UNITS

Bibliography

SHIFFER, M. M., and BOWDEN, L. *The Role of Mathematics in Science* (Mathematical Association of America, Washington, DC, 1984).

ROBERT C. HILBORN

SCIENTIFIC REVOLUTION

The Scientific Revolution of the sixteenth and seventeen centuries, sometimes dated more precisely between 1543 (the publication of Nicolaus Copernicus's *De Revolutionibus*) and 1687 (the publication of Isaac Newton's *Principia*), witnessed the thorough transformation of the existing tradition of natural philosophy in Western Europe and the establishment of a new tradition, modern science. The previous tradition had been based on the revival of Aristotelian natural philosophy that formed the core of the curriculum in the medieval universities. Although it is impossible to imagine the Scientific Revolution without the background of rigorous investigation of nature that medieval Aristotelianism provided, that tradition was so completely rejected or transformed that it is difficult to find its traces in the science that reigned in Europe at the end of the seventeenth century. The whole of modern science has developed directly from the new tradition created during the Scientific Revolution.

Nearly everyone accepts the publication of Copernicus's book as the opening engagement of the Scientific Revolution. To solve a number of recognized problems in astronomy, which effectively meant the planetary system, Copernicus proposed that the Sun rather than Earth was at its center and that Earth was one of six planets, revolving like the others in an orbit around the Sun and also rotating daily upon its axis. In this system the puzzling relation of the Sun to the theories of the other planets in Ptolemaic astronomy and the peculiar periodic retrograde motions of the other planets emerged as mere appearances caused by the annual motion of Earth, and the planets acquired a necessary and harmonious order. Since Copernicus continued to share the mystique that heavenly motions can be explained only by compounding uniform motions in the perfect figure, the circle, he had to make use of epicyclic devices just as Ptolemaic astronomers had, and in fact his system did not (and could not) achieve a higher degree of accuracy than the geocentric system, using analogous combinations of epicycles, that he sought to replace.

In the second half of the sixteenth century the observations of the Danish astronomer, Tycho Brahe, amassed a body of data both more extensive and more accurate than any available before. Tycho himself could not believe that Earth is in motion, but his observations passed into the hands of a convinced Copernican, Johannes Kepler, his successor as Imperial Astronomer to the Holy Roman Emperor, who employed the observational data to transform and perfect the heliocentric system. Kepler believed that Tycho's observations of the great comet of 1572 had proved that there are no crystalline orbs, as established natural philosophy held, to carry planets around in their orbits. He concluded that astronomy had to stop adding up the circular motions of multiple orbs and to start considering physical causes, similar to those that move terrestrial bodies, as they operate to move the planets and to hold them in their paths through the immensity of empty space.

Following this program, Kepler arrived at two laws of planetary motion, discovered initially in respect to Mars but generalized to apply equally to the other five planets, which he published in *Astonomia Nova* in 1609. The first law states that planets move, not in circles, but in ellipses with the Sun located at one focus, and the second law that the motions vary so that the radius vector between a planet and the Sun sweeps out areas proportional to elapsed time. Later Kepler added a third law binding the planets into a mathematically defined system: For all the planets, the ratios of the cubes of the mean radii of their orbits to the squares of their periods are identical. These were the first of the mathematical laws of modern science. The redefinition of the old concept of natural law to refer to a mathematical description of a body's motion was another dimension of the Scientific Revolution.

Intimately related to the new astronomy was a new science of mechanics. Without it heliocentric astronomy was impossible, for many of the motions we observe about us, such as the vertical fall of heavy bodies, could not possibly happen on a moving Earth as we observe them to happen if the Aristotelian conception of motion were correct. Early in the seventeenth century, spurred in part by the problem set by heliocentric astronomy, Galileo

Galilei began to rethink the concept of motion, a central category in any natural philosophy. He concluded that motion does not require a cause, contrary to what Aristotle maintained. A body in motion tends to remain in motion; only changes of motion require a cause. We know this concept as the principle of inertia, although Galileo did not use that word and did not conceive of the concept precisely in the form we now accept. Philosophers regard it as the fundamental concept in modern science. Galileo used the new conception of motion to explain away apparent problems arising from the motion of Earth.

Building on his conception of motion, Galileo went on to create something that no system of mechanics before that time had possessed—a mathematical kinematics of motion, of uniform motion in a horizontal plane, of uniformly accelerated motion in a vertical plane, and of the combination of the two in projectile motion. Although Galileo did not express his kinematics in the form of laws, we can regard his system as the second set of mathematical laws in modern science. Before the century was out there would be a number of others, such as the sine law of refraction of light and Boyle's Law relating the pressure and volume of a confined gas.

The new astronomy and the new mechanics contradicted central tenets of Aristotelian natural philosophy, to the extent that the philosophy became untenable if they were accepted as true. It is not surprising, then, that a new natural philosophy, which came to be called the mechanical philosophy, replaced the old ideas in the minds of leaders of the new science shortly before the middle of the seventeenth century. About this time, independently of each other, several philosophers proposed mechanistic natural philosophies that were quite similar to each other. The most influential among them was the philosophy of René Descartes, suggested in his *Discourse on Method* (1637) and published in full in later works. Defining mind as thinking substance and matter as extended substance, Descartes rigorously separated the two, effectively excluding all nonmaterial agency from the operations of nature and leaving the natural order to the blind, inexorable operation of mechanical necessity.

The mechanical philosophy, not just in its Cartesian form, shared a number of things in common with the new astronomy and the new mechanics. It was heliocentric; Descartes imagined a great whirlpool of matter, a vortex, around the Sun bearing the planets, all in the same direction and the same

plane, like wooden balls floating in a stream of water. The philosophy was inconceivable without the new conception of motion; it pictured a system of material particles set in motion originally by God but kept in motion by the fact that motion itself perseveres. The philosophy generalized the assault on common sense. Aristotelian natural philosophy had been a sophisticated elaboration of common sense, which was challenged both by heliocentric astronomy and by the new mechanics. In effect, Descartes added that not just the solar system and not just phenomena of motion, but everything, is different from what it seems. We see about us a world filled with life and qualities. They are all illusions. Particles of matter can join together in structures that display all the phenomena of life. Particles can impinge on nerves, giving rise to sensations that philosophers have mistakenly projected onto the external world. There is nothing out there but particles of inert matter in motion. The world could hardly be more different from what it appears to be.

In another respect, however, the mechanical philosophy was profoundly in tension with the mathematical character of Keplerian astronomy and Galilean mechanics. In their conviction that all the phenomena of nature are produced by particles of matter in motion, mechanical philosophers allowed themselves free rein in imagining mechanisms of theoretical particles that could not be observed. The problem was that the mechanisms did not yield Kepler's and Galileo's mathematical laws. Descartes's vortices were incompatible with Kepler's laws of planetary motion. The various mechanisms invoked to explain why bodies are heavy and fall toward the earth could not produce uniformly accelerated motion. At the end of the century Newton resolved the tension by transforming the mechanical philosophy, expanding its ontology of material particles to include forces of attraction and repulsion between particles. The forces were mathematically defined and became the means by which a universe conceived as particles of matter in motion submitted to precise mathematical treatment. In Newton's *Mathematical Principles of Natural Philosophy* (the *Principia*) the character of modern science was permanently set.

The *Principia* opened by defining a mathematical science of dynamics that completed the new science of mechanics. Newton's three laws of motion, the best known of the mathematical laws enunciated during the Scientific Revolution and still accepted today as the foundation of modern physics, brought together Kepler's kinematics of celestial motion and Galileo's kinematics of terrestrial motion, which both emerged as necessary consequences of Newton's dynamics. Book I of the *Principia* was devoted primarily to idealized orbital dynamics of point masses revolving around hypothetical centers of force. Book II inaugurated the mathematical treatment of bodies moving through resisting media. In Book III Newton applied the conclusions from Book I to the real world as observation and experiment present it and derived the law of universal gravitation. He then employed the law to explicate in precise quantitative terms a number of phenomena not used in the law's derivation—perturbations of the Moon's orbit caused by the attraction of the Sun, a slow conical motion of Earth's axis that gives rise to an appearance known as precession of the equinoxes, the phenomena of tides, and the great comet of 1680–1681, which he treated as a planet-like body orbiting the Sun in a conical path. By synthesizing the major prior achievements of the new science and raising them to a higher level of sophistication, Newton marked the culmination of the Scientific Revolution and established the pattern for the whole of modern science.

The seventeenth century witnessed significant other work in the physical sciences, especially in optics and chemistry, and significant work in the life sciences. Nevertheless, the heart of the Scientific Revolution, which undermined and rejected Aristotelian natural philosophy and replaced it with a radically different image of nature and of scientific knowledge, lay in the allied sciences of heliocentric astronomy and mechanics.

There was also a methodological dimension to the Scientific Revolution, the establishment of experimentation as the distinctive method of science. Experimentation was not an invention of the seventeenth century. Nevertheless, when the century opened, no one would have ventured to assert that experimentation was the characteristic procedure of scientific investigation. During the century a number of investigations demonstrated both the power of experimental procedure and the growing awareness of that power. Beginning with Galileo's discussion of why siphons would not operate over a rise of more than about thirty feet, and passing across Europe through the endeavors of Torricelli, Pascal, and Boyle, the probing of phenomena related to the barometer led to the mathematical law that bears Boyle's name. Newton relied on elaborate experimentation to establish the heterogeneity of light and a new theory of the origin of colors. If there had

been experiments before the seventeenth century, there had never been sustained investigations like these. In the future there would be very few investigations in the physical sciences that were not like them, and increasingly the same was true of the life sciences.

At least one other change of immense importance was an essential aspect of the Scientific Revolution. During the time when Copernicus was active, no one in Western Europe doubted that natural philosophy, like all human acitivites, pursued its course within limits set by Christianity. Certain passages in Scripture constituted one of the major obstacles to the heliocentric system, and early in the seventeenth century the Catholic Church condemned it because it was at odds with the overt meaning of these passages. Compare this action with a correspondence between Newton and Thomas Burnet in 1681 about Burnet's book, *The Sacred Theory of the Earth.* From his observations of Earth's surface, Burnet had convinced himself that the biblical account of creation could not be accepted as scientifically valid and that it had to be regarded as a fiction composed by Moses for political purposes. Newton sought to defend *Genesis,* arguing that its account of creation was what science, which was primarily chemistry in this letter, would lead us to expect. Both Burnet and Newton had exactly reversed the earlier locus of authority; instead of using Scripture to judge what was valid in science, they used science to judge what was valid in Scripture. By the end of the seventeenth century, science had emancipated itself from the control of Christianity and vindicated its autonomy. It had done more than this; it had begun to assert its own authority as the dominant enterprise in Western civilization. A once Christian civilization had become a scientific one. Perhaps nothing better expresses the importance of the Scientific Revolution in Western history.

See also: COPERNICAN REVOLUTION; COPERNICUS, NICOLAUS; GALILEI, GALILEO; KEPLER, JOHANNES; KEPLER'S LAWS; KINEMATICS; NEWTON, ISAAC; NEWTONIAN MECHANICS; NEWTONIAN SYNTHESIS; NEWTON'S LAWS

Bibliography

BUTTERFIELD, H. *The Origins of Modern Science, 1300–1800* (Bell, London, 1950).

COHEN, I. B. *The Birth of a New Physics,* rev. ed. (W. W. Norton, New York, 1985).

COHEN, I. B. *Revolution in Science* (Harvard University Press, Cambridge, MA, 1985).

HALL, A. R. *The Revolution in Science, 1500–1750* (Longman, London, 1983).

KUHN, T. S. *The Copernican Revolution* (Harvard University Press, Cambridge, MA, 1957).

WESTFALL, R. S. *The Construction of Modern Science* (Wiley, New York, 1971).

RICHARD S. WESTFALL

SCINTILLATION COUNTER

Scintillation counters are widely used in particle and nuclear physics to detect, count, and measure the energy of charged and neutral elementary particles. Although there are many variations of the basic design, all scintillation counters consist of a scintillating material and a light sensitive detector, such as a photomultiplier tube, which converts the scintillation light into an electrical pulse.

Commonly used scintillation materials include plastics and liquids doped with an organic scintillator, such as p-Terphenyl ($C_{18}H_{14}$), and inorganic crystals, such as thallium-doped sodium iodide NaI(Tl). As charged particles move through these scintillation materials, they give up energy to the atomic electrons in the scintillator. Transitions of these electrons from excited states to their ground state produce the scintillation light. Typically, the wavelength of the emitted light is about 400 nm, which is well matched to the wavelength of maximum quantum efficiency of many photomultiplier tubes. Organic scintillators produce a light output of about one photon for each 100 eV of deposited energy in pulses less than 5 ns in duration and are typically used to detect charged particles. Inorganic crystals, which produce approximately 4 times as much light as organic scintillators in pulses several hundred nanoseconds long, are widely used in applications in which accurate energy determination is more important than speed.

Scintillation counters also detect neutral particles that interact with electrons or undergo nuclear interactions in the scintillation material. Gamma radiation generates light in scintillation material by means of the photoelectric effect, Compton scattering, and pair production. Neutrons can be detected when they undergo interactions with the nuclei of the scintillation material to produce charged, moving, nuclear fragments.

The type of scintillation material used in a particular scintillator counter depends on the specific application of the counter. NaI(Tl), which has a large number of atomic electrons and hence a relatively high probability of a gamma-electron interaction, is commonly used to characterize radioactive sources and to measure the energy of gamma radiation in atomic and nuclear physics experiments. A typical counter assembly consists of a cylindrically shaped, hygroscopic NaI(Tl) crystal 3 in. in diameter and 3 in. long, hermetically sealed in a highly reflective container with a transparent window viewed by a 3-in. photomultiplier tube. The full-width-at-half-maximum energy resolution is about 5 percent for 1-MeV gamma radiation in this type of detector.

Plastic or liquid scintillator counters are widely used in large-area elementary particle physics experiments where it is important simply to detect the passage of a charged particle in a variety of geometries. A typical plastic scintillator assembly consists of a polished and wrapped piece of scintillation plastic optically epoxied along an edge to a clear plastic lightguide viewed by a photomultiplier tube. Because of their very fast signals, large arrays of these detectors have been used extensively to determine whether scattered particles produced in fixed target or colliding beam elementary particle physics experiments satisfy crude geometric patterns of interest and to trigger slower detector systems with much higher position resolution, such as planes of wire chambers, when the conditions are met.

See also: COMPTON EFFECT; PHOTOELECTRIC EFFECT

Bibliography

KNOLL, G. F. *Radiation Detection and Measurement* (Wiley, New York, 1979).

LEO, W. R. *Techniques for Nuclear and Particle Physics Experiments* (Springer-Verlag, Berlin, 1987).

HOWARD NICHOLSON

SEASONS

While Earth revolves around the Sun in a period of one year, it also rotates on its axis producing the daily cycle of night and day. If the rotational axis of Earth were exactly perpendicular to its orbital

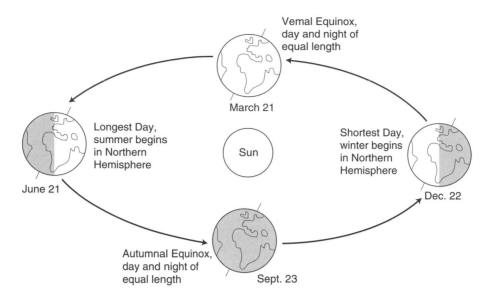

Figure 1   The four key days in Earth's orbit about the Sun.

plane, then each day would be nearly identical to every other day. Solar energy striking Earth perpendicularly at the equator would produce a warm tropic zone. The same amount of solar energy spreading over progressively wider zones at high northerly and southerly latitudes would result in temperate and arctic zones. At a given latitude, however, the solar heating of each day would be identical to that of every other day throughout the course of the year. As a direct consequence there would be no annual variation of temperature, and therefore, no seasons would occur anywhere on Earth.

The real Earth, however, has a rotational axis that is tilted at an angle, known as the obliquity, of 23.5° to the perpendicular to the plane of its orbit (see Fig. 1). The celestial equator therefore is not coincident with the ecliptic. Both are great circles upon the celestial sphere, and they cross each other at two positions on opposite sides of the sky. At the present time the first intersection is in the constellation of Pisces and the other is across the sky in the constellation of Virgo. Halfway between the intersections, at the positions of their maximum angular separation, the ecliptic and the equator are 23.5° apart on the sky. Over the course of a year, as the Sun moves around the ecliptic, it is thus seen to oscillate in latitude north of the celestial equator to a maximum angle of 23.5° and south to a maximum southern latitude of −23.5°. Twice during the year the Sun

appears coincident in position with the celestial equator.

The two times of the year when the Sun is found at the intersections of the ecliptic with the celestial equator are known as the equinoxes (literally "equal nights"). Due to Earth's rotation, the Sun's daily path across the sky at these times coincides with the celestial equator, which is one-half above the horizon and one-half below, making the day and night periods of equal duration. The first equinox occurs each year about March 21 when the Sun is moving from the southern sky into the northern sky; both the time of occurrence as well as the position on the sky where the Sun crosses the celestial equator are termed the vernal equinox. The fall or autumnal equinox (again used for both a time and a position on the sky) occurs six months later, about September 23, when the Sun crosses the equator from north to south. These two dates also mark the beginning of the northern spring and northern autumn, respectively.

By about June 21, the Sun appears as far north in the sky as it can move. Its northerly motion slows to a stop. This time is called the summer solstice (literally "standing still") and marks the beginning of the northern summer. A seasonal change marked by warmer temperatures and other weather variations occurs because solar heating is greatest when the Sun is highest in the sky. One also observes that the Sun rises north of due east, moves high across the southern sky, and sets north of due west. More than one-half of the daily path of the Sun around the sky is above the horizon, and hence, the daylight hours are longer than the hours of night, a second factor that contributes to the warmth of the summer. In contrast, at the time of the winter solstice, which occurs about December 22 and marks the start of the northern winter, the Sun rises south of due east, moves across the sky low to the south, and sets south of due west. Less than one-half of its apparent daily path around the sky is above the horizon, and hence, the length of the day is short. In addition, the position of the Sun low in the sky also contributes to minimizing the insolation (solar heating in terms of energy per second per unit of area) over the daily cycle.

To an observer in the Southern Hemisphere, the Sun is seen relatively high in the sky and the days are long when a Northern Hemisphere inhabitant experiences just the opposite. Thus the seasons of the Southern Hemisphere are the reverse of those of the Northern Hemisphere. As the yearly cycle progresses, however, equatorial inhabitants see the solar position at noon oscillating north and south about the zenith position. The change in daily solar heating is relatively small and hence the seasonal cycle of temperature variation is minimal.

The yearly seasons are also affected by one other factor involving Earth's orbital motion about the Sun. Earth's orbit is slightly elliptical, and hence, its motion along the orbit varies slightly (a consequence of Kepler's second law of planetary motion). Each year at perihelion, January 3, Earth is moving faster about the Sun. Consequently, the northern winter (the time between winter solstice and vernal equinox) is slightly shorter than the northern summer, which occurs when Earth passes through aphelion and is moving more slowly about its orbit. The opposite is true for the southern seasons.

See also: ECLIPSE; KEPLER'S LAWS; MOON, PHASES OF; NEWTON'S LAWS; SUN

Bibliography

ASIMOV, I. *The Clock We Live On* (Abelard-Schuman, New York, 1965).

KRUPP, E. C. "A Sky for All Seasons" in *In Search of Ancient Astronomies,* edited by E. C. Krupp (Doubleday, New York, 1978).

CHARLES J. PETERSON

SEISMIC WAVE

Seismic waves are elastic disturbances that are generated whenever a transient stress imbalance is produced within or on the surface of an elastic medium. A great variety of physical phenomena within the earth involve sudden deformation and thus excite seismic waves. The most common seismic source is earthquake faulting; other sources include such things as buried explosions, wind, landslides, and meteorite impacts. The properties of the seismic waves are governed by the theory of elastodynamics, which provides a mathematical relationship between stresses (internal forces in the medium) and strains (small elastic deformations).

The equations of motion for a continuum give rise to the three-dimensional homogeneous vector wave equation, which governs the behavior of seismic waves:

$$\rho \ddot{\mathbf{u}} = (\lambda + 2\mu)\nabla(\nabla \cdot \mathbf{u}) - (\mu\nabla \times \nabla \times \mathbf{u}) \quad (1)$$

where $\mathbf{u}$ is the displacement of the material initiated by some seismic source. The variable ρ is the density of the material, while λ and μ are elastic moduli that define the material properties such as resistance to shear or compression. We can use Helmholtz's theorem to represent the displacement field as

$$\mathbf{u} = \nabla\phi + \nabla \times \boldsymbol{\psi}, \quad (2)$$

where ϕ is the curl-free scalar potential field and $\boldsymbol{\psi}$ is the divergenceless vector field. Physically, a curl-free field involves no shearing or particle rotation, and a divergence field involves no change in volume. Substitution of Eq. (2) into Eq. (1) gives two independent equations:

$$\nabla^2\phi - (1/\alpha^2)\ddot{\phi} = 0$$
$$\nabla^2\psi - (1/\beta^2)\ddot{\psi} = 0, \quad (3)$$

where

$$\alpha = \sqrt{(\lambda + 2\mu)/\rho}$$
$$\beta = \sqrt{\mu/\rho}. \quad (4)$$

The variables α and β are the velocities of the two wave types. The solution to Eq. (3) gives rise to the two fundamental types of seismic waves: P and S waves. P waves (or primary waves) travel as compressional motions and volumetric changes. S waves (or secondary waves) involve shearing motions without volume changes. Since the elastic moduli are nonnegative, P waves, which travel with a velocity α, always arrive before S waves. The shear modulus μ is zero for a fluid; thus S waves do not exist in a fluid. P and S waves are the only transient solutions for a homogeneous whole space and thus provide a complete solution to the displacement equation of motion.

Nonhomogeneous media result in more complex seismic wave fields. When a P or S wave encounters a discontinuity at which the elastic moduli change, the waves reflect or refract. A free surface, or boundary between an elastic medium and a vacuum, generates a special case of seismic wave known as a surface wave. The free surface of an elastic medium has the special stress environment defined by zero surface tractions. The interaction of P and S waves at the surface gives rise to Rayleigh waves (named after Lord Rayleigh, the former John W. Stutt, an English mathematician). Rayleigh waves travel along the surface and have particle motions that decay rapidly below the free surface. Total reflection of S waves at the free surface combined with an increase in S wave velocity with depth below the surface generates a second class of surface wave known as Love waves (named after A. E. Love, another English mathematician). A final class of surface wave is the tsunami, which is a gravitationally controlled wave in water.

See also: ELASTICITY; ELASTIC MODULI AND CONSTANTS; GRAVITATIONAL WAVE; SEISMOLOGY; STRAIN; STRESS

Bibliography

BOLT, B. A. *Earthquakes* (W. H. Freeman, San Francisco, 1988).

LAY, T., and WALLACE, T. C. *Modern Global Seismology* (Academic Press, San Diego, CA, 1995).

T. C. WALLACE

SEISMOLOGY

Seismology is the study of the generation, propagation, and recording of elastic waves in the earth. These elastic waves, or seismic waves, are generated whenever there is a sudden stress imbalance introduced within, or on, the earth. Seismic waves travel as mechanical vibrations that can be measured with ground-motion recording instruments called seismometers; recordings of ground motions as a function of time are known as seismograms. Seismograms are the basic data that seismologists use to study earthquakes and the internal structure of the earth.

One of the principal sources of seismic energy is shear faulting associated with earthquakes. After the 1906 San Francisco earthquake, Harry Reid developed the theory of elastic rebound to explain most faulting behavior. This theory states that crustal stresses, generally resulting from large-scale regional crustal shearing motions, cause strain to accumulate in the immediate vicinity of faults, which are quasiplanar breaks in the crust across which some pre-existing displacement has occurred and which are hence relatively weak. When the strain accumulates to some threshold defined by the material properties of the fault, abrupt frictional sliding occurs. Much of the strain energy is consumed in heating and fracturing of the rock, but a portion is converted to seismic waves, which travel at speeds of the order of kilometers per second. The nature of the seismic waves that are generated depends on the material properties of the rock, the dynamics of the fault slip, and the size of the fault involved in the slip. A tremendous range in scales is required to describe the waves generated during an earthquake. The smallest detectable micro-earthquake has a seismic moment (the product of the fault surface area, average displacement on the fault, and the rigidity, or "strength" of the fault) of the order of 10^5 N·m, while great earthquakes have seismic moments as large as 10^{23} N·m. The amplitudes of seismic-wave motions are directly proportional to the seismic moment and hence span a tremendous range. The frequency content of seismic waves varies from tens of hertz to thousands of seconds; the frequency band of interest spans a range of approximately 10^7 Hz.

The tremendous range in scales for seismic waves poses a problem in designing seismometers that can cover the frequency range (bandwidth) and amplitude range (dynamic range). Prior to 1980 no single instrument could span these ranges, and seismometers were designed to record a pass band of interest. The seismometers were inertial pendulum systems that had a natural frequency of oscillation. By choosing an appropriate natural frequency and damping constants, seismometers can be tuned to

Table 1 Primary Magnitude Scales

Symbol	Name	Period of Measurement (in seconds)
M_L	Richter magnitude	0.1–1.0
m_b	body wave magnitude	1.0–5.0
M_S	surface wave magnitude	20
M_W	moment magnitude	> 200

record a particular bandpass, or a limited frequency range. Body waves (P and S waves) are of smaller amplitude and higher frequency than surface waves (Rayleigh and Love waves), so combinations of instruments of limited bandpass were used to record the range of seismic wave phenomena. The diversity of instruments that record different wave types has led to the development of many different scales for comparing the relative size of earthquakes based on seismic waves, typically called seismic magnitudes. Almost all magnitude scales are based on the logarithmic amplitude of a particular seismic wave on a particular seismometer, with corrections for distance between the source and seismometer. Table 1 gives the primary magnitude scales. The nature of the seismic waves means that any one earthquake can have many different seismic magnitudes. This has led to confusion in the news media, where a given earthquake is expected to have a single magnitude (usually the Richter magnitude, named after Charles F. Richter, who first invented seismic magnitude scales in the mid-1930s).

After 1980 a new class of seismic instruments, called force-feedback seismometers, were introduced and allowed the recording of a very wide frequency band on a single instrument. The broadband seismometers provide seismologists with a full-fidelity recording of seismic wave types that allows analysis of details of the seismic source. Fault slip involves three main stages: (1) initiation of fault sliding (or formation of a crack), (2) growth of the slip zone, or rupture front expansion, and (3) termination of the rupture process. The details of the fault slip impose a signature on the seismic wave forms. The point of initiation of an earthquake is known as the hypocenter (usually given in terms of latitude, longitude, and depth below the surface; the epicenter is the surface projection of the hypocenter). Rupture front growth is controlled by the dynamics of frictional sliding and depends on the material properties, temperature, and state of stress on the fault. In general, the rup-

ture front advances with a velocity of approximately 0.8β (the S-wave velocity). The largest earthquakes have fault lengths of several hundred kilometers.

Earthquakes occur when local strain accumulation exceeds the frictional strength of a fault. This strain only accumulates where there is a significant differential stress field (inhomogeneous stress). The source of most differential stress occurs along major geologic boundaries separating plates of mobile lithosphere. The interaction of these plates is a main principle of the theory of plate tectonics. Seismicity is largely concentrated in narrow bands along plate boundaries. Three basic types of plate boundary are characterized by different modes of plate interaction: divergent, convergent, and transcurrent. Divergent boundaries, where two plates are moving apart, are characterized by normal faulting (i.e., slipping along a fault with one side of the fault dropping down relative to the other. At convergent boundaries, the lithosphere is thickened or consumed by sinking into the mantle. Subduction zones, the most common convergent boundary, are characterized by thrust faulting. Transcurrent boundaries occur where plates move past one another without convergence or divergence. The type of faulting which occurs at transcurrent boundaries is called strike-slip faulting.

The yearly earthquake budget is usually measured in seismic moment release. Convergent boundaries account for 80 to 85 percent of the yearly total and are dominated by the largest earthquakes. For example, the May 1960 Chilean earthquake, which had a moment magnitude (M_W) of 9.6, accounts for 35 percent of the total seismic moment in the twentieth century. Earthquake size is distributed logarithmically; globally, we expect one earthquake per year with an M_W greater than 8.0, ten events with an M_W between 7.0 and 8.0, and more than one hundred events with an M_W between 6.0 and 7.0.

See also. EARTHQUAKE, SEISMIC WAVE, VOLCANO

Bibliography

BOLT, B. A. *Earthquakes* (W. H. Freeman, San Francisco, 1988).

GUBBINS, D. *Seismology and Plate Tectonics* (Cambridge University Press, Cambridge, Eng., 1990).

LAY, T., and WALLACE, T. C. *Modern Global Seismology* (Academic Press, San Diego, CA, 1995).

T. C. WALLACE

SELECTION RULE

Selection rules are used to determine the possible electromagnetic transitions between specified quantum states within a system. In common usage, the term "selection rule" refers to electric dipole transitions between states, although selection rules also apply to other types of radiation (e.g., magnetic dipole and electric quadrupole transitions).

Electric dipole transitions in a hydrogen atom are used to illustrate the concept of selection rules. Electric dipole transitions promote a single electron from one quantum state to another (e.g., from the $1s$ ground state to the $2p$ first excited state). For an electric dipole transition to occur, the following spatial integral must be nonzero:

$$\int \Psi_f^* x \, \Psi_i \, dV,$$

where Ψ_i, Ψ_f are the initial and final state wave functions and x represents the electric dipole operator. Equivalently, y or z can be used to represent the electric dipole transition, since the choice of axis is arbitrary. In the discussion that follows, symmetric (antisymmetric) means that the quantity remains unchanged (becomes negative) with spatial inversion through the origin ($x \to -x$, $y \to -y$, $z \to -z$). Since x is antisymmetric, the product $\Psi_i \Psi_f$ must also be antisymmetric in order for the integral to be nonzero and the transition to be *allowed*. The symmetry properties of Ψ_i and Ψ_f are determined by their quantum numbers: n (principal quantum number), l (orbital angular momentum), s (spin angular momentum), J (total angular momentum), m (projection of the total angular momentum on the z quantization axis). For a hydrogen atom the wave function is symmetric for even values of l and antisymmetric for odd values of l. Thus, electric dipole transitions are allowed only between states of even and odd l. This is the origin of the stringent selection rule on parity, known as Laporte's rule: Parity changes in a transition. Another stringent restriction on electric dipole transitions originates from the need for conservation of angular momentum. The total angular momentum of the photon and atom before the absorption must equal that of the atom after absorption. Since the electric dipole photon carries one unit of angular momentum, $\Delta J = 0, \pm 1$. ΔJ is not constrained to be ± 1 because J is formed by the vector (not arithmetic) sum of l and s. Finally, the change in the z component of the angular momentum of the atom is simply the z component of angular momentum added by the photon. For a photon angular momentum of one, as in electric dipole transitions, the z component may be $0, \pm 1$. Thus, the selection rule for m is $\Delta m = 0, \pm 1$. These three rules are rigorous for electric dipole transitions between states of well-defined parity.

Since the symmetry and angular momentum properties for an electric quadrupole radiation field differ from those of an electric dipole, different selection rules are operative. Specifically, the total angular momentum of the electric quadrupole photon is two, and the behavior of an electric quadrupole with respect to inversion at the origin is symmetric. Therefore, the selection rules in this case are no parity change; $\Delta J = 0, \pm 1, \pm 2$; and $\Delta m = 0, \pm 1, \pm 2$. Similar rules can be derived for all types of multipole radiation.

See also: DIPOLE MOMENT; SPECTROSCOPY; SYMMETRY

Bibliography

CORNEY, A. *Atomic and Laser Spectroscopy* (Clarendon, Oxford, Eng., 1977).

KARPLUS, M., and PORTER, R. N. *Atoms and Molecules* (W. A. Benjamin, Menlo Park, CA, 1971).

LINDA YOUNG

SELF-INDUCTANCE

The self-inductance L of a circuit is the proportionality constant between the EMF induced in the circuit and the rate of change of current in the circuit:

$$\text{EMF} = L \, di/dt. \tag{1}$$

In SI units, EMF is given in volts, di/dt is given in amperes per second, and L is given in henrys.

In principle, self-inductance is a property of an entire circuit, but when part of the circuit is coiled up (which greatly increases its inductance), we associate the self-inductance with the coil and call it an inductor.

The magnetic field inside an inductor is enhanced, because the fields due to current in the many turns of the coil point in the same direction and add together, providing a magnetic flux within the coil proportional to the number of turns. Furthermore, this flux will link the circuit many times, since most of it links most turns of the coil.

The self-inductance of an empty solenoid with N turns, cross-sectional area A, and length $l << A^{1/2}$ is given approximately by

$$L = \frac{\mu_0 N^2 A}{l}, \qquad (2)$$

where $\mu_0 = 4\pi \times 10^{-7}$ H/m.

For example, if $N = 1,000$, $A = 0.001$ m^2, and $l = 0.1$ m, then L is about 10 mH.

Self-inductances about 1,000 times greater are obtained by filling the coil with a ferromagnetic core and providing a ferromagnetic return path outside the coil for the magnetic flux.

Since increasing the current in an inductor generates a back EMF, work is required to push current through the inductor while the current is being increased. The work needed to build up the current from 0 to i through an inductor of self-inductance L is

$$W = \frac{Li^2}{2}. \qquad (3)$$

This work goes into stored magnetic energy, and it comes back out as work done *by* the inductor when the current is reduced. This stored energy can cause problems when the current through a solenoid is suddenly switched off. An alternate path, through a diode for example, may be needed to dissipate the energy gradually.

Applications of self-inductance include tuned resonant circuits in transmitters and receivers, filter circuits to block ac signals while passing dc current, and transient energy storage in switching power supplies. Self-inductance affects the propagation of signals in coaxial cables and waveguides. Strategies to reduce inductance effects must be employed in any circuits where very fast-rising pulses are used.

See also: COAXIAL CABLE; ELECTROMAGNETIC INDUCTION; FERROMAGNETISM; FIELD, MAGNETIC; INDUCTANCE; INDUCTANCE, MUTUAL; INDUCTOR; LENZ'S LAW; MAGNETIC FLUX; SOLENOID; WAVEGUIDE

Bibliography

FEYNMAN, R. P.; LEIGHTON, R. B.; SANDS, M. *The Feynman Lectures on Physics,* Vol. 2 (Addison-Wesley, Reading, MA, 1964).

TIPLER, P. A. *Physics for Scientists and Engineers,* 3rd ed. (Worth, New York, 1991).

DAVID A. DOBSON

SEMICONDUCTOR

If one classifies solid materials based on electrical conductivity (σ), they can be put into three groups: metal, semiconductor, and insulator. The resistivities ($\rho \equiv \sigma^{-1}$) of typical metals such as silver, copper, or aluminum range from 10^{-5} to 10^{-6} Ω cm. [The resistance R of a bar of material of length L and cross-sectional area A is related to its resistivity by the relation $R = \rho L / A$. For example, a bar of metal of resistivity $\rho = 10^{-6}$ Ω-cm with length 10 cm and cross-sectional area 2 cm^2 is $R = (10^{-6}\ \Omega\,\text{cm})\ (10\ \text{cm})/(2\ \text{cm}^2) = 5 \times 10^{-6}$ Ω, a resistance which is much too small to measure with a typical ohmmeter.] On the other hand, insulators such as glass, diamond, and quartz have resistivities ranging from 10^{10} to as high as 10^{18} Ω cm. Semiconductors, as the name implies, have resistivities in between the extremes of metals and insulators. Moreover, while resistivity increases with temperature in metals, it decreases in semiconductors. However, the resistivities of semiconductors are not the only things that set them apart from metals and insulators. An important aspect is that a given semiconductor such as silicon (Si) can be made to have very low resistivity similar to a metal, or very high resistivity like an insulator. Additionally, semiconductors can be made to have electrical carriers that have either negative or positive charge. When the carriers are negative, the semiconductor is called n type and electrons carry the electrical current. When the carriers are positive, the semiconductor is said to be p type, and the current-carrying entities are called holes.

Basic Physics of Semiconductors

To understand the physical properties of semiconductors, it is useful to have a basic understanding of the nature of electrons on a very small scale. Near the beginning of the twentieth century, it was demonstrated experimentally that the electrons in atoms can exist only in certain states of energy. This was demonstrated by measuring the transmission of light through a container of a certain type of gas, such as hydrogen. It was found that certain frequencies (colors) of light get absorbed by the gas, whereas wide ranges of other frequencies pass through without being absorbed. It was separately found that light comes in bunches of energy called photons. The frequency v of a photon is related to its energy E by $E = hv$, where h (equal to 6.626 J·s) is Planck's constant. The reason why light of only very particular frequencies gets absorbed by the atoms is that the electrons in atoms can exist in only very particular states of energy. During absorption of a photon, an electron in an atom of the gas makes a transition from a state of energy $E_{initial}$ to a state of higher energy E_{final}. The energy of the photon E_{photon}, which disappears in the process, must be equal to the energy difference between the energies of the final and initial states of the electron: $E_{photon} = E_{final} - E_{initial}$. The set of absorption frequencies (absorption spectra) is unique to each particular gas and can be used as sort of a fingerprint to identify an unknown gas. In fact, by comparing the spectra of light that comes from far away stars and galaxies to the absorption spectra of known gases that have been measured in the laboratory, astronomers can determine what types of gases exist in space that cause the absorption.

Pauli exclusion principle. It is also known that electrons must obey the Pauli exclusion principle. The Pauli exclusion principle states that no two electrons can exist in the same state. For our purposes, we can think of a state as being characterized by the energy of the electron and a second property called spin. The spin can take on two possible values which, for lack of better words, are called up and down. More complicated situations can occur. For example, sometimes many states can have the same energy, in which case there is some other physical property that electrons can have which will uniquely define the state, such as the states associated with two separate but identical atoms. A given electron can go into a state of energy E on one atom, or into an identical state on the other atom. The states associated with each atom are identical in every way, but they are still considered to be different because they are on two separate atoms.

In order to describe the Pauli exclusion principle, let us suppose we could build up a Si atom by adding consecutively one electron at a time. Initially we start with a bare Si nucleus (i.e., a Si^{+14} ion). If we throw one electron onto the Si ion and let it settle down, the electron will go to the lowest possible energy state. Let us call the energy of this state E_1. If we then add a second electron, it will settle into the lowest energy state that it can get to—a state identical to that of the first electron, except that the second electron will have the opposite spin. Its energy will also be E_1. Now when we add the third electron, it cannot go into a state with the same energy as the first two electrons. The Pauli exclusion principle excludes this possibility, so the third electron must settle into the next higher energy state. Let us call the energy of this state E_2. If we continue this, the fourth will have the same energy as the third (E_2), the sixth electron will have the same energy as the fifth (E_3), and so forth, until we have added the fourteenth electron at energy E_7. Although there are also available states at higher energies (E_8, E_9, . . .), these are not occupied when the Si atom has its electrons in the lowest possible energy states.

Energy bands. Now let us consider a crystal of Si. In this situation, the Si atoms are quite close to each other. It turns out that the lower energy states of electrons in Si atoms that are in a crystal are nearly identical to the states of electrons in a single isolated Si atom. This is more true for the electrons in the very lowest energy states because they typically hug the nucleus very closely and are not influenced by the neighboring Si atoms. The energies of states $E_1, . . . , E_6$ are nearly the same as they are in the isolated Si atoms. To characterize the state of an electron uniquely in one of these states, it is enough to specify its energy and spin and the location of the Si atom with which it is associated.

The highest energy electrons, the ones that come from the states of energy E_7, do not live very close to the nucleus. These are strongly influenced by the neighboring atoms. It is no longer useful to characterize the state of an electron by defining the atom with which it is associated, because electrons in these states are not associated with any particular Si atom when the atoms are arranged in a crystal. These electrons can hop from atom to atom rather freely and are better characterized by momentum rather than location. In this case, to define uniquely these states of electrons in a Si crystal, we need to specify the energy E_7, the spin, and the momentum $\mathbf{p}$ of the electron. There are two properties of the momentum states: (1) There is a maximum allowable momentum that is proportional to a^{-1}, where a is the spacing between neighboring Si atoms, and (2) there will be as many states of different allowed values of momentum as there are Si atoms in the crystal. Two electrons can have the same momentum, one with spin up, the other with spin down. The actual energy of an electron in one of these states will be $E_7 + f(\mathbf{p})$, where $f(\mathbf{p})$ is some function of the momentum $\mathbf{p}$. These states are spread out into a band of different energies. This band of states is called the valence band. It is useful to label the energy of the highest energy state in the valence band as E_V.

Semiconductor Doping

For a perfect crystal of Si, when all the electrons are in the lowest possible states, the valence band is completely filled with electrons. There are as many electrons with momentum in any given direction as there are with momentum in the opposite direction. In order for the Si crystal to pass an electrical current, it would have to have more electrons going in one direction than in the opposite direction. If we attempt to drive a current by applying a small voltage drop along the x direction, the electrons in the valence band will feel a force in the x direction. However, they cannot become accelerated to different momentum states because, in order for an electron to accelerate from one momentum state to another, the second momentum state must be empty. The Pauli exclusion principle does not allow it to be otherwise. In a perfect crystal of Si, the valence band is totally filled, therefore no electrons can become accelerated, and no current can be made to flow. A perfect crystal of Si, therefore, acts as an insulator.

n-type doping. Let us now consider what happens when we replace one Si atom with a phosphorus (P) atom. This process is an example of doping a semiconductor to be *n* type. P atoms are almost identical to Si atoms except that there are fifteen electrons, one more than in Si. The lowest fourteen electrons will go into identical states as the fourteen electrons from the Si atom it replaced. However, the fifteenth electron cannot go into any of the states associated with the states labeled $E_1, ..., E_7$. They are already filled and the Pauli exclusion principle does not allow it. The fifteenth electron must go into the next highest state of energy E_8. Just as the states asso-

ciated with E_7 form a band of states depending on momentum, there is also a band of states associated with E_8. This band is called the conduction band. It is useful to label the energy of the lowest state in the conduction band as E_C. There are no states between E_C and E_V. The difference in energy between the two states is called the energy gap $E_G = E_C - E_V$. In Si at room temperature, $E_G = 1.12$ eV[2]. [An electronvolt (1 eV $= 1.602 \times 10^{-19}$ J) is defined as the amount of energy a free electron would acquire if it is accelerated through a voltage of 1V.]

If, for example, we dope the Si crystal with P at a level of two out of 10^6, each P atom will contribute one electron to the conduction band. The total number of momentum states in the conduction band is equal to the total number of atoms in the crystal, and there are two unique states associated with each momentum value (spin up and down); therefore the total number of states in the conduction band is twice the total number of atoms in the crystal. Hence only one state out of the 10^6 states in the conduction band will be filled. In this case, if we attempt to drive a current by applying a small voltage drop along the x direction, the electrons in the conduction band *can* become accelerated, because there are an enormous number of empty momentum states into which they can accelerate. In this case the semiconductor acts like a conductor. When we turn off the voltage, all of the electrons will attempt to go into the lowest possible energy states. In this case, the electrons in the conduction band will settle down to the bottom one of the 10^6 states in the conduction band.

p-type doping. Let us now consider what happens when we replace two out of 10^6 Si atoms with aluminum (Al) atoms rather than P atoms. This process is an example of doping a semiconductor to be *p* type. Al has thirteen electrons, one less than Si has. Therefore, one out of the 10^6 states in the valence band will be empty. The empty states in the valence band are called holes. When the electrons in the valence band settle into their lowest possible states in energy, the empty states (holes) will be at the top of the valence band. It is useful to draw an analogy between holes in the valence band and air bubbles in water, with the water representing electrons in the valence band. An empty state (hole) far below the top of the valence band will tend to rise as electrons sequentially fall into it, just as an air bubble in water tends to rise as the water above flows into the air pocket. It is rather cumbersome to describe the motion of an air bubble by saying that it moves because the water keeps flowing into it. It is more preferable to simply call it a bubble and acquire an intuitive feel for what the bubble tends to. Similarly, rather than describing motion of empty states in the valence band in terms of electrons sequentially moving into empty states, it is more intuitive to call the empty states holes and follow their motions. Holes described in this way act like they have the opposite charge of electrons because the application of a voltage that pushes electrons to the left causes the holes to be pushed to the right.

p-n Junction Diode

One of the simplest semiconductor devices that we can understand in terms of the above picture is the p-n junction diode. A possible way to make such a diode is to begin with a substrate of Si, which is a doped p type. If phosphorus is diffused into a region on top of the crystal, then the region where there is a significant amount of phosphorus is made to be n type. Let us consider what occurs at the interface between the p and n regions. The electrons in a system are constantly seeking to find lower energy states into which they can go. Therefore, electrons from the conduction band on the n side would be quite happy to cross into the p side where there are many empty states in the lower-lying valence band. Some of the electrons from the n side will indeed do this; they will find their ways into the p side and fill up the holes in the valence band there. However, once some of them have done this, there will be a region in the n side that has fewer electrons than it had previously. The n-type semiconductor previously had no net charge because for each electron in the conduction band with a charge of -1, there was a phosphorus atom with a nuclear charge of $+15$ and electronic charge of -14, which we can think of as a P^{+1} ion. Each electron that leaves the n side and fills up a hole on the p side leaves behind a P^{+1} ion. Similarly, for each hole in the valence band with a $+1$ charge, there is an Al ion with a -1 charge. Each hole that gets filled in the valence band leaves behind an Al^{-1} ion. Eventually, the electrons from the n side do not gain any energy by traveling into the p side to recombine with holes, because to do so requires energy to move away from the attractive P^{+1} ions and go toward the repulsive Al^{-1} ions. At this point, the system has reached equilibrium and all of the electrons are in their lowest possible energy states. In equilibrium, there is a region in the n side next to the junction with the p side that has only P^{+1}

ions and no electrons. Similarly, there is a region on the p side next to the junction with the n side that has only Al^{-1} ions and no holes. These two regions together are called the depletion region.

If we apply a negative voltage to the n side with respect to the p side, which is called forward biasing the junction, then electrons in the conduction band on the n side and holes in the valence band on the p side will be pushed toward the junction. In this case, the depletion region becomes narrower and it is relatively easy for a net current of electrons to continually flow from the n to the p side and recombine. If we apply the opposite voltage (i.e., reverse bias the junction), electrons are pulled back from the p to the n side. In this case, the depletion region becomes wider and a small amount of electrons can flow from the p to the n side. When forward biasing the junction a large current can flow, which increases with forward bias. Reverse biasing the junction causes a small current to flow in the reverse direction. This current does not increase much as the reverse bias is increased. This phenomenon is called rectification.

See also: CONDUCTOR; CRYSTAL STRUCTURE; ELECTRICAL CONDUCTIVITY; ELECTRON; ENERGY LEVELS; HOLES IN SOLIDS; INSULATOR; METAL; PAULI'S EXCLUSION PRINCIPLE; PHOTON; QUANTUM MECHANICS; SPIN; SPIN, ELECTRON

Bibliography

KROEMER, H. *Quantum Mechanics for Engineering, Materials Science, and Applied Physics* (Prentice Hall, Englewood Cliffs, NJ, 1994).

SZE, S. M. *Physics of Semiconductor Devices* (Wiley, New York, 1981).

SZE, S. M. *Semiconductor Devices Physics and Technology* (Prentice Hall, Englewood Cliffs, NJ, 1985).

YANG, E. S. *Microelectronic Devices* (McGraw-Hill, New York, 1988).

J. SPECTOR

SERVOMECHANISM

A servomechanism is an error-correcting, power-amplifying, closed-loop feedback-control system in

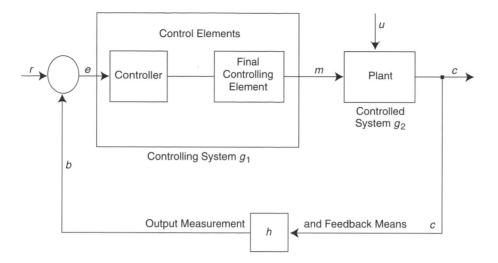

Figure 1   Block diagram of a servomechanism.

which the time-dependent input-command variable v is a mechanical position or its time derivative (e.g., velocity, acceleration, torque). Closed-loop control is dependent on output, whereas open-loop feedback control is independent of output. The primary function of a servomechanism is to cause the output of the system to follow a varying input. The directly controlled variable output c is measured continuously or sampled digitally (see Fig. 1). The feedback signal b is a function of c and is algebraically summed with the reference input r to obtain the actuating signal e. The v is usually equal to r, but a transducer may be required between r and v. The c changes as a result of the algebraic comparison of b with r so as to reduce the error, $e - r - b$, by the action of the negative feedback loop.

The purpose of this closed-feedback loop is to bring the value of c as close as possible to the value specified by r in spite of disturbances u. The disturbance u is an undesired input signal that affects the value of c. It may enter the controlled system by summation with m or at an intermediate point. The manipulated variable or controlled signal m is the quantity that the elements of the controlling system g_1 apply to the plant or controlled system g_2. The forward path of the loop is from e to the controlled output c, while the feedback path is from c to the feedback signal b. The feedback elements h are the components required to establish the functional relationship between b and c. Fig. 1 is a block diagram illustrating the principle of operation of the servomechanism. With discrete-time control, the output c is monitored and compared with r only at the sampling times.

Integral and differential equations arise in the theory of automatic control systems. A series of analytic and synthesizing processes is available for application in control engineering. Figure 1, with its time-dependent signals denoted by lowercase letters, can be transformed into the transform function of the system, shown in Fig. 2, simply by substituting uppercase letters signifying the corresponding Laplace transforms. From the ratio of output to input signals c/r, one calculates the following: C/R (the control ratio) $\equiv$ the closed-loop transfer function; G (the direct-transfer function) $\equiv$ the forward-transfer function; $H \equiv$ the feedback transfer function; GH (the loop-transfer function) $\equiv$ the open-loop-transfer function; E/R (the actuating sig-

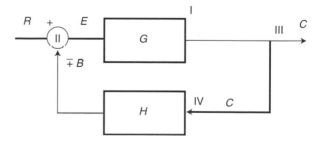

Figure 2   Canonical form of a feedback-control system: (I) algebraic and transfer functions for block, (II) summing points, (III) takeoff points, and (IV) unidirectional signal-flow arrows.

nal) ≡ the error ratio; and B/R ≡ the primary feedback ratio. The equations governing the feedback system are

$$C/R = G/(1 \pm GH), \qquad (1)$$

$$E/R = 1/(1 \pm GH), \qquad (2)$$

and

$$B/R = GH/(1 \pm GH). \qquad (3)$$

These equations result from the following relations: $E = R \mp B$, $B = HC$, and $C = GE$. The positive sign in the denominator refers to a negative-feed-

back system, and the negative sign in the denominator refers to a positive-feedback system.

A simple example of a servomechanism for controlling the angular position θ_0 of an output shaft, with viscous damping acting on it, with respect to the angular position θ_i of an input shaft is shown in Fig. 3a. The θ_0 is transmitted to a differential gear system by a feedback loop, which is shaft integral with the output shaft. The difference, $\theta_i - \theta_0$, is the error signal e, which actuates the controller. The controller applies a torque to the output shaft to bring it into angular correspondence with the input shaft. Fig. 3b is the functional form of Fig. 3a and is comparable to Fig. 2. In analyzing the system to determine steady-state behavior, the angular velocity of the output shaft is directly proportional to the output torque since the inertial term, proportional to

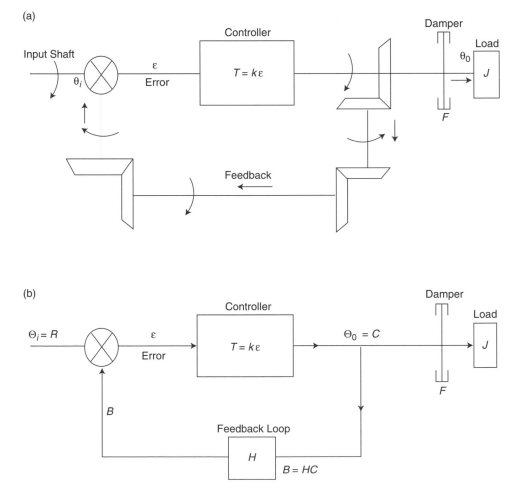

Figure 3 (a) A servomechanism for controlling position of output shaft θ_0 and (b) the related functional form.

the angular acceleration, is zero. With no angular acceleration, the torques on the shaft must balance out. Thus, corresponding to a constant error in angular velocity, there will be a counterbalancing torque from the controller, which implies a steady-state error in angle ϵ_{ss} for this system. It would be given by $\epsilon_{ss} = F\omega_1/\kappa$, where F is frictional torque per unit angular velocity, and κ is output torque per unit error in angle.

See also: ACCELERATION, ANGULAR; VELOCITY, ANGULAR

Bibliography

CHURCHILL, R. V. *Operational Mathematics* (McGraw-Hill, New York, 1958).

FINK, D. G., and MCKENZIE, A. A. eds. *Electronic Engineers' Handbook* (McGraw-Hill, New York, 1975).

LAUER, H.; LESNICK, R. N.; and MATSON, L. E. *Servomechanism Fundamentals* (McGraw-Hill, New York, 1960).

PHILLIPS, C. L., and NAGLE, H. T., JR. *Digital Control System Analysis and Design* (Prentice Hall, New York, 1984).

CAROL ZWICK ROSEN

SHOCK WAVE

A shock wave represents the propagation of a discontinuous change in any state variable, such as pressure or density, at a speed faster than that of sound. Sonic booms from aircraft are familiar examples of shock waves, but the crack of a lightning flash is the most frequently encountered naturally occurring shock. The temperature of air is normally about 300 K. Strong dissipation of electrical current, generated by charge separation and subsequent ion flow, heats the air to temperatures in excess of 10,000 K with the attendant increase in pressure. The expansion of the cylindrical column occurs supersonically and eventually ends in sound generation, or thunder. Bullets have supersonic muzzle velocities and consequently form Mach cones that extend from the tip, precluding the upstream propagation of a sound wave to warn of the impending impact.

The characteristic speed of a disturbance in a gas generated by a pressure or density variation is the sound speed. It depends on the gas equation of state, $c_s = (\partial p/\partial \rho)^{1/2}$. Here p is the gas pressure and ρ is its density. For an ideal gas $c_s = (\gamma p/\rho)^{1/2}$, and thus the sound speed depends only on γ, the ratio of the specific heat at constant pressure to that at constant volume ($\gamma = C_p/C_v$), and the temperature T. Any pressure variation can equilibrate over some length L in a typical timescale $t_s = L/c_s$. If for any reason the pressure, or any other thermodynamic state variable, changes discontinuously, there is no length small enough for a sound wave to smoothly adjust the conditions. Consequently, the front cannot communicate with material upstream. Another way of saying this is that any material moving faster than the sound speed overtakes any sound waves it generates before they can cross out of the region of the front and, therefore, interacts ballistically with the medium ahead of it.

The shock strength is measured in terms of the "Mach number" ($M = v/c_s$), the ratio of the fluid or source speed to the sound speed. The properties of the shock are set by the initial conditions in what is called a "Riemann problem." The speed of the shock is determined by its strength, measured as p_2/p_1. A sound wave may turn into a shock if its amplitude is large enough. This can happen in several ways, the easiest being the propagation of a strong pressure disturbance into an environment with a steeply decreasing density, like an isothermal atmosphere (where the density falls exponentially). The phase speed of the sound wave depends on its amplitude in the nonlinear limit, so the peak actually overtakes the trough, much like a breaking wave on a beach, and the density locally becomes double-valued at the front. Since this is physically unsupportable, the wave dissipates energy and forms a discontinuity. This is an essential feature of shocks; they are dissipative in the sense that the entropy always increases in the postshock region.

The mass flux $\rho \mathbf{v} \cdot \mathbf{n}$, momentum flux $\rho v^2 + p$, and energy flux $\rho \mathbf{v} \cdot \mathbf{n}(\frac{1}{2}v^2 + C_p T)$ are all equal on opposite sides of the shock front. Postshock cooling may alter the energy condition, however. Here $\mathbf{n}$ is the surface normal unit vector and v is the gas velocity. These are specified in the frame in which the front is at rest, so the gas appears to be flowing through a stationary front. However, a front also can form around a stationary body, like the bow shock in front of an obstacle.

Since the gas cannot reach equilibrium on crossing the front, it slowly relaxes on decompression. The shock heating of the gas depends on the compression ratio. The cooling of a nonadiabatic shock depends on the available atomic and molecular species. The more efficient the coolant, the quicker the density again increases and the temperature drops.

The conservation equations are also called the Rankine–Hugoniot conditions. Labeling with 1 the variables upstream of the shock and with 2 the variables immediately behind the front, the density compression and pressure jumps computed in terms of the Mach number are

$$\frac{p_2}{p_1} = \frac{2\gamma M^2 - (\gamma - 1)}{\gamma + 1}, \qquad (1)$$

$$\frac{\rho_2}{\rho_1} = \frac{(\gamma + 1) M^2}{(\gamma - 1) M^2 + 2}. \qquad (2)$$

Then $T_2/T_1 = (p_2/p_1)/(\rho_2/\rho_1)$ for an ideal gas.

Point explosions produce blast waves. These are a very special class of shock front because they propagate self-similarly. This means that their radius changes in time in such a way as to maintain some physical property constant. L. Sedov, G. Taylor, and J. von Neumann were primarily responsible for general developments of the theory of such shocks using techniques of dimensional analysis. Take for instance a blast that is so strong, and expands so quickly, that its temperature only drops adiabatically. Its internal energy is therefore constant and, since the energy dimensionally relates a length to a time scale, we find that

$$R(t) \approx \left(\frac{E_0}{\rho_0}\right)^{1/5} t^{2/5}, \qquad (3)$$

where E_0 is the initial energy and ρ_0 is the density of the medium into which the blast is moving. This is the Sedov–Taylor solution, and it well describes phenomena as different as supernova remnant expansion and the pressure blast from detonation of a nuclear weapon. Since the internal pressure drops due to expansion of the front, the blast wave eventually stalls. This happens when the internal and ambient pressures are equal, once the blast velocity becomes subsonic. This stalling radius R_s is the upper limit on the effective size of the shock; it scales as $R_s \sim E_0^{1/3}$

Oblique shocks are well-known from explosions in air. Consider a spherical blast wave or a sonic boom that reflects off the ground. The speed of sound behind the front is greater than the preshock value, and the shock is weaker. It therefore moves into the postshocked gas to form a secondary front. A line perpendicular to the ground forms, called a "Mach collar," that moves outward from the source of the wave at a speed greater than that of sound. The over-pressure behind this collar is greater than the initial shock.

Detonation waves are another special type of shock. Unlike blast waves, which are freely propagating, detonations power their own expansion through the release of energy in the postshocked gas. Chemical explosions, like TNT detonations, illustrate this.

The first physical investigations of strong sound waves were undertaken by Bernhard Riemann (1860), William Rankine (1870), and Henri Hugoniot (1889). The first systematic description of the physics of shock waves was by Ernst Mach (1879), whose attention was first drawn to the subject in connection with ballistics. Mach also developed many of the precursors of the modern flow visualization techniques for studying shock phenomena, in particular use of interferometry (the discontinuous change in the index of refraction of a gas across the front renders it visible in monochromatic light). Much of the modern work on shocks began with the Manhattan Project during World War II and with engineering studies of supersonic aircraft flight.

See also: MACH, ERNST; SOUND; WAVE MOTION

Bibliography

COURANT, R., and FRIEDRICHS, K. *Supersonic Flows and Shock Waves* (Interscience, New York, 1948).

LANDAU, L. D., and LIFSHITZ, E. M. *Fluid Mechanics,* 3rd ed. (Pergamon, New York, 1985).

SHORE, S. N. *An Introduction to Astrophysical Hydrodynamics* (Academic Press, San Diego, CA, 1992).

ZELDOVICH, YA. B., and RAZER, Y. *High Temperature Flows and Shock Phenomena* (Academic Press, San Diego, CA, 1966).

STEVEN N. SHORE

SHORT CIRCUIT

A short circuit is an unintended low-resistance path that bypasses a load in an electrical circuit. A large current flows through this newly created path and may also cause high currents to flow through branches feeding into it. These high currents can exceed the capacity of the elements involved and damage them.

In household circuits, a short circuit usually occurs through the accidental contact of two wires that are normally insulated from each other. Common causes are damaged insulation or a broken plug. Under normal conditions the household wiring is the least resistive part of an electrical circuit and has a very small voltage drop across it. When a short circuit occurs, the wiring becomes the most resistive part of the circuit, and the voltage across it is virtually the entire line voltage. The power P dissipated as heat in a resistor is $P = V^2/R$, where V is the line voltage and R is the small resistance of the household wiring. Absent any safety mechanisms, the wiring heats up and its temperature may become high enough to ignite any combustible materials surrounding the wire.

In electronic circuits, a short circuit may cause large currents to flow through components that have limited current-carrying capability. When these components fail, other components may fail, resulting in a massive destruction of the electronic device. Short circuits can also occur in power lines, usually resulting from a downed power line, the failure of an insulator, or the failure of a transformer.

Fuses or automatic circuit breakers are used to prevent damage to power circuits, household circuits, electrical appliances, and electronic devices. A fuse consists of a piece of material that melts easily. This "fusible" material is placed in series with the element that it protects. When the current flowing through the element is within a safe range, the material is a normal conductor but, if the current exceeds some threshold value, the material melts quickly. This breaks the circuit, averting any further damage due to a short circuit.

The melting of the material is usually violent, with a portion of the material vaporizing. To prevent the hot, molten material from becoming a source of fire when the fuse "blows," the fusible material is usually enclosed in a fireproof container.

An alternative safety device is the automatic circuit breaker, which consists of a switch that opens the circuit either because of a high temperature or a high current. In a heat-triggered breaker, a bimetallic strip is part of the circuit. Heating the strip causes it to bend and, if it bends enough, it opens the circuit. The high-current version uses an electromagnet that attracts a magnetic part that opens the circuit when the current is high enough. Both types have spring-loaded mechanisms that prevent them from reconnecting unless they are reset. In the case of power lines, circuit breakers are often arranged to reroute the circuit through a safe alternative path so that the ordinary user is not aware that an interruption has taken place.

See also: CIRCUIT, AC; CIRCUIT, DC; CIRCUIT, PARALLEL; CIRCUIT, SERIES; CURRENT, ALTERNATING; CURRENT, DIRECT; INSULATOR

Bibliography

GREENWALD, E. K. *Electrical Hazards and Accidents* (Van Nostrand Reinhold, New York, 1991).

OLIVER, K. G. *Basic Industrial Electricity* (Industrial Press, New York, 1991).

GIULIO VENEZIAN

SIGNAL

A signal S is the value of a physical parameter which conveys information about the phenomena being studied. The temperature of the air outside and its daily variation are both signals. Signals can be acoustical as a bird's song played through a hi-fi speaker; optical chemical as the photographic image of a bug taken through a microscope; electro-optical as the CAT scan's image of a human brain; electrical as an electrocardiogram; electro-acoustical as the clicks on a Geiger counter detecting radioactivity.

Signals are the result of a measurement made by a detector (transducer). They usually involve electricity at some point because signals are either electrical to start with or are converted to electrical variations by a transducer. Signal values are often displayed on the measuring instrument itself—voltmeters, thermometers, altimeters, lightmeters, speedometers, wattmeters. Both the instantaneous value and the time variation of the signal carry information.

Some signals are naturally analog such as the deflection of a meter needle or a strip chart pen that indicates the voltage V of a battery, the brightness B of a light, the temperature T of an oven, the weight W of a baby, or loudness L of a rock-and-roll band.

Some signals are naturally digital, especially those that arise from a counting process. Such measurements produce a number n, which can be shown on a liquid crystal display (LCD) or a counter. Digital signals might represent the number of fish in a pond, trees in a forest, lightning flashes during a four-hour thunderstorm, cars crossing a bridge per hour, cosmic rays passing through your head each second. A scale weighing a quart of sand would produce an analog signal for the weight W, whereas the number n of sand grains in the quart would be digital (exactly countable).

Some measuring instruments convert naturally analog signals to digital signals (a number) for display. For clocks, speedometers, and voltmeters the number displayed does not arise from a counting process. In all cases, the signal—acoustical, optical, electrical, mechanical, or counts—contains useful information.

The sensors of the human body evolved to react to some physical properties of the outside world and create signals. The eye detects light and converts it to signals called images. The ear reacts to periodic air pressure vibrations to create sound signals. The nose and tongue react to chemicals to create smell and taste signals. Fingers react to heat, pressure, and voltage to create signals known as the sensations of touch and pain.

Detectors (photodiodes, microphones, thermometers, barometers) are artificial sensors developed to produce signals far beyond the detectable range of our human senses. For example, exotic light detectors (photomultipliers, photodiodes, photographic plates) used by high energy physicists and astronomers can detect optical signals over an extraordinary energy range—from the highest energy gamma rays to the low energy infrared and microwaves—a range billions of times larger than the range detected by the eye.

The development of detectors (devices that react to a stimulus) and transducers (devices that convert any signal to a voltage or count rate for display on a meter, counter, or computer) is one of the frontiers of modern technology. All detectors are characterized by their useful range, sensitivity, stability, accuracy, and by the noise they contribute to the desired signal S.

See also: COSMIC RAY; ELECTRICITY; ENERGY; GEIGER COUNTER; NOISE; PRESSURE, SOUND; RADIOACTIVITY; SIGNAL-TO-NOISE RATIO; TRANSDUCER

Bibliography

DERENAIK, E. L., and CROWE, D. G. *Optical Radiation Detectors* (Wiley, New York, 1984).

GRUM, F., and BECHERER, R. J. *Optical Radiation Measurements* (Academic Press, San Diego, CA, 1979).

WILLIAM BICKEL

SIGNAL-TO-NOISE RATIO

All physical measurements M are the sum of the desired signal S and noise N. When the noise N is known, the signal is calculated from $S = (M - N)$. The signal-to-noise ratio R is simply

$$R = \frac{S}{N} = \frac{M - N}{N}.$$

It is not M/N. The following examples show the relationships between N, S, $M = (S + N)$, and $R = S/N$.

The radioactivity at a superfund site produces $M = 600$ counts/s in a Geiger counter. When the Geiger counter is placed in a lead shielded box, the noise "signal" N is 100 counts/s. The actual signal S is therefore $(M - N) = (600 \text{ counts/s} - 100 \text{ counts/s}) = 500$ counts/s. The signal-to-noise ratio $R = S/N = (500 \text{ counts/s})/(100 \text{ counts/s}) = 5$. Signal-to-noise ratios are dimensionless. A higher quality—more sensitive, less noisy—Geiger counter might produce $M = 8,000$, $N = 20$ with $S = (M - N) = (8,000 - 20) = 7,980$. Then $R = S/N = 7,980/20 = 399$. It is desirable to strive for the highest signal-to-noise ratios possible.

A tape recording of an orchestral performance produces a measured loudness of $M = 3.46 \text{ W/m}^2$ at the loudspeaker. The empty tape (no recording) generates a noise $N = 0.02 \text{ W/m}^2$. The signal $S = (M - N) = (3.46 - 0.02) \text{ W/m}^2 = 3.44 \text{ W/m}^2$. The signal-to-noise ratio $R = S/N = (3.46 \text{ W/m}^2)/(0.02 \text{ W/m}^2) = 173$.

A photographic film produces $M = 20,400$ grains/cm^2 in the image of a comet tail. The unexposed film when developed produces a background fogging of $N = 400$ grains/cm^2. The signal $S = (M - N) = (20,400 - 400) = 20,000$ grains/cm^2. The $S/N = 20,000/400 = 50$.

A fish counter counts $M = 750$ fish/h swimming through a pipe. When no fish swim through the pipe the counter still counts $N = 5$ fish/h. The signal $S = (M - N) = (750 - 5) = 745$ fish/h. The signal-to-noise ratio $R = S/N = 745/5 = 173$.

Sources of noise are varied. Noise can be generated by poor experiments, instrumentation, and technique. With care, noise can be reduced but never lower than the value set by the fundamental limit of measurement. Ongoing technology strives to develop detectors and instrumentation to give the highest signal-to-noise ratios. On the one hand, atomic physics experiments that employ photon counting can easily achieve S/N ratios as high as 10^8. On the other hand, in high energy physics, where millions of events must be sorted through to confirm the existence of a single up quark, the S/N ratios are as small as 10^{-10}.

The importance of the signal-to-noise ratio is shown as follows: We have $M = S + N$ and $R = S/N$. From these we get

$$S = \frac{M}{1 + \dfrac{1}{R}}.$$

This shows that for large values of R, the true signal S is approximately equal to the measured value M. For low noise values, R is essentially zero and noise corrections are insignificant.

See also: ATOMIC PHYSICS; GEIGER COUNTER; NOISE; RADIOACTIVITY; SIGNAL; SOUND

Bibliography

DERENIAK, E. L., and CROWE, D. G. *Optical Radiation Detectors* (Wiley, New York, 1984).

GRUM, F., and BECHERER, R. J. *Optical Radiation Measurements* (Academic Press, New York, 1979).

WILLIAM BICKEL

SIGNIFICANT FIGURES

The familiar number π is both real and irrational; to express it as a decimal number without error, one would need to write down an infinite number of dig-

its. Indeed, mathematicians and computer scientists have devised algorithms that, in principle, can calculate arbitrary numbers of digits in the decimal expansions of this and many other irrational real numbers. Recent calculations have produced well in excess of 2 billion digits of π.

As impressive as these achievements are, they are of little practical import. Recall that the circumference of a circle of radius r is $2\pi r$. With an apparatus that could measure arbitrarily large lengths to an accuracy of one-tenth of a millimeter, one would have to measure the radius and circumference of a near-perfect circle larger than about 500,000 km in radius before an error in just the thirteenth digit of π could be discovered. This is larger than the average radius of the orbit of the earth's moon. To detect an error in only the thirtieth digit would require an essentially perfect circle larger in size than the observable universe. The digits of π beyond the first several are simply not significant in most physical applications.

Most measurable physical quantities are represented by real numbers. But unlike the pure number π, the digits of physical quantities are accessible only by measurements, and not by formulas or algorithms. The limitations of physical measurements permit accurate knowledge of only a finite number of digits of a physical quantity. The number of digits believed to be accurately known is called the number of significant figures.

Scientists adhere to the convention of quoting only the significant figures of the results of measurements and calculations as a shorthand for communicating the accuracy of their results. Every digit in a number is considered significant unless it is a zero whose only purpose is to fix the position of a decimal point. Thus all of the digits in 76.50 are significant, but only the digits 7, 6, and 5 in 0.0765 are significant. Sometimes the number of significant digits is not clear in values greater than one. For example, the final zero in 7,650 may or may not be significant, depending on whether it is known to be zero or whether its function is merely to mark the place of the decimal point. To eliminate such ambiguity, it is best to express values in scientific notation, in which case all of the digits of the mantissa (which must be between 1 and 10) are considered significant. In scientific notation, the first two examples are 7.650×10^1 and 7.65×10^{-2}. The third example would be written as 7.650×10^3 if the trailing zero is significant, and as 7.65×10^3 if it is not.

Very few physical quantities are known to many significant figures; the electron's gyromagnetic ratio (known to eleven significant figures) and the period of the radio pulsar PSR 1937 + 214 (known to fourteen significant figures) are examples of uncommonly accurate measurements. More commonly, physical quantities are known to only a few significant figures. For example, the electron's mass is known to six significant figures, and Newton's constant of gravitation is known to only four.

As already noted, use of significant figures is merely a shorthand for expressing the accuracy of a value. A more precise quantification is provided by quoting the uncertainty of the value along with the value itself. When this is done, it is common to quote one or two digits beyond those that are significant to avoid inaccuracies from rounding off the value to the number of significant digits. For example, suppose one measured the mass of a sample with a scale that provided digits to the nearest milligram and that repeated measurements fluctuated in the last digit, revealing the scale to be accurate to ±3 mg. If the scale indicated a mass of 3.257 g, then a summary of the measurement using significant figures would be 3.26 g, telling the reader only that the true value lies between 3.255 g and 3.265 g. A summary that included the uncertainty would instead be 3.257 ± 0.003 g, a different, smaller range than that inferred from only the significant figures.

One must be careful when combining numbers known with finite accuracy. Calculations can change the number of significant figures available in subtle ways. For example, although 8.677 and 8.642 each have four significant figures, their difference, 0.035, has only two significant figures (that is, it is not 0.03500). Their sum, 17.32, has four significant figures, although it does not have as many digits to the right of the decimal point. Most calculations either reduce the number of significant figures or leave it unchanged; only a few types of calculation (such as taking roots, like the square root) can increase the number of significant figures. One can best account for uncertainties in calculations by including a measure of uncertainty with each value and using the theory of probability to determine how these uncertainties affect the final results. Such calculations are called propagation of errors.

The significant figures scientists quote are those *believed* to be accurately known. Scientists determine the number of significant digits based on the sources of experimental error known to them. If undetected or inaccurately quantified sources of error exist, a result will be less accurate than quoted. For example, three experimental teams recently measured Newton's gravitational constant with greater precision than had been obtained in previous experiments. However, their results differ in their significant figures, both from each other and from the previously measured value. Most likely, some or all of the teams have neglected or underestimated sources of systematic error in their measurements, a danger that all scientists face.

See also: ACCURACY AND PRECISION; ERROR, EXPERIMENTAL; SCIENTIFIC NOTATION

Bibliography

TAYLOR, J. R. *An Introduction to Error Analysis: The Study of Uncertainties in Physical Measurements* (University Science Books, Mill Valley, CA, 1982).

THOMAS J. LOREDO

SI UNITS

SI, short for the French name *Le Système International d'Unités,* is sometimes called the Modernized Metric System. The international character of the metric system was established in 1875 by the Treaty of the Meter (seventeen countries subscribing, including the United States). SI was created in 1960, primarily by making modifications to one of the meter-kilogram-second (MKS) systems.

Generally accepted units of measurement facilitate communication and trade across national borders. Scientists, who need to be understood worldwide, have always used metric units, except in some specialized applications. Companies engaged in international trade use SI, and SI is increasingly used by the U.S. Government. In 1988 the U.S. Congress designated SI as the preferred system of measurement. U.S. Customary units are based on SI. The inch and the pound are defined in terms of the meter and the kilogram; other units, such as electrical units, have been adopted from SI.

Main Features of the SI

Many features give the SI distinct advantages over other units, and after a little practice, most users praise its simplicity.

Table 1 SI Base Units

Quantity	Unit Name	Unit Symbol
Length	meter	m
Mass	kilogram	kg
Time	second	s
Electric current	ampere	A
Temperature	kelvin	K
Amount of substance	mole	mol
Luminous intensity	candela	cd

There are seven SI base units (Table 1), which are used to form all other so-called derived units. The unit for quantity is given in terms of base units by the formulas of physics and geometry, which relate the quantity to the base quantities. For example, the unit for area is the square meter (m^2); it is formed by two "meter" factors since areas are obtained essentially by multiplying two length factors—as in multiplying the length and width of a rectangle, or having the square of the radius in the formula for the area of a circle, $A_c = \pi r^2$.

The units for quantities in all fields, such as electricity, heat, mechanics, and so on, are part of the system.

There is only one unit for each kind of quantity. This is in contrast, for example, to the many units for length in U.S. Customary units (e.g., inch, foot, yard, mile, furlong, fathom, chain, etc.) which are related to each other by various conversion factors. By using SI units consistently, one knows the unit of any calculated quantity (coherence). For example, in order to calculate the work done in compressing a gas, one multiplies the pressure (for simplicity, assumed to be constant) by the change of volume. This would not give a familiar energy unit if one uses the atmosphere (atm) as the pressure unit and the liter as the volume unit; while measuring pressure in pascals and volume in cubic meters will give work in joules.

The multiples and submultiples of the units provide the equivalent of larger or smaller units for a given quantity. They are designated by prefixes which can be attached to any unit having a special name. The prefixes indicate the factor by which the multiple or submultiple differs from the unit, that is, by how many places the decimal point has to be shifted.

Data from measurements can immediately be used in calculations because of the decimal nature of both the prefixes and the common number system. There is no need to remove common fractions or use a variety of conversion factors to combine the units for a given quantity.

With data and calculations in decimal form one can easily give an approximate indication of the precision of the information by the number of digits carried. For example, if the length of a bench is given as 2 m, one does not know whether the measurement is an approximation or has been carefully established. By giving the length as 2.00 m one can show that it has been measured with centimeter precision.

The few specific facts that one needs to know in using SI can be presented in a few tables, and cover applications in all sciences, technology, commerce, and so on. For general use the parts shown in boldface in Tables 1 and 2 are often sufficient, and most users need only a few units from the lists in Tables 3 and 4.

Prefixes

Table 2 lists the prefixes, their symbols, and power-of-ten equivalents. The multiples and submultiples of the units are generally in steps of 1,000.

Table 2 SI Prefixes

Factor	Prefix	Symbol
10^{24}	yotta	Y
10^{21}	zetta	Z
10^{18}	exa	E
10^{15}	peta	P
10^{12}	tera	T
10^{9}	giga	G
10^{6}	mega	M
10^{3}	kilo	k
10^{2}	hecto	h
10^{1}	deca (U.S.: deka)	da
10^{-1}	deci	d
10^{-2}	centi	c
10^{-3}	milli	m
10^{-6}	micro	μ
10^{-9}	nano	n
10^{-12}	pico	p
10^{-15}	femto	f
10^{-18}	atto	a
10^{-21}	zepto	z
10^{-24}	yocto	y

However, for greater flexibility in everyday applications, there are also prefixes for factors of 10.

One can avoid the use of prefixes by substituting power-of-ten notation. For example, one can substitute 2×10^3 m for 2 km.

Changing to different multiples and submultiples requires only a shift of the decimal point. It is well to realize that going down the table to smaller multiples and submultiples results in larger numerical values, that is, moving the decimal point toward the right, as in 2.345 km = 2,345 m.

The prefix becomes a part of the new multiple or submultiple of the unit, and should not be separated from the unit by a space or hyphen in either the name or the symbols. This is important, for example, when a unit with a prefix is raised to a power. The meaning can be clarified by using parentheses, as in the explanatory steps of the following example:

$$5 \text{ cm}^2 = 5(\text{cm})^2 = 5(10^{-2} \text{ m})^2 = 5 \times 10^{-4} \text{ m}^2.$$

In substituting data into an equation, it may happen that there are several prefixes and power-of-ten factors. Normally, one would combine all such factors and express the final result with only one power-of-ten factor or a single prefix. For example, calculating the gravitational force between two lead spheres with masses of $M = 4$ kg and $m = 9$ g, at a distance of $d = 7$ cm between centers, might look like the following equations, where the tabulated value of the gravitational constant is $G = 6.7 \times 10^{-11}$ m^3/(kg·s^2):

$$F = \frac{G \cdot M \cdot m}{d^2}$$

$$= \frac{6.7 \times 10^{-11} \text{ m}^3}{\text{kg·s}^2} \times \frac{4.0 \text{ kg} \times 9.0 \text{ g}}{(7 \text{ cm})^2}.$$

Multiplying by the conversion factors 1 kg/10^3 g and $(10^2$ cm/m$)^2$, we obtain

$$F = \frac{6.7 \times 4.0 \times 9.0 \times 10^{-10} \text{ m·kg}}{49 \text{ s}^2}$$

$$= 4.9 \times 10^{-10} \text{ N} = 0.49 \text{ nN}.$$

In order to use units already in use in older metric systems, the kilogram was chosen as a base unit (in spite of the fact that it already has a prefix). Prefixes are normally applied to base units; however, in the case of the mass unit, prefixes are attached to the "gram," as in milligram (mg). When one consolidates the various prefixes and powers-of-ten in a calculation, (as in the preceding example), mass units should be changed to "kilogram."

Special Unit Names

Table 3 lists all derived units that have special names. Their equivalent in terms of other derived units or base units may be used. Such use often becomes necessary when one wants to cancel or combine units.

In some cases, the names serve important purposes. When prefixes are used, names are simpler than the expression in terms of base units. Names are frequently preferred for units that occur in many different fields and when the relation to the base units is not important. Some names were well established, and others replaced obsolete units.

The joule (J) is the unit of energy, and is encountered in many fields. It also serves to distinguish the units for energy and torque (moment of force), since both are measured in N·m or m^2·kg·s^{-2}.

The hertz (Hz) is the unit for frequency of periodic processes. With a prefix it is better understood than "cycles per second" (e.g., one megahertz equals one cycle per microsecond).

The becquerel (Bq) is another reciprocal time unit. It measures the activity, the number of "disintegrations per second," of radioactive materials.

Two other radiologic units, the unit for absorbed dose, the gray (Gy), and the unit for dose equivalent, the sievert (Sv), have special names for reasons of safety. In order to distinguish these quantities, these names should be used instead of J/kg, which measures the energy supplied by ionizing radiation per kilogram of the irradiated material. The biological effect of radiation depends on both the amount of energy that the radiation deposits, and on the kind of radiation and the energy of the photons or other particles. The equivalent dose (in sieverts) received in a given irradiation event is obtained by multiplying the dose (in grays) by a quality factor (also called relative biological effectiveness) with values from about 1 to 20.

Table 3 SI-Derived Units with Special Names

Quantity	Name	Symbol	Expression in Terms of SI Base Units	Some Expressions in Terms of Other SI Units
Force	newton	N	$m \cdot kg \cdot s^{-2}$	
Energy, work, heat	joule	J	$m^2 \cdot kg \cdot s^{-2}$	$N \cdot m$
Power	watt	W	$m^2 \cdot kg \cdot s^{-3}$	J/s
Pressure, stress	pascal	Pa	$m^{-1} \cdot kg \cdot s^{-2}$	N/m^2
Frequency (periodic)	hertz	Hz	$1/s$	
Activity (decay rate in radioactivity)	becquerel	Bq	$1/s$	
Absorbed dose	grey	Gy	$m^2 \cdot s^{-2}$	J/kg
Dose equivalent	sievert	Sv	$m^2 \cdot s^{-2}$	J/kg
Electric charge	coulomb	C	$s \cdot A$	
Electric potential	volt	V	$m^2 \cdot kg \cdot s^{-3} \cdot A^{-1}$	$W/A, J/C$
Electrical resistance	ohm	Ω	$m^2 \cdot kg \cdot s^{-3} \cdot A^{-2}$	$V/A,$
Electrical conductance	siemens	S	$m^{-2} \cdot kg^{-1} \cdot s^3 \cdot A^2$	$A/V, \Omega^{-1}$
Capacitance	farad	F	$m^{-2} \cdot kg^{-1} \cdot s^4 \cdot A^2$	C/V
Inductance	henry	H	$m^2 \cdot kg \cdot s^{-2} \cdot A^{-2}$	Wb/A
Magnetic flux	weber	Wb	$m^2 \cdot kg \cdot s^{-2} \cdot A^{-1}$	$V \cdot s$
Magnetic flux density	tesla	T	$kg \cdot s^{-2} \cdot A^{-1}$	$Wb/m^2, N \cdot m^{-1} \cdot A^{-1}$
Plane angle	radian	rad	$m/m = 1$	
Solid angle	steradian	sr	$m^2/m^2 = 1$	
Luminous flux	lumen	lm	$cd \cdot sr$	
Illuminance	lux	lx	$m^{-2} \cdot cd \cdot sr$	lm/m^2
Celsius temperature	degree Celsius	°C	K	

Many electrical and magnetic units have special names that were in use before SI was established. The relation to other electrical and magnetic units is more apparent, and is often more important than the relation to base units, as shown in Table 3.

The radian and steradian are units of plane angle and solid angle, respectively. They were sometimes considered as a different class of units. They have the property that their expression in base units is "one" ($m/m = 1$, and $m^2/m^2 = 1$). The units can be used when their use contributes to greater clarity, or can be omitted when not needed. These units should be used explicitly, when the quantity under consideration does contain the angle in its usual definition, as in angle (rad), angular speed (rad/s), angular acceleration (rad/s²), torsion constant (N·m/rad), and in several radiation quantities, such as radiant intensity (W/sr).

Writing Rules and Recommendations

In writing compound units, where symbols are to be multiplied or divided, one should exercise caution that there is no ambiguity in what operation is intended or whether a symbol represents a unit or a prefix. This can be done by using multiplication or division signs for the operations, parentheses, or positive or negative exponents.

Although it is permissible to omit a multiplication sign and use a space, or even no space, between the unit symbols, in the United States the centered dot (multiplication dot) is recommended. For example, since m may stand for the prefix milli- or for the unit meter, it is better to write m·N, or Nm instead of m N, because the space might be overlooked and the compound unit misunderstood as mN (millinewton).

There should be no multiplication or division signs on the same line following a solidus (slanted division sign), especially not another solidus, unless parentheses make the operations unambiguous. For example, use $(m/s)/s$ or m/s^2 or $m \cdot s^{-2}$, but not $m/s/s$. Although $kg/m \cdot s^2$ may be admitted by some, $kg/(m \cdot s^2)$ or $m^{-1} \cdot kg \cdot s^{-2}$ or N/m^2 or Pa are preferred.

One should never use two prefixes applied to the same unit. For example, do not use $m\mu m$ (millimicrometer) for nm (nanometer).

Prefixes should not be used without a unit; that is, do not use 1 k or 1 kilo for 1 kg; do not write 1 M/s for 1 MHz $= 1/\mu s$. Prefixes should not be used on derived units in compound form; for example, do not use $m(m \cdot kg/s^2)$ for $10^{-3} \ m \cdot kg/s^2 = 1 \ mN$.

More rules and recommendations for the correct use of units of measure are as follows:

- The symbols for units and prefixes should be printed in roman (upright) type and without the plural "s" or abbreviation periods.
- All units, including those named after persons, should be written with a lowercase initial letter (except at the beginning of a sentence and "degree Celsius" and °C).
- Use the appropriate lowercase or capital letters for symbols as shown in the Tables 1–4.
- Half-spaces may be used to separate numbers with more than four digits on either side of the decimal point, in groups of three. Commas should not be used, because the comma is the decimal marker in some countries.

- A zero should be placed in front of the decimal point if there are only decimal fractions (e.g., 0.454 kg).
- There should usually be a space between the numerical value and the unit symbol, except for plane angles (e.g., 10° 24′ = 10.4°).
- Spelling and pronunciation differ in various countries but the symbols are the same everywhere.

Non-SI Units

A few non-SI units are officially in use with SI (see Table 4). Their use, however, destroys some of the advantages of SI, such as the coherence and the existence of only one unit for each quantity.

There are several units that are temporarily in use with SI. However, they are not needed, since there are SI units available.

Comments About Base Units

Users of SI seldom need to know how the base units (Table 1) are defined; instead, they rely on calibrated measuring instruments. The definitions of some of the base units appear simple in principle, but are experimentally too complicated to use directly. Simpler experiments are often used for actual calibrations, using theoretical or experimental modifications and corrections.

The meter was defined in 1983 as the length of the path light travels in vacuum in a specified time. The time was chosen so that the meter comes as close as

Table 4 Units in Use with the SI

Quantity	Unit Name	Unit Symbol	SI Equivalent
Time	minute	min	1 min = 60 s
	hour	h	1 h = 3,600 s
	day	d	1 d = 86,400 s
Plane angle	degree	°	$1° = (\pi/180)$ rad
	minute	′	$1′ = [\pi/(180 \times 60)]$ rad
	second	″	$1″ = [\pi/(180 \times 60 \times 60)]$ rad
Volume	liter	l or L (U.S.)	$1 \ L = 1 \ dm^3 = 10^{-3} \ m^3$
Mass	tonne (U.S.: metric ton)	t	1 t = 1,000 kg
Energy (atomic)	electron volt	eV	$1 \ eV \approx 1.602 \times 10^{-19} \ J$
Mass (atomic)	unified atomic mass unit	u	$1 \ u \approx 1.660 \times 10^{-27} \ kg$

possible to the length unit previously defined, so there is no need to correct earlier measurements.

The kilogram is defined as the mass of the prototype kilogram kept at Sevres, France. It is the only base unit not yet defined in terms of physical processes.

The second is defined as the duration of a specified number of periods of the radiation corresponding to a specified transition of atoms of cesium-133. Atomic clocks are more uniform than the earth's motion, which was the original basis of the definition of the second. In order to keep these two ways of timing in step, a few seconds are added to, or subtracted from, the astronomical year, twice a year if necessary.

The ampere is defined in terms of the magnetic forces between parallel currents, and allows all electrical and magnetic units to become part of the system.

The kelvin or "thermodynamic temperature" scale is defined by the relation that the ratio of the temperatures between which an ideal heat engine (Carnot cycle) operates is equal to the ratio of the amount of heat supplied to the amount wasted. To complete the definition, one temperature value has to be specified. The temperature of the triple point of water has been set at $T_T = 273.16$ K. This scale also establishes absolute zero, which coincides with the absolute zero of the ideal gas law. The zero of the Celsius scale is defined to be at 273.15 K. These definitions place the freezing point of water and the boiling point of water at a pressure of 101.325 kPa at approximately 0 °C and 100 °C, respectively. A temperature interval of 1 K is the same as 1 °C. One measures both temperatures and temperature intervals in kelvin (K) or degrees Celsius (°C).

The mole is the base unit of "amount of substance." This is a way to measure the amount of a "substance" (atoms, or molecules, or electrons, etc.) by the number of particles. One mole is the number of particles equal to the number of atoms in 0.012 kg of carbon-12. That number, known as Avogadro's number, has been determined to be about $N_A \approx 6.022137 \times 10^{23}$ particles per mole.

The candela is defined in terms of a monochromatic light source of specified wavelength and power radiated per steradian. In order to make measurements on sources of various colors, one must refer to generally accepted average spectral sensitivity curves of dark- and light-adapted human eyes.

Conclusion

SI is continually being modified because increased precision is demanded and made possible by improved technology, or because new developments of measurement science allow more consistent approaches. The latest official status is found in a frequently updated booklet published by the international metric committees.

Bibliography

INTERNATIONAL ORGANIZATION FOR STANDARDIZATION. *International Standard ISO 31: Quantities and Units* (ISO, Geneva, 1992).

INTERNATIONAL ORGANIZATION FOR STANDARDIZATION. *International Standard ISO 1000* (ISO, Geneva, 1992).

NATIONAL INSTITUTE OF STANDARDS AND TECHNOLOGY. *The International System of Units (SI)*, NIST Special Publication 330 (U.S. Government Printing Office, Washington, DC, 1991).

NATIONAL INSTITUTE OF STANDARDS AND TECHNOLOGY. *Guide for the Use of the International System of Units (SI)*, NIST Special Publication 811 (U.S. Government Printing Office, Washington, DC, 1995).

MARIO IONA

SKIN EFFECT

The amplitude of an electromagnetic (EM) wave in a conductive medium is attenuated more or less exponentially in the direction of propagation. The attenuation is measured by the skin depth δ, which is defined as the distance of penetration at which the amplitude is reduced to $1/e$ of its initial value. For a good conductor,

$$\delta \approx (\omega\sigma\mu)^{-1/2},$$

where ω is the angular frequency of the wave ($\omega = 2\pi f$, where f is the ordinary frequency), σ the conductivity of the medium, and μ its permeability. Since δ varies inversely as the square root of ω, high frequency waves penetrate less than low-frequency waves; electric currents produced by the wave are therefore concentrated nearer the surface of a conductor in the high-frequency case. With copper

$[\sigma \approx 6 \times 10^7 \ (\Omega \ \text{m})^{-1}$ and $\mu \approx \mu_0 = 4\pi \times 10^{-7}$ $\Omega \ \text{s/m}]$, for example, a line current with a frequency of 60 Hz has a skin depth of 6 mm, while radio waves with a frequency of 1 MHz have a skin depth of 0.05 mm and microwaves with a frequency of 10 GHz have a skin depth of 0.5 μm.

Low-frequency current, such as ordinary line current, is rather uniformly distributed over the cross section of a typical wire because the radius of the wire is usually small compared with the skin depth. At radio frequencies, however, the current is concentrated near the surface of a wire, thus reducing its effective cross section and increasing its resistance; this is called the skin effect.

At microwave frequencies, the skin depth is so small that current exists virtually on the surface of a wire. Moreover, energy is essentially carried by the electromagnetic wave that surrounds the wire, or as is usually the case, within a hollow, often rectangular, conductor called a waveguide. A relatively low-loss microwave guide, therefore, can be economically made by plating, say brass, with a good conductor like silver.

Theory

For a linear, homogeneous, isotropic, conducting medium in which the current density $\mathbf{j}$ is proportional to the electric field $\mathbf{E}$ (i.e., $\mathbf{j} = \sigma\mathbf{E}$), Maxwell's equations can be combined to yield a wave equation in $\mathbf{E}$. Specifically, if we consider a plane wave traveling in the z direction, we can write $\mathbf{E} = \mathbf{E}(z)\exp(i\omega t)$; then

$$\frac{d^2\mathbf{E}(z)}{dz^2} + (\omega^2\varepsilon\mu + i\omega\sigma\mu)\mathbf{E}(z) = 0,$$

where ε is the permittivity of the medium and $i = \sqrt{-1}$. Writing $\mathbf{E}(z) = \mathbf{E}_0\exp(i\kappa z)$, where κ is a constant, and substituting this form of $\mathbf{E}$ into the above differential equation, we find that

$$-\kappa^2 + \omega^2\varepsilon\mu + i\omega\sigma\mu = 0.$$

Thus κ is a complex number whose real and imaginary parts can be determined using the algebra of complex numbers:

$$\text{Re}(\kappa) = \pm\omega\sqrt{\varepsilon\mu/2}\left(1 \pm \sqrt{1 + (\sigma/\omega\varepsilon)^2}\right)^{1/2},$$

$$\text{Im}(\kappa) = \frac{\omega\sigma\mu}{2\text{Re}(\kappa)}.$$

The real part of κ is the propagation constant such that $\text{Re}(\kappa) = 2\pi/\lambda$, where λ is the wavelength. The imaginary part gives the attenuation of the wave (i.e., the loss of amplitude and thus energy of the wave in the direction of propagation); $\text{Im}(\kappa) = 1/\delta$, which defines the skin depth exactly. Therefore,

$$\mathbf{E} = \mathbf{E}_0 \exp\left[-z/\delta + 2\pi i \ (z/\lambda - ft)\right],$$

which represents a plane wave propagating in the z direction with wavelength λ, frequency f, and amplitude decaying exponentially with penetration depth δ.

A good conductor can be defined by the condition $(\sigma/\omega\varepsilon) \gg 1$. From the equations for the real and imaginary parts of κ, we find, after some approximation, that $\text{Re}(\kappa) \approx \text{Im}(\kappa) \approx (\omega\sigma\mu/2)^{1/2}$, which justifies our initial expression for the skin depth. From the relationships above we can show that $\sigma/\omega\varepsilon = 2(\lambda/2\pi\delta)^2$; thus, in a good conductor the penetration depth is small compared to the wavelength of the penetrating wave.

See also: CONDUCTION; CONDUCTOR; ELECTRICAL CONDUCTIVITY; ELECTROMAGNETISM; RADIO WAVE

Bibliography

GRIFFITHS, D. J. *Introduction to Electrodynamics,* 2nd ed. (Prentice Hall, Englewood Cliffs, NJ, 1981).

REITZ, J. R., and MILFORD, F. J. *Foundations of Electromagnetic Theory,* 2nd ed. (Addison-Wesley, Reading, MA, 1967).

WANGSNESS, R. K. *Electromagnetic Fields* (Wiley, New York, 1979).

F. R. YEATTS

SKY, COLOR OF

The blue color of the clear, daytime sky is one of the most striking and ubiquitous examples in nature of the interaction of light with matter. The first physical explanation of the effect was given in 1871 by the famous British scientist Lord Rayleigh (John

William Strutt, third Baron Rayleigh). Ever since that time, the phenomenon that produces this blue color has been known as Rayleigh scattering. Rayleigh's explanation, employing sound physical intuition and dimensional analysis, is so clear and general that it is worth paraphrasing herein.

Rayleigh reasoned that there are small particles in the atmosphere, much smaller than even the shortest wavelength of light, that intercept light coming from the sun and scatter it in all directions. He set out to find the ratio of amplitude of the scattered wave to that of the incident wave, A_s/A_i, for one such particle. His intuition told him that the only quantities with dimensions that should affect this ratio are V, the volume of the scattering particle; r, the distance from the scattering particle to the point where the scattered light is observed; λ, the wavelength of the light; c, the speed of light; and ρ and ρ', the densities of the surrounding medium and particle, respectively. Dimensionless quantities, such as angle, were ignored. Considering the fundamental dimensions of mass, length, and time, he noted that the two densities were the only quantities in the list of six that contain mass. Since the final ratio has no dimensions of mass, these two can only enter the final expression as a ratio (so that mass cancels out): ρ/ρ'. This ratio is itself a dimensionless constant and was dropped from any further consideration. He next noted that c is the only quantity with dimensions of time contained in it, and, therefore, because the final ratio is time-independent, it must not enter the final expression. This left him with a dependence of A_s/A_i on V, r, and λ. However, the ratio is proportional to V and inversely proportional to r (the amplitude of a wave spreading out in three-dimensional space decreases as $1/r$, if the observer is more than a few wavelengths away). Therefore, λ must enter the final expression so as to make the ratio dimensionless and have A_s/A_i proportional to $V/\lambda^2 r$. Now the intensity I of a wave (power per unit area) is proportional to amplitude squared, so

$$I_s/I_i \propto V^2/(\lambda^4 r^2). \tag{1}$$

This result, obtained with remarkably little effort and no analysis of the details of the scattering process itself, correctly predicts the dependence of scattered light on particle size, distance, and wavelength, at least insofar as the scattering particles are much smaller than a wavelength. The part of the expression for the ratio of intensities that is of the most importance here is the proportionality of λ^{-4}, and this dependence is confirmed by later analyses that more specifically consider the mechanism of the scattering. As Rayleigh suspected, the particles in the atmosphere that give rise to this type of scattering are mainly the air molecules of nitrogen and oxygen themselves: N_2 and O_2. These easily satisfy the condition of being much smaller than a wavelength of light, each being only about 0.1 nm in diameter, whereas light wavelengths are thousands of times larger. The electrons in these air molecules act much like little oscillators, like small masses on springs, when acted upon by an outside force. Every such oscillator has "natural" or "resonant" frequencies with which it vibrates when briefly disturbed and then left to move on its own. The resonant frequencies for these electrons are very high, corresponding to ultraviolet frequencies of electromagnetic radiation far above the frequency of light. Because the electrons are electrically charged, they feel a force when an electromagnetic wave such as light passes by. The force is periodic, with a frequency of a light wave, and because this frequency is well below the resonant frequency for the electrons, their response is to oscillate weakly at the same frequency as the light. The amplitude of vibration is very nearly the same no matter what the frequency of light, because it is far below resonance. However, electromagnetic theory says that any accelerating charge also radiates an electromagnetic wave, and any oscillating particle is continually accelerating. The strength of the electric field in this wave radiated from a charge is proportional to the acceleration, $E \propto a$. It also is known that acceleration in this type of simple harmonic motion is proportional to frequency squared times the displacement of the particle from equilibrium, $a \propto f^2 x$. Combining these proportionalities produces $E \propto f^2 x$. The intensity of an electromagnetic wave is proportional to field squared, so $I \propto f^4 x^2$. Both the electron position and the field strength are changing very rapidly (with the frequency of the incident light), and, therefore, so is the radiated wave intensity at any point. However, the main interest lies in average or mean values, and although the mean position of the oscillating electron may be zero, the mean *squared* position is not. Thus, it may be concluded that the mean intensity of light radiated from these oscillating electrons is proportional to f^4. This intensity corresponds to the I_s of Rayleigh's treatment because it is the intensity of the light reradiated in all directions by the disturbed electrons: the scattered light. As frequency and wavelength are inversely related by

$$f = c/\lambda, \qquad (2)$$

it can finally be stated that $I_s \propto \lambda^{-4}$. A complete analysis along these lines, which includes the electromagnetic nature of the interaction between light and matter, also will reveal the dependence of the scattered light intensity on angle and polarization, but all that is needed to explain the blue sky is the λ^{-4} dependence.

The expression for scattered intensity implies that the *shortest* wavelengths will be scattered most strongly. Now the wavelengths of visible light range from about 400 nm to about 700 nm, with the shortest wavelength appearing violet and the longest appearing red to the human eye, and the intermediate wavelengths each producing the sensation of one of the other colors of the spectrum or the rainbow: blue, blue-green, green, yellow, orange, and so on. Sunlight contains all wavelengths at approximately equal intensities and such light appears white to the human eye. As sunlight streams through the atmosphere in a nearly parallel beam, power is continuously removed from the direct beam and scattered in all directions by Rayleigh scattering. The above reasoning indicates that more of the violet light will be scattered than the blue, more blue than green, more green than yellow, and so forth to the conclusion that red light will be scattered least of all. Since the whole atmosphere within the field-of-view of any earthbound observer is bathed in sunlight when the Sun is above the horizon, and the atmospheric particles scatter in all directions, the observer will see deep-blue light coming from all directions in the sky, the color of which is that of the sunlight mixture heavily weighted toward the blue end of the spectrum by the λ^{-4} dependence. The ratio of Eq. (1) is quite small, even for blue light, so it is difficult to see the color of Rayleigh-scattered light unless it is viewed against a dark background. However, the background for sky light is the blackness of outer space, so that condition is fulfilled.

The red color of the sunrise or sunset is a lighting effect complementary to the blue of the sky. The direct, unscattered, light from the sun is nearly white when entering the atmosphere, and then has progressively more of the violet, blue, green, and so on removed by Rayleigh scattering along its path. Therefore, the light remaining after a long atmospheric path is orange to red in appearance. Any observer views direct sunlight through the longest atmospheric path when the sun appears just on the horizon, sunrise or sunset, so the Sun itself appears reddish.

In this explanation, it has been assumed that the scattered intensity from many particles is essentially just like that from one particle, only scaled up by the number of particles doing the scattering. This assumption is true if the individual scattering particles are acting independently, in which case the light is said to be incoherent and total scattered intensity is the sum of intensities from individual scatterers. In a gas, the molecules are moving around quite randomly, little influenced by one another, and emitting light independently. But the same cannot be said for condensed states of matter. The most notable example of condensed matter in the atmosphere is small suspended droplets of water (small solid or liquid particles suspended in the atmosphere are often referred to as an aerosol). When the droplets are very small, smaller than a wavelength of light, each can still be considered as a single scattering particle in either the general argument of Rayleigh or the electromagnetic reasoning, so they would still give rise to Rayleigh scattering with its propensity for blue light. For this reason, an aerosol of very small particles can increase the Rayleigh scattering of the atmosphere over that obtained from the air molecules alone. When fine dust is added to the atmosphere by volcanic explosions, sunsets may appear more vividly red for a period of time. However, when the aerosol particles become as large as or larger than a wavelength of light, cooperative effects begin to make a difference: light from molecules within the larger particle begins to add in a partially coherent manner. In this case, the amplitude of the wave being radiated by the entire surface of the particle toward the observer is just the same as if it had come only from oscillators acting together in a circular zone on the surface whose area is proportional to wavelength (known as the first Fresnel zone); the effect of oscillators outside this zone is nil. Now the depth within the droplet from which molecules contribute to the scattered wave also is proportional to wavelength, so the total volume of oscillators within the droplet contributing to the scattered wave is proportional to λ^2. For a uniform density, the number of oscillators contributing also must be proportional to λ^2, and, therefore, $E \propto \lambda^2$, $I_s \propto \lambda^4$. However, the intensity already had a λ^{-4} dependence from each oscillator, and thus this proportionality of the number of cooperatively radiating oscillators to λ^4 just cancels out the previous effect! For large scattering particles, there is no wavelength dependence and white-light scattering results.

This is the reason that clouds appear white: Clouds are made up of suspended water droplets that are larger than a wavelength of light, and those droplets scatter all visible wavelengths equally. Individuals watching a wisp at the edge of a cloud apparently disappearing into the blue sky are really seeing the change from white-light scattering to Rayleigh scattering as the water droplets evaporate to a size smaller than a wavelength of light. One may use this knowledge to judge the size of haze droplets, which may range in radius from 10 nm to 1,000 nm. A bluish haze must have particles toward the lower end of the size range, whereas a white haze must consist of the larger particles. Another example of color change with scattering particle size can be seen in cigarette smoke. If the smoke rising from the burning tip is observed against a dark background, it has a definite bluish tinge, indicating small smoke particles. However, the smoke from the other end is noticeably whiter due to the increase in smoke particle size from the addition of moisture and tars as the smoke travels the length of the cigarette. The bluish tinge of skimmed milk is a Rayleigh scattering effect caused by the small size of the suspended butterfat particles; whole milk has a larger butterfat content and correspondingly larger suspended particles that give white light scattering. Finally, even blue eyes are due to Rayleigh scattering of pigment particles smaller than a wavelength in the iris. In this case, the small intensity of the scattered light is made visible by the darkness of the interior of the eye, against which the scattered light is viewed. If the particles of pigment in the iris are larger, then they can absorb part of the light and produce brown or green eyes, the latter color arising from a combination of Rayleigh scattering and absorption.

See also: DIFFRACTION, FRESNEL; ELECTROMAGNETIC SPECTRUM; ELECTROMAGNETIC WAVE; LIGHT; LIGHT, ELECTROMAGNETIC THEORY OF; LIGHT, WAVE THEORY OF; OSCILLATION; RAINBOW; RESONANCE; SCATTERING, RAYLEIGH

Bibliography

BRAGG, W. *The Universe of Light* (Dover, New York, 1959).
FALK, D.; BRILL, D.; and STORK, D. *Seeing the Light* (Harper & Row, New York, 1986).
MINNAERT, M. *The Nature of Light and Colour in the Open Air* (Dover, New York, 1954).
WALDMAN, G. *Introduction to Light* (Prentice Hall, Englewood Cliffs, NJ, 1983).
WEISSKOPF, V. "How Light Interacts with Matter" in *Lasers and Light: Readings from Scientific American*, with introductions by A. L. Schawlow (W. H. Freeman, San Francisco, 1968).
WILLIAMSON, S., and CUMMINS, H. *Light and Color in Nature and Art* (Wiley, New York, 1983).

GARY WALDMAN

SNELL'S LAW

Whenever an electromagnetic wave, which includes visible light, ultraviolet and infrared rays, and microwaves, traveling in one medium is incident at the juncture with another medium, part of the ray is reflected back into the same medium and part is transmitted into the other medium, as shown in Fig. 1. The transmitted ray is also called the refracted ray; this phenomenon is known as refraction. Just as in the law of reflection, which relates the angle of incidence to the angle of reflection—the angles that the respective rays make with the normal to the interface between the two mediums—there is a definite relationship between the angle of incidence α

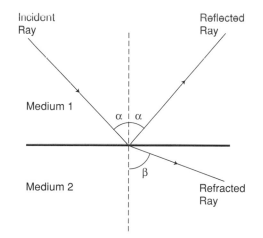

Figure 1 The geometry of an electromagnetic wave experiencing reflection and refraction as it is transmitted from one medium to another.

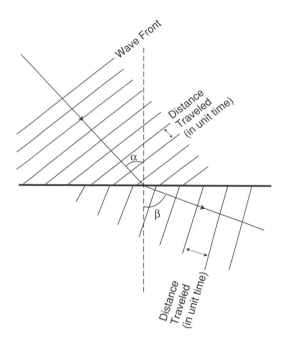

Figure 2 Variation in distance traveled by a wave front as it passes from one medium to another.

and the angle of refraction β, which depends on the relative characteristics of the two mediums. The physical basis for this relationship stems from the difference in the velocities with which electromagnetic waves propagate in the two mediums. The following relationship between the speeds v_1 and v_2 of the wave fronts in the two mediums satisfies the boundary condition for these waves:

$$\frac{v_1}{v_2} = \frac{\sin\alpha}{\sin\beta}. \tag{1}$$

The speed of propagation of the wave front in a medium is governed by the refractive index n of the medium, which is defined as

$$n = \frac{\text{speed of wave fronts in a vacuum}}{\text{speed of wave fronts in a medium}}. \tag{2}$$

For these purposes, $n_1 = c/v_1$ and $n_2 = c/v_2$, where c is the speed of light in the vacuum (3×10^8 m/s), and n_1 and n_2 are refractive indices of mediums 1 and 2, respectively. Hence

$$n_2 \sin\beta = n_1 \sin\alpha. \tag{3}$$

This relationship between the indices of refraction and the angles of incidence and refraction is known as Snell's law.

Figures 1 and 2 illustrate some of the consequences of this law. In Fig. 1, the angle of refraction is larger than the angle of incidence. This can only happen if $n_2 < n_1$; that is, if $v_2 > v_1$, which implies that the wave front travels a larger distance in unit time in medium 2 compared to that in medium 1, as in Fig. 2. For this case of an electromagnetic wave incident from a medium of higher refractive index to a lower one (like light traveling in water incident at the interface with air), Snell's law explains that for a particular angle of incidence α_o the angle of refraction becomes 90°. At this stage, the incidence ray undergoes total internal reflection, and there is no more transmission in medium 2. The angle α_c is called the critical angle. For angles of incidence equal to or larger than α_c, there is no more refraction. Therefore, $\alpha_c = \sin^{-1}(n_2/n_1)$.

See also: ELECTROMAGNETIC WAVE; REFLECTION; REFRACTION; REFRACTION, INDEX OF

TALAT RAHMAN

SOCIAL RESPONSIBILITY

In 1986, Soviet scientists and technicians were performing an unauthorized experiment at the Chernobyl nuclear power station. They accidentally cut off the water supply, triggering a massive reactor meltdown, explosion, and fire that spewed radioactive materials into the atmosphere. Experts predict that these materials, circulated around the globe, will cause between 30,000 and 475,500 additional cancer deaths, worldwide, by the year 2040.

Between 1951 and 1963, the U.S. Atomic Energy Commission performed more than one hundred above-ground weapons tests that will cause, worldwide, two million premature cancer deaths. Because U.S. scientists and politicians suppressed records showing fallout damage, Congress did not authorize compensation of test victims until 1990.

Both of these examples suggest that, independent of their duties to perform unbiased research, all scientists also bear responsibility for the social consequences of their work. The three main groups to whom they have social responsibility are employers or clients, third parties (members of the public), and other scientists or professionals.

Responsibilities to Three Groups

According to ethicist Michael Bayles, because of the employer-employee contract, scientists have at least six responsibilities to their clients: honesty, candor, competence, diligence, loyalty, and discretion. Because scientists' work has consequences for public welfare, they also have responsibilities to third parties: truthfulness, nonmaleficence, and fairness. To the degree that taxpayers ultimately fund scientific work, clients also include members of the public. Because fellow scientists control their education, licensing, and memberships, scientists likewise have responsibilities to other professionals: responsibilities to do candid and independent research, to reform the profession (so that it serves the public good), and to promote respect for the profession. Most ethicists justify all three scientists' responsibilities, in part, because they are necessary to promote the values of a liberal society. They reason that, if all members of society have an interest in life, bodily integrity, and personal property, then all people—so far as they are able—have good reasons for promoting the values of a liberal society: governance by law, freedom, protection from injury, equality of opportunity, privacy, and welfare. To the extent that scientists have greater abilities to promote these social values, they have greater responsibilities to do so to serve the public interest.

Three Duties

Regardless of how we define "the public interest," all scientists have basic duties to (1) avoid doing biased research, (2) promote nonbiased use of scholarly results, and (3) avoid harming present and future inhabitants of the planet. Scientists have the first two duties because lack of objectivity can harm those who use, or who are affected by, scientific work. Deliberate lack of objectivity also thwarts the purpose of science. The third duty is necessary to guarantee citizens' rights, such as free informed consent to decisions affecting their welfare. These three duties also are necessary because scientists—as professionals with economic, political, and intellectual power—control much of what happens in society. Their power arises from their special knowledge and the dependence of the public on them. Given scientists' special power and our highly sophisticated and technocratic society, scientists' social responsibilities are much greater than those of nonscientists.

Scientists also have greater responsibility because, as professionals, they exercise a monopoly over the services they provide. Because of this monopoly, the pressures of a competitive marketplace cannot function to check abuses of scientists' power. As a result, scientists have special knowledge and ability—often shared by few people—that lends them a degree of immunity from being discovered to be doing wrong. Because of this immunity, society depends on other scientists—fellow travellers along the lonely byways of knowledge—to protect the public interest.

Scientists who withhold potentially harmful information from the public ignore the fact that the ultimate power in a democracy ought to reside with individual citizens. Denying citizens information pertinent to their welfare effectively deprives them of the rights of citizenship. James Madison warned that knowledge always governs ignorance, and that a popular government—without popular means of acquiring information—will fail.

Albert Einstein likewise warned scientists that the right to search for truth also implies a duty not to conceal it. Even though taxpayer monies fund much research, governments often suppress scientific results and violate this duty. For example, in the 1950s the United States commissioned the Brookhaven Report (WASH-740) to investigate whether commercial nuclear power was safe and economical. When the experts concluded that a catastrophic nuclear accident could wipe out an area the size of Pennsylvania, cost more than $17 billion in property damage, and cause 45,000 immediate deaths and 100,000 later fatalities, government suppressed the taxpayer-funded report, lest its conclusions frighten the public. The government (the taxpayers) nevertheless underwrote insurance for the nuclear industry, both because private insurers refused to do so (at a cost-effective rate) and because utilities feared bankruptcy in the event of a catastrophic reactor accident. The Brookhaven Report was not released until nearly twenty years later, when it was made available as a result of the Freedom of Information Act.

Whistleblowing

Scientists have a responsibility to serve the public interest, to disseminate important policy-relevant results to those likely to be affected by them. Because scientists have this responsibility, they sometimes have a duty to "go public" with research—especially taxpayer-funded research—when employers or the government do not do so.

Whistleblowing is an act of organizational disobedience, performed by an employee—such as a scientist—in an effort to change organizational policies so that they protect the public interest. Some of the many constraints on ethical use of whistleblowing include the employee's reasonable beliefs that a potentially unethical policy cannot be overturned internally, that the public interest is seriously threatened, and that whistleblowing is likely to be effective. Because whistleblowing could hurt innocent people, scientists must assess each situation carefully before taking action.

See also: ERROR AND FRAUD; ETHICS

Bibliography

AMERICAN ASSOCIATION FOR THE ADVANCEMENT OF SCIENCE (AAAS). *Principles of Scientific Freedom and Responsibility,* revised draft (AAAS, Washington, DC, 1980).

BAYLES, M. *Professional Ethics* (Wadsworth, Belmont, CA, 1981).

GLAZER, M., and GLAZER, P. *The Whistleblowers* (Basic Books, New York, 1989).

MICELI, M., and NEAR, J. *Blowing the Whistle* (Macmillan, New York, 1992).

SHEA, W. R., and SITTER, B., eds. *Scientists and Their Responsibility* (Watson, Canton, MA, 1989).

SHRADER-FRECHETTE, K. S. *Nuclear Power and Public Policy* (Kluwer, Boston, 1983).

SHRADER-FRECHETTE, K. S. *Ethics of Scientific Research* (Rowman and Littlefield, Lanham, MD, 1994).

SIGMA XI, THE SCIENTIFIC RESEARCH SOCIETY. *Honor in Science* (Sigma Xi, New Haven, CT, 1986).

UNGER, S. H. *Controlling Technology: Ethics and the Responsible Engineer,* 2nd ed. (Wiley, New York, 1994).

KRISTIN SHRADER-FRECHETTE

SOCIETY, PHYSICS AND

What is the main driving force of history? Historians might answer that it is a combination of pan-ethnic nationalism (ancient Rome, modern Serbia), the great men of history (Napoleon, Winston Churchill), comparative economics (capitalism versus communism), and democracy versus despotic dictatorships (NATO versus the Warsaw Pact). Another view is that such historic drives are extremely important, but rather it is science and technology that have made and will continue to make the largest difference in what happens on Earth. The automobile frees us from the labor of walking, but it has changed landscapes and the sociology of the cities. Modern medicines certainly have saved lives, but they will help propel world population to 10 billion by 2050. Electricity is clearly a requirement for modern society, but its production creates carbon dioxide, which might warm the globe, and nuclear wastes, which continue to remain on-site. Even though the number of nuclear weapons is still more than 30,000, the major threats of the Cold War seem to be over. However, questions remain on maintaining guard over existing Russian plutonium, Iraqi nuclear desires, and North Korean nuclear ambitions. Thus, it appears that for each technological benefit, there are other costs that must be considered.

Universities

Because the study of the impact of science on society is a broad application of physics, most university physics departments have only developed a token approach to the subdiscipline of physics and society. One cannot argue with this approach, since a bachelor's degree in physics is the prerequisite to either a Ph.D. or a job in industry, both requiring a solid foundation in physics. However, it should be the role of university physics departments to offer a few courses and colloquia that would acquaint students with the interaction of science and the applied topics of energy, military, and environmental matters. Serious graduate level studies on these matters are not usually carried out in physics departments, but rather at specialized institutes, such as Stanford's Center for International Security and Arms Control, Lawrence Berkeley Laboratory's Center for Building Studies, or Princeton's Center for Energy and Environmental Studies.

The U.S. Congress

The U.S. Congress plays a major role in science and technology because laws that deal with science and technology must be passed and funds for research and demonstration projects must be appropriated. Because the Congress and its staff are primarily from nontechnical disciplines, Congress has often had to rely on the executive branch for much of its technical information. These complex issues are usually clouded and very interdisciplinary, with economic, political, and social trade-offs. For example, raising the automotive corporate average fuel economy (CAFE) standards to 40 miles per gallon is indeed a trade off between saving a million barrels of petroleum a day (one-half the production of the Alaskan pipeline) and various economic factors that affect the U.S. automobile industry. The simple physics answer of higher CAFE standards or a $3 per gallon tax (the same as Europe and Japan) will alone not carry the day.

Over the past two decades, Congress has been strengthened in several ways. In 1973 the congressional Office of Technology Assessment (OTA) was created to carry out broadly based studies on the many issues of technology and society. Usually OTA, which was closed in 1995, did not directly conclude that one technology or policy choice should be preferred to another. OTA preferred to present the costs and benefits of various policies, with their uncertainties, and let the senators and congressmen make the decision. For the case of determining the best basing mode for the Peacekeeper/MX missile, OTA gave no preference, but merely described the downsides for each of the modes, including deep underground mobile basing (DUMB). The president and the Congress ultimately decided to place the MX on railway cars, but this was terminated at the close of the Cold War. In order to avoid too much dependence on the executive branch, the Congress also relies on information from Congressional Research Service, the General Accounting Office, the National Academy of Sciences, the universities, industry, think-tanks, and the national laboratories.

Also in 1973, the American Physical Society joined a half-dozen other professional science societies in funding congressional science fellowships. Each year about 10 percent of the 30 new congressional fellows are physicists. Perhaps one-half of these physicists remain in Washington, D.C., changing their occupation because of this experience, some of them rising to staff directors of important congressional committees or executive branch offices. At any one time, there are about a six Ph.D. physicists on "the hill," forming a bipartisan network on physics and society information. Some of the results of these physicists can be gleaned by examining records of hearings, reading the pointed questions from the senators to the executive branch, or reading the relevant statutes. Of course, this process is not perfect, but it can be substantial.

The Executive Branch

If a national technical issue arises, such as what should be done with 100 tons of surplus weapons-grade plutonium, the president will probably sign an executive order ordering the relevant federal agencies to produce a report on the policy options. For the case of plutonium disposition, President George Bush requested the National Academy of Sciences to examine the options. The choice of the lead agencies can make a large difference in the direction and quality of the analysis and conclusions. If agencies disagree with the conclusion of the report, then minority views can be expressed to the president before he makes his final decision. Sometimes interesting voting patterns can be observed. For example, the Departments of Energy and State and the Central Intelligence Agency determined that the Soviets were in compliance with the nuclear Threshold Test Ban Treaty (with the caveat that a couple of tests could have slightly exceeded the yield limit, which also was true for U.S. testing). On the other hand, the Arms Control and Disarmament Agency and the Pentagon charged that a likely violation existed. With such split decisions, the issue was referred to President Ronald Reagan, who voted for the charge of a "likely" violation. Ultimately, U.S. measurements at the Soviet test site confirmed the State–DOE–CIA position. Politics can have an impact on decisions, but if there is a measurable answer, the truth can ultimately be determined, but perhaps when the importance of the issue has passed. Most examples of science and social policy issues are less measurable, and often involve value judgments and "the dismal science" of economics. Lastly, it is the duty of the executive branch to promulgate regulations to carry out the legal dictates of the Congress. These regulations are determined after executive branch hearings or studies and waiting a period of time after publishing the draft regulations in the *Federal Register*. Many consider this regulatory process to be about one-half of the actual process necessary to make laws.

The Social Responsibility of Scientists

In order to minimize mindless political impacts on science and technology issues, it is very important to pre-study an issue before members of Congress are forced to make a political decision on the issue. Once politicians have locked into a position, it is politically hurtful for them to change their minds. Because scientists have special knowledge of such diverse topics as space-based weapons or global warming, their views are valued during the debates in Congress and in the executive branch. Needless to say, there is a great responsibility for scientists to accurately explain their findings with a statement on what they know and don't know, with a full declaration of the assumptions and uncertainties. An error of omission can be as unethical as an error of commission. The physics community does not require that newly frocked Ph.D. take a "Hippocratic oath" to always keep clients "from harm and injustice." However, such a Hippocratic oath is implied in science because of the openness of science and the peer review process. The current congressional hearings are often flawed because many of the hard questions are not asked in hearings, and the questions for the record are often not treated seriously and arrive too late to affect the outcome.

Thus, other venues should be explored to improve the process. The debate can only be advanced by an interchange between the opposing points of view. The concept of a "science court" was advanced in the 1970s, but it has not yet made an impact on the process. More recent versions of the science court also would convene juries of nonscientists to act in parallel with the scientist jurors. The American Physical Society and the American Association for the Advancement of Science have held numerous sessions with opposing points of view, but they are not held in a debate mode, and do not debate the issue of admissible evidence. There is a larger role for these professional societies to enhance the quality of science and society debates in directions that would clarify the assumptions and submit the data to more critical analysis. The National Academy of Sciences produces reports from diverse points of view, but the debates within the Academy are not open, and, therefore, the Academy reports may, on some occasions, not be as broad as needed.

Probabilistic Risk Assessment and Cost-Benefit Analysis

There is no one simple answer or process to ensure that technology will only be used in a pleas-ant, benign, and optimal manner. However, we might lessen the negative impacts with some other approaches.

DOE cleanup. Several studies have indicated that the United States will need some 100 to 200 billion dollars to restore the radioactive sites where nuclear weapons were developed and produced. Because funding of this magnitude is unlikely, it would be useful to carry out probabilistic risk assessments that approximately quantify the reduction in human mortality, as well as the cost that must be spent to mitigate the damage. There is a wide diversity of opinion on the migration rates for underground radioactivity, but measurements can be made to determine the approximate truth. A prioritization should be based on the approximate cost to save a life. If the cost is millions of dollars per life saved, then the environmental dollars should be spent on other, more pressing environmental problems. If the cost is low, then speedy action should be required. Although the United States is spending some $5 billion each year on DOE cleanup, the U.S. program appears to lack direction.

Comprehensive Test Ban Treaty. In 1992 the executive branch stated that it was necessary to continue testing nuclear weapons in order to enhance the safety of the weapons. Legislation called for the executive branch to determine the costs and benefits of testing and installing these safety features on new nuclear weapons. Several studies indicated that it would cost about $300 million to save a life. Because of the large costs, neither the Air Force nor the Navy were interested in diverting funds to rebuild the U.S. nuclear force structure for safety reasons. The legislative call for a cost-benefit analysis reduced the drive of the executive branch for additional testing for safety measures, thus allowing the CTB negotiations to begin in 1993.

Cost-benefit analyses also would help on such difficult issues as (1) the merit of the Environmental Protection Agency proposal to lower the radon level in houses to 4 pCi/liter at a cost of 20 to 100 billion dollars, and (2) whether "prudent avoidance" of electromagnetic fields from electricity, costing billions of dollars, was cost-effective. These cost-benefit analyses should then be compared, for example, with the cost-benefit figures for the cleanup of America's chemical legacy.

See also: ETHICS; SOCIAL RESPONSIBILITY

Bibliography

FAINBERG, A., ed. *From the Lab to the Hill: Essays Celebrating 20 Years of Congressional Science and Engineering Fellows* (American Association for the Advancement of Science, Washington, DC, 1994).

HAFEMEISTER, D., ed. *Physics and Nuclear Arms Today: Readings from Physics Today* (American Institute of Physics Press, New York, 1991).

KANTROWITZ, A. "Controlling Technology Democratically." *American Scientist* 63, 505–509 (1975).

KANTROWITZ, A. "The Science Court Experiment." *Science* **193,** 653–656 (1976).

REDMAN, E. *The Dance of Legislation* (Simon & Schuster, New York, 1973).

DAVID HAFEMEISTER

SOLAR CELL

Solar or photovoltaic cells are electronic devices which convert light (photons) directly into electrical current and voltage using the "photovoltaic" effect. The first solar cell was fabricated by scientists at Bell Telephone Laboratories in 1954 using the semiconductor material, silicon.

Scientists and engineers quickly realized the value of solar cells for supplying power for space satellites because they have low mass and involve no mechanically moving parts. The first U.S. satellite in space was equipped with solar cells made from silicon and today silicon photovoltaics still power almost all spacecraft except for space probes which penetrate to the outer reaches of the solar system and beyond where sunlight is too weak.

The original solar cells were made from single crystal silicon (Si) which is too expensive for general use in large scale, flat panel power generation. Although SiO_2 the raw material for Si is abundant, refining the sand and purifying the Si sufficiently for solar cells is costly; furthermore, slicing the single crystal boules into thin wafers requires diamond sawing, further polishing, and then several additional steps to add the appropriate impurities.

One possible way to reduce costs with expensive crystalline materials such as Si and more recently gallium arsenide (GaAs) is to use a concentrator arrangement with a large, inexpensive Fresnel lens to focus the light onto a small cell. Concentration factors of 25 to 1,000 have been used successfully, although concentrator designs require careful two-axis tracking of the Sun during the day.

Another very promising design for photovoltaics lies in the use of very thin films deposited on cheap substrates such as glass or stainless steel. Three materials have achieved good photovoltaic results as thin films (roughly 1 to 3 μm thick): hydrogenated amorphous silicon (*a*-Si:H), copper indium diselenide ($CuInSe_2$ or simply CIS), and cadmium telluride (CdTe). *a*-Si:H is used as an amorphous film, while CIS and CdTe are used as polycrystalline films with grain sizes of about 1 μm.

The photovoltaic process in a CdTe solar cell is illustrated in Fig. 1. A quantum of light (the photon) has the energy hf, where h is Planck's constant and f is the light frequency ($f = c/\lambda$, where c is the speed and λ is the wavelength of light). If the photon energy is greater than the semiconductor energy gap (separation between the valence and conduction bands), then it will be absorbed and will excite an electron from the valence band to the conduction band where it can freely move through the crystal. The electron has a negative charge but the vacancy created in the valence band has a positive charge (called a "hole"). Unless the electron and hole are quickly separated, the electron will be attracted to the positive hole and be annihilated with no current being produced. Therefore it is necessary to build in an electric field that will separate the charges. This is done by adding small numbers of impurities or "doping" the semiconductor to make a junction between *n*-type (negative charge carrier) and *p*-type (positive charge carrier) regions. In Fig. 1 the junction region is a *hetero*junction between *n*-type cadmium sulfide

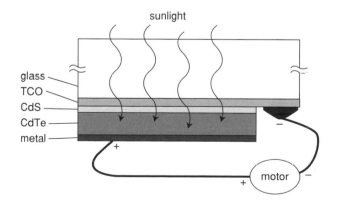

Figure 1 The CdS/CdTe thin-film solar cell.

(CdS) and *p*-type CdTe. The photovoltaic process is most efficient if the photon creates electron–hole pairs near this *n-p* junction where the electric field is strong. The solar cell now needs only appropriate metal contacts to bond wires which allow the current to flow through an external device. For the CdS/CdTe cell of Fig. 1, tin oxide (SnO_2) serves as the transparent conducting oxide (TCO) for contact to CdS and nickel, graphite, or gold are used for contact to the CdTe.

Typically the solar cell will generate a peak voltage which is about two-thirds of the energy gap of the semiconductor. Optimum energy gaps are 1.0 to 1.7 eV. On a clear day with the Sun overhead the intensity of sunlight is about 1,000 W/m^2. A one square meter solar module with 10 percent efficiency will generate 100 W of power in bright sunshine. With clear sunshine for an average of six hours per day, 60 m^2 of solar modules would produce about 1,000 kW h of electricity per month—about equal to that used by a typical American family.

See also: Doping; Light; Photon; Planck Constant; Semiconductor; Thin Film

Bibliography

Zweibel, K. *Basic Photovoltaic Principles and Methods* (Van Nostrand Reinhold, New York, 1984).
Zweibel, K. *Harnessing Solar Power: The Photovoltaic Challenge* (Plenum, New York, 1990).

Alvin D. Compaan

SOLAR ENERGY

See Energy, Solar

SOLAR NEUTRINO

See Neutrino, Solar

SOLAR SYSTEM

The inventory of the solar system contains a large variety of objects, with size ranging over a factor of 10^{12}. In descending order of size, the solar system consists of nine planets (radius: 1,000–72,000 km), more than sixty planetary satellites (radius: 10–2,600 km), approximately 10^6 asteroids (from several meters to 500 km in size), 10^{12} comets (from kilometers to tens of kilometers in size), and a multitude of meteoroids (from several centimeters to several meters in size). The bulk physical properties of the planets and satellites are reasonably well known and are listed in Table 1. Smaller than the meteoroids are fine dust grains, which are concentrated at certain regions in the solar system, like the zodiacal light. The Sun outweighs everything else in the solar system—all the planets put together would weigh only 0.0014 M_{Sun} ($M_{Sun} = 10^{30}$ kg, the mass of the Sun). Everything orbits around the Sun except for the planetary satellites, which move in orbits around their respective planets. All the planets travel in *direct* orbits, that is, counterclockwise as seen from above the orbital plane of Earth. They also rotate about their axis in the same sense. Except for Pluto, the inclinations of the planets' orbital planes are always less than or equal to 16°; this means that the planets' orbits are never tilted more than 16° from the Earth's equatorial plane. Finally, except for Mercury and Pluto, the planets' orbits have very small eccentricities (< 0.1), meaning that the orbits are nearly circular. Distances in the solar system are measured in astronomical units (AU). An AU is equal to the distance between the Earth and the Sun, or 1.496 $\times$ 10^8 km. The contents of the solar system objects are spread out in an uneven fashion over a scale of some 10^5 AU, starting from Mercury at 0.39 AU, to comets in the Oort cloud at 50,000–100,000 AU.

The Terrestrial Planets

Closest to the Sun lies Mercury, the smallest of the terrestrial planets. A bit further on lies Venus, followed by Earth, then Mars. These four planets are commonly referred to as the terrestrial planets, since they are known to have solid, rocky interiors. (In contrast, the giant planets—Jupiter, Saturn, Uranus, and Neptune—have interiors consisting mostly of hydrogen and helium.) All four of the ter-

Table 1 Physical Data of Terrestrial Planets

Planet	Radius (km)	Mass (kg)	Semimajor Axis (AU)	Orbital Period (yr)	Density ($kg \cdot m^{-3}$)	Temperature (Kelvin)
Mercury	2,439	0.33×10^{24}	0.39	0.241	5,420	100–700
Venus	6,051	4.87×10^{24}	0.72	0.615	5,240	700
Earth	6,378	5.98×10^{24}	1.00	1.000	5,520	250–300
Mars	3,398	0.64×10^{24}	1.52	1.88	3,940	210–390
Jupiter	71,600	1.90×10^{24}	5.20	11.86	1,326	110–150
Saturn	57,550	5.69×10^{26}	9.54	29.46	686	95
Uranus	25,050	8.67×10^{25}	19.18	84.01	1,267	58
Neptune	24,700	1.03×10^{26}	30.06	164.8	1,640	56
Pluto	1,151	1.36×10^{22}[a]	39.44	248.6	2,029[a]	40

[a]Refers to the Pluto-Charon pair.

restrial planets have high densities, ranging from 3,750 $kg \cdot m^{-3}$ (Mars) to 5,000 $kg \cdot m^{-3}$ (Mercury), a testimony to the rocky interiors. Like most solid surfaces in the solar system, the surfaces of the terrestrial planets are cratered by meteorite impacts, and the number of craters allows us to determine the cratering records and the ages of the cratered surfaces. Other surface features besides craters include highlands, lowlands, and lava flows. From cratering records, Mercury has the least modified surface, followed by Mars, Venus, and Earth.

The surface of Mercury is dark and has similar features as the Moon's, but it also possesses many cliffs (scarps) produced by faults in the surface. These cliffs can be as long as hundreds of kilometers and as high as 2 km. The surface of Venus is hidden beneath two layers of cloud of sulfuric acid and water and cannot be seen from Earth. However, it has been mapped with the help of spacecraft landers and radar signals, and these show that Venus is relatively flat with the exception of a few highland regions as high as 12 km. The northern and southern hemispheres of Venus are vastly different from each other: the north is mountainous but uncratered, while the south is relatively flat, uncratered terrain. Volcanoes are present on both halves and may still be active. A few long and deep canyons also scar the surface of Venus; these are thought to have been caused by sections of the crust drifting apart.

Even from Earth, Mars is easily recognized by its vivid reddish-orange color. Data brought back by the Viking landers indicated that silicate minerals was the major component of the surface composition at approximately 44 percent; about 19 percent of the surface is iron oxide (Fe_2O_3), which gives the planet its color. The surface of Mars is battered by fierce dust storms stirred up by strong winds with speeds greater than 100 km/h. During a dust storm, the dust clouds can rise as high as 50 km, then take many months for the dust to settle down. The dust deposits are very thin, cover the entire planet, and are constantly reworked by winds.

All the terrestrial planets have atmospheres, although these are quite different from each other. Mercury has an extremely thin, almost nonexistent, atmosphere of helium and hydrogen. The atmospheres of Venus and Mars are quite similar and contain mostly carbon dioxide (CO_2), and that of the Earth consists mostly of molecular nitrogen (N_2) and oxygen (O_2).

The Giant Planets

The giant planets are often called the Jovian planets or gas giants, with the latter name deriving from their mainly gaseous interiors. The predominance of gas in the planets' interiors is inferred from their low densities (690–1,660 $kg \cdot m^{-3}$). In contrast to the terrestrial planets, the solid cores of the giant planets are tiny compared to the gaseous and liquid material that surround them. The principal composition of Jupiter and Saturn is hydrogen ($\sim 75\%$) and helium ($\sim 23\%$), with other molecules such as ammonia making up the remaining few percent. Most of the hydrogen is in the liquid state. The visible features seen on the Jupiter disk are clouds lying beneath a thin, transparent atmosphere. The most striking feature is the Great Red Spot, a high pressure region that deflects clouds around it. There are actually three cloud layers, the top layer being ammonia, the next one ammonia and hydrogen sulfide, and the bottom layer water ice. Saturn shares most of these features, although its clouds are less prominent and lie lower in the atmosphere. Saturn makes up for its less dramatic clouds with its bright rings and many moons.

Uranus and Neptune would more accurately be called "ice giants," since they consist roughly of 15 percent hydrogen and helium, 60 percent various types of ice (water, methane, and ammonia), and 25 percent rocky materials (silicates). They both have a slightly green color due to the absorption of sunlight by methane. Sunlight penetrates the atmosphere, where the red component is absorbed and the green component is reflected back. Cloud bands are present in both atmospheres.

Pluto-Charon and the Kuiper Belt

The most distant planet, Pluto, does not fit in with the giant planets nor does it fit in with the terrestrial planets. Its satellite, Charon, is in such a tight orbit around the planet that it was only discovered in 1978 when astronomers noticed a "bump" on top of Chiron's image. Their very small separation makes it difficult to study the two objects individually and for that reason, astronomers often refer to properties of Pluto-Charon combined. Pluto is only two times as large as Charon, and the mass of the pair combined is only about 19 percent of the mass of the Moon—minuscule compared to its giant neighbors. Pluto's density (1,800–2,000 kg·m^{-3}) implies a higher rock/ice ratio than the satellites of Jupiter and Saturn, and most likely contains a silicate core. Nitrogen ice dominates Pluto's surface and atmosphere. Pluto's atmosphere is a seasonal phenomenon: it exists when Pluto is near perihelion (when it is closest to the Sun) and therefore warm enough that nitrogen can exist in gaseous form. When Pluto is furthest from the Sun and therefore cold, the atmosphere freezes into ice. Thus the atmosphere forms and collapses depending on Pluto's position around the Sun. Interestingly, the surface composition of Charon is quite different from that of Pluto; it is most likely coated with water ice, and methane is conspicuously absent. No atmosphere is expected on Charon.

With its unusual properties, Pluto does not so much resemble the giant or the terrestrial planets, but another group of icy objects located beyond Neptune called the Kuiper belt. The existence of the Kuiper belt was predicted by Gerard Kuiper in 1951 but only discovered in 1992. Pluto's orbit lies in a special region called the 2:3 resonance, which is safe from Neptune's gravitational perturbations. The 2:3 resonance lies squarely in the middle of the Kuiper belt, and in fact, other Kuiper belt members have been found to be trapped in the same region. The new findings strongly suggest that Pluto is just another, probably one of the largest, Kuiper belt objects trapped into its current orbit during the early stages of the solar system.

Not much is known yet about the Kuiper belt, but it may soon prove to be a wealth of information on the early solar system. It contains at least 10^6 objects, and is probably the source of the short-period comets, as well as the origin of Pluto, Charon, and the Neptunian satellite Triton. It is most likely "leftover" material that was not incorporated into a planet, and as such is a primordial remnant from the formation of the planetary system. Its exploration should yield valuable information on the accretion process in our solar system.

Satellites and Rings

The giant planets lay claim to at least fifty satellites (not counting Charon), or almost all of the known planetary satellites. Besides these moons, the giant planets can also boast of a great number of micron- to meter-size particles that form rings around them. In contrast, Mercury and Venus have no satellite, while Earth has one (the Moon), and Mars has two (Phobos and Deimos). It is believed that the Martian moons are asteroids that were captured by Mars, while the Moon may have been formed from the remnants of a single large impactor that collided with Earth.

The satellite systems of the giant planets are all very different from each other, but most satellites are in synchronous rotation, meaning that they keep the same face toward their planet. Most also have low densities (650–3,600 kg·m^{-3}), consistent with a composition of rock and ice. Jupiter's satellites are at least sixteen in number, with the four Galilean satellites (Io, Europa, Ganymede, and Callisto) being the largest and the closest. The rest of Jupiter's moons are asteroid-like objects and were probably captured from the nearby asteroid belt. Saturn has at least seventeen moons: Titan is by far the largest (radius: ~ 2,575 km), followed by six medium-size moons (Mimas, Enceladus, Tethys, Dione, Rhea, Iapetus), and ten much smaller moons (including Phoebe and

Hyperion). All have lower densities than the Jovian satellites, implying a higher ice content. Uranus is surrounded by five large moons (Miranda, Ariel, Umbriel, Titania, and Oberon) and at least ten small moons. The Uranian satellites in general have higher densities ($\sim 1,500$ kg·m^{-3}) than the Saturnian ones. Their most interesting characteristic is that many have young surfaces, meaning that their surfaces have been reworked, possibly by some internal heat source. Only two Neptunian satellites were known before the Voyager 2 encounter with Neptune: Triton (radius: $\sim 1,352$ km) and Nereid (radius: ~ 175 km). Voyager discovered six smaller moons, ranging from 30 to 210 km. Little is known about the smaller moons, but the unusual physical and dynamical properties of Triton and Nereid suggest that these are captured satellites.

The ring systems of the giant planets prove to be as diverse as the satellites. The Jovian rings are thin (<30 km), tenuous and made up of micro-size particles. Saturn's spectacular rings are also thin (~ 1 km thick), but wide (the largest extends 70,000–140,000 km from Saturn). Some of the rings are kept narrow by shepherd satellites which restrict the range of orbits of the rings. Saturnian ring particles are either made of water ice or coated by water ice, 3–5 m in size on the average, although some larger particles and fine dust (0.1–10 μm) also exist. Uranus has nine narrow rings, each a few kilometers wide and approximately 10 m thick, consisting of dark micron-size particles. The four Neptunian rings are much smaller than the Uranian rings, but are most unusual in that the outer ring contains thickened arc segments a few degrees in length. Why the ring material has not spread out uniformly around the ring is not known.

Comets and Asteroids

There are about 5,000 asteroids with well-known orbits and many more ($\sim 10^6$) smaller, unknown asteroids. Asteroids are generally confined to the region between Mars and Jupiter, an area known as the main asteroid belt. A few thousands more asteroids are trapped in two smaller clouds located along the orbit of Jupiter, one preceding and one following the planet; these are called Trojan asteroids. The largest asteroid, 1 Ceres, is 480 km in radius and it alone contains about one-third of the mass of the entire asteroid belt. Most of the asteroids travel on well-behaved orbits that are stable over the age of the solar system.

Comets are icy interlopers of the solar system. There are two types of comets: the short-period comets, with orbital periods $P \leq 200$ years, and the long-period comets with $P > 200$ years. Their dramatic appearance, a fuzzy cloud (the coma) sometimes accompanied by one or two tails, is caused by sublimation of surface ices. Sublimation is the process where ice is converted directly into gas; it occurs when ices are heated in a low pressure environment (e.g., when cometary ices are heated by the Sun). As the ices turn into gas, the molecules escape from the nucleus, carrying off dust particles. For this reason the coma consists of dust and gas. From their orbital characteristics, we know that the long-period comets come from a reservoir of comets called the Oort cloud. The Oort cloud contains approximately 10^{12} comets and lies at about 50,000 AU, basically the edge of the solar system. The short-period comets most likely come from the Kuiper belt, the ring of comets located beyond Neptune.

In contrast to the relatively predictable asteroids, comets travel on unstable orbits, the chaotic nature of which prevents the determination of their future fate. The lifetimes of comets in the inner planetary region are short (a few thousand years) and are usually ended by the comets either being ejected out of the solar system or colliding with the Sun or a planet. It is possible that comets eventually lose the ability to sublimate by building up a rocky crust on their surface. This raises the question of whether some comets have in fact "turned into" asteroids and are now part of the asteroid population, but such "extinct" comets have not been identified.

Meteoroids and Interplanetary Dust

The solar system contains a significant amount of interplanetary debris. When a piece of debris (called a meteoroid) enters the atmosphere, it makes a fiery streak and is called a meteor. If it hits the ground, it is called a meteorite. Meteoroids mostly come from comets and asteroids and most do not survive the plunge into the atmosphere. Meteorites consist mostly of some combination of iron, nickel, and silicate materials, like terrestrial stones. Many meteorites (called chondrites) contain silicate spheres called chondrules. The most unusual chondrite is the dark carbonaceous chondrite, which may be primitive material from the early solar system.

The smallest meteorites form the zodiacal particles, a diffuse cloud of dust particles orbiting in the ecliptic plane. These dust particles consist of silicates, iron, and nickel, and reflect sunlight, resulting in the zodiacal light.

See also: PLANETARY MAGNETISM; PLANETARY SYSTEMS; PLANET FORMATION; SUN

Bibliography

TAYLOR, S. R. *Solar System Evolution* (Cambridge University Press, Cambridge, Eng., 1992).

ZEILICK, M., and SMITH, E. v. P. *Introductory Astronomy and Astrophysics*, 2nd ed. (Saunders, Philadelphia, 1987).

JANE LUU

SOLAR WIND

"Solar wind" is the name given to the continual outward supersonic wind from the Sun. The solar wind blows outward in all directions from the Sun, as first indicated by the anti-solar pointing of comet tails, irrespective of the direction of motion and the heliocentric latitude of the comet. The wind is now observed directly with instruments carried on spacecraft outside the sheltering magnetic field of Earth. Consequently, the solar wind has been studied in the greatest detail near the equatorial plane of the Sun at a distance of 1 AU from the Sun (1 AU = Earth-Sun distance of 1.5×10^{13} cm, or about 8 light-minutes), but instruments have in fact observed the wind as close to the Sun as 0.3 AU and as far out as 50 AU. Solar wind speeds are typically 300–500 km/s near the equatorial plane of the Sun, making the journey from the Sun to the orbit of Earth in about 4 days. However, speeds as low as 200 km/s and as high as 1,200 km/s have been recorded on occasion. The density of the solar wind at 1 AU is typically about 5 atoms/cm³, but it ranges to an occasional high of 20 atoms/cm³ or more in a blast wave from a coronal mass ejection and during times of low wind velocity. Densities may fall as low as 1 atom/cm³ in high wind velocities. The wind is made up of fully ionized hydrogen (electrons and protons) with a fully ionized helium component, usually 2–3 percent by number, but occasionally as much as 50 percent for brief periods in association with an outburst on the Sun. Heavier ions (e.g., C, N, O), some only partially ionized, are also present

in small numbers, giving an idea of the conditions in which the solar wind arises at the Sun.

Radio scintillation measurements of distant radio sources, and now the Ulysses spacecraft passing at about 2 AU over the poles of the Sun, show a fast steady wind of 700–800 km/s at high heliocentric latitudes.

The mean velocity v of the solar wind in any given direction from the Sun varies but little once the gas is well away from the Sun. Hence, for a radial flow, the gas density ρ declines outward as $1/r^2$. Somewhere in the vicinity of 100 AU, the ram pressure ρv^2 of the wind falls to values on the order of 10^{-12} dynes/cm², comparable to the pressure of the interstellar gas, magnetic field, and galactic cosmic rays. Consequently, it is expected that at some such distance the supersonic solar wind crashes through a shock transition into a subsonic flow, thereafter trailing off in the prevailing 20 km/s interstellar wind to form a downstream interstellar wake of hot tenuous solar gas and field.

The solar wind originates as the gentle outward hydrodynamic expansion of the very hot outer atmosphere—the corona—of the Sun. The means by which the outer atmosphere is heated (typically, 1.5×10^6 K and 10^8 atoms/cm³, to be contrasted with the visible surface at 5,600 K and 10^{17} atoms/cm³) is not clear, even after decades of investigation. But the fact is that approximately 10^6 erg·cm⁻²·s⁻¹ (about 1 kW/m², comparable to the intensity of sunlight at Earth, or 1.6×10^{-5} of the surface emission of the Sun) are supplied to the corona in regions of weak magnetic field $B \lesssim 10$ G. This small heat input raises the temperature enormously, because the outer atmosphere is too tenuous to radiate and cool effectively. So there is no significant cooling except for thermal conduction back down into the Sun and outward into space and, of course, the continual expansion of the gas to form the solar wind.

The coronal gas close to the Sun is strongly bound by the enormous gravitational attraction of the Sun, so the gas is not free to expand away into space. Specifically, the mean thermal energy $3kT$ per atom (ion-electron pair) is 6×10^{-10} erg at T = 1.5×10^6 K (the Boltzmann constant $k = 1.38 \times 10^{-16}$ erg/K), whereas the gravitational binding energy $GM_\odot M/R_\odot$ is about five times larger ($G = 6.66 \times 10^{-8}$ cm³·g⁻¹·s⁻², $M_\odot = 2 \times 10^{33}$ g, $M = 1.66 \times 10^{-24}$ g, and $R_\odot = 7 \times 10^{10}$ cm), so the gas cannot escape directly into space. The escape is more subtle and is based on the fact that the temperature of the gas declines but little with distance from the Sun because of the high thermal conductivity of the hot gas, and because the heat source, whatever it may be, appears to provide active heating out to distances of $10R_\odot$ or more. On the other hand, the gas density falls off substantially in the strong gravitational field with increasing distance r from the Sun while the gravitational binding energy $GM_\odot M/r$ declines inversely with distance r. Hence, at a distance of the order $10R_\odot$, the thermal energy exceeds the gravitational binding energy, and the gas expands outward into space. The escape is a hydrodynamic phenomenon, and it is a straight forward calculation to show that the outward flow is very slow (~ 1 km/s) near the Sun ($r \cong R_\odot$), gradually accelerating to the speed of sound (~ 100 km/s) at a distance of several solar radii, and to 200–600 km/s at very large distances as the gas expands in the presence of continuing heat input.

The solar wind is often highly variable with large rapid fluctuations (over minutes and hours) in velocity, density, and particularly magnetic field direction. Unfortunately, the absence of an understanding of the coronal heating prevents any direct quantitative association of solar wind speed, density, and temperature with specific conditions of magnetic activity and turbulent convection at the Sun. One infers that the faster outflows of gas [e.g., the fast streams (> 400 km/s) in the solar wind, and the transient coronal mass ejections that produce a blast wave in the solar wind] may be boosted to such high speeds by the pressure of Alfven waves in the magnetic fields in the wind. But curiously, while the coronal mass ejections are associated with strong magnetic fields, the fast streams arise in regions of particularly weak field at the Sun in the so-called coronal holes.

The continuing outflow of coronal gas to provide the solar wind carries the weak large-scale magnetic field of the Sun along with it so that the magnetic field extends in the wind out through the solar system. The field extends radially, falling off as $1/r^2$, were it not for the rotation of the Sun, which winds the field configuration into an expanding rotating Archimedean spiral form around the Sun. The magnetic field is typically 4×10^{-5} G at the orbit of Earth, where the spiral has an inclination of about $45°$ to the radial direction. Far beyond the orbit of Earth the field is nearly in the azimuthal direction and, accordingly, falls off only as $1/r$, while the radial component continues to decline as $1/r^2$.

The outward sweep of the spiral magnetic field near the equatorial plane of the spinning Sun pushes back the galactic cosmic rays to a significant degree, providing variable depression of the galactic cosmic ray intensity at Earth. It remains for the Ulysses spacecraft to determine the extent to which cosmic rays are swept back in the nearly radial magnetic fields extending outward in the fast solar wind from the north and south polar regions of the Sun.

The Sun is a rather ordinary main sequence star with regions of magnetically confined x-ray emitting corona and regions of open expanding corona that provide the solar wind. Most other stars exhibit x-ray emission and by inference are expected to have stellar winds of the same general nature as the Sun.

See also: ALFVEN WAVE; COSMIC RAY; FIELD, MAGNETIC; MAGNETOHYDRODYNAMICS; SOLAR SYSTEM; SUN

Bibliography

FOUKAL, P. *Solar Astrophysics* (Wiley, New York, 1990).

HUNDHAUSEN, A. J. *Coronal Expansion and the Solar Wind* (Springer-Verlag, New York, 1972).

PARKER, E. N. *Interplanetary Dynamical Processes* (Interscience New York, 1963).

E. N. PARKER

SOLENOID

One of the most practical ways to create a controlled magnetic field is to construct a solenoid. A solenoid is a long cylinder upon which is wound a uniform coil of wire. When a current is sent through the wire, a magnetic field is created inside the cylinder.

The usual solenoid has a length several times its diameter. The wire is closely wound around the outside of a long cylinder in the form of a helix with a small pitch. The magnetic field created inside the cylinder is quite uniform, especially far from the ends of the solenoid. The larger the ratio of the length to the diameter, the more uniform the field near the middle.

The approximate value of the magnetic field is given by

$$B = \mu_0 n I,$$

where B is the magnetic field, μ_0 the permeability of free space, n is the number of turns of wire per unit length, and I the current through the wire. This relationship would hold exactly if the solenoid were infinitely long. A more precise calculation shows that the above relationship is within 2 percent of the correct value at the center of a solenoid if the ratio of the length to the diameter is five or greater.

This equation shows that one way to increase B is to increase I. But, because all wire has resistance, this procedure requires an increase in voltage across the solenoid and results in more heat being generated by the resistance of the wire. Another way to increase B is to increase n. But this increase can only be accomplished by decreasing the wire size (if the solenoid, as is usually the case, has turns wound as closely as possible), resulting in an increase in resistance and an increase in the voltage required for a given current, as well as an increase in heat generated by the resistance of the wire. An alternative way to increase n is to wind several layers of wire. This procedure increases the resistance of the wire, adds insulation problems, and decreases the length to diameter ratio. The selection of the appropriate trade-offs is the principle problem that must be solved by the solenoid designer.

If a soft iron rod is placed partly inside a solenoid and the current turned on, the rod will be drawn into the solenoid by the resulting magnetic field. This motion can be used to actuate a lever, unlock a door, or operate a relay. In this way the operation of a small electric switch can produce a large mechanical action at a remote location.

It is worth noting that the iron core has to be placed at the end of the solenoid where the field is nonuniform for it to move. Furthermore, it is not necessary for the current to flow in one direction only. An alternating current will work also.

The magnetic field of a solenoid can also be used directly. It is used to deflect the beam of electrons in a television tube. Solenoids are also used to provide the magnetic field for magnetic resonance imaging.

Physics textbooks often use solenoids in problems about magnetic fields because the field produced by the solenoid is easily calculated and is easy to visualize.

See also: ELECTRICAL RESISTANCE; FIELD, MAGNETIC; JOULE HEATING

Bibliography

HECHT, E. *Physics* (Brooks/Cole, Pacific Grove, CA, 1996).

A. F. BURR

SOLID

Solid and liquid are condensed phases of matter, as opposed to the rarefied gas phase. A solid tends to retain its shape, and can support a shearing stress, whereas a liquid flows and takes the shape of its container. At a microscopic level, in a solid the atoms are restricted in their motion, oscillating about fixed equilibrium positions, while in a liquid the atoms move around each other, though they are almost as close together as in the solid. Most materials become solids at sufficiently low temperatures.

Solids are classified according to structure and type of binding, as well as mechanical, thermal, electrical, optical, and magnetic properties. In crystalline solids the atoms form a regular array over a long range. In amorphous and glassy solids, the atoms are disordered on a large scale, but have local order and bonding arrangements. For example, in silicon oxide, oxygen atoms form bridges between pairs of silicon atoms. In quartz the atoms are on a crystalline lattice, while in glass there is a disordered network of bonds. A polycrystalline solid consists of many small crystal grains with varying orientations. Simple solids are pure substances, compounds, and alloys, which are mixtures of elements. Recently, layered structures called superlattices have been produced, consisting of thin layers of alternating materials, such as the semiconductors GaAs and AlAs. Polymers contain long chains of molecules that are responsible for the properties of plastics and rubber.

Types of Binding

The most weakly bound solids are formed of rare gases such as argon, which are held together by van der Waals forces. In ionic crystals such as NaCl the positive and negative ions are held together by electrostatic forces. Diamond and many semiconductors, as well as polymers, are held together by covalent bonds, or electron pair bonds. Hydrogen bonds are important in ice. In metals the conduction electrons contribute to the cohesion of the crystal.

Mechanical Properties

The rigid body used in physics textbooks is an idealization. Actual solids deform when subjected to forces, specifically to stresses such as pressure, tension, and shear. If the stress, say a tension, is small, the body undergoes elastic deformation, which means that it returns to its original shape when the stress is removed. With a larger stress, beyond the elastic limit, there is plastic deformation, a permanent change in shape. When the stress exceeds the strength of the body, it breaks. Crystalline materials often contain defects, such as impurities, vacant sites, and dislocations, or mistakes in the lattice matching of crystals. These defects can influence the mechanical properties; for example, plastic deformation (work hardening) can strengthen a metal. Metals tend to be ductile, that is, to undergo plastic deformation without breaking, while ceramics tend to be brittle. The mechanical properties of polymers depend on the size of the macromolecules and the intermolecular forces.

Thermal Properties

The lattice vibrations of a crystal (phonons) are important in determining the thermal properties, including specific heat, thermal conductivity, and thermal expansion. Phonons can transport heat, and are primarily responsible for the specific heat. In metals, electrons also transport heat and contribute to the specific heat.

Electrical Properties

Insulators are materials that do not conduct an electrical current. Metals are good conductors of electricity. Semiconductors such as Si are important electronic materials whose conductivity depends on temperature and impurity content. At very low temperatures certain metals become superconductors, in which current can flow without any resistance. A new class of oxide materials exhibits superconductivity at higher temperatures. The electrical properties of materials are greatly dependent on their electronic structure. According to the energy band theory, the quantum states of electrons in solids consist of bands of energy in which electrons can move throughout the crystal, separated by forbidden energy gaps. Insulators have filled energy bands and large forbidden energy gaps, so there are no electrons free to conduct electricity, while metals have partly filled energy bands that contribute many carriers for conduction. In between are semiconductors, which have a filled energy band, the valence band, corresponding to the covalent bonds between atoms, and an empty conduction band separated from the filled bands by a small energy gap. Electrons can be excited from the valence band to the conduction band by heating the sample, and both the electrons and the holes they leave behind can conduct electricity. Electrons and holes can also be introduced through impurities.

Optical Properties

The optical absorption of solids depends on the electronic structure and to some extent the lattice vibrations. The transparency of diamonds as well as glass is due to the large forbidden energy gap, because according to quantum theory, light of frequency f can only be absorbed in quanta of energy hf, where h is Planck's constant, and visible light quanta do not have sufficient energy to excite electrons across the energy gap. Metals absorb light because the electrons are free to take up the energy of the light. Semiconductors absorb visible light but are transparent in the infrared. Transparent materials propagate light at a reduced speed depending on the dielectric constant. The lattice vibrations of ionic crystals produce optical anomalies in the infrared.

Magnetic Properties

In paramagnets and diamagnets, a magnetic moment is induced in the same or opposite direction, respectively, to an applied magnetic field. Ferromagnets such as iron, cobalt, nickel, and gadolinium, have a permanent magnetization at sufficiently low temperatures, as do ferrites, which are magnetic insulators. These effects are due to the behavior of electron orbital and spin angular momentum in atoms.

See also: ALLOY; CONDUCTION; CRYSTAL; ELECTRICAL CONDUCTIVITY; ELECTRICAL RESISTANCE; ELECTRICAL RESISTIVITY; ELECTRON, CONDUCTION; INSULATOR; METAL; PLANCK CONSTANT; SEMICONDUCTOR; SPECIFIC

HEAT; STRESS; SUPERCONDUCTIVITY; SUPERCONDUCTIVITY, HIGH-TEMPERATURE

Bibliography

HALLIDAY, D., and RESNICK, R. *Fundamentals of Physics,* 4th ed. (Wiley, New York, 1992).

KITTEL, C. *Introduction to Solid-State Physics,* 6th ed. (Wiley, New York, 1986).

LAURA M. ROTH

SOLID-STATE PHYSICS

See CONDENSED MATTER PHYSICS

SOLITON

"Soliton" is a term that was introduced in the 1960s to describe a special type of solution to certain partial differential equations that were found at that time to possess unexpectedly simple and interesting properties. The equations involved are of the type that arise in the study of various phenomena in such subjects as hydrodynamics and electrodynamics. Consequently, these solutions provide simple analytical descriptions of certain physical effects that occur in these fields.

Although heightened interest in this subject has occurred only since the 1960s, the first encounter with the subject took place long ago and is best summarized by the 1834 description given by J. Scott-Russell:

> I was observing the motion of a boat which was rapidly drawn along a narrow channel by a pair of horses, when the boat suddenly stopped—not so the mass of water in the channel which had been put in motion; it accumulated round the prow of the vessel in a state of violent agitation, then suddenly leaving it behind, rolled forward with great velocity, assuming the form of a large solitary elevation, a rounded smooth and well defined heap of water, which continued its course along the channel apparently without change of form or diminution of speed. I followed it on horseback, and overtook it still rolling on at a rate of some eight or nine miles an hour, preserving its original figure some thirty feet long and a foot to a foot and a half in height. Its height gradually diminished, and after a chase of one or two miles I lost it in the windings of the channel. Such, in the month of August 1834, was my first chance interview with that singular and beautiful phenomenon ["Reports on Progress in Waves." *Proc. Roy. Soc. Edinburgh* 1834, 319–320].

The "large solitary elevation" mentioned here is an example of what is now referred to as a soliton. In the context of water waves, the soliton represents a balance between two competing effects. On the one hand, the equation that describes surface waves predicts that waves tend to steepen and even break as they propagate. On the other hand, the governing equation also contains a term that represents dispersion, an effect that leads to the spreading out of a localized disturbance as it propagates. The steady shape of the soliton results from a balance between these two competing effects. Similar competition between pulse steepening and pulse spreading occurs in other physical situations as well and, as in the water wave instance described above, provides a means for transporting energy (and thus information) over unexpectedly large distances. One such example is that of light pulses in optical fibers.

Although one of the most common equations that exhibit soliton behavior has been known since the end of the nineteenth century, only the single soliton solution of that equation was available for a long time. The mathematical description of an individual soliton takes the form of an analytical expression that is localized in both space and time (i.e., it is a pulse). An example of such an expression is $\operatorname{sech}^2\left[(x - vt)/L\right]$. This pulse has a width of approximately $2L$ and moves with a constant velocity v in a positive x direction. With an appropriate choice of the physical parameters, it describes the "well defined heap of water" observed by Scott-Russell. It was the results displayed by numerical solutions of some of these equations in modern times that uncovered the interesting effects associated with the interaction of two or more solitons. In particular, it was found that not only do solitons behave like particles, since they preserve their identity upon interaction, but also that there are simple analytical expressions that describe this interaction. An example of the overtaking of a slow soliton by a more rapidly moving one is provided by the relation

$$u(x,t) = 12 \frac{4\cosh(2x - 8t) + \cosh(4x - 64t) + 3}{[3\cosh(x - 28t) + \cosh(3x - 36t)]^2}.$$

A graph of this result appears in Fig. 1. The above expression is a solution of the Korteweg–deVries (or KdV) equation. This equation, derived in 1895, has a solution that describes the water wave soliton observed by Scott-Russell. The equation has the form

$$\frac{\partial u}{\partial t} + u\frac{\partial u}{\partial x} + \frac{\partial^3 u}{\partial x^3} = 0,$$

where $u(x,t)$ represents the height of a water wave above the undisturbed surface of the liquid as a function of position x and time t. The second and third terms in this equation, respectively, are responsible for the wave steepening and dispersive effects referred to above. The product $u\partial u/x$ in the second term places this equation in a category referred to as nonlinear. In general such equations are extremely difficult to solve, if they can be solved at all by analytical means, and their solutions frequently yield results that are counter to one's intuition. For example, Fig. 1 shows that when the two solitons overlap at $t = 0$ the combined amplitude of the two solitons is *less* than that of the more rapidly moving of the two solitons when they are separate.

The key to the analytical solution of the nonlinear KdV equation was the realization that its solution $u(x,t)$ could be related to a linear differential equation of the form

$$\frac{d^2\psi}{dx^2} + [k^2 - u(x,t)]\psi = 0.$$

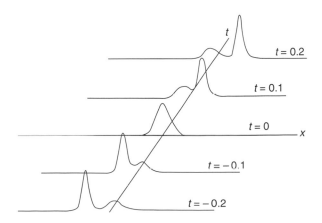

Figure 1

This equation arises in many fields of *linear* wave motion and is thus more fully understood. In linear wave propagation the term $u(x,t)$ in the equation for ψ plays the role of a refractive index or, in quantum theory, an atomic potential. [It should be emphasized that here t is merely a label for a free parameter that may be used to change the shape of $u(x,t)$. The equation is thus *not* the time-dependent Schrödinger equation.] When u is independent of a parameter such as t, the term k is a constant in the linear equation. In the present instance, then, the value of k could be expected to depend upon t. It can be shown, however, that there are certain expressions for $u(x,t)$ for which k remains independent of t. Such expressions for $u(x,t)$ are found to be governed by various partial differential equations, one of which is the KdV equation. This relation to a linear equation can then be exploited to obtain solutions of the nonlinear equation. (Solution of a nonlinear equation through recognition of an underlying linearity is also encountered in the study of elementary differential equations in the context of solving the Riccati equation.)

Considerable progress has been made in expanding the list of equations that have soliton solutions and in discerning the physical processes in which soliton behavior takes place. In particular, these extensions now include equations that describe wave motion in more than one space dimension.

See also: HYDRODYNAMICS; OPTICAL FIBER; SCHRÖDINGER EQUATION; WAVE MOTION

Bibliography

KIVSHAR, Y. S., and MALOMED, B. A. "Dynamics of Solitons in Nearly Integrable Systems." *Rev. Mod. Phys.* **61**, 763–915 (1989).

SCOTT, A. C.; CHU, F. Y. F.; and McLAUGHLIN, D. W. "The Soliton, A New Concept in Applied Science." *Proc. IEEE* **63**, 1443–1483 (1973).

G. L. LAMB JR.

SOUND

The word "sound" can have two meanings: an audible sensation in the ear, or the disturbance in a medium that can cause this sensation. (Making this distinction answers the age-old question, If a tree falls in a forest and no one is there to hear it, does it make a sound?) Sound is carried by waves that propagate through elastic materials and cause alterations in pressure.

The most familiar medium for propagating sound waves is air. The pressure changes that occur when a sound wave propagates in air are generally much smaller than atmospheric pressure. The minimum pressure fluctuation to which the ear can respond is less than one billionth (10^{-9}) of atmospheric pressure. This threshold of audibility, which varies from person to person, corresponds to a sound pressure amplitude of about 2×10^{-5} N/m^2 at a frequency of 1,000 Hz. The threshold of pain corresponds to a pressure amplitude approximately one million (10^6) times greater, but still less than 1/1,000 of atmospheric pressure.

In a gas or liquid, the local vibrations are always parallel to the direction of wave travel, so sound waves are classified as longitudinal waves. A solid material can transmit shearing or bending stresses and thus can support transverse as well as longitudinal vibrations, but generally the term "sound" refers only to longitudinal waves.

The speed of sound waves in air is about 343 m/s; it increases about 0.6 m/s for each degree Celsius. Wavelengths of audible sound span the range of about 2 cm to 7 m. Sound waves travel much faster in liquids and solids than they do in gases (approximately 1,410 m/s in water and 5,100 m/s in steel).

Sound sources are of many types, including vibrating bodies, such as the head of a drum; time-dependent flow (pulsations, turbulence), such as the sound of the wind or a high-speed jet; time-dependent heat sources, such as a spark or a bolt of lightning (thunder); and supersonic flow, such as the shock waves from an aircraft flying at supersonic speed. Unwanted sound is sometimes characterized as noise.

Because of the wide range of pressure stimuli, it is convenient to measure sound pressures on a logarithmic scale, called the decibel (dB) scale. The sound pressure level (SPL) of a sound (in dB) is expressed as SPL = $20 \log p/p_0$, where p is the sound pressure and $p_0 = 20$ μPa (2×10^{-5} N/m^2) is a reference pressure. Sound pressure level is measured with a sound level meter (it should not be called a decibel meter, because other quantities, such as sound power level and sound intensity level are expressed in decibels as well).

Other important parameters in describing sound are the acoustic velocity and the intensity. The acoustic velocity is the excess particle velocity (in addition to thermal motion) due to the passage of a sound wave. The acoustic impedance is defined as the ratio of sound pressure to acoustic velocity. The acoustic impedance of air is about 400 Pa/m. The sound intensity, measured in a specified direction at a point, is the average rate at which energy is transmitted across a unit area perpendicular to the wave direction.

When a sound wave encounters a change in the medium in which it is propagating, it may experience reflection, refraction, or scattering. At an interface between two media, the ratio of the reflected intensity to the incident intensity is given by

$$\frac{I_r}{I_o} = \left(\frac{z_2 - z_1}{z_2 + z_1} \right)^2,$$

where z_1 and z_2 are the impedances of the two media. The transmitted intensity I_t is given by

$$\frac{I_t}{I_o} = \frac{4z_2 z_1}{(z_2 + z_1)^2}.$$

Thus, if there is a large acoustic mismatch at the interface ($z_2 >> z_1$ or $z_2 << z_1$), most of the sound intensity is reflected.

The three principal loss mechanisms for a sound wave propagating in a fluid are viscosity, thermal conduction, and molecular relaxation.

Sound waves of very large amplitude exhibit nonlinear behavior. Regions of compression (where the temperature is higher) move slightly faster than rarefactions, and thus sound waves of very large amplitude can steepen and eventually form shock waves (much as water waves steepen and "break" as they approach the shore).

Attributes used to describe sounds include loudness, pitch, timbre, and duration, and each of the subjective qualities depends on one or more physical parameters such as sound pressure, frequency, spectrum, physical duration, and amplitude envelope. Loudness depends upon sound pressure level, but to a lesser extent it also depends on frequency; hearing sensitivity reaches its maximum around 3,500 to 4,000 Hz and decreases considerably below about 200 Hz. Pitch depends on frequency, but to a lesser extent it depends on the sound pressure level and the spectrum as well. Timbre is a term we use to describe the tone quality or tone color of a sound.

One of the most important uses of sound is in communication. Although many members of the animal kingdom have the ability to communicate by means of sound, human beings alone have the power of articulate speech. The human voice and the human ear are very well matched to each other. The ear has its maximum sensitivity in the frequency range 1,000 to 4,000 Hz, and that is the range of frequency in which the resonances of the vocal tract, which are the acoustical bases for most speech sounds, occur.

The terms ultrasonics and infrasonics refer to sound that is too high in frequency or too low in frequency to be audible. Acoustic imaging using ultrasound has many important medical and industrial applications. Ultrasonic microscopes using wavelengths as short as 0.03 μm are able to achieve high resolution.

Music and speech are not the only contributions humans have made to the world of sound. With few exceptions, advances in technology, such as the development of labor-saving machines, have resulted in a steady increase in the amount of unwanted sound, which we call noise. Noise has been receiving increased recognition as one of our critical environmental pollution problems. Like air and water pollution, noise pollution increases with population density; in our urban areas, it is a serious threat to our quality of life. Noise-induced hearing loss is a major health problem for millions of people employed in noisy environments. Besides actual hearing loss, however, human beings are affected in many other ways by high levels of noise; interference with speech, interruption of sleep, and other physiological and psychological effects of noise have been the subject of considerable study.

See also: ACOUSTICS; NOISE; PRESSURE, SOUND; SOUND, MUSICAL; SOUND ABSORPTION; ULTRASONICS; WAVE MOTION

Bibliography

HALL, D. E. *Basic Acoustics* (Harper & Row, New York, 1987).

KINSLER, L. E.; FREY, A. R.; COPPENS, A. B.; and SANDERS, J. V. *Fundamentals of Acoustics*, 3rd ed. (Wiley, New York, 1982).

ROSSING, T. D. *The Science of Sound*, 2nd ed. (Addison-Wesley, Reading, MA, 1990).

ROSSING, T. D., and FLETCHER, N. H. *Principles of Vibration and Sound* (Springer-Verlag, New York, 1994).

THOMAS D. ROSSING

SOUND, MUSICAL

Sound waves are longitudinal waves that travel in a solid, liquid, or gas. They can carry speech, music, or warning sounds from the source to the listener, but they also transmit noise. Whether a given sound is considered "music" or "noise" often depends on the listener's taste, the cultural setting, and the context.

Four attributes are frequently used to describe sound, especially musical sound: loudness, pitch, timbre, and duration. Each of these subjective qualities depends on one or more physical parameters than can be measured. Loudness, for example, depends mainly on sound pressure but also on the spectrum of the partials and the physical duration of the sound. Pitch depends mainly on frequency, but also shows lesser dependence on sound pressure and envelope. Timbre includes those attributes that serve to distinguish two sounds with the same pitch and loudness. Table 1 relates subjective qualities to measurable physical parameters.

Loudness

Although sounds with a greater sound pressure level usually sound louder, this is not always the case; the sensitivity of the ear varies with the frequency, the spectrum of partials, and other parameters (see Table 1). Hearing sensitivity reaches its maximum around 3,500 to 4,000 Hz and decreases considerably below about 200 Hz. In 1933 Harvey Fletcher and W. A. Munson determined curves of equal loudness level for tones of a single frequency. The contours of equal loudness level are labeled in units called phons, the level in phons being numerically equal to the sound pressure level in decibels at $f = 1,000$ Hz. In an effort to obtain a quantity proportional to the actual loudness sensation, a loudness scale was developed in which the unit of

Table 1 Dependence of Subjective Qualities of Sound on Physical Parameters

Physical Parameter	Subjective Quality			
	Loudness	Pitch	Timbre	Duration
Pressure	+++	+	+	+
Frequency	+	+++	++	+
Spectrum	+	+	+++	+
Duration	+	+	+	+++
Envelope	+	+	++	+

+ = weakly dependent; ++ = moderately dependent; +++ = strongly dependent.

loudness is called the sone. One sone is defined as the loudness of a 1,000-Hz tone at a sound level of 40 dB (a loudness level of 40 phons). For loudness levels of 40 phons or greater, the relationship between loudness S in sones and loudness level L_L in phons recommended by the International Standards Organization (ISO) is $S = 2^{(L_L - 40)/10}$.

Determining the loudness of the complex sounds in music is somewhat more difficult compared with sounds of a single frequency. The perceived loudness depends on the frequency bandwidth of the sound. Several techniques have been suggested for estimating the loudness of complex sounds; most of them begin by measuring the sound pressure level in several frequency bands (octave bands or $\frac{1}{3}$-octave bands).

The range of sound level in musical performance (the dynamic range) may vary widely, depending on the music. Composers use dynamic symbols to indicate the desired loudness; six levels, from softest to the loudest, are denoted by the symbols *pp*, *p*, *mp*, *mf*, *f*, and *ff* (occasionally *ppp* and *fff* are added). Measurements of sound intensity of a number of instrumentalists have shown, however, that seldom do musical performers actually play at as many as six distinguishable dynamic levels.

Pitch

Pitch is the characteristic of a musical sound that makes it sound high or low or that determines position on a scale. For a pure (sinusoidal) tone, the pitch is determined largely by its frequency, although parameters such as sound pressure and spectrum also play a role (see Table 1). The pitch of complex tones, however, is considerably more complicated.

When one listens to a musical tone composed of exact harmonics, the perceived pitch will generally correspond to the lowest common factor in their frequencies, which is called the fundamental. The ear identifies the pitch of the fundamental, even if the fundamental is very weak or missing altogether. The ability of the auditory system to determine a virtual pitch when the fundamental is missing makes it possible, for example, for small loudspeakers to produce bass tones.

When the partials of a complex tone are not harmonic, however, the determination of pitch is more subtle. The ear apparently picks out a series of nearly harmonic partials somewhere near the center of the audible range and determines the pitch to be the largest near-common factor in the series. Musical examples of the ability of the auditory system to arrive at a virtual pitch from "near harmonics" in a complex tone are found in the sounds of bells and chimes. In each case the pitch of the "strike tone" is determined mainly by three partials that have frequencies almost in the ratio 2:3:4.

Timbre

Timbre refers to the "tone quality" or "tone color" of a sound. The timbre of a musical sound is determined partly by the spectrum of the partials, but the sound pressure, the envelope, the waveform, and other parameters contribute as well. A piano sound played backward (so that the attack transient occurs at the end of the sound), for example, sounds quite unlike a piano even though the spectrum remains unchanged.

Timbre is sometimes described as a "multidimensional attribute" of sound; it is impossible to construct a single subjective scale of timbre of the type used for loudness or pitch. Scales such as "dull" to "sharp," "cold" to "warm," and "pure" to "rich" have been used to characterize the timbre of musical sounds. Still, one authority is of the opinion that "understanding timbre is perhaps the most challenging problem facing the musical community at the present time."

Rhythm

Rhythm is one of the most fundamental elements of music. In assigning a rhythmic interpretation to a musical passage, a listener will generally be influenced by many different kinds of clues. One of the most important of these clues, the relative durations of the notes, appears to be available even when the musical sound is devoid of accent, phrasing, or rubato. A key question addressed in recent research is: How should music be performed in order to elicit the desired rhythm response?

See also: ACOUSTICS; PRESSURE, SOUND; SOUND; SOUND ABSORPTION

Bibliography

BENGTSSON, I., and GABRIELSSON, A. "Analysis and Synthesis of Musical Rhythm" in *Studies of Music Performance,* edited by J. Sundberg (Royal Academy of Music, Stockholm, 1983).

HOUTSMA, A. J. M.; ROSSING, T. D.; and WAGENAARS, W. M. *Auditory Demonstrations* (Acoustic Society of America, Woodbury, NY, 1988).

KRUMHANSL, C. L. "Why is Musical Timbre so Hard to Understand?" in *Structure and Perception of Electroacoustic Sound and Music,* edited by S. Nielzén and O. Olsson (Excerpta Medica, Amsterdam, 1989).

ROSSING, T. D. *The Science of Sound,* 2nd ed. (Addison-Wesley, Reading, MA, 1990).

STEVENS, S. S., and STEVENS, G. *Psychophysics: Introduction to its Perceptual, Neural, and Social Prospects* (Wiley, New York, 1975).

ZWICKER, E. "Procedure for Calculating Loudness of Temporally Variable Sounds" *J. Acoust. Soc. Am.* **62,** 675–682 (1977).

TIIOMAS D. ROSSING

SOUND ABSORPTION

Sound waves carry energy. Ultimately this energy is dissipated or converted into heat. Part of this dissipation takes place in the transmitting medium and part of it at the boundaries of the medium.

Absorption of Sound in Fluids

It is customary to characterize the absorption of sound by a coefficient α, so that the wave amplitude of a plane wave decays as $e^{-\alpha x}$, while that of a spherical wave decays as $(1/r)e^{-\alpha x}$. When $x = 1/x$, the pressure amplitude of a plane wave has dropped to $1/e$ of its initial value. The change in sound pressure level (SPL) is given by $8.7\alpha x$.

The three principle loss mechanisms for a sound wave propagating in a fluid are viscosity, thermal conduction, and molecular relaxation. The first two are sometimes referred to collectively as the viscothermal loss or the classical absorption. In a free field, viscothermal losses are small and are found to vary approximately as the square of the frequency.

Loss due to molecular thermal relaxation takes place at frequencies where the period of a sound wave is comparable to the time for energy to be exchanged between molecular translational motion and internal states, such as vibration and rotation. The frequency at which maximum molecular absorption occurs in air depends on temperature and humidity—especially on humidity. Collisions between water and oxygen molecules are over 1,000 times more effective in converting translational energy to vibrational energy, as compared with collisions between two oxygen molecules. Thus the molecular absorption range moves to higher frequency as the humidity increases. For relative humidity of 20 percent, α is increased by as much as ten times over the audible frequency range; in large concert halls, this gives a noticeable reduction in brightness of the sound in the rear part of the hall.

Although viscothermal loss is very small in a free field, viscous loss can become large near a boundary where there is a stagnant layer; in a small pipe, viscous absorption of sound may be large. Similarly, loss due to thermal conductivity can become substantial in a pipe with walls of a material that is a good thermal conductor.

Absorption of Sound at Boundaries

When sound waves fall on a surface or object, their energy is partially reflected, partially transmitted, and partially absorbed. The relationship between reflected, transmitted, and absorbed energy depends on the angle of incidence, so for most sound-absorbing materials a different absorption coefficient is associated with each angle of incidence. The most commonly used absorption coefficient is a statistical one that assumes random incidence of sound waves (i.e., a diffuse sound field).

The sound absorption coefficient of most materials also depends on frequency. Porous materials tend to absorb best at high frequency, whereas materials that flex (such as wood or window glass) absorb best at low frequency. Since the reverberation time of a room is inversely proportional to the total sound absorption, the reverberation time of a concert hall can be quite different at high and low frequencies.

See also: PRESSURE, SOUND; SOUND

Bibliography

KINSLER, L. E.; FREY, A. R.; COPPENS, A. B.; and SANDERS, J. V. *Fundamentals of Acoustics,* 3rd ed. (Wiley, New York, 1982).

ROSSING, T. D. and FLETCHER, N. H. *Principles of Vibration and Sound* (Springer-Verlag, New York, 1994).

THOMAS D. ROSSING

SOUND PRESSURE

See PRESSURE, SOUND

SPACE

The most obvious occupants of space are self-luminous stars; larger units, such as galaxies, are luminous due to the stars they contain although other possible emissions, for example from compact objects in their centers and from emission nebulas, may also be important. Galileo's telescope resolved the Milky Way into individual stars that were too dim to be discerned with the naked eye. Galileo's contemporary, Johannes Kepler, remarking that the night sky was generally dark, used this datum as evidence that the universe was finite. In an infinite universe every line of sight will ultimately intersect a star; and, if the stars are distributed uniformly, this means that the sky should be uniformly as bright as a typical star, such as the Sun. An infinite Euclidean universe was a popular concept in the eighteenth and nineteenth centuries; thus there was concern about this contradiction, now known as Olbers's paradox. In modern cosmology Olbers's paradox is not a problem because (1) in the expanding universe, distant contributions are redshifted to lower energy, and (2) for a universe with a finite age, light from distant stars has not yet had time to reach us.

William Herschel, by carefully counting the stars visible to his telescope in different directions, was able to chart the first map of our galaxy in the late eighteenth century; but it was not until Harlow Shapley's work on the space distribution of globular clusters—spherical systems of stars located outside the main portion of the Galaxy—that the true size and shape of the Milky Way was finally revealed in the 1920s. Arguments over the nature of the diffuse spiral nebulas observed by astronomers were settled when Edwin Hubble was able to show that they were other galaxies rather than objects in the Milky Way. Research with constantly improving detectors has revealed billions of galaxies that are grouped in clusters and superclusters which, themselves, define a structure that has been compared to the surfaces of a mass of contiguous soap bubbles.

Space most often refers to the regions between the material bodies such as stars and planets. Most manned space activity has taken place in near-Earth space, a region that is still in a real sense part of Earth's atmosphere. The portion of the atmosphere where collisions between molecules are sufficiently rare that atoms move on ballistic trajectories is called the exosphere and occurs above an altitude of 500 km. The density at this level is still more than one billion particles per cubic centimeter; though more tenuous than the best vacuum obtainable on Earth, this is still enough to affect the orbits of satellites such as the Hubble Space Telescope (at 600-km altitude), so that boosts are needed periodically to maintain satellite altitudes.

Interplanetary space is considerably more empty than this, but there is still particulate matter between the planets. Small dust grains concentrated in the ecliptic plane give rise to the phenomena of "gegenschein" and "zodiacal light" due to scattering of sunlight from these micrometer-sized particles in the backward and forward directions, respectively. Drag due to interaction with solar radiation (Poynting–Robertson drag) limits the lifetimes of these particles by causing them to rapidly spiral into the Sun; thus they must be continuously replenished, presumably through constant erosion of comets and asteroids. Solar wind particles that originate in the expanding corona of the Sun also permeate the solar system; at Earth's distance the density of solar wind particles is about 5 cm^3. Most of the supersonic solar wind particles are deflected around Earth's magnetosphere, the region in which the planetary magnetic field dominates; but some are trapped, forming the Van Allen radiation belts that separate the top atmospheric layers from interplanetary space.

Space between the stars contains neutral gas, ionized gas, and small particulate matter or dust. William Herschel, the first astronomer to carefully study the distribution of stars in the sky, noticed voids in the distribution of stars in the late eighteenth century. Although the most plausible explanation was absorption of light from distant stars by intervening material (called extinction), conclusive proof was not obtained until 1930. The interstellar dust in our galaxy is composed of silicates, various forms of crystalline and amorphous carbon, ices, and other nonvolatile material. The typical particles are smaller than the wavelengths of visible light, which is known because they are observed to scatter blue light more strongly than red, resulting in "reddening" of starlight of stars at increasing distances. On the other hand, the extinction efficiency implies that they are not much smaller, probably $r \sim 0.1$ μm. They are therefore more like smoke particles than like terrestrial dust grains. The density of particles that is required to explain the observed reddening is very small, only roughly a thousand dust grains in a cubic kilometer of space.

A second component of the interstellar medium in the Galaxy is neutral and ionized gas, which is concentrated near the galactic plane. The mass of the gas in interstellar space is about 100 times that of the dust component, and the average density near the galactic plane is roughly 0.6 atoms/cm^3. The presence of the gas is revealed by its absorption of light from background stars; the first evidence was obtained by J. Hartmann in 1904 when he noticed a non-Doppler shifted component in spectral lines from a spectroscopic binary—a pair of stars that cannot be visually resolved as double but which are revealed by the periodic Doppler shifts of the lines from the individual stars. Most of the gas component in the Galaxy is in the form of large clouds of neutral atomic or molecular hydrogen, typically at temperatures between 10 K and 100 K. Other atoms beside hydrogen occur in the clouds; most atoms with atomic number $Z < 30$ have been seen, and heavier atoms such as selenium and arsenic have been found through their UV spectra. Abundances are similar to those in the solar system when allowance is made for incorporation of the more refractory atoms in dust grains, thereby depleting the gas component. Neutral atomic hydrogen is revealed by the hyperfine transition in the hydrogen atoms at 21 cm. Study of the colder (10–20 K) clouds of molecular hydrogen is more complicated; rotational absorption lines of simple molecular species such as OH, CH, and CN are alternate markers, and more recently UV absorptions have revealed H$_2$ directly. Dust in giant molecular clouds screens the hydrogen molecules from dissociation by UV radiation and catalyzes hydrogen combination into molecules. These relatively dense clouds (100 to 10,000 per cm^3) are very important because they are the regions in which star formation occurs.

Clouds of ionized hydrogen, referred to as HII regions or emission nebulas, are also common, especially in regions of recent star formation. The material in these clouds is maintained in the ionized state by the UV flux from young O- and B-type stars that have recently formed from large, neutral hydrogen clouds. The material in the clouds fluoresces as an equilibrium between photodissociation and recombination is reached. The reddish color of these spectacular objects is mainly due to the red Balmer emission line from recombining hydrogen atoms. Metastable states of heavier atoms are formed by collisions in these high temperature nebulas; they are able to decay radiatively because of the low probability of further collisions in the tenuous clouds. The green emission from twice-ionized oxygen is a classic example of such a forbidden transition that is prominent in emission nebulas; this transition is an important astronomic marker for hot, ionized gas.

In addition to matter in the form of gas and dust, the interstellar medium is also characterized by an interstellar magnetic field whose strength is roughly 1 μG. The magnetic field aligns the dust grains that are responsible for interstellar reddening, revealing its presence through polarization of the reddened starlight. Even this weak field is able, on the galactic scale, to confine relativistic protons and electrons to the Galaxy by deflecting them to spiral around magnetic field lines. The protons are the major galactic component of cosmic rays, and the spiraling electrons are revealed by synchrotron radio emission.

Though the gravitational field of any individual star becomes very small as the distance increases, the net gravitational effects of the many objects in the Galaxy produce a gravitational field that controls the motion of the individual stars therein. There is a roughly spherical concentration of stars in the galactic nucleus which causes Keplerian motion of stars; the Sun orbits the galactic center with a period of about 240,000,000 years, corresponding to an acceleration toward the galactic center of $1/1,000,000$ m/s^2. In addition, the concentration of mass into the galactic plane gives rise to an additional force component normal to the plane, which is approximately linear with distance; the Sun oscillates perpendicular to this plane with an amplitude of 100 parsecs and a period of about 60,000,000 years. The Sun's actual motion is a complicated superposition of these two effects.

It is clear that many galaxies have gas and dust like the Milky Way, but the question of gas and dust between the galaxies is less clear cut. Many galaxies are gravitationally bound into clusters, the largest of which contain thousands of galaxies and are called rich clusters. X-ray emission from rich clusters has revealed large amounts of hot, intergalactic gas with a mass roughly equal to the luminous constituent galaxies. Studies of large redshift quasars has revealed absorption features at smaller red shifts, which are attributed to Lyman α absorptions of hard UV photons by intervening clouds of hydrogen gas. Although it is possible that these absorptions, referred to as the "Lyman α forest," are due to intergalactic gas clouds, it is also possible that these absorptions occur in the extended halos of intervening galaxies.

The distribution of mass in the Milky Way and in other galaxies is calculated from the relation between the periods of stars orbiting the galactic centers and their distances. Although stars near the center have the behavior expected for a mass concentration in the nucleus, for larger distances the rotation curve flattens out so that the tangential velocities are independent of distance. This implies that the mass enclosed increases roughly in proportion to the radius in regions where the luminosity (due to stars) is falling off rapidly. Some nonluminous form of matter, dark matter that is distributed more uniformly than the luminous mass, seems to

be required by the rotational dynamics. The same problem appears when the dynamics of large clusters of galaxies are studied. Even allowing for the large component of gas in these clusters, the total observable mass falls far short of what is needed to explain the observed spatial and velocity distributions. Again, some nonluminous form of matter seems to be required.

Space is also permeated by radiation. In addition to the obvious photons originating in the discrete sources such as stars, there is a general isotropic cosmic background component of radiation corresponding to a blackbody with a temperature of 2.7 K. This is the redshifted remnant of the radiation that filled the cosmos 300,000 years after the big bang. At that time the temperature of the universe had dropped to about 4,000 K, and protons and electrons combined to form atoms. Radiation and matter, which had been kept in equilibrium by Thompson scattering from the free charges, effectively decoupled from each other. From that time on the radiation field has expanded with the universe and been redshifted until reaching its currently observed distribution.

Space is clearly not the "empty void" it is sometimes pictured to be. Many aspects of space and its contents are areas of current research about which much more will be known in the near future.

See also: BIG BANG THEORY; DARK MATTER; KEPLER'S LAWS; OLBERS'S PARADOX; SOLAR WIND; VAN ALLEN BELTS

Bibliography

BOK, B., and BOK, P. *The Milky Way*, 5th ed. (Harvard University Press, Cambridge, MA, 1981).

SPITZER, L., JR. *Physical Processes in the Interstellar Medium* (Wiley, New York, 1978).

PHILIP B. JAMES

SPACE AND TIME

Prior to Isaac Newton, discussions of space and time had been the province of philosophers and theologians. Newton's laws of motion are statements about acceleration and velocity, which are defined in terms of position and time. As a practical matter, therefore, applications of Newton's laws require measurements of both spatial location, which must be measured relative to a frame of reference, and of time.

Reference Frames

Our concepts of position are based on relative spatial relationships. A reference frame is defined by a collection of objects at rest with respect to each other (e.g., a set of rigid, orthogonal axes); positions of other objects are quantitatively identified by specifying their location relative to these using standard measuring rods for comparison. One can visualize many different reference frames moving, rotating, and accelerating relative to each other. The special reference systems in which the equations of motion assume their simplest form, Newton's laws, are called inertial or Galilean frames. Newton's first law may be used to define a Galilean reference system as one in which a test body upon which no external forces act moves with a constant velocity; if such a system can be found, the other two laws of motion will also be valid therein.

If one Galilean reference frame has been identified, any other reference system that is moving with a constant velocity with respect to that system is also inertial because of the fact that the equation of motion involves only changes in the velocity of the object. This property of the equations of motion is called Galilean invariance, or the principle of Newtonian relativity. Finding the first inertial system is not a trivial matter, however, and most mechanics problems are solved in reference frames that are only approximately inertial. For example, the equations of motion on the surface of the rotating Earth include centrifugal and Coriolis terms; in many situations, however, these terms in the equations of motion can be neglected so that they reduce to Newton's law as a very good approximation. The surface of the rotating Earth can be used as an approximate inertial system for the purpose of computing the trajectory of a tennis ball, but would not be appropriate for predicting the trajectory of a ballistic missile, where the additional terms cannot be ignored. Similarly, a reference frame at rest relative to the center of the sun is a good frame to use for celestial mechanics in the solar system, but the acceleration of the sun toward the center of the galaxy disqualifies it as a candidate for an inertial frame for problems in galactic mechanics.

What then determines which frames (if any) are true (as opposed to approximate) inertial frames? Newton postulated that there must exist an absolute space and that inertial frames are those at rest or moving with constant velocity with respect to this preferred reference frame. He attributed observable effects of rotation, such as the polar flattening of Jupiter due to centrifugal forces, to rotation relative to this absolute space. Ernst Mach, among others, attacked the concept of an absolute space that was unobservable except for its effects on bodies rotating with respect to it; he postulated that these effects were produced by an interaction with the masses of the earth and other celestial bodies in the universe. In general relativity, inertial frames are determined by the distribution of all of the matter in the universe and, in the absence of nearby mass concentrations, are in a state of uniform motion with respect to the stars, consistent with Mach's hypothesis. On the other hand, Mach's principle predicts differences in accelerations in different directions with respect to nearby mass concentrations, while in relativity the laws of motion in the inertial frames are unaffected by nearby masses. So relativity theory is not totally consistent with Mach's principle, either; in fact, the Brans–Dicke theory was developed to provide an alternative to general relativity which is consistent with Mach's principle.

Length Measurement

Application of the equations of motion requires a coordinate system that is fixed relative to our chosen inertial frame, and a system of self-consistent units that include a standard measuring rod. The standard unit of distance in the SI system, the meter, was originally defined to be 10^{-7} of the distance from the equator to the north pole of the earth along the meridian of Paris. This standard of distance was maintained for practical use on accurately scribed metal bars. When it was discovered that the terrestrial measure used to define the meter was in error, the original definition was abandoned in favor of the distance marked on a "master" bar that was kept near Paris.

The desirability of defining the meter in terms of a natural standard rather than a man-made standard that was potentially vulnerable led in 1960 to the adoption of a definition of the meter in terms of the wavelength of light. This standard was itself abandoned in 1983 in favor of a definition relying on the standard time unit, the second, and the speed of light; the meter is now defined to be 1/299,792,458 times the distance traveled by light in a vacuum during one second. The precision allowed by this definition exceeds that which could be obtained with the independent wavelength standard.

Time

Our concept of time is based on sequential relationships of events; event A precedes event B, follows event B, or is simultaneous with event B. Newtonian mechanics assumes that there is an absolute time that can be defined independent of an observer's frame or position within that frame. The acceleration and the subsequent motion of an object depend on both defining a standard unit for time and creating a means to measure it. This is achieved by using repetitive events, such as swings of a pendulum, to define a clock. The time of an event will be determined by the particular "tick" on the clock that is simultaneous with the event; and the time interval between two events can be defined in terms of the number of intervening ticks on the clock. One can imagine a set of identical clocks placed throughout our reference frame to provide a measure of time for events; Newton assumed that when these clocks were synchronized they would provide an absolute time that would be equally valid in any inertial frame. In effect, this is equivalent to the assumption that events that are simultaneous in one frame will be observed as simultaneous in other frames.

Measurement of Time

The regular succession of day and night brought about by the rotation of the earth is the most natural repetitive event to use as a time measure, and whatever system is adopted for defining our time measurements must ultimately be brought into phase with this natural cycle. A celestial object is said to transit when it crosses an observer's meridian. Within the accuracy imposed by the degree to which the earth's rotation rate is constant, the time interval between transits of a fixed celestial object, such as a star, is constant and can be used as a time reference; the resulting sidereal time is useful for astronomers but is not in phase with the cycle defined by solar transits. The Sun is not fixed but appears to move relative to the background stars, and the situa-

tion is complicated by the rate of this motion not being constant.

Johannes Kepler showed that Earth does not move at a constant speed in its orbit about the Sun; this causes the rate of apparent solar motion relative to the background stars to vary. The time interval between successive solar transits is smaller in January, when Earth is close to the Sun and moves faster than its average speed, than it is in July. Because of the inclination of Earth's axis to its orbital plane, the path of the Sun relative to the stars is inclined relative to the celestial equator. Thus even if Earth moved at a constant rate in its orbit, the easterly component of the Sun's motion would appear to vary periodically through the year; the west to east component would be maximum at the solstices, when the Sun's motion is parallel to the celestial equator, and least at the equinoxes, when the Sun's path crosses the equator.

Because of these two effects, the length of the solar day, defined by consecutive transits of the Sun, varies throughout the year. In order to define a constant unit of time, astronomers introduced the concept of the "mean sun," a fictitious sun that moves in a west to east direction at a constant rate equal to the average rate of the real sun over the course of one year. The difference between this "mean solar time" and real solar time, as read for example on a sundial, is called the "equation of time"; it is sometimes positive, sometimes negative, and can be as large as sixteen minutes. The "analemma," the mysterious figure eight that decorated many older globes, is a graphical representation of this difference.

Definition of the basic time unit, the second, to be 1/86,400 of a mean solar day is sufficient for many commercial and navigational purposes but is not accurate enough for precise scientific work. There are small variations in the rotation rate of the earth which affect the length of a solar day due to seasonal weather changes, polar wandering, phenomena in the interior of the earth, and a secular angular deceleration of the earth caused by tides. In an attempt to retain a definition of time in terms of astronomical events, the second was for a while defined as a fraction of a Tropical year (length of time between equinoxes); but this proved to be too cumbersome, so an alternative standard was set.

In 1967 the astronomical definition of the second was abandoned in favor of a new standard—the atomic second. The basic unit of time in SI units, the second, was defined to be 9,192,631,770 periods of the radiation resulting from the transition between the hyperfine levels of the ground state of the cesium 133 atom. These two states are distinguished by the spins of the cesium 133 nucleus and of the unpaired valence electron, which are parallel in one case and antiparallel in the other. In an atomic clock, a magnetic field isolates one of the states; maximizing transitions to the other state, which are induced by absorption of radio-frequency (rf) radiation, is used to tune an rf oscillator.

Although the definition of the time interval no longer depends on astronomy, it is still necessary to maintain a relation between atomic time and universal time, the mean solar time at the Greenwich Meridian. Times on the two scales were defined to be equal on January 1, 1958. As the two scales drift apart due to the various effects discussed above, leap seconds are added or subtracted in order to keep the two scales within 0.9 s of each other. Time is therefore still in phase with the Sun.

The Newtonian relativity principle was challenged by James Maxwell's electromagnetic theory, in which there was a preferred frame in which the speed of light is the same in all directions. If the medium in which the electromagnetic waves propagated, the ether, pervaded all space, it seemed natural to assume that it was at rest or moving with constant velocity relative to Newton's absolute space. Therefore, detection of motion relative to the ether could be interpreted in favor of the Newtonian viewpoint. The experiment of Albert Michelson and Edward Morley was unable to detect any motion of the earth relative to this ether and therefore subject to the assumption above, is evidence against absolute space. Einstein showed that the principle of relativity could be recovered by using the set of Lorentz transformations in place of the Galilean transformations. In the process, the intuitive idea of an absolute time that is the same for all inertial observers was abandoned. Time and space coordinates are interwoven by the Lorentz transformation equations.

See also: ATOMIC CLOCK; KEPLER'S LAWS; MACH'S PRINCIPLE; MICHELSON–MORLEY EXPERIMENT; NEWTON'S LAWS; RELATIVITY, GENERAL THEORY OF; RELATIVITY, SPECIAL THEORY OF; SPACE; SPACETIME; TIME

Bibliography

CLOTFELTER, B. E., *Reference Systems and Inertia: The Nature of Space* (Iowa State University Press, Ames, 1970).

HOWSE, D. *Greenwich Time* (Oxford University Press, Oxford, Eng., 1980).

WEINBERG, S. *Gravitation and Cosmology* (Wiley, New York, 1972).

PHILIP B. JAMES

SPACETIME

In both the special and general theories of relativity, the three dimensions of space and one dimension of time are imagined to be but parts of a unified, four-dimensional whole called spacetime. Both theories mathematically describe the geometry of spacetime using the same concepts and tools that one would use to describe geometry of a two-dimensional surface. This geometrical metaphor lies at the very heart of relativity theory.

Events, Coordinates, and Spacetime Diagrams

Figure 1a shows a map of a two-dimensional patch of land. The cartesian coordinate axes allow us to assign coordinates x and y to various points on the map (or plot points on the map given their coordinates). Figure 1b shows an analogous map of spacetime, called a spacetime diagram. The vertical axis on this diagram represents time and the horizontal axis represents position along the x direction in space (the y and z dimensions are ignored in this diagram to enable us to represent four-dimensional spacetime with a two-dimensional drawing). The points on this diagram actually represent events (such as the collision of two particles or the decay of a radioactive atom) that mark not only a specific location in space but also a certain instant of time. Just as the map depicts the spatial relationships between points on the field, so a spacetime diagram depicts the relationships between events in spacetime.

In a spacetime diagram, we actually plot not t versus x but ct verses x (as shown), where c is the speed of light. Just as we would not draw a map with the vertical and horizontal axes labeled in miles and meters respectively, it does not make sense to mark the vertical axis in a spacetime diagram in seconds while we label the horizontal axis in meters. Note that in SI units ct is measured in meters, where 1 m of ct corre-

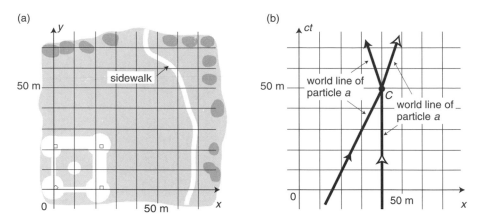

Figure 1 (a) A map of a field. The Cartesian coordinate grid superimposed on the diagram allows us to assign coordinates to points on the field. (b) A map of spacetime, called a spacetime diagram. A reference frame enables us to superimpose a grid on spacetime, allowing us to assign coordinates to events. Particle *a* is initially moving at a constant speed of about $0.5c$ in the $+x$ direction, while particle *b* is initially at rest. At event *C,* the two particles collide. They subsequently move away from the collision in the negative and positive *x* directions, respectively, at speeds of about $0.25c$.

sponds to the time required (≈ 3.3 ns) for light to travel 1 m. So if we plot ct versus x, both axes on the spacetime diagram have the same units. Since c always has the same value in every inertial reference frame in relativity, it provides an unambiguous means for expressing times in distance units.

A footpath wandering through the field would be represented on the map by a connected sequence of points called a curve. Analogously, we represent the path of a particle on a spacetime diagram as a connected series of events called a world line, which is really no more than a graph of the particle's *x* coordinate position versus time. The world line of a particle at rest will be a vertical line on the spacetime diagram, while the world line of a particle moving in the $+x$ direction in space will be tilted to the right on the diagram at an angle that increases as the particle's speed increases. Since no particle can travel faster than the speed of light, no particle can travel more than 1 m of distance in 1 m of light-travel-time ct, so the angle that any particle's world line makes with the vertical cannot be greater than $45°$.

Different Inertial Frames Are Like Rotated Coordinate Systems

In plane geometry, a coordinate system is a grid that we superimpose on a plane so that we can as-

sign an *x* and *y* coordinate to any point on the surface. Similarly, a reference frame in relativity is both a spatial and temporal grid that we superimpose on space and time so that we can assign position coordinates *x*, *y*, *z* and a time coordinate *t* to any event in spacetime.

When we draw a map, we are free to orient our cartesian coordinate system any way that we please because all orientations are physically equivalent. Similarly, the theory of relativity asserts that we can describe spacetime using any inertial reference frame that we like, since all inertial frames are physically equivalent. Figure 2a shows a map where we have superimposed two differently oriented coordinate systems on the same plot of land. Now, consider two inertial reference frames *S* and *S′* that move relative to each other at a constant speed along the spatial *x* direction. If we superimpose the time and space axes for these frames on the same spacetime diagram, it turns out that we get the map shown in Fig. 2b.

How do we know that Fig. 2b should look this way? By definition, the time axis on a spacetime diagram for a given reference frame connects all events happening at the origin ($x = 0$) of that frame; it thus represents the world line of that frame's origin. If the *S′* frame is moving in the $+x$ direction relative to *S*, then the world line of its origin should be a straight line tilted to the right, as shown. (Conversely, you can see that relative to the *S′* coordinate grid, the t axis of the S frame is a straight line tilted to the left, indicating that S is moving in the $-x$ direction relative to S'.) Thus, the t and t' axes on the spacetime diagram must be tilted relative to each other if the frames are in relative motion.

Comparing Figs. 2a and 2b, we see inertial frames in relative motion in spacetime are analogous to differently oriented coordinate systems in plane geometry. The analogy is not exact; the spatial x' for frame S' axis on the spacetime diagram (which connects all events occurring at the same time $t' = 0$ in that frame) is tilted up relative to the same for frame S (as shown in Fig. 2b) rather than the same angle down (as shown in Fig. 2a). This follows from the requirement that the speed of light have the same value in both frames (note that particle traveling along a world line tilted at a $45°$ angle on the diagram travels 1 m right or left in 1 m of ct time as measured in either frame).

Figure 2a makes it clear that the coordinate differences Δx and Δy between two given points P and Q on the map depend on your choice of coordinate systems. Similarly, Fig. 2b makes it clear that the spatial separation Δx and elapsed time Δt measured between two given events P and Q depend on your choice of inertial frame. In particular, note that P and Q are simultaneous in the S' frame ($\Delta t' = 0$) but not in the S frame. The relativity of simultaneity and elapsed times are famous consequences of special relativity.

Distance and Spacetime Interval

There is a way of quantifying the separation between two points on a plot of land without using a coordinate system at all; we can simply measure the distance Δr between the points with a tape measure laid in a straight line. The Pythagorean theorem is useful because it allows us to compute this coordinate-independent distance using the coordinate-dependent coordinate differences Δx and Δy between the points:

$$\Delta r^2 = \Delta x^2 + \Delta y^2. \tag{1}$$

No matter what coordinate system we use to measure Δx and Δy, we get the same distance Δr.

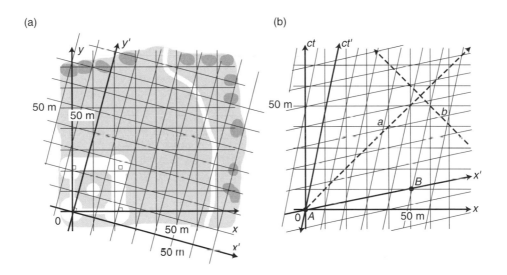

Figure 2 (a) Two coordinate grids, one rotated with respect to the other, are superimposed on the same map. Note that $\Delta x = 0$ between first and second base on the softball field in the upright grid, but $\Delta x \neq 0$ in the rotated grid. (b) Two coordinate grids for different inertial reference frames S and S' are superimposed on the same spacetime. Frame S' is moving in the $+x$ direction with a speed of $0.20c$ with respect to S. Note that events A and B are simultaneous in frame S' ($\Delta t' = 0$), but $\Delta t \neq 0$ in frame S. The dotted lines A and B show world lines of photons moving at the speed of light in the positive and negative x directions, respectively. Note that in both frames, these photons cover 1 m of distance in 1 m of ct time.

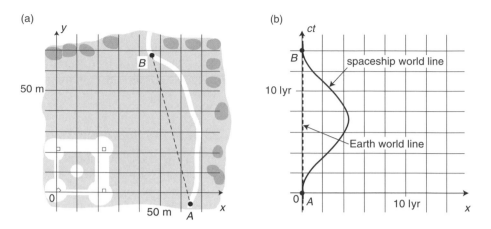

Figure 3 (a) The pathlength measured along the curved sidewalk path from point A to B is longer than that measured along the straight path between those points (dotted line). (b) A person riding in a spaceship going from Earth to Alpha Centauri and back would measure less proper time along the ship's curved world line between the departure and arrival events A and B than a person who stays home on Earth (less time rather than more time because of the minus signs in the spacetime metric equation).

Like the tape measure laid straight between points, a clock that travels from one event to another at a constant velocity quantifies the separation between those events in a unique and frame-independent way (every observer will agree that the clock travels at a constant velocity and what its face reads as it passes each event). We define the elapsed time between events measured by such a clock to be the spacetime interval Δs between the events. Just as we can calculate the distance Δr from the coordinate-dependent differences Δx and Δy, the frame-independent spacetime interval can be calculated from the frame-dependent coordinate differences Δx, Δy, Δz, and Δt using an equation similar to the Pythagorean theorem:

$$\Delta s^2 = (c\Delta t)^2 - \Delta x^2 - \Delta y^2 - \Delta z^2. \quad (2)$$

This equation is called the metric equation for flat spacetime. The main difference between it and the Pythagorean theorem (besides the number of dimensions involved) is the minus signs; these also turn out to be necessary to keep the speed of light frame-independent.

We can also measure the frame-independent pathlength between two points on our plot of land along a given footpath that travels between the points by laying our flexible tape measure along the path. Analogously, we might measure a frame-independent time interval between two events along a certain particle's world line simply by attaching a clock to that particle and seeing what it measures; we call this the particle's proper time (in the sense of "proprietary") along its world line. Just as it is not surprising that the pathlength along two different paths between the same two points on a plot of land is different, so it should not be surprising that the elapsed proper time measured along two different world lines between the same two events in spacetime should be different. This analogy to pathlength provides a natural resolution of the famous Twin Paradox.

Curved Spacetime

The straightest possible lines on a given surface are called geodesics. On a flat piece of paper, geodesics are simply straight lines. On the curved surface of a globe, the geodesics are no longer straight, but rather great circles. The pilot of a plane flying above Earth's equator would believe the plane to be flying in a straight line, but an observer at the North Pole would see the plane following a circular orbit around the pole. Similarly, some geodesics near the throat of a funnel like the one shown in Fig. 4 follow orbits around the funnel's throat.

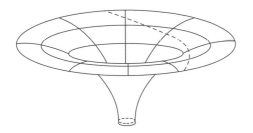

Figure 4 Some geodesics (dotted lines) on the surface of a funnel.

The core of the general theory of relativity is the geodesic hypothesis, which asserts that a free particle (one that is acted on by no forces except gravity) always follows a geodesic through spacetime. A massive object curves the spacetime around it so that geodesics near that object are no longer simple straight lines but curve toward or around the massive object.

On a curved two-dimensional surface, the Pythagorean theorem has to be replaced by the more general equation

$$dr^2 = g_{xx}dx^2 + g_{xy}dxdy + g_{yx}dydx + g_{yy}dy^2, \quad (3)$$

where dr is the distance between two infinitesimally separated points on the surface and dx, dy are the coordinate separations between those points. The four quantities g_{xx}, g_{xy}, g_{yx}, and g_{yy} are components of what we call the surface's metric; taken together, these quantities (which may vary with position on the curved surface) completely describe the surface's curvature in the neighborhood of the points in question.

By direct analogy, the metric equation for curved spacetime is

$$ds^2 = g_{tt}dt^2 + g_{tx}dtdx + g_{ty}dtdy + \ldots + g_{zz}dz^2, \quad (4)$$

where ds is the spacetime interval between two infinitesimally separated events. The sixteen metric components g_{tt}, g_{tx}, $g_{ty}, \ldots, g_{zz}$ (one for each possible combination of two of the four coordinate differentials dt, dx, dy, and dz) together completely specify the curvature of spacetime in the neighborhood of the events in question. The Einstein field equations of general relativity mathematically link these metric components with the presence of mass.

Thus, in general relativity, there really is no gravitational force acting directly between two objects; rather, a massive object curves the spacetime around it, and particles near the massive object then follow the curved geodesics defined by that spacetime. In John A. Wheeler's poetic description, "space tells matter how to move; matter tells space how to curve" (Misner, Thorne, and Wheeler, 1973, p. 5).

Conclusion

We have seen how the idea of spacetime, as a geometric unity, is based on a detailed analogy with the geometry of ordinary two-dimensional surfaces. This analogy is useful and powerful not only because it works (all of the predictions of the geometric analogies in both special and general relativity have been consistently supported by experiment) but because it makes the difficult concepts of relativity easier to visualize and understand.

See also: EVENT; FRAME OF REFERENCE, INERTIAL; PROPER TIME; RELATIVITY, GENERAL THEORY OF; RELATIVITY, SPECIAL THEORY OF; SPACE AND TIME; TIME DILATION; TWIN PARADOX

Bibliography

ELLIS, G. F. R., and WILLIAMS, R. M. *Flat and Curved Space-Times* (Clarendon Press, Oxford, Eng., 1988).

MISNER, C. W.; THORNE, K. S.; and WHEELER, J. A. *Gravitation* (W. H. Freeman, San Francisco, 1973).

MOORE, T. A. *A Traveler's Guide to Spacetime* (McGraw-Hill, New York, 1996).

TAYLOR, E. F., and WHEELER, J. A. *Spacetime Physics* (W. H. Freeman, New York, 1992).

THOMAS A. MOORE

SPACE TRAVEL

Space travel has been a subject of fiction for more than a century, and since the late 1950s, it has been a historical reality. Space travel can be viewed as a continuation of the process that has caused humanity to spread from a single continent to inhabit every land body on Earth. The reasons for expansion have been territorial, economic, and military.

The military need for long-range missile bombardment led to the German development of the V2 missile during World War II and to ballistic missile development during the Cold War. Long-range missile systems provided launch vehicles for most of the initial satellite launches and manned space flights during the late 1950s and early 1960s.

The existence of vast resources of material and energy within the solar system provide economic motivation for space travel. Communication systems, using satellite-based equipment, provide another. Military applications also create incentives for space development.

Perhaps the most important resource for the near future is energy. Gerard O'Neil of Princeton University and others have proposed the creation of large solar power stations in orbit around Earth, which would beam power to the surface using microwaves. Such a power system would be relatively free of environmental hazards.

Another important resource is knowledge. Information about physical conditions and processes in space is important for its own sake, and for applications to practical problems in technology and science. Knowledge of hazardous conditions, such as the presence of comets or asteroids on eventual collision course with Earth, could enable us to avoid disastrous future events.

Finally, in the future we may be able to use space beyond Earth as living space for ourselves and the rest of Earth's biosphere.

Conditions in Space

Near the surface, Earth's atmosphere consists mostly of nitrogen and oxygen at a pressure of about 10^5 N/m^2 and temperature of about 300 K. Atmospheric density decreases by roughly a factor of e (2.718 ...) for each increase of about 8 km in altitude above the surface up to the exosphere ("outer space"), which begins about 500 km above Earth's surface, and is characterized by hard vacuum, with atmospheric pressure less than 10^{-10} N/m^2. The gravitational field, about 10 m/s^2 at the surface, decreases as the inverse square of the distance from the center of Earth until it eventually becomes dominated by contributions from other astronomical bodies, such as the Sun, Moon, and other planets.

Orbital Principles

The motion of objects in space is governed by Newton's laws of motion, given the gravitational and other forces exerted on the objects. For a spacecraft outside the atmosphere, gravity and the spacecraft's propulsion system are the only significant forces. To a good approximation, the motion of an object in space, without propulsion, is described by Kepler's three laws of planetary motion:

1. The orbit of a planet is an ellipse with the Sun at one focus.
2. The motion of a planet is such that a line between the planet and the Sun sweeps out area at a constant rate.
3. The orbital period of a planet is proportional to the 3/2 power of the semi-major axis of its orbit.

In the case of an object orbiting around a body other than the Sun, Kepler's laws also apply, except that the distances and other parameters are those relating to the other body; thus satellites of Earth travel in elliptical paths with Earth at a focus, and so on.

Most current space propulsion systems are designed for short duration; they apply only brief thrusts to the spacecraft. Therefore, except for planetary landing or takeoff, maneuvers in space generally involve transfers from one elliptical orbit to another. Typically, orbital transfers are performed to change altitude (semi-major axis) or eccentricity of the orbit, or to change the body about which the craft is orbiting, as in going from Earth's orbit to the orbit of Mars (see Fig. 1).

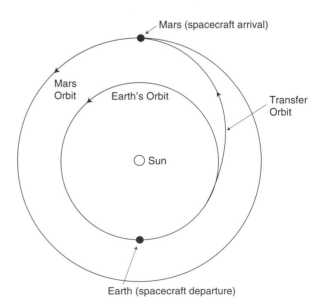

Figure 1   Transfer orbit from Earth to Mars.

The combination of Kepler's third law and the increasing scale of distances of astronomical objects implies that each increasingly distant category of destination requires a disproportionately longer travel time. Thus distances on the surface of Earth, on the order of 10^4 km, require travel times of less than an hour by orbit; the Moon, several days; interplanetary travel requires about half a year (for a nearby planet such as Venus) to several years for more distant planets such as Jupiter, to a decade for the outer planets such as Neptune or Pluto.

For yet more distant objects travel times are extremely large. Interstellar distances are of the order of 10^{14} km or greater. At speeds approaching that of light, distant interstellar or intergalactic voyages might be possible. Due to relativistic time dilation, however, the crew of such a voyage would return to an Earth whose civilization or even biology may have evolved radically.

Transportation Principles

The absence of a large, readily available, reaction mass creates serious engineering difficulties for space travel. In the case of terrestrial transportation the reaction mass consists entirely, or in part, of some environmental object or medium, such as Earth's solid component, the ocean water, or the gaseous atmosphere. In the Newtonian range of velocities, the energy imparted to the reaction mass is proportional to the ratio of craft mass to reaction mass:

$$K_r = \frac{K_c \, m_c}{m_r},$$

where m_c and m_r are the craft mass and reaction mass, and K_c and K_r the craft kinetic energy and reaction mass kinetic energy, respectively. Thus a large reaction mass implies minimal waste of energy.

These considerations make it desirable to employ as large a reaction mass as possible. Available masses include the Sun, planets, satellites, and other stars. To use a mass as reaction mass, however, it is necessary to exert a force on it. Space travel implies that eventually the craft will be far from any large mass, and thus it is necessary to employ a long-range force to use a planet or other astronomical body as reaction mass. The only known practical long-range force for this purpose is gravity; its use in space travel is described later in this entry in connection with the gravitational slingshot. Otherwise, it is necessary to maintain contact with a large mass in order to use it for reaction. Because this is usually impossible, rocket propulsion is necessary.

The first goal of space travel is to attain orbital velocity. Orbital velocity in the vicinity of Earth's surface is approximately 27,000 km/h; at this speed the atmosphere at low altitude exerts very large and destructive forces, accompanied by extreme heat, making orbit at low altitude a practical impossibility.

To attain orbital velocity, therefore, requires an altitude of roughly 100 km or more above the surface of Earth. Since the atmosphere at such altitudes is too thin to exert large forces, Earth's atmosphere cannot be used as reaction mass there. Thus, normally any spacecraft must be powered to orbit in part by rocket propulsion. One alternative, to use Earth's magnetic field as a means of thrusting against Earth, would require superconducting magnets of strength far beyond present technology. The other long-range force, gravity, is not useable for attaining orbit.

Given these engineering limitations, the standard solution is to use rocket propulsion exclusively to attain orbit. Hybrid solutions are also under study, such as the use of supersonic ram (SCRAM) jet propulsion while in the atmosphere, followed by rocket propulsion at above SCRAM jet operating altitudes.

The Russian theoretician Constantin Tsilkovski appears to have been the first to systematically investigate using rocket propulsion for space travel. Rocket propulsion is based on Newton's third law of motion, which states that for every force exerted on a given object, there must be a total force of equal magnitude, in the opposite direction, exerted on some other mass (the reaction mass). Tsilkovski's approach was to use rocket propulsion, in which the propulsion system carries along its own reaction mass. The initial development of the modern, liquid-fueled rocket was carried out in the United States by Robert Goddard during the 1920s and 1930s.

A rocket works by continually ejecting material (exhaust) from one end, so that the rocket accelerates in the other direction. Usually the exhaust is ejected at a fixed speed v_e relative to the rocket. In the absence of any external force, the result of ejecting a given amount of exhaust is that the rocket changes speed by an amount

$$\Delta v = v_e \ln\left(\frac{m_0}{m_1}\right),$$

where m_0/m_1, the ratio of initial (fueled) over final (empty) mass, is called the mass ratio. Since a rocket must carry its own reaction mass, which adds to the mass of the rocket until it is ejected, there is a diminishing returns effect that is expressed in the logarithmic factor in the rocket formula, that is, each increase in final velocity by an amount v_e of the rocket requires a factor of $e = 2.718...$ (the base of the natural logarithms) increase in the mass ratio.

Furthermore, the presence of an external force, such as the force of gravity, adds another term to the rocket equation:

$$\Delta v = v_e \ln\left(\frac{m_0}{m_1}\right) - g \,\Delta t,$$

making it necessary to exhaust reaction mass rapidly when a rocket is taking off, to avoid loss of velocity due to gravity.

Chemical Propulsion Systems

Chemical rocket engines use an oxidation-reduction reaction to generate energy in the form of heat. The chemicals, or propellant, consist of two components, oxidizer and fuel. These are chemically combined in a combustion chamber; the combined product of the reaction exits the combustion chamber through a nozzle. The rocket engine converts the random heat energy of the gas to a directed stream in which all molecules are traveling at their thermal velocity in the same direction (Fig. 2).

The exhaust velocity of a chemical rocket engine is determined ideally by the chemical energy in the combustion reaction, and by the molecular mass of the reaction product. The exhaust velocity times the mass of propellant burned equals the total momentum transferred to the spacecraft, which is also known as the impulse. Thus the exhaust velocity, expressed in terms of impulse per unit mass, is also known as the specific impulse. Specific impulses for a few propellant combinations are given below.

Nuclear Propulsion Systems

Since chemical rocket propellants are limited in specific impulse to approximately 135 m/s, engineers have considered nonchemical rocket propulsion systems, such as nuclear rockets. The SNAP system used a gaseous propellant forced through a fission reaction chamber to heat it to high temperature. Disadvantages to this approach include radioactivity in the exhaust, an environmental danger. While a SNAP-type system could be used above the atmosphere, current international controls on orbiting radioactives render this approach impracticable.

Another nuclear-power scheme, named Project Orion, uses nuclear explosions to propel a spacecraft in a series of impulsive shoves. The spacecraft would periodically release a nuclear bomb, allowing it to drift to a certain distance from the craft, where it would be detonated. A large pressure plate on the back of the craft would absorb the force of the explosion. This system would obviously need to operate far from Earth's atmosphere.

Ion drive systems take advantage of an abundant source of energy, either nuclear or solar, to make efficient use of reaction mass. An ion drive accelerates ionized reaction mass to high velocity using a linear accelerator. Specific impulses of ion drives can be very high.

Photon drive systems are similar to ion drive systems, except that the exhaust is composed of photons instead of charged particles. A photon drive system would be appropriate in a craft powered by matter-antimatter reaction in which all rest mass of the propellant is converted to energy. In this case, the specific impulse would be c, the speed of light.

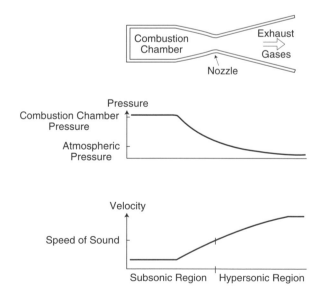

Figure 2 Pressure and flow of gases in a chemical rocket engine.

Other Propulsion Systems

The solar sail is a propulsion system for extraterrestrial travel that uses light pressure from the Sun for thrust. Efficient solar sails require very large, light, strong reflective sheets and are vulnerable to puncture by micrometeorites.

The gravitational slingshot is a method of borrowing momentum from a planet or satellite by going into a hyperbolic orbit past it. Space probes such as Pioneer and Voyager have used this technique to explore the outer solar system.

Magnetohydrodynamic (MHD) propulsion uses magnetic fields to accelerate a plasma to high speeds, attaining very high specific impulse. MHD propulsion is advantageous when high thrust is needed, as in attaining initial orbit, and when a large external source of power is available. Possible means of supplying power include beamed microwaves or lasers.

See also: ESCAPE VELOCITY; GRAVITATIONAL ASSIST; IMPULSE; KEPLER'S LAWS; NEWTON'S LAWS; SPACE

Bibliography

ADELMAN, S. J., and ADELMAN, B. *Bound For the Stars* (Prentice Hall, Englewood Cliffs, NJ, 1981).

DYSON, F. J. "21st-Century Spacecraft." *Sci. Am.* **273** (3), 114–116 (1995).

REICHHARDT, T. "Gravity's Overdrive." *Air and Space* March, 73 (1994).

SHKLOVSKII, I. S., and SAGAN, C. *Intelligent Life in the Universe* (Holden-Day, New York 1966).

STINE, G. H. *Rocket Power and Space Flight* (Henry Holt, New York, 1957).

RUSSELL J. DUBISCH

SPALLATION

Astrophysical spallation—the process of breaking up more massive nuclei to create smaller nuclei—was suggested in the early 1960s to be the dominant component of cosmic-ray nucleosynthesis of the light elements lithium (Li), beryllium (Be), and boron (B). Unlike the nucleosynthesis that occurred during the big bang and that occurs in stellar interiors, cosmic-ray nucleosynthesis occurs at relatively low particle densities so that its fragile light-element by-products can survive rather than be quickly destroyed by collisions with other nuclei as they were in the big bang and are in stars.

In cosmic-ray nucleosynthesis, high-energy cosmic rays—primarily protons and alpha particles (helium-4 nuclei) along with a few carbon (C), nitrogen (N), and oxygen (O) nuclei—collide with target nuclei—protons, alphas, and CNO nuclei—resting in the ambient interstellar medium (ISM), producing Li-Be-B nuclei by both spallation of the CNO nuclei (e.g., $p + {}^{12}C \rightarrow {}^{10}B + n + 2p$) and fusion of the alpha nuclei (e.g., $\alpha + \alpha \rightarrow {}^6Li + n + p$). Depending on the incident cosmic ray's energy, the fragments spalled or fused during these collisions are either added to the cosmic-ray spectrum (so-called secondary cosmic rays) or are sufficiently slowed to come to rest in the ISM. In this way, the ISM abundances of Li-Be-B nuclei build up over the history of the Milky Way Galaxy and the cosmic ray Li-Be-B abundances are enhanced. The building blocks of the cosmic-ray-nucleosynthesis theory are: (1) the flux of cosmic rays as a function of time; (2) the density of target nuclei in the ISM as a function of time; (3) the Li-Be-B spallation and fusion yields for each type of collision; and (4) a model that describes the interactions of the Li-Be-B fragments with the Galaxy. The predictions of cosmic-ray nucleosynthesis are then compared to observational data to test the theory.

The abundances of light elements in cosmic rays strongly support the astrophysical spallation mechanism. The light elements Li, Be, and B are roughly a million times more abundant in cosmic rays than they are in the solar system. This enhancement is due to astrophysical spallation that contributes spalled Li-Be-B secondaries to the primary cosmic-ray spectrum, which is assumed to be similar in composition to the ISM. In addition, the products of astrophysical spallation that come to rest over the lifetime of the Galaxy can explain the ISM abundances of Be and B. The cosmic-ray-nucleosynthesis yield of Li, in particular, its most stable isotope, lithium-7, falls short of its observed abundance, but enough lithium-7 is made in the big bang to account for the discrepancy.

Until the 1980s, confirmation of astrophysical spallation rested in the observation of cosmic-ray secondaries and measurements of Be and B in meteorites. Such measurements reflect the abundances as they are at the current epoch or just prior to the formation of the solar system, and astrophysical spallation provided a reasonably consistent explanation of these data. During the early 1980s, lithium-7 was observed in some of the older stars of the Galaxy, where its abundance (roughly one part in 10^{10} per hydrogen atom), though barely detectable, was ten times more than that expected from cosmic-ray nucleosynthesis. The early 1990s brought observations of Be and B in these same stars, which provides evidence for astrophysical spallation in the early Galaxy. With these data has emerged a multicomponent Li-Be-B nucleosynthesis model: Be and B are produced solely by cosmic-ray spallation; and Li was produced mainly in the big bang, with an additional 10 percent contribution from cosmic-ray spallation and fusion. Future tests of this theory will include observations of Be, B, and lithium-6 in the oldest stars of the Galaxy.

See also: ASTROPHYSICS; BIG BANG THEORY; COSMIC RAY; NUCLEOSYNTHESIS

TERRY P. WALKER

SPECIFIC GRAVITY

Specific gravity is defined as the ratio of the mass of a volume of substance to an equal volume of reference substance or, in other words, the ratios of the densities. Since specific gravity is a ratio, there are no dimensions or units associated with it, and one only needs to know what reference substance is being used. It was to alleviate the problem of having to deal with many different systems of units that the idea of specific gravity was introduced around 1025 C.E. by the Persian scientist and historian al-Biruni. In the case of liquids and solids, the reference substance is nowadays usually taken as water at 4°C, at which temperature water has its maximum density. Since, in SI units, the density of water at this temperature is 1,000 kg/m^3, the specific gravity of a substance is equal to the density in SI units divided by one thousand. For the case of gases, there can be several other reference substances, including dry air and hydrogen gas. The specific gravities of gases are expressed under the same conditions of temperature and pressure (e.g., standard temperature and pressure) and one may also note that, as a consequence of Avogadro's Law, the specific gravity of a

gas is equal to the ratio of the molecular weights of the two gases.

There are several methods for determining specific gravity. In the case of liquids and solids, the most famous is through Archimedes' principle, where the relative weights of solids in air and immersed in liquid are obtained. Once the specific gravity of a solid has been determined, specific gravities of other liquids can then be inferred from the solid gravity. Rapid assessment of liquid specific gravities can also be made using the hydrometer and, although not very accurate, this method is widely used in the food industry to assess the alcohol and sugar content of liquids and to gauge the condition of sulphuric acid in car batteries. The determination of gas densities and specific gravities can be made by weighing evacuated glass bulbs, which are then filled with the gas under investigation and reweighed, a technique known as Regnault's method.

The term "specific gravity" derives from the now obsolete use of the word "gravity" to mean heaviness or weight; hence, it was the weight specific to a given volume of material. Nowadays, the more meaningful term "relative density" is often used. The specific gravities of some well-known substances are platinum, 21.4; gold, 19.3; lead, 11.3; silver, 10.5; iron, 7.8; aluminum, 2.7; ethanol, 0.81; and air 1.29 $\times$ 10^{-3}.

See also: ARCHIMEDES' PRINCIPLE; AVOGADRO NUMBER; DENSITY; HYDROMETER

Bibliography

HECHT, E. *Physics* (Brookes/Cole, New York, 1994).

JOHN P. SHARPE

SPECIFIC HEAT

Suppose you have a certain object—a solid, a body of liquid, or gas—that you want to heat. The amount of heat you must supply depends on the mass of the object, m, the desired change in temperature $\Delta T = T_f - T_i$, and the material of which the object is made. It is easier to heat some materials than others. For example, a great deal more heat is needed to raise the temperature of 1 kg of water by 1°C (or

Table 1 Common Specific Heats

Substance	Specific Heat c J/(kg · °C)	Molar Heat Capacity C J/(mol· °C)
Lead	128	26.5
Silver	236	25.5
Aluminum	910	24.6
Granite	790	
Glass	840	
Ice (at −10°C)	2,220	
Mercury	140	27.7
Ethylene glycol	2,386	
Water	4,186	
Helium (at constant volume)		12.5
Nitrogen (at constant volume)		20.7
Carbon dioxide (at constant volume)		29.7

1 K) than is needed to raise the temperature of 1 kg of cooking oil by the same amount.

The specific heat c of a substance is defined as the amount of heat required to raise the temperature of 1 kg of the substance by 1°C. Heat is energy transferred due to a temperature difference and is measured in joules in the Standard International System of units, so c is measured in units of J/(kg·°C). Sometimes, for historical reasons, c is expressed in units of cal/(kg·°C), where 1 cal is, by definition, 4.186 J.

Thus, if you have an object of mass m and wish to raise its temperature by ΔT, you must supply heat Q, where

$$Q = mc\Delta T.$$

In general the value of c for any particular substance depends on the ambient temperature and pressure. Table 1 shows the specific heats of a few common solids and liquids and gases at room temperature with atmospheric pressure. According to these figures, 41,860 J is needed to raise the temperature of 1 kg of water by 10°C, but only 1,280 J would be needed to heat 1 kg of lead by 10°C.

Sometimes specific heat is expressed as the amount of heat required to raise the temperature of 1 mol of a substance by 1°C, and this is called the molar heat capacity, C. It is especially significant for elemental solids and gases, and Table 1 also shows the values of C for some of these. The values of C for simple metals lie close together, at about

25 J/(mol·K). This observation is called the Dulong–Petit rule, named for its discoverers.

The specific heat of a substance varies with temperature, and on the conditions under which heat is added. For most solids and liquids the specific heat is measured while the pressure is kept constant (usually at atmospheric pressure). However, it would be possible to measure c while keeping the volume of the sample constant instead, and this would give a different value of specific heat. This is especially important for gases.

The specific heat c and molar heat capacity C depend on ambient temperature and pressure. For example, the specific heat of ice at $T = -10°C$ and 1 atm is 2220 J/(kg·°C) as quoted in Table 1, but at low temperatures c is smaller. At $T = -180°C$, the c for ice is 833 J/kg·°C. The amount of heat needed to raise the temperature of m kilograms of a substance from initial temperature T_i to final temperature T_f, taking into account that c depends on T, and without the substance changing phase, is then

$$Q = \int_{T_i}^{T_f} m\, c(T)\, dT.$$

See also: HEAT CAPACITY; SPECIFIC HEAT, EINSTEIN THEORY OF; SPECIFIC HEAT OF SOLIDS

Bibliography

WEAST, R.C., and ASTLE, M. J. *Handbook of Chemistry and Physics,* 68th ed. (CRC Press, Boca Raton, FL, 1992).
YOUNG, H. D. *University Physics,* 8th ed. (Addison-Wesley, New York, 1992).

ROBERT H. DICKERSON

GAYLE COOK

SPECIFIC HEAT, EINSTEIN THEORY OF

Albert Einstein's theory of specific heat, which appeared in 1907, was primarily a theory for the specific heat of solid but also included molecules, and it was chronologically the third major development in the history of quantum mechanics; Max Planck's introduction of the energy quantum in 1900 and Einstein's explanation of the photoelectric effect in

1905 were the first two. An earlier derivation by Planck of his own blackbody radiation formula had utilized simple harmonic oscillators (resonators) that exchanged energy with the radiation field in energy quanta $h\nu$, where ν denotes a frequency contained in the radiation and h is Planck's constant. The motivation for Einstein's theory is expressed in his 1907 paper, in which he acknowledges Planck's derivation:

> I believe that we must not content ourselves with this result [Planck's derivation]. For the question arises: If the elementary structures that are to be assumed in the theory of energy exchange between radiation and matter cannot be perceived in terms of the current molecular-kinetic theory, are we then not obliged also to modify the theory for the other periodically oscillating structures considered in the molecular theory of heat? In my opinion the answer is not in doubt [p. 184].

Einstein remarked in this paper that although Newtonian physics was applicable to matter of ordinary occurrences, the quantum hypothesis, namely, that only discrete energies were admissible (despite the absence of any theory explaining why that must be true), is applicable to matter on the scale of atoms. In fact, serious difficulties had existed for a long time concerning the classical (prequantum) theory of specific heat. According to several historical accounts, it was the success of Einstein's specific heat theory that convinced many of the leading physicists to accept the quantum hypothesis, for the well-established wave properties of light made the earlier light quantum difficult to accept.

Both the classical and Einstein theories of a solid were based on the so-called harmonic approximation—that the expansion of the potential energy of the crystal in powers of displacements of atoms from equilibrium positions can be truncated at quadratic terms. The classical theory for the specific heat of solids had been given by Ludwig Boltzmann in the 1870s in terms of the equipartition theorem. The equipartition theorem leads to $C_V = 3Nk = 5.96$ cal·mol^{-1}·K^{-1}, where C_V is the heat capacity at constant volume, N is Avogadro's number, and k is Boltzmann's constant. The theory supported the law proposed in 1819 by Pierre Dulong and Alexis Petit that the molar heat capacity is approximately 6 cal·mol^{-1}·K^{-1} for all monatomic solids and at all temperatures. The Dulong–Petit law was an empirical law based on room-temperature experiments. Deviations from the law were noticed at an early date; specific heats of light atomic mass solids (e.g., boron, carbon) at room temperature had significantly lower values than required, and before the beginning of the twentieth century there was evidence that the specific heat of a solid was temperature dependent.

The Einstein specific heat theory has three important features: a simplifying model for the vibrations of atoms in solids, the restriction of vibrational energies to discrete values proportional to the frequency of vibration (quantum hypothesis), and the use of statistical mechanics. As stated in his 1907 paper, Einstein made the simplest possible approximation for the atomic vibrations of a solid: He assumed that each atom vibrates about its equilibrium position in simple harmonic motion and independently of the motion of the remaining atoms. Therefore, a monatomic solid of no anisotropy (associated with the geometrical arrangement of atoms) has only one vibrational frequency, ν, within the Einstein model. Furthermore, the vibrational energy (kinetic + potential) per mole is equivalent to that of $3N$ independent simple harmonic oscillators. Einstein considered the time-averaged energy $<e_{SHO}>$ of a simple harmonic oscillator of frequency ν in thermal equilibrium at temperature T, and he used the statistical mechanical method of the canonical ensemble that—unaware of Josiah Gibbs's 1902 book—he had derived himself: According to the quantum hypothesis the oscillator's possible energies are the discrete values $nh\nu$, with $n = 0,1,2,\ldots$. The correct quantum theory of a harmonic oscillator shows that the allowed energies are $(n + 1/2)h\nu$, where $h\nu/2$ is called the zero-point energy. Therefore

$$<e_{SHO}> = \frac{\sum_{n=0}^{\infty}\left(n + \frac{1}{2}\right)h\nu e^{-\left(n+\frac{1}{2}\right)\beta h\nu}}{\sum_{n=0}^{\infty} e^{-\left(n+\frac{1}{2}\right)\beta h\nu}}$$

$$= \frac{1}{2}h\nu + h\nu\frac{\sum_{n=0}^{\infty} n e^{-n\beta h\nu}}{\sum_{n=0}^{\infty} e^{-n\beta h\nu}}, \qquad (1)$$

which leads to the expression,

$$<e> = 3N<e_{SHO}> = 3N\left(\frac{1}{2}h\nu + \frac{h\nu}{e^{\beta h\nu} - 1}\right) \qquad (2)$$

for the total vibrational energy of a solid within the Einstein model. In this expression $\beta = 1/kT$. (The same formula is arrived at by applying Boltzmann statistics to a system of independent, quantized, simple harmonic oscillators, as done by Planck.) According to thermodynamics,

$$C_V = (\partial \langle e \rangle / \partial T)_V = 3Nk \frac{x^2 e^x}{(e^x - 1)^2}; \; x \equiv \frac{h\nu}{kT}. \quad (3)$$

In the derivation, the zero-point energy did not effect the formula for C_V. If more than one frequency is present, then the formulas in Eqs. (2) and (3) must be replaced by a sum or an integral over frequencies.

An Einstein temperature $\theta_E (\equiv h\nu/k)$ sets the scale of temperatures within the theory. The Einstein specific heat formula gives $C \to 0$ for $T \to 0$ K (large θ_E/T) and the Dulong–Petit value in the high temperature limit (small θ_E/T). The comparison of the formula with data for several monatomic solids is made in Fig. 1 in a similar fashion to Einstein's comparison. The comparison is made to heat capacity at constant pressure C_P, since that is what is directly measured. For each solid an Einstein frequency, ν, was computed that gives the measured temperature at which C_P is approximately 1.84 cal·mol^{-1}·K^{-1}.

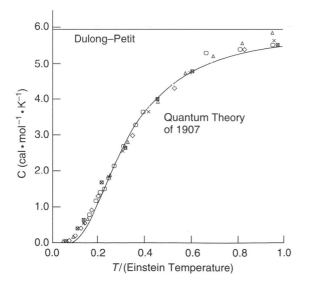

Figure 1 Heat capacity vs "scaled" temperature. Experimental C_P values for diamond ($\bigcirc$, $\Diamond$), aluminum ($\times$), nickel ($\triangle$), and lead ($\boxtimes$). The Einstein temperatures used to plot the points are the second row of values in Table 1. The circles represent the data quoted in Einstein's 1907 paper.

Table 1 Frequencies of Vibration Used in Fig. 1

	Diamond	Aluminum	Nickel	Lead
ν (THz)[a]	27.7	5.85	5.65	1.38
θ_E (K)	1,325	280	270	66

[a] 1 THz = 10^{12} s^{-1}

Those frequencies are shown in Table 1 and were used to obtain Fig. 1. The results shown in Table 1 are plausible on the basis of simple harmonic oscillators of fixed spring constant; heavy (light) atomic mass materials have low (high) Einstein frequencies. Einstein also showed that the frequencies that were extracted from his theory were roughly in agreement with optical measurements on compounds, for Paul Drude had earlier interpreted observed optical dispersion features in the infrared in terms of vibrational frequencies of atoms. Figure 1 shows that the Einstein theory was a vast improvement over the classical theory (Dulong–Petit). Moreover, there are corrections that can be applied to the data in order to obtain an even better comparison—metals show a contribution from the conduction electrons, and measured C_P data have been used rather than C_V—and those corrections substantially improve the agreement between theory and experiment at high temperatures. That the Einstein theory gives too small values of the specific heat at low temperatures was clearly indicated in 1911 through the measurements by Walter Nernst and his students at liquid hydrogen temperatures, and it was apparent at that time that the approximation of a single vibrational frequency was at fault. The Einstein theory also helped establish Nernst's third law of thermodynamics since it was the only theory that predicted that the specific heat of solids is zero at 0 K.

In 1912 two major theories were introduced that extended Einstein's theory. Within the Debye theory an elastic continuum model replaces the solid, and atomicity is accounted for by an assumed maximum frequency called the Debye frequency. The Debye temperature is defined as $\theta_D \equiv h\nu_D/k$. The model leads to a parabolic frequency distribution function, $G(\nu)$, and the Debye frequency is chosen by equating the number of "elastic" waves to the number of degrees of freedom. These are the correct standing elastic waves at low frequency but are an approximation to the nature of the true vibrations at high frequencies. For $T \to 0$ K this theory yields a T^3 temperature dependence of C_V that was subsequently observed in crystals, whereas the Einstein theory yields a $(1/T^2)e^{-h\nu/kT}$ dependence. Experimental results for the specific heat are often presented as an effective Debye temperature, $\theta_D(V,T)$. Today, the Born–von Karman theory is the accepted fundamental theory for the atomic vibrations in a solid within the harmonic approximation. The enormous number of subsequent related studies, both experimental and theoretical, resulted in a discipline of physics called lattice dynamics. This theory properly includes the effects of terms (in the potential energy) coupling the displacement of an atom with those of its neighboring atoms and leads to "normal modes" of vibration in which all the atoms of the crystal participate. In order to obtain the Einstein theory it is necessary to make the unrealistic assumption that those coupling terms are zero. Bertram N. Brockhouse shared the 1994 Nobel Prize in physics for his pioneering work on the measurement of lattice dynamical properties of crystals through inelastic neutron scattering experiments. Brockhouse's experiments provided measurements of the frequency versus wave number relationships, or "dispersion curves," of the normal modes of vibration. Combined theoretical and neutron scattering results provide the most accurate determination of the frequency distribution function.

See also: EINSTEIN, ALBERT; EQUIPARTITION THEOREM; HEAT CAPACITY; OSCILLATOR, HARMONIC; PHOTOELECTRIC EFFECT; QUANTUM MECHANICS; SPECIFIC HEAT; SPECIFIC HEAT OF SOLIDS; STATISTICAL MECHANICS; THERMODYNAMICS

Bibliography

CHANDLER, D. *Introduction to Modern Statistical Mechanics* (Oxford University Press, New York, 1987).

EINSTEIN, A. "Planck's Theory of Radiation and the Theory of Specific Heat," trans. by A. Berg. *Ann. Phys.* (*Leipzig*) **22**, 180–190 (1907).

KITTEL, C. *Introduction to Solid-State Physics,* 6th ed. (Wiley, New York, 1986).

KLEIN, M. J. "Einstein, Specific Heats, and the Early Quantum Theory." *Science* **148**, 173–180 (1965).

LANCZOS, C. *The Einstein Decade: 1905–1915* (Academic Press, New York, 1974).

STACHEL, J.; CASSIDY, D. C.; and SCHULMANN, R., eds. *The Collected Papers of Albert Einstein,* Vol. 2 (Princeton University Press, Princeton, NJ, 1989).

JOSEPH L. FELDMAN

SPECIFIC HEAT OF SOLIDS

With only a few exceptions, such as graphite and boron, specific heats of most simple solids at room temperature have about the same value, 26 J·mol^{-1}·K^{-1} or approximately $3R$ ($R = 8.31$ J·mol^{-1}·K^{-1}). This rule is known as the Dulong–Petit law. Another empirical finding known as the Neumann–Kopp law states that the molar specific heat of a solid at room temperature can be expressed approximately as the sum of the molar specific heats of its constituent elements. As the temperature is lowered, however, it has been observed that the specific heat of all solids diminish and as the temperature approaches 0 K it also approaches zero. At very low temperature the molar specific heat of solids (C_V) was found to approach zero as T^3 (see Fig. 1).

On the basis of the equipartition law of classical statistical mechanics, each degree of freedom in solid carries equal thermal energy $\frac{1}{2}kT$. Since one mole of simple solid has $6N_A$ degrees of freedom, the total internal energy of the solid is $3RT$. (N_A is Avogadro's number and $kN_A = R$, the universal gas constant.) The molar specific heat then is

$$C_V = dU/dT = 3R,$$

which agrees well with the Dulong–Petit law. The classical theory, however, cannot account for the low temperature behavior and, in addition, for metals, could not explain the apparent absence of contribution from conduction electrons that should share in the equipartition of energy since it has up to $3N_A$ degrees of freedom.

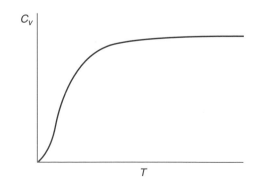

Figure 1 Measure of molar specific heat as it varies with temperature.

Einstein and Debye Theory of Specific Heat

As a way to resolve the apparent contradiction between observation and the classical theory of specific heat, Albert Einstein in 1907 proposed a simplified quantum model of solids. He represented the thermal vibration of a mole of solid to consist of $3N_A$ harmonic oscillators and, for the sake of simplicity, assumed all the oscillators to have the same frequency ν. According to the quantum hypothesis, each oscillator has the energy

$$E_n = (n + \tfrac{1}{2})h\nu, \qquad n = 0, 1, 2, 3, \ldots.$$

It can been seen schematically why a simple quantum model such as this can lead to the low temperature behavior qualitatively in agreement with the observation. Figure 2 is the comparison of the classical and quantum models. Let us say that the assembly of harmonic oscillators is in contact with a heat reservoir at very low temperature T. Each oscillator receives energy from the reservoir and the average energy transferred is kT. In the classical model the allowed energy is a continuum. Regardless of how small the value of T, an oscillator can make a transition to an exited state. A quantum oscillator, however, cannot make this transition if kT is smaller than the interval $h\nu$ between successive energy levels. At a very low temperature, these oscillators have difficulty jumping from the ground state of energy ($\tfrac{1}{2}h\nu$) to the exited state of energy $\tfrac{3}{2}h\nu$ that lies immediately above, and thus many oscillators remain in ground state. Compared to the classical model, therefore, the internal energy of a quantum solid is considerably lower. (Quantum oscillators are frozen.)

All it takes at this point is to invoke statistical mechanics to calculate the average energy of Einstein oscillators at temperature T. This yields the expression for

$$<E>_{AV} = \tfrac{1}{2}h\nu + h\nu/(e^{h\nu/kT} - 1).$$

The ratio $h\nu/k$ is defined as the Einstein characteristic temperature or Einstein temperature and is often designated as Θ_E. The internal energy U is

$$U = 3N<E>_{AV} = \tfrac{3}{2}Nh\nu + 3Nh\nu/(e^{h\nu/kT} - 1).$$

The specific heat at constant volume C_V is obtained by differentiation as

$$C_V = (\partial U/\partial T)_V = 3Nk(h\nu/kT)^2(e^{h\nu/kT}/e^{h\nu/kT} - 1)^2.$$

At very low temperature, this expression indicates C_V to vary as $(1/T^2)\exp(-h\nu/kT)$ and the exponential term dominates as T becomes very small. This does not agree with the observed T^3 dependence.

In 1912 Peter Debye proposed an improvement to the Einstein model. Debye analyzed the elastic waves (phonons) spectra in a solid and arrived at a more realistic normal mode distribution. His model has a normal mode distribution proportional to the square of the frequency ν up to a maximum cut-off frequency ν_D (Debye frequency). This model leads to the desired T^3 behavior at very low temperature, and $h\nu_D/k = \Theta_D$ is called the Debye characteristic temperature or the temperature.

The Electronic Contribution

The problem of electronic contribution to the specific heat of solid is also resolved. The electronic contribution depends on how free the electrons are to gain energy from a heat reservoir just as for a lattice phonon (quantized normal mode of crystal lattice vibration) at low temperature. The reservoir for the electrons is actually the system of phonons. The number of electrons that are allowed to gain thermal energy kT are limited to those near the maximum (E_F) energy distribution, that is, the Fermi

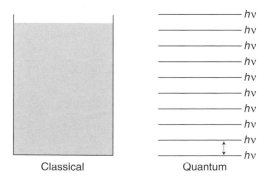

Figure 2 Comparison of classical and quantum models of specific heat.

Classical   Quantum

surface. This is because all electrons have filled states above them except at the highest energy states (at the Fermi surface). Thus the electron contribution to the specific heat is limited to those within kT of E_F. One can thus assume that the number (n) of electrons participating is of the order of $N_A(kT/E_F)$ or $N_A(T/T_F)$, where T_F is the Fermi temperature (E_F/k). If we designate C_{el} as the electronic specific heat, $C_{el} \sim (3/2)nk = (3/2)N_A k(T/T_F)$. Since for most metals T_F is in the neighborhood of 50,000 K, T/T_F is very small up to the melting point of metals. This explains why the electronic contribution to the specific heat is very small for metals.

See also: FERMI SURFACE; SPECIFIC HEAT; SPECIFIC HEAT, EINSTEIN THEORY OF

Bibliography

SEITZ, F. *Modern Theory of Solids* (McGraw-Hill, New York, 1940).

TIPLER, P. A. *Foundations of Modern Physics* (Worth, New York, 1991).

CARL T. TOMIZUKA

SPECTRAL SERIES

When matter is heated it emits radiation. If the matter is dense, as in the case of a liquid or solid, it will emit all frequencies (or wavelengths) at any temperature above absolute zero. The intensity of the radiation will vary; very high and very low frequency radiation will occur at low intensities. This radiation represents the collective behavior of a large number of interacting atoms thus obscuring the radiative behavior of isolated single atoms.

A rarefied collection of pure atoms, however, will be far enough apart so that radiation emanating from this entity when excited will be characteristic of the properties of the particles themselves rather than the interactions among the particles. This condition is fulfilled by a pure gas, such as hydrogen or helium, at a pressure below atmospheric. When this gas is excited by a steady bombardment of electrons—as in a current—the radiation emitted consists of a set of discrete wavelengths.

To observe the set of individual wavelengths—or what is referred to as the line spectrum—the radiation is collimated and passed through a diffraction grating that separates each discrete wavelength. The radiation is then intercepted by a screen or suitable detector (Fig. 1).

Each element emits a unique set of lines that serve as a tool to identify the substance and to understand the properties of the atomic structure. It was discovered that the wavelengths occurring in an atomic spectrum fall into sets of particular series. Each series of wavelengths are specified by empirical equations that are relatively simple in structure and similar to one another. For example, the wavelengths emitted from hydrogen fall into series described by

$$1/\lambda_{N,n} = R(1/N^2 - 1/n^2),$$

where n and N are positive integers and satisfy the condition

$$n \geq N + 1.$$

The quantity R is the Rydberg constant. Its value is $R = 1.097 \times 10^{-7}$ m^{-1} or 1.097×10^{-3} Å^{-1}. When $N = 1$, for example, n can be 2, 3, 4, . . . , ∞, making the series of wavelengths related by

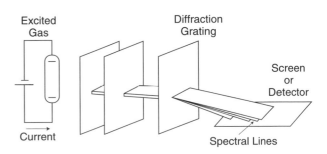

Figure 1 Radiation from an excited gas diffracted and collected at a screen or detector.

$$1/\lambda_{1,n} = R(1/1^2 - 1/n^2)$$

or

$$1/\lambda_{1,2} = R(1 - 1/2^2) \quad = 3R/4$$

$$1/\lambda_{1,3} = R(1 - 1/3^2) \quad = 8R/9$$

$$\begin{array}{ccc} \cdot & \cdot & \cdot \\ \cdot & \cdot & \cdot \\ \cdot & \cdot & \cdot \end{array}$$

$$1/\lambda_{1,\infty} = \lim_{n \to \infty} R(1 - 1/n) = R.$$

The wavelengths, thus, for the series $N = 1$ are given by

$$\lambda_{1,2} = 4/3R$$

$$\lambda_{1,3} = 9/8R$$

$$\cdot$$

$$\cdot$$

$$\cdot$$

$$\lambda_{1,\infty} = 1/R.$$

This series of wavelengths, named after its discoverer, is referred to as the Lyman series. The wavelengths in this series fall in the ultraviolet range. The series of wavelengths for $N = 2$ was discovered in 1885 by Johann J. Balmer. The wavelengths of the Balmer series fall in the visible light range. The next three series are generated for $N = 3$, 4, and 5. The wavelengths for these series is given by

$$\lambda_{3,n} = 9n^2/(n^2 - 9)R \quad (n = 4, 5, \ldots)$$

$$\lambda_{4,n} = 16n^2/(n^2 - 16)R \quad (n = 5, 6, \ldots)$$

$$\lambda_{5,n} = 25n^2/(n^2 - 25)R \quad (n = 6, 7 \ldots).$$

These series, respectively referred to as the Paschen, Brackett, and Pfund series, all have wavelengths that lie in the infrared range of the spectrum.

A plot of the series of the spectral lines for hydrogen appears as shown in Fig. 2. Some of the wavelengths of the Pfund and Brackett series overlap as do some wavelengths of the Brackett and Paschen series.

The structure of the spectral series for hydrogen and other elements would have to be explained by any model of the atom. This occurred after the discovery of the spectral series when Neils Bohr (1913) proposed a model of the hydrogen atom that predicted the wavelengths of radiation emitted from the atom when its excited electron falls from any higher to lower energy levels of the atom. These wavelengths are identical with those found empirically for the spectral series.

In the Bohr model the energy levels of the hydrogen atom are discrete, changing in steps by $1/n^2$, starting from the lowest energy level where $n = 1$, to the highest energy where n approaches infinity. The spectral series are generated as excited electrons fall

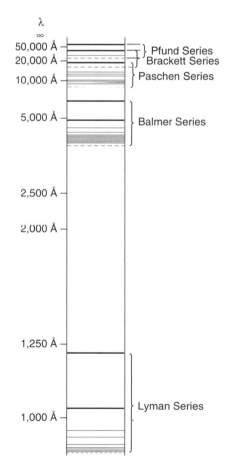

Figure 2 Spectral series for hydrogen.

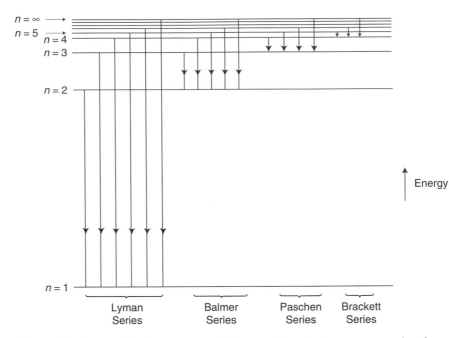

Figure 3 Spectral series generated by transition between energy levels.

from all higher levels to a particular lower energy level as shown in Fig. 3.

See also: BOHR'S ATOMIC THEORY; DIFFRACTION; ENERGY LEVELS; GRATING, DIFFRACTION; LINE SPECTRUM; RYDBERG CONSTANT; WAVELENGTH

Bibliography

BEISER, A. *Concepts of Modern Physics* (McGraw-Hill, New York, 1981).

SERWAY, R. A. *Principles of Physics* (Saunders, Fort Worth, TX, 1994).

EDWIN GOLDIN

SPECTROMETER

See MASS SPECTROMETER

SPECTROPHOTOMETRY

Spectrophotometry is a widely used method for the quantitative analysis of chemical substances that ab-

sorb radiation in the ultraviolet, visible, or infrared regions of the electromagnetic spectrum. Since the introduction of reliable commercial instruments for spectrophotometric analysis around 1935, the method has become one of the most important analytical tools available for the measurement of chemical concentrations in solutions. Spectrophotometry is rapid, precise, and relatively simple to perform.

The basic principles of spectrophotometry are illustrated in Fig. 1. The radiant power P (or intensity) of light that passes through a sample of the substance under investigation is measured and com-

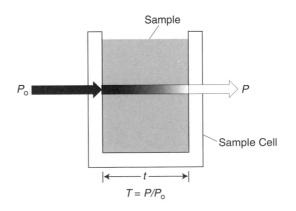

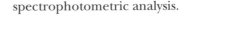

Figure 1 Diagram illustrating the absorption of a light beam as it passes through a sample during spectrophotometric analysis.

pared to the incident radiant power P_0. Two quantities of importance are the transmittance T, defined as the ratio P/P_0, and the absorbance A, defined as $\log(1/T)$. The utility of spectrophotometry for quantitative analysis stems from the Beer–Lambert law, which states that the absorbance is directly proportional to the product of the sample thickness, t, and its concentration, C:

$$A = ktC,$$

where k is a proportionality constant whose value is a characteristic of the absorbing substance.

Consider, for example, the spectrophotometric analysis of an aqueous solution of copper sulfate, $CuSO_4$. The hydrated Cu^{2+} ions in the solution absorb orange light and are transparent to other colors of visible light, causing the solution to appear blue (the complementary color of orange). Therefore, the concentration of Cu^{2+} may be determined by measuring the absorbance of orange light passing through a sample of the solution under standardized conditions. In the simplest application of the method, this is accomplished in two steps. The radiant power, P, of orange light emerging from a standard cell (made of glass) containing a sample of the Cu^{2+} solution is measured in the first step. The Cu^{2+} solution is then replaced with a sample of pure water in the second step and the measurement is repeated to obtain P_0. By performing the same series of measurements on Cu^{2+} solutions prepared in known concentrations (i.e., standard solutions), the value of the proportionality constant, k, in the Beer–Lambert law may be determined from the slope of the straight line obtained by plotting absorbance versus concentration.

A schematic diagram showing the components of a typical spectrophotometer, the instrument used to perform spectrophotometric analysis, is presented in Fig. 2. The incident radiation is generated by the source, either a tungsten filament lamp (visible region), a hydrogen discharge tube or mercury-vapor lamp (ultraviolet region), or an electrically heated rod (infrared region). The radiation is formed into a narrow parallel beam by means of a lens and set of entrance slits and is directed onto a wavelength dispersing element consisting of either a prism or a diffraction grating. The part of the assembly consisting of the entrance slits, the dispersing element, and the exit slits is called a monochromator. The function of the monochromator is to diffract the continuous range of wave-

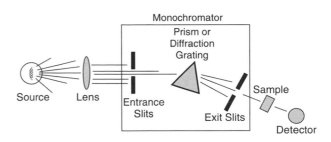

Figure 2 Schematic diagram showing the major components of a typical spectrophotometer.

lengths in the incident beam through different angles so that a very narrow band of wavelengths can be selected to pass through the exit slits for use in the measurements. By rotating the dispersing element, the band of wavelengths incident on the sample can be varied continuously over the range of wavelengths produced by the radiation source. After passing through the sample cell, the transmitted radiation arrives at the detector where its radiant power is measured and recorded. As with the dispersing element, the type of detector employed is dependent upon the wavelength region. In the visible and ultraviolet regions, photocells and photomultiplier tubes are commonly used.

Spectrophotometers of the type shown in Fig. 2 measure only one band of wavelengths at a time and hence multiple measurements must be performed if assays at other wavelengths are required. The advent of solid-state photodiodes sensitive to radiation over a wide spectral range spanning from the ultraviolet through the visible region recently has led to the development of a new type of diode array spectrophotometer capable of recording the radiant power of all transmitted wavelengths (in this range) simultaneously.

See also: DISPERSION; ELECTROMAGNETIC SPECTRUM; GRATING, DIFFRACTION; SPECTROSCOPY; SPECTROSCOPY, ULTRAVIOLET; SPECTROSCOPY, VISIBLE

Bibliography

EWING, G. W. *Instrumental Methods of Chemical Analysis*, 4th ed. (McGraw-Hill, New York, 1975).

OLSEN, E. D. *Modern Optical Methods of Analysis* (McGraw-Hill, New York, 1975).

SAWYER, D. T.; HEINEMAN, W. R.; and BEEBE, J. M. *Chemistry Experiments for Instrumental Methods* (Wiley, New York, 1984).

RAND L. WATSON

SPECTROSCOPY

The term "spectroscopy" relates traditionally to the quantitative study of the absorption or emission of light by matter, where the light beam, after passing through, is usually broken up into a rainbow of colors by a glass prism or a diffraction grating. The colors of visible light, for example, are associated with different wavelengths of electromagnetic radiation. For example, red light corresponds to wavelengths in the 600–650 nm (10^{-9} m) range, and blue light corresponds to shorter wavelengths in the 450–490 nm range. A graph of the relative light intensity absorbed, scattered, or emitted by a matter sample versus wavelength is called a spectrum (from the Latin word for appearance). The study and interpretation of such graphs is called spectroscopy from the combination of spectrum and the Greek word "skopein," meaning "to see." Spectroscopy is often used in chemical analysis to provide an optical "fingerprint" for identification of the presence of various elements or compounds in a sample. It may also be used in forensics and for many research and practical applications in chemistry, biology, physics, astronomy, and medicine.

The history of spectroscopy goes back to Isaac Newton's creation of an artificial rainbow (ca. 1664) by using a prism to break up a beam of sunlight into a spectrum of colors from red to violet (see Fig. 1). Spectroscopy has provided crucial clues to understanding the structure of matter from the simplest atom of hydrogen to complex biological molecules, such as DNA. At the end of the twentieth century, new forms of spectroscopy, far outside the range of visible-light wavelengths, were still being invented. Examples include x-ray spectroscopy, gamma-ray spectroscopy, microwave spectroscopy, nuclear-magnetic-resonance spectroscopy, laser spectroscopy, Fourier transform infrared (FTIR) spectroscopy of molecular bond vibrations, and spectroscopy involving measurements on beams of charged particles, such as electron spectroscopy for chemical analysis (ESCA) and mass spectroscopy. Spectroscopy is one of the principal research tools available for the study of the structure and properties of atoms, molecules, nuclei, liquids, and solids and for the remote sensing of atmospheric pollutants and the analysis of light from astronomical objects, such as stars and galaxies. For determining the composition and atomic-crystal structure of materials, spectroscopic techniques are used in place of classical methods of chemical analysis, along with such methods as x-ray diffraction and neutron diffraction.

In visible-light optical spectroscopy, a spectroscope or spectrometer is often used to observe the wavelengths of light waves emitted when light from a glowing electric discharge in a monatomic gas, such as helium, neon, or mercury, is separated into individual colors by a prism or grating. The light-analyzing instrument is called a spectrograph when electronic or photographic recording is used instead of the naked eye. Spectroscopy in astrophysics covers the full range of the electromagnetic spectrum from radio waves, with wavelengths in the meter to centimeter range observed by using radio telescopes, through the infrared and visible range, to the ultraviolet (using the Hubble space telescope), x-ray, and gamma-ray range (using high-altitude balloons and satellites). Laser spectroscopy, using monochromatic light from a tunable laser source, is used for studying chemical reactions, atomic and molecular structure, environmental pollution, and the development of frequency and time standards.

The history of atomic spectroscopy closely parallels the development of the modern understanding of the atomic structure of matter. In 1802 William Hyde Wollaston used a prism in a refinement of Newton's method to observe the rainbow spectrum of sunlight. By focusing the sunlight onto a narrow slit, followed by a telescope to make the rays parallel, and observing the spectrum after passing through the prism via a second telescope, which formed a

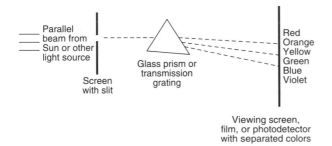

Parallel beam from Sun or other light source

Screen with slit

Glass prism or transmission grating

Red
Orange
Yellow
Green
Blue
Violet

Viewing screen, film, or photodetector with separated colors

Figure 1 Essential elements of a simple spectrometer/spectrograph. Projected colored images of the slit appear at the viewing screen, film, or detector. Distance along the screen depends in a nonlinear way on wavelength, so calibration is necessary. The optical path may be folded if a diffraction grating is used in reflection rather than transmission.

colored image of the slit, dark and narrow lines appeared in the otherwise continuous rainbow spectrum. These dark lines were rediscovered and first correctly interpreted by Joseph von Fraunhofer in Bavaria about 1815. Several hundred of these dark Fraunhofer lines in the solar spectrum were cataloged and found to correspond to absorption lines (due to the cooler outer layers of the Sun's atmosphere) at the same visible wavelengths as the bright emission lines later observed from vaporized samples in hot flames of common terrestrial chemical elements and in light emitted from gas discharges. The most pronounced of the Fraunhofer lines in the solar spectrum (labeled by single letters of the alphabet) correspond to wavelengths that are like fingerprints for atomic hydrogen (C and F lines, later called H_α and H_β), oxygen (A and B lines), sodium (D), iron (E and G), and calcium (H and K). Thus, the chemical elements of the glowing solar photosphere were from the same set of known elements abundant on Earth. In 1878, the element helium was discovered, first in a spectrum from the Sun and seventeen years later on Earth.

At the turn of the twentieth century, the discovery of radioactivity and alpha-particle decay (alpha particles are bare helium nuclei) of heavy elements led to Ernest Rutherford's alpha-scattering experiments and to discovery of the atomic nucleus. This, in turn, led to the development by Rutherford's protégé, Niels Bohr, of the planetary model of the simplest atom (hydrogen) containing one proton in its nucleus and one orbiting electron surrounding it. Bohr's successful interpretation in 1913 of the simple formula for the wavelengths in the Balmer series of spectral lines of hydrogen, and his prediction of other spectral series of lines observed later in the ultraviolet (Lyman series) and infrared (Paschen series) regions, led to the development of quantum mechanics in the 1920s, which provides a detailed quantitative description of atomic and molecular structure, with its discrete sets of quantized electronic energy levels.

By applying the concept of the light quantum or photon with energy $E = hf$ (h is Planck's constant and f is the frequency of the light), first proposed by Max Planck in 1900 to explain the continuous spectrum of blackbody radiation from an incandescent object, and adding the concepts of quantized energy levels and conservation of energy when light is emitted or absorbed, Bohr laid the groundwork for the modern quantum theoretical explanation of atomic and molecular electronic structure

and spectra (along with many features of x-ray spectra, nuclear-gamma-ray spectra, and the Rydberg atom). The Bohr frequency condition is: photon energy $E = hf = E_2 - E_1$, where the two energies $E_{2,1}$ are the upper and lower quantized energy levels (stationary states), respectively, of the electrons in the hydrogen atom. Photons, according to Bohr, have both wavelike properties (wavelength λ and frequency f, with velocity $c = \lambda f$) and particle-like properties (localization and energy). Bohr's frequency condition can be extended to the general connection $hc/\lambda = E_2 - E_1$ between the wavelength of any emitted or absorbed light and the energy levels of the microscopic quantum system that emits or absorbs the photons. This equation is applicable to essentially all branches of spectroscopy and is the essence of the Ritz combination principle. This simple principle allows a large number of wavelengths in the observed spectrum of an atom or molecule to be fitted to the differences between a much smaller set of energy levels or spectral term values and allows the approximate determination of a consistent set of these energy levels from the measured wavelengths of the characteristic spectral lines. Knowledge of the energy levels is then connected to information about the structure of the atom, molecule, and nucleus via comparison with the quantum theory.

In the analysis of spectra, not all differences between energy levels of the electrons in an atomic or molecular system give rise to observed lines or wavelengths in the spectrum. That is because of two factors: At normal temperatures, the electrons in an atom or molecule are primarily in the lowest energy level or ground state, so that light absorption occurs only when an electron makes a transition, or quantum jump, from this lowest level to one of the higher levels; and certain selection rules forbid or inhibit photon emission or absorption between some of the possible pairs of energy levels of the atom or molecule. For example, the electronic energy levels in an atom or molecule are also characterized by certain quantum numbers associated with other conserved quantities, such as electron spin, orbital angular momentum, and parity. Ordinarily, a photon carries an angular momentum of one unit of Planck's constant divided by 2π, leading to the selection rule that the difference in angular momentum between quantum states E_2 and E_1 in a photon-emitting transition cannot be larger than one unit. In molecular vibrational spectra, the quantized energy levels are approximated by a harmonic oscillator (two atomic masses connected by a springlike chemical bond) with a set of energy levels $E_V = (v + 1/2)\hbar\omega/2\pi$, where v is the vibrational quantum number, $v = 0, 1, 2, \ldots$ The selection rules for pure vibrational molecular spectra require a change in quantum number v, so that $\Delta v = \pm 1$.

Experimental work in infrared, visible, or ultraviolet spectroscopy requires consideration of appropriate light sources, analyzing instruments (spectrometers or spectroscopes), detectors, and wavelength-calibration methods. In a neutral or ionized gas, the thermal velocity distribution of the atoms or molecules causes shifts and broadening of spectral lines via the Doppler effect, just as a moving transmitter or receiver alters the pitch of a sound wave, decreasing the precision with which the wavelengths can be determined. By confining the atoms in an atomic trap or using special techniques of laser spectroscopy, Doppler broadening effects can be very much reduced, and extremely high precision measurements of atomic emission and absorption wavelengths can be made (to one part in 10^{14} or better). This is likely to lead to new types of atomic clocks and better time standards.

Light Sources for Spectroscopy

Aside from the Sun and natural phenomena like the aurora borealis or lightning, artificial light sources for spectroscopy and chemical analysis include introducing a sample into a flame; incandescent lamps; electrically heated graphite tubes or furnaces with samples inside; electric arcs and sparks; low-pressure electric discharges; the hollow-cathode gas discharge (devised by Paschen), using a hollow cylindrical cathode and a low pressure of a noble gas such as argon; various types of lasers; and circular electron accelerators producing synchrotron radiation. Of these, laser sources usually have by far the highest spectral brightness (photons per second per unit of solid angle per unit wavelength interval). This is counterbalanced by the limited wavelength-tuning range of many lasers. Semiconductor diode lasers on a microchip, such as those in a compact disc, are being developed for fiber-optics communications and other purposes. Diode lasers operate mainly in the infrared and long-wavelength visible range, but new types are rapidly being developed in the blue-green and even the ultraviolet spectral ranges. Some experts predict that many of today's electronic devices, including some types of comput-

ers, will be supplanted in the future by photonic devices based on semiconductor-diode-laser and optical-fiber technology.

Analyzing Instruments

The wavelength resolution of a prism spectroscope is limited by the size of the entrance slit that comes before the prism and by the dispersion or rate of change of the index of refraction of the glass with wavelength. Transmission- or reflection-diffraction gratings often replace the prism as the wavelength-separating element. The grating spectrometer or spectrograph has the advantage of greater wavelength resolution, along with the possibility of being used, particularly with a reflection grating, far into the ultraviolet region, where a glass prism would absorb the incident light. The grating is basically a mirror or screen with many fine ($\sim 10,000$ or more) grooves or rulings per centimeter that individually scatter or diffract the light waves so that they interfere constructively at angles θ given by the grating equation for normal incidence: $n\lambda = d \sin \theta$, where d is the spacing between adjacent grooves of the grating, and n is an integer called the diffraction order number. The resolving power $\lambda/\Delta\lambda = nN$, where n is the order number, and N is the total number of grating grooves illuminated by the light. In a grating instrument, the spacing d and the resolving power can be controlled for the purpose at hand. A monochromator is a spectrometer designed to transmit a high-intensity beam of a well-determined wavelength. Other analyzing devices used for high wavelength resolution in spectroscopy include Albert Michelson's interferometer and the Fabry–Pérot interferometer. The transmission of both of these devices is a periodic function of wavelength (multiple orders), so they are often combined in series with a prism or grating to select a wavelength range. Periodic-diffraction-grating structures may be burned into optical fibers for making specialized compact-wavelength sensors for chemical analysis, optical strain gauges, and other photonic-device applications.

See also: DIFFRACTION, ELECTRON; DIFFRACTION, FRAUNHOFER; DIFFRACTION, FRESNEL; GRATING, DIFFRACTION; INTERFEROMETER, FABRY–PÉROT; INTERFEROMETRY; MASS SPECTROMETER; SPECTRAL SERIES; SPECTROSCOPY, ATOMIC; SPECTROSCOPY, LASER; SPECTROSCOPY, MASS;

Spectroscopy, Microwave; Spectroscopy, Ultraviolet; Spectroscopy, Visible; Spectroscopy, X-Ray

Bibliography

Bass, M., ed. *Handbook of Optics*, vol. 1, 2nd ed. (McGraw-Hill, New York, 1995).

Herzberg, G. *Atomic Spectra and Atomic Structure* (Dover, New York, 1945).

Steinfeld, J. I. *Molecules and Radiation: An Introduction to Modern Molecular Spectroscopy*, 2nd ed. (MIT Press, Cambridge, MA, 1985).

Weisskopf, V. F. *Physics in the Twentieth Century: Selected Essays* (MIT Press, Cambridge, MA, 1972).

Winthrop W. Smith

SPECTROSCOPY, ATOMIC

Atomic spectroscopy is that branch of atomic physics which studies and interprets the distribution of energy in the radiation emitted or absorbed by isolated atoms or ions. This radiation generally is of electromagnetic origin (i.e., photons), but can sometimes be made up of particles (electrons). The present article treats both theoretical concepts and experimental aspects of atomic spectroscopy. According to the wavelength of the electromagnetic radiation involved, atomic spectroscopy also has important techniques in common with the special fields of microwave, visible, ultraviolet, and x-ray spectroscopy.

Historically atomic spectroscopy was the way much of the insight into the electronic structure of the atom was gained and it was on the basis of spectroscopic information that Niels Bohr in 1913 formulated his planetary model as an alternative to the Rutherford atom. Atomic spectroscopic data was also the starting point for the development of the quantum mechanical theory by Werner Heisenberg, Erwin Schrödinger, Paul Dirac, and others around 1925. Quantum electrodynamics (QED), the theory of interaction between matter and radiation, was formulated by Richard Feynman, Julian Schwinger, Sin-Itiro Tomonaga, and others in the 1940s in close connection to atomic spectroscopic observations. Today atomic spectroscopists are, for example, looking for a breakdown of perturbative QED in the strong nuclear Coulomb fields of highly charged ions and for possible violations of the standard model of elementary particles in heavy neutral atoms, activities which possibly might lead to further breakthroughs in the fundamentals of theoretical physics.

But atomic spectroscopy is not pursued mainly for such fundamental reasons, but to a much larger extent to fit together important pieces of the complicated jigsaw puzzle that on many different scales gives a picture of the world we live in. One example is the detailed laboratory atomic spectroscopy that is needed to convert new astronomical observations made from the Hubble Space Telescope, into physical statements about element abundances in the stars. Another example is the basic spectroscopy of highly charged ions needed for diagnostics of the transport properties in the hot plasmas of fusion tokamaks. A third example is the broad range of spectroscopic fingerprints needed for spectro-chemical element analysis in connection with environmental pollution problems.

Reflecting the importance of atomic spectroscopy as a subfield of physics as a whole, in the twentieth century a number of Nobel Prizes for physics have been awarded for discoveries or inventions related to atomic spectroscopy. Among the scientists to have received the award are Manne Siegbahn (1924), Isidor Isaac Rabi (1944), Willis Eugene Lamb (1955), Alfred Kastler (1966), and Kai Siegbahn (1981).

According to quantum mechanics the energies of the bound electrons in free atoms or ions are quantized and can only take discrete values $\{E_n\}$. In atomic hydrogen or hydrogen-like one-electron ions these energies can be approximated by the non-relativistic quantum mechanical expression $E_n = -RhcZ^2/n^2$, where $n = 1,2,3,...$ Here n is the principal quantum number, R is the Rydberg constant, h is Planck's constant, c is the velocity of light in vacuum, and Z is the nuclear charge. Each n defines an energy shell denoted according to the maximum orbital angular momentum the electron can have in the shell. Traditionally the designations for $l = 0,1,2,...,$ are $s,p,d,f,...$ In the alkali atoms or in alkali-like ions, the hydrogenic energies split according to the angular momentum, for example, for $n = 3$ the splitting is into $3s$, $3p$, and $3d$. Atomic spectra derive from energy-changing transitions in or between these electronic shells. A transition from an initial state E_i to a final state E_f of lower (higher) energy can be accompanied by the emission (absorption) of a photon or an electron of energy $\Delta E_{if} = E_i - E_f$. An emitted photon has wavelength λ (in vacuum) and frequency ν given by $\Delta E_{if} = hc/\lambda = h\nu$, where h is Planck's constant and c the velocity of light in vacuum. For an electron to be emitted the initial state has to be multiply excited, that is, more than one electron must be excited. This is, for example, the case for a multielectron atom or ion in which an inner electron has been removed.

An atomic transition is not only characterized by the energy of the emitted radiation, that is, the energy difference $\Delta E_{if} = E_i - E_f$ between the initial and final state. An important property is the transition probability A_{if}, which reflects the willingness of the excited state to decay spontaneously. The transition probability A_{if} is related to the intensity of the corresponding spectral line as compared to other lines in the same spectrum. The strongest lines in a photon spectrum, the so-called resonance lines, typically involve transitions to the lowest energy level, the ground state, and give rise to electromagnetic radiation having the same distribution pattern as that of an oscillating electric dipole. Weak lines may derive from transitions connecting states that for symmetry reasons must give radiation according to more complex distribution patterns, such as that of an oscillating magnetic dipole or an electric quadrupole. The lifetime τ of an excited state is equal to the inverse of the sum of transition probabilities to all energy levels lower than the initial one.

An important property of spectral lines is their width. For an isolated atom or ion the natural line width, through Heisenberg's time-energy uncertainty relation $\delta E \cdot \delta t \approx h$, reflects the time needed for the transition (i.e., the inverse A_{if}^{-1} of the transition probability). By measuring line widths under ideal conditions, the lifetimes of excited states can be derived. If a spectrum is taken from an ensemble of atoms or ions at nonzero temperature, the lines will acquire a width due to the Doppler effect of the nonzero thermal random velocities (Doppler broadening). Experimental determinations of reliable lifetimes are notoriously more difficult than the corresponding determination of energy levels. The amount of experimental information gathered on lifetimes is accordingly much smaller than on energy levels.

From the theoretical point of view, the set of values $\{E_n\}$ is a characteristic of the whole system of electrons and can in principle be computed from quantum theory. But, even using nonrelativistic quantum mechanics, it is only for the most simple cases that this can be done exactly (one-electron atoms and ions). In practice, some more or less sophisticated approximation scheme has to be used. A very useful simple scheme is the central-field approximation. In this scheme all electrons are at first considered to be independent and the energy levels of one of the electrons in the average field of all other electrons is computed. An approximate description of a many-electron atom can now be built up by designing electrons to the energy levels according to Pauli's exclusion principle. Each such listing, or configuration, of electrons is the basis for a number of spectroscopic states, which are deduced by coupling the orbital and spin angular momenta of the electrons. The energies of these states can be calculated in different approximation schemes. For few-electron atoms and ions the calculations can be done with high precision, but for many-electron systems the approximations become more drastic and have to be checked carefully against measurements. This is also true of the lifetimes of excited states. A particular difficulty pertains to the lifetimes of multiply excited states. The development of reliable computational schemes for the electronic properties of atoms and ions is an iterative procedure to which both atomic theoreticians and experimentalists contribute.

In the traditional atomic spectroscopic experiment the electromagnetic line radiation emitted from an ensemble of excited neutral atoms or singly charged ions in a gas discharge is studied with a spectrometer. In the spectrometer the radiation is dispersed into its monoenergetic elements and can then be registered on a detector as a spectrum (i.e., as a function giving intensity versus energy). Another kind of atomic spectroscopy relies on the absorption of broadband radiation by an ensemble of atoms or ions. This is, for example, often what happens naturally in astronomical objects, when the hot central region of a star may act as light source behind a cooler atmosphere (cf. Fraunhofer lines).

An important way to produce radiation from more highly charged ions is to set up a hot plasma by a spark discharge in vacuum between electrodes of the element to be studied. This was the method developed and perfected by Manne Siegbahn and his collaborators in the 1920s and 1930s. A modern version of the spark discharge plasma is the laser produced plasma. A high power pulsed laser beam is focused on a small spot of a solid material, thereby producing an expanding hot plasma. Another development, the electron beam ion trap (EBIT), has been shown to yield line emission from very highly charged ions. In the EBIT, an intense electron beam passes through a strong solenoidal magnetic field and ionizes and excites atoms and ions. The ions are trapped in the electromagnetic field generated by the compressed electron beam and the solenoidal magnet. In this way ions become reionized to higher and higher charge states, and are finally stripped of all their electrons. Line emission can result from electron impact excitation of core electrons, electron capture in collisions with the background gas, or from recombination collisions with free electrons.

A very general source of line radiation from atoms and ions, which also can be used to study the time-dependence of the decay of the excitation (i.e., the lifetime) is the beam-foil source introduced in the early 1960s by Stanley Bashkin and Laurence Kay. In the experiment a beam of fast ions from an accelerator is passed through a thin solid foil, thereby exciting or ionizing bound electrons in the projectiles. Since recombination may also occur, the beam exiting the foil will consist of a mixture of neutrals and ions of different charge and excitation states (negative ions can also be produced). Because of the very short excitation times involved, defining a zero on the time scale with high accuracy, and the possibility of converting time to distance by moving the detector, the beam-foil method is also well suited for lifetime measurements.

In a completely different kind of spectroscopic method, the atomic beam resonance method invented by Rabi in the 1930s, a beam of neutral atoms is passed through two inhomogeneous magnetic fields and is perturbed by radiofrequency electromagnetic radiation in between. The inhomogeneous magnetic field will split the beam of atoms into states of different magnetism (cf. the Stern–Gerlach experiment). When the frequency of the perturbing field is in resonance with a transition in the atom, the enhanced excitation of the atoms can be detected as a deflection of the beam. This method is the one used by Lamb in the 1940s. In the optical resonance method introduced by Kastler in 1950, the dependence of the transmission of polarized light through a gas cell on an applied radiofrequency field is used to find the resonance condition.

Electrons may be emitted from atoms or ions by the process of photoionization or by the impact of neutral or charged particles. The kinetic energy of an electron emitted in a direct knock-out process will reflect its binding energy in the initial state, but also the energy of the photon or particle that produced the ionization. For practical reasons it is thus convenient if the latter has a well-defined energy that is completely given up in the ionization process. This can be realized for photoionization by using a strong source of line radiation or a monochromatized beam from a continuum source, for example, a synchrotron. Electron spectrometers use electric or magnetic fields to disperse the particles. Because of the low intensity of emitted electrons, several attempts to increase the effectiveness of electron spectrometers have been tried. An important milestone was the introduction of the double-focusing magnetic spectrometer, developed and perfected by Kai Siegbahn in the 1940s.

See also: ATOM TRAP; BOHR, NIELS HENRIK DAVID; DIRAC, PAUL ADRIEN MAURICE; DOPPLER EFFECT; FEYNMAN, RICHARD PHILLIPS; HEISENBERG, WERNER KARL; PAULI'S EXCLUSION PRINCIPLE; QUANTUM ELECTRODYNAMICS; QUANTUM MECHANICS; RABI, ISIDOR ISAAC; RUTHERFORD, ERNEST; SCHRÖDINGER, ERWIN; SPECTROSCOPY; SPECTROSCOPY, LASER; SPECTROSCOPY, MICROWAVE; SPECTROSCOPY, ULTRAVIOLET; SPECTROSCOPY, VISIBLE; SPECTROSCOPY, X-RAY

Bibliography

BRANSDEN, B. H., and JOACHAIN, C. J. *Physics of Atoms and Molecules* (Longman, New York, 1983).

HANLE, W., and KLEINPOPPEN, H. *Progress in Atomic Spectroscopy* (Plenum, New York, 1978).

LINDGREN, I.; MARTINSON, I.; and SCHUCH, R., eds. "Heavy-Ion Spectroscopy and QED Effects in Atomic Systems." *Phy. Scripta* **T46**, 1–272 (1993).

MARTINSON, I., and GAUPP, A. "Atomic Physics with Ion Accelerators: Beam-Foil Spectroscopy." *Phy. Rep.* **15C**, 113–180 (1974).

SVANBERG, S. *Atomic and Molecular Spectroscopy: Basic Aspects and Practical Applications* (Springer-Verlag, Berlin, 1991).

ANDERS BÁRÁNY

SPECTROSCOPY, LASER

Laser spectroscopy is the use of intense monochromatic light to probe the frequency response of matter. The use of a laser in spectroscopy results in improved sensitivity because of its intensity and resolution, and because of its monochromaticity. Laser light interacts with atoms, individually or in bulk matter, by being either absorbed or scattered. Absorption occurs when the laser photon energy, $E_p = h\nu$, where h is Planck's constant, and ν is the frequency of the laser light, equals the energy separation between two atomic-energy levels. Otherwise, atoms scatter laser light. Absorption and scattering are the basis of the three most common forms of laser spectroscopy: laser-absorption spectroscopy, laser-induced fluorescence, and laser Raman scattering. The uses of these techniques range from basic scientific studies in physics, chemistry, and biology, to commercial applications in medical diagnostics and industrial-process monitoring and control.

Optical spectroscopy has a long and distinguished history in science and technology. Most of the knowledge about atomic and molecular energy levels, which ultimately led to the invention of the laser, resulted from nonlaser optical spectroscopy.

The sensitivity and resolution of nonlaser optical spectroscopy, however, is limited because of low-intensity polychromatic light sources. The invention of the laser in 1960 altered this situation. The laser is a source of high-intensity monochromatic light. Early lasers emitted light at only one or a few fixed colors determined by the energy levels of the lasing medium, which restricted spectroscopic studies to materials with energy levels that were fortuitously coincident with the available laser wavelengths. Laser light needed to be tunable to any desired frequency (color) to be most useful.

The dye laser realized the spectroscopist's need for a tunable laser. In 1966 Peter Sorokin at IBM discovered that solutions containing organic dye molecules could be used as a laser medium with a broad range of wavelengths. In 1970 Theodor W. Hänsch devised a dye laser, based on Sorokin's work. The Hänsch laser consists of a dye solution inserted between a diffraction grating and a partially reflecting mirror. The solution is excited into a lasing state by light from a fixed-frequency laser, and rotation of the grating tunes the dye laser output.

To a spectroscopist, a laser provides many identical photons with the same wavelength and traveling in the same direction. The frequency response of matter is probed by tuning the frequency, $\nu = c/\lambda$, of the photons and detecting absorption, fluorescence, or scattering. The spectral location and intensity of the frequency response provide structural information about both the individual atoms—energy levels and coupling strength—and the properties of the bulk matter, such as gas concentration and temperature. For clarity and brevity, spectroscopy of atoms will serve as an example.

Atoms that interact with laser photons either absorb or scatter those photons. Atoms absorb photons when the photon energy, $E = h\nu$, equals the energy separation between two atomic-energy levels, as first described by the Bohr atom model. An atom that has absorbed a laser photon may spontaneously emit another photon and decay to a lower-lying energy level. Both the absorption frequency and the emission frequency (fluorescence), which are not necessarily the same, provide structural information about the internal energy levels of the atom.

The intensity of the emitted fluorescence and/or the intensity of the transmitted light is proportional to the coupling between two internal energy levels and the density of atoms. A typical laser-spectroscopy experiment for monitoring absorption, fluorescence, or scattering is shown in Fig. 1. If laser light of intensity I_0 and resonant frequency ν is incident on a sample, then atoms will absorb photons. A photodiode monitors the transmitted beam and detects the absorption as a decrease in the laser intensity I_x. A spectrometer at right angles to the sample can detect scattered or fluorescent light emitted by the atoms.

A specific example of laser-absorption spectroscopy in physics is the measurement of the hyperfine splitting in rubidium atoms. The hyperfine interaction is a coupling between the total spin of

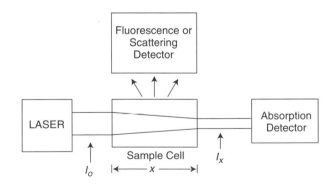

Figure 1 A typical laser-spectroscopy experiment for monitoring absorption, fluorescence, or scattering.

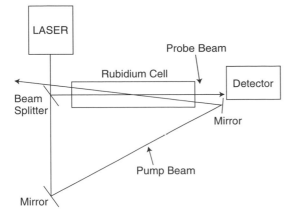

Figure 2 Set-up for the measurement of the hyperfine splitting in rubidium atoms.

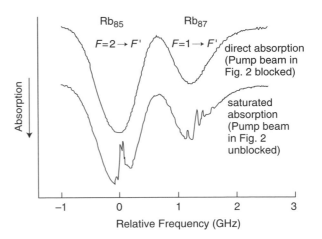

Figure 3 Hyperfine spectroscopy of rubidium.

nuclear particles (protons, neutrons) and the electron spin. The interaction causes a splitting of atomic-energy levels by amounts unresolvable with traditional infrared spectroscopic techniques. Figure 2 shows a vapor cell of rubidium atoms, all in their ground-energy level, and a laser beam split in two by a piece of glass. The transmitted (pump) beam, which is approximately 10 times stronger than the reflected beam (about 4 percent of the laser light is reflected from each surface of the glass slide), is used to saturate the rubidium-resonance transition. The weaker reflected (probe) beam is then counterpropagated against the pump beam through the vapor, tuned in frequency, and detected by a photodetector, which converts light to electricity. The use of two counterpropagating beams eliminates the effect of the motion of the atoms in the sample. This motion, the Doppler effect, tends to broaden spectral signals, as shown in the upper trace of Fig. 3, and reduces the measurement resolution. The saturated absorption spectrum is shown in the lower trace of Fig. 3. The spacing between features is megahertz (MHz), whereas the resolution of traditional spectrometers is gigahertz (GHz), a resolution enhancement of three orders of magnitude.

In medical diagnostics, laser-absorption spectroscopy is used, for example, to identify an ulcer-causing bacteria in a patient's stomach by monitoring the concentration ratio of $^{13}CO_2$:$^{12}CO_2$ in exhaled breath. A doctor may administer to a patient suspected of having an ulcer a substance containing ^{13}C, a nonradioactive, naturally occurring isotope of carbon. An enzyme associated with the ulcer-causing

bacteria will metabolize the ^{13}C-containing substance and increase the amount of $^{13}CO_2$ exhaled by the patient. The breath is collected in a glass cell, and laser-absorption spectroscopy is used to monitor the concentration ratio of $^{13}CO_2$:$^{12}CO_2$ by tuning the laser frequency to match an internal molecular transition of each isotope. The high resolution possible with laser spectroscopy allows each isotope to be monitored separately.

See also: ENERGY LEVELS; GRATING, DIFFRACTION; LASER; SCATTERING, RAMAN; SPECTROSCOPY

Bibliography

BROMBERG, J. L. "The Birth of the Laser." *Phys. Today* **41** (10), 26–33 (1988).

COOPER, D. E.; MARTINELLI, R. U.; CARLISLE, C. B.; RIRIS, H.; BOUR, D. B.; and MENNA, R. J. "Measurement of $^{12}CO_2$:$^{13}CO_2$ Ratios for Medical Diagnostics with 1.6μm Distributed Feedback Semiconductor Diode Lasers." *Appl. Opt.* **32**, 6727–6731 (1993).

HÄNSCH, T. W.; SHAWLOW, A. L.; and SERIES, G. W. "The Spectrum of Atomic Hydrogen." *Sci. Am.* **240** (3), 94–110 (1979).

HARNWELL, G. P., and LIVENGOOD, J. J. *Experimental Atomic Physics* (McGraw-Hill, New York, 1993).

RADZIEMSKI, L. J.; SOLARZ, R. W.; and PAISNER, J. A. *Laser Spectroscopy and Its Applications* (Marcel Dekker, New York, 1987).

JAMES VEALE

WILLIAM ANDERSON

THOMAS GALLAGHER

SPECTROSCOPY, MASS

Mass spectroscopy is a technique for the study of a substance by ionizing it and determining the relative numbers of each ionic mass present. The relative numbers of ions of each mass is sometimes called the intensity because it is frequently measured as a current; when relative numbers of ions are displayed as a function of mass, it is called a mass spectrum. The mass spectrum of a sample can be used to determine isotopic composition, chemical composition, and molecular structure.

Mass spectroscopy originated with Joseph J. Thomson's 1912 study of the motion of canal rays, the positively charged ions in a gas discharge which pass through a hole or "canal" in the cathode and then perpendicularly through a region of parallel electric and magnetic fields. The deflection of the beam of positive ions along the electric field and perpendicular to the magnetic field causes ions, with different velocities but of a given charge to mass ratio, to fall along a parabola when they reach a photographic plate after the electric and magnetic field regions are traversed. Each ion with a different charge to mass ratio falls on a different parabola. If the ion charge is known its mass is thus determined. The resolving power at a specific mass, the mass of the ion divided by the mass difference to the closest mass ion which can just be distinguished, was limited to a value of ten by the angular spread of the beam of ions in Thomson's apparatus. Introducing different gases into his discharge tube allowed Thomson to make a case for the existence of two stable isotopes of neon, one having an atomic weight of twenty and another having an atomic weight of twenty-two, as well as to determine the atomic weights of a number of other gaseous elements.

We owe the name "mass spectrograph" to Francis W. Aston, who was encouraged by Thomson to try other ways of measuring the atomic weights of stable isotopes. As a result, Aston developed an instrument which also used ions from a gas discharge tube but reduced the angular spread of the beam of ions by a set of narrow slits. Aston's instrument was arranged so that the ions were first deflected in a uniform electric field then passed into a circular region of uniform magnetic field oriented so as to cause deflection in the opposite direction. This arrangement causes ions of the same charge to mass ratio to be brought to the same position regardless of initial velocity. The positions where different

charge to mass ions are focused lie in a plane where ions can be detected on a photographic plate. This velocity focusing increases the measurable intensity in Aston's instrument, which he called a mass spectrograph. Aston's instrument had a resolving power of about 130.

From these early efforts, a large number of instruments were developed with higher resolving power and ease of operation. Present day mass spectrometers consist of three major parts. The first part is a source which can ionize the sample to be studied and form the ions into a beam for injection into the second part. The second part is a mass dispersion device which separates ions of different mass or charge-to-mass ratios into separate beams. This mass analyzer is controlled so that either the beams are brought to a focal plane where a detector can scan and measure the ion current for each mass, or the detector is fixed and the parameters of the mass analyzer are varied to bring the beams for each mass ion onto the detector in sequence and the ion current for that mass determined. The third part is the detector, which must be capable of measuring very small ion currents. Detectors can be simple electrometers or rather sophisticated ion counting devices, but in any case the sensitivity of the detector will determine the smallest ion current which can be detected.

From about 1915 to the early 1950s mass spectroscopy was employed primarily in the determination of isotopic masses of atoms. Mass spectrometers were operated by physicists who spent much time in maintaining, calibrating, and improving these instruments. The impetus for much of the improvement in mass spectroscopy came from the effort to understand the structure and stability of the atomic nucleus. The mass of a stable nucleus is less than the sum of the masses of its parts; the decrease in mass is related to the "binding energy" of the nucleus through the Einstein mass-energy equivalence relationship. By 1951 the resolution of mass spectrometers and the use of comparison techniques yielded mass measurements of sufficient accuracy to be useful in the study of nuclear binding. The resolving power of these instruments ranged as high as 500,000.

Starting in the early 1950s, designs had progressed sufficiently that commercial instruments began to be available. These commercial instruments were more easily maintained and calibrated so that scientists in fields other than nuclear physics began to apply mass spectroscopy as a tool. One of the first applications was the development of the vacuum leak detector. A small mass spectrometer set to detect ^{4}He is connected to the outlet of the pump on the vacuum system to be tested. Helium gas is sprayed on suspected leak sites and if a leak is present the helium that gets into the system will be detected. The larger the leak the larger the detected signal. Another mass spectroscopy tool used in vacuum trouble shooting is the residual gas analyzer, which consists of a mass spectrometer capable of scanning a fairly large mass range. When this device is connected to a vacuum system and the residual gas is ionized and injected into the mass analyzer, a mass scan indicates the gases and vapors that remain in the system, yielding helpful clues to eliminate vacuum problems.

The ability of mass spectrometers to measure isotope ratios accurately in samples which can be vaporized and ionized has encouraged their wide use in isotope-age dating in geology. If a rock contains radioactive elements, its isotopic ratios will change with time. This occurs because those isotopes which come from radioactive decay will increase while nonradiogenic isotopes will not change. Since the original amounts of isotopes present are not known, the time behavior of several isotope ratios must be used to infer the "age" of the rock, that is the time since its composition changed by adding radioactive material from its surroundings.

Mass spectroscopy has found wide use in chemistry. An early application was the determination of molecular ionization potentials by subjecting the vapor of the material of interest to a variable monoenergetic electron beam bombardment. The electron beam energy when the molecular ions of interest are first detected yields the desired ionization potential. In organic chemistry the use of mass spectroscopy on samples purified by gas chromatography has led to the elucidation of many organic molecular structures. One technique is to admit the elutant from a gas chromatography column into an ionization chamber where it is ionized by electron bombardment. The molecules break up into ions whose structures can be identified from their masses. The investigator is then left with the puzzle of deciding what molecular structure would give rise to fragments with the observed masses. Additional clues can be obtained by changing the energy of the ionizing electron beam and by using what has been called "chemical ionization." In this technique a gas, typically methane, is ionized and these ions are allowed to interact through low-energy collisions with

the material to be analyzed. These collisions frequently remove a hydrogen atom from a molecule of interest and the redistribution of energy and subsequent break up of the molecule gives a different ion fragmentation pattern, and thus provides additional information from which a molecular structure can be deduced.

With every development of a new way to produce an ionized sample for mass analysis, new applications arise. The use of lasers to vaporize, ionize, or desorb molecules from surfaces has led to a myriad of applications in solid state and surface physics as well as studies of large desorbed molecules.

See also: IONIZATION; ISOTOPES; MASS SPECTROMETER; NUCLEAR BINDING ENERGY; RADIOACTIVE DATING; SPECTROPHOTOMETRY; THOMSON, JOSEPH JOHN

Bibliography

COOKS, R. G.; BUSCH, K. L.; and GISH, G. L. "Mass Spectrometer: Analytical Capabilities and Potentials." *Science* **222**, 273–291 (1983).

DUCKWORTH, H. E.; BARBER, R. C.; and VENKATASUBRIAMANIAN, V. S. *Mass Spectroscopy*, 2nd ed. (Cambridge University Press, Cambridge, Eng., 1986).

LUBMAN, D. M., ed. *Lasers and Mass Spectroscopy* (Oxford University Press, New York, 1990).

BASIL CURNUTTE

SPECTROSCOPY, MICROWAVE

Microwaves are the cousins of visible light; both belong to the family of electromagnetic waves. Visible light has wavelengths on the order of 1,000 Å ($1Å = 10^{-10}$ m), while microwaves have much longer wavelengths (or lower frequency) ranging from millimeters to centimeters. An alternate way of distinguishing between light and microwaves is in terms of energy: visible light, with its high frequency, is the high-energy cousin of low-frequency, low-energy microwaves.

When either microwaves or visible light shine on molecules, some of the energy of the electromagnetic waves is absorbed by the molecules; however, the absorption occurs in very different fashions. The study and analysis of how electromagnetic waves (or electromagnetic energy) interact with matter is called spectroscopy.

When visible light is incident on a gaseous collection of molecules, the interaction that occurs is between the light and the atomic electrons that bind the atoms together in molecular form. The lower-energy microwaves do not significantly influence the electrons; rather, the microwaves interact with each molecule by making the molecule, as a whole, rotate like a top. In order to do this, however, the molecule must have something for the microwave to grab onto; namely, an electric dipole moment. The water molecule (H_2O) has a dipole moment because the oxygen end of the molecule is positively charged relative to the hydrogen end. In other words, molecules in which the centers of positive and negative charges are slightly separated have a dipole moment.

When an object rotates (for example, a molecule), there is energy associated with the rotation. It is called rotational energy. Two factors influence the magnitude of the molecular rotational energy due to the interaction with microwaves: (1) The way the mass is distributed in the molecule; the more spread out the mass is, the slower the molecule rotates. The measure of the mass distribution of the molecule is given by the moment of inertia of the molecule. (2) The energy associated with the rotational energy of a molecule is governed by the rules of quantum mechanics so that only certain rotational energies are allowed. To understand each of these factors, we shall consider a gaseous collection of diatomic molecules like hydrochloric acid (HCl).

Each atom of the HCl molecule has a mass and these masses are separated by the length of the chemical bond between them. Somewhere between the two atoms is the center of mass, which is closer to the much heavier chlorine atom. When microwaves interact with the HCl molecule, it rotates around an axis passing between the two atoms through the center of mass. The rotational energy depends on the two masses, hydrogen and chlorine, and their respective distances from the axis of rotation. Specifically,

$$\text{rotational energy} \propto \frac{1}{\text{moment of inertia}}.$$

The moment of inertia for HCl is given by

$$\text{moment of inertia} = I_{HCl} = m_H r_H^2 + m_{Cl} r_{Cl}^2,$$

where m_H and m_{Cl} are the masses of the two atoms and r_H and r_{Cl} are their respective distances from the center of mass. We shall pause here and consider the second influencing factor, the quantum mechanical rules.

As indicated earlier, a molecule cannot have an arbitrary rotational energy. Rotational energy at the molecular level is quantized, which means that only select rotational energy states are allowed. The allowed energy states (or energy levels) for a diatomic molecule like HCl are as follows:

$$E_J = \frac{h^2}{8\pi^2 I_{HCl}} J(J+1),$$

where h is Planck's constant and J is an integer that takes the values 1, 2, 3, . . . and so on. Thus, for $J = 1$,

$$E_1 = \frac{h^2}{8\pi^2 I_{HCl}} (1)(1+1) = \frac{h^2}{4\pi^2 I_{HCl}}.$$

For $J = 2$,

$$E_2 = \frac{h^2}{8\pi^2 I_{HCl}} (2)(2+1) = \frac{3h^2}{4\pi^2 I_{HCl}},$$

and so on for larger values of J. It is on this basis that microwave spectroscopy derives its practical usefulness.

In all spectroscopic experiments electromagnetic waves bring energy to a system of atoms or molecules, and energy is transferred from the electromagnetic waves to the atoms or molecules. Again, however, the rules of quantum mechanics apply. Electromagnetic waves have both wave-like and particle-like behaviors. A particle of electromagnetic energy is called a photon and its energy is

$$E = h\nu,$$

where ν is the frequency of the electromagnetic wave. In order for a molecule to absorb the energy of a photon, the energy of the photon must exactly equal the difference between two allowed energy states of the molecule. In terms of the symbols above,

$$h\nu = E_{(J+1)} - E_J.$$

The microwave spectroscopist passes microwave radiation through a gaseous sample and slowly varies the frequency of the microwave radiation. When the frequency of the microwaves is such that it satisfies a condition like that above, the molecules absorb energy from the radiation, and the frequency at which this absorption occurs can be measured to a very high degree of accuracy. With a knowledge of this frequency, one can deduce information about the molecule.

To see how this works, we return to the molecule HCl. Assume the frequency at which the sample of HCl absorbs has been measured, and further assume that this absorption can be identified with the $J = 1$ to the $J = 2$ transition of the HCl molecules. Then we have the condition

$$hv = E_2 - E_1$$

$$= \frac{3h^2}{4\pi^2 I_{\text{HCl}}} - \frac{h^2}{4\pi^2 I_{\text{HCl}}}$$

$$= \frac{h^2}{2\pi^2 I_{\text{HCl}}}.$$

Note that everything in the last equation above is known except the moment of inertia I_{HCl}. Therefore, this equation can be solved for the unknown I_{HCl} and, if we know the masses of the hydrogen and chlorine atoms, the distance between the hydrogen and chlorine atoms (the bond length) can be determined.

This example demonstrates one of the most powerful applications of microwave spectroscopy; namely, the determination of molecular structure: bond lengths and, for more complicated molecules, bond angles as well. In addition to precise structural information, other properties of a molecule can be measured. By applying an electric field to the sample of molecules, the molecular dipole moment can be measured. Furthermore, some atomic nuclei possess inherent angular momentum, called spin, and those nuclei with spin greater than $1/2$ also have nonspherical shapes and possess a property called an electric quadrupole moment. The presence of the nuclear quadrupole moment alters the energy states of a molecule and, as a result, both the spin and the quadrupole moment can be measured. Moreover, a quadrupolar nucleus is sensitive to the way electrons are distributed around it, and from the microwave spectrum we can learn about elec-trons in the molecule near such nuclei. Dynamic features of molecules also can be learned from an analysis of microwave spectra. For example, one part of a molecule can rotate around a single bond relative to another part, and the energy opposing such internal rotation can be measured.

Microwave spectroscopy provides an open window into many properties of molecules and allows these properties to be measured with great accuracy and precision.

See also: DIPOLE MOMENT; ELECTROMAGNETIC SPECTRUM; ELECTROMAGNETIC WAVE; ENERGY LEVELS; INERTIA, MOMENT OF; PHOTON; QUANTUM MECHANICS; SPECTROSCOPY

Bibliography

GORDY, W., and COOK, R. L. *Microwave Spectroscopy and Molecular Spectra* (Interscience, New York, 1970).

SUGDEN, T. M., and KENNEY, C. N. *Microwave Spectroscopy of Gases* (Van Nostrand, London, 1965).

TOWNES, C. H., and SCHAWLOW, A. L. *Microwave Spectroscopy* (McGraw-Hill, New York, 1955).

JOHN S. RIGDEN

SPECTROSCOPY, ULTRAVIOLET

The ultraviolet (uv) region of the electromagnetic spectrum spans the frequency range from approximately 7.5×10^{14} s^{-1} to 3×10^{16} s^{-1}, the wave-number range from 2.5×10^4 cm^{-1} to 1×10^6 cm^{-1}, and the wavelength range from 400 nm to 10 nm. The spectroscopy associated with the uv region involves transitions between the electronic energy levels of the outer electrons in atoms and molecules. Important examples of atomic transitions in the uv include the decay of an excited helium $2p$ electron to the $1s^2$ ground state (58.43 nm) and the decay of an excited mercury $6p$ electron to the $6s^2$ ground state (184.95 nm). Both of these transitions provide useful laboratory sources of uv radiation, and the mercury transition also is employed to generate fluorescent (visible) light in mercury street lamps. Examples of uv transitions in molecules are excitations of electrons from π bonding orbitals to π^* anti-bonding orbitals in compounds containing carbon-

carbon (~180 nm) and carbon-oxygen (~290 nm) double bonds.

Spectrophotometers that cover both the visible and uv regions of the spectrum are quite common. For operation in the uv, optical components must be made from quartz because uv radiation is highly absorbed by glass.

An important application of uv radiation is in uv-photoelectron spectroscopy. This technique uses the photoelectric effect to determine the ionization energies of valence electrons in atoms and molecules. Monochromatic photons of uv light are absorbed by atoms of a sample, causing the ejection of electrons from their quantum states. The kinetic energies of the ejected electrons (photoelectrons) are precisely measured in an electron spectrometer and converted to ionization energies via the photoelectric equation $I_i = h\nu - E_i$, where $h\nu$ is the energy of the incident photon and E_i is the measured kinetic energy of the ejected electron. Because the ionization energies of an atom are influenced by surrounding atoms, photoelectron spectra provide valuable information concerning the chemical composition of a substance. The technique is especially useful for investigating the chemical and physical properties of surfaces since most of the photoelectrons that are ejected from atoms below the surface of a sample are absorbed or lose much of their energy due to scattering. In the study of molecules in the gas phase by uv-photoelectron spectroscopy, it is possible to observe additional structures associated with vibrational energy levels. During the process of photoionization, the molecule may undergo a transition to an excited vibrational state. The energy for this additional excitation comes from the incident photon, and hence the kinetic energy of the photoelectron is lowered by an amount exactly equal to the vibrational transition energy.

The most common source of uv radiation for uv-photoelectron spectroscopy is the $2p \rightarrow 1s$ transition in helium. However, synchrotron-radiation facilities have greatly expanded the technique's capabilities and range of applications. Some modern synchrotron light sources produce extremely high intensities of radiation with a spectrum that is continuously distributed across the whole range of uv wavelengths. Synchrotron radiation is also polarized and highly focused.

The effect on living organisms of increasing levels of uv radiation impinging on the earth from the Sun has been a matter of growing concern. Most uv radiation is absorbed by diatomic oxygen molecules (O_2) and triatomic ozone molecules (O_3) in the atmosphere. Absorption by O_2 molecules, however, occurs only for wavelengths of 242 nm or less, whereas O_3 molecules play a critical role in shielding the earth from potentially damaging uv radiation in the 242 to 320 nm range. A number of scientific studies have concluded that the steady-state ozone concentration in the stratosphere is decreasing at a faster rate than can be explained by natural processes. A class of commercially produced chemical compounds, called chlorofluorocarbons (CFCs), has been identified as the most probable cause of ozone depletion. Compelling evidence of a direct link between increasing concentrations of CFCs and decreasing concentrations of ozone comes from studies of the ozone hole that has developed over Antarctica.

See also: PHOTOELECTRIC EFFECT; RADIATION, SYNCHROTRON; SPECTROPHOTOMETRY; SPECTROSCOPY, VISIBLE

Bibliography

BAKER, A. D., and BETTERIDGE, D. *Photoelectron Spectroscopy* (Pergamon, Oxford, Eng., 1977).

HERZBERG, G. *Molecular Spectra and Molecular Structure III: Electronic Spectra and Electronic Structure of Polyatomic Molecules* (Van Nostrand Reinhold, New York, 1966).

HOLLAS, J. M. *Modern Spectroscopy* (Wiley, New York, 1987).

SCHWARTZ, A. T.; BUNCE, D. M.; SILBERMAN, R. G.; STANITSKI, C. L.; STRATTON, W. J.; and ZIPP, A. P. *Chemistry in Context: Applying Chemistry to Society* (Wm. C. Brown, Dubuque, IA, 1994).

RAND L. WATSON

SPECTROSCOPY, VISIBLE

The general term "spectroscopy" refers to the study of wavelengths (or frequencies) and intensities of electromagnetic radiation emitted, absorbed, and scattered by atoms and molecules. Visible spectroscopy is the branch of spectroscopy that examines the part of the electromagnetic spectrum visible to the human eye. The standard unit for expressing wavelength in the visible region is the nanometer (nm) which is equal to 1×10^{-9} m or 10 Å. The visible spectrum, as shown in Fig. 1, extends over the wavelength region from approximately 400 nm (violet light) to 750 nm (red light). In terms of frequency ν, which is related to wavelength λ by the formula $\nu = c/\lambda$, where c is the speed of light, the visible spectrum extends from 7.5×10^{14} s^{-1} (violet) to 4.0×10^{14} s^{-1} (red).

Because the energies of atoms and molecules are quantized, discrete amounts of energy are required to raise or lower them from one energy state to another. The process of changing from an initial energy state to a final energy state is called a transition. The energy state of an atom or molecule may be raised or lowered by respectively absorbing or emitting electromagnetic radiation of energy equal to the difference in energy ($E_f - E_i$) between the two states involved. Since the energy of electromagnetic radiation may be expressed by the formula $E = h\nu$, where h is Planck's constant, the wavelength of light either absorbed or emitted in such a transition is given by

$$\lambda = \frac{hc}{E_f - E_i}.$$

Since the energy differences have unique and characteristic values, which depend on various properties of the particular atom or molecule, so do the wavelengths of the absorbed or emitted radiation. It is this feature that makes spectroscopy so useful for the identification and quantitative analysis of atoms and molecules (atomic absorption spectroscopy, spectrophotometry), and for the elucidation of their structure.

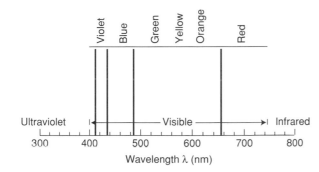

Figure 1 The visible region of the electromagnetic spectrum. The colors corresponding to the different wavelength regions are shown along the top. The lines depict the visible spectrum of atomic hydrogen.

Transitions in the visible region occur primarily as a result of changes in the electronic energies of atoms and molecules, as opposed to other types of energy changes, such as those associated with molecular vibrations and rotations, which occur in the infrared and microwave regions of the electromagnetic spectrum, respectively. However, electronic energy changes in molecules are always accompanied by vibrational and rotational energy changes, and this property causes molecular spectra to display broadbands extending over wide ranges of wavelengths instead of narrow lines, which are characteristic of the spectra of free atoms.

Free atoms exhibit extremely rich spectra in the visible region because generally an atom possesses numerous electronic energy levels with the required energy spacings that may be populated by exciting the outermost electron. For example, in the hydrogen atom, a series of four transitions from energy levels having principal quantum number $n = 3, 4, 5,$ and 6 to the $n = 2$ energy level (part of the Balmer series) fall in the visible region at the wavelengths indicated in Fig. 1. The uranium atom displays more than 70 lines in its visible spectrum. Molecules, on the other hand, have more limited spectroscopic activity in the visible region since most valence electron transitions of molecules occur in the ultraviolet. Notable exceptions to this generalization are transition–metal coordination complexes. Bonding in these compounds involves the five d orbitals of the metal ion and causes their energies to differ, depending on the nature of the complexing agent and the symmetry of the resultant complex. For example, in the octahedral symmetry of the hexa-aqua complex of Cr^{3+}, $[Cr(H_2O)_6]^{3+}$, the d orbitals are split into two sets of energy levels whose difference is equal to the energy of yellow light. Consequently this complex absorbs yellow light by raising d electrons from the lower energy levels to the upper energy levels; hence its color is violet, the complement of yellow (i.e., white minus yellow gives violet). Many molecular ions and free radicals, such as CN, also absorb and emit visible light.

Absorption measurements in the visible conventionally employ either an incandescent lamp or a high pressure xenon arc lamp as the light source, a diffraction grating as the wavelength dispersing element, and a photomultiplier tube as the detector. Some modern instruments for visible spectroscopy now utilize holographic gratings and photodiode array detectors. The advent of tunable lasers has caused a renaissance in visible spectroscopy as numerous applications of these unique sources of radiation have rapidly evolved. High resolution spectra are obtained by either measuring the attenuation of the incident laser radiation by the sample as a function of the laser frequency or by monitoring secondary processes that directly follow excitation of the sample by the laser, such as fluorescence, dissociation, or ionization.

See also: COLOR; ELECTROMAGNETIC RADIATION; ELECTROMAGNETIC SPECTRUM; GRATING, DIFFRACTION; LIGHT, ELECTROMAGNETIC THEORY OF; SPECTRAL SERIES; SPECTROPHOTOMETRY; SPECTROSCOPY

Bibliography

ATKINS, P. W. *Physical Chemistry*, 5th ed. (W. H. Freeman, New York, 1994).

DEMTRÖDER, W. *Laser Spectroscopy: Basic Concepts and Instrumentation* (Springer-Verlag, Berlin, 1982).

HOLLAS, J. M. *High Resolution Spectroscopy* (Butterworth, London, 1982).

RAND L. WATSON

SPECTROSCOPY, X-RAY

X-ray spectroscopy is the study of radiant intensity of short wavelength (10^{-8} to 10^{-11} m) electromagnetic radiation ordered according to wavelength through the use of an instrument called a spectrometer. X-ray spectroscopy is an important way to analyze the composition of materials and to study the electronic properties of matter. When x rays were discovered by Wilhelm Conrad Röntgen as he was investigating a high voltage discharge between two electrodes in a partially evacuated tube, the electromagnetic nature of the phenomenon was not known. In a short time, after only a few key experiments, the electromagnetic nature of x rays clearly emerged. Once it was known that x rays were part of the electromagnetic spectrum, scientists began to characterize x rays in terms of intensity and wavelength. It was during the course of these early investigations that x-ray spectroscopy began to emerge in the early years of the twentieth century.

Max von Laue and his coworkers demonstrated that atoms arranged in a regular array called a crystal could act to diffract x rays in a way similar to the diffraction of visible radiation by a system of slits, because the spacing between the planes of atoms is approximately the same as the x-ray wavelength. An explanation of these results was offered by William L. Bragg, who showed that x rays of wavelength λ, expressed in meters, would be preferentially diffracted into an angle θ according to the simple relationship $n\lambda = 2d \sin \theta$. In this formula, n is an integer called the order, d is the spacing of the atomic planes, and θ is the angle the x-ray beam makes with respect to the atomic planes, as shown in Fig. 1.

Bragg applied the principle of diffraction outlined in the previous paragraph to the construction of a simple x-ray spectrometer, shown in Fig. 2. With this equipment he obtained the first x-ray spectrum from a platinum target. If a different target is substituted for platinum, the spectral features appear at different angles because the wavelength of the emitted radiation depends on the element, and if the crystal is replaced by another and the target remains the same, the original spectrum will be reproduced at a different angle because the spacing of the atomic planes is different for different crystals.

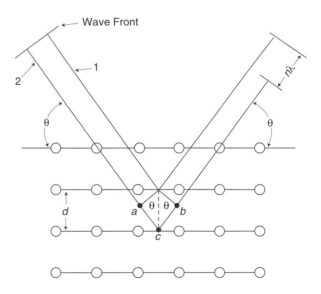

Figure 1 Rays 1 and 2 reflect from planes containing atoms in a crystalline solid. Ray 2 travels a greater distance ($ac + cb = 2d \sin \theta$) than ray 1. The two rays experience constructive interference when their path difference, $ac + cb$, equals an integer number of wavelengths, λ.

The spectrometer developed by Bragg in 1912 has proven to be so elegantly simple that new x-ray spectrometers have retained the fundamental elements of the design. These characteristics can easily be seen in the schematic representation of a modern two-crystal x-ray spectrometer shown in Fig. 3.

By carefully studying the elements using the spectrometer of the type developed by Bragg, Henry G. J. Mosley became one of the early leaders in the field of x-ray spectroscopy. From his and subsequent work it became clear that the electrons in atoms were arranged in shells, that were denoted K, L, M, and so on. Through a systematic study of the wavelength of many of these x-ray emission lines, one may deduce the amount of energy E, called the binding energy, that is required to remove an electron from a particular shell in the atom. The emission of x rays from the atom is caused by electrons jumping from one shell to another, emitting an x-ray photon of wavelength λ that could be calculated from the formula: $hc/\lambda = E_K - E_L$. This formula equates the photon energy hc/λ with the difference in the binding energy for the K and the L shells in this example. The quantities h and c are symbols for Planck's constant ($h = 6.626 \times 10^{-34}$ J·s) and the velocity of light ($c = 2.997 \times 10^8$ m·s^{-1}), respectively. A typical high resolution x-ray emission spectrum for the rare gas argon obtained from the spectrometer illustrated in Fig. 3 is shown in Fig. 4a. Only four spectral lines of the many are shown, two that are very intense, $K\alpha_1$ and $K\alpha_2$, and two that are quite weak, $K\alpha_3$ and $K\alpha_4$. The intense lines arise from the electron jumping from the subshell L orbits ($2p_{3/2}$ and $2p_{1/2}$ levels in spectroscopic notation) to the K shell (1s level in spectroscopic notation). The weak features denoted $K\alpha_3$ and $K\alpha_4$ are due to the excitation of two electrons, one in the L shell and one in the K shell.

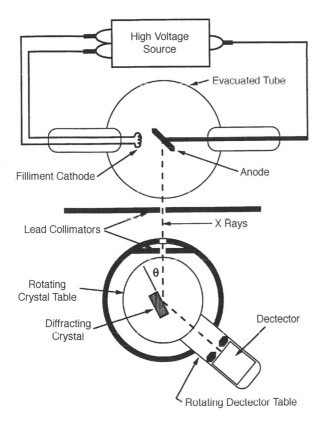

Figure 2 Schematic diagram of a simple Bragg x-ray spectrometer. The wavelength is changed by rotating the table containing the crystal to different values of the angle θ. The detector rotates at double the angle of the crystal.

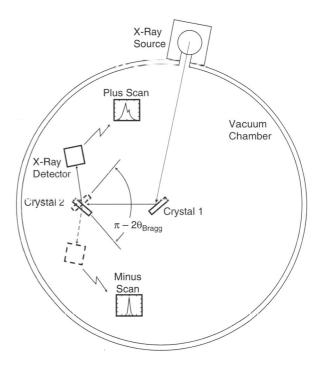

Figure 3 Schematic Diagram of a two-crystal vacuum Bragg x-ray spectrometer. The wavelength is changed by rotating crystal 2 to different values of the angle θ. The x-ray detector rotates at double the angle of the crystal. The "minus scan" produces a reflectivity curve of the crystal, and the "plus scan" produces a spectrum.

The origin of these emission features is shown in the energy level diagram shown in Fig. 4b.

The vast majority of research using x rays has been conducted with a simple x-ray tube source. While the x-ray tube is still an important source, it was replaced in the later decades of the twentieth century by a very powerful source that generates x rays by the acceleration of very high energy electrons, in a machine called a synchrotron.

It is through the use of these x-ray sources that a great deal of research is being conducted to learn about the structure and function of biological compounds, and for the development of new materials that may serve as chemical catalysts or high-efficiency conductors of electricity.

See also: ATOM; BRAGG'S LAW; DIFFRACTION; ELECTROMAGNETIC RADIATION; *K* CAPTURE; NUCLEAR SHELL MODEL; NUCLEAR STRUCTURE; RÖNTGEN, WILHELM CONRAD; SPECTROSCOPY; SYNCHROTRON; X RAY; X RAY, DISCOVERY OF

Bibliography

BERTIN, E. P. *Introduction to X-Ray Spectrometric Analysis* (Plenum, New York, 1978).

BRAGG, W. L. "The Diffraction of Short Electromagnetic Waves by a Crystal." *Proc. Cambridge Philos. Soc.* **17,** 43 (1912).

COMPTON, A. H., and ALLISON, S. K. *X Rays in Theory and Experiment* (Van Nostrand, New York, 1935).

DYSON, N. A. *X Rays in Atomic and Nuclear Physics,* 2nd ed. (Cambridge University Press, Cambridge, Eng., 1990).

JENKINS, R., and DEVRIES, J. L. *Practical X-Ray Spectrometry* (Springer-Verlag, Berlin, 1975).

MOSLEY, H. G. J. "The High-Frequency Spectra of the Elements." *Philos. Mag.* **26,** 1024 (1913).

DAVID L. EDERER

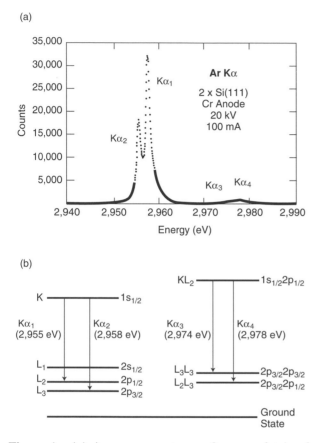

Figure 4 (a) An x-ray spectrum of argon obtained using the apparatus shown in Fig. 3. Two intense transitions—the $K\alpha_1$ and the $K\alpha_2$—originate when an electron from the $2p$ or L shell fills a hole in the K or $1s$ shell. Because of rules governing the de-excitation of the atom, no x ray is produced when a $2s$ or L_1 electron fills the vacancy in the K shell. The $K\alpha_3$ and the $K\alpha_4$ arise because in some instances two electrons are removed from the atom in the excitation process. (b) Schematic diagram of the four x-ray transitions shown in (a). Not all of the core atomic levels are shown for argon. The complete x-ray spectrum contains many more transitions. Note that the energy scale is greatly exaggerated for clarity. The photon energies of the x-ray transitions are indicated in the units of energy, electron volt, and can be calculated from the wavelength using the formula $hc/\lambda = E,$ as shown in the text.

SPHERICAL ABERRATION

See ABERRATION, SPHERICAL

SPHERICAL HARMONICS

See HARMONICS, SPHERICAL

SPIN

The law of conservation of angular momentum, which is deeply tied to the invariance of physical law under rotations, is found to be valid in quantum mechanics, just as it is in classical mechanics. In quantum mechanics, however, the concept of angular momentum is considerably subtler than in classical mechanics and richer in its consequences. Among these consequences is the existence of an important new intrinsic property of particles, their spin.

Qualitative Phenomena

In reaching a qualitative appreciation of why it is necessary to introduce spin, and of how this concept is used, there is no better starting point than to consider the classic Stern–Gerlach experiment. If a collection of electrons initially at rest is subjected to the field of a strong bar magnet by bringing the north pole of the magnet nearby, the electrons separate into two sharply defined populations, a group that is attracted to the pole and a group that is repelled. Within each population, the electrons all move at the same velocity. If one repeats this sort of experiment with particles other than electrons, one often finds similar results. For instance, collections of protons or of neutrons will also separate into two populations, although the velocities will be much smaller. In other cases (e.g., helium atoms), one finds that the particles do not separate, and in still other cases, the particles separate into *more* than two populations—for example, diatomic oxygen splits into three populations. (Strictly speaking, this applies only to isotopically pure ^{4}He and ^{16}O.)

This sort of experiment has revealed an intrinsic property distinguishing otherwise identical particles. For reasons that will soon emerge, we identify this new property as their spin. Thus, we say that our particle has spin s if it produces $2s + 1$ populations in the type of experiment just described. Thus, electrons, protons, and neutrons have spin $\frac{1}{2}$, while helium atoms have spin 0 and diatomic oxygen has spin 1. Evidently, according to this definition, the spin will be either a whole number, or half of an odd whole number. The different populations are said to have different values of spin around an axis aligned in the north-south direction, with values s, $s - 1$, ..., $-s$.

The physical meaning of spin, as identified operationally above, can be elucidated by further investigat-ing differences among the particles in the various populations. A particularly striking difference becomes evident if the particles being analyzed happen to be unstable, so that one can observe their decay. One then observes that the angular distribution of the decay products can be quite different for the different populations. As a concrete example, suppose we consider ρ^+ mesons, which separate into three populations and are therefore spin-1 particles according to our definition. One finds that in the decay $\rho^+ \rightarrow \pi^+ + \pi^0$ the probability for either of the pions to emerge at an angle θ from north (as defined by the magnetic field previously described) is proportional to $\sin^2 \theta$ if they emerge from decays of $s = 1$ or $s = -1$ ρ^+ meson populations, but the probability is independent of θ if they emerge from the $s = 0$ population. Very roughly speaking, this can be understood as the effect that the ρs with $s = \pm 1$ are spinning, so the π mesons are hurled away from the axis.

One major job of the quantum theory of angular momentum is to correlate in a precise way such angular distributions of decay products with the spin of the particles involved. In general, the answer is complicated and richly structured. A beautiful branch of mathematics, group representation theory, has been crafted for the task.

Aspects of the Mathematical Theory

The quantum theory of angular momentum was first constructed, and is still most easily understood, by suitably modifying the classical theory. Let us consider first the simplest idealized case of a single isolated body. In classical mechanics, there are two contributions to the angular momentum of such a body, having somewhat distinct characters. The orbital angular momentum **L** around a given point is associated with motion of the body as a whole; it is equal to the vector product of the position of the body **R** (the position of its center of mass) with its momentum **P**: $\mathbf{L} = \mathbf{R} \times \mathbf{P}$. The rotational, intrinsic, or spin angular momentum is associated with the rotation of the body about an axis fixed in the body. Thus, for example, the total angular momentum of Earth with respect to the Sun is the sum of an orbital part associated with its yearly revolution and a spin part associated with its daily rotation. Notice that while the value of the orbital angular momentum depends on the choice of reference point, the value of the spin angular momentum does not—it is an intrinsic property of the body.

In quantum mechanics, this division of the total angular momentum into orbital and spin parts remains valid. In either form of mechanics, we may write the equation

$$J = L + S = R \times P + S, \qquad (1)$$

expressing the total angular momentum J as a sum of orbital angular momentum L and spin angular momentum S.

The quantum theory differs from the classical theory, however, in one crucial respect. Whereas in the classical theory the magnitudes of the components of J, L, and S (as well as R and P) are described by ordinary real numbers, in the quantum theory they are described by operators that have a very particular set of algebraic properties quite different from ordinary numbers. The fundamental equations of the quantum theory of spin and their simplest solutions have two striking physical consequences: the irreducible uncertainty in spin alignment, and the discreteness of possible spin values.

Equations. The fundamental equations of the quantum theory of spin are the commutation relations among its components S_x, S_y, S_z along the three axes:

$$S_x S_y - S_y S_x = i\hbar S_z$$
$$S_y S_z - S_z S_y = i\hbar S_x \qquad (2)$$
$$S_z S_x - S_x S_z = i\hbar S_y,$$

where $\hbar \equiv h/2\pi$ is the reduced Planck constant and $i = \sqrt{-1}$. These equations can be written in an equivalent but more compact form using a vector product notation:

$$S \times S = i\hbar S. \qquad (3)$$

Similar equations hold for the orbital angular momentum operators, and thus they also hold for the total angular momentum operators. [Note that the peculiar algebraic property that angular momentum operators do not commute ($S_x S_y - S_y S_x \neq 0$) is related to the fact that rotations do not commute. To see this, you can perform a simple experiment with any book. Hold it face up, rotate it $90°$ about two perpendicular axes (say, one vertical and one hori-

zontal straight in front of you). Observe the book's final position. Now repeat the process, except reverse the order of the two rotations. You will find the result is quite different.]

Solutions. Mathematically, one simple solution of these equations is provided by the matrices

$$S_x^{(1/2)} = \frac{\hbar}{2} \begin{pmatrix} 0 & 1 \\ 1 & 0 \end{pmatrix}$$

$$S_y^{(1/2)} = \frac{\hbar}{2} \begin{pmatrix} 0 & -i \\ i & 0 \end{pmatrix} \qquad (4)$$

$$S_z^{(1/2)} = \frac{\hbar}{2} \begin{pmatrix} 1 & 0 \\ 0 & -1 \end{pmatrix},$$

and another by the matrices

$$S_x^{(1)} = \frac{\hbar}{\sqrt{2}} \begin{pmatrix} 0 & 1 & 0 \\ 1 & 0 & 1 \\ 0 & 1 & 0 \end{pmatrix}$$

$$S_y^{(1)} = \frac{\hbar}{\sqrt{2}} \begin{pmatrix} 0 & -i & 0 \\ i & 0 & -i \\ 0 & i & 0 \end{pmatrix} \qquad (5)$$

$$S_z^{(1)} = \hbar \begin{pmatrix} 1 & 0 & 0 \\ 0 & 0 & 0 \\ 0 & 0 & -1 \end{pmatrix}.$$

Uncertainty. The fact that different components of the spin vector do not commute has a profound physical meaning. It means that the values of these components, in any state, cannot both have definite numerical values. This is an analog, for spin, of the famous Heisenberg uncertainty relation between position and momentum.

Discreteness. According to the general theory of quantum mechanics, observables are represented by (Hermitean) operators. Again according to this theory, the result of a measurement of an observable in a state is equal to one of the eigenvalues of the operator. The probability for the measurement to yield any particular eigenvalue is determined by the state. Our solutions in Eqs. (4) and (5) are well adapted to discussing the observable S_z. In the case of a particle described by Eq. (4), the possible values resulting from its measurement are the eigenvalues $\hbar/2$ and $-\hbar/2$. In the case of a particle described by Eq. (5), the possible values resulting from its measurement are $\hbar$, 0, $-\hbar$. Thus, these solutions embody the qualitative behaviors described earlier for spin-$\frac{1}{2}$ and spin-1 particles, respectively.

It is remarkable that for a spin-$\frac{1}{2}$ particle one never measures 0 for the spin angular momentum—in any direction. This illustrates the difficulties facing any attempt to visualize spin in terms of a classical model invoking rotating objects. Quantum mechanical spin appears to be an irreducible property that in general cannot be explained in terms of anything simpler.

By purely mathematical reasoning, one can classify all solutions of the commutation relations in Eq. (2) that have sensible physical interpretations. All such solutions exhibit the feature of discreteness we just saw in the simplest cases. This allows us to understand in a general way the emergence of a finite number of populations in the Stern–Gerlach procedure. Further development of the theory allows one to describe additional details of their behavior.

Ramifications

There is a remarkable correlation between the spin of an elementary particle and its quantum statistics. Particles whose spin is half an odd integer obey Fermi statistics (and are called fermions), while particles whose spin is an integer obey Bose statistics (and are called bosons).

The spin of electrons interacts strongly with external magnetic fields, as does the spin of atomic nuclei. One can exploit this coupling to manipulate and sense the direction of such spins; this is the basis of magnetic resonance technique. The spin of photons is manifested in the polarization of the light they constitute. The direction of a photon's spin can strongly influence its interaction with matter. Polarizers are made from material that preferentially absorbs photons with particular polarization (i.e., in a particular spin state).

The description of different states of otherwise identical particles by ascribing to them different values of spin, encourages one to inquire whether other apparently different particles can be understood as fundamentally identical, but with different values of some additional spin-like variable. Isospin, as its name hints, was an early and still quite useful idea to understand protons and neutrons as different aspects of one particle—the nucleon—in this way. In some recent speculations, additional spin-

like variables differentiating fundamental particles actually are quantum angular momenta—around axes in additional, curled-up dimensions.

See also: EIGENFUNCTION AND EIGENVALUE; FERMIONS AND BOSONS; MOMENTUM; MOMENTUM, CONSERVATION OF; NUCLEON; POLARIZED LIGHT; SPIN, ELECTRON; SPIN AND STATISTICS; STERN–GERLACH EXPERIMENT; SYMMETRY; UNCERTAINTY PRINCIPLE

Bibliography

EDMONDS, A. *Angular Momentum in Quantum Mechanics* (Princeton University Press, Princeton, NJ, 1957).

FEYNMAN, R. P.; LEIGHTON, R. B.; and SANDS, M. *The Feynman Lectures in Physics,* 3 vols. (Addison-Wesley, Reading, MA, 1963–1965).

FRANK WILCZEK

SPIN, ELECTRON

Spin is an internal attribute of particles. It is associated with their having nonzero angular momentum when at rest. The fact that electrons carry spin is uniquely important. Electron spin plays a fundamental role in chemistry and in several aspects of the behavior of ordinary matter, especially magnetic phenomena.

Electrons carry spin $\frac{1}{2}$, which means that a measurement of the angular momentum, around a given axis, of a stationary electron will yield one of two possible results, that is $\pm\hbar/2$, where $\hbar = h/2\pi$ is the reduced Planck's constant.

There are two main physical effects of electron spin. First, it makes electrons into microscopic magnets that both generate and respond to magnetic fields. Second, it provides an additional internal degree of freedom for electrons. This is especially important in view of the Pauli exclusion principle, which states that no two electrons can occupy the same quantum state, a property that itself depends on the fact that electrons are fermions. In specifying the possible quantum states of an electron, we must allow for two directions of spin; thus, two electrons (with opposite spin orientations) are allowed to occupy a state that otherwise could accommodate just one, such as the lowest energy level in an atom.

Spin and Magnetism

According to classical electromagnetic theory, a rotating ball of electrically charged material will act as a magnetic dipole. It will generate a magnetic field, and conversely it will be perturbed by an imposed magnetic field.

The nature of this interaction with magnetic fields can be predicted, with astonishing precision, from fundamental theory. It leads to the expression

$$H = g\left(\frac{e}{2mc}\right)\mathbf{S} \cdot \mathbf{B} \qquad (1)$$

for the Hamiltonian, or energy operator, of the electron spin $\mathbf{S}$ in magnetic field $\mathbf{B}$. Here m is the mass of the electron, and g is a number (the g-factor), equal to

$$g = 2 + 2.31934400(80) \times 10^{-4} \text{ (experimental)}$$
$$= 2 + 2.31930492(200) \times 10^{-4} \text{ (theoretical)}. \quad (2)$$

The g-factor of an elementary point electron would be 2; numerically small, but fundamentally important, corrections to this value arise from quantum interactions between the magnetic field and the electron fields (so-called radiative corrections). The spectacular agreement between experimental determinations and the theoretical prediction marks one of the pinnacles of twentieth-century physics.

An immediate consequence of Eq. (1) is that in a magnetic field, the spin states with definite energy will be those in which the component of spin in the direction of $\mathbf{B}$ takes a definite value. The energy of one of these two states will be raised, and the energy of the other lowered, by an amount proportional to the magnitude of $\mathbf{B}$. Thus, spectral lines arising from transitions into or out of these states will be different from one another by an amount proportional to the magnitude of B. This is known as the Zeeman effect. This effect can be used, for example, to measure the strength of magnetic fields on the surface of the Sun.

One can also read Eq. (1) the other way—not only does a given magnetic field affect the electron, but the electron affects the field. Indeed, one finds that each spin acts as an elementary dipole (i.e., like a tiny bar magnet), contributing a field

$$\mathbf{B}(r) = \frac{ge}{2mc}\left(\frac{r^2\mathbf{S} - 3\mathbf{r}(\mathbf{S} \cdot \mathbf{r})}{|r|^5}\right) \qquad (3)$$

at position $\mathbf{r}$, measured from the electron as origin. The field of a single electron is miniscule, and when many spins are randomly aligned, their fields tend to cancel. However, if a large number of electrons line up in the same direction, their cumulative field can be significant. This is the source of ferromagnetism; the magnetic field of any permanent magnet is due to the alignment of the spins of some fraction of the electrons in the material.

Spin and Exclusion

To illustrate the significance of electron spin for chemistry, it is instructive to compare the properties of the first few atoms. A hydrogen atom contains a single electron. In the ground state its spatial wave function is in the lowest energy, $1s$ configuration. A (neutral) helium atom has two electrons. The Pauli exclusion principle states that these electrons cannot be in the same quantum state. Hence, if both are to take advantage of the lowest energy $1s$ configuration, they must have opposite spins. A lithium atom has three electrons, and they cannot all be accommodated in the $1s$ configuration. Thus, the lowest energy configuration for the electrons in lithium consists of a filled $1s$ configuration, with two electrons of opposite spin, and a single electron in the higher energy $2p$ shell. While the electrons in the inner shell are tightly bound and chemically inert, the electron in the outer shell is only loosely bound, and its orbit may be altered, or it may even be stripped off the atom altogether under the influence of other nearby atoms. This sort of argument starts to explain the unit valence of lithium. With many elaborations and refinements, similar ideas can be used to understand at least in a rough way the properties of atoms throughout the periodic table.

A beautiful, subtle interplay of spin and statistics leads to the existence of an additional, metastable form of helium (parahelium) and more generally to metastable spin-triplet states, which play an important role in many chemical and biological processes.

See also: ELECTROMAGNETISM; ELECTRON; ENERGY LEVELS; FERROMAGNETISM; PAULI'S EXCLUSION PRINCIPLE; SPIN; SPIN AND STATISTICS; ZEEMAN EFFECT

Bibliography

BETHE, H. A., and JACKIW, R. *Intermediate Quantum Mechanics,* 3rd ed. (Benjamin-Cummings, Menlo Park, CA, 1986).

KARPLUS, M., and PORTER, R. N. *Atoms and Molecules: An Introduction for Students of Physical Chemistry* (W. A. Benjamin, New York, 1970).

FRANK WILCZEK

SPIN AND STATISTICS

Spin and statistics, in the sense used in this entry, are two important, essentially quantum-mechanical, properties of elementary particles. The spin of such a particle is a measure of its intrinsic angular momentum, that is, the irreducible angular momentum it possesses when its center of mass is at rest. The quantum statistics of a given kind of particle (e.g., an electron) controls important aspects of the behavior of matter containing many indistinguishable particles of that kind (e.g., a uranium atom or a lump of metal containing many electrons). There are profound connections between spin and statistics.

Quantum Statistics

A fundamental rule of quantum mechanics instructs us to add the probability amplitudes for alternative pathways to the same final state. This rule marks a sharp difference between quantum mechanics and classical theory, since the classical theory would tell us to add the probabilities themselves, rather than the amplitudes. (Recall that the probability is the absolute square of the probability amplitude.)

The quantum rule for adding amplitudes has remarkable implications for the description of indistinguishable particles. To see this, consider a simple process wherein two indistinguishable particles begin at points A and B and arrive at points X and Y. Clearly, there are two ways that this might occur—the particle initially at A could arrive at X, and the one initially at B at Y (we write: $AB \rightarrow XY$); or alternatively, the particle starting at A could arrive at Y, with the one starting at B arriving at X ($AB \rightarrow YX$). According to the aforementioned rule, since the final state—particles at X and Y—is the same in both cases, one must add the amplitudes for these two alternatives. Similarly, if we have many identical particles, we must add the amplitudes for all processes taking the initial particles (in any order) into the given final configuration.

There is a very important variant on this procedure. The rule given above, that to obtain the total amplitude for final configuration X, Y one adds the amplitude for $AB \rightarrow XY$ to that for $AB \rightarrow YX$, is characteristic of only one class of particles, that is, bosons. For another class of particles, namely fermions, the procedure is instead to subtract these sub-amplitudes. More generally, for processes involving many fermions, the rule is to add amplitudes after attaching a change of sign if there have been an odd number of interchanges. Thus, for example, for fermions one would add the amplitudes for

$$ABC \rightarrow XYZ$$
$$ABC \rightarrow YZX$$
$$ABC \rightarrow ZXY$$

and subtract the amplitudes for

$$ABC \rightarrow YXZ$$
$$ABC \rightarrow ZYX$$
$$ABC \rightarrow XZY.$$

The Relation of Spin and Statistics

A particle is said to have spin s when a measurement of its spin angular momentum around an axis is constrained to give one of the values $s, s - 1, \ldots - s$ times the reduced Planck's constant $\hbar$. The spin can be a whole number $(0, 1, 2, \ldots)$ or alternatively half of an odd number $(\frac{1}{2}, \frac{3}{2}, \frac{5}{2}, \ldots)$. A most remarkable regularity is observed in nature: Particles of the first type are invariably bosons, while particles of the second type are invariably fermions.

This spin-statistics connection is one of the deepest general results of relativistic quantum field theory.

Spin and Exchange

The elementary rules for adding amplitudes are reflected in differing rules for the quantum-mechanical wave functions for assemblies of indistinguishable bosons and fermions. (For any system of particles, the quantum mechanical quantity known as the wave function is a position-dependent amplitude, the absolute square of which represents the probability distribution for the location and spin orientation of the particles.) The wave function for bosons is required to be unchanged by the interchange of two particles, while the wave function for fermions is required to change sign. One says the wave functions are symmetric or antisymmetric, respectively, in these two cases. An important, immediate consequence is the Pauli exclusion principle for fermions: Two indistinguishable fermions cannot be in the same quantum state. If they were, then interchanging them would not affect the overall physical state, yet the interchange must change the sign of the wave function. Thus, this wave function must therefore be equal to its own negative, which means it vanishes.

In the preceding discussion, it is important that the interchanges trade all the properties of the particles involved, including specifically their spin direction, not only their position. Thus, if two electrons are in a symmetric state (i.e., unchanged under interchange) for their spins, then their spatial wave function must be antisymmetric (i.e., changes sign under interchange), and vice versa, since electrons are fermions. Under many circumstances, the interactions that cause electrons to reorient their spins are small, and processes that depend on spins reorienting themselves are correspondingly slow. Thus, the lowest energy state of atomic helium in which the two electrons have symmetric spin, though it is higher in energy than the true ground state with antisymmetric spin, decays into the ground state only very slowly. Dilute helium gas therefore contains a mixture of these two distinct components, which are called parahelium and orthohelium. Heisenberg's theoretical elucidation of this puzzling behavior was one of the earliest successes of quantum mechanics. Metastable spin triplet states (symmetric in spin) of other molecules play an important role in photochemistry and biology, since any process that excites them provides a means for storing and transporting chemical energy.

See also: ELEMENTARY PARTICLES; FERMIONS AND BOSONS; PAULI'S EXCLUSION PRINCIPLE; SPIN; SPIN, ELECTRON; SYMMETRY; WAVE FUNCTION

Bibliography

DIRAC, P. A. M. *The Principles of Quantum Mechanics,* 2nd ed. (Clarendon Press, Oxford, Eng., 1935).

FEYNMAN, R. P., and WEINBERG, S. *Elementary Particles and the Laws of Physics: The 1986 Dirac Memorial Lectures* (Cambridge University Press, Cambridge, Eng., 1987).

FRANK WILCZEK

SPIN GLASS

Spin glasses are disordered magnetic materials. They comprise a relatively new class of magnetic systems with unusual and often puzzling behavior. Investigation of their properties has led to new ways of thinking about the relationships among thermodynamics, symmetry, and order, and has also revealed new insights into seemingly unrelated problems ranging from neural networks to optimization of multivariable systems.

Magnetic materials are composed of atoms which individually behave like tiny bar magnets (arising from electrons in incompletely filled inner atomic shells). When these atomic magnets interact with one another, large-scale magnetic phenomena can result.

The most familiar of these is called ferromagnetism. This is the kind of magnetism seen in permanent magnets, occurring as well in solid iron, nickel, cobalt, and other materials. Ferromagnetism arises when the interactions among nearby atomic magnets favor alignment, so that the total energy is lowest when all north poles are pointing in the same direction.

However, there are other possible ordered arrangements of atomic magnets (or spins, the electron property from which atomic magnetism ultimately arises). In antiferromagnets, the interaction between neighboring spins favors an antiparallel orientation, so that the energy is lowest when the south pole of one atomic magnet is pointing in the same direction as the north pole of its nearest neighbor. Antiferromagnetism is found in chromium, the oxides of certain metals, and many other compounds.

Spin glasses represent a peculiar mixture of the two, in which neighboring atomic magnets may prefer either to align, as in a ferromagnet, or antialign, as in an antiferromagnet, with roughly equal probability. Moreover, the ferromagnetic and antiferromagnetic interactions occur randomly throughout the material (or are situated in a complicated enough way as to be effectively random). This has been found to occur in certain dilute magnetic alloys and other compounds; the result is a new kind of magnetic system.

In a spin glass the atomic magnets, or spins, appear to be frozen in random orientations. Hence the name "spin glass": In ordinary glass, the atoms are frozen in random positions (see Fig. 1).

Unlike ferromagnets, a spin glass cannot find a configuration (i.e., arrangement of spins) that satisfies the alignment preferences between all pairs of neighboring spins. To illustrate, consider the simple case of only four spins arranged on a square, as in Fig. 2. Which spin configuration will satisfy *all* of the interactions? The answer is *none;* at least one interaction will always be violated. This conflict of internal interactions is called frustration, a concept whose applications stretch far beyond spin glass physics.

Frustration is not unique to spin glasses, but the combination of both frustration and the random placement of ferromagnetic and antiferromagnetic couplings (that is, the disorder) results in a magnetic solid with bizarre experimental features, as well as a singularly difficult system to analyze theoretically.

One such difficulty concerns the nature of the spin glass ground state. The ground state is the minimum energy configuration—ferromagnetic and antiferromagnetic ground states are shown in Fig. 1. While ferromagnets and unfrustrated antiferromagnets have a unique ground state (excluding uniform rotations of all the spins at once), certain mathematical models of spin glasses have been found to have many ground states. It is not yet known whether the

unusual feature of having many ground states applies to real spin glasses. Another central question of spin glass physics remains unresolved—whether the spin glass phase truly represents a new state of matter, like ferromagnetism or antiferromagnetism. (However, most physicists believe it does.)

Experimentally, spin glasses possess a number of intriguing (and again poorly understood) properties. When perturbed (e.g., by turning a magnetic field on and off), they respond extremely slowly. They often show memory effects—that is, a spin glass sample seems to "remember" the manner in which it was prepared. Thermodynamic measurements often seem to contradict one another, sometimes indicating that the change from paramagnet to spin glass is a true phase transition (like, for example, liquid to solid) and other times indicating the opposite. Much of the problem here stems from the difficulty of knowing when or if a spin glass has reached thermal equilibrium; this in turn is related to the very sluggish response of spin glasses to changes in external conditions.

Spin glasses are very complicated systems, but, as with many other things, their chief vices are also their main virtues—the dirtiness and messiness of a spin glass lend it quite readily to the mathematical modeling of interesting systems from neural networks, computer science, and biology.

What are the common features between spin glasses and these other systems? For one, the real world is "dirty"; many systems do not have simple, uniform interactions between their parts. Furthermore, not all of their internal constraints can be satisfied simultaneously, in analogy to the frustrated magnetic interactions in a spin glass. Finally, many problems exhibit many possible solutions, none of

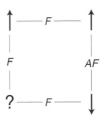

Figure 2 Frustrated interactions. The spin at the lower left corner cannot satisfy both its interactions simultaneously. Here F denotes a ferromagnetic interaction and AF denotes an antiferromagnetic interaction.

Figure 1 Ground state spin configurations for (a) a ferromagnet, (b) an antiferromagnet, and (c) a spin glass.

which are "perfect" (in the sense of satisfying all constraints). The study of spin glasses may result not only in a new way of looking at order and symmetry in physics, but also may serve as a bridge to other fields.

See also: ANTIFERROMAGNETISM; FERROMAGNETISM; MAGNETIC MATERIAL; MAGNETIZATION; PARAMAGNETISM

Bibliography

ANDERSON, P. W. "Spin Glass Hamiltonians: A Bridge Between Biology, Statistical Mechanics, and Computer Science" in *Emerging Syntheses in Science,* edited by D. Pines (Addison-Wesley, Redwood City, CA, 1988).

BINDER, K., and YOUNG, A. P. "Spin Glasses." *Rev. Mod. Phys.* **58**, 801–976 (1986).

CHOWDHURY, D. *Spin Glasses and Other Frustrated Systems* (World Scientific, Singapore, 1986).

MEZARD, M.; PARISI, G.; and VIRASORO, M. A. *Spin Glass Theory and Beyond* (World Scientific, Singapore, 1986).

STEIN, D. L. "Spin Glasses." *Sci. Am.* **260**, 52–59 (1989).

STEIN, D. L. *Spin Glasses and Biology* (World Scientific, Singapore, 1992).

DANIEL L. STEIN

SPINOR

A spinor is a pair of complex numbers used in quantum mechanics and was extended by Roger Penrose to the description of speed-of-light propagation of wave phenomenon. The concept of a spinor was introduced in quantum mechanics by Wolfgang Pauli to explain electron spin. It provides the mathematical basis to describe the "classical two-valuedness" observed in spin systems. The Pauli exclusion principle follows mathematically from this description. The two-valuedness arises because, for a spin system, rotation about any axis through 360° does not return the system to its original state; a full two rotations (720°) is necessary. The description of a spinor also requires the introduction of complex numbers (based on the concept that -1 has a square root, $i = \sqrt{-1}$, so $i \times i = -1$). Thus they have a natural importance in quantum mechanics, which is based on a complex number formulation. Although Erwin

Schrödinger's original description of quantum mechanics was based on a single complex number at each point of space (a single complex field), spin requires the introduction of a spinor described as a pair of complex numbers at every point of space.

The value of a spinor changes in a mathematically precise way under rotations. We may mathematically describe the rotation of physical quantities or objects. Objects we typically think of rotating correspond to vectors. For instance, the position of a point x, y, z in space is a vector; a rotation changes this vector in a certain way, which can be described by a rotation matrix. A rotation through the angle ϕ (radians) around the z axis gives a new position x', y', z' by $\sqrt{x'^2 + y'^2 + z'^2}$

$$\begin{pmatrix} x' \\ y' \\ z' \end{pmatrix} = \begin{pmatrix} \cos\phi & \sin\phi & 0 \\ -\sin\phi & \cos\phi & 0 \\ 0 & 0 & 1 \end{pmatrix} \begin{pmatrix} x \\ y \\ z \end{pmatrix}, \qquad (1)$$

which, by matrix algebra, gives for the new coordinants

$$x' = x\cos\phi + y\sin\phi$$
$$y' = -x\sin\phi + y\cos\phi \qquad (2)$$
$$z' = z.$$

The rotation leaves the z position unchanged as it should, and it also leaves the new point at the same distance from the origin as was the old point: $\sqrt{x'^2 + y'^2 + z'^2} = \sqrt{x^2 + y^2 + z^2}$. When a spinor undergoes rotation, a similar matrix operation occurs, which is simpler because the spinor has only two components, which we can denote by ζ^1, ζ^2

$$\begin{pmatrix} \zeta'^1 \\ \zeta'^2 \end{pmatrix} = \begin{pmatrix} u_1^1 & u_1^2 \\ u_1^2 & u_2^2 \end{pmatrix} \begin{pmatrix} \zeta^1 \\ \zeta^2 \end{pmatrix}. \qquad (3)$$

Thus $\zeta'^1 = u_1^1 \zeta^1 + u_2^1 \zeta^2$ for instance. The rotation around the z axis is very simple:

$$\begin{pmatrix} \zeta'^1 \\ \zeta'^2 \end{pmatrix} = \begin{pmatrix} e^{i\phi/2} & 0 \\ 0 & e^{i\phi/2} \end{pmatrix} \begin{pmatrix} \zeta^1 \\ \zeta^2 \end{pmatrix}, \qquad (4)$$

or $\zeta'^1 = e^{i\phi/2}\zeta^1$ and $\zeta'^2 = e^{i\phi/2}\zeta^2$. Notice that the half angle $\phi/2$ appears in the expression, and the complex number i is an essential part of the description. In a notation that emphasizes the components,

$$\zeta'^A = \sum_{B=1}^{2} U^A_B \zeta^B, \tag{5}$$

where $\Sigma^2_{B=1}$ means a sum of the terms for $B = 1$ and for $B = 2$. An important, at first sight innocuous, feature of this equation is that it relates quantities that inherently require complex numbers for their description. This means that the matrix equation

$$\zeta' = U\zeta \tag{6}$$

can be related to the complex conjugated equation

$$\overline{\zeta}' = \overline{U}\overline{\zeta}, \tag{7}$$

with the overbars indicating complex conjugation (complex conjunction replaces i by $-i$ everywhere).

There is more to physical transformations than simply rotations. Motion at high velocities (comparable to the speed of light) requires a description in terms of special relativity. The special theory of relativity demands that additionally we consider boosts, which are changes from one state of linear motion to the other. For vectors, this means considering time t as an additional component; one then has a four-dimensional matrix (a Lorentz Transformation matrix) acting on a four-dimensional point (three spatial dimensions plus time). Pauli introduced matrices that allow a connection between vectors and spinors. This relationship to vectors can be described by connecting a vector in four-dimension, x^α ($\alpha = 0, 1, 2, 3$, corresponding to t, x, y, z), to a pair of spinors, η^A, γ^B. Here A, B range over 1, 2, the number of components of a spinor. The explicit connection is

$$x^\alpha = \sum_{Z,B=1}^{2} \sigma^\alpha_{A\overline{B}}\, \eta^A \gamma^{\overline{B}} \quad x^\alpha \leftrightarrow \eta^A \gamma^{\overline{B}}, \tag{8}$$

where $\sigma^\alpha_{A\overline{B}}$ is a Pauli matrix and the bar over B indicates that one uses the complex coordinate transformation $\overline{U}$ to describe changes of $\gamma^{\overline{B}}$.

In general two spinors, as here with $\eta^A \gamma^{\overline{B}}$ are required. For the special case that x^α is a null vector

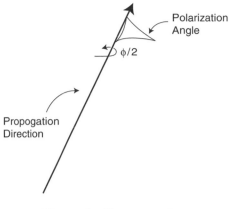

Figure 1   Penrose spinor.

(meaning it can be used to parameterize the direction of a light ray), then only one spinor is necessary to describe the vector

$$x^\alpha \leftrightarrow \zeta^A\, \overline{\zeta}^{\overline{A}} \tag{9}$$

if x^α is null.

The expression involves a spinor ζ, and its complex conjugate $\overline{\zeta}$. ($\overline{\zeta}^A$ is obtained from the fundamental spinor ζ^A simply by complex conjugating ζ^A, the components of ζ.) From this point of view we have replaced the four components of the null vector with the two components of a spinor. All analysis on radiation that travels at the speed of light (including gravitational radiation) then is greatly simplified because only half as many components need to be treated in the analysis.

Furthermore, the spinor ζ^A itself allows us to encode more information about the radiation field. Electromagnetic radiation (for instance, light) has a polarization as well as a propagation direction. First define a standard spinor; then rotate it around the propagation direction, as in Eq. (4). Then the complex phase of the spinor (the $i\phi/2$ from above) encodes the angle of polarization. Penrose thus draws a picture of a spinor as a flagpole pointing in the direction of the propagation direction, with a pennant that shows the angle of the polarization of the radiation, as shown in Fig. 1.

See also: LORENTZ TRANSFORMATION; PAULI'S EXCLUSION PRINCIPLE; QUANTUM MECHANICS; SCHRÖDINGER EQUATION

Bibliography

COHEN-TONNOUDJA, C.; DIU, B.; and LALOË, F. *Quantum Mechanics* (Wiley, New York, 1977).

MATZNER, R. A., and SHEPLEY, L. C. *Classical Mechanics* (Prentice Hall, Englewood Cliffs, NJ, 1991).

MISNER, C. W.; THORNE, K. S.; and WHEELER, J. A. *Gravitation* (W. H. Freeman, San Francisco, 1973).

PENROSE, R., and RINDLER, W. *Spinors and Space-Time* (Cambridge University Press, Cambridge, Eng., 1986).

RICHARD A. MATZNER

SPONTANEOUS SYMMETRY BREAKING

See SYMMETRY BREAKING, SPONTANEOUS

SQUID

See SUPERCONDUCTING QUANTUM INTERFERENCE DEVICE

STANDARD TEMPERATURE AND PRESSURE

In thermodynamics and chemical physics, it is frequently necessary to list a compact set of physical and chemical quantities that vary with temperature and pressure, such as density of air, thermal expansion coefficient of copper, or a certain chemical reaction rate. In such instances it is commonplace to list these quantities at a certain agreed-upon pressure and temperature, the standard temperature and pressure (STP). Almost invariably such an agreed-upon pressure is 1 atm, or 101,325 $N \cdot m^{-2}$, and this is referred to as the standard pressure. For temperature, even though the standard temperature is defined as 0°C (273.15 K), there are notable instances where the temperature at which these quantities are listed differs from 0°C.

Typically, quantities of significance at room temperature, such as thermal expansion coefficients of common metals and alloys, tend to be listed at room temperature and 1 atm. Properties of gases, on the other hand, are usually listed at STP. There are, however, exceptions. In some cases, such as the enthalpy of formation in the field of chemical thermodynamics, the standard temperature is generally taken as 25°C (298.15 K) and the standard pressure is 0.1 MPa (10^5 $N \cdot m^{-2}$), which is approximately equal to 1 atm.

See also: PRESSURE; TEMPERATURE

CARL T. TOMIZUKA

STANDING WAVE

When a stretched string is plucked, a complicated motion begins that quickly settles into a simple back-and-forth motion of the whole string. This is an example of a standing wave. The pattern of the oscillation in space depends on the length of the string and determines the frequency. Oscillation in a standing wave is not always visible: When a wind instrument is blown, a standing wave is set up in which the pattern of the pressure variation in space is determined by the shape of the instrument and determines the frequency. In all standing waves, a motion is excited in a confined space, and most of it damps out quickly, leaving a standing wave whose spatial pattern depends on the boundary and whose frequency is fixed by the spatial pattern. The mathematical description of the stretched string exhibits features of most standing waves, so it is useful as an example.

A point on the string can be designated by its distance x from one end and its displacement h from equilibrium. This displacement varies with both x and time t and, as long as it is not too large, can be written

$$h(x,t) = A \sin(2\pi x/\lambda) \cos(2\pi ft). \quad (1)$$

In this expression, A is the amplitude and is the maximum displacement from equilibrium; f is the frequency; and λ is the wavelength. The effect of the boundary may be described in the following way: If the length of the string is L, then $h(L, t) = 0$ because the ends do not move. Thus $\sin(2\pi L/\lambda) = 0$, so the wavelength must be

$$\lambda = 2L/n, \tag{2}$$

for $n = 1, 2, 3,\ldots$. Points that do not move are called nodes. In the simplest pattern, the fundamental, $n = 1$. Only the end points are nodes, while the rest of the string oscillates. In the first harmonic, $n = 2$, so the midpoint of the string is also a node while the two halves oscillate.

The expression for $h(x, t)$ can be rewritten using an identity from trigonometry:

$$h(x,t) = (A/2) \sin 2\pi(x/\lambda - ft)$$
$$+ (A/2) \sin 2\pi(x/\lambda - ft). \tag{3}$$

The standing wave is a sum of two traveling waves moving in opposite directions, both having speed v with

$$v = f\lambda. \tag{4}$$

Thus the spatial pattern, which is characterized by λ, fixes the frequency of the oscillation:

$$f = nf_1, \tag{5}$$

where $f_1 = v/2L$.

The physical mechanism that forms any standing wave can now be seen. When the string is plucked or any medium is excited, traveling waves race out toward the fixed boundary. Their motion conforms to Newton's laws, which fix the value of the speed. When the waves reach the boundary, any motion that tries to move the fixed boundary loses energy and is damped. Those motions that have a node at the boundary are simply reflected. After a few trips back and forth, only those waves with nodes at the boundaries remain, the standing waves. The nodes at the boundary allow only certain patterns to persist, and the frequency of the standing wave is fixed by this pattern. The explicit expression for these allowed frequencies is usually more complicated than the simple integer proportionality in Eq. (5).

See also: ELASTICITY; FOURIER SERIES AND FOURIER TRANSFORM; MOTION, HARMONIC; OSCILLATION; OSCILLATOR, HARMONIC; WAVE MOTION

Bibliography

PIERCE, J. R. *The Science of Musical Sound* (Scientific American Books, New York, 1983).

LARRY WEAVER

STARK EFFECT

The effect of an external uniform and constant electric field on the spectra of atoms was discovered by Johannes Stark in 1913 for the Balmer lines of atomic hydrogen. The investigation was prompted by the 1897 discovery of the splitting of atomic spectra by uniform magnetic fields, the Zeeman effect. It was soon given a theoretical explanation by Paul Epstein and Karl Schwarzschild in 1916 on the basis of Niels Bohr's "old quantum theory" of the hydrogen atom and was probably the greatest success of that theory. It is now understood as the effect of an electric field on the electron(s) as obtained from a solution of the Schrödinger equation, the basis of modern quantum theory.

If the shift of the atomic energy level (or spectral line frequency) is proportional to F, the magnitude of the electric field, then this is known as the linear Stark effect. Otherwise, for weak fields, the shift is proportional to F^2 and is the quadratic Stark effect. The linear effect can only occur when an unperturbed energy level, with angular momentum quantum number l, lies close to another level with either $(l + 1)$ or $(l - 1)$. Here "close" means that their energy difference is not much larger than the shift of either level due to the field. Excited states of atomic hydrogen fall into this class and provide the simplest example of the linear Stark effect. For example, in the first excited level (principal quantum number $n = 2$) the states whose energies depart from the unperturbed value symmetrically with a magnitude of 1.59×10^{-10} eV $= 2.5 \times 10^{-29}$ J for a field of 1 V/m. Evidently this is a small effect and

Stark needed fields of at least 10^7 V/m in order to observe the shifts. This explains why attempts to detect the effect about fourteen years earlier were unsuccessful.

The quadratic Stark effect is more common in atomic spectra and its simplest occurrence is in the ground state of atomic hydrogen. Its detailed explanation can only be given in the context of modern quantum theory, but a qualitative explanation follows: In the absence of the field the hydrogen ground state is spherically symmetric but the field causes equal but oppositely directed forces on the electron and proton in the atom. This distorts the atom resulting in an electric dipole moment whose magnitude is proportional to the field strength. The dipole then interacts with the field resulting in an energy shift which is proportional to the square of the field strength. This shift is written as

$$\Delta W = -\tfrac{1}{2}\alpha F^2, \tag{1}$$

where α is called the dipole polarizability of the state. For the hydrogenic ground state the shift is 2.34×10^{-20} eV $= 3.74 \times 10^{-39}$ J for an electric field of 1 V/m. The negative sign in the equation indicates that the shift is downward for this state as it is for any other ground state.

Calculations and measurements of the Stark shift for more complex atoms exist and in general they are somewhat larger than those in hydrogen.

More recently, a generalization of this phenomenon to time-dependent electric fields has been predicted and observed. This is the "dynamic Stark effect." The fields usually have sinusoidal time dependence with a period which is very long compared to the period of the electronic motion in an atom. Therefore it is a good approximation to treat the field as essentially constant as far as the electrons are concerned and Eq. (1) for the quadratic Stark effect still applies but the F occurring there is time-dependent. The time scale of the observation of the shift is long compared to that of the field so the observation is, in effect, a time average of Eq. (1). For a simple sinusoidal time dependence of the field this results in the interpretation of F, in Eq. (1), as the root-mean-square amplitude of the field.

Modern lasers can produce electric field with amplitudes of 10^{12} V/m and higher so observation of the quadratic and higher orders is common.

See also: FIELD, ELECTRIC; LASER; QUANTUM THEORY OF MEASUREMENT; SCHRÖDINGER EQUATION; SPECTROSCOPY, ATOMIC; ZEEMAN EFFECT

Bibliography

BRAMSDEN, B. H., and JOACHAIN, C. J. *Physics of Atoms and Molecules* (Longman, London, 1983).

COHEN-TANNOUDJI, C.; DIU, B.; and LALÖE, F. *Quantum Mechanics* (Wiley, New York, 1977).

MARVIN H. MITTLEMAN

STARS AND STELLAR STRUCTURE

From times before antiquity, people looked to the night sky and noted the positions, brightnesses, and colors of the glistening points called stars. With the first parallax measurements by Friedrich Wilhelm Bessel in 1838, distances were determined, and the way was set to begin understanding these objects. Combining apparent brightness and distance measurements, astronomers determine the rate at which a star radiates energy, its luminosity. The color, or spectrum, establishes the effective temperature of a star's surface. With the luminosity and effective temperature known, the radius can be found through the Stefan–Boltzmann relation. In binary systems (where two stars orbit around each other), Newton's laws and observations of the orbits give the masses. Finally, the absorption lines in a star's spectrum prescribe its surface composition. The elements that appear in stellar spectra vary tremendously with the surface temperature. However, analysis of the ionization and excitation state of the stellar surface (using the Saha and Boltzmann equations) shows the composition to be mostly hydrogen (70 to 76 percent by mass) and helium (24 to 28 percent by mass), with all other elements typically amounting to 2 percent or less of a star's mass.

More than a century before these measurements were made, astronomers suspected that the Sun was a typical star. As a common star, the Sun's luminosity, surface temperature, radius, and mass provide useful units for describing other stars:

$$L_{sun} = 3.89 \times 10^{33} \text{ erg/s}$$

$$T_{eff} = 5760 \text{ K}$$

$$R_{sun} = 6.95 \times 10^{10} \text{ cm}$$

$$M_{sun} = 1.99 \times 10^{33} \text{ g.}$$

Stars were found to be quite diverse, with stellar radii and luminosities ranging from less than 1 percent of the solar values to well over 1,000 times those of the Sun. The mass range is less dramatic, with few stars seen with less than half of the Sun's mass or more than 10 solar masses. The surface temperatures of these objects ranged from a few thousand kelvins for the reddest stars to well over 20,000 K for the bluish-white ones.

Stars with very large radii are called giants or supergiants. Giant stars are commonly redder than the Sun, and those having temperatures below about 4,500 K are known as red giants. Other stars were found to have radii near that of Earth, yet to be nearly as massive as the Sun. These small, hot, faint objects became known as white dwarfs. With average densities of more than 1 ton/cm^3, they presented physicists of the 1920s with a dilemma of how atoms could be packed so closely together. It was only with the development of Fermi statistics and degeneracy pressure that this problem was resolved. While stars were seen with extreme sizes, most were found to have radii between a half and a few times the radius of the Sun. When plotted on a diagram of intrinsic luminosity versus temperature (or color), these stars form a diagonal band from the hot luminous corner to the cool faint corner (see Fig. 1). This band became known as the main sequence.

With this information, astronomers could ask why the stars along the main sequence differed from each other, and how stars of the same mass could appear as a giant, a main sequence star, or a white dwarf. Answering these questions required a physical understanding of a star's interior structure. The high surface temperatures and composition required them to be gaseous, so an equation of state (a thermodynamic relation among the temperature, pressure, density, and composition) constrains the conditions found in stars. In most stars, the equation of state is near that of a perfect gas, but giants and white dwarfs may require a more sophisticated treatment, including the effects of degeneracy. Neutron stars required an even more exotic equation of state to account for the effects of the strong force on densely packed nucleons.

While some stars were observed to pulsate, most stars were seen to be very stable. Even the pulsating stars appeared to be oscillating about an equilibrium configuration. This stability can be expressed by the equations of hydrostatic equilibrium. The first of these equations is derived from Newton's law relating forces and acceleration. For a star to be stable, there must be no accelerations; all of the forces must balance each other. At *each point* in the star the inward pulling force of gravity must equal the outward pushing pressure gradient, the pressure difference between the gas interior to that point and exterior to it. This is written with a differential equation and if the balance is not maintained the radius changes in a matter of hours to days. In the center of the star, the pressure must be high enough to support all of the star's mass against the pull of gravity, so the pressure is highest at the center. This balance fails weakly in the outer regions of pulsating variables and more dramatically in eruptive variables like novas. It fails completely when a star evolves to a point where it becomes a supernova. Detailed modeling of unstable stars requires an equation in which acceleration and momentum terms are included. A second equation for hydrostatic equilibrium describes the material distribution in the star.

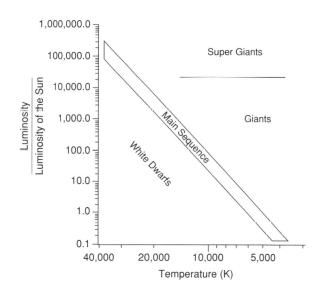

Figure 1 Astronomers call a plot of the luminosity versus temperature (or color) an HR diagram, after Einar Hertzsprung and Henry Norris Russell. Nearly 90 percent of the stars lie along the band called the main sequence. Giants and supergiants lie above the main sequence, while white dwarfs are below.

This equation relates the mass, volume, and density in each portion of the star. Stability requires the density to continuously decrease from the center of the star to its surface, so a particular density exists only in a small region of a star. As a result, this equation is also a differential equation relating the density to changes in volume (or radius in a spherical star) and mass.

Inside a star, the local luminosity is the rate at which energy flows past any point. Conservation of energy requires that changes in that luminosity are equal to the local energy production (or loss) rates. The equation balancing changes in the luminosity with local energy production is called the equation of thermal equilibrium. The importance of nuclear energy generation by fusion as an energy source is inarguably attested to by the surface abundances of some stars and the observed neutrino emissions from the Sun. The neutrino emission rate of the Sun is not exactly at the predicted value, but it is sufficiently close to require that nearly all of the solar luminosity results from fusion. In fact, the difference in neutrino emission rates may not result from small errors in the calculation of the solar interior, but from currently unknown properties of neutrinos (masses, mixing angles). The slow composition change associated with nuclear fusion requires stars to evolve. Calculating a temporal sequence of stellar structures that includes this composition change is called stellar evolution, and this theory has been remarkably successful in linking the various types of stars as evolutionary phases. Depending on the composition structure, a star of 1 solar mass may be a pre–main sequence star, a main sequence star, a red giant star, a horizontal branch star, or a white dwarf.

Another source of energy that can be important for short periods is gravitational potential energy. This source is insufficient to provide the energy of a star for more than a few thousand to 10 million years (depending on the star), but whenever a star's luminosity is not equal to its nuclear energy production rate, gravitational energy becomes important. When a main sequence star expands to become a giant, the material in its outer regions absorbs some of the excess nuclear energy and expands. This lifts the mass against gravity, storing potential energy. Conversely, when nuclear energy generation is insufficient to provide the energy radiated by a star, the star's material is compressed and heated by gravity. The additional energy is added to the luminosity. Gravitational energy is also important in some types of supernovas. When stability fails in the core of a massive star, it collapses to form a neutron star, or a black hole. The sudden collapse liberates a tremendous amount of gravitational energy ($> 10^{53}$ erg) in a matter of seconds.

For fusion to provide the energy that stars radiate into space, stars must maintain internal temperatures of more than 10 million K. This energy production occurs in the deep interiors of stars and must be transported to the cooler surfaces. This energy transport can be done by the diffusion of radiation from the hot interior to the cooler exterior. In stars where the energy production is too vigorous to be transported by diffusion, or where the material is too opaque for radiation diffusion to be efficient, the material will heat, and hot bubbles of material become buoyant. These bubbles rise up, carrying the energy in a process called convection. In stars like white dwarfs, where the electrons become degenerate, conduction can also contribute to the energy transport. At each position in the star, an equation is chosen to represent the dominant mode of energy transport.

A star must satisfy these relations at every point in its interior. The four differential equations can be differenced with respect to a star's mass or radius. When the differences are taken with respect to mass, the equations are in Lagrangian form; when taken with respect to radius, they are in Eulerian form. The choice of differencing method depends on the method of integration, the question being addressed, and personal preference. When calculating a set of stellar structures for an evolutionary sequence, the mass remains constant, while the radius changes. Lagrangian coordinates are more convenient for this type of calculation. Eulerian coordinates may be preferred when studying a particular star of known radius.

Solving first-order differential equations requires a boundary condition for each equation. In stars, two of these conditions are determined at the center, where the mass and luminosity go to zero (there can be nothing interior to $r = 0$, so at this point $m = 0$ and $L = 0$). At the surface of the star, the mass is equal to the total mass of the star. Here, the pressure and temperature must drop to zero ($P = T = 0$), as there is no more material. The visible surface of the star is slightly inside of this boundary, at a point where the Stefan–Boltzmann equation relates the temperature to the luminosity and radius.

To summarize the problem, there are seven variables defining each point of a star's interior: pres-

Table 1 Stellar Models[a]

Mass (solar masses)	Radius (solar radii)	Luminosity (solar luminosities)	$T_{surface}$ (K)	$T_{central}$ (million K)	Central Density (gm/cm^3)
Homogeneous (Main Sequence) Models					
0.6	0.56	0.10	4,381	10.1	69
0.8	0.68	0.24	4,872	11.5	76
1.0[b]	0.89	0.68	5,565	13.3	79
4.0	2.49	223.0	14,138	24.7	26
10.0	4.09	5,463.0	24,490	31.0	8
Inhomogeneous (Red Giant) Model					
1.0[c]	92.70	1,340.0	3,630	69.1	697,000

[a]Composition (by mass): 70 percent hydrogen, 28 percent helium, and 2 percent all other elements.

[b]This model is appropriate for the *early* Sun, not for the present Sun; the Sun has evolved for 4.5 billion years and is no longer homogeneous.

[c]This model has a degenerate helium core of 0.43 solar masses with a hydrogen-rich envelope of 0.57 solar masses.

sure, temperature, density, luminosity, radius, mass, and composition. Choosing mass or radius as the coordinate for the differential equations makes one of them a dependent variable, reducing the problem to six independent variables. With the five equations described (four differential equations plus an equation of state), a solution to these equations can be found by specifying one of the remaining independent variables. The composition of a star's surface can be observed, and an assumption of homogeneity is reasonable for stars that have just formed from a cloud of interstellar gas. For a specified composition and total mass, these equations can be integrated to determine the pressure, temperature, density, luminosity, radius, and mass at any position in the star. These results are usually called a stellar model.

Calculating homogeneous stellar models in which the nuclear energy generation just equals the radiated luminosity reproduces the stars of the main sequence. Stars with lower masses than the Sun lie at the faint cool end, while stars with higher mass are at the bright hot end of this diagonal band. Some results of such calculations are presented in Table 1. Careful observations of pressure waves on the surface of the Sun have permitted a seismic probing of the Sun's structure in the outer half of its radius (outer 20 percent of its mass). These observations are in very good agreement with the calculated structure. Continued observations will ultimately determine the Sun's structure in deeper regions. It is not necessary to use a homogeneous composition, and some

structure calculations assume that fusion has converted all of the hydrogen in the center of the star into a core of helium. The structure calculated for these inhomogeneous stars have huge radii like giant stars. The more mass that is assumed to be in the core, the larger and brighter the giant. Such models are often used as a starting place for understanding pulsating giants like Cepheids.

Nearly all stellar structure calculations are made with the assumption that stars are spherically symmetric. In the absence of rapid rotation, or the tidal effects of a close companion, this is an excellent approximation and sufficient to understand observed stellar behavior. There are, however, stars distorted by rotating near their breakup velocity and stars in close binary systems. While calculations that assume spherical symmetry may provide a general understanding of the structure of these stars, the assumption of sphericity may compromise our understanding of some aspects of these stars. Nevertheless, stellar structure calculations remain a powerful tool for understanding an individual star or class of stars.

See also: BLACK HOLE; NEUTRINO, SOLAR; NEUTRON STAR; NOVA; PARALLAX; RED GIANT; STEFAN–BOLTZMANN LAW; STELLAR EVOLUTION; SUN; SUPERNOVA

Bibliography

CHANDRASEKHAR, S. *An Introduction to the Study of Stellar Structure* (Dover, New York, 1967).

COX, J. P., and GIULI, R. T. *Principles of Stellar Structure* (Gordon and Breach, New York, 1968).

SCHWARZSCHILD, M. *Structure and Evolution of the Stars* (Princeton University Press, Princeton, NJ, 1958).

DAVID S. P. DEARBORN

STATE, EQUATION OF

The thermodynamic state of a system is characterized by a set of directly observable quantities that specify the system completely. These quantities are called the state variables. An equation of state describes the relationship between the state variables. For example, the state of an ideal gas is determined by its pressure P, volume V, mole number n, and temperature T. The equation of state of an ideal gas is $PV = nRT$, where T must be expressed as absolute temperature and R is a universal constant of nature called the gas constant. The gas constant is defined per mole gas substance and has a value of $R = 8.314$ $J \cdot mol^{-1} \cdot K^{-1}$. Because of the equation of state, the state of an ideal gas is already determined when three of the above state variables are given. The fourth state variable can be calculated from these three variables. By introducing the molar volume $v = V/n$, the ideal gas equation of state can be written more briefly as $Pv = RT$.

Two physical quantities that are easily accessible to measurement can be derived from the equation of state by differentiation: the coefficient of volume thermal expansion, $\beta = (1/V) \, \partial V / \partial T$, and the compressibility, $\kappa = (1/V) \, \partial V / \partial P$. For elastic properties of solids the quantity reciprocal to κ, that is the elastic bulk modulus $B = \kappa^{-1}$ rather than the compressibility is commonly used. By measuring the quantities β and κ one can obtain (through integration) empirical equations of state for any substance.

The ideal gas equation of state can be derived with the kinetic theory of gases by applying the laws of classical mechanics to gas molecules subject to two idealizing assumptions. These assumptions are (1) that the molecules have no size (point particles), and (2) that no forces act between the molecules. Consequently, the molar volume v of an ideal gas results only from the motion of the point particles, and the pressure P results from elastic impact forces of the point particles on the walls of the gas container.

When any actual gas (commonly called a real gas), such as oxygen, nitrogen, or water vapor, is much diluted, it approaches the properties of an ideal gas. On a conceptual level this is easy to see. The molecules of a real gas do, of course, have a size and they do interact with each other through intermolecular forces. However, when a real gas is very diluted, the size of the molecules that comprise the gas is *relatively* small, and therefore negligible, compared to the volume between the molecules. Also, the intermolecular forces, always decreasing with larger intermolecular distance, become negligibly weak in a diluted real gas because of the wide separation of the molecules.

The success of the ideal gas concept indicates what kind of improvements are necessary to obtain an equation of state for a real (nondiluted) gas. The improvements must take into account the self-volume of the molecules and the intermolecular forces. Since intermolecular forces are only approximately known, there are various ways for formulating real gas equations of state depending on intended emphasis and accuracy. One such equation of state for real gases is the van der Waals equation of state $(P + a/v^2) (v - b) = RT$. This equation of state was empirically derived and contains empirical constants a and b. The term a/v^2, sometimes called self-pressure, is a correction due to the intermolecular forces. The other term, b, is called the self-volume and is closely related to the molecular size. Historically, the van der Waals equation of state was a major step in the development of thermodynamics because its validity extends even to the phase transition between gases and liquids, that is, to condensation and boiling.

Very sophisticated equations of state, providing a link between thermodynamic properties of a system (state variables) and molecular properties of the system's molecules, can be derived with the methods of statistical mechanics. In its most general form the equation of state of a gas is given as a power series, $Pv = RT [1 + B(T)/v + C(T)/v^2 + \ldots]$, called the virial equation of state. The temperature-dependent quantities $B(T)$ and $C(T)$ are the virial coefficients. They contain information about intermolecular forces. Notice that neglecting the intermolecular forces amounts to vanishing virial coefficients, $B(T) = 0$, $C(T) = 0$, and so on, which reduces the virial equation of state to the one of the ideal gas.

Studies of gases use the ideal gas as a reference. For the study of liquids a different, idealizing model that contains the dominant features of liquids serves as a reference. This is the hard-sphere model of fluids where the intermolecular forces are assumed to be (1) infinitely strong to prevent molecular deformation of molecules in contact, and (2) zero beyond molecular contact. From these assumptions a hard-sphere equation of state can be derived, $Pv = RT (1 + y + y^2 = y^3)/(1 - y^3)$, where $y = \pi N_A d^3/(6v)$, N_A is the Avogadro number, and d is the diameter of the sphere. For $d = 0$ the ideal gas equation of state is retrieved.

Studies of the equation of state of solids use the Debye model of lattice vibrations as a reference system. In that model it is assumed that the crystal can be represented as an assembly of harmonic oscillators with oscillator frequencies ν up to some maximum value ν^*. The maximum (or cutoff) frequency is determined by the number of standing lattice waves (modes) that are possible for the system. The explicit equation of state is too complicated to exhibit here. The maximum frequency of the Debye model is used to define a temperature, the Debye temperature, $\Theta_D = h\nu^*/k_B$. The Debye temperature serves as a convenient thermal characterization of a solid since it can be readily inferred from heat-capacity measurements. If the temperature of a solid is above its Debye temperature, $T > \Theta_D$, then the thermal properties of the solid are classical. If $T < \Theta_D$, quantum-mechanical effects are involved. More accurate theories of solids modify the Debye model by calculating harmonic, or even anharmonic, oscillator frequencies from lattice interaction parameters.

See also: GAS; GAS CONSTANT; IDEAL GAS LAW; KINETIC THEORY; SPECIFIC HEAT OF SOLIDS; THERMODYNAMICS, HISTORY OF; VAN DER WAALS FORCE

Bibliography

SEARS, F. W., and SALINGER, G. L. *Thermodynamics*, 3rd ed. (Addison-Wesley, Reading, MA, 1975).

MANFRED BUCHER

STATES, DENSITY OF

Density of states is a concept used in the quantum mechanical description of properties. Density alone is a familiar concept. A common, general definition is the amount of a given entity per spatial unit. Thus, the density of a solid is expressed as mass per unit volume; the density of a string is expressed as mass per unit length; and a population density is expressed as the number of people per unit area. A study of quantum mechanics teaches us that entities do not exist in some continuous distribution; instead, they are associated with specific quantum states. Quantum mechanics also indicates that as the energy of a quantum system of states becomes less precisely known, then the lifetime of the system correspondingly increases. In the macroscopic world of our common experiences both the scale of final energy and the total number of states needed to produce an observed entity astronomically exceed the corresponding quantities for a single state. Thus, density is found by counting the long-lived, observed entities per spatial unit.

In the microscopic world of quantum mechanics counting must take a different form. Long-lived entities and well-defined energy states are still useful concepts but the entities of interest can make transitions between these states. Thus, any description of properties must involve both the number of entities involved and the states that they occupy. In addition, since the entities may change states as time progresses, the occupancy of states must be described by some form of statistical average. Entities like electrons obey Fermi–Dirac statistics and only one electron of each spin can occupy a state. Entities like photons (a quantum unit of light) obey Bose–Einstein statistics and there is no limit to the number of photons that can occupy a state. For entities of either type, descriptions of properties and the necessary averaging are expedited by use of a density of states which is usually the number of states per unit energy. Any property of interest is related to the density of filled states multiplied by the probability of a transition to an empty state multiplied by the density of empty states available to be occupied. This product of three terms is then summed over the energy range that is available for transitions.

A brief discussion of several examples of electronic properties may help clarify the ideas involved. Consider the movement of electrons within materials. All materials contain electrons and thus there is a density of occupied states. An applied electric field exerts a force upon an electron which changes its energy and creates the probability of making transitions to new states. But materials differ in the availability of empty mobile electron states. Good conductors like metals have a large density of empty mobile states even for very small energy changes; semiconductors have a zero density of empty mobile states for small energy changes and a small density of these states for larger energy changes; insulators have a zero density of empty mobile states for a wide range of energy changes and thus are very poor conductors. Consider the excitation of electrons within materials; that is, the transition of electrons into localized states. Once again a density of occupied states exists and the exciting stimulus causes an energy change and produces a transition probability. However, an actual transition only occurs if there is a nonzero density of empty states at the energy change caused by the stimulus. Materials are optical transparent when the needed density of empty states is small and few transitions occur (weak absorption); materials are opaque when that density is large and causes many transitions (strong absorption). Lasers require a coherent transition between two localized states and the density of states is an important parameter in determining the power of the laser.

See also: CONDUCTION; ELECTRON; EXCITED STATE; LASER; PHOTON; QUANTUM MECHANICS; SEMICONDUCTOR; THERMAL CONDUCTIVITY

Bibliography

MENDELSSOHN, K. *Quest for Absolute Zero* (Halsey, New York, 1977).

SCURLOCK, R. G. *Low-Temperature Behaviour of Solids* (Dover, New York, 1966).

C. L. FOILES

STATICS

Statics is the branch of mechanics that deals with the forces on nonrotating rigid bodies at rest or in equilibrium. As such, it is distinguished from the other main branch of mechanics, called dynamics, which deals with the motions of bodies subject to external forces. Although it may seem strange to distinguish the special case where there is no motion (or more properly, no acceleration), this case is of considerable importance since many man-made structures such as bridges and buildings are and should re-

main static. Statics is thus often studied along with the strength of materials since it allows one to calculate the forces that these materials will be subjected to in engineering structures.

There are two requirements to be satisfied so that a rigid body is static. First, there should be no net acceleration of the center of mass of the body. Using Newton's second law, this requirement can be restated as the sum of the forces on the body must be equal to zero. The second condition is that there should be no net angular acceleration about any point. This means that there is no net torque on the body. The fundamental tool used for analyzing static systems is that of vector analysis of forces, which allows one to add and subtract forces in a consistent manner.

As an example of statics calculation consider the system shown in Fig. 1, where a shelf is hinged at the wall and supported by a string attached 40 cm above. If the shelf is made of a uniform material of mass $m = 10$ kg and is 30 cm wide, one can calculate the force on the shelf due to the wall and the minimum load that the string must be able to bear in order to support the shelf without any other objects on it. Taking the forces in order, there is first the weight of the shelf, given by the mass multiplied by the acceleration due to gravity (g). This acts through

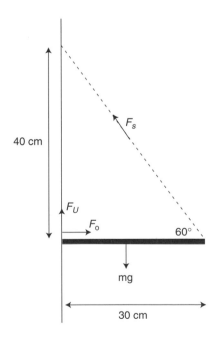

Figure 1 Illustration for statics calculation of shelf hinged to a wall and supported by a string.

the center of mass, which, since the shelf is uniform, occurs at the shelf midpoint. There is also the force on the shelf due to the wall, which can be resolved into two perpendicular components F_O and F_U. Finally there is the force due to the tension of the string F_S. Resolving the forces in the vertical and horizontal directions and requiring a balance of forces in each direction gives

$$F_s \sin(60°) + F_U = mg$$

and

$$F_S \cos(60°) = F_O,$$

respectively.

There also must be zero net torque due to these forces. It can be shown that for a body that is not accelerating, if the torque is zero about any one arbitrary point, then it is zero about any other point. Choosing the hinge as the arbitrary point leads to

$$0.3 \times F_S \sin(60°) = 0.15 \times mg.$$

These equations are sufficient to solve for all the unknown forces to yield $F_S = 56.64$ N, $F_O = 28.32$ N and $F_U = 49.05$ N.

See also: CENTER OF MASS; CENTER-OF-MASS SYSTEM; EQUILIBRIUM; FORCE; GRAVITATIONAL FORCE LAW; NEWTON'S LAWS; RIGID BODY; WEIGHT

Bibliography

FISHBANE, P. M.; GASIOROWICZ, S.; and THORNTON, S. T. *Physics for Scientists and Engineers* (Prentice Hall, Englewood Cliffs, NJ, 1993).

JOHN P. SHARPE

STATIONARY STATE

A stationary state is one whose probability of existing is independent of time. The term is most often used in quantum mechanics or wave mechanics to describe one property of an energy level of an atom or atomic nucleus. In a more general context, stationary states also exist as standing waves for any wave phenomenon, such as an acoustic wave in a tube or an electromagnetic wave in a waveguide.

To picture a stationary state, consider the following analogy from the physics of sound. Imagine that you bow a violin (or other simple stringed instrument) and try to play a single note. A wave motion forms on the string because of the pulling action of the bow. If just the right note is struck, the pattern of this wave will be a standing wave, with its greatest amplitude where the string was bowed and no amplitude of vibration at the ends of the string. If no energy escapes from the vibrating string, then there is no sound and the vibration will be that of a stationary state. When there is a sound, some energy escapes and the state is not completely independent of time.

Thus, stationary states of systems, such as atoms, their nuclei, or violin strings, are, strictly speaking, only *quasi*-stationary. That is, either in the remote past they did not exist, or in the distant future they will not exist. To see why this is so, consider a very ancient rock found on Earth. The molecules in the rock cannot be much older than Earth, and its atoms cannot be older than the nucleosynthesis stellar material from which Earth was formed. On the other hand, if a quasi-stationary state does not interact with something else, or decay into some detectable remnants (as in radioactivity), or emit light (electromagnetic radiation), then there is no way of knowing that it exists. From the viewpoint of quantum mechanics, there is no way to measure that it has existence.

The relationship between the lifetime of a (quasi-) stationary state and the lower limit to the uncertainty with which its energy can be measured is given by Heisenberg's uncertainty principle. A long-lived stationary state can have a very small uncertainty in energy and vice versa.

See also: ATOM; ENERGY LEVELS; QUANTUM MECHANICS; RADIOACTIVITY; STANDING WAVE; UNCERTAINTY PRINCIPLE; WAVE MECHANICS

Bibliography

LANDAU, R. H. *Quantum Mechanics II*, 2nd ed. (Wiley, New York, 1996).
MESSIAH, A. *Quantum Mechanics* (Wiley, New York, 1961).

WILLIAM J. THOMPSON

STATISTICAL MECHANICS

The purpose of statistical mechanics is the description of the macroscopic properties of systems made up of a large number N of atoms or molecules. Statistical mechanics grew out of the nineteenth century kinetic theory of gases which sought to provide a microscopic, molecular interpretation of the laws of thermodynamics. The objectives of statistical mechanics include: (1) finding expressions for macroscopic quantities such as pressure, temperature, internal energy, and entropy in terms of microscopic properties such as molecular mass, velocity, and potential energy; (2) deriving equations of state for specific materials; (3) determining measured thermodynamic quantities in terms of fundamental microscopic constants; and (4) determining relaxation rates for nonequilibrium processes.

As an equilibrium example, consider n moles of an ideal gas in volume V at pressure P and temperature T. The thermodynamic equation of state found empirically is

$$PV = nRT, \qquad (1)$$

in which R is the measured gas constant: $R = 8.3145$ $\text{J·K}^{-1}\text{·mol}^{-1}$. Statistical mechanics adds the molecular interpretation that

$$R = N_A k, \qquad (2)$$

where $N_A = 6.0221 \times 10^{23}$ is Avogadro's number and $k = 1.3807 \times 10^{-23}$ J/K is Boltzmann's constant [the total number of molecules in Eq. (1) is $N = nN_A$]. This interpretation is arrived at by performing an equilibrium statistical mechanical calculation based on the fundamental probabilistic centerpiece of the theory, the partition function Z. Associated with an N molecule system is a Hamiltonian energy function H that depends on the molecular coordinates and their conjugate momenta. The partition function Z is defined by

$$Z = \sum \exp(-H/kT), \qquad (3)$$

in which $\sum$ symbolizes either a continuous integral or a discrete sum as determined by which type of variables is appropriate in a particular case. This definition works equally well for classical mechanical and quantum mechanical descriptions. In the former case, one usually has integrals, in which case $\sum$ is divided by certain constant factors that make Z dimensionless, whereas in the latter case one usually has discrete summations that represent the trace operation of linear algebra since the quantum H is an operator. The volume V of the system explicitly enters Z through either the limits of coordinate integration in the classical case or through the energy eigenvalues of H in the quantum mechanical case. Therefore, Z is explicitly a function of N, T, and V. The thermodynamic quantities, such as internal energy U and entropy S, are determined by thermodynamic formulas from the Helmholtz free energy F defined in terms of Z by

$$F = -kT \ln Z. \qquad (4)$$

The difficult step in implementing this prescription in general is the execution of $\sum$ in Eq. (3). For an ideal gas, $\sum$ is elementary and one easily derives the equation of state in Eq. (1) with R given as in Eq. (2).

The heart of the partition function definition, Eq. (3), is the Boltzmann factor, $\exp(-H/kT)$. The kinetic energy portion of this factor is proportional to the Maxwell distribution for the momenta of molecules in thermal equilibrium. From this distribution, we obtain an expression for the temperature T in terms of the average value of the kinetic energy per molecule. The potential energy portion of the Boltzmann factor is proportional to the Boltzmann distribution for the coordin-ates of the molecules in thermal equilibrium. From this distribution, we obtain an expression for a contribution to the pressure P in terms of the intermolecular potential energy (a kinetic energy contribution also arises from the Maxwell distribution). These distributions are valid for gases, liquids, and solids.

An example of the determination of a measured thermodynamic quantity in terms of fundamental constants is given by the Stefan–Boltzmann law for blackbody radiation. Ludwig Boltzmann used the first law of thermodynamics, that is, conservation of energy, and two empirical laws for blackbody radiation to deduce on purely thermodynamic grounds that the energy density of the radiation is proportional to the fourth power of the temperature:

$$\frac{U}{V} = CT^4 \qquad (5)$$

in which C is an empirical constant of proportionality. From thermodynamics alone, it is impossible to determine C. A measurement must be done. The two empirical blackbody laws are that the pressure is one-third times the energy density and that the energy density is a function of temperature only. These laws imply the blackbody radiation equation of state but they cannot be justified on purely thermodynamic grounds. However, statistical mechanics not only enables us to derive both empirical laws (by using the Planck distribution for electromagnetic energy), but it also yields an explicit expression for C in terms of fundamental microscopic constants. In parallel with Eq. (5), the flux of energy (ergs per square centimeter per second) J depends on temperature T according to the Stefan–Boltzmann law

$$J = \sigma T^4 \qquad (6)$$

in which the Stefan–Boltzmann constant, $\sigma = 5.671 \times 10^{-8}\ \text{W}\cdot\text{m}^{-2}\cdot\text{K}^{-4}$, is $c/4$ times C:

$$\sigma = \frac{2}{15}\frac{\pi^5 k^4}{c^2 h^3} \qquad (7)$$

in which $c = 2.9979 \times 10^8\ \text{m}\cdot\text{s}^{-1}$ is the speed of light in a vacuum and $h = 6.6261 \times 10^{-34}\ \text{J}\cdot\text{s}$ is Planck's constant. This reduction of a measured quantity to a formula in fundamental constants is one of the outstanding achievements of statistical mechanics.

Statistical mechanics also explains nonequilibrium thermodynamic phenomena. The prototype example is Brownian motion, a phenomenon in which a small particle immersed in a fluid experiences a random force caused by collisions with the fluid molecules and executes a random motion. A collection of Brownian particles with an arbitrary initial distribution of velocities will evolve in time to a collection with a Maxwellian distribution of velocities. The rate at which this transition occurs may be determined from statistical mechanics. The rate is intimately related to the random forces caused by the fluid molecules interacting with the Brownian particles. The mean square correlation strength of these force fluctuations is proportional to the rate. This rate is called the dissipation rate since the redistribution of velocities is accompanied by an overall increase in entropy and converts whatever coherent initial motion the collection might have had into heat. The proportionality between fluctuation correlation strength and dissipation rate is called the fluctuation-dissipation relation. Such a fluctuation-dissipation relation underlies every relaxation process observed in macroscopic nonequilibrium processes.

In electrical systems, the fluctuation–dissipation relation connects current fluctuations (or voltage fluctuations) with the electrical resistance of the circuit. In fluid systems, analogous connections exist connecting momentum flux fluctuations with viscosity and heat flux fluctuations with thermal conductivity. In chemical systems, fluctuations in reaction-progress-variable velocities are connected with reaction rates. These are a few of the examples of the generality of the fluctuation-dissipation relation perspective for nonequilibrium processes.

Microscopic molecular fluctuations provide a deep insight into thermodynamic processes and properties. One especially dramatic display of this fact is given by light scattering from a fluid in thermodynamic equilibrium. From a purely macroscopic point of view, an equilibrium fluid exhibits no change, but from a microscopic, statistical mechanical viewpoint, an equilibrium fluid exhibits incessant molecular fluctuations. Light scattering detects spatial and temporal correlations in these fluctuations. Because the fluctuation-dissipation relation connects equilibrium fluctuations with nonequilibrium, dissipative rate parameters, it is possible to determine these rates with light scattering from an equilibrium fluid. Such light scattering yields the Rayleigh–Brillouin spectrum from which one quantitatively deduces values for the coefficients of viscosity and heat conductivity, for the speed of sound and for the sound attenuation coefficient. Otherwise, determination of these values requires macroscopic measurements on nonequilibrium states of the fluid. Similarly, in a fluid mixture of chemically reactive species, light scattering can determine the reaction rates even when the fluid mixture is in complete thermodynamic and chemical equilibrium.

Many substances can exist in distinct phases such as gas, liquid, or solid. Transitions between pairs of these phases are called phase transitions and their properties have been extensively studied both with thermodynamics and statistical mechanics.

Thermodynamics can describe these transitions in terms of equations of state that are determined empirically. The van der Waals equation of state for nonideal gases is an example. Instead of the ideal gas equation of state, Eq. (1), one has

$$\left(P + \frac{aN^2}{V^2}\right)\left(\frac{V}{N} - b\right) = kT \qquad (8)$$

in which a and b are empirical constants. The gas-liquid phase transition can be explained with this equation of state. Statistical mechanics permits one to see how this equation arises as an approximation to the partition function prescription, and it provides one with physical interpretations for a and b (e.g., b is four times the volume of a hard sphere gas molecule) with explicit values for specific substances.

In addition to explaining the existence of phase transitions, statistical mechanics explains anomalous fluctuational behavior in thermodynamic parameter regimes close to phase transition parameter values. These fluctuation anomalies exhibit themselves in a variety of ways in different systems. For example, a ferromagnet will exhibit spontaneous magnetization below a critical temperature and no magnetization above it. The value of the magnetization approaches zero as the temperature approaches the critical temperature from below. This approach is characterized by a power law relating the value of the magnetic susceptibility to a power of the deviation of the temperature from the critical temperature. The magnetic susceptibility is also directly related to the anomalous magnetic fluctuations through their variance. The power law exponent is called the critical exponent. Statistical mechanics has been applied extensively to the study of critical phenomena. The existence of universality classes of different systems sharing the same set of critical exponents has been established.

Another way in which fluctuations manifest themselves is in the nucleation of a phase transition, or of a transition of a driven state from stability to instability (often, as one state becomes unstable the system develops a new stable state). As an example of the latter kind of transition, consider the behavior of a layer of fluid heated from below in a gravitational field. At low levels of heating, heat is conducted from below to the upper layer of the fluid by thermal conduction and there is no associated mass motion. The heat conduction process is simply thermal diffusion through the motionless fluid. However, as the heating level is increased, a transition to thermal convection ensues, and at even higher heating levels there is full blown turbulence. Thermal convection involves macroscopic mass motion. What makes the transition from conduction to convection take place? Analysis of the quantitative properties of the fluid for these different levels of heating shows that a stability parameter, a certain combination of physical quantities (including nonequilibrium ones such as viscosity), attains a value implying an instability for a critical level of heating. But how does the quiescent, conductive fluid "know" that this value has been reached so that the transition occurs? How does it know the values of the nonequilibrium stability parameters while it is stationary? The answer is that incessant intrinsic molecular fluctuations nucleate the transition. Fluctuations in the fluid are constantly "measuring" the values of the stability parameters. Statistical mechanics describes these fluctuations in detail but thermodynamics alone cannot.

Many phenomena require statistical mechanics for part of their explanation. Usually, it is the Boltzmann factor that is invoked. This is true for the theories of superfluids and superconductors as well as for the theory of the laser. Our understanding of semiconductors and the transitor is another outstanding example. Indeed, modern solid-state physics, now called condensed matter physics, subsumes statistical mechanics as a major, essential component. Statistical mechanical ideas also underlie our understanding of many biological phenomena such as the self-assembly of macromolecular complexes and membranes, polymer folding, macromolecular rotors and motors, and biochemical energy transductions (e.g., proton translocations during chemiosmosis). It is now clear that the vitality of biological systems owes much to the thermal agitation we call Brownian motion. Thermodynamics alone cannot explain these remarkable biological processes, but statistical mechanics enables us to use thermostatistical reasoning to treat individual molecular events if they are embedded within a larger thermal environment. Statistical mechanical thinking continues to be applied to these and other fields with considerable success.

See also: AVOGADRO NUMBER; BOLTZMANN DISTRIBUTION; ENTROPY; MOTION, BROWNIAN; PHASE TRANSITION; PLANCK CONSTANT; RADIATION, BLACKBODY; STEFAN–BOLTZMANN LAW; THERMODYNAMICS

Bibliography

BERNE, B. J., and PECORA, R. *Dynamic Light Scattering* (Wiley-Interscience, New York, 1976).

LIFSHITZ, E. M., and PITAEVSKII, L. P. *Statistical Physics* (Pergamon, Oxford, Eng., 1980).

RONALD F. FOX

STEFAN–BOLTZMANN LAW

The Stefan–Boltzmann law relates the temperature of an object to its brightness. The brightness or radiancy of an object is equal to the amount of energy it radiates per unit time divided by the area over which it emits that energy. The Stefan–Boltzmann law states that the radiancy of an ideal blackbody is proportional to the fourth power of its absolute temperature. That is, $\varepsilon = \sigma T^4$, where ε is the radiancy of the blackbody, σ is Stefan's constant ($\sigma = 5.67 \times 10^{-8} \, W/m^2K^4$), and T is the absolute temperature of the blackbody. Doubling the temperature of a blackbody increases its radiancy by a factor of sixteen. The total power radiated by a blackbody is also proportional to its temperature raised to the fourth power.

A blackbody is any object that completely absorbs all frequencies of electromagnetic radiation. It is also a perfect emitter of radiation. The amount of radiation emitted by a blackbody at any particular frequency depends only on its temperature. An ideal blackbody condition can be achieved by constructing a cavity whose interior is totally reflective of electromagnetic radiation. A small hole in the cavity permits observation and measurement. A white-hot or incandescent wire acts approximately like a blackbody. The stars also act like blackbodies.

Josef Stefan discovered the relationship between the temperatures of blackbodies and their radiancies in 1879. Stefan measured the radiancy of a glowing platinum wire. He made these measurements over a wide range of temperatures. He then deduced the experimental law relating a wire's temperature to its brilliance.

One application of the Stefan–Boltzmann law is known as radiometry. This technique requires the measurement of the radiancy of an object. A calculation based on the Stefan–Boltzmann law and this measured radiancy yields the temperature of the object. It is often easier to calculate a temperature than to measure it directly. Stefan used this technique to estimate the Sun's surface temperature.

A few years after Stefan's discovery, Ludwig Boltzmann derived the same relationship (1884). He used arguments based on the principles of classical thermodynamics. Electromagnetic radiation exerts a pressure on surfaces. Since radiation exerts a pressure it can do work. This means it can power an engine. Boltzmann calculated the amount of radiant energy supplied to a Carnot engine. He then found out how much useful work that engine could do. Finally, he showed that the power radiated by a blackbody had to be proportional to its temperature raised to the fourth power.

The Stefan–Boltzmann law gives us information about the total amount of energy a body radiates. It does not tell us anything about the amount of energy radiated at a particular frequency. Attempts to predict this based on classical physics failed. In 1900 Max Planck finally proposed a formula that fitted the experimental data. His work led to the idea that radiation comes in packets known as quanta. Planck's radiation law gives the amount of radiation emitted at a particular frequency. The total amount of energy radiated is the sum of the amounts of energy radiated at each frequency. This approach yields the Stefan–Boltzmann law and relates Stefan's constant to more fundamental physical constants. On the basis of Planck's theory, σ can be expressed as $\pi^2 k_B^4 / 60 c^2 \hbar^3$, where k_B is the Boltzmann constant, c is the velocity of light, and $\hbar$ is Planck's constant divided by 2π.

See also: BOLTZMANN, LUDWIG; BOLTZMANN CONSTANT; ENERGY, RADIANT; PLANCK, MAX KARL ERNST LUDWIG; RADIATION, BLACKBODY

Bibliography

LONGAIR, M. S. *Theoretical Concepts in Physics* (Cambridge University Press, Cambridge, Eng., 1984).

STEHLE, P. *Order, Chaos, Order: The Transition from Classical to Quantum Physics* (Oxford University Press, Oxford, Eng., 1994).

PATRICIA RANKIN

STELLAR EVOLUTION

Stars are very diverse objects, with types ranging from cool red giants to hot white dwarfs. The theory of stellar evolution links the different stellar types as distinct phases in the lifetimes of individual stars. Evolution between each phase is driven by the energy that a star loses when it radiates. The theory rests on evidence that most of the energy emitted by stars originates from nuclear fusion. As this fusion slowly changes the interior composition of a star, the star's structure and appearance alter. Stellar evolution theory is extremely successful in predicting the time that a star spends in each stage of evolution, the changes in composition that are seen when the products of nuclear fusion are mixed to the surface, and the different ways in which stars end their lives. It has also provided useful constraints on the properties of fundamental particles, like the neutrino magnetic moment or the coupling strengths of hypothetical particles like axions. Finally, as the source of most elements other than hydrogen and helium, the results of stellar evolution are fundamental for understanding the chemical evolution of our galaxy, and others.

Understanding stars begins with determining their intrinsic properties. By measuring the brightness and distance of nearby stars, astronomers find their true luminosities. The Wien displacement law can be used to relate the color or spectrum of a star to the surface temperature. The luminosity and temperature can then be used with the Stefan–Boltzman law to find a star's radius. In binary systems (where two stars orbit around each other), Newton's laws can be applied to determine the masses of the individual stars.

As this data was gathered, astronomers found a tremendous range of luminosities, temperatures, radii, and masses. This information was organized by plotting each star on a diagram of intrinsic luminosity and temperature (or color). Such a plot is commonly called an HR diagram after Einar Hertzsprung and Henry Norris Russell. In an HR diagram, most stars are seen to lie along a diagonal band called the main sequence (see Figure 1). A smaller number of stars are much more luminous and cooler (redder) than the main sequence stars. They have huge radii, and are known as either red giants or supergiants. In older star clusters, it is evident that most of the red giants were grouped at a particular luminosity, with the remaining giants tracing a path connecting this group to the main sequence.

On the other side of the size spectrum, some stars were found to be faint and hot. The radii of these objects had to be much smaller than stars of the main sequence, and they became known as white dwarfs. White dwarfs were found to have a small range of radii, typically a little larger than that of Earth. However, their masses were sometimes as much as that of the Sun, requiring incredibly high densities. In addition to differences in appearance, some stars distinguished themselves through activi-

ties including brightness variations, mass ejections, and explosions.

Understanding this diversity of stellar types and activities begins with the equations that determine stellar structure. One equation expresses the condition of hydrostatic equilibrium, a balance between gravity and pressure necessary for a stable star. Local conservation of energy is defined in an equation of thermal equilibrium, and energy produced at the center of stars must be transported to the surface where it is radiated. This requires either an equation to represent the diffusion of energy by radiation or one to describe the transport of energy by convection. In some phases of evolution, even electron conduction can be important for transporting energy. Finally, an equation of state provides a thermodynamic relation among the temperature, pressure, density, and composition. For a specified composition and total mass, the solution to these equations determines the pressure, temperature, luminosity and radius at any mass point in a star. Evolution oc-

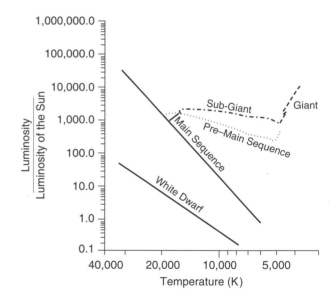

Figure 1 The evolutionary path of a star 6 times more massive than the Sun is shown. It begins in the pre–main sequence collapse phase. As the interior warms, nuclear fusion begins and stabilizes the star on the main sequence, where it spends most of its life. A line shows the position of the main sequence for stars of other masses. After the main sequence, a star evolves to the giant branch, where this star burns helium in the core. Finally, the envelope escapes, and the core remains as a cooling white dwarf.

curs because the stellar surface is hot and radiates energy. As this energy is lost from the star, the interior structure must change, and the change depends on the energy sources available.

In the early twentieth century, physicists and astronomers thought that the gravitational potential of a star was its sole source of energy. When energy is lost (radiated) from the surface of a star, its gas falls farther into the gravitational potential well, releasing gravitational energy. Application of the virial theorem, a relation between the potential and kinetic energies of a stable system, shows that half of this gravitational energy is radiated, and the other half heats the gas. Early calculations by the nineteenth century physicist Lord Kelvin found that it required approximately 10 million years for a star like the Sun to contract from a large cloud of gas to the present size. This seemed long enough to many scientists of the time, but geologists thought it too short for the age of Earth. Astronomers also encountered problems as they attempted to calculate the evolution of stars with only gravitational energy. At this time, red giants were thought to be young, contracting stars. Cepheids, a type of giant star, pulsate with a period that depends on the sound travel time through the star. The period of these pulsations was expected to decrease as a Cepheid contracted. However, observations found that the pulsation periods changed much more slowly than expected, and sometimes they actually increased. Another source of energy was needed.

The discovery of a relationship between mass and energy, coupled with measurements that helium had less mass than the four hydrogen nuclei from which it formed (a mass defect) led to the idea that the energy of stars came from fusion. The CNO cycle, in which hydrogen is converted to helium in a series of captures on isotopes of carbon, nitrogen, and oxygen was proposed independently by Hans Bethe and Richard von Weizsacker in 1938. This is the main source of energy in stars more massive than the Sun. In 1939 Bethe realized that a weak interaction can convert a proton into a neutron during a scattering event, allowing two protons to form deuterium. This is the first step in the chain of nuclear reactions that are the dominant source of energy in the Sun and lower mass stars. With an understanding of the nuclear reactions that convert hydrogen to helium, an energy source was available that would permit a star like the Sun to last billions of years instead of millions.

Summarizing the phases of stellar evolution, a star begins as cloud of interstellar gas. There is still uncertainty in the processes that trigger gas clouds to begin collapsing, but radio and infrared observations show objects forming in such clouds. In these pre–main sequence stars, gravitational potential energy supplies the radiated luminosity and increases the interior temperature. Eventually, a temperature is reached where hydrogen fusion occurs, and the nuclear energy released stabilizes a star's structure. Calculations identify this hydrogen burning phase with stars on the main sequence. Mass is the primary difference between various main sequence stars. In agreement with the masses determined from binaries, those stars more massive than the Sun are found at the hotter (bluer), brighter end of the main sequence, and lower mass stars are on the cooler (redder) fainter end.

In addition to producing energy, the slow fusion of hydrogen into helium reduces the number of particles per gram of material in the core of a star. This lowers the pressure; to maintain the balance between pressure and gravity the central regions of a star must contract and heat. The rising core temperature enhances the rate of nuclear reactions, resulting in more energy for the star to radiate. In star clusters, this luminosity increase is seen in those stars that are about to deplete their hydrogen and leave the main sequence. The large number of stars seen to be on the main sequence agrees with the stellar evolution result that stars spend about 90 percent of their lifetimes there. The time to deplete hydrogen in the core of a star like the Sun is about 10 billion years. Stellar structure calculations require main sequence stars to have a luminosity that is approximately proportional to the fourth power of the mass ($L \propto M^4$). The fuel available for nuclear fusion increases only linearly as the mass, so the lifetimes of a more massive main sequence star decreases sharply (lifetime $\propto 1/M^3$).

When the hydrogen is depleted in the center of a star, a helium core remains, surrounded by a shell in which hydrogen continues to burn. Without a source of nuclear energy, the helium core begins to contract. The increasing gravity of the core causes the temperature and luminosity of the hydrogen burning shell to increase. Unable to transport the higher luminosity to the surface, the material surrounding the burning shell absorbs the energy and expands. As the overall radius of the star increases, the surface temperature decreases, and the star increases, the surface temperature decreases, and the star becomes a red giant. During this time, the helium core continues to grow. When the temperature and density of the core are sufficient, helium fusion into carbon begins.

Core helium burning supports a star for a period that is nearly 10 percent of the main sequence lifetime, so most stars that are not on the main sequence are in this core helium burning phase. In HR diagrams of older clusters with many stars, core helium burning stars lie in a clump on the red giant branch, or they are spread out to the blue in a horizontal branch. The luminosity of clump and horizontal branch stars is about the same, but the surface temperature depends on the precise composition of the envelope and the amount of mass in the star. While the initial stages of helium burning produce only carbon, as the carbon abundance increases, oxygen is also produced.

The advanced stages of stellar evolution depend on a star's original mass. In stars with a mass less than 9 times that of the Sun, helium depletion results in a carbon and oxygen core that contracts and becomes degenerate to electrons. If the star was not in the clump on the red giant branch during core helium burning, it returns as the helium is depleted. Stars with carbon-oxygen cores are called asymptotic giant branch (AGB) stars. The high luminosity and low surface gravity of a star in this stage results in mass loss through stellar winds. This mass loss can remove the entire envelope of a star, leaving behind only the core. As the last bits of the envelope are removed, the star appears to shrink rapidly (10,000 years or less), becoming hotter and bluer. The core is degenerate, hot and small. Because the structure of the core is supported by degenerate electrons, it cannot contract and heat to burn carbon. The star then cools as it radiates the remaining heat stored in its material. These stars are known as white dwarfs. Observations of white dwarfs in clusters indicate that most stars with masses below 8 or 9 solar masses lose their envelope and become white dwarfs.

If mass loss does not remove the material surrounding the core, its mass and gravity increase. Gravity forces the carbon nuclei closer together. When the core grows to near 1.4 solar masses, the density is high enough that the nuclear force overcomes the Coulomb force and fusion begins, resulting in an explosion called a supernova of type I. Stars more massive than 9 solar masses ignite carbon without becoming degenerate and have successive stages of neon, oxygen, and silicon burning. When iron, the most stable nucleus in nature, is formed, fusion can provide no more energy. The core again becomes degenerate and approaches 1.4

solar masses. At this point, gravity overwhelms the internal pressure, and the core begins to collapse in on itself, converting gravitational potential energy to kinetic energy. The pressure becomes so high that electrons combine with nuclei to form neutrons. When the center is so dense that the neutrons become degenerate, then the pressure in this tiny new core can halt the collapse. The kinetic energy of the inward falling material is converted to heat and a shock wave. This shock wave, coupled with the outflow of hot neutrinos from the high temperature core, explosively ejects the exterior of the star. This explosion is also called a supernova (type II). The core remains as a neutron star, or if the star was too massive, as a black hole.

The theory of stellar evolution permits an understanding of the myriad stellar types as various stages in the evolution of stars with different initial masses. It also predicts the yields of elements produced during the various phases of evolution, including those elements above iron. During the advanced burning phases, neutrons will be produced and captured to synthesize the full suite of elements observed in nature. Research continues in stellar evolution to refine our understanding of complex systems like binary stars, and to provide a basis for studying galactic evolution.

See also: BLACK HOLE; NEUTRON STAR; NOVA; RED GIANT; STARS AND STELLAR STRUCTURE; SUN; SUPERNOVA

Bibliography

CLAYTON, D. D. *Principles of Stellar Evolution and Nucleosynthesis* (McGraw-Hill, New York, 1968).

SCHWARZSCHILD, M. *Structure and Evolution of the Stars* (Princeton University Press, Princeton, NJ, 1958).

DAVID S. P. DEARBORN

STERN–GERLACH EXPERIMENT

Otto Stern, then a young professor at the University of Frankfurt, proposed in 1921 a novel experiment, "which if successful, will decide unequivocally between the quantum theoretical and classical views." This experiment, performed in 1922 in collaboration with Walther Gerlach, is celebrated both for its dramatic historical impact and as the conceptual ancestor of a host of subsequent "state-selection" methods applied in many fields of physics.

The original experiment was designed to test one of the most perplexing aspects of what is now called the "old quantum theory." According to the atomic model of Niels Bohr, only certain discrete orbits of atomic electrons were allowed. In an attempt to explain the splitting of atomic spectral lines by a magnetic field (known as the Zeeman effect), Arnold Sommerfeld and, independently, Peter Debye postulated that the Bohr orbits also could have only certain discrete spatial orientations with respect to the direction of the magnetic field. This notion, introduced in 1916, was termed "space quantization." The drastic contrast with classical theory, in which all spatial orientations of electron orbits would be allowed, led Stern to devise his crucial experiment. His key idea was to look for space quantization by using the magnetism of an atom as a probe. Since the orbital motion of an electron produces a magnetic moment normal to the orbit, an isolated atom acts like a tiny bar magnet. The experimental challenge was to determine whether in an external field such atomic magnets point only in discrete directions.

Figure 1 illustrates the chief features of the Stern–Gerlach apparatus. Within a vacuum chamber, silver atoms evaporate from a hot oven and are collimated into a narrow beam by passing through small holes. The beam is so dilute that individual atoms sail through the apparatus without interacting with other atoms. After traveling between the pole pieces of a magnet, the atoms land on a cold glass plate to which they adhere and thereby exhibit the beam intensity profile. One of the magnet pole pieces has a sharp edge, the other a broad notch; this makes the magnetic field stronger near the edge and weaker near the notch. In this nonuniform field, perpendicular to the beam path, an atom is subjected to a transverse deflecting force proportional to $\cos \theta$, with θ the angle between the magnetic moment of the atom and the external field direction. Atoms whose magnetic moments are tilted toward ($\theta < 90°$) or away from ($\theta > 90°$) the field direction are attracted to or repelled from the stronger field region, respectively. The trajectories of atoms emerging from the deflecting magnet, as recorded by deposits on the glass plate, thus reveal the spatial orientation of the atomic magnetic moments.

The silver atoms evaporating from the oven have their magnetic moments randomly oriented; there-fore, the number of atoms with a given value of θ is proportional to $\sin \theta$. According to classical theory, this random distribution also would pertain to the external field region. In that case, the beam emerging from the magnet would have its maximum intensity at $\theta = 90°$, corresponding to zero deflection, and the beam would merely become somewhat broader than its original intensity profile. However, according to the Sommerfeld–Debye space quantization, only orientations parallel ($\theta = 0°$) and antiparallel ($\theta = 180°$) to the external field are allowed, so the beam should split into two distinct components of equal intensity. This twofold splitting was in fact found in the Stern–Gerlach experiment.

The simple elegance of the method, the skill and audacity required for the original experiment (in which the deflections were only about 0.1 mm), and the compelling evidence obtained for space quantization have captivated generations of scientists. Yet an ironic aspect should be noted. From careful analysis of the beam splitting, Stern and Gerlach were able to determine the size of the magnetic moment

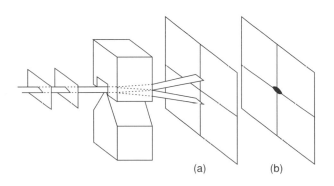

Figure 1 Schematic view of the Stern–Gerlach apparatus, indicating (a) the observed beam splitting, and (b) the unsplit outcome predicted by classical mechanics. The beam of silver atoms, produced by effusion of metallic vapor from an oven heated to 1,000°C, is collimated by two slits (30 μm wide in the vertical direction). The beam passes through an inhomogeneous magnetic field about 3.5 cm long; its direction and gradient are vertical, the field strength is about 0.1 T, and the gradient is 10 T/cm. The transmitted beam is deposited on a cold glass plate. The magnitude of the splitting is only 200 μm. For the sake of clarity, in the figure the splitting is much exaggerated and the broadening of the deposits caused by the thermal distribution of velocities in the beam is omitted.

of the silver atom (with an accuracy of about 10 percent). It was in gratifying but misleading agreement with the old quantum theory, which attributed the atomic magnetic moment to the orbital motion of the valence electron with one quantum of angular momentum (in units of $h/2\pi$, where h is Planck's constant). The correct interpretation did not emerge until 1925, after the discovery of electron spin and the "new" quantum theory of angular momentum. For the silver atom, the electronic orbital angular momentum is actually zero; the magnetic moment is instead due to one-half unit of spin angular momentum. This gives a magnetic moment of the same size as would one unit of orbital momentum, by virtue of a factor of 2 arising from a relativistic effect not recognized until 1926. Stern described the experiment as "a question put to Nature," and Nature's beguiling answer proved to be subtle.

Beyond demonstrating the reality of space quantization, the Stern–Gerlach experiment showed how to use external fields to analyze quantum states. Its descendants thus include many of the most seminal techniques of modern physics. Among these are molecular beam and nuclear magnetic resonance methods, atomic clocks, masers and lasers, and much else. By splitting a narrow atomic beam, Stern and Gerlach brought conceptual unity to wide domains of physics.

See also: ATOM, RUTHERFORD–BOHR; MAGNETIC MOMENT; QUANTUM THEORY, ORIGINS OF; ZEEMAN EFFECT

Bibliography

FEYNMAN, R. P.; LEIGHTON, R. B.; and SANDS, M. *The Feynman Lectures on Physics,* Vol. 2 (Addison-Wesley, New York, 1964).

HERSCHBACH, D., ed. "An Homage to Otto Stern." *Zeitschrift für Physik D* **10,** 109–392 (1988).

BRETISLAV FRIEDRICH

DUDLEY HERSCHBACH

STOCHASTIC PROCESSES

Happenings determined by chance and probability but which obey known physical laws are stochastic processes. The word "stochastic" stems from the Greek word $\sigma\tau o\chi o\sigma$, meaning to aim at or to guess. Such processes may take many forms, from the random arrival of rain drops on a tin roof, or of electrons on an electrode of an old-fashioned vacuum tube, to the irregular motions of microscopic particles suspended in a fluid (Brownian motion).

The first theory of a stochastic process was developed by Albert Einstein in 1905 to explain the effects of thermal fluctuations on small particles suspended in a fluid at room temperature. The molecules of the fluid have, on average, kinetic energy equal to $(3/2)k_BT$, where k_B is Boltzmann's constant and T is the absolute temperature, but the energy of any individual molecule is a random number. Hence, with small, but nevertheless nonzero, probability, a fluid molecule may have quite a large energy. It may also happen by chance that a number of molecules with large energies may collide with a much larger but microscopic particle and impart to it a measurably large velocity in a given direction. The larger particle will continue in that direction for a time and over a distance which are also random numbers, before its direction and velocity are again changed by collision with another collection of fluid molecules with large thermal energies. The motion of the larger particle, which can easily be viewed under a microscope, might look like that depicted in Fig. 1, where each dot represents a successive position. Note that each individual flight of the particle is completely unpredictable, and that this unpredictability stems from the very large number of fluid molecules involved in the motion of a single particle. In this case we say that the process is "high dimensional," each fluid molecule constituting a set of dimensions of its own quite independent of the other molecules. The most notable characteristic of this example of stochastic motion is that as time progresses from $t = 0$, the particle, on average, migrates further and further from its starting point, shown by the dot at the center of the circles. Regarding this motion, several quantities are of interest to calculate: the relation between the average distance from the starting point $\langle r \rangle$, and t, the time after starting; the average distance between collisions $\langle \ell \rangle$, called the mean free path; the average time $\langle t_B \rangle$ for the particle to arrive at some boundary, as shown by the large solid circle, called the mean first passage time. All of these can be calculated from Einstein's theory, but we will give only the most famous result here: $\langle r \rangle = \sqrt{2Dt}$, where D is a constant called the coefficient of diffusion, which depends on the temperature, the size and shape of the particle, and the viscosity of the fluid. This prediction—that the average distance from the starting point is proportional to the square root of the time—is easily checked in a variety of experiments.

In nature, one finds myriad stochastic processes. In essence, any phenomenon that operates according to known scientific laws, but whose motion or future is unpredictable, can be traced to an underlying or overt stochastic process. Examples include the climate, lasers, chemical reactions and fluid dynamics, biology, economics, and even the rate of Earth's rotation, to name but a few. Since it is impossible to discuss all of these in detail here, we shall look instead at one example that is currently attracting considerable interest in virtually every area of science: stochastic resonance.

This process deals with the flow of information in a stochastic environment. Since the early days of radio, engineers have regarded the stochastic processes inherent in their electronic devices and transmission lines as a kind of contamination that interferes with the detection or transmission of useful information; and so it does, in the linear systems with which we have conventionally dealt. Stochastic resonance deals with the remarkable property of certain nonlinear systems to actively make use of the stochasticity in order to detect or transmit coherent information. Since time immemorial, we have considered stochastic processes to be the destroyers of information, so how can it be that the "noise" can increase our ability to detect or process information?

An extremely simple example can clarify this very counterintuitive assertion. Consider a system which can output a pulse only when some internal threshold Δ is crossed, and suppose that a "weak" signal is input as shown in Fig. 2a. We imagine that the signal is hidden from our view, and further, that we know nothing about what happens inside the "black box." As observers, we can only look at the output. The signal amplitude is smaller than the threshold; consequently, no information about the signal is available to an observer looking at the output. Now suppose that a stochastic process is added to the signal, as shown in Fig. 2b. The stochastic process could be input by the observer at the port shown, or it could be generated internally by the system. The stochastic process adds to the information-carrying signal so that the threshold is crossed frequently, as shown. What is important is

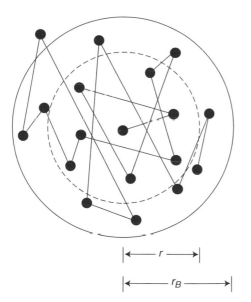

Figure 1 A depiction of Brownian motion. The particle begins at the dot at the center of the circles at time $t = 0$. Each successive location of the particle is shown by a dot. The average distance r from the starting point is shown by the dashed circle, and some boundary r_B is marked by the solid circle.

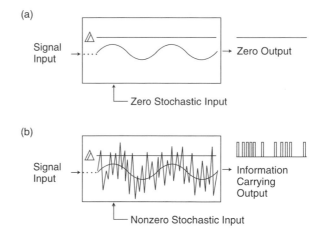

Figure 2 (a) A box representing a threshold detection process with a weak or subthreshold information carrying signal at the input. There is no output because there are no threshold crossings. (b) The addition of a stochastic process causes threshold crossings and consequently an information-carrying output in the form of a train of pulses that can be observed. The threshold is marked by Δ.

that there are more threshold crossings near the maxima of the signal and fewer near the minima. The output pulse *rate* thus carries information about the signal that was absent before; this is entirely the result of the added stochastic process. Of course, if the added stochastic intensity is too large, the information content of the output is degraded, but if too small, little information is detected due to too few threshold crossings. This means that there exists an optimum stochastic intensity that maximizes the information flow through the system. This process has recently been shown to play a significant role in the remarkable sensitivity of biological sensory neurons.

See also: CHAOS; FLUID DYNAMICS; LASER; MEAN FREE PATH; MOTION, BROWNIAN; NOISE; SIGNAL

Bibliography

DOUGLASS, J. K.; WILKENS, L.; PANTAZELOU, E.; and MOSS, F. "Noise Enhancement of Information Transfer in Crayfish Mechanoreceptors by Stochastic Resonance." *Nature* **365,** 337–340 (1993).

DUFFIE, D. *Security Markets, Stochastic Models* (Academic Press, San Diego, 1988).

EINSTEIN, A. *Investigations on the Theory of Brownian Movement,* edited by R. Fürth and A. D. Cowper (Dover, New York, 1956).

GHIL, M., and CHILDRESS, S. *Topics in Geophysical Fluid Dynamics* (Springer-Verlag, Berlin, 1987).

HORSTHEMKE, W., and KONDEPUDI, D. K., eds. *Fluctuations and Sensitivity in Nonequilibrium Systems* (Springer-Verlag, Berlin, 1984).

HORSTHEMKE, W., and LEFEVER, R. *Noise-Induced Transitions,* (Springer-Verlag, Berlin, 1980).

LAMBECK, K. *The Earth's Variable Rotation* (Cambridge University Press, Cambridge, Eng., 1980).

MADDOX, J. "Towards the Brain-Computer's Code?" *Nature* **352,** 469 (1991).

MADDOX, J. "Bringing More Order Out of Noisiness." *Nature* **369,** 271 (1994).

MOSS, F. "Stochastic Resonance: From the Ice Ages to the Monkey's Ear" in *Contemporary Problems in Statistical Physics,* edited by G. H. Weiss (SIAM, Philadelphia, 1994).

MOSS, F.; LUGIATO, L. A.; and SCHLEICH, W., eds. *Noise and Chaos in Nonlinear Dynamical Systems* (Cambridge University Press, Cambridge, Eng., 1990).

RUELLE, D. *Chance and Chaos* (Princeton University Press, Princeton, NJ, 1991).

TUCKWELL, H. C. *Stochastic Processes in the Neurosciences* (SIAM, Philadelphia, 1989).

FRANK MOSS

STRAIN

The term "strain" refers to a change in the relative positions of points in a body that has been deformed. The deformation may occur by the imposition of external forces (mechanical, electrical, or magnetic) or from nonuniform deformation in parts of the body (as around defects, such as dislocations, or included second phases, such as precipitates). Strains may be either extensions—changes in length along a line in the body—or shears—changes in position of points in two parallel planes in the body. Geometries of these two types of strains are shown in Fig. 1.

Strains that are immediately recoverable after removal of the stress are called elastic. They result from mere stretching of the bonds between neighboring atoms of the body. They are related to the imposed stress by Hooke's law—whose proportionality constant is called the elastic constant. Components of some recoverable strains, though, have a time-dependent component, both for their imposition and recovery. Those components result from reversible reorientation of particular atomic units within the body—as the reorientation of anisotropic defects in ionic crystals, short-range diffusion of elements such as carbon in body-centered-cubic (bcc) iron or reorientation of small parts of macromolecular chains in polymers. Such strain components are called anelastic. Nonrecoverable strain may occur

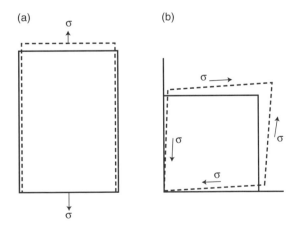

Figure 1 (a) Stresses normal to the surface of a body produce linear extension and lateral contraction. (b) Shear stresses, as couples, deform a square section of a body into a rhombus.

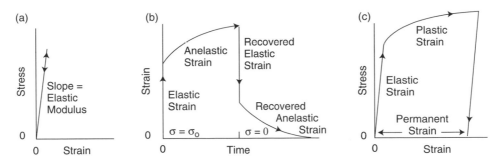

Figure 2 (a) Small stresses produce linear strain in a body; the slope of the line is the elastic modulus. (b) Certain solids undergo a reversible elongation (under the action of a constant stress) in addition to the elastic strain. The elastic strain is recovered instantaneously upon removal of the stress and the additional elongation is also recovered with time. Such solids are called anelastic. (c) Stresses above a certain value produce a plastic strain, which is not recovered upon removal of the stress.

if permanent geometrical changes occur—such strains are called plastic. These three types of strain are illustrated in Fig. 2.

Strains of an isotropic body are of three independent types: The extensional strains in the direction of the applied stress, a lateral contraction (termed Poisson's contraction), and a pure shear. Thus three components are required to characterize the elastic behavior. Crystals of lower symmetry possess more independent components of strain, up to six for the triclinic. These crystals of lower symmetry thus have more elastic constants, up to twenty-one for the triclinic. Compressional strain occurs if a body is acted upon by hydraulic forces. However, that strain may be expressed in terms of the extension and shear components just described.

Usually, strain is described in terms of deformation from mechanical forces. However, strains resulting from other types of forces are also technologically important: magnetostrictive effects (which produce transformer hum) and piezoelectric effects (which make quartz clocks possible).

Precipitates in alloys and ceramic solids often produce internal compressive strains, which are, as noted above, resolvable into tensile and shear strains. Such strain components may retard dislocation and boundary motion under the action of external stesses, thereby increasing strength, creep resistance, fatigue life, and hardness. Carbides are introduced into steels for this purpose, as are fine precipitates of copper, zinc, silicon, and other elements in aluminum and its alloys. Tangles of dislocations produced by large deformation may produce internal strains that provide further strengthening in such alloys during subsequent use, as well as in brass and many stainless steels, even in the absence of precipitates.

See also: ALLOY; CREEP; CRYSTAL; CRYSTAL STRUCTURE; ELASTICITY; ELASTIC MODULI AND CONSTANTS; HOOKE'S LAW; MAGNETOSTRICTION; PIEZOELECTRIC EFFECT; SOLID; STRESS

CHARLES A. WERT

STRESS

Stress may be defined as a force per unit area exerted by a part of a body on one side of a surface upon another part of a body on the other side. The force can be resolved into a normal part, a pressure, and a tangential part, a shearing stress. If the body is in equilibrium, an equal and opposite stress must exist in the other direction, so the stresses come in pairs. Nine components of stress must exist, three for each coordinate direction; they are sketched for an elementary cube in Fig. 1. For the body to be in equilibrium, equal and opposite stresses are assumed on the back faces. Furthermore, the shear components must be equal in pairs: $\sigma_{xy} = \sigma_{yx}$, $\sigma_{xz} = \sigma_{zx}$, and $\sigma_{yz} = \sigma_{zy}$.

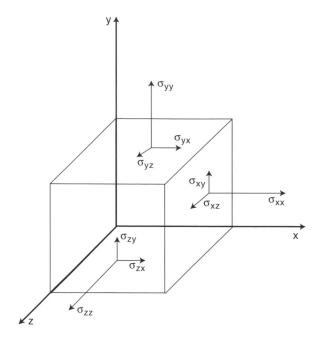

Figure 1 The nine components of stress are shown of the faces of a unit cube.

The normal stresses and the shear stresses are components of a stress tensor, usually written as

$$\sigma = \begin{array}{ccc} \sigma_{xx} & \sigma_{xy} & \sigma_{xz} \\ \sigma_{xy} & \sigma_{yy} & \sigma_{yz} \\ \sigma^{xz} & \sigma_{yz} & \sigma_{zz} \end{array}.$$

Although nine components of stress exist, only six are independent. This stress tensor σ is related to the strain tensor ε by the generalized Hooke's law:

$$\sigma_{ij} = \sum_{k,\ell} c_{ijkl} * \varepsilon_{kl}.$$

It might seem that eighty-one components of the stiffness constants c_{ijkl} might exist. However, symmetries of the stress and strain tensors, as well as conservation of energy requirements, permit only twenty-one independent components of the c's to exist, even for triclinic crystals. For crystals of higher symmetry, even fewer exist—for cubic crystals, only three.

Special states of stress may be defined. A uniaxial stress has only one component, σ_{xx}; it is produced in a long rod by a weight hanging at one end. A biaxial stress has two components, σ_{xx} and σ_{yy}. A triaxial stress has three components, σ_{xx}, σ_{yy}, and σ_{zz}. A hydrostatic pressure is a special case of a triaxial stress with all components equal and negative.

Finally, a pure shear may be expressed in alternate forms:

$$\begin{array}{ccc} -\sigma_{xx} & 0 & 0 \\ 0 & \sigma_{xx} & 0 \\ 0 & 0 & 0 \end{array} \qquad \begin{array}{ccc} 0 & \sigma_{xx} & 0 \\ \sigma_{xx} & 0 & 0 \\ 0 & 0 & 0 \end{array}.$$

The geometry of these configurations is shown in Fig. 2.

See also: CRYSTAL; CRYSTAL STRUCTURE; ELASTICITY; ELASTIC MODULI AND CONSTANTS; EQUILIBRIUM; FORCE; HOOKE'S LAW; STRAIN; SYMMETRY; TENSOR

CHARLES A. WERT

Figure 2 The pair of normal stresses, as applied on the left-hand side, may be resolved into a pair of shear stresses by rotation of axes by 45°.

STRONG INTERACTION

See INTERACTION, STRONG

SUN

Although astronomers regard the Sun as a perfectly ordinary (G2) main sequence star, it is of central importance to many aspects of more immediate human concern: The Sun is by far the preeminent source of energy within the solar system; it contains approximately 99.7 percent of the total mass of the solar system; and its constantly varying activity relates to important terrestrial effects, many of which remain to be understood in detail and are still of great controversy.

In astrophysics, the Sun is widely regarded as a Rosetta stone: It allows for the connection of theories of nuclear-power generation in stars, stellar evolution, and magnetic field–related stellar activity with an astronomical object that can be observed in great detail. As a consequence, the astrophysics of stars rests on far surer footing than theories of more exotic objects, such as pulsars and quasars, for which no nearby astronomical counterpart exists. For these reasons, the Sun, as an astronomical object, is of central importance to astronomy and astrophysics. The basic facts about the Sun are given in Table 1.

Stellar Structure

The Sun is, to first approximation, a self-gravitating gaseous sphere, with an internal structure governed by hydrostatic equilibrium, that is, by the balance of forces due to gravity and gas-pressure gradients. Because of gravitational contraction, the Sun's deep interior is far hotter than its surface, reaching temperatures of 15 million degrees in the core. These temperatures are sufficiently high to cause nuclear burning of the core's hydrogen; this burning process, which consumes hydrogen to yield helium (the so-called proton-proton, or pp, chain),

maintains the luminosity of the Sun. The dominant reaction chain involves three steps: The first step directly consumes hydrogen (p) to yield deuterium (^{2}H), positrons (e^+), and electron neutrinos (ν_e):

$$p + p \rightarrow {}^2\text{H} + e^+ + \nu_e. \tag{1}$$

The next step involves the consumption of this deuterium to form an isotope of helium (^{3}He) and a gamma ray (γ),

$$^2\text{H} + p \rightarrow {}^3\text{He} + \gamma. \tag{2}$$

The final step involves the consumption of the helium isotope to form an alpha particle (e.g., a stable helium nucleus, $\alpha = {}^4$He) and two protons,

$$^3\text{He} + {}^3\text{He} \rightarrow {}^4\text{He} + 2p. \tag{3}$$

The net result is then to start with four protons (e.g., four hydrogen nuclei) and to terminate with one helium nucleus,

$$4p \rightarrow {}^4\text{He} + 2e^+ + 2\nu_e + \gamma, \tag{4}$$

together with a total energy release of 26.73 MeV per pp chain reaction; the electron neutrinos produced by this chain are relatively low energy (maximum energy 0.420 MeV). Roughly 85 percent of the total energy produced in the Sun's core by nuclear reactions is a result of this three-step burning pro-

Table 1   Basic Facts for the Sun

Feature	Measurement
Mean diameter (D_{Sun})	$D_{\text{Sun}} \simeq 1.392 \times 10^{11}$ cm $\simeq 110 \times D_{\text{Earth}}$
Mass (M_{Sun})	$M_{\text{Sun}} \simeq 1.9891 \times 10^{33}$ g $\simeq 330{,}000 \times M_{\text{Earth}}$
Mean density (ρ_{Sun})	$\rho_{\text{Sun}} \simeq 1.41$ g·cm$^{-3} \simeq 0.26 \times \rho_{\text{Earth}}$
Surface escape speed (v_{Sun})	$v_{\text{Sun}} \simeq 617$ km·s$^{-1} \simeq 55 \times v_{\text{Earth}}$
Effective surface temperature (T_{Sun})	$T_{\text{Sun}} \simeq 5{,}770$ K
Relative elemental composition	H: 10^{12}; He: 6×10^{10}; "Metals" (including Li, C, O, Si, Fe, . . .): $< 10^9$
Mean distance (Sun-Earth) ($R_{\text{Sun-Earth}}$)	$R_{\text{Sun-Earth}} = 1$ AU $\simeq 1.5 \times 10^{13}$ cm
Luminosity (L_{Sun})	$L_{\text{Sun}} \simeq 3.826 \times 10^{33}$ ergs·s^{-1}
Solar constant (f_{Sun})	$f_{\text{Sun}} \simeq 1.368$ kW·m^{-2}
Spatial scale	1 arc second at Earth $\simeq 720$ km at the Sun

cess; the remaining 15 percent is produced by two branch processes, which replace the second and third steps of the pp chain with alternative reactions. One of these side chains, which yields only approximately 0.02 percent of the total energy released, involves the chain of reactions

$$^3He + {}^4He \rightarrow {}^7Be + \gamma; \, p + {}^7Be \rightarrow {}^8B + \gamma;$$

$$^8B \rightarrow {}^8Be + e^+ + \nu_e. \quad (5)$$

The final decay of boron B yields a very energetic (maximum energy, 15 MeV) electron neutrino, which can be relatively easily detected at Earth and has played a key role in founding the field of neutrino astrophysics.

The energy liberated as a result of nuclear burning is carried outward from the core by photons, which diffuse toward the Sun's surface. This diffusion process is slow: The outward random walk takes 10 million years. If nuclear burning were to be turned off in the Sun's interior, humans would not be aware of this crucial event until some 10 million years after its occurrence. As one moves toward the Sun's surface from the deep interior, the interior temperature decreases in concert with the outward photon diffusion; in addition, the opacity of the solar gas increases as the temperature drops (it becomes less and less transparent). As a consequence, outward energy transport becomes less and less efficient as one approaches the solar surface. When one reaches roughly two-thirds of the radial distance to the surface, where the interior temperature has decreased to approximately 2 million degrees, energy transport by radiation decreases to the point that energy transport by convection (i.e., by physical motions upward and downward of the heated gas) is more efficient and therefore physically preferred; this process is similar to the transition from conductive heat transport to convective heat transport seen in a pot of heated water. As a consequence, the outer one-third of the Sun is in a constant state of turbulent convection, which persists virtually to the visible solar surface; and the radial temperature variation in this convection zone is very close to adiabatic.

Until quite recently, this picture of the Sun's interior was largely based on theory and on comparisons to theoretical predictions for the interior structure and evolution of other stars with observations of these stars. This successful comparison, which led to a physical explanation of the Hertzsprung–Russell diagram, is one of the triumphs of modern stellar astrophysics. However, the question remained as to whether one could directly observe the nuclear burning in the Sun's core and compare these observations with the standard solar model. This question was answered affirmatively in the early 1970s by Raymond Davis and collaborators, who demonstrated that it is possible to detect the expected neutrino flux from the nuclear burning process by using a chlorine compound (^{37}Cl) (a cleaning fluid named perchloroethylene) to capture electron neutrinos from the boron-decay side chain reaction:

$$^8B \rightarrow {}^8Be + e^+ + \nu_e. \quad (6)$$

The remarkable result was that the observed neutrino-capture ratio of 2.05 ± 0.3 solar-neutrino units (SNU) was well below the expected rate of 7.9 ± 2.6 SNU. Later experiments based on capture of the energetic boron-decay neutrinos by water (the Japanese Kamiokande II experiment) and capture of the far less energetic neutrinos from the primary pp chain [the SAGE (Soviet-American Gallium Experiment) and GALLEX (Gallium Experiment) experimental collaborations, which measured the conversion rate of gallium to germanium, $\nu_e + {}^{71}Ga \rightarrow {}^{71}Ge + e^-$], also produced significantly lower neutrino-capture rates than predicted by the standard solar model. The gallium-germanium conversion experiment has been considered especially troubling because it tests directly the primary reaction chain responsible for the Sun's luminosity. These results suggest that either there is a problem with the standard solar model or with our understanding of neutrino physics.

It has become possible to explore the internal temperature and density stratification of the Sun by means of helioseismology, the counterpart of terrestrial seismology applied to the Sun. This observational technique entails measurement of the frequencies of global modes of oscillation of the entire Sun; these global modes are sound waves (p-modes) trapped in the solar interior. These waves have periods in the range of approximately five minutes, with most of the power lying in the frequency range of 2.5 to 4.5 MHz. Longtime series observations of these modes also allow measurement of their frequency splitting, an effect that permits measurement of the rotation properties of the solar interior. In 1994–1995 an experiment sponsored by the National Science Foundation led to the creation of the Global Oscillations Network Group (GONG), which placed helioseismographic observation stations around the globe to maximize the chances of obtaining uninterrupted long-duration solar observations. In addition, the joint European–U.S. SOHO (Solar and Heliospheric Observatory) satellite carries onboard helioseismographic experiments. With these experiments and a flood of new data, a new view of the solar interior can be expected to emerge.

Rotation

Galileo Galilei inferred the rotation of the Sun by observing the motion of sunspots across the solar surface. Observations indicate that the surface rotation is not uniform but rather substantially faster near the solar equator than near the solar poles: The sidereal rotation period varies from twenty-five days near the equator to over thirty days near the poles. Thus, the Sun does not rotate as a solid body, but rather rotates differentially. Until recently, little was known about the interior solar-rotation rate, but with the aid of helioseismology, it has been possible to determine that the rate is roughly constant on radial lines within the solar convection zone and that there is a substantial gradient in angular rotation at the base of this zone. Little is known about the rotation rate of the deep interior, where nuclear burning takes place, because the p-modes are not very sensitive to the rotation of the deep core. However, it has been possible to use helioseismological data to exclude the extreme rotation periods—ranging down to a few days—suggested by some observers in the 1970s. (These suggestions were based on tentative measurements of solar oblateness, or departures from spherical symmetry of the solar surface; these oblateness measurements are extremely difficult to interpret in terms of actual rotational distortions of the solar figure.)

Surface Layers

The visible surface of the Sun—the photosphere—is where energy transport within the Sun changes from convective transport to transport by radiation (i.e., through photons). This changeover in the energy-transport mechanism occurs over a very short distance (a few hundred kilometers), which is the fundamental reason that the Sun's limb (edge) appears so sharp and well-defined when viewed from Earth. Thus, the photosphere is not part of the solar-convection zone, but is instead a region of convective overshoot, that is, a region where energy transport occurs by a combination of convection and radiation. This convective overshoot can be observed directly by imaging of the surface at visible wavelengths with high angular resolution (e.g., one arc second or better); one can then see the so-called granulation, a network of convective cells (typically 500–1,000 km in diameter) with rising centers that are hotter and brighter than the immediately surrounding descending matter in the intergranular lanes. Surface convection can also be seen by observing the Doppler shift associated with horizontal solar-surface motions. Doppler images obtained in this way have shown the existence of a larger-scale surface-convection pattern (the so-called supergranulation), which has a spatial scale of order 10,000 km.

In addition to the surface inhomogeneities associated with convection, the photosphere reveals sunspots. Sunspots are associated with the presence of very strong magnetic fields at the solar surface and are believed to be a consequence of the ability of these magnetic fields (whose strength can range up to 3,000 G) to suppress convection—and therefore suppress energy transport—in the photosphere. Thus, sunspots are substantially cooler than the surrounding nonmagnetic photosphere, with typical effective temperatures of order 4,000 K, more than 1,000 degrees below that of the nonmagnetic photosphere. Sunspots are only the most prominent of an entire spectrum of magnetically related features in the photosphere, whose size scales range down to dimensions well below those directly observable from Earth: Spacelab observations of the photosphere show magnetic flux elements down to spatial scales of a few hundred kilometers. The relationship of these small-flux elements to the larger sunspot fields, and to a possible weak and more homogeneous background magnetic field, is not well understood and is an active field of investigation.

The emergence of sunspots at the solar surface from the interior is ordered both in time and space: Sunspots typically emerge in pairs with opposite magnetic polarity, with the leading (westward) spot emerging closer to the equator; the polarities of the leading and following spots are usually reversed in the Northern and Southern Hemispheres. These general properties are often referred to as the Hale polarity laws. The solar latitude of emergence also changes on a systematic basis, starting at high (pole-ward) latitudes and descending to the equatorial regions; this change is referred to as the butterfly diagram. This emergence cycle has roughly an eleven-year period, after which the polarities of the leading and following spots switch in the Northern and Southern Hemispheres, and sunspot emergence begins again at high solar latitudes. Thus, a full sunspot cycle takes roughly twenty-two years to complete. The physical mechanism underlying this cyclical behavior was not understood until the mid-1950s; afterward, it was thought to involve a self-regenerative magnetic dynamo, which is maintained by a combination of convection and rotation within or just below the convection zone. The detailed workings of this dynamo process remained mysterious, however, not because the basic physical principles were lacking, but because the highly nonlinear character of the dynamo process made detailed calculations extremely difficult.

Anyone who has experienced a solar eclipse (when the moon passes in front of the solar disk) knows that the Sun's atmosphere extends well beyond the visible photosphere. By the 1940s it was known that this extended atmosphere (consisting of, in radial order outward, the chromosphere, the transition region, and the corona) was substantially hotter than the photosphere, reaching temperatures in the corona of up to 10 million degrees; the puzzle was how the Sun reversed the decrease in temperature with radius that characterizes the solar interior, leading to a sharp upward jump in temperature just above the solar surface. Now it is believed that the magnetic fields associated with magnetic elements observed at the photospheric level, which penetrate into this overlying atmosphere, are active agents in plasma-heating processes leading to these high temperatures and act as a means of containing these hot plasmas, which would otherwise escape from the Sun.

This simple division of the extended outer atmosphere into chromosphere, transition region, and corona (based on horizontally averaged temperature properties) is highly deceptive because it hides the enormous morphological complexity of this atmosphere. This complexity was not well appreciated until it became possible to observe the Sun's atmosphere from space in the mid-1960s: Because of the high temperature of the gases in this atmosphere, the optimal way of observing them is at wavelengths in the ultraviolet or shorter yet (e.g., extreme ultraviolet and x rays), but, unfortunately, Earth's atmosphere is an excellent absorber at these short wavelengths. Extreme ultraviolet and x-ray images of

the chromosphere, transition region, and corona show a complex plasma geometry, dominated by loop-like plasma structures whose shape is presumably determined by magnetic fields anchored in the underlying photosphere. These structures are also highly dynamic, changing on time scales ranging from seconds to days; at the shorter end of this temporal dynamic range lies the most spectacular dynamical event on the Sun, the solar flare. The luminosity of a solar flare can easily exceed the luminosity of the entire quiescent extended atmosphere. This dynamical behavior is thought to be a consequence of the physical processes that lead to dissipation of magnetic fields and consequent (at times, impulsive) plasma heating. The heating process that is responsible for this dynamic extended atmosphere is not especially prominent in the overall energy budget of the Sun. For example, the mean heating levels of the solar corona and transition region are only roughly one-millionth of the total (bolometric) luminosity of the Sun.

The notion that magnetic fields act to contain and restrain the coronal plasma from escaping the Sun finds very strong support in the observation that in regions in the solar outer atmosphere, in which the magnetic field is believed to be open to the interplanetary medium, there is a strong depletion of x-ray-emitting plasma in the corona (the so-called coronal holes), together with evidence of a strong outflow (the high-speed solar wind, flowing at rates of up to 800 km·s^{-1}) coming from this depleted coronal region. These outflows were studied in great detail by the Ulysses spacecraft, which orbited over the solar poles in 1994–1995, and thus passed through the high-speed wind streams that commonly emerge from the solar polar regions.

Magnetic Fields, Solar Activity, and Stellar Activity

The level of dynamical activity in the solar outer atmosphere closely follows the rhythm of the sunspot cycle: At sunspot maximum, the level of extreme ultraviolet and x-ray emission peaks; at sunspot minimum, the level of radiative emission from this atmosphere dips to a minimum. The dynamic range of these variations in short-wavelength emissions is extremely large and becomes more and more pronounced as the wavelength of the emissions decreases; it is not unusual to observe a factor of two or more fluctuations in x-ray emission. These cyclical variations in radiative output have also been seen in other stars and are the subject of study of the astronomical field known as the solar-stellar connection. One objective of these studies is to observe stars of mass similar to that of the Sun and then to determine how the rotation rate and activity levels of these stars depend on (for example) stellar age. By this means, astronomers are able to test theories for the solar magnetic cycle despite the impossibility of carrying out laboratory-style experiments on the Sun itself.

Terrestrial Effects

The most obvious solar effect on the earth is radiation, roughly 1.4 kW/m^2 (the so-called solar constant); this radiation almost entirely accounts for the heat input to the earth's atmosphere and surface and leads to everyday phenomena, such as the weather.

A long-standing question is whether changes in the Sun's energy output lead to measurable effects on the earth. For example, do changes in the solar constant and in the spectrum of sunlight (its spectral irradiance) during the course of the solar-sunspot cycle have significant effects on Earth's climate and weather? This subject has been controversial since its beginnings, largely because on short time scales, the possible effects are small and easily swamped by noise. Nevertheless, it is essential to establish this connection because a number of physical processes in the terrestrial atmosphere are likely to be affected by solar variability and have significant human impact. An important example is the effect of changes in spectral irradiance (especially in the ultraviolet) on ozone in the upper atmosphere. Ozone is an essential absorber of solar ultraviolet light and thus acts to protect life on or near the terrestrial surface from the damaging effects of this radiation; in contrast, increases in the incident flux of short-wavelength ultraviolet and x-ray emission can lead to increased dissociation, and a depletion, of ozone. The significance of such photochemical effects on time scales comparable to, and somewhat longer than, the solar-cycle-activity period ($\sim$ 11 years) is not firmly established. Other terrestrial effects—especially those related to solar flares and coronal mass ejections—are firmly established; these effects range from disruption of long-distance (short-wave) communication to the interruption of continent-scale electrical-power-distribution networks. In addition, operators of terrestrial satellites, especially those outside the terrestrial magnetosphere, are concerned about space weather, the energetic-particle and electromagnetic-fields environment near the earth's orbit. For example, energetic particles from the Sun, when present in sufficient numbers, can lead to premature destruction of semiconductor-based electronics onboard these satellites and, hence, to failure of these extremely expensive missions.

Because the Sun evolves as a star, its total radiative output varies with time, but on time scales much longer than the variations alluded to in the context of solar activity and with amplitudes far in excess of those associated with this activity. For example, since the time some 4.5 billion years ago that the Sun began nuclear burning via the *pp* chain, its luminosity has increased by roughly 30 percent; thus, the solar constant 4.5 billion years ago was of order 1 kW/m^2. This low value of the solar constant during the earth's youth is widely regarded by scientists as a major challenge for models of the young earth's atmosphere because mean terrestrial-surface temperatures would then have been low enough to freeze water over much of the earth's surface, thereby significantly increasing the earth's albedo (reflectivity); thus, how the earth avoided a permanently frozen state is considered an unsolved puzzle by many scientists.

See also: NEUTRINO, SOLAR; PLANETARY SYSTEMS; SOLAR SYSTEM; SOLAR WIND; STARS AND STELLAR STRUCTURE; STELLAR EVOLUTION

Bibliography

BAHCALL, J. N. *Neutrino Astrophysics* (Cambridge University Press, Cambridge, Eng., 1989).

COX, A. N.; LIVINGSTON, W. C.; and MATTHEWS, M. S., eds. *Solar Interior and Atmosphere* (University of Arizona Press, Tucson, 1991).

FOUKAL, P. V. *Solar Astrophysics* (Wiley, New York, 1990).

HARVEY, K. L., ed. *The Solar Cycle* (Astronomical Society of the Pacific, San Francisco, CA, 1992).

LEIBACHER, J.; NOYES, R.; TOOMRE, J.; and ULRICH, R. "Helioseismology." *Sci. Am.* **253**, 48 (1985).

PHILLIPS, A. C. *The Physics of Stars* (Wiley, Chichester, Eng., 1994).

SONETT, C. P.; GIAMPAPA, M. S.; and MATTHEWS, M. S., eds. *The Sun in Time* (University of Arizona Press, Tucson, 1991).

STURROCK, P. A.; HOLZER, T. E.; MIHALAS, D. M.; and ULRICH, R. K., eds. *Physics of the Sun* (Reidel, Dordrecht, 1986).

ZIRIN, H. *Astrophysics of the Sun* (Cambridge University Press, Cambridge, Eng., 1988).

ROBERT ROSNER

SUPERCONDUCTING QUANTUM INTERFERENCE DEVICE

The Superconducting Quantum Interference Device (SQUID) is the most commonly used version of a class of new superconducting measurement devices that has emerged following Brian Josephson's discovery of coherent superconducting tunneling in 1962. The SQUID exploits the macroscopic phase coherence of superconducting electrons around a small loop to make the most precise low-frequency measurements possible in physics, as described below. This has lead to many new opportunities in medicine, geophysics, and fundamental physics that would be impossible without the SQUID.

The SQUID is the most sensitive magnetometer ever developed for making low-frequency measurements. A typical commercial SQUID is capable of measuring changes in magnetic flux as small as one part in 10^{12} (one trillionth) of Earth's magnetic field through a 1-cm^2 pickup loop in a 1-Hz bandwidth. This makes the SQUID roughly a thousand times more sensitive to changes in magnetic flux than a typical flux gate magnetometer. The SQUID is so extremely sensitive that its proper use generally requires the utmost care in shielding, grounding, and data reduction in order to assure that the intended SQUID-based measurement is not swamped by external noise sources. The SQUID only detects changes in magnetic flux that are coupled to the SQUID loop; it is not sensitive to the absolute magnetic flux, as are most other magnetometers. The SQUID may be thought of as an extremely low-noise, high-gain cryogenic preamplifier with extremely low input inductance. The low-frequency variation of any physical quantity that can be converted to magnetic flux may be measured to very high precision with the SQUID. Although SQUIDs continue to function at higher frequencies (greater than 10 kHz), other magnetometers become competitive in sensitivity with the SQUID in this range.

The SQUID consists of a loop of superconducting material broken in at least one place by a thin, non-superconducting layer, which is called the "Josephson junction." Some of the conduction electrons in superconductors form Cooper pairs and macroscopically occupy the lowest accessible energy state of the conduction band. This lowest energy state, which typically contains about 10^{20} Cooper pairs per cm^3, is described by a well-defined order parameter, or wave function, which has both an amplitude and a phase. For the SQUID to support a superconducting current around its loop there must exist an integer number of periods of the wave function around the loop. When this occurs, the total magnetic flux threading the SQUID loop must be an integer number of flux quanta, where the flux quantum is Planck's constant divided by the charge of the Cooper pair ($2e$), or about 2×10^{-7} G cm^2. If we attempt to place more magnetic flux into the SQUID loop, then the superconducting current in the SQUID will increase to cancel this flux that we are trying to put through the SQUID, hence keeping the SQUID flux constant. This is known as the Meissner effect. As this superconducting current through the Josephson junction changes, so does the phase shift in the wave function across the Josephson junction. Josephson shared the 1973 Nobel Prize in part for his discovery that this phase shift across the junction is equal to the arcsine of the superconducting current, normalized to the critical current of the junction. This critical current is the maximum current that the Josephson junction may support and still remain superconducting. Hence the interference of the superconducting wave function at the Josephson junction is an extremely sensitive indicator of small changes in magnetic flux coupled to the SQUID loop, directly analogous to the change in optical interference fringes in an interferometer when one optical path changes length relative to the other. One of many possible readout circuits may then be used to measure any change in this phase shift at the junction, and thus the change in magnetic flux coupled to the SQUID loop. The rf and dc SQUID readout techniques are the two most popular techniques in use today.

Applications of the SQUID have revolutionized medicine, fundamental science, and geophysics. As many as 122 SQUIDs are used in a single commercial medical imaging apparatus designed to measure the tiny magnetic fields created when our brain functions, with a noise level as low as just a few picoGauss (10^{-12} G) in a 1 Hz measurement bandwidth. This has lead to a revolution in neurological diagnostics and in our fundamental understanding of the human cognitive process. SQUIDs have been applied in a number of fundamental science missions that either have, or will soon, fly in Earth orbit. Such fundamental science applications include the Gravity Probe B mission, which will test the general theory of relativity in a polar Earth orbit. The mission will use SQUIDs to read the rotation of superconducting gyroscopes. Also, superfluid helium experiments have been, and will be, conducted on Earth orbit to explore the fundamental physics of phase transitions. In this application SQUIDs will be used within the cargo bay of the space shuttle to read thermometers with noise levels as low as 0.2 nK. SQUID-based systems are being used in ultraprecise superconducting gravity meters and gravity gradiometers to study deep-Earth dynamics and to explore for oil and minerals, as well as in measurement equipment to determine the fundamental constants and the physical units with unprecedented accuracy.

The SQUID remains the most sensitive and lowest noise sensor available in experimental physics for making low-frequency (near dc) measurements of any quantity that may be converted to magnetic flux. With the advent of high-transition temperature superconducting materials, new SQUID designs are being developed and applied at temperatures as high as 80 K. This promises to have a revolutionary impact on many fields, most notably biophysics, physiology, and medicine.

See also: COOPER PAIR; INTERFERENCE; INTERFEROMETRY; MAGNETIC RESONANCE IMAGING; MAGNETIC FLUX; SUPERCONDUCTIVITY

Bibliography

FEYNMAN, R. P.; LEIGHTON, R. B.; and SANDS, M. *The Feynman Lectures on Physics*, Vol. 3 (Addison-Wesley, Reading, MA, 1965).

KOCH, H., and LUBBIG, H. eds. *Superconducting Devices and Their Applications* (Springer-Verlag, Berlin, 1992).

LOUNASMAA, O. V. *Experimental Principles and Methods Below 1 K* (Academic Press, London, 1974).

ROBERT V. DUNCAN

SUPERCONDUCTIVITY

Superconductivity is a property of many metals and alloys in which the electrical resistance abruptly disappears at some characteristic temperature far below room temperature. The effect was discovered in 1911 when Heike Kammerlingh Onnes showed that at 4.36 K, the electrical resistance of a mercury wire dropped to a value too small to measure at 4.35 K. Subsequently, sophisticated measurements

have shown that the resistivity drops more than 15 factors of 10, from about 10^{-6} Ω cm to less than 10^{-21} Ω cm. It is a remarkable phase change in the electron gas of a metal in which the electrons transform from a normal state where the electrons act as independent particles to a superconducting state where the electrons act as a coherent unit much like a giant molecule containing many billions of electrons. This coherent gas of electrons moves through the metal without the scattering from defects and energy loss that accompanies this scattering. To understand superconductivity in more detail, it is helpful to know what types of materials show this zero electrical resistance effect and to know which forces are important in causing the transformation to a coherent state.

Superconductivity is a very common phenomenon, especially among nonmagnetic metals. Roughly half the elements of the periodic table and a wide range of alloys and intermetallic compounds show the effect. For some elements, the superconducting transition occurs simply by cooling a sample at atmospheric pressure. Examples are Nb at 9.25 K, Pb at 7.25 K, Sn at 3.72 K, Al at 1.18 K, and W at 0.015 K. Many other elements that are semiconductors or insulators at atmospheric pressure can be transformed into metals at high pressure, and they then become superconducting. For example, antimony is an insulator at one atmosphere pressure but becomes metallic at 115,000 atm and superconducting at 5.35 K. Probably the most widely used alloy is a highly ductile Nb-Ti conductor that is the material of choice for large-scale magnets up to 7 T operating at 4.2 K. The magnets associated with the magnetic resonance imaging (MRI) unit at your local hospital is probably made of this alloy. Among the most widely used intermetallic superconducting compounds is Nb_3Sn. This material has higher performance characteristics, but it is rather brittle and more difficult to make into a magnet. One of the most recent applications of Nb_3Sn is for a MRI magnet that operates at 0.5 T and 10 K on a closed cycle refrigerator that requires no liquid helium. It is large enough to accommodate a surgeon operating on a patient, imaging a tumor as the surgeon cuts toward it. To use superconductivity in practical applications has always required a substantial investment in refrigeration to work below 20 K.

A full understanding of superconductivity requires the principles of quantum mechanics, but there are many classical analogies that permit us to understand how the electrons behave and why the zero resistance phenomenon occurs. In a normal metal such as a Pb wire at 8 K, the electrons behave as individual particles that are free to hop from atom to atom and carry electrical current. As the electrons move, they scatter from irregularities in the lattice and cause energy dissipation and heat. If this Pb wire is cooled below the superconducting transition temperature, the electrons undergo a phase transition temperature, the electrons undergo a phase transition to a state in which they behave as a giant, coherent collection of particles that moves through the metal as a unit without scattering. A classical analogy that might help to give the picture is to think of a highway surface made of pebbles and tar. If you roll a small coin across the surface, it will scatter because the size of the pebble is comparable to the size of the coin. If you roll a giant truck tire over the surface, it does not scatter because the tire is so large. The suppression of scattering in the electron gas is a little like this. John Bardeen often referred to the coherent state of the superconducting electrons as a macromolecule.

The next stage in understanding superconductivity is to determine the cause of the coherence. Why do the electrons lock together and act as a unit? For most classical superconductors, the electrons interact with one another by the coherent exchange of phonons or lattice waves, the so-called electron-phonon interaction. In this process, two electrons communicate by exchanging a phonon. An electron moving through the crystal emits a phonon (bumps into an ion and disturbs its position) creating a local charge fluctuation and then moves on with a different momentum. Another electron is attracted to the charge fluctuation and then moves on with a different momentum. Another electron is attracted to the charge fluctuation and absorbs the phonon restoring the crystal to its original configuration. This pair of electrons is called a Cooper pair. This coherent exchange of phonons lowers the energy of the electron gas and gives a kind of cadence counting that causes the electrons to move such that they all have the same phase. Scattering of the electrons by defects in the crystal would disrupt the orderly phonon exchange and raise the energy of the system. Thus the scattering is suppressed in order to give a lower energy state. In a very short temperature interval below the transition temperature, often less than 0.001 K, a sufficient number of Cooper pairs form to completely eliminate the scattering.

Parenthetically, we might add that the lowest energy state is obtained when the two electrons of the Cooper pair have equal and opposite momentum. This particular kind of pair is favored because Fermi surface symmetry gives this combination the maximum amount of phonon exchange. Similarly, the spin of the two electrons of the Cooper pair are opposite because of a quantum mechanical effect called exchange symmetry that permits two electrons with opposite spin to be closer together in space so that they can electron-phonon scatter more often.

Once the electrons condense into a phase coherent state, some truly remarkable features become apparent. The first is the Meissner effect, a tendency of the material to have zero magnetic field in the interior of a specimen. If a magnetic field is applied to a superconductor, it is energetically favored for the material to establish screening currents around the surface to cancel the field so that $B = 0$ inside the sample. There is no scattering, so these supercurrents dissipate no energy. In the surface layer where the screening currents flow, the magnetic field decays to zero in a distance of about 100 nm called the penetration depth. There are, in fact, two types of superconductors depending on the size of the penetration depth relative to the size of the Cooper pair called the coherence distance. If the penetration distance is smaller than the coherence distance, then the superconductor is said to be type I. For this class of material, $B = 0$ for all fields up to a thermodynamic critical field H_c, where the flux suddenly collapses into the sample in a first order transition and the material returns to the normal state. If the penetration depth is longer than the coherence distance, then the superconductor is said to be type II. For this class of material, $B = 0$ up to some lower critical field H_{c1}, where magnetic flux begins to enter the sample gradually in the form of quantized vortices, tiny whirlpools of electrons. Because the Cooper pairs are phase coherent, when they go around in a circle in the vortex, they must have a single valued wave function and obey the Bohr–Sommerfeld quantization condition, just as do electrons moving around a hydrogen atom. This quantization of the angular momentum of the Cooper pair leads directly to the fact that superconducting vortices carry an elementary quantum of flux equal to $\Phi_0 = 2.07 \times 10^{-7}$ G cm^2. As the magnetic field is raised further above H_{c1}, more and more vortices pack into the sample and eventually the sample undergoes a second order transition to the normal state at the upper critical field H_{c2}. Generally speaking, clean superconductors are type I and dirty materials are type II. You can shorten the coherence distance or the size of the Cooper pair by adding impurities so you can convert a type I to a type II by shortening the electron mean-free-path. Most practical materials are type II.

The presence of vortices in a material has a profound effect on the response of a superconductor to the presence of a transport current. A current flowing in a thin film or wire containing vortices will exert a Lorentz force on the vortex and push it sideways. If the vortex moves in response to this force, it creates a time-varying magnetic field that, by Faraday's law, gives a voltage in the direction of the transport current. This voltage times the transport current gives a power dissipation, which is just what we are trying to avoid. Hence, for a practical superconductor to have effectively zero resistance, the vortices must be pinned.

To pin a superconducting vortex, it is necessary to have an irregularity in the material where it is energetically favorable for the vortex to be located. Often the irregularity or defect is a normal or insulating inclusion; sometimes it is simply a grain boundary where the electron mean free path is shorter than in the bulk. Because the core of a vortex acts like a cylinder of normal material, it is energetically favorable for the normal core to sit on the defect and be pinned to it. Hence, a very high performance Nb-Ti wire will have a very fine dispersion of α-Ti precipitates spaced about 10 to 100 atomic spacings apart to serve as pinning centers for the vortex lattice.

A genuine revolution occurred in the field with the discovery of superconductivity in a new class of copper oxide materials by Georg Bednorz and Alex Mueller. Throughout the first seventy-five years that the phenomenon had been known, there was a fairly regular discovery of superconductivity at ever higher temperatures starting from the original discovery in mercury at 4.35 K in 1911, and progressing to Nb_3Ge at 23 K in 1968. Then, in 1986, La_2CuO_4 doped with Ca was found to be superconducting at 35 K and soon after $Y_1Ba_2Cu_3O_{7-\delta}$ was discovered to be superconducting at 92 K. This opened whole new areas of research, not only because the superconducting transition temperature was high but also because these materials were a new class of metals. They were composed of an oxygen deficient crystal structure with highly anisotropic bonding. There is a very characteristic laminar structure in which various combinations of CuO_2 sheets, alkaline earth-oxide sheets, and other layers stack to form the crystal structure. This class of materials often has a parent compound that is an antiferromagnetic insulator, but it can be made metallic and superconducting by using the oxygen or metal ion content to control the density of electrons or holes. This, in turn, controls whether it is a metal and whether it goes superconducting.

With the discovery of much higher transition temperatures and higher critical fields, there is the potential for far superior performance in practical devices. To realistically assess the opportunities for practical applications of these materials, it is helpful to understand the similarities and differences between these materials and the classical superconductors. First the similarities. We know that flux is quantized in units of $hc/2e$ so that the fundamental entity in the superfluid is a Cooper pair. Second, measurements of the difference in energy between the superconducting and normal state has the same temperature and magnetic field dependence as for the classical superconductors. Whatever theories or models are proposed, the thermodynamic properties and flux quantization properties have to reduce to the same result as for the classical materials. A first major difference between these copper oxide materials and most classical materials is the high anisotropy in chemical bonding and the transport properties. In some of the materials the electrical coupling between planes is much weaker than the in-plane coupling. This means that the vortices tend to decouple into "pancakes" of circulating supercurrents in the a-b plane so that the vortices tend to tilt and bend much more easily. A second major difference is that the size of the Cooper pairs goes inversely as the transition temperature and is only about 4 or 5 atomic spacings long for those having a transition temperature of about 100 K. This means that any one Cooper pair only overlaps about a dozen other Cooper pairs, so the phase locking is much more fragile than in the classical materials, where there are millions of Cooper pairs overlapping any one Cooper pair.

See also: COHERENCE; COOPER PAIR; ELECTRICAL RESISTANCE; MAGNETIC FLUX; MAGNETIC RESONANCE IMAGING; SUPERCONDUCTING QUANTUM INTERFERENCE DEVICE; SUPERCONDUCTIVITY, HIGH-TEMPERATURE

Bibliography

SCHRIEFFER, J. R. *Theory of Superconductivity* (W. A. Benjamin, New York, 1964).

TINKHAM, M. *Introduction to Superconductivity* (McGraw-Hill, New York, 1975).

DOUGLAS K. FINNEMORE

SUPERCONDUCTIVITY, HIGH-TEMPERATURE

Arguably, one of the most extraordinary and unexpected events in physics in the last half of the twentieth century was the discovery of high-temperature ("high T_c") superconductivity in 1986. In 1911 it was discovered that the electrical resistance in purified mercury effectively vanishes below a temperature of 4.2 K. The loss of resistance was sudden, and a similar disappearance of resistance was observed in a number of metals and alloys. Superconductivity developed from its initial, almost chance observation, into a significant branch of solid-state physics. This development culminated in the theoretical understanding provided by the Bardeen, Cooper, Schrieffer (BCS) pairing theory in 1957, which integrated superconductivity into the general framework of solid-state physics. The highest temperature at which superconductivity was observed at that time was about 28 K. The phenomena in this temperature domain (0–30 K) are summarized as the field of low T_c superconductivity. Associated with the vanishing of the resistance are a number of radical changes in the electric, magnetic, and thermal behavior, while the mechanical, elastic, and crystallographic properties changed very little.

In 1951 Fritz London made the brilliant guess that superconductivity was a genuine quantum phenomenon which resulted in a quantized magnetic flux in superconductors, quantized in units of hc/e (h is Planck's constant, c is the velocity of light, and e is the charge of the electron). Two ideas were central in the understanding of superconductivity in the BCS theory. The first idea came from a careful and detailed quantum mechanical analysis of the various interactions which led to the insight of an overall weak attraction between electrons. The second was the recognition that as a consequence of this interaction, bound electron pairs, called Cooper pairs, were formed, which at sufficiently low temperature could move through the solid without losing or gaining any energy. These insights led to an impressive description of superconductivity, which explained both the qualitative aspects and numerous quantitative agreements. One consequence was that the transition temperature T_c should vary with the isotopic mass M as $T_c \sim 1/\sqrt{M}$. Another was that since the Cooper pairs were the entities moving through the solid without friction, the unit of flux quantization should be $hc/2e$. Both were confirmed by many experiments. Although not proven, there were all kinds of arguments suggesting that the Cooper pairs would become unstable and dissolve at temperatures above 25 K. Indeed, the highest critical temperature known before 1986 was one alloy, Nb_3Ge, with a T_c of 23.2 K.

In 1986 J. G. Bednorz and K. A. Muller, studying cuprates (Copper oxides) such as La_2CuO_4, found that by replacing some of the La atoms by ions of Ba, Sr or Ca, new materials were obtained which, surprisingly, were superconductors with quite high transition temperatures. For example $(La_{2-2c}\ Sr_{2c})CuO_4$ has a T_c of 38 K, an increase in T_c of about 40 percent. In spite of the somewhat unlikely material, a poorly conducting brittle material of complex structure, this started an explosive development of producing high T_c materials.

While low T_c materials are either metals such as Tb, Sn, and Al, with T_c anywhere from 1–12 K, or simple alloys such as V_3 Si and Nb–Ti, with T_c between 7 and 23 K, the high T_c materials are more complicated compounds, and often ceramics. The manufacture of $YBa_2Cu_3O_{7.8}$ (the first so-called 1-2-3 compounds) caused enormous excitement. Its T_c was 92 K, well above the boiling point of nitrogen (which is 77 K). Clearly, producing a superconductive material with liquid nitrogen (10¢ a liter) is much cheaper than using liquid helium (at $5.00 a liter).

A large and growing number of compounds exhibit high T_c superconductivity—$Bi_2Sr_2CaCu_2U_8$ with a T_c of 85 K and $Te_2Ba_2Ca_2Cu_3U_{10}$ with a T_c of 125 K. Most of the compounds are Copper oxides. The low T_c superconductors occur in two rather distinct classes—type I and type II. Most of the superconductive elements Sn, Al, are type I, and most of the alloys are type II. When placed in an external field, a type I superconductor acts like a perfect diamagnet, the magnetic lines of force are pushed out and are restricted to a very thin layer near the surface. The width of this layer (called λ, the penetration depth) varies with material and temperatures between 100 Å and 10,000 Å. For lead at 3 K, the penetration depth λ is 600 Å. This expulsion of the magnetic field is the Meissner effect. For magnetic fields larger than a critical value (the critical field), the material reverts back to its normal state and the electrical resistance reappears. For type I superconductors, the critical fields are usually less than 1,000 G.

Type II materials behave quite differently. There is again a critical field, but it is much larger—hundreds of thousands of gauss. For small external fields, there is again an expulsion, a Meissner effect. For larger fields there is a mixed or vortex state where the magnetic field penetrates certain locations in discrete vortices, while other parts of the superconductor remain field free.

There is another parameter—the coherence length ξ—which is important in describing superconductors. The current at a point in the superconductor depends not only on the electric field at that same point (as it does in Ohm's law), but it depends on the electric field in a region of size ξ. For usual metallic superconductors, ξ varies between 1,000 and 5,000 Å, it could be as high as 10,000 Å. The coherence length ξ is also a measure of the spatial separation of the two electrons in a Cooper pair.

For type I superconductors $\lambda < \xi$, the coherence extends much beyond the magnetic penetration depth.

For type II superconductors $\lambda > \xi$, the magnetic field can penetrate well beyond the coherence length. All the high T_c superconductors are of type II, and they have very large critical fields. A very important characterization of a high T_c superconductor is that its coherence length is a lot smaller than in any low T_c superconductor. It is often of the order, or less than 30 Å.

Geometrically, almost all high T_c materials contain a series of parallel planes in which the Cu-O atoms are located. The Cu-O distance is rather short, about 1.9 Å. The distance between two nearest-neighbor Cu-O planes is rather large, about 6.6 Å. Sandwiched between these planes are planes containing other atoms, rare-earth ions, and oxides. The charge transport and the superconductive properties are primarily confined to the Cu-O planes. In both high and low T_c superconductors, Cooper pairs are believed to be carriers of the frictionless transport. The measured flux quantum in high and low T_c superconductors is the same. On the other hand, the isotope effect $T_c \sim 1/\sqrt{M}$ is quite different in high and low T_c materials.

The practical and technological applications of high T_c superconductivity all depend on the manufacture of materials which can maintain large currents; their critical fields must be quite high. Just as there is a critical field strength, there is also a critical current density J_c. For larger currents, the resistance reappears again. Thus, one needs materials with high T_c, high J_c, and high critical fields. Furthermore, they should be mechanically strong, not brittle. It should be possible to make wires, tapes, shields, and films from these materials. Not all of this has been achieved. The highest T_c so far confirmed is 133 K, and the highest critical field is 7×10^6 G.

If the material science problems (mainly manufacturing problems) can be solved, there are many immediate and obvious uses of these materials, such as high-speed computing, the production of strong magnets for extraction and separation processes, magnetic shielding, power transmission, superconducting storage of energy by circulating currents, and medical imaging.

But perhaps the most tempting research direction is to obtain such a deep understanding of superconductivity that it becomes possible to design superconductive materials to order. If that materializes, it may even be possible to design room-temperature superconductors, with prescribed mechanical properties.

See also: COHERENCE; CONDUCTION; CONDUCTOR; COOPER PAIR; ELECTRICAL CONDUCTIVITY; ELECTRICAL RESISTANCE; SUPERCONDUCTIVITY

Bibliography

BEDNORZ, J. G., and MULLER, K. A., eds. *Earlier and Recent Aspects of Superconductivity* (Springer-Verlag, New York, 1990).

LYNN, J. W., ed. *High-Temperature Superconductivity* (Springer-Verlag, New York, 1990).

MAX DRESDEN

SUPERGRAVITY

Supergravity is a conjectured theory of basic physics that combines supersymmetry and general relativity. One of the guiding principles in fundamental physics is the search for symmetries that relate the properties of different particles when they are transformed into one another. Supersymmetry is a new class of symmetry that relates particles with different amounts of internal angular momentum, or spin. Particles with integer amounts of spin, such as the photon or graviton, are called bosons, while particles with half-integer spins, such as the electron or neutrino, are called fermions. Theories with just one type of supersymmetry transformation relate bosons and fermions (see Table 1), and theories with more than one type of supersymmetry transformation also relate bosons at different spins.

In general, symmetries may be either global, in which case all particles are transformed in the same way wherever they are in space and time, or local, in which case particles located at different spacetime points are transformed independently. The underlying symmetries of general relativity and the standard model are of the more powerful local type. In general relativity, the spacetime coordinates may be changed in different places, a symmetry called general covariance. In the standard model, the phases of the particle-wave functions may vary locally, a symmetry called gauge invariance. Like all previously established symmetries, these local symmetries only relate particles of the same spin; in particular, bosons of integer spin are unrelated to fermions of half-integer spin. All local symmetries involve interactions that are carried by intermediate bosonic particles, such as the graviton of general relativity, the photon of quantum electrodynamics, the W and Z bosons of weak interactions, and the gluons of strong interactions (see Table 1).

There are two strong reasons to elevate supersymmetry to a local symmetry. One is the analogy with the successful theories of general relativity and the standard model, and the other is the hope of constructing a unified theory of all particle interactions. This hope is in part because supersymmetry might relate the force-carrying graviton, photon, and other bosons to fermions, such as the electron and neutrino, and because any pair of supersymmetry transformations combines to transform spacetime coordinates. Thus, local supersymmetry transformation combine to yield general coordinate transformations of the type underlying general relativity, and a locally supersymmetric theory necessarily incorporates general relativity.

The first theory of supergravity was formulated by Sergio Ferrara, Daniel Freedman, and Peter van Nieuwenhuizen in 1976, followed by Stanley Desor and Bruno Zumino using a different approach. In this theory, the new intermediate particle required by local supersymmetry is a spin-$\frac{3}{2}$ fermionic particle, called the gravitino, that is the supersymmetric partner of the graviton (see Table 1). Subsequently, generalizations with more types of supersymmetry were discovered, culminating in the theory with eight types of local supersymmetry developed by Eugène Cremmer, Bernard Julia, Bernard de Wit, and Hermann Nicolai. The most attractive formulation of this and other supergravity theories was in a spacetime with more than four dimensions, as studied by Joel Scherk and others. In particular, the maximally symmetric theory of de Wit and Nicolai could be obtained most naturally from a supergravity theory with just one type of local supersymmetry transformation in eleven dimensions. This realiza-

Table 1 Particles and Their Conjectured Supersymmetric Partners

Ordinary Particles			Supersymmetric Particles		
	Spin	Mass (GeV)		Spin	Mass (GeV)
Intermediate bosons					
photon	1	0	photino	$\frac{1}{2}$	> 12
W	1	80	Wino	$\frac{1}{2}$	> 64
Z	1	91	Zino	$\frac{1}{2}$	> 12
gluon	1	0	gluino	$\frac{1}{2}$	> 175
graviton	2	0	gravitino	$\frac{3}{2}$	?
Matter fermions					
electron	$\frac{1}{2}$	0.0005	selectron	0	> 60
neutrino	$\frac{1}{2}$	0?	sneutrino	0	> 43
quark	$\frac{1}{2}$	0.005 to 170	squark	0	> 60
Higgs boson	0	> 65	higgsino	$\frac{1}{2}$	>12

tion stimulated new interest in the old idea of Matjaz Kaluza and Oskar Klein that the laws of physics could be obtained from an underlying higher-dimensional theory.

Initially, it was hoped that the unique maximally supersymmetric theory with eight types of supersymmetry transformation would provide a suitable framework for unifying all the elementary particles. However, no way was found of accommodating the left-right asymmetry (parity violation) observed in weak interactions. Moreover, quantum corrections to known supergravity theories are suspected to be infinite in such a way as to make meaningful calculations impossible. For these and other reasons, hopes for a unified theory of all the elementary particles and their interactions have now largely been transferred to superstring theory. However, many theoretical physicists believe that supergravity plays a key role by providing an effective theory of fundamental physics at energies below the Planck energy of about 10^{19} GeV.

In the initial formulations of supergravity theory, the gravitino appeared massless like the graviton, reflecting unbroken, exact supersymmetry. However, just as the massive W and Z boson particles of the standard model are believed to acquire their masses from a mechanism in which the corresponding local symmetry is spontaneously broken, or hidden, so the gravitino is believed to become massive through a spontaneous breakdown of local supersymmetry. Supersymmetry must be broken in nature, since no known particles have supersymmetric partners with the same masses (lower limits on their masses are also shown in Table 1), and this spontaneous mechanism is the only consistent way of breaking local supersymmetry. It is also possible to break global supersymmetry spontaneously but only at the expense of a large density of energy in empty space, corresponding to an unacceptably large cosmological constant in general relativity.

This problem is avoided in the supergravity theory discovered by Cremmer, Ferrara, Costas Kounnas, and Dimitri Nanopoulos, and generalized by John Ellis, Kounnas, and Nanopoulos, in which supersymmetry may be broken with an arbitrary value of the gravitino mass and no cosmological constant in a first approximation. It is hoped that, within such a no-scale supergravity theory, particle masses may be determined dynamically by quantum effects.

Superstring theory is the favored candidate for a "Theory of Everything" comprising all elementary particles and fundamental interactions. According to

superstring theory, physics at energies smaller than the Planck mass of about 10^{19} GeV, or distances greater than the Planck length of about 10^{-33} cm, is described by an effective field theory of the no-scale supergravity type, as was first demonstrated by Edward Witten. Thus, no-scale supergravity and ideas associated with it may play a role in describing nature, though there is no experimental evidence for this belief. Supergravity theories suggest relations between particle masses and couplings that could be tested directly if supersymmetric particles are found in experiments using accelerators. The gravitinos are only very weakly coupled to ordinary matter, so detecting them is expected to be difficult. However, the gravitino is one possible candidate for the dark matter believed to be present throughout the universe, though it might be one of the other electrically uncharged and weakly interacting supersymmetric particles listed in Table 1.

See also: DARK MATTER; ELEMENTARY PARTICLES; FERMIONS AND BOSONS; RELATIVITY, GENERAL THEORY OF; SUPERSTRING; SUPERSYMMETRY; SYMMETRY; SYMMETRY BREAKING, SPONTANEOUS

Bibliography

SALAM, A., and SEZGIN, E., eds. *Supergravities in Diverse Dimensions* (North-Holland, Amsterdam, 1989).

WESS, J., and BAGGER, J. *Supersymmetry and Supergravity* (Princeton University Press, Princeton, NJ, 1983).

WEST, P. C. *Introduction to Supersymmetry and Supergravity* (World Scientific, Singapore, 1990).

JOHN ELLIS

SUPERNOVA

Supernovas represent stellar explosions that mark the end of the life of some normal stars. A mass from 1 to 10 times the mass of the Sun is ejected with velocities typically 1 to 3 percent of the speed of light. The corresponding kinetic energy, about 10^{51} ergs, is comparable to the gravitational binding energy of the star and hence evidence of the disruptive nature of the explosion. Some compact remnant, a neutron star or a black hole, may survive in some cases.

Supernovas have been observed in our galaxy, but only in the historic past. The last clearly observed with the naked eye was reported by Johannes Kepler in 1604. Other galactic events are marked by the expanding supernova remnants created when the supernova ejecta collide with the interstellar medium. More evidence is contained in the pulsars, the rotating, magnetic neutron stars that were presumably born in supernova explosions. No supernova has been witnessed in our galaxy in the era of modern astronomy that began with the invention of the telescope. All contemporary supernovas have been discovered in other galaxies. The nearest and best studied was the event Supernova 1987A in the Large Magellanic Cloud, a small companion galaxy to our own. This galaxy is only 150,000 light-years away. More typical supernovas, discovered at the rate of about 50 per year, occur in galaxies at distances of 10 to 100 million light-years away. Supernovas occur on average about once per 100 years in a galaxy like the Milky Way, and hence, we are statistically overdue. A galactic supernova could be discovered at any time.

Observationally, supernovas are characterized by the nature of their spectra and by their light curves, the pattern of their brightness as it rises and falls in different wavelength bands. Supernovas typically rise to maximum light in about two weeks, at which time they can be nearly as bright as their host galaxy, containing 10 to 100 billion stars like the Sun. The light output then decays on time scales of months, the pattern varying from event to event. There are two broad observational categories of supernovas, called type I and type II. Type I show no (or very little) evidence of hydrogen in their spectra at any phase. Type II show clear evidence for hydrogen near maximum light.

There are two principal mechanisms proposed by theory to account for the explosions. One is a thermonuclear explosion that is thought to disrupt the star completely, leaving no compact remnant. The other mechanism involves the collapse of an evolved stellar core in the middle of the star to form a neutron star. Some of the gravitational energy released in the collapse is thought to power the explosion. These two mechanisms do not correlate in any simple way with the basic observational categories of type I and type II.

Continued observational study has shown that supernovas can be further differentiated. Some type I supernovas show evidence for intermediate mass elements such as oxygen, magnesium, and calcium near maximum and for iron later on. These have been defined as type Ia. They are, on average, the brightest type of supernova. Other type I supernovas show varying evidence for helium in their ejecta near maximum and strong emission lines of intermediate mass elements at later times. These are currently called type Ib for the case with strong helium, and type Ic for the events with little observed helium. Some supernovas show evidence for hydrogen near maximum light, but little or none at later times.

Supernovas have been observed in polarized light on a few occasions. Although data are sparse, all type Ia events have revealed little detectable polarization, indicating that the ejecta are nearly spherically symmetric at the level of resolution available. All type II observed have shown some intrinsic polarization, suggesting that they are not spherically symmetric in some way. The cause is not clear.

Type Ia supernovas probably arise from an explosion in a binary star system. This class is rather homogeneous, and the spectral and photometric evolution can be explained by thermonuclear combustion of a white dwarf of the Chandrasekhar-mass (about 1.4 times the mass of the Sun) composed of carbon and oxygen and supported by the pressure of degenerate electrons. Stellar evolution theory predicts that this type of white dwarf is formed in a star with original mass less than about 8 times the mass of the Sun. Such a configuration is very volatile when thermonuclear carbon burning is initiated, but a companion star of some kind is thought to be necessary to add mass to the white dwarf to bring it to the point of nuclear ignition. This type of supernova is generally associated with an older stellar population, which is consistent with the idea that there is a delay while the companion star evolves and begins to transfer mass to the white dwarf. No direct evidence for stellar duplicity has ever been obtained.

The precise nature of the explosion of type Ia is still under investigation. Complex, dynamical fluid flows are probably involved, and these are just now becoming amenable to numerical computation in sufficient detail. The most advanced models predict that the nuclear burning starts as a subsonic flame. This configuration is subject to the Rayleigh–Taylor instability that will cause the burning to become turbulent. At some point, conditions are right such that a transition is made to a supersonic detonation mediated by a shock front. This type of explosion leaves intermediate mass elements on the outside, in keeping with the observation near maximum light. On the inside, the matter is transformed to nickel-56, the element with the highest nuclear binding energy per nucleon that has equal numbers of protons and neutrons. This element is unstable to decay into cobalt-56 and then into stable iron-56. The decay releases gamma rays that are presumed to power the light output of this kind of supernova. Some variation has been seen within this class. Some type Ia are brighter and have broader light curves with hotter radiation; others are somewhat dimmer and have narrower light curves with cooler radiation. Both extremes have nearly the same velocity and hence probably similar kinetic energy. This behavior is consistent with models in which some type Ia make the transition to detonation later and produce less nickel. They are cooler and hence have less opacity and narrower light curves. Theory predicts that no compact remnant will be left in this type of explosion, consistent with available observations.

Essentially all other observed types of supernovas are thought to arise from the gravitational collapse mechanism. The basic mechanism is that massive stars, more than about 12 times the mass of the Sun, burn a series of nuclear fuels in their hot, dense cores until they form iron. The arrangement of neutrons and protons in iron nuclei give it the highest nuclear binding energy per nucleon of any common element. For this reason, iron can only absorb energy from the star by breaking up into lighter elements or by fusing to form even heavier elements. When iron is compressed it undergoes these processes and thus removes energy from the star that is required to provide support against gravity. The result is the catastrophic collapse of the iron core to form a neutron star. Stars with initial masses from about 8 to 12 times the solar mass may form electron degenerate cores of oxygen, neon, and magnesium. These are also believed likely to collapse, leading to a situation similar to iron-core collapse. The processes that turn this collapse into an explosion are still not totally clear.

The problem is that while the collapse of the iron core to form a neutron star releases 100 times more energy than is necessary to disrupt the star, most of that energy is lost to neutrinos. Neutrinos are particles of little or no mass that have no charge and interact only by means of the weak force. They can therefore flow out of the star virtually unimpeded. The neutrinos are produced in the collapse as the protons of the iron nuclei are converted by the weak force into neutrons, the predominant component of the newly formed neutron star, and by other physical processes. The neutrinos are trapped in the densest parts of the newly formed neutron star, but stream out easily from the infalling matter. The question is whether about 1 percent of the available neutrino energy can be trapped in the star in such a way as to trigger the explosion. The original collapse is halted when the stiff resistance of the neutrons is encountered. The overcompression and rebound of the neutron star creates a shock that travels back "upstream" in the infalling matter, slowing and even reversing its flow. Current studies show, however, that the momentum of the inflow and the property of the infalling iron nuclei that they disintegrate and absorb energy combine to rob this shock of its energy, and it stalls. Some other process must enter to enhance the outward flow of matter. Once again, there is a growing realization that key processes may involve multidimensional dynamics, only now becoming computationally feasible. A mixing, convective-like process may carry trapped neutrinos outward where they can more effectively deposit their energy. If the process fails, as it may in some cases, then the new neutron star will continue to accrete matter from the infall and collapse to form a black hole. Whether or not this will prevent the supernova explosion is not known.

The basic correctness of this picture was established with the detection of neutrinos from Supernova 1987A. There were not sufficient data from that event, however, to determine the precise nature of the explosion mechanism. No confirmed evidence for a neutron star has been published, so the question of whether the collapse ultimately left a neutron star or a black hole is still open. Any neutron star in Supernova 1987A is producing a total power less than the 1,000-year-old pulsar in the Crab nebula that is the remnant of the Galactic supernova of 1054.

Type II supernovas are associated with young stellar populations. They are thus presumed to arise in short-lived massive stars and hence to result from core collapse in analogy with Supernova 1987A, for which the original mass was about 20 solar masses. Type II explode in stars that retain their extended, hydrogen-rich, red giant envelopes. The light emitted at maximum is thought to be from the shock heating of this large envelope, but the late time decay most probably again arises from the decay of nickel and cobalt produced in the explosion in smaller quantities than for type Ia. This process of radioactive decay was also confirmed in Supernova 1987A. One variety of type II is especially bright, and there is some speculation that they may arise from a thermonuclear explosion but still within a blanket of hydrogen.

Types Ib and Ic and the hybrid types that show hydrogen at early, but not late, times are also associated with young stellar populations and hence thought to come from massive stars by means of core collapse. The varying degrees of hydrogen deficiency probably come from loss of outer layers to a binary companion or by means of a stellar wind, but again no direct evidence for duplicity has been obtained. The loss of the envelope means that the progenitors tend to be small in radius, akin to those of type Ia, and hence the initial shock energy is dissipated in the expansion. The dominant source of light is radioactive decay of an ejected nickel mass comparable to that of type II. Some events classified as type Ic have relatively shallow late-time decay typical of type Ib, and others have very steep declines. The spectral classification is insufficient to categorize this behavior and so a complete record of an event must consist of both spectral and photometric observations.

See also: GALAXIES AND GALACTIC STRUCTURE; NEUTRINO, SOLAR; NEUTRON STAR; NOVA; PULSAR; STARS AND STELLAR STRUCTURE; STELLAR EVOLUTION

Bibliography

KIRSHNER, R. P. "Death of a Star." *National Geographic* **173** (5), 618–647 (1988).

MARSCHALL, L. A. *The Supernova Story* (Plenum, New York, 1988).

MURDIN, P., and MURDIN, L. *Supernovae* (Cambridge University Press, Cambridge, Eng., 1985).

WHEELER, J. C., and HARKNESS, R. P. "Helium-Rich Supernovas." *Sci. Am.* **257** (5), 50–58 (1987).

J. CRAIG WHEELER

SUPERSTRING

Traditional studies of relativistic quantum physics describe elementary particles as mathematical points without any spatial extension. This approach has had impressive success, but it breaks down at extremely high energies or short distances, where gravitational forces between particles become comparable in strength to the nuclear and electromagnetic forces. In 1974 Joël Scherk and John H. Schwarz proposed overcoming this limitation by basing a unified description of elementary particles on fundamental one-dimensional curves, called strings. String theories appear to be free from the inconsistencies that have plagued all previous attempts to construct a unified theory describing gravity together with the other forces. Superstring theories, which contain a special kind of symmetry called supersymmetry, show the most promise for giving realistic results.

There are many mathematically consistent quantum theories for point particles, although none of them contains gravity. On the other hand, there are very few mathematically consistent quantum theories of elementary extended objects. In the case of strings, which are one-dimensional, consistency requires gravity. It is not known whether there are consistent theories for objects of more than one dimension, such as two-dimensional membranes, but this appears to be unlikely. The existence of quantum string theories depends on special features that do not generalize to higher-dimensional objects.

Typically, string theory solutions have a particle spectrum that includes exactly one massless spin-2 graviton, the particle that transmits the gravitational force. Furthermore, this graviton interacts in accord with Albert Einstein's general theory of relativity at distances large compared to the typical length of the strings, which is the Planck length (L_p). [The Planck length is formed from fundamental constants—Planck's constant ($\hbar$), the speed of light (c), and the gravitational constant (G). Specifically, $L_p = (\hbar G/c^3)^{1/2} \sim 1.6 \times 10^{-33}$ cm.] Requiring the gravitational force between static well-separated strings to have the usual Newtonian strength determines this incredibly short length.

For each solution to the underlying equations of string theory there is a specific spectrum of elementary particles. Each of the particles in this spectrum corresponds to a particular quantum mechanical state (or normal mode) of the string. Rotational and vibrational excitations, as well as excitations of various internal degrees of freedom that reside along the string, characterize the possibilities for string states. The internal excitations describe Lie group symmetries, such as those that appear in the standard model of elementary particles, as well as more speculative properties such as supersymmetry. Thus, string theory provides a unified view of the rich world of elementary particles as different modes of a single fundamental string. There are a finite number (typically about 100 to 1,000, depending on the solution under consideration) of string states in the spectrum that have mass much below the Planck mass (the mass formed from $\hbar$, c, and G). These are the ones that should correspond to observed particles, since all known elementary particles have incredibly tiny masses compared to the Planck mass. The spectrum also contains an infinite number of string states whose mass is comparable to or larger than the Planck mass. Even though such particles presumably do exist, they are too heavy to make at accelerators (by converting energy into mass). Also, they are unstable and decay rapidly into the light particles, except when they carry some exotic property such as magnetic charge or fractional electric charge, whose conservation can ensure stability.

It is very exciting to think that we may be close to knowing the fundamental theory of elementary particles, but this is not our only goal. Knowing a theory means knowing the basic equations, whereas only *solutions* to equations can describe nature. The relevant quantum solutions are the one of lowest energy (called the vacuum) and ones in which particles are added to the vacuum. When a theory has many different possible vacuums, one must make a specific choice before confronting the experimental data. In the case of string theory, there are very many candidate vacuums, and it is not known whether there is a theoretical principle that singles out a particular choice. If we must make the choice phenomenologically (i.e., by choosing the one that works), that would be disappointing. After all, the goal of string theory is to explain as much as possible from first principles. Thus, many string theorists speculate that nonperturbative effects rule out all but one, or perhaps a few, of the vacuums. An interesting alternative is that each choice has a certain a priori probability of occurring when a universe is created. However the correct choice is selected, it should not only account for the spectrum of elementary particles and their properties but for the cosmological evolution of the universe as well.

Since string theory requires gravity, its dynamics determines the geometry of spacetime (including its dimension) as part of the characterization of the vacuum. In fact, there are perturbatively consistent solutions for any number of spatial dimensions up to and including nine plus one time dimension. Thus, the dimension of spacetime is a property of the solution and not of the theory itself. Many of the known solutions with four-dimensional spacetime actually describe a ten-dimensional spacetime manifold in which six spatial dimensions form a very tiny compact space that is invisible at ordinary energies. There are other classes of four-dimensional solutions that do not admit such an interpretation.

A standard method of studying quantum theories is by means of a power series expansion in Planck's constant. In this perturbative approach, Feynman diagrams, which consist of networks of lines, represent point-particle interactions. The history of the motion of a particle is a trajectory in spacetime called the world line of the particle. Feynman diagrams represent interactions by joining or bifurcating world lines. A sum of contributions associated with all allowed Feynman diagrams gives the complete interaction amplitude, whose square gives the interaction probability. The allowed diagrams, which include all possible interactions appropriate to the theory in question, are classified by their topology. The contribution from any particular diagram is usually infinite, but in renormalizable theories there is a well-defined prescription for extracting finite results unambiguously.

String theory interactions are formulated in an analogous manner. The spacetime trajectory of a string is a two-dimensional surface called the world sheet of the string. Once again, there is a topological classification of the Feynman diagrams, which are now two-dimensional surfaces. (String theorists describe string world sheets as Riemann surfaces using mathematical techniques of complex analysis.) Theories of oriented closed strings (loops) have a single fundamental interaction, which is described by a diagram with the topology of a pair of pants. When a plane (representing an instant in time) intersects the legs of the pants diagram, there are two closed strings. Intersecting the surface closer to the waist reveals just one closed string. Clearly, at intermediate times the two closed strings approach one another, touch, and join.

The pants diagram describes an interaction structure that differs in fundamental respects from interactions in point-particle theories. In each case, we can ask at what spacetime point the interaction that turns two particles into one takes place. In the point-particle theory there is a definite point at which the interaction occurs. In the string case, on the other hand, the string world sheet is a smooth manifold with no preferred points. The fact that it describes interaction is purely a consequence of the topology of the surface. Thus the noninteracting theory completely determines the details of the interacting theory with none of the arbitrariness that exists for point-particle theories.

The topological classification of the Feynman diagrams is especially simple in the case of closed string theories. Points (or punctures) on the surface represent absorption or emission of external strings. The number of handles attached to the surface, called the genus, characterizes the topology of the world sheets. The genus corresponds to the power of $\hbar$ in the perturbation expansion. It is remarkable that there is just one diagram at each order of the perturbation expansion, especially as their number in point-particle theories is very large indeed. (Recent work has used string theory methods to simplify the evaluation of field theory Feynman diagrams by describing the latter as a low-energy limit of the former.) Not only is the number of diagrams much fewer than in ordinary quantum field theory, but the convergence properties of the associated integrals are much better. The only infinities that occur are ones of very well-understood and inevitable origin. The types of divergences that result in parameters becoming arbitrary in renormalizable quantum field theories, or amplitudes becoming completely undefined in nonrenormalizable field theories, have no counterparts in string theory.

Can string theory be tested? Some people express pessimism because the most distinctive features of string theory only emerge at the Planck energy, which is far out of reach experimentally. Nevertheless, there are several promising possibilities. The reconciliation of gravity and quantum mechanics is already a remarkable success. No other approach is known that can do this. Moreover, it should be possible to use the theory to derive properties of elementary particles. After all, if the theory is unique and its solutions do not have too much freedom, then a great deal of particle physics data should be calculable. This has not been done yet, but large classes of solutions with many realistic features have been found. Each of these solutions requires the existence of supersymmetry particles with masses not far above the present experimental limits. Therefore, if string theory is correct, it is likely that supersymmetry particles will be discovered in the early twenty-first century. By itself, this would not prove that string theory is correct, but it certainly would be very encouraging.

A more remote possibility, alluded to earlier, is that the big bang created some Planck mass particles (such as magnetic monopoles) that survive to the present epoch as observable stable entities. A related possibility is that a successful understanding of the cosmology of the very early universe requires characteristic features of superstring theory. For example, string theory naturally includes several of the most interesting candidates for the mysterious invisible dark matter that accounts for most of the mass in the universe. These include certain supersymmetry particles, called neutralinos, as well as massive neutrinos and axions. Experimental searches currently underway could shed light on the dark matter.

Even though the present understanding of string theory is insufficient to make definitive testable predictions in any of these areas, the rate of progress is very impressive. Pessimism about eventual testability is probably unwarranted. As Edward Witten has noted, general relativity gave rise to various predictions that seemed quite hopeless to verify when they were made (around 1915). These included the existence of neutron stars, black holes, gravitational radiation, and gravitational lenses. There is now substantial observational evidence for all of these.

The history of string theory differs in interesting ways from that of general relativity. In that case, Einstein began by formulating certain far-reaching principles—the equivalence principle and general covariance—then (with the help of others) he found their proper mathematical embodiment in the language of Riemannian geometry. This led to dynamical equations and successful experimental predictions. In string theory, the fundamental principles have not yet been identified that generalize the equivalence principle and general coordinate invariance, though these must surely exist since general relativity is a low-energy (long-distance) approximation to string theory. These principles, whatever they are, are likely to require a new kind of geometry, perhaps an infinite-dimensional generalization of Riemannian geometry, for their implementation. The recent literature contains some specific suggestions along these lines, but understanding is still far from complete.

Once the correct geometric formulation incorporating the fundamental principles of string theory in a comprehensible form is achieved, it will be interesting to study how string theory modifies classical general relativity at short distances. In particular, there is a great deal of interest in studying the implications of string theory for the properties of black holes. Stephen Hawking has suggested that the existence of black holes implies the breakdown of quantum mechanics, but there are indications that this is not the case in string theory.

Many clever people are working hard on string theory and progress is rapid. Even so, one should not expect too much too soon. To obtain a satisfactory understanding of what string theory is really all about will require substantial advances in mathematics. Also, new experimental results are likely to play an important role in shaping ideas.

See also: BLACK HOLE; COSMIC STRING; DARK MATTER; ELEMENTARY PARTICLES; FERMIONS AND BOSONS; GRAVITON; MAGNETIC MONOPOLE; NEUTRINO; RELATIVITY, GENERAL THEORY OF; SPACETIME; SUPERSYMMETRY

Bibliography

BELAVIN, A. A.; POLYAKOV, A. M.; and ZAMOLODCHIKOV, A. B. "Infinite Conformal Symmetry in Two-Dimensional Quantum Field Theory." *Nucl. Phys. B* **241**, 333–380 (1984).

CANDELAS, P.; HOROWITZ, G.; STROMINGER, A.; and WITTEN, E. "Vacuum Configurations for Superstrings." *Nucl. Phys. B* **258**, 46–74 (1985).

GREEN, M. B., and SCHWARZ, J. H. "Anomaly Cancellations in Supersymmetric D = 10 Gauge Theory and Superstring Theory." *Phys. Lett. B* **149**, 117–122 (1984).

GREEN, M. B.; SCHWARZ, J. H.; and WITTEN, E. *Superstring Theory* (Cambridge University Press, Cambridge, Eng., 1987).

LÜST, D., and THEISEN, S. *Lectures on String Theory* (Springer-Verlag, Berlin, 1989).

POLYAKOV, A. M. "Quantum Geometry of Bosonic Strings." *Phys. Lett. B* **103**, 207–210 (1981).

POLYAKOV, A. M. "Quantum Geometry of Fermionic Strings." *Phys. Lett. B* **103**, 211–213 (1981).

RAMOND. P. "Dual Theory for Free Fermions." *Phys. Rev. D* **3**, 2415–2418 (1971).

RAMOND. P.; NEVEU, A.; and SCHWARZ, J. H. "Factorizable Dual Model of Pions." *Nucl. Phys. B* **31**, 86–112 (1971).

SCHERK, J., and SCHWARZ, J. H. "Dual Models for Non-Hadrons." *Nucl. Phys. B* **81**, 118–144 (1974).

JOHN H. SCHWARZ

SUPERSYMMETRY

The name "supersymmetry" is given to any symmetry that seeks to relate fermions and bosons, particles with different types of spin. In nature, all matter consists of these two types of elementary particles. The precepts of quantum mechanics, together with Albert Einstein's theory of special relativity, call for all elementary particles to be endowed with (at least) two intrinsic properties: mass and spin. Mass is a familiar property of all matter, which applies equally well to macroscopic everyday objects, as well as to the smallest constituents of matter. Spin is more subtle and is not easily recognized in macroscopic objects. In fact, spin was discovered only in the twentieth century to explain the anomalous behavior of electrons in a magnetic field. Particles with spin act like tiny magnets, and spin measures the force on an elementary particle in a varying magnetic field. The natural magnetism of macroscopic objects, such as iron, is now understood as a manifestation of the spin of their constituents.

Masses are allowed to range over continuous values, but spin only comes in integer quanta of half of the fundamental constant of quantum mechanics, Planck's constant, $\hbar$. There are two broad classes of particles: those with integer spin, called bosons, and those with half integer spin, called fermions. Electrons, which make up the outer layers of atoms, and the quarks, the constituents of atomic nuclei, each have half a unit of spin; they are fermions. On the other hand, the photon, the particle associated with light that generates the electromagnetic force, has one unit of spin; it is a boson. Similarly, the particles that cause the other forces in nature, the gluons, which mediate the nuclear force, and the weak bosons, which are responsible for beta radioactivity, all have one unit of spin, are examples of bosons. The graviton, which is thought to mediate the force of gravity, is a boson with two units of spin.

Supersymmetry has been suggested as a fundamental symmetry of nature. According to this proposal, for each elementary constituent of matter there exists another particle, its superpartner, with exactly the same properties (e.g., mass, electric charge), but differing from the constituent only by its spin, displaced by half a unit. Thus, to the spin-$\frac{1}{2}$ electron (fermion) we add the spin-0 selectron (boson), and to the spin-$\frac{1}{2}$ quarks, we add the spin-0 squarks. The superpartner of the spin-1 photon is the spin-$\frac{1}{2}$ photino, those of the spin-1 gluons are the spin-$\frac{1}{2}$ gluinos, and so on. Presently, there is no experimental evidence for the existence of these superpartners. Rather than concluding that this proposal is wrong, many prefer to believe that the superpartners are so very heavy that the particle accelerators with the highest collision energies, at Fermilab and SLAC in the United States and at CERN in Europe, do not have enough energy to produce them in collisions of elementary particles. The latter implies that supersymmetry appears only as a broken symmetry. This concept is still very powerful, since it doubles the number of constituents of matter by predicting the existence of the superpartners, albeit with larger masses.

It is not the first time that symmetries have led physicists to make such predictions. In 1927, in his relativistic description of the electron, the British physicist P. A. M. Dirac showed that the electron might have its own antiparticle (with the same mass and spin, but opposite charge). The positron, the antiparticle of the electron, was found shortly after in experiments, but only after enough energy was available to create an electron-positron pair. While the existence of antimatter was unanticipated, antiparticles of all types are produced today and stored in laboratories the world over. Supersymmetry, which generalizes the symmetries of special relativity, also predicts a new form of matter, the superpartners. However, their masses can be much heavier, indicating that supersymmetry is not an exact symmetry. Superpartners can be produced in the laboratory with accelerators powerful enough to create them in pairs. This requires an energy (according to Einstein, mass is equivalent to energy) of at least twice their masses. Once produced, the superpartners will quickly decay sequentially into particles of lesser mass until the particle with the lowest mass is reached, at which point the decay chain is stopped. In the simplest version of supersymmetry, this particle is a superpartner, predicting a new stable form of matter.

High-energy accelerators recreate the conditions prevalent in the early days of the universe, shortly after the big bang. If supersymmetry is correct, the early cosmic soup contained the superpartners as well. As the universe cooled, these decayed into the lightest of their kind, leaving a stable remnant of supersymmetry in the universe. Some speculate that it is the main component of the dark matter observed in the halos of galaxies.

Supersymmetry can be generalized to the Einstein theory of gravity, yielding the theory of supergravity, with the spin-2 graviton joined by its spin-$\frac{3}{2}$ superpartner, the gravitino. While the graviton is massless, to account for the long-range force of gravity, the gravitino has a mass, which serves as a measure of supersymmetry breaking. The origins of this mass is the subject of intense theoretical research.

There are powerful aesthetic arguments in favor of supersymmetry. Theories that seek to unify all the forces of nature, such as the so-called theory of everything, naturally incorporate supersymmetry. A prime example is superstring theory, where the constraint of supersymmetry restricts the theory to be formulated in a space with nine spatial dimensions, leading to speculations that this reflected the conditions of the universe at its creation.

See also: ANTIMATTER; DARK MATTER; ELEMENTARY PARTICLES; FERMIONS AND BOSONS; GRAVITON; MASS; POSITRON; SPIN; SUPERGRAVITY; SUPERSTRING

PIERRE RAMOND

SURFACE TENSION

A variety of natural phenomena suggest that the molecules in the surface of a liquid are under tension, and the surface acts like a stretched membrane. Some insects can walk on the surface of a pond. A needle can float on water if carefully placed on the surface. Small water droplets and soap bubbles are spherical, showing that water and soap films have a tendency to minimize their surface area. Hence, forces must act between the surface molecules that help support the weight of the insect and the needle and act to minimize surface area.

A loop of thin thread placed in a soap film will be stretched into a circle, if the film inside the thread is pierced. A circle has the maximum area for a given circumference, which implies that the soap film has minimized its surface area. Different liquids have different surface tensions, which can easily be demonstrated by sprinkling powder on the surface of water and then adding a drop of soap solution in the center. The soap film will expand rapidly and the powder is pulled outward into a large circle or to the edges of the container. Water has a larger surface tension than soap so the tension on the outside of the soap film stretches the film to within a molecule thickness. The water thereby reduces its surface area.

Units

From the thread example above, it is clear that a force exists in the surface of a soap film (or any liquid) acting at right angles to the thread along its circumference. Therefore, we can define surface tension as the force acting in the surface at right angles to a line of unit length. Surface tension γ equals F/ℓ and has units of newtons per meter (N·m^{-1}). Since 1 N is a rather large unit of force, surface tensions are often quoted in dynes per centimeter, where 1 dyn = 10^{-5} N, and 1 dyn·cm^{-1} = 10^{-3} N·m^{-1}. Surface tension can also be defined in terms of the isothermal (no change in temperature) work done (or energy) required to increase the surface area of the liquid by unity, which has units in joules per square meter (J·m^{-2}). This has the same dimensions as before since energy is a force times a distance. We may talk of surface energy as an alternative expression for surface tension.

Surface tension depends on temperature and pressure. As a liquid is heated the net attractive forces between the molecules are lowered decreasing surface tension. The surface tension of most liquids is between 20×10^{-3} N·m^{-1} and 40×10^{-3} N·m^{-1} at room temperature. Water has a quite high surface tension of 72.7×10^{-3} N·m^{-1} at 20°C. By comparison, mercury has a surface tension, at the same temperature, of 465×10^{-3} N·m^{-1}. Condensed gas at low temperatures generally has very low surface tension. For example, liquid helium at 4.3 K has a surface tension of 9.8×10^{-5} N·m^{-1}.

Usually surface tension acts on both sides of an imaginary line drawn in the surface of a liquid. To see the effects of surface tension, the liquid must be absent from one side of the line. For example, if we consider a wire frame with a metal slider holding a soap film, as in Fig. 1, we must apply a force of $2\gamma\ell$ to the right in order to prevent the soap film from collapsing. (A film has two surfaces, hence the factor of two.) Surface tension also occurs in solids; however, in rigid bodies, stretching of the surface is hard to observe. In heated solids, whose surface molecules are mobile, surface tension can be observed.

More generally, surface tension, or interfacial tension, exists between the boundary of two immiscible fluids or at a density discontinuity.

Microscopic Explanation

The molecules in the surface of a liquid are further apart on average than the molecules in the bulk of the liquid. The change from liquid to vapor is not a sudden discontinuity. The density of molecules changes gradually through the surface so there are fewer molecules at the surface. Molecules exert both attractive and repulsive forces on each other, the magnitude of the forces depending on their separation. At an equilibrium separation the net force is zero. When the molecules get too close the force between them is repulsive and when the molecules are too far apart the force is attractive. The time averaged force on molecules in the bulk of the liquid is zero, even though there are random collisions and diffusion displacements going on. There are no forces acting on a given molecule for a long period of time. The situation is different on the surface. There are far fewer molecules above the surface so that a net attractive force acts downward into the body of the liquid. These centrally directed forces cause liquid drops to take up a spherical shape. Also the molecules in the surface are further apart because of the liquid-vapor transition so there are forces acting along the surface causing these molecules to act as though under tension.

Wetting and Capillarity

Surface forces, generally interfacial forces, govern wetting or nonwetting of solids by liquids. A liquid is said to wet a solid if the angle of contact (measured through the liquid) between the liquid and solid is less than 90° (see Fig. 2). An example is water on glass; the water spreads over the surface of

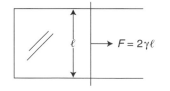

Figure 1 Wire frame with a metal slider holding a soap film.

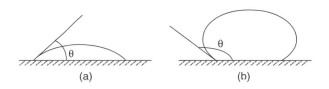

Figure 2 The (a) wetting and (b) nonwetting of a solid.

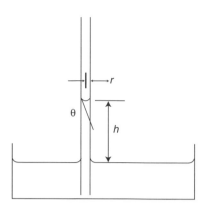

Figure 3 Forces governing the rise of a liquid in a capillary tube.

the glass. For clean glass the angle of contact is zero. If the contact angle is greater than 90° then the liquid does not wet the solid. Mercury, for example, is seen to form small globules (or beads) on the glass and does not spread.

Surface tension is responsible for the rise (contact angle < 90°) or fall (> 90°) of a liquid in a very thin (capillary) tube above or below the level outside. This is caused by the vertical component of surface tension forces in the meniscus formed (due to the angle of contact) at the liquid surface. The vertical component of the force, around the circumference of the tube, supports the weight of a column of liquid (see Fig. 3). If the density of the liquid is ρ, the surface tension γ, the height of the column h, and the radius of the tube at the liquid surface r, then using g as the force due to gravity

$$\pi r^2 h \rho g = \gamma \cos \theta \times 2 \pi r,$$

where θ is the contact angle. If $\theta < 90°$ then the liquid inside a glass tube will rise above the level of the liquid outside the tube (e.g., water). If $\theta > 90°$ then the liquid level in the tube will drop below the level outside the tube (e.g., mercury). By measuring this capillary action we may determine the surface tension γ.

The pressure inside a soap bubble can be derived to be $4\gamma/r$, where the surface tension of the film forming the bubble is γ. For a liquid drop in air, or an air bubble in a liquid, the excess pressure inside is one half this because a soap film has two sides but air bubbles or liquid drops have only one.

Applications

In oil fired burners, fast efficient burning of vapor is enhanced by droplet formation. Soaps and detergents need to spread over a solid to remove dirt particles. These substances have a low surface tension so they can wet solids. Paint also requires wetting agents to prevent the paint forming droplets and assist in the spreading of the paint over a solid surface. For a strong soldered joint, molten metal solder (tin-lead alloy) must be spread over the two metals to be joined. A wetting agent called a flux (e.g., resin) is applied first to help the spreading of the solder over the joint. Capillarity also helps the metal solder get into the cracks in the metal forming a stronger joint. Anti-frothing and waterproofing agents tend to increase surface tension to prevent wetting. They also prevent bubbles from forming in the surface by increasing surface tension, and hence the energy required to increase surface area. Capillarity is a mechanism used in biological organisms to carry blood to organs in the body. It also explains how blotting paper soaks up ink. Bubble formation is important in the expanded plastics industry for producing styrofoam (polystyrene).

See also: LIQUID; MOLECULE

Bibliography

DUNCAN, T. *Physics: A Textbook for Advanced Level Students* (John Murray, London, 1982).

FEYNMAN, R. P.; LEIGHTON, R. B.; and SANDS, M. *The Feynman Lectures on Physics*, Vol. 2 (Addison-Wesley, Reading, MA, 1964).

HEIDI FEARN

SYMMETRY

Natural objects or laws are said to have a symmetry if they remain unchanged after some operation has been performed on them. Examples are crystals or ideal snowflakes that appear unchanged after having been rotated through a particular angle. Symmetries are classified as "discrete" or "continuous." For discrete symmetries the operation involved yields a finite (usually small) number of equivalent versions of the original. Thus a perfect six-pronged snowflake has a discrete sixfold symmetry. For continuous symmetries the operation yields an indefinite number of equivalent versions. An example would be a perfect sphere that remains unchanged as one continuously rotates it.

Symmetries have played a variety of roles in physics. They are used to classify different types of crystals. Symmetries that are properties of established physical laws are used as aids in finding solutions. Postulated symmetries have been used to derive proposed new physical laws.

Mathematical discussions of symmetry involve the language of "group theory." A symmetry group consists of all the symmetry operations that leave an object unchanged; these are called "elements" of the group. Since the produce of two such operations must also leave the object unchanged, the product of two elements is also an element. In this way one defines a group algebra that characterizes the group. In the case of discrete symmetries, such as those used to classify crystals, the symmetry group has a finite number of elements. In the case of continuous symmetries the group has an infinite number of elements characterized by one or more continuous parameters.

Not all symmetries of importance in physics are exact. There may be approximate symmetries that hold in the limit that some small parameter of the theory vanishes. It may then be possible to calculate results by perturbation about the symmetric solution. It is also possible that even if a theory possesses an exact symmetry, the solutions do not display this symmetry. This happens if the ground state or the vacuum state of the system is degenerate. A particular choice of ground state may then destroy the symmetry. An example would be a spherical ball of magnetic material that becomes permanently magnetized in one direction, thus breaking the rotational symmetry. Such cases are referred to as spontaneously broken symmetry.

The laws of classical physics do not distinguish any points in space or time. This can be expressed as a continuous symmetry with respect to a translation in space or time. Mathematically this means the equations of classical physics are invariant to a change of coordinate $\mathbf{x} \to \mathbf{x} + \Delta\mathbf{x}$ or $t \to t + \Delta t$. An example is Newton's second law with the force given by Newton's law of gravitation. Similarly, classical laws do not define an axis in space. This can be expressed as a symmetry with respect to a rotation of the coordinate system.

There is a close relation between symmetries and conservation laws. The symmetry with respect to space (time) translation ensures the conservation of momentum (energy). Rotational symmetry has as a consequence the conservation of angular momentum.

In 1905 Albert Einstein postulated that all physical laws were symmetrical with respect to a transformation to a new reference frame moving with an arbitrary constant velocity $\mathbf{v}$. This symmetry is the basis of the special theory of relativity. Under this transformation the new space and time coordinates are related to the old by the Lorentz transformation.

There is a fundamental historical distinction in the role of symmetry in the case of special relativity in contrast to the case of classical Newtonian physics. In the case of classical physics the fundamental laws came first and the symmetries were noted later and proved very useful in applications of the laws. In the case of special relativity Einstein first postulated the basic relativistic symmetry and from this derived new laws of mechanics that were later verified.

Three discrete symmetries have played an important role in quantum theory and in particle physics. These are P, parity; T, time reversal; and C, particle-antiparticle conjugation. The T symmetry states the invariance of physical laws under the transformation $t \to -t$. This holds already for classical Newtonian motion; the time reverse of a motion allowed by Newton's laws is also an allowed motion. The P symmetry states invariance with respect to space reflection. The C symmetry states invariance when all particles are replaced by antiparticles.

The P and T symmetry of the Schrödinger equation has important consequences for atomic and molecular physics. There exist molecules that have a definite handedness as demonstrated by the fact that plane-polarized light transmitted through them has the plane of polarization rotated to the left or right. The P symmetry requires that given a "left-handed" molecule there must be the possibility of the mirror image "right-handed" molecule with the same energy levels. Examples are the sugars dextrose and levulose. Atomic energy levels typically transform into themselves under P and are classified parity even or parity odd, corresponding to whether the wave function is multiplied by $+1$ or -1 under the parity transformation.

The magnetic field $\mathbf{B}$ due to currents changes sign under the T transformation, but the electric field $\mathbf{E}$ due to charges stays the same. The spin vector or angular momentum vector $\mathbf{J}$ reverses under T. As a result, states with opposite values of $\mathbf{J} \cdot \mathbf{B}$ can have different energies as is well known from the Zeeman effect, but states with opposite values of $\mathbf{J} \cdot \mathbf{E}$ must have the same energy. This latter is known as the Kramers degeneracy and was derived via the T symmetry by Eugene Wigner. It also follows that elementary particles cannot have an electric dipole moment d_e.

The C symmetry states that for every state there must exist a C-conjugate state with the same energy levels. In the case of a neutral system the C-conjugate state may be the original state, in which case the system must be either C-even or C-odd. Thus, given the hydrogen atom made of an electron and proton, the C-symmetry states that there is a possibility of a system of a positron and antiproton with the same energy levels. Under the C symmetry the photon transforms into itself and is C-odd. The bound state of an electron and a positron is called positronium. Under the C symmetry the ground $^1S_0$ state of positronium is C-even but the $^3S_1$ state can be shown to be C-odd. As a result the $^1S_0$ state can annihilate into two photons but the $^3S_1$ state must go to three photons.

In 1957 it was discovered that the P symmetry is badly violated in the weak interactions. An example is nuclear beta decay in which an electron e^- and an antineutrino $\bar{\nu}_e$ are emitted. The emitted $\bar{\nu}_e$ is in a right-handed state, meaning that its spin is parallel to its momentum, whereas the e^- are predominantly left-handed. Since the original nuclear state has no handedness, the P symmetry predicted the final e^- and $\bar{\nu}_e$ would have no handedness.

There is no problem in constructing interaction laws that violate the C or P or T symmetries. However, it has been shown that for local relativistic quantum field theory the product symmetry CPT always holds. The theory of weak interactions developed after 1957 involved a large violation of the P and C symmetries but retained the CP and T symmetries. However, in 1964 it was discovered that the CP symmetry was violated in the decay of the strange particle K^0. Many experiments have verified this effect and the quantitative analysis of these experiments implies that T is also violated and that CPT is indeed a good symmetry. However, so far CP violation has been observed only in the K^0 system and evidence for T violation is indirect.

Nuclear forces, to a good approximation, are the same for protons and neutrons. This leads to "isospin" symmetry. Mathematically this is expressed by considering protons and neutrons as two states of the particle called the nucleon, and the isospin transformation is the most general unitary transformation [denoted by $SU(2)$] on this two-component object. The mathematics, but not the physics, is identical to that giving the rotation of the two-component Pauli spinor describing a particle with spin $-\frac{1}{2}$. Isospin symmetry is not exact for two main reasons: (1) electromagnetic interactions clearly distinguish protons and neutrons; and (2) neutrons are heavier than protons primarily because down quarks are heavier than up quarks.

The strong forces that bind quarks together, described by the theory called quantum chromodynamics (QCD), are believed to be the same for all quarks. This is referred to as "flavor symmetry" and is the basis for isospin symmetry. Extending this to the three lightest quarks (u, d, s) leads to the $SU(3)$ symmetry first proposed by Murray Gell-Mann and Yuval Neeman in 1961. This symmetry is broken by the large mass of the s quark compared with u and d and so is expected to be good only to about 20 percent in general.

A more abstract symmetry that has played a major role in particle physics is "gauge symmetry." This arises first in classical electrodynamics as the invariance of the physics to a change in the choice of the vector potential that leaves the electromagnetic fields unchanged. Mathematically it corresponds to the transformation of the four-vector potential A_μ to $A_\mu + (\partial/\partial x_\mu)\Lambda$, where Λ is a fairly arbitrary scalar function. The importance of this symmetry shows up in quantum electrodynamics (QED) because it greatly simplifies calculations and proves to be the basis for the renormalization of the theory. The standard model of particle physics is based on the extension of the gauge invariance idea to strong and weak interactions. The new gauge transformations involve the fields that describe the gluons for the strong interactions and the W and Z bosons for the weak interactions. Exact gauge symmetry requires that the quanta of the fields, the photon in QED and the gluons in QCD, be massless. It has been well known since the time of Enrico Fermi and Hideki Yukawa that the weak force has a very short range so that, if it were transmitted by bosons, these would be very massive. For this reason it seemed impossible to apply the gauge symmetry to the weak interactions. In the case of the present standard model the weak gauge symmetry is spontaneously broken by the Higgs mechanism, allowing the W and Z bosons to be massive. In spite of the breaking of the symmetry the derivation of the theory starting with a gauge symmetry leads to the possibility of renormalizing the theory.

Symmetry principles have played a major role in present-day thinking about fundamental physical laws. Our ideas about the universe depend on the general cosmologic principle that the universe on a large scale appears the same independent of the location of the observer. Proposals for theories of particle physics that go beyond the standard model are nearly all based on postulated symmetries.

See also: PARTICLE PHYSICS; QUANTUM CHROMODYNAMICS; QUANTUM ELECTRODYNAMICS; SYMMETRY BREAKING, SPONTANEOUS

Bibliography

FEYNMAN, R. P. *The Character of Physical Law* (MIT Press, Cambridge, MA, 1965).

FIELD, M., and GOLUBITSKY, M. *Symmetry in Chaos* (Oxford University Press, Oxford, Eng., 1992).

FRAUENFELDER, H., and HENLEY, E. M. *Nuclear and Particle Physics* (W. J. Benjamin, Reading, MA, 1975).

GIBSON, W. M., and POLLARD, B. R. *Symmetry Principles in Elementary Particle Physics* (Cambridge University Press, Cambridge, Eng., 1976).

HO-KIM, Q.; KUMAR, N.; and LAM, C. S. *Invitation to Contemporary Physics* (World Scientific, Singapore, 1991).

ZEE, A. *Fearful Symmetry* (Macmillan, New York, 1986).

LINCOLN WOLFENSTEIN

SYMMETRY BREAKING, SPONTANEOUS

Many physical laws embody symmetry principles of nature. For instance, the description of interactions between two bodies in terms of a central force potential that depends only on the relative distance between these objects, leads to an equation of motion that is invariant under rotations of the system of reference. This invariance is simple to understand. Under rotations the relative distance between the bodies is not altered. Hence, the equation of motion in a rotated frame coincides with that in the original frame. However, invariance of the equations of motion of a system under a set of symmetry transformations is not a guarantee that the resulting motion respects this symmetry. If it does, then one speaks of the symmetry as being manifest, while in the contrary case one has a spontaneously broken symmetry.

Historically, the first example of a spontaneously broken symmetry was provided by the Bardeen–Cooper–Schrieffer (BCS) theory of superconductivity. Although electron number is a conserved quantity in the theory, the energetically favored BCS solution does not respect this symmetry. In this case, the spontaneous breakdown of electron number is associated with the dynamical formation in the superconductor of condensates of pairs of electrons of opposite spin—the so-called Cooper pairs. This is a general characteristic of spontaneously broken symmetries. For spontaneous breakdown of a symmetry to occur, there must be interactions associated with the phenomena in question that lead to the formation of condensates carrying nontrivial quantum numbers under the symmetry. It is the presence of these condensates, which determine some preferred direction in symmetry space, that leads to the breakdown of the symmetry. The symmetry breakdown is called "spontaneous" because, as a result of the formation of symmetry breaking condensates, the symmetry present in the equations of the theory is not reflected in their solutions.

For relativistic invariant theories, there is an important consequence of having a spontaneously broken symmetry. In this case, one can show that for every broken symmetry in the theory there is an associated massless excitation. These particles are called Nambu–Goldstone bosons. The proof of this statement relies on the two aspects of broken symmetries mentioned above. Namely, that broken symmetries are associated with condensate formation and that these condensates, although they transform nontrivially under the symmetry, have a nonvanishing expectation value in the ground state (vacuum state) of the theory. It is a general property of quantities that transform nontrivially under a symmetry that they can always be obtained by applying a symmetry transformation on some other (conjugate) quantities in the theory. This connection provides the crucial ingredient for establishing the existence of Nambu–Goldstone bosons. Basically, the relation between the objects that condense and their conjugates allows for a nonvanishing expectation value for the condensates only if the object conjugate to them connects the vacuum state with that of a massless particle state. Since condensate formation is necessary for spontaneous symmetry breaking, so are Nambu–Goldstone bosons.

Although no examples of exactly massless Nambu–Goldstone bosons are known in nature, the particles responsible for the long-range part of the nuclear force—the π mesons—are approximate Nambu–Goldstone bosons. In the limit of vanishing quark masses the theory describing the strong interactions, quantum chromodynamics, possesses a larger symmetry. This symmetry, however, is not apparent in the spectrum of bound-state particles of the theory and, therefore, is presumed to be spontaneously broken. The Nambu–Goldstone bosons associated with this broken symmetry are identified with the π mesons. These particles, in reality, have a small mass because the quarks are not exactly massless. Detailed calculations show that, except for this fact, π mesons indeed behave precisely in the ways one expects Nambu–Goldstone bosons to behave.

The reason why there are not more Nambu–Goldstone bosons in nature is due, in part, to an important exception to the theorem that associates a Nambu–Goldstone boson to each spontaneously broken symmetry. This theorem ceases to apply when the symmetries in question, rather than being global symmetries, are local symmetries. Local symmetries, often called gauge symmetries, require invariance of the theory under transformations that can differ, in different points of spacetime. For this to obtain, there must exist in the theory a set of spin-1 particles that, through their presence, serve to compensate for the symmetry transformation not being the same at different points. These excitations are known as gauge bosons, or Yang–Mills particles. Not surprisingly perhaps, due to their compensatory nature, there is one gauge boson for each independent local symmetry transformation in the theory. To preserve the local symmetry, it turns out that no mass term can be included for these excitations. As a result, if the local symmetry is manifest in nature, then the associated gauge boson is massless. This is the case, for example, for the phase transformations associated with electrodynamics, whose massless gauge bosons are the familiar photons. Remarkably, if the local symmetry is spontaneously broken this ceases to be so. In this case, two interlinked phenomena occur: the gauge bosons associated with the broken symmetry acquire a mass, and the expected Nambu–Goldstone bosons disappear from the theory. This is the celebrated Higgs mechanism.

Physically, one can understand the origin of the Higgs mechanism by focusing on the degrees of freedom associated with spin-1 particles. If these particles are massless, then they possess only two degrees of freedom (e.g., for the photon these are its two independent polarizations). Massive spin-1 particles, on the other hand, have three degrees of freedom. The Higgs mechanism, in effect, makes use of the Nambu–Goldstone bosons to augment the degrees of freedom of the putatively massless gauge particles to produce a massive spin-1 particle. The scale of masses produced by the Higgs mechanism is related to the scale that characterizes the symmetry breaking condensates. A physically important example of a spontaneously broken symmetry in which the Higgs mechanism is operative is the electroweak theory of Sheldon Glashow, Abdus Salam, and Steven Weinberg. This theory describes both electrodynamics and the weak interactions. In the absence of symmetry breakdown the weak gauge bosons, W and Z, are massless and degenerate with the photon. The breakdown of the electroweak symmetry, however, gives the weak gauge bosons mass, keeping the photon massless.

See also: BOSON, HIGGS; BOSON, NAMBU–GOLDSTONE; BOSON, W; BOSON, Z; FERMIONS AND BOSONS; INTERACTION, ELECTROWEAK; SUPERCONDUCTIVITY; SUPERSYMMETRY; SYMMETRY

Bibliography

VELTMAN, M. J. G. "The Higgs Boson." *Sci. Am.* **255** (Nov.), 76 (1986).

ROBERTO D. PECCEI

SYNCHROTRON

A synchrotron is a machine designed to accelerate particles to high energies while containing them in a circular orbit. They are an advance over earlier machines called cyclotrons.

A practical way of overcoming the energy limit from machines operating on the cyclotron principle was pointed out simultaneously by V. I. Veksler in the Soviet Union and Edward M. McMillan in the United States in 1945. This is based on the recognition of the property of phase stability, which is inherent in cyclotron operation. This property guarantees that particles arriving at a radio-frequency-driven accelerating region at different times (due to their difference in energy) receive energy increases from the field in that region. These energy increases cause the particles to move closer to the so-called synchronous particle, which executes its orbit in exactly the right time and with the right energy to cross the accelerating region at the same phase on its next, and subsequent, orbits. The equation defining the property of synchronism is

$$\frac{v}{r} = 2\pi f = \frac{eB}{m},$$

where m is the mass in grams, e is the charge in absolute electromagnetic units, B is the applied magnetic field strength in gauss, v is the particle velocity, f is the applied frequency (equal to the number of times per second around the orbit), and r is the radius of the orbit.

Using the equation one can see that it is possible to design a machine where the mass (or energy) of the particle can be increased while maintaining a constant orbital length if both the magnetic field strength and the applied frequency are varied with time. Such a machine is called a "synchrotron" and can be used to accelerate both electrons and protons (or ions).

Electrons are well adapted to acceleration in a ring-shaped magnet since they acquire a velocity essentially equal to the velocity of light at relatively low energies ($v = 0.98c$ at 2 MeV); for higher energies they circulate about an orbit of fixed radius at constant frequency gaining energy by interaction with the applied electric field developed in an acceleration gap.

The first electron synchrotron (for 8 MeV) was built in England in 1946 to test the principle of phase-stable acceleration. By 1956 more than twenty synchrotrons of energies between 50 and 500 MeV were in use as research tools in many countries. The electron synchrotron has a unique property that leads to a practical upper limit of energy. When deflected in a magnetic field, relativistic electrons radiate electromagnetic energy in a continuous spectrum extending into the soft x-ray region with an intensity that increases as the third power of the electron energy, divided by the rest mass. At very high energies the radiation disturbs particle orbits, causing the electrons to strike the wall of the enclosing vacuum vessel. The Cambridge Electron Accelerator, a joint project of the Massachusetts Institute of Technology and Harvard University, was designed in the early 1960s to produce electrons at an energy of 6 GeV, which approached the practical energy limit for its radius.

Proton synchrotrons have also been designed. Because of the larger proton rest, mass synchrotron radiation is not a problem in proton synchrotrons, so much higher energies can be achieved. Figure 1 shows the layout of the 3-GeV proton synchrotron called the Cosmotron, which was constructed at the Brookhaven National Laboratory in Upton, New York, in 1952. Note that a ring magnet is also used since the orbit radius can be maintained constant by varying the frequency of the applied electric field as the particle velocity increases. Protons are first preaccelerated in an electrostatic generator to 4 MeV and inflected into the orbit when the magnetic field is at the right value for the injection orbit to have the correct radius. The magnet is formed of four quadrants, each spaced by 10-ft straight sections forming a distorted circle with a 75-ft diameter. One straight section is used for injection, and a ferrite loaded radio frequency (rf) resonant accelerating cavity situated in another straight section supplies about 3,000 V per turn for acceleration and is modulated between 0.37 and 4.20 MHz. The magnet cycles from a few gauss to about 10,000 G and back once every five seconds, thus producing bursts of protons at five-second intervals. In the early 1960s, these "constant gradient synchrotrons," which required large-aperture magnets and thus required very large and costly magnets, became obsolete due to the invention at Brookhaven by Ernest D. Courant and Hartland S. Snyder of the alternating gradient principle of magnetic focusing. This method provides much stronger focusing to the ion beam and allows smaller and less costly magnets with smaller apertures to be utilized. The 33-GeV Alternating Gradient Synchrotron (AGS) at Brookhaven was one of the first machines to use this focusing method that is still used today for all high-energy synchrotrons.

The highest energy machines generally utilize the "storage ring" method whereby particles are stored in circular orbit by repeatedly injecting them from a conventional synchrotron into the same stable orbit. After the desired stored charge has been accumulated, the particles are accelerated to the final operating energy.

The highest energy storage rings built to date are the Large Electron Proton (LEP) storage ring at the European Center for Nuclear Research (CERN),

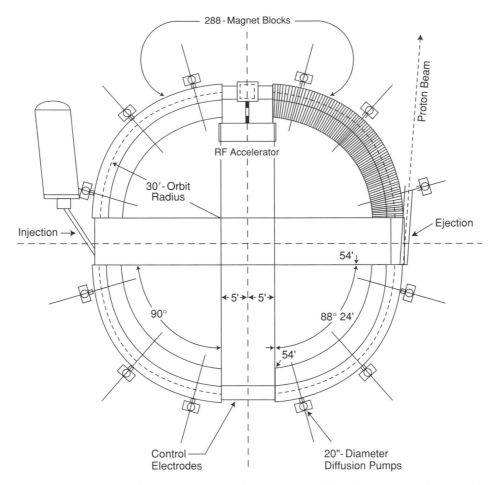

Figure 1 Plan view of the Cosmotron, the first operational proton synchrotron in the United States.

near Geneva, Switzerland, which has a circumference of 26.6 km and contains electrons (and counter-circulating positrons) with up to 50 GeV of energy per particle, and, for protons, the TeVatron at the Fermi National Acceleration Laboratory, which stores 1-TeV (1,000-GeV) protons and counter-circulating antiprotons in a 6.3-km circumference ring. Plans to build the large hadron collider (LHC), a 7-TeV proton storage ring in the LEP tunnel at CERN, has been approved.

See also: ACCELERATOR; ACCELERATOR, HISTORY OF; CYCLOTRON; RADIATION, SYNCHROTRON

Bibliography

COURANT, E. D., and SNYDER, H. S. "Theory of the Alternating Gradient Synchrotron." *Ann. Phys.* **3,** 1–48 (1958).

KENNETH BATCHELOR

SYNCHROTRON RADIATION

See RADIATION, SYNCHROTRON

SYSTEMS

The idea of a system is an artificial construct that allows a scientist to isolate conceptually the objects, the arena of study, and the scales of interest in the study from the rest of the surrounding world and from processes and structures that occur at very different temporal and spatial scales. The concept of a system and its subsystems is used in all scientific study, not just in physics. We study the solar system, weather systems, ecosystems, societies, the human body, and so on using the same conceptual framework.

At the start of any study it is important to define the area of study—what system is to be examined. To define a system we need to answer two questions: "What are the boundaries and scales of the system under study?" and "What are the constituents of the system?" Then to study the behavior of the system we need to examine two further questions: "What are the interactions between the constituents of the system?" and "What flows into and out of the system?" (Namely, what is the effect of the environment on the system, and vice versa. Particular attention should be given to energy flow.)

Asking and answering these questions about the system under study helps to clarify exactly which problem we plan to examine. Not only do we limit attention to a certain spatial region, but it is also limited to certain time periods and certain scales. The constituents or subsystems on one scale may later need to be examined as systems in their own right when we approach problems on another scale. Processes that occur on very different size or time scales can be ignored as the system under study is examined. When we study a process, such as the respiration of birds, that takes place over seconds, we do not need to worry about the effect of the seasons. Likewise, when we study seasonal migration of birds, we do not need to know the details of processes that occur on the scale of seconds in a bird's body. When we deal with objects on the scale of meters, for example, to design a bridge, we do not need to worry about the atomic structure of matter in any detail; we can summarize it by a bulk description of the materials to be used (their tensile strength, density, and so on). However, when we want to discover a better kind of steel with which to build the bridge, we can forget the bridge design and the scale of meters and study only how the detailed atomic structure of a metal affects its bulk properties.

This process of artificial separation of the problem of interest from all other problems is known as the reductionist approach. It is a very powerful tool because it allows us to focus only on one restricted and well-defined problem at a time. This method always involves making some approximations to the physics of other scales. We must understand what approximations are being made and under what conditions these approximations will need to be further examined.

In any scientific experiment it is important to define the boundaries of the system under study. This must be done to be sure that the conditions of the experiment are well defined and repeatable. This is much easier to do when we deal with benchtop experiments in the physics laboratory than when we deal with large-scale natural or social systems.

The method of approaching problems by defining what is or is not part of the system under study clearly works best when the system of interest can effectively be isolated from all other systems, at least at the conceptual level, and the flows in and out of the system can be well understood and controlled. In an experimental situation, the degree to which a system needs to be isolated from its surroundings depends to some extent on the accuracy of the measurements being made.

Even though it may not be easily achieved in reality, the concept of an isolated system is a useful abstraction that allows one to solve a simple problem. Interactions with the surrounding environment that alter the condition of the system slowly or by small amounts can then be treated as corrections to the original calculations in a controlled way. Thus, a range of conditions can be understood.

The underlying assumption of this approach, that a small change in the conditions leads to a small change in the behavior of the system, is not always true. There are a class of problems for which very small changes in the conditions of the system can lead to completely different results after some time has passed. Systems in such conditions are called chaotic systems. Our ability to predict the future behavior of a chaotic system is quite limited.

In general in science when we ask the question "Why?" about the behavior of a system, the answer is to be found by understanding the nature of its subsystems at a smaller scale. It is interesting to notice that when we work our way down to the smallest building blocks of matter, the fundamental particles and their interactions, physics provides only a description of *what* happens, never any answer to *why* this is the way it is. There is no longer a smaller scale that can be examined. Thus, fundamental particle physics appears at first glance to be unlike the remainder of science. It simply gives a set of rules with no explanation other than that the theory predicts the observed behaviors.

In fact we never answer the question "Why?" in any deep sense in science; what we actually answer is the question "What is the mechanism for this process?" For systems at every scale, the fundamental conservation laws of physics (such as conservation of energy or of electric charge) are part of the answer that is never explained. These laws are imposed as observed facts of nature. (Of course we may learn at some future time that these are not exact laws, because we find certain very rare processes to which they do not apply.) We cannot explain why the fundamental laws of physics apply, we can only state that observations of all systems are consistent with these laws.

See also: APPROXIMATION AND IDEALIZATION; CONSERVATION LAWS; EXPERIMENTAL PHYSICS

Bibliography

AMERICAN ASSOCIATION FOR THE ADVANCEMENT OF SCIENCE, PROJECT 2061. *Benchmarks for Science Literacy* (Oxford University Press, New York, 1993).

HELEN R. QUINN

T

TACHYON

All of the known objects and fundamental particles of the physical world travel slower than light, but it is possible in principle to have particles that travel faster than light. Such a particle is given the name "tachyon," from the Greek word meaning "swift." In the 1960s and early 1970s physicists became very interested in whether tachyons exist. There are strong reasons they should not.

If a bullet breaks a bottle, we can say that the firing of the bullet was the cause and the breaking of the bottle was the effect. Clearly a cause must precede an effect, but according to Albert Einstein's special theory of relativity, the time between two events depends on the motion of the observer. Two events are said to be timelike if (as in the bullet-bottle example) they are connected by the motion of a slower-than-light particle. It turns out that the order of timelike events is the same for all observers; there is no problem with cause and effect. For events with spacelike separation, events that could be connected by a faster-than-light particle, the order of events is different for different observers. If the bullet were a tachyon, some observers would see it being fired *after* the bottle breaks. If tachyons exist we must abandon simple ideas about causality.

Relativity does not allow bullets or any other objects to be accelerated past the speed of light. The resistance to acceleration becomes infinite as the speed of light is approached. Bullets then cannot become tachyons. But this does *not* rule out the existence of particles that *always* go faster than light and could never be slowed down to the speed of light.

Do such particles exist? A number of experimental searches were carried out in the late 1960s. One difficulty in these searches was the indefinite nature of the goal. The experimentalists had no clear knowledge of the properties tachyons might have, whether they would be electrically charged, whether they could only be produced in pairs, and so on. Some experiments specifically sought electrically charged tachyons and assumed that they would produce a kind of electromagnetic shock wave called Cerenkov radiation. Other experiments did not look directly for the tachyons and were less sensitive to assumptions about their properties. By studying bubble chamber tracks of particles from high-energy accelerators, physicists measure the momentum and energy of particles resulting from collisions. From the conservation laws of energy and momentum they can infer the energy, momentum, and speed of the particles that originally collided. In this way a faster-than-light particle can be detected even if it leaves no track. In those searches, and to this day, no experimental evidence has been found for the existence of tachyons.

See also: BUBBLE CHAMBER; EVENT; RELATIVITY, SPECIAL THEORY OF

Bibliography

FEINBERG, G. "Particles that Go Faster-Than-Light." *Sci. Am.* **222,** 68–77 (1970).

FELDMAN, L. M. "Short Bibliography on Faster-Than-Light Particles (Tachyons)." *Am. J. Phys.* **42,** 179–181 (1974).

RICHARD H. PRICE

TAU LEPTON

See LEPTON, TAU

TELESCOPE

The telescope is an optical instrument that allows the human eye to observe distant objects or scenes distinctly. A telescope increases the size of an image and improves image definition. The increase in image size makes distant objects appear closer. A telescope also increases the brightness in images of stars. These three effects are dramatic in well-designed and well-built telescopes.

A telescope consists of an optical system, a mounting, and accessories. The main optical components are the objective lens and the eyepiece, as illustrated in Fig. 1. The objective lens is located closer to the object or scene under observation, and the eyepiece is where the viewer puts his or her eye; the objective is generally larger in diameter than the eyepiece. Telescopes are classified as terrestrial and astronomical. In terrestrial telescopes, the image always appears erect to the eye. This is often achieved with an additional system of prisms or lenses. In as-

tronomical telescopes, the image may be inverted. When the astronomical telescope is used in scientific research, the eyepiece is replaced by an instrument that measures and records specific data of the object under study. The objectives of telescopes are divided into three major classes depending on whether they are made up of lenses (refractors, dioptric), mirrors (reflective, catoptric), or a combination of lenses and mirrors (catadioptric). The telescopes made by Galileo Galilei and Isaac Newton were refracting and reflecting types, respectively.

The objective in a telescope forms an image of an object, which in turn is magnified by the eyepiece. A telescope is an afocal optical system in which parallel light rays arriving at it leave it as parallel light rays. In practice, this is accomplished by making the focal points of the objective and eyepiece coincident in space. The telescope increases the angular subtend of the light beam arriving from the object and also reduces the beam cross section; these effects are illustrated in Figs. 1 and 2. The image size created by the unaided eye is proportional to the angular subtend of the object. Since the telescope increases this subtend, the image in the eye is correspondingly increased in size. The ratio of the image subtend to the object subtend is called the magnifying power, which is equal to the ratio of the focal length of the objective to the focal length of the eyepiece. Typical magnifying powers vary from 2–60 in small telescopes to 300–3,000 in large ones.

The resolution, or capability to define detail, depends on the diameter of the objective: the larger the diameter, the more detail that can be observed in a distant object. The magnifying power does not determine the capability of a telescope to provide image definition. Thus, excessive magnifying powers do not improve image quality. The theoretical resolution of a telescope with an objective 70 mm in diameter is 2.1 arc sec. In comparison, the resolution of the normal eye is 60 arc sec. Since telescopes generally have objectives with large diameters, a light-gathering power is associated with telescopes. The light-gathering power does not increase the image

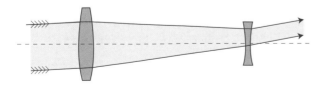

Figure 1 Galilean telescope.

Figure 2 Keplerian telescope.

brightness of objects that are extended because the image correspondingly increases in size. For objects that do not have a significant angular subtend in comparison to the resolution of the eye, such as stars, an increase of brightness is distinctly perceived. The angular field of view of a telescope is the angular extent of the object or scene the telescope can image. The field of view depends on the quality of the objective and eyepiece design. Typically, the field of view ranges from a few arc minutes to a few degrees. Many telescopes for visual use are designed to cover the angular subtend of the Moon, which is 30 arc min.

The objective lens is the largest optical component in a telescope, and its quality is critical to obtaining well-defined images. The goal in objective design is to minimize optical defects that decrease image definition and contrast. These defects are called optical aberrations and arise from the spherical form of lenses, optical dispersion, and manufacturing errors. The main aberrations are chromatic, spherical, comatic, astigmatic, and distortional. Most objective lenses used in refracting telescopes are doublets formed by a positive and a negative lens. These lenses are made with different types of glass (crown and flint) and selected curvatures to correct for aberrations. The type of glass and the optical power of each lens are used to correct for chromatic aberrations, and the lens curvatures are used to correct for spherical and comatic aberrations. In a reflective telescope, there are no chromatic aberrations due to the objective because light is not dispersed upon reflection. In the Newtonian telescope, spherical aberration is corrected by making the primary mirror a paraboloid. Image degradation can also occur from stray light and spu-

rious images. To avoid stray or unwanted light, diaphragms, light baffles, and lens coatings are integrated into the telescope design. The eyepiece is smaller than the objective and made only with lenses. Simple eyepieces consist of a field lens and a magnifying lens. The field lens helps to increase the field of view, and the magnifying lens enlarges the intermediate image formed by the objective.

Because of the diverse ways that lenses and mirrors can be arranged, there are many possible optical configurations in a telescope. The telescope application and the size of the objective usually determine which optical configuration to use. In the Galilean arrangement shown in Fig. 1, the objective is a positive lens and the eyepiece is a negative lens. This arrangement is compact and maintains the image in the eye erect. Opera glasses and camera viewers are often designed with the Galilean configuration. In comparison, the Keplerian telescope shown in Fig. 2 uses a positive lens for the eyepiece. As a result, the image in the eye is inverted, and the telescope length is increased. Many pairs of binoculars use this configuration with a system of prisms to reinvert the image.

Before the invention of lens doublets corrected for chromatic aberration, refracting telescopes were very long in order to minimize the effects of such aberration. An alternate solution, both to shorten the length of telescopes and to avoid chromatic aberration, is the use of mirrors to form the objective of the telescope. Thus, different reflective arrangements have been devised; the most popular are the Newtonian (Fig. 3), the Cassegranian (Fig. 4), and the Gregorian (Fig. 5). In these arrangements, the primary image is formed by a paraboloid mirror. The Newtonian system uses a flat mirror to fold the reflected beam and gain access to the image. The Cassegranian telescope uses a convex, hyperbolic secondary mirror to relay the image to

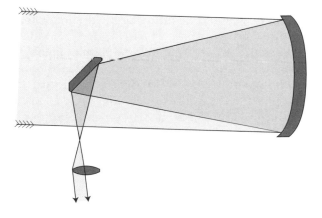

Figure 3   Newtonian telescope.

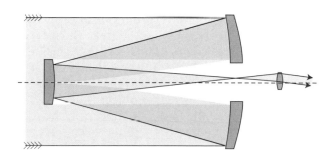

Figure 4   Cassegranian telescope.

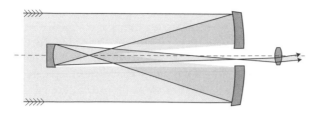

Figure 5 Gregorian telescope.

the back of the primary mirror. In the Gregorian arrangement, the secondary mirror is a concave ellipsoid, and the image orientation is preserved as in the Galilean telescope. The convex and concave secondary mirrors provide additional magnifying power to the telescope.

An essential part of a telescope is the mechanical mount, which supports the optics and permits aiming. Telescope mountings have evolved from simple tripods supporting the telescope with limited aiming capabilities to complex multiaxis mounts that are computer controlled. There are two basic types of mountings: the equatorial and the altazimuth. Both mountings have two perpendicular axes of rotation. The equatorial mount has one axis (right ascension) parallel to the axis of rotation of Earth so that only one movement is needed to follow a star in the sky. The other axis (declination) provides the second degree of freedom to aim the telescope. In contrast, the altazimuth mounting requires movement of both azimuth (vertical) and altitude (horizontal) axes to track a star. Desirable features in a mount are stability of pointing and guidance mechanisms. Most large astronomical telescopes have equatorial mounts. However, some large telescopes are built with altazimuth mounts controlled by computers. This change in the choice of mounting permits smaller and more stable telescopes for a given objective diameter.

Accessories make telescopes easy to use and accommodating to different conditions of observing. The most useful accessory is a finder, which facilitates aiming the telescope. The finder is a small telescope with a field of view of several degrees. The optical axes of the telescope and finder are parallel to each other. Thus, when an object is centered in the field of view of the finder, it appears in the field of view of the main telescope. Other accessories include image erectors, beam-folding prisms to permit a comfortable viewing position, eyepieces to provide different magnifications, and filters to discriminate

light or enhance the image.

In astronomy, the amount of light collected and the resolution of a telescope are important. These characteristics permit the astronomer to identify and distinguish dim celestial bodies and their details. Astronomical telescopes for scientific research tend to use large lenses and mirrors for their objectives. In the twentieth century, reflective telescopes have been preferred because mirrors can be supported and made in very large sizes. For example, the Mount Palomar 5-m telescope and the 10-m Keck telescope in Hawaii could not have been built with a refracting objective because of the technological difficulties of producing large high-quality glass disks, the structural problems in supporting large lenses, and the overall telescope size that results from using a refracting objective.

In scientific research, the eyepiece is often replaced by instruments that measure and analyze the information conveyed by light and collected by the objective. Among these instruments are photographic cameras, photometers, spectroscopes, and CCD (charge-coupled device) arrays. The Hubble Space Telescope has been equipped with several instruments, including the faint-object camera, the faint-object spectrograph, the wide-field and planetary camera, and the Goddard high-resolution spectrograph. The results of analyzing the information gathered by a telescope and its instruments are used to answer some of the fundamental questions about the origin, evolution, and structure of the universe.

The quality of celestial images formed with ground-based telescopes is degraded by the effects of the earth's atmosphere. Most large telescopes are located on mountaintops to diminish such seeing effects. Light waves that pass through the air are distorted to the extent that the resolution of telescopes is limited to about one-half of one arc second. The distortion is caused by inhomogeneities in air temperature and pressure, which produce variations in the index of refraction. New developments in astronomical optics now make it possible to compensate for the errors introduced by the earth's atmosphere. In large telescopes, this optical compensation allows the astronomer to obtain close to the theoretical resolution. This innovation is a significant achievement in modern technology. Other advances in large-telescope technology are large mirrors, optimized supporting structures, precise guidance controls, and understanding and management of the telescope site effects.

See also: HUBBLE SPACE TELESCOPE; REFLECTION; REFRACTION; OPTICS, ADAPTIVE; TELESCOPE, HISTORY OF

Bibliography

HECHT E., and ZAJAC A. *Optics* (Addison-Wesley, Reading, MA, 1974).

KING, H. C. *The History of the Telescope* (Dover, New York, 1979).

MANLY, P. L. *Unusual Telescopes* (Cambridge University Press, Cambridge, Eng., 1991).

RUTTEN, H. G. J., and VAN VENROOIJ, M. A. M. *Telescope Optics: Evaluation and Design* (Willmann-Bell, Richmond, VA, 1988).

SCHROEDER, D. J. *Astronomical Optics* (Academic Press, San Diego, CA, 1987).

TEXEREAU, J. *How to Make a Telescope* (Willmann-Bell, Richmond, VA, 1984).

JOSE M. SASIAN

TELESCOPE, HISTORY OF

Telescopes are the instruments on which astronomy depends. It is an observational science, for it is impossible for us on Earth to do experiments on the scale of stars, nebulas, galaxies and the universe. Each increase in the light gathering power of telescopes has led to new, unexpected discoveries, which theorists have then studied, interpreted, and built on, thus increasing our knowledge of the universe in which we live.

The first telescope was a small refractor in which one lens (the objective) collected light from a star and brought it toward a focus and a second lens (the eyepiece) made the light rays parallel again to enter the eye. It was invented in Holland in 1608, very probably by spectacle maker Hans Lippershey. A year later Galileo Galilei, professor of physics at Padua, heard a rumor of the invention. Once he had learned of the idea, Galileo quickly duplicated the instrument and made his first small telescope in May 1609. He made successively larger ones, and with them saw that the Moon had a rough, mountainous surface and that Jupiter had a disk and was not simply a point of light like a star. By January 1610 he had seen that four "stars," always near Jupiter in the sky, in fact were satellites moving about Jupiter in periodic orbits. Wherever Galileo looked in the sky through his telescope, he saw many more faint stars than he could see with his naked eye. He also saw that the Milky Way, apparently a cloud, was in reality made up of many faint stars, too faint to be seen individually with the unaided eye. Not long afterward, Galileo saw the phases of Venus and noticed sunspots, which showed him that the Sun rotates about an axis in one month. These observations, which Galileo made with his refracting telescope with a diameter of about two inches, were the beginning of observational physical astronomy. Since the human eye can accept a light beam only about one third of an inch in diameter (from a faint star), his telescope collected light over an area about 36 times larger than his naked eye, allowing him to see objects that much fainter.

In Galileo's first telescope, the front (objective) lens was convex to focus the light, while the eyepiece lens, placed inside the focus, was concave. Johannes Kepler in 1611 discovered theoretically that a better system is to place a second convex lens behind the focus of the first as an eyepiece; Christopher Scheiner first used this system in 1617. Since glass refracts blue light more strongly than red, these simple refracting telescopes could only be in focus for one color; that is, they suffered from chromatic aberration. This defect can be reduced by making the telescope very long, so that the amount of refraction is small. The refractor with which Christiaan Huygens discovered Titan, the brightest satellite of Saturn, in 1653 was 12 ft long, and in 1656 he discovered the true nature of Saturn's rings (which Galileo had seen but not understood) with a 123-ft telescope. It was very awkward to use.

In 1663 James Gregory proposed a reflecting telescope that would not suffer from chromatic aberration, since reflection treats all colors equally. The primary mirror, a concave paraboloid, was to bring the light to a focus, and then past that focus a concave ellipsoidal mirror would send the light back through a hole in the primary to a second focus with an eyepiece behind it. Gregory was unable to make satisfactorily curved mirrors ground to put this system into practice. Isaac Newton made a reflecting telescope in 1668 with a spherical primary and a flat mirror mounted at an angle of 45° in the convergent beam to bring the light out at a right angle to an eyepiece just outside the tube. The usable diameter of the primary mirror, made of a shiny metal alloy, was only $1\frac{1}{3}$ in., and it did not bring all the light to one focus. A paraboloid is required to do that, but Newton did not know how to grind the mirror to that form. In France in 1672 Guillame Cassegrain made a two-mirror system in which the primary was a paraboloid and the secondary a convex hyperboloid, which again directed the light back through a hole in the primary to a focus behind it. These three types are the predecessors of modern reflecting telescopes.

Around 1773 William Herschel, a professional musician in Bath, England, began making reflecting telescopes with which he surveyed the heavens. With a 6-in. Newtonian he had made, he discovered many double stars, and in 1781 he discovered the planet Uranus, the first to be found since antiquity. King George III, who was impressed, provided him with enough funds to become a full-time astronomer. Herschel conducted several surveys with a 12-in. Newtonian and then progressed to a 19-in. and a 48-in. telescopes. The latter paraboloids did not use secondary mirrors; the primary mirror was instead slightly tipped to bring the light out to an off-axis eyepiece. His mountings for these telescopes were very awkward, and for this reason the 48-in. reflector was not as useful as the 19-in. reflector. Herschel discovered two satellites of Uranus with the 19-in. and two satellites of Saturn with the 48-in.; more important, in his systematic surveys he discovered and listed numerous clusters and nebulas (many of the latter actually known today to be galaxies, each composed of myriads of stars). In the next century William Parsons, Earl of Rosse, made and used still larger reflecting telescopes of this type at his estate in Ireland, culminating in a 72-in., the Leviathan of Parsonstown, completed in 1845.

Refracting telescopes became more practical after Charles Moor Hall, an English attorney and amateur optical experimenter, conceived the idea of achromatic lenses, made by combining a convex lens of one type of glass with a concave lens of a second type. It was possible to design the system so that the combination brought light to a focus, but with minimum chromatic aberration for the wavelengths around yellow light to which the human eye was most sensitive. Quite independently, the Swiss mathematician Leonhard Euler worked out the theory of this type of refractor and published it in 1747. The optician John Dolland, in London, learned of this design, developed it empirically, and began selling achromatic telescope lenses in the late 1750s. Even though these telescopes were quite successful, they were limited to relatively small apertures, 5 or 6 in. at most, by the difficulties of getting larger pieces of clear glass.

In the years around 1800, the Swiss Pierre Louis Guinand greatly improved the process of making large, clear glass blanks. In Munich, Joseph Fraunhofer used such disks to make excellent refracting telescopes; the largest was the $9\frac{1}{2}$-in. used by Wilhelm Struve at Dorpat Observatory in Estonia, then a province of Russia. Fraunhofer also perfected the equatorial type of mounting, in which the telescope, driven by a clock drive about an axis parallel to the axis of the earth, accurately followed the stars across the sky. With his telescope Struve surveyed the entire sky north of $-15°$ declination (analogous to latitude on the earth) and measured more than 3,000 double stars.

In America Henry Fitz, an excellent telescope maker in New York, produced many refractors up to the time of the Civil War. For Lewis M. Rutherfurd, an amateur, he made an 11-in. achromatized for blue light, rather than for yellow, to use for astronomical photography, as the early photographic plates were only sensitive to blue and violet radiation. With this telescope, in 1864, Rutherfurd pioneered in stellar photography. The great American lens makers were Alvan Clark and his son Alvan G. Clark. The father, originally an artist, began with an 8-in. refracting telescope in 1858 and then made an $18\frac{1}{2}$-in. for the University of Mississippi, which went instead to Dearborn Observatory in Chicago. While testing this telescope at Alvan Clark & Sons' shop in Cambridgeport, Massachusetts, Alvan G. Clark discovered the faint companion star to Sirius, confirming the prediction Friedrich W. Bessel had made that it was a double star. The Clarks proceeded to build larger and larger refractors by essentially empirical methods, scaling up their basic design a few inches each time. These telescopes reached their apotheosis in the Lick Observatory 36-in. refractor, completed in 1888, and the Yerkes 40-in., completed in 1897. The Cleveland firm of Warner and Swasey made the mountings for both these large refractors, which were close to the upper size limit for such telescopes, because of the sagging of the lenses supported only at their edges. With the Lick 36-in., on the first night it was used, James E. Keeler discovered the very narrow, dark, outer division in the rings of Saturn, and in 1893 Edward E. Barnard discovered the faint fifth satellite of Jupiter, the first of its moons to be found since Galileo's time.

A new era in reflecting telescopes opened after the German chemist Justus von Liebig developed the method of depositing a metallic silver coat on glass in the 1850s. Carl August von Steinheil in Munich and Leon Foucault in Paris soon applied it to making telescope mirrors of glass, which could be ground and figured to the required surface much more accurately and easily than a metal mirror. Silver-on-glass reflectors, which could be resilvered as often as necessary, soon swept the field. George Calver, in England, made many such mirrors, including the 36-in. diameter paraboloid that Andrew A. Common mounted as a Newtonian reflector in 1879. With it he began photographing nebulas, comets, and planets. Because they are perfectly achromatic and can be made with relatively fast focal ratios (familiar from hand cameras as the ratio of the diameter of the objective to the focal length of the system), reflecting telescopes proved ideal for photography. With a 20-in. reflector Isaac Roberts in the 1880s obtained photographs of nebulas, including one in 1887 that showed the spiral form of the Andromeda "nebula" (actually a galaxy of stars, analogous to the Milky Way Galaxy).

However, James E. Keeler obtained far better photographs with the 36-in. reflector that Common had made for wealthy Edward Crossley, who eventually gave it to Lick Observatory. There, on Mount Hamilton, California, the first permanent clear-sky, mountaintop observatory site of the type advocated years before by Charles Piazzi Smyth, and later independently by George Davidson, Keeler used this reflector, which he had rebuilt in 1898 to obtain many excellent long-exposure photographs. They revealed as never before the true forms and complexity of many nebulas, including large numbers of spirals, of all sizes from Andromeda down to the smallest limit of resolution. By 1900 Keeler recognized them as objects of essentially similar physical size and structure, seen at all distances, important as numerous constituents of the universe, although he did not realize that they were galaxies. His results convinced many American astronomers that reflectors, not refractors, would be the "monster telescopes of the future," as Howard Grubb, the Irish telescope-maker called them.

George Willis Ritchey, at Yerkes Observatory, then constructed the very fast 24-in. reflector with which he took an even better series of direct photographs of nebulas and galaxies. Moving west to help George Ellery Hale start Mount Wilson Observatory in Southern California, Ritchey built the 60-in. reflector completed in 1908. It was a great success. Then he ground and figured the paraboloidal mirror for the 100-in. telescope completed in 1919. With the 100-in., Edwin Hubble proved that spiral nebulas are

galaxies of stars and discovered the expansion of the universe. Hale raised the funds to build the outstanding 200-in. Palomar reflecting telescope, named for him when it went into operation in 1948. With it Maarten Schmidt, Jesse L. Greenstein and J. Beverly Oke discovered in 1963 the true nature of quasars (quasi-stellar radio sources), objects that look like stars but are among the most luminous and distant objects in the universe. By then aluminum deposited in vacuum had replaced silver as the preferred reflecting surface for glass telescope mirrors.

The 200-in. was the largest telescope in the world until the Soviet 6-m (236-in.) reflector at the Special Astrophysical Observatory was completed in the Caucasus in 1976. The first mirror used in it did not have a good figure, and the site was plagued by clouds and an unsteady atmosphere, but some good spectroscopic results were obtained with it. It was the first large research optical telescope constructed with an alt-azimuth mounting and controlled by a computer instead of an equatorial mounting. A small flat mirror can bring the light beam out to either side of the telescope through a horizontal axis about which it rotates. This system was originated by James Nasmyth in 1845 for his 20-in. Cassegrain telescope at his home near Manchester, England.

In 1910 Ritchey, with Henri Chrétien, had invented the wide-field Cassegrain telescope in which both the primary and the secondary are hyperboloids. Unlike a conventional Cassegrain or Newtonian reflector, which suffer from the natural aberration or defect of coma, making the off-axis images blurred, a Ritchey–Chrétien telescope can record a large angular field on one exposure; it is thus superior for photography. Ritchey made the first telescope of this type, a 20-in., in Paris in 1927. He completed a 40-in. research telescope in 1934 for the U.S. Naval Observatory in Washington. It was never a success there, but when moved to Flagstaff, Arizona, it proved an outstanding photographic instrument in 1956 in the hands of John S. Hall and Arthur A. Hoag. Aden Meinel, director of the Kitt Peak National Observatory, near Tucson, decided to make its 84-in. reflector a Ritchey–Chrétien in 1958, and since then most large telescopes have been constructed in that form. The largest is the 10-m (400-in.) Keck telescope built and operated on Mauna Kea, Hawaii, by the California Institute of Technology and the University of California. It went into operation in 1993. Its primary mirror is not a single glass disk but a mosaic of glass segments, each a hexagon 1.8 m (72 in.) in diameter, ground and figured to the proper portion of the correct hyperboloid. The positions of the segments are constantly measured and adjusted by a complicated computer system to counteract whatever distortions gravity, wind, and thermal changes might otherwise cause. A second, identical Keck II telescope was completed and went into operation on the same site in 1996. The 94-in. Hubble Space Telescope, launched in 1992, is also a Ritchey–Chrétien reflector; its primary is a single, lightweight disk.

See also: ABERRATION, CHROMATIC; GALAXIES AND GALACTIC STRUCTURE; GALILEI, GALILEO; HUBBLE, EDWIN POWELL; HUBBLE SPACE TELESCOPE; HUYGENS, CHRISTIAAN; KEPLER, JOHANNES; QUASAR; TELESCOPE; UNIVERSE, EXPANSION OF, DISCOVERY OF

Bibliography

ASIMOV, I. *Eyes on the Universe: A History of the Telescope* (Houghton Mifflin, Boston, 1975).

DIMITROFF, G. Z., and BAKER, J. G. *Telescopes and Accessories* (Blakiston, Philadelphia, 1945).

FLORENCE, R. *The Perfect Machine: Building the Palomar Telescope* (HarperCollins, New York, 1994).

KING, H. C. *The History of the Telescope* (Dover, New York, [1955] 1979).

KIRBY-SMITH, H. T. *U.S. Observatories: A Directory and Travel Guide* (Van Nostrand Reinhold, New York, 1976).

KUIPER, G. P., and MIDDLEHURST, B. M., eds. *Telescopes and Accessories* (University of Chicago Press, Chicago, 1961).

OSTERBROCK, D. E. *James E. Keeler, Pioneer American Astrophysicist: And the Early Development of American Astrophysics* (Cambridge University Press, Cambridge, Eng., 1984).

OSTERBROCK, D. E. *Pauper & Prince: Ritchey, Hale, & Big American Telescopes* (University of Arizona Press, Tucson, 1993).

WARNER, D. J., and ARIAIL, R. B. *Alvan Clark & Sons: Artists in Optics,* 2nd ed. (Willmann-Bell, Richmond, VA, 1995).

DONALD E. OSTERBROCK

TEMPERATURE

Temperature is one of the fundamental quantities in classical and modern physics. The concept of hot and cold has been present throughout our civilization. Temperature is the quantification of this sensation and the indicator of thermal equilibrium. The zeroth law of thermodynamics guarantees the existence of such an indicator. The zeroth law states that if bodies *A* and *B* are each separately in thermal equilibrium with a third body *C*, then *A* and *B* are in thermal equilibrium with each other. If *C* is a thermometer in this case, the zeroth law guarantees the two objects *A* and *B*, which are at the same temperature as the thermometer C, to be in thermal equilibrium with each other.

The proof that an indicator function for equilibrium exists as a consequence of the zeroth law is an interesting example of the type of logic frequently employed in the field of thermodynamics. Let us say that the systems *A, B,* and *C* are specified by two parameters, *p* (pressure) and *V* (volume). This will be the case with a system like the ideal gas. When *A* and *C* are in thermal equilibrium, there is a relationship among the quantities that characterize the two systems in their respective states. Thus an equation like the following should hold:

$$F_1(p_A, V_A, p_C, V_C) = 0. \tag{1}$$

Or we solve this for p_c to obtain

$$p_C = f_1(p_A, V_A, V_C) \tag{1'}$$

Likewise, from the condition that *B* and *C* are in thermal equilibrium, we have a relation of the form

$$F_2(p_B, V_B, p_C, V_C) = 0 \tag{2}$$

or

$$p_C = f_2(p_B, V_B, V_C), \tag{2'}$$

Combining Eqs. (1′) and (2′) we obtain

$$f_1(p_A, V_A, V_C) = f_2(p_B, V_B, V_C). \tag{3}$$

At this point we invoke the zeroth law, which states that the thermal equilibrium conditions given by Eqs. (1) and (2) leads to the equilibrium between *A* and *B*. This means that there is also an expression equivalent to Eq. (3), but it has the form

$$F_3(p_A, V_A, p_B, V_B) = 0. \tag{4}$$

Equations (3) and (4) should describe the same equilibrium between A and B. Yet Eq. (3) contains the variable V_C. This must mean that terms or factors containing V_C in expressions f_1 and f_2 canceled out of Eq. (3) to produce Eq. (4). In other words, Eq. (3) should look like the following: $g_1(p_A, V_A) h(V_C) = g_2(p_B, V_B) h(V_C)$, where $h(V_C)$ is an arbitrary function of V_C. (Strictly speaking, we could also have an arbitrary identical additive term on each side.) Then we see that Eq. (3), and consequently Eq. (4), has the form $g_1(p_A, V_A) = g_2(p_B, V_B)$. We can use the same reasoning to extend this to obtain

$$g_1(p_A, V_A) = g_2(p_B, V_B) = g_3(p_C, V_C), \tag{5}$$

and so on to all the systems that are in thermal equilibrium with C.

Note that function g_1 contains only the parameters of system A, and g_2 contains only the parameters of B (and likewise for system C). These functions are the functions characteristic of each system and each depends only on its own state variables. In thermal equilibrium these functions, g_1, g_2, g_3, . . . , all have the same numerical value as seen from Eq. (5). These functions then are the indicators of thermal equilibrium and the function g for each system is called its empirical temperature Θ, that is, $g(p, V) = \Theta$. The function $g(p, V)$ for a system can be any single-valued function in principle. It is convenient to assign a simple function such as $\Theta = pV/NR$, or $pV = NR\Theta$, where N and R are constants. For ideal gas this is commonly known as the equation of state of an ideal gas and R is the universal gas constant ($R = 8.314 \, \text{J} \cdot \text{mol}^{-1} \cdot \text{K}^{-1}$) and N is the mole number (number of moles of gas molecules present).

The absolute temperature scale is defined in terms of the Carnot (engine) cycle. The efficiency ε of the Carnot engine is defined as the amount of work output W divided by the quantity of heat Q_1 absorbed from a reservoir (a large heat source or sink) at a high temperature T_1 as $\varepsilon = W/Q_1$. The engine exhausts a quantity of heat Q_2 to another reservoir at lower temperature T_2, which is usually the temperature of the atmosphere. According to the law of conservation of energy (i.e., the first law of thermodynamics, which states that the energy of a closed system is conserved if heat is taken into account) we must have $Q_1 = W + Q_2$. This can be rewritten as $\varepsilon = (Q_1 - Q_2)/Q_1 = 1 - Q_2/Q_1$.

The absolute (or Kelvin) temperature is defined by setting the ratio of the two temperatures equal to the ratio of the quantities of heat energy involved in the engine operation as:

$$T_2/T_1 = Q_2/Q_1. \tag{6}$$

Now the primary standard of temperature scale is the temperature at the triple point of water. It is defined as $T_3 = 273.16$ K. This numerical value of T_3 and Eq. (6) are sufficient to give the absolute temperature scale by heat (i.e., energy) measurements. The efficiency of the Carnot engine then is expressed as $\varepsilon = 1 - T_2/T_1$.

Thermodynamics theory establishes the identity of the two temperature scales, the Kelvin scale and the ideal gas scale, by operating a Carnot engine that uses an ideal gas as the working substance.

Temperature and Entropy

Historically, the concept of temperature entered into the theoretical framework of thermodynamics through its second law, which, in one of its many forms, states that no process is possible whose sole result is the complete conversion of heat into work (the Kelvin statement). The second law as applied to the Carnot cycle leads to the justification of the Kelvin scale of temperature as described above. This logical progression eventually leads to the introduction of the concept of entropy. More precisely, entropy S enters the exposition as an infinitesimal quantity:

$$ds = đQ/T,$$

where $đQ$ is the infinitesimal quantity of heat entering the system at temperature T. The notation d with a bar across the top portion of the differential notation, $đ$, signifies an inexact differential which means that Q is not a function of the parameters describing an equilibrium state. In other words, $đQ$ cannot be integrated to yield a function Q, since the quantity Q (and this also applies to work W) depends not only on the state but also on the path of the thermodynamic process through which the system arrived at that state. Dividing $đQ$ by T, however, makes it possible to integrate the expression to obtain a state function S, the entropy of the state. For this reason temperature is sometimes thought of as an integrating denominator. (The so-called Carathéodory's formulation of the second law renders this aspect mathematically meaningful but is beyond the scope of this entry.)

Temperature enters into the axiomatic construction of thermodynamics (which is an alternative to the historical and traditional exposition) as a derivative of the internal energy function U with respect to the entropy parameter as $T = (\partial U/\partial S)_{V,N}$, where the symbol $(\partial\ /\partial\ )$ denotes operation of partial differentiation and the subscripts indicate parameters to be held constant during partial differentiation. The first derivative of an energy function with respect to an extensive parameter such as entropy is an intensive parameter. Thus temperature is an intensive parameter and as such does not depend on the size of the system as long as it is in thermodynamic equilibrium. Intensive parameters such as temperature and pressure are thus more convenient to measure than extensive parameters such as entropy and volume. One only needs to probe the boundary region of the system and obtain the temperature or pressure reading guaranteed to be that of the interior.

Microscopic Interpretation of Temperature

Since matter is made of atoms and molecules, the concept of temperature needs to be interpreted microscopically in terms of the dynamics of these particles comprising the system. Such a kinetic consideration leads to the interpretation of temperature as a measure of average kinetic energy of internal (microscopic) motions of atoms or molecules. Specifically, for a single-component monatomic ideal gas one can apply mechanical consideration to a system of idealized particles to obtain the relationship: $(3/2)\,k_B T = (1/2)\,m\bar{v}^2$, where k_B is the Boltzmann's constant ($k_B = 1.38 \times 10^{-23}$ J/K), m is the mass of the particle, and $\bar{v}$ is its average velocity. Higher temperature corresponds to faster molecular motion. In solids such as copper crystals or silicon wafers, higher temperature represents larger amplitudes of atomic or molecular vibrations. When two bodies, one hot and the other cold, are brought in contact with each other, the kinetic energy of the body at higher temperature is gradually transferred to the molecules of the body at lower temperature

thereby increasing the temperature of the colder body and cooling the body at higher temperature until thermal equilibrium is reached. The kinetic energy of the combined system then is uniformly distributed on the average to all the molecules.

When a system is at a finite (nonzero) temperature, some of its constituent atoms or molecules acquire sufficient thermal energy to jump to higher quantum states. For the sake of simplicity, let us assume there are only two quantum states easily accessible to an atom and the other states are sufficiently higher to render them insignificant for our purpose. The lower of these two states is the ground state that is occupied by all the atoms of the system at 0 K. As the temperature is raised some of the atoms begin to acquire energy to jump to the higher (exited) state. The occupation ratio by the atoms of these energy levels is a function of temperature. If the population of the ground state is N_1 and that of the excited state is N_2, the temperature dependence is given by

$$N_2/N_1 = \exp\left(-E/k_B T\right), \qquad (7)$$

where E is the energy difference between the excited state and the ground state. This can be regarded as the definition of temperature of the two-level system (i.e., aggregate of atoms with two energy levels). When the temperature is low (e.g., a fraction of a degree above 0 K), the negative exponent of e is very large (in absolute value) and the ratio N_2/N_1 is a very small number. In other words, very few atoms are excited from the ground state to the excited state. When the temperature is high, on the other hand, the ratio N_2/N_1 becomes larger and finally, at very high temperatures, approaches 1. Then the population of the excited state approaches that of the ground state. In some cases where atoms are artificially pumped by external supply of energy to be forced into the excited state, N_2 becomes larger than N_1. This is called population inversion. When this happens the ratio N_2/N_1 becomes larger than 1. If we define temperature by the population ratio using the above expression, this corresponds to the case of "negative temperature." It should be noted that this is not an equilibrium state. As we can see in this case, the temperature concept is frequently used for states not in equilibrium as long as the state lasts sufficiently long compared to time required for observation. Weakly interacting nuclear spin moments in the host crystal lattice is a case in point. Manipulation of this population inversion of atomic systems is the basic operating principle of laser action.

Since the product $k_B T$ has the unit of energy and has the order of magnitude of the thermal energy per atom, certain characteristic energies related to various phenomena or properties of matter are frequently expressed in terms of temperature in lieu of its energy equivalent. For example, Fermi energy ε_F signifies the maximum energy of an electron in a solid at 0 K. This is sometimes expressed in terms of Fermi temperature T_F to describe the distribution of electron energy at a finite temperature ($k_B T_F = \varepsilon_F$).

Temperature and pressure are the variables one manipulates most frequently to investigate the properties of matter. Of these, temperature parameter has been more extensively employed. Modern experimental techniques have made it possible to attain temperature as low as a few micro Kelvin and as high as a few thousand degrees.

See also: CURIE TEMPERATURE; ENTROPY; STANDARD TEMPERATURE AND PRESSURE; STATE, EQUATION OF; TEMPERATURE SCALE, CELSIUS; TEMPERATURE SCALE, FAHRENHEIT; TEMPERATURE SCALE, KELVIN; THERMOMETER; THERMOMETRY

Bibliography

ADKINS, C. J. *Equilibrium Thermodynamics* (McGraw-Hill, London, 1968).

CALLEN, H. B. *Thermodynamics and Introduction to Thermostatistics*, 2nd ed. (Wiley, New York, 1985).

HOLTON, G., and BRUSH, S. G. *Introduction to Concepts and Theories in Physical Science* (Addison-Wesley, Reading, MA, 1973).

CARL T. TOMIZUKA

TEMPERATURE SCALE, CELSIUS

Temperature scales provide a quantitative measure of the hotness or coldness of a system. They are established by assigning numbers to a series of states corresponding to different amounts of hotness or coldness. The Celsius temperature scale was devised in 1742 by the Swedish astronomer Anders C. Celsius. He defined zero degrees Celsius as the temperature of a mixture of water and ice in equilibrium at standard atmospheric pressure, and one hundred degrees Celsius as the temperature of a mixture of water and steam at standard atmospheric pressure. The one hundred divisions (degrees) between these two fixed points are equal.

Scientists throughout the world use the Celsius temperature scale. The Celsius scale was formerly called the centigrade scale in the United States and Great Britain because of the one hundred units between the boiling and freezing points of water. Most of the non-English-speaking world, however, has always used the term "Celsius scale". During the Ninth General Conference on Weights and Measures in 1948, the United States formally adopted the name Celsius in place of centigrade. Great Britain changed to the name Celsius in 1962. The Celsius and centigrade scales are the same.

Temperature scales are no longer defined by the standard ice point and steam point. By international agreement, temperature scales are now defined by absolute zero and the triple point of water. The International Practical Temperature Scale of 1968 establishes the triple point of water at standard atmospheric pressure as 0.01°C. Absolute zero is −273.15°C. This revised definition of the Celsius

Table 1 Fixed-Point Temperatures

Fixed Point	T_C (°C)	T_K (K)
Triple point of oxygen	−218.79	54.36
Boiling point of oxygen	−182.96	90.19
Freezing point of water	0.00	273.15
Triple point of water	0.01	273.16
Boiling point of water	100.00	373.15
Freezing point of zinc	419.58	692.73
Freezing point of silver	961.93	1,235.08
Freezing point of gold	1,064.43	1,337.58

scale was selected so there would be little practical difference between the old and the new.

A temperature scale whose zero point is the same as absolute zero is called an absolute temperature scale. A second characteristic of an absolute temperature scale is that it is independent of the property of any substance. The Kelvin temperature scale is such a scale. Celsius degrees (°C) are of the same magnitude as the degree employed in the Kelvin scale (K). The relationship between the two scales is

$$T_C = T_K - 273.15,$$

where T_C and T_K represent temperature in degrees Celsius and degrees Kelvin, respectively. Absolute temperatures must be used in the gas laws.

Two other temperature scales in common use are the Fahrenheit (United States) and Rankine (Great Britain) scales. They are related to the Celsius scale as follows:

$$T_C = \frac{5}{9}(T_F - 32),$$
$$T_C = \frac{5}{9}T_R - 273.15,$$

since

$$T_K = \frac{5}{9}T_R,$$

where T_F and T_R are measured in degrees Fahrenheit and degrees Rankine, respectively. The magnitude of the Fahrenheit and Rankine degrees is the same and is larger than that of the Celsius and Kelvin degrees.

Table 1 gives assigned temperature values of some fixed points associated with common substances. All values are at standard atmospheric pressure.

See also: ABSOLUTE ZERO; STANDARD TEMPERATURE AND PRESSURE; TEMPERATURE; TEMPERATURE SCALE, FAHRENHEIT; TEMPERATURE SCALE, KELVIN; TRIPLE POINT; WATER

Bibliography

KITTEL, C., and KROEMER, H. *Thermal Physics,* 2nd ed. (W. H. Freeman, New York, 1980).

McGEE, T. D. *Principles and Methods of Temperature Measurement* (Wiley, New York, 1988).

WOLFSON, R., and PASACHOFF, J. M. *Physics* (Scott Foresman/Little Brown Higher Education, Glenview, IL, 1990).

ELIZABETH S. IVEY

TEMPERATURE SCALE, FAHRENHEIT

The first thermometer, the air thermoscope, was invented by Galileo Galilei around 1592, but it was affected by changes in atmospheric pressure—a disadvantage he soon overcame with sealed liquid-in-glass thermometers. In 1701 Isaac Newton proposed a temperature scale based on fixed points; 0° for the freezing point of water and 12° for body temperature, although there was doubt at that time that the freezing point of water was constant. Around 1713 Gabriel Daniel Fahrenheit, a German instrument maker born in Danzig who lived most of his life in England and Holland, proposed as the zero point the lowest temperature achievable with salt, ice, and water (a eutectic point), and 12° for body temperature. The scale was soon expanded by a factor of eight, which made body temperature 96°F. [The close coincidence of body temperature, which is now taken as 98.6°F (oral) or 99.6°F (rectal) was thus accidental.]

Fahrenheit soon showed that the variation in freezing point of pure water was a consequence of supercooling. After the initial dip in temperature, the thermal energy released in freezing restored the temperature to a fixed point, which was read on his thermometer as 32°. The boiling point of water had been suggested as a fixed point by Ole Rømer, Edmund Halley, and others. Fahrenheit showed that the observed variations in boiling point could be attributed to variations in atmospheric pressure. By about the time of his death in 1736, the fixed points were taken as the ice point, at 32°F, and the normal boiling point, at 212°F. Neither point can be measured experimentally to the accuracy required for modern thermometric definitions.

No temperature scale has real advantages over any other scale for a limited range. However, there are strong advantages to ready conversion to the scientific (Kelvin) scale and to agreement across political boundaries. The Fahrenheit scale has therefore largely disappeared, except in the United States, in favor of the Celsius scale.

Between the ice point and boiling point, there are 180°F, compared to 100°C, a ratio of 180/100 = 9/5. Thus, to convert from °F to °C, or vice versa, one simply multiplies by 5/9 or 9/5, respectively (remembering that there are more Fahrenheit degrees), subtracting or adding 32°F on the Fahrenheit value to correct for the value of the ice point. For example, starting with 75°F gives (75°F − 32°F) × (5°C/9°F) = 24°C, and starting with 24°C gives 24°C × (9°F/5°C) + 32°F = 75°F.

There is also an absolute temperature scale based on the Fahrenheit scale. This absolute temperature scale is called the Rankine scale and differs from the Fahrenheit scale by the constant value of 459.67; that is, the absolute zero is 0°R = −459.67°F.

See also: TEMPERATURE; TEMPERATURE SCALE, CELSIUS; TEMPERATURE SCALE, KELVIN

Bibliography

HALL, J. A. *The Measurement of Temperature* (Chapman and Hall, London, 1966).

MIDDLETON, W. E. K. *A History of the Thermometer and Its Use in Meteorology* (Johns Hopkins University Press, Baltimore, MD, 1966).

ROBERT P. BAUMAN

TEMPERATURE SCALE, KELVIN

Joseph Gay-Lussac, Jacques Charles, and John Dalton independently recognized that common gases have nearly identical values for the coefficient of expansion (the percentage change in volume for a given change in temperature) at a fixed pressure. The value is nearly independent of the fixed pressure. This implies that the volume of a gas is a linear function of temperature, which becomes a proportionality for a suitable choice of zero temperature. (The volume relationship must fail at very low temperatures; otherwise, the volume of the gas would become zero and then negative.)

The zero of temperature is called absolute zero, and the temperature is then called an absolute temperature. When combined with Avogadro's hypothesis that equal volumes of different gases at the same temperature and pressure contain the same number of particles or molecules, the relationship can be expressed in the form $PV = nRT$. This is called the ideal gas law, in which P, V, and T are the pressure, volume, and temperature, n is the number of molecules expressed in units of moles (6.022×10^{23} particles/mol), and R is a universal constant ($8.31441 \text{ J·mol}^{-1}\text{·K}^{-1} \equiv 8.31441 \text{ Pa·m}^3\text{·mol}^{-1}\text{·K}^{-1}$) called the gas constant.

Because real gases deviate from this ideal gas equation, measurements of the temperature based on this absolute scale with real gases give variable results depending on the choice of gas. It is easily shown that any monotonic scale provides an adequate measure of temperature, but there are advantages to having a unique scale that agrees with the absolute (gas) scale for sufficiently low gas pressures.

William Thomson, the future Lord Kelvin, proposed a scale in 1847 based on Carnot's theory of heat engines. For any reversible heat engine, operating between fixed high and low temperatures, T_H and T_C, on Kelvin's thermodynamic scale, the amounts of thermal energy transferred to or from the system must be in the ratio $Q_H/Q_C = T_H/T_C$, independent of the nature of the working fluid in the engine.

This leaves only the size of the degree to be determined by fixing a single point (other than the inherent absolute zero). Choosing the triple point of water to be 273.16 K (0.01°C) sets the unit, called the kelvin, equal to the Celsius degree. The scale is known as the Kelvin scale. (A comparable absolute scale, with a unit 5/9 as great, is known as the Rankine scale.) Temperatures on the Celsius scale are equal to the Kelvin temperature minus 273.15.

The Kelvin scale has been incorporated into the International System of Units (SI). In principle, no other defined temperature values are permitted or required. In practice, it is found convenient to define an International Practical Temperature Scale (IPTS), believed to be experimentally consistent with the Kelvin scale, that identifies fixed temperature points (such as the triple point and boiling point of H_2, the boiling point of O_2, and the freezing point of gold) and assigns values to them, indicating the particular measurement scheme by which values are to be interpolated between the fixed values.

See also: ABSOLUTE ZERO; GAS CONSTANT; IDEAL GAS LAW; KELVIN, LORD; TEMPERATURE; TEMPERATURE SCALE, CELSIUS; TEMPERATURE SCALE, FAHRENHEIT

Bibliography

AMERICAN SOCIETY FOR TESTING AND MATERIALS. *ASTM Special Technical Publication 565: Evolution of the International Practical Temperature Scale of 1968* (American Society for Testing and Materials, Philadelphia, 1974).

HALL, J. A. *The Measurement of Temperature* (Chapman and Hall, London, 1966).

ROBERT P. BAUMAN

TENSOR

Tensors are an extension of the vector concept. They have two major applications in physics: (1) second-rank three-tensors, such as the inertia tensor and the electromagnetic stress tensor, and (2) four-tensors of various ranks used in special and general relativity. A tensor of zero-rank is a scalar, and a tensor of first-rank is a vector.

The inertia tensor $\mathbf{I}$ for a rigid body relates the angular momentum vector $\mathbf{L}$ to the angular velocity vector ω ($\mathbf{L} = \mathbf{I} \cdot \omega$) and is determined by the mass distribution of the body. Since there are three components of the angular momentum and each is related to the three components of the angular velocity, the inertia tensor must have nine components. The component forms of the angular momentum–angular velocity relations are $L_x = I_{xx}\omega_x + I_{xy}\omega_y + I_{xz}\omega_z$, $L_y = I_{yx}\omega_x + I_{yy}\omega_y + I_{yz}\omega_z$, and $L_z = I_{zx}\omega_x + I_{zy}\omega_y + I_{zz}\omega_z$. (Actually, only six inertia tensor components are independent, since the inertia tensor is symmetric: $I_{yx} = I_{xy}$, $I_{zy} = I_{yz}$, and $I_{xz} = I_{zx}$.)

A more compact notation is afforded by the use of indices: $i = 1$, 2, or 3, and $j = 1$, 2, or 3, with 1 indicating x, 2 indicating y, and 3 indicating z. So $\mathbf{L} = \mathbf{I} \cdot \omega$ becomes $L_i = I_{ij}\omega_j$, where i may be 1, 2, or 3, and the fact that j appears twice (repeated index) implies summation over $j = 1$, 2, and 3.

Using index notation, the inertia tensor for a set of n particles, with the αth particle having mass m_α and position r_α, is $I_{ij} = \sum_{\alpha=1}^{n} m_\alpha [r_\alpha^2 \delta_{ij} - (r_\alpha)_i (r_\alpha)_j]$. Here δ_{ij} is the Kroneker delta: $\delta_{ij} = 1$ if $i = j$ and $\delta_{ij} = 0$ if $i \neq j$. Such a set of particles may be regarded as an approximation to a rigid body, or the expression for the inertia tensor may be converted to an integral.

The kinetic energy of rotation of a rigid body may be written: $K = \frac{1}{2}\omega \cdot \mathbf{I} \cdot \omega$, $K = \frac{1}{2}I_{ij}\omega_i\omega_j$, or, extensively, $K = \frac{1}{2}(I_{xx}\omega_x\omega_x + I_{xy}\omega_x\omega_y + I_{xz}\omega_x\omega_z + I_{yx}\omega_y\omega_x + I_{yy}\omega_y\omega_y + I_{yz}\omega_y\omega_z + I_{zx}\omega_z\omega_x + I_{zy}\omega_z\omega_y + I_{zz}\omega_z\omega_z)$. Note that each of these expressions for K is actually the same nine term sum.

Since the kinetic energy is a scalar, any coordinate system may be used to evaluate $\mathbf{I}$ and ω (albeit, the same for both) when calculating K. For a rotating body, a particular coordinate system (principal axes) that is fixed relative to the body, makes all the components of $\mathbf{I}$ zero except I_{xx}, I_{yy}, and I_{zz}. Using principal axes greatly reduces the complexity in expressions involving the inertia tensor and simplifies the calculation of the kinetic energy. (This feature can be applied whenever a tensor is symmetric.)

The electromagnetic stress tensor describes the flow of energy and momentum in electromagnetic fields. Its components are defined in terms of the electric and magnetic field vectors.

As with three-vectors, three-tensors must transform appropriately when the coordinates are rotated. First consider vector transformations associated with coordinate rotations in three dimensions. If a vector $\mathbf{p}$ has components p_1, p_2, and p_3 in the initial coordinates and p'_1, p'_2, and p'_3 in the rotated coordinates, then $p'_i = R_{ij}p_j$, where R_{ij} is the rotation matrix (a set of nine constants determined by the angle and axis of rotation). Likewise, for another vector $\mathbf{q}$, $q'_i = R_{ij}q_j$. But the scalar product of $\mathbf{p}$ and $\mathbf{q}$ is unchanged by the coordinate rotation so $p'_i q'_i = p_i q_i$, that is, $R_{im}p_m R_{in}q_n = \delta_{mn}p_m q_n$. Since $\mathbf{p}$ and $\mathbf{q}$ are arbitrary, this requires that the rotation matrix satisfy $R_{im}R_{in} = \delta_{mn}$, a set of nine equations. However, interchanging m and n gives the same equation, so only six conditions are obtained. Any R_{ij} that satisfies $R_{im}R_{in} = \delta_{mn}$ represents a rotation (or a rotation and a reflection).

A second-rank three-tensor, I_{ij}, must transform according to $I'_{ij} = R_{im}R_{jn}I_{mn}$, a third-rank three-tensor, Q_{ijk}, must transform according to $Q'_{ijk} = R_{im}R_{jn}R_{kh}Q_{mnh}$, and so on.

In special and general relativity, the concept of three-tensors is extended to four-tensors. The primitive four-vector is the event vector $(ct, \mathbf{r})$ where c is the speed of light, t is the time, and $\mathbf{r}$ is the three-vector position. A general four-vector is denoted (q^0, q^1, q^2, q^3) or q^μ, where $\mu = 0$, 1, 2, and 3; in particular, $(ct, \mathbf{r})$ is written as r^μ. The components q^1, q^2, and q^3, must be a three-vector $\mathbf{q}$ and transform appropriately under spatial rotations. The new feature is that q^0 and $\mathbf{q}$ must also obey the Lorentz transformation relating the components of a four-vector in one reference frame with those in another frame moving with constant velocity with respect to the first (inertial frames). Since the rotational property of $\mathbf{q}$ can be used to reorient the spatial axes, the relative velocity is taken to be v in the x direction. Then the Lorentz transformation of q^{μ} to q'^{μ} (primes indicate the new reference frame) is $q'^{\mu} = \Lambda^{\mu}_{\nu} q^{\nu}$ (summation for $\nu = 0, 1, 2$, and 3), where $\beta = v/c$, $\gamma = (1 - \beta^2)^{-1/2}$, $\Lambda^0_0 = \Lambda^1_1 = \gamma$, $\Lambda^0_1 = \Lambda^1_0 = -\gamma\beta$, $\Lambda^2_2 = \Lambda^3_3 = 1$, and the other ten components of Λ are zero. This transformation was proposed by Hendrick A. Lorentz, but the underlying physical concepts were developed by Albert Einstein. The Lorentz transformation ensures that the speed of light is the same in all reference frames. Note that the sums and differences of four-vectors are also four-vectors, and so are their differentials (limits of differences) with respect to four-scalar quantities.

The primitive four-scalar associated with a particle is the time τ registered on a clock that travels with the particle. In a reference frame where the particle has velocity $\mathbf{v}$, time increments are $\Delta t = \gamma \Delta \tau$ (time dilation). The power of tensor analysis now becomes apparent. Define $p^{\mu} = m dr^{\mu}/d\tau$, where m is the particle mass (sometimes referred to as the rest mass). Then p^{μ} must be a four-tensor. Its components are $(\gamma mc, \gamma m\mathbf{v})$. In the non-relativistic limit (v less than about 10^6 mph), γ is very close to 1 and p^{μ} becomes $[(K + mc^2)/c, m\mathbf{v}]$, where K is the particle's kinetic energy and $m\mathbf{v}$ is its momentum. It follows that p^{μ} must be the correct relativistic form of the energy and momentum with $p^0 = E/c$. Here E is the total energy and includes the rest energy, mc^2.

The scalar product in special relativity is more complicated than that in three-space since some minus signs are involved. These are usually handled by introducing the metric tensor $g_{\mu\nu}$, with $g_{00} = 1$, $g_{11} = g_{22} = g_{33} = -1$, and the other twelve components of g being zero (this simple form of the metric tensor is radically changed in general relativity). Then a covariant vector q_{μ}, companion to the contravariant vector q^{μ}, is defined as $q_{\mu} = g_{\mu\nu} q^{\nu}$ and the scalar product of q^{μ} and another vector s^{μ}, say, is $q_{\mu} s^{\mu}$, or equivalently, $g_{\mu\nu} q^{\mu} s^{\nu}$. In particular, $r_{\mu} r^{\mu} = (ct)^2 - \mathbf{r} \cdot \mathbf{r} = (c\tau)^2$, $p_{\mu} p^{\mu} = (E/c)^2 - \mathbf{p} \cdot \mathbf{p} = (mc)^2$, and $r_{\mu} p^{\mu} = Et - \mathbf{r} \cdot \mathbf{p}$.

By defining all new quantities in terms of four-tensors, a complete theory may be developed that is in full accord with the Lorentz transformation requirements.

See also: FRAME OF REFERENCE, INERTIAL; LORENTZ TRANSFORMATION; MOMENTUM; MOTION, ROTATIONAL; RELATIVITY, GENERAL THEORY OF; RELATIVITY, SPECIAL THEORY OF; RIGID BODY; SCALAR; TIME DILATION; VECTOR; VELOCITY, ANGULAR

Bibliography

GRIFFITHS, D. J. *Introduction to Electrodynamics*, 2nd ed. (Prentice Hall, Englewood Cliffs, NJ, 1981).

MARION, J. B. *Classical Dynamics* (Academic Press, San Diego, CA, 1970).

RINDLER, W. *Introduction to Special Relativity*, 2nd ed. (Clarendon Press, Oxford, Eng., 1991).

IAN R. GATLAND

TERMINAL VELOCITY

See VELOCITY, TERMINAL

THEORETICAL PHYSICS

The explosion of knowledge and activity in science and the length of training required to join the professional scientific community has made it almost impossible for most practicing scientists to participate fully in all fields and modes of the scientific investigation. The most notable feature of modern science is its rapid tendency toward specialization.

Specialization in Science

The study of science began when people started to observe, collect, and organize data about the natural world and to discover patterns in this data. In modern times the pursuit of scientific knowledge has tended to follow a cyclical procedure of hypothesis formulation and experimental verification known as the scientific method. The objective of the scientific method is to construct predictive and experimentally verifiable scientific theories. The scientific method is a powerful tool for making rapid scientific advances. As the body of scientific knowledge has grown, it has become subdivided into many branches including astronomy, biology, chemistry, geology, medical science, and physics.

Physics itself is such a large field that most professional physicists tend to specialize in one distinct area (e.g., atmospheric physics or molecular physics). Some physicists work at the boundary of physics and another branch of science (e.g., astrophysics, biophysics, chemical physics). This specialization is expressed clearly by the format of *Physical Review,* one of the world's foremost journals devoted to reporting new discoveries in physics. This journal, published by The American Physical Society, appears in five separate monthly issues: *Physical Review A* (atomic, molecular, and optical physics), *Physical Review B* (condensed matter physics), *Physical Review C* (nuclear physics), *Physical Review D* (particle physics, gravitation, and cosmology), and *Physical Review E* (statistical physics, plasma physics, and fluids).

Physicists specialize on yet another level. Experimental equipment has become extremely sophisticated and delicate, sometimes taking years to build and calibrate. Modern physical theories have become increasingly mathematical and abstract. Some physicists prefer to design experiments, assemble experimental apparatus, and write computer programs for processing vast collections of data; such physicists are called experimental physicists. Other physicists are more interested in formulation, verification, and examination of theories; such physicists are called theoretical physicists.

Experimental Versus Theoretical Physics

The current theory of gravitation, discovered by Albert Einstein, is known as general relativity. Since the 1960s physicists have been preparing an extremely difficult experiment to test the accuracy and validity of this theory by observing the precession of a spinning gyroscope in orbit around the earth.

Theorists contribute to this experiment by formulating and solving Einstein's equations of gravity to determine the curvature of space in the vicinity of the orbit. They use this result to predict the rate of precession of the gyroscope. Theorists also try to predict the signal-to-noise ratio for this experiment; that is, they try to determine how other physical phenomena might affect the magnitude of the precession. Experimentalists, on the other hand, design and build the experimental components. The gyro-scope itself is a rapidly rotating homogeneous ball of quartz about 4 cm in diameter. The ball must be perfectly spherical to a tolerance of 1 part in 10 million and must operate at liquid-helium temperature. The orbiting apparatus uses an extremely precise telescope as well as superconducting electronic circuitry to orient the gyroscope relative to the fixed stars. The experimental equipment must be extremely stable; it must withstand the stresses associated with a rocket launch and be able to give an uninterrupted stream of data for several years.

Classic Examples of Theoretical Physics

Although separated by more than a century, the spectacular discoveries of the planet Neptune in 1846 and an elementary particle called the neutrino in 1956 are remarkably similar. They were both predicted by theoretical physicists to account for anomalous experimental data.

The planet Uranus was discovered by William Herschel in 1781. Its orbit is complicated because it is perturbed by the large planets Jupiter and Saturn. However, in the early 1840s theoretical calculations by John Couch Adams in England and Urbain Le-Verrier in France showed that even taking these perturbations into account, the only way to explain the observed anomalous orbit of Uranus was to postulate the existence of an as yet unobserved planet beyond Uranus. Adams and LeVerrier were able to predict the orbit of Neptune using Isaac Newton's theory of gravitation. Neptune was first seen by Johann G. Galle in 1846; its position in the sky was almost exactly what Adams and LeVerrier had predicted.

In the early 1930s experimentalists making accurate measurements of the energy and momentum of particles produced in radioactive decay observed an anomaly: Electrically charged particles coming from beta decay seemed to violate a fundamental principle of physics: namely, the conservation of energy and momentum. Wolfgang Pauli, a theoretical physicist, then pointed out that this anomaly could be explained if, in addition to the charged particles, there were an as yet unobserved, electrically neutral particle. This particle, called the neutrino, was observed in 1956 by Frederick Reines and Clyde Cowan.

Three Different Approaches

Theoretical physicists contribute to scientific progress in three distinct ways. Some theoreticians study anomalous experimental data that seems to conflict with currently accepted scientific theories. By resolving the conflicts they advance science; often, the resolution involves the prediction of new and unexpected phenomena that are subsequently observed. This kind of theoretical physics led to the discovery of Neptune and the neutrino.

Other theoreticians prefer to test the validity of accepted theories of physics. They probe theories by using them to predict phenomena that have not yet been observed experimentally. They then propose experiments designed to observe such phenomena. Measuring the precession of a gyroscope due to general relativistic effects is one example of such an experiment. The outcome of this experiment will either strengthen the currently accepted theory of gravitation or else provide evidence that this theory is inadequate and requires revision. Another example of this kind of approach to theoretical physics is the laser. Developed in the early 1960s, the laser is a device that is predicted by the theory of quantum mechanics; it provides dramatic evidence for the existence of quantized energy levels.

The boldest theoreticians seek to unify the prevailing theories governing the natural world. For example, James Clerk Maxwell examined the experimental and theoretical situation in three apparently unrelated areas: electricity, magnetism, and light. Maxwell showed that electricity, magnetism, and light are manifestations of a single phenomenon called electromagnetism.

Modern Examples of Unification

The dream of Albert Einstein was to find a single theory that provides a unified description of all four fundamental forces: strong, weak, electromagnetic, and gravitational. Although this problem has not yet been solved, in the late twentieth century there has been much progress toward this goal.

In the 1960s and 1970s, Steven Weinberg and Abdus Salam proposed the electroweak theory, a unified theory of electromagnetism and weak interactions. (Weak interactions are the forces responsible for beta decay.) Electroweak theory predicted the existence of two particles, W and Z, which are nearly 100 times as massive as protons and neutrons. These particles were observed experimentally in the early 1980s.

A unified theory of strong forces, which hold the nuclei of atoms together, was developed by Mur-

ray Gell-Mann, Sheldon Glashow, and other distinguished theoretical physicists. In this theory, called quantum chromodynamics, the strong force is described in terms of quarks.

The standard model is a unified picture of electroweak and strong forces and the elementary particles associated with them. However, attempts to unify these two theories into a grand unified theory (GUT) have thus far been unsuccessful because GUTs predict two phenomena that have not yet been observed: proton decay and magnetic monopoles.

Phenomenological Versus Theoretical Theory

The past two decades have witnessed another level of specialization in theoretical physics. Many theoretical physicists continue to pursue the more traditional approach, looking for anomalies in experimental data, making predictions based on current theories, and suggesting experiments. Because these physicists closely follow the latest experiments, they are called phenomenological theorists or phenomenologists.

The increasing mathematical sophistication and abstraction in modern theories of physics have spawned a new class of theoretical physicists, who could be called theoretical theoreticians. These theorists are less interested in specific details of the latest data; they prefer to investigate the mathematical structure and internal consistency of physical theories. These physicists often formulate and study simplified theoretical models, which are sometimes even physically unrealistic, to obtain a deeper understanding of the fundamental laws and symmetries that govern the universe. Theoretical theoreticians have developed such beautiful mathematical models as superstring theory.

Computational Physics

With the development of fast computers, another specialization in theoretical physics has emerged: computational physics. Computers enable physicists to obtain approximate numerical solutions to highly complicated theories. Using computers to perform simulations, computational physicists study turbulence in fluids, collisions of black holes, masses and decay rates of elementary particles, nuclear energy levels, supernovae, the motion of an impurity in a crystal lattice, and chaos in dynamic systems.

Soliton scattering was first observed in a computer simulation.

See also: COMPUTATIONAL PHYSICS; EXPERIMENTAL PHYSICS; GRAND UNIFIED THEORY; MAXWELL'S EQUATIONS; NEUTRINO, HISTORY OF; PRECESSION; QUANTUM CHROMODYNAMICS; SCIENTIFIC METHOD; SCIENTIFIC REVOLUTION

Bibliography

FEYNMAN, R. P. *Surely You're Joking, Mr. Feynman: Adventures of a Curious Character* (W. W. Norton, New York, 1985).
GELL-MANN, M. *The Quark and the Jaguar: Adventures in the Simple and the Complex* (W. H. Freeman, New York, 1994).
GLASHOW, S. *From Alchemy to Quarks: The Study of Physics as a Liberal Art* (Brooks/Cole, Pacific Grove, CA, 1994).
HAWKING, S. W. *A Brief History of Time: From the Big Bang to Black Holes* (Bantam Books, Toronto, Can., 1988).
HEWITT, P. G. *Conceptual Physics* (HarperCollins, New York, 1993).
HOBSON, A. *Physics: Concepts and Connections* (Prentice Hall, Englewood Cliffs, NJ, 1995).
WILL, C. M. *Was Einstein Right?* (HarperCollins, New York, 1986).

CARL M. BENDER

THERMAL CONDUCTIVITY

When there is a temperature difference between two bodies in contact or a temperature gradient within a single body, heat is transferred by conduction through the body. Thermal conductivity is the measure of the ease with which heat is transferred.

Thermal conduction can be described quantitatively in the following way: A material to be measured is made into a slab of area A and thickness Δx. One face (of area A) is in contact with a heat reservoir at temperature T and the other face with another reservoir at $T + \Delta T$. In the presence of this temperature gradient $\Delta T/\Delta x$, a certain quantity of heat Q is transferred through the slab from the reservoir at higher temperature to the one held at lower temperature in time $\Delta \tau$. If the temperature gradient is not very large, an approximate relation

$$Q/\Delta\tau = KA(\Delta T/\Delta x)$$

holds with a constant factor K. This expression states that the heat conducted in unit time is proportional to the cross-sectional area and the temperature gradient. In the limit that the ratio $\Delta T/\Delta x$ becomes that of two infinitesimal quantities, the above relation is exact. So the limit-going process yields the relation

$$dQ/d\tau = -\kappa A dT/dx,$$

where the constant κ is called the thermal conductivity and has units $J \cdot s^{-1} \cdot m^{-1} \cdot K^{-1}$. This relation is called Fourier's law (1822). The negative sign in the above expression means that the heat flows in the downhill direction, that is, the direction of negative temperature gradient.

In insulators the lattice vibration (phonons) are primarily responsible for thermal conduction. In metals conduction electrons play the major role. These are the same electrons that contribute to electrical conduction. In fact, an empirical relation exists between electrical conductivity σ and thermal conductivity κ. The ratio $\kappa/\sigma T$ is approximately constant independent of the metal. This relation can also be theoretically derived by the free electron model of metals as

$$\kappa/\sigma T = \pi^2 k_B^2/3e^2,$$

where e is the electron charge. This is known as the Wiedemann–Franz law, and it is fairly well obeyed except at low temperatures.

There are some notable exceptions to the conventional behavior of thermal conduction and the most remarkable example can be see in liquid helium.

See also: CONDUCTION; CONDUCTOR; HEAT TRANSFER; INSULATOR; LIQUID HELIUM

Bibliography

RESNICK, R.; HALLIDAY, D.; and KRANE, K. S. *Physics,* 4th ed. (Wiley, New York, 1992).

CARL T. TOMIZUKA

THERMAL EXPANSION

A change in the volume of a material due to a change in temperature is known as thermal expansion. For an infinitesimally small change in temperature of a substance, the ratio of the corresponding change in the volume ΔV to the change in temperature ΔT divided by the substance volume V is the coefficient of thermal expansion β:

$$\beta = \frac{1}{V}\left(\frac{\Delta V}{\Delta T}\right)_p .$$

The subscript p indicates that the pressure is held constant. Most substances expand with increasing temperature. A negative coefficient of thermal expansion is anomalous, but has been observed, for instance, in the common substance water at temperatures near freezing (0 to 4°C).

The ideal gas law indicates that the value of β for an ideal gas at constant pressure is the inverse of its absolute temperature (i.e., $\beta = T^{-1}$). The thermal expansion coefficient of an ideal gas at a temperature of 0°C has a value of 3,661 × 10^{-6} (°C)$^{-1}$. A thermometer based on the thermal expansion of a real gas at low pressure could be constructed, as the temperature dependence of β is very close to that of an ideal gas. In practice, gas thermometers are more likely to be held at constant volume rather than at constant pressure. Liquids are more commonly used in thermometers based upon thermal expansion. This is true despite the fact that the physical behavior of liquids is more complex than that of gases, and generally only an empirical characterization of the temperature dependence of the thermal expansion of liquids is available.

To construct a thermometer based upon the phenomenon of thermal expansion, a glass bulb may be filled with a liquid such as mercury and connected to a capillary tube. As the temperature increases, the mercury expands into the tube. Because the thermal expansion coefficient of mercury is nearly constant over a wide temperature range near room temperature, a linear scale can be used to measure the extent of the expansion and thus the temperature of the mercury. The extent of thermal expansion of this liquid provides a measure of the temperature of anything that is in thermal equilibrium with the mercury, for instance, a person's mouth holding a mercury thermometer.

The thermal expansion of solids reflects changes in the configuration of the atoms in the material. Atoms in crystalline solids arrange themselves in periodic structures, with regular spacings between atoms. Atoms in solids oscillate about their equilibrium positions. Harmonic oscillators such as a pendulum or a mass on a spring are macroscopic analogs of this situation. A mass in a harmonic oscillator vibrates about an equilibrium position with an amplitude that depends upon the energy of the system. The motion of an atom in a solid is in many ways similar to that of a harmonic oscillator (some of the deviations from this approximation offer an exciting view of quantum mechanics). However, in contrast to the vibrations of an atom, the time-averaged position of a mass in a harmonic oscillator is a constant, independent of oscillation amplitude. Thermal expansion of solids results because the forces pushing the atoms back toward their equilibrium positions are slightly different than those of a

Table 1 Values of β or α for a Variety of Substances

Material	phase	$\beta\ 10^{-6}(°C)^{-1}$	$\alpha\ 10^{-6}(°C)^{-1}$
Polystyrene	solid	–	60–80
NaCl (table salt)	solid	–	40
Al, Aluminum	solid	–	24
Steel	solid	–	11
Concrete	solid	–	12
SiO$_2$	glass	–	4
Hg, Mercury	liquid	182	–
Gasoline	liquid	96	–
Water	liquid	194	–

harmonic oscillator. The forces that pull atoms back together as they move apart generally are slightly less than those that push the atoms apart as they move toward each other from their equilibrium positions. In this case, as the temperature of a solid increases and the atoms in the solid vibrate with larger amplitudes, the average separation of the atoms increases. The thermal expansion of a solid reflects that these atomic spacings have changed.

Engineers often consider the linear coefficient, α, of the thermal expansion of solids, where

$$\alpha = \frac{1}{l}\left(\frac{\Delta l}{\Delta T}\right)_p.$$

Here l is the length of a sample, and Δl is the change in its length corresponding to an infinitesimally small change in temperature ΔT. For isotropic solids, that is, those that behave the same way in all directions, $\beta = 3\alpha$. One of the reasons for the simplicity of this relationship is that the values of α and β for solids are much less than one. For example, common steel has a value of $\alpha = 11 \times 10^{-6}$ $(°C)^{-1}$. A change in volume ΔV for an isotropic solid cube can be related to a change in length Δl with $\Delta V = (l + \Delta l)^3 - V$. Since α, and thus Δl, is small, ΔV is very close to $3\Delta l$, and $\beta = 3\alpha$ is an excellent approximation.

Despite the small values of α, the thermal expansion of solids influences many engineering designs. It is true that steel alloys commonly used in building construction increase their length by only about 0.05 percent when the temperature increases from $-20°C$ to $30°C$. But for a steel member 10 m in length, this means a length increase of about 6 mm. Structural designers generally must allow for these changes in length because they result in very large stresses in a beam that is clamped at both ends. In some buildings designers include connections that are not fixed, but consist of a roller configuration that allows a beam to move upon thermal expansion. Allowances for thermal expansion can be observed in the configuration of railways. Generally a gap is left between rails to allow for the change in length of the rails upon temperature swings. Such expansion joints are also found between slabs of concrete in highways. Any mismatch in the thermal expansion coefficients of materials joined together is generally of concern to the designer. This is particularly true for cryogenic engineers, who must design for temperature changes of up to 300°C, from

room temperature down to the temperature of liquid nitrogen or liquid helium. One solution is to configure joints so that they tighten rather than loosen upon cooling, for instance, cylindrical joints with a tube with a relatively large value of β surrounding another tube with a smaller value of β.

For solids near room temperature the coefficient of thermal expansion exhibits a small temperature variation. For most considerations this variation is negligible. Values of thermal expansion coefficients are provided in Table 1 for a variety of substances near room temperature.

See also: CRYOGENICS; IDEAL GAS LAW; OSCILLATOR, HARMONIC; THERMAL CONDUCTIVITY; THERMOMETER; THERMOMETRY

Bibliography

CLARK, A. F. "Thermal Expansion" in *Materials at Low Temperature*, edited by R. P. Reed and A. F. Clark (American Society for Metals, Metals Park, OH, 1983).

KITTEL, C. *Introduction to Solid-State Physics* (Wiley, New York, 1986).

ERIC J. COTTS

THERMAL RADIATION

See RADIATION, THERMAL

THERMIONIC EMISSION

See EMISSION, THERMIONIC

THERMOCOUPLE

A thermocouple is a differential thermometer whose output is voltage. Stated in more physical terms, a thermocouple is a sensor that uses two materials with different Seebeck effects to convert a temperature difference into a voltage difference. Figure 1a is an ideal thermocouple arrangement with isothermal regions while Fig. 1b is the practical arrangement frequently used. The open-circuit voltage V_{12} of Fig. 1a is

$$V_{12} = \int_{T_1}^{T_2} [S_A(T) - S_B(T)]\, dT,$$

where $S_m(T)$ is the Seebeck effect, or thermopower, of material m at temperature T, and t_i denotes the temperature of an isothermal region. For homogeneous materials and good isothermal regions the voltage V_{12} is independent of how the temperature

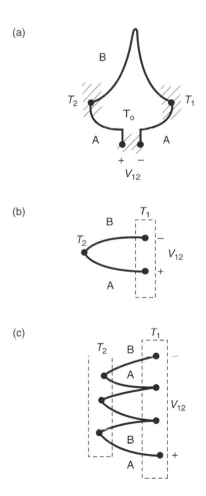

Figure 1 Three thermocouple arrangements using materials A and B: (a) an ideal thermocouple, (b) the practical arrangement commonly used, and (c) a thermopile. The shaded areas denote isothermal regions of temperature T_i, and the dashed lines identify temperature regions of interest.

varies between T_2 and T_1; only the temperature difference is important. Specifically, if two identical thermocouples of Fig. 1a were used but the middle of material B for one thermocouple was in a high temperature oven while the middle of material B for the second thermocouple was in a cryogenic liquid, the two thermocouple voltages would be identical.

The practical thermocouple arrangement of Fig. 1b will give the same results as the ideal arrangement if several precautions are taken. First, there must be no temperature gradient in the A-B junction located at T_2. This condition can be achieved by forming the materials into wires and making good thermal contact of the junction and a portion of each wire to the object being measured. Second, having different wires at T_1 where the voltage is measured makes it essential that T_1 is a known, isothermal region. In earlier times this condition was met by connecting the thermocouple and voltmeter in reference baths such as a stirred mixture of ice and water or a boiling cryogenic liquid. Modern instruments often make the connection in regions whose temperature is electronically controlled. Third, it is essential that the thermopower of each material forming the thermocouple not be altered by the range of temperatures being measured or by impurities that might be present in the measuring environment. A possible violation of this condition is oxidation of one or both materials. The use of transition metal alloys for thermocouple materials provides a good match to all these conditions. Assembling a thermocouple by using one alloy with a positive thermopower and one with a negative thermopower gives a larger voltage output, or sensitivity, for a given temperature difference.

A thermopile is a collection of thermocouples that are connected in parallel thermally and in series electrically (see Fig. 1c). Thermopiles are used when larger voltages are needed. The detection of temperature differences caused by the absorption of optical power and the design of voltage sources are two examples of such a need.

See also: ELECTROMOTIVE FORCE; TEMPERATURE; THERMOELECTRIC EFFECT

Bibliography

ASTM COMMITTEE E-20. *Manual on the Use of Thermocouples in Temperature Measurements* (ASTM, Philadelphia, 1974).

OMEGA TECHNOLOGIES. *The Temperature Handbook* (OMEGA Technologies, Stamford, CT, 1990).

POLLOCK, D. D. *The Theory and Properties of Thermocouple Elements* (ASTM, Philadelphia, 1971).

C. L. FOILES

THERMODYNAMICS

Heat is an everyday phenomenon. Temperature is a measure of the hotness of a body. The body becomes hotter when heat produced from fuel is added to it. But what is heat and what is temperature?

In the late eighteenth century there were two theories of heat: the caloric (a substance) theory and the mechanical theory. The former was discredited by the experiments of Benjamin Rumford and Humphry Davy, which supported the latter. But the caloric theory was supported by Nicolas Carnot's work on the efficiency of heat engines in 1824. At that time the steam engine had been in use for half a century. Its efficiency was an important concern. Carnot derived a theorem bearing his name based on the caloric theory. The theorem was very useful for the then budding energy industry.

Thus the two theories stood side by side and scientists used one or the other as they saw fit until 1850. In the 1840s James Prescott Joule did a series of experiments determining a precise mechanical equivalent of heat: 4.2 J for 1 cal of heat. Hence we have a general theorem of conservation of energy with heat as one form of energy, confirming the mechanical theory of heat. But, unlike other energies in the conservation equation, heat cannot be fully converted back to mechanical energy. There can be some conversion, but there is a limit, as specified by the Carnot theorem. Obviously something important was missing in the mechanical theory.

It was Rudolf Clausius and Lord Kelvin who realized that there must be two fundamental laws controlling the behavior of heat. One is the conservation of energy with heat as a form of energy. The other deals with the conversion of heat to mechanical energy, with which the Carnot theorem can be derived on the basis of the mechanical theory instead of the caloric theory. They succeeded in finding such a law. These two fundamental laws are called the first and second laws of thermodynamics. Thus began a new branch of science, thermodynamics, dealing with the interaction of heat and mechanics.

The easiest way to introduce the two laws is through the notion of a perpetual motion machine. Since time immemorial, and particularly since the steam engine, society's thirst for energy has been obvious. Any invention that could produce energy (through motion) without cost would be welcome. The perpetual motion machine was pursued with a zeal comparable to alchemy, which tried to make gold out of base metals, and with a fate just the same.

The perpetual motion machine of the first kind was to generate energy out of nothing, which was ruled out by the energy conservation principle. More subtle was the machine of the second kind. There is plenty of heat energy in ocean water. If by any means this heat could be transported from the cold spot (ocean) to the hot spot (boiler of a steam engine), then it could generate energy (such as electricity) without one having to pay for the cost of coal consumed in the boiler. Indeed, there is a machine, the refrigerator, which does just that, but it consumes energy (electricity) to operate, which must be paid for. Now consider combining a refrigerator and a heat engine, the latter generating electrical energy to run the refrigerator. *If* it should have a little electric energy left over after running the refrigerator, then we would have a perpetual motion machine of the second kind by repeating the process endlessly.

It would be an energy bonanza. In addition we would have a means to make a hot spot hotter by collecting all heat and adding to it without any cost. Only by using a few pieces of dead hardware could we collect all heat in the universe together in one spot, create the big bang, and start the history of the universe all over again without any cost. This would be preposterous.

Thus it would be reasonable to assert that the perpetual motion machine of the second kind is never possible. Indeed, the two laws of thermodynamics may be established, respectively, by stating that the perpetual motion machines of the first and the second kinds are impossible.

It is important to notice that such an assumption does lead us to a derivation of the Carnot theorem, this time based on the mechanical theory of heat instead of the caloric theory. Thus the last missing link of our study of the nature of heat is closed. With the two laws we have a complete theory of heat that can be applied directly to the engineering problem of the efficiency of heat engines. More important to pure science is that we have a complete theory to study the properties of matter—thermodynamics is a basic part of physics and chemistry. Moreover, together with the law of conservation of mass, we have a complete set of laws to establish the new environmental science and energy science, a sideline not elaborated here.

The behavior of nature dictated by the second law is obviously related to the fact that heat naturally flows from the hot to the cold. This has been the main drama of our universe since the big bang. Clearly, the transport of heat is an important concern. Clausius, after establishing the second law, introduced the concept of entropy (Greek for transport) years later and formulated a principle of increase of entropy as another statement of the second law.

Clausius's entropy turns out to be a property of materials systems and is related to many thermal properties of matter. As a result, thermodynamics goes beyond engineering and provides an avenue to study the properties of matter and thus is important to physics and chemistry. Yet it remains a macroscopic theory of matter that does not refer to atomic structure.

After Clausius, the next question was, What is entropy and the nature of the entropy principle? For many years scientists unsuccessfully attempted to derive the entropy principle from Newtonian mechanics—the fountainhead of all sciences. Finally, Ludwig Boltzmann interpreted entropy in terms of probability in the microscopic (atomic) theory of matter, thus going beyond Newtonianism. He introduced the famous equation that became his epitaph: $S = k \log W$, where S is entropy, W is probability, and k is the Boltzmann constant (i.e., the universal gas constant per molecule, R/N_0). The entropy principle then turns out to be just the probability principle that systems evolve to reach states of maximum probability. Thus the originally macroscopic thermodynamics now has a microscopic interpretation and can be combined with statistical mechanics in a statistical thermodynamics that has wider applications, in particular, to calculate the macroscopic properties of matter from the microscopic atomic theory based only on molecular properties.

In this view the macroscopic phenomenon that underlies the second law that heat flows from hot to cold is the property that interacting systems tend toward states that maximize the total probability. The final state of equal temperatures represents the state of thermal equilibrium in which energy is equally distributed to all degrees of freedom with $(1/2)kT$ to each, where T is the absolute temperature (the principle of equipartition of energy). This also gives us the ultimate meaning of temperature.

Thus the outline of the theoretical structure of thermodynamics is completed and it seems that only applications remain. However, significant mopping actions remain. They concern the impossibility of perpetual motion machines and the classical formulation of the theory.

The statement that perpetual motion machines are impossible is a sweeping one, covering all kinds of natural phenomena issuing from different fundamental laws of nature. Is the second law a super law that supersedes all other natural laws, as Albert Einstein contended, or is it, like other laws, determined by the physics of the system and thus might be occasionally excepted, as Ilya Prigogine maintained? This is one of the most fundamental problems in physics. A modest approach is to consider special examples.

The first and foremost example to challenge the second law is Maxwell's demon. An intelligent demon, by opening and closing a trap door separating two chambers, can recognize and separate high energy molecules from those with low energy and thus create a temperature difference between the two chambers, thereby running a heat engine as a perpetual motion machine to violate the second law. From that we are endowed with the phrase "inanimate material agency" in the parlance of thermodynamics to exorcise demons. Intelligence is excluded in the second law.

However, it is possible to sort out energies of molecules by inanimate material agency, for example, by a porous membrane of specific pore size. The size will let diatomic molecules of low vibration energy pass but stop molecules of high vibration energy that are associated with larger molecular sizes. However, the membrane will not violate the second law. The low energy molecules will pass through the pores of the membrane back to the hotter side and cool it down. Eventually, the Maxwell–Boltzmann distribution will guarantee equal temperatures on both sides.

Thus, what makes the demon work is the one-way action, not the intelligence for energy selection. Any one-way action for molecular movement would violate the second law by creating a density difference.

The most obvious one-way mechanism is the spring-lock. You can close the room door by pushing it, but once the door is closed, you cannot open it by pulling. It works so because of the friction dissipation of kinetic energy of the spring lock. Without energy dissipation it will not lock. On the microscopic level there is no friction and laws of mechanics are time reversible. Thus there can be no one-way mechanism to violate the second law.

Consider the pressure valve. Molecules coming from one side slam the valve shut, which stops them from passing. From the other side molecules slam the valve open and pass through. Thus it seems that the pressure on one side can be pumped up by this one-way mechanism. It works because of the energy dissipation in the collisions. With elastic collisions the kinetic energy will make the valve flip up and down repeatedly without stopping, and the valve is effectively open both ways. It cannot do the demon's job.

Another example more commonly discussed is the ratchet mechanism that generates a one-way motion, such as in jacking up an automobile for changing a tire. Richard Feynman spent one chapter in his *Lectures on Physics* to prove that the ratchet will not work to rectify the random motions of molecules to make a perpetual motion machine. Actually, it can be explained simply by recognizing that the ratchet works because of the dissipation of kinetic energy generated from the dropping of the pawl. In order to advance the ratchet wheel, the energy from the slamming of one molecule, $(3/2)kT$, must be greater than the gravity energy to lift the pawl over one tooth of the wheel. But the pawl, considered as a giant molecule, has an average energy of $(3/2)kT$, sufficient to overcome the gravity energy difference of one tooth and to jump out of the tooth in a frictionless setting. Thus the ratchet will not lock and will not produce directional motion.

The second law works so far because molecules can move both ways with equal ease due to the time reversibility of the laws of Newtonian mechanics. However, the force of a magnetic field on a charge, known as the Lorentz force, is not time reversible—its velocity-dependent part changes direction when velocity is reversed. There might be a possibility of generating one-way motion. Indeed there is one.

In the 1950s, in the heyday of nuclear tests, an experiment code named Argus was carried out with a nuclear explosion set off at a northern latitude. The electrons generated were traced to move in spirals along Earth's magnetic lines of force, converging on the image point on the Southern Hemisphere. Of interest to us is that in addition to the north-south movement there is also a net eastward movement of the electrons due to the nonuniformity of Earth's magnetic field. Can one use this one-way motion to drive a machine?

To do so, the electrons must be confined in a giant donut-shaped container with a piston set up to receive the impact of the eastward motion of the electrons. The surprise result is that once an impact is made the electrons will never be free again. They will keep on colliding on the piston and on the container wall in a backward (westward) movement all the way, circling the donut to the other side of the piston with an impact cancelling out the original one. No directional motion *of the piston* can be generated.

More intriguing is the magnetic plasma machine shown in Fig. 1. Two chambers containing ionized gases are connected by a curved tube. A magnetic field is applied to select a group of high energy particles to move from one chamber to the other, thus increasing the energy and density of the latter, violating the second law. These particles cannot move backward because when the velocity is reversed, the Lorentz force changes sign and so does the curvature of the trajectory. The particles will be stopped by the tube.

F. J. Belinfante undertook a detailed kinetic theory calculation to find out the quantitative change of the temperature and density. At first, approximations were used and finite differences were obtained, suggesting violation of the second law. Finally he developed the exact theory to calculate without any approximation, and to his surprise the differences turned out to be exactly zero. The second law triumphed again. In spite of the apparent difference the particles can move back through the curved tube through multiple collisions on the tube walls *with equal ease* as the direct motion without collisions.

This unbelievable result may be traced back to the cyclotron principle, which makes the Boltzmann distribution invariant under a magnetic field. But the cyclotron principle breaks down at relativistic velocities, and there seems to be a last hope to topple

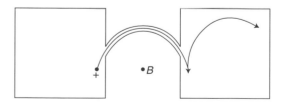

Figure 1   Magnetic plasma machine.

the second law at high energies. However, at that energy the ionized gas will be in equilibrium with its own radiation field, which can move back and forth through the tube with equal ease, and equilibrium will be restored. Again there is no violation.

Eugene Wigner was not the least surprised by the results of Belinfante's calculation and commented that "I learned statistical mechanics from Einstein and Einstein said only a time dependent Hamiltonian can destroy the Boltzmann distribution." Any inanimate material agency cannot destroy the second law regardless of whatever apparent asymmetry that Hamiltonian may possess that might suggest an exception.

After the discovery of the violation of time reversal invariance in elementary particles physics, the possibility of violation of the second law surfaced again. The point was raised by Edward Teller and was investigated by high energy physicists. Nothing new was found.

It is now apparent that the impossibility of the perpetual motion machine is not a simple, self-evident axiom that may be used as the basic principle to begin a new branch of science, as Clausius did in his formulation. It is rather a complicated principle that involves all branches of science. We cannot wait to study thermodynamics until we finish the study of all other sciences.

The traditional formulation of thermodynamics based on the heat engine has been criticized by many, since the engine is a human contrivance created for profit, not the basis of a natural law. With these criticisms in mind, many reformulations have been and continue to be proposed to bypass the heat engine.

However, the original Clausius formulation of the second law, and its derivation of the Carnot theorem, are unimpeachable; his profound insight, often misunderstood, should not be under-rated. He recognized that heat always flows from the hot to the cold and there seems to be a fundamental law behind the fact. This fact would not change if we threw in a bunch of nuts and bolts, pistons and cylinders, and would remain so if the latter organized themselves into heat engines and refrigerators. Thus his second law that heat cannot move from the cold to the hot by inanimate material agency is a self-evident axiom stating a common-sense criterion suitable for use as the foundation of a new science, even though the thermodynamics so established may not be the most general. The emphasis is on a fundamental law of heat transport rather than on making money from a machine. Also, Clausius did not consider *all* perpetual motion machines under the sun, thus avoiding the bottomless pit we encountered earlier; the impossibility refers to a special type of machine concerning the heat transport, which is perfectly under control. He then pursued his point through the concept of entropy and the principle of increase of entropy.

The general principle of increase of entropy does include elements beyond the originally conceived fundamental law on heat transport (e.g., the inclusion of the diffusion process), which is completely unrelated to heat transport. Thus the general entropy principle does not follow logically from the Clausius formulation. It has left the secure confines of Clausius and ventured into uncharted waters. It is a brand new animal; to identify it with the old animal is logically impermissible. It is much more general; it covers new grounds in physics and chemistry beyond engineering (i.e., the spontaneous processes such as chemical equilibria). It is essentially a new law sneaked in through the back door, which does not do justice to the new law. Any reformulation without addressing this point is futile.

The Leiden School of physicists contended that there are three separate parts of the second law (i.e., there should be three laws): (1) Entropy does not increase in reversible processes. (2) Entropy does increase in irreversible processes. (3) Separate from the above contrived processes, there are in nature spontaneous processes in which entropy always increases. The third part obviously does not follow from the first two parts.

Just to say the third part is a new assumption or a generalization is not enough, because it contains brand new material and there is no logical ground upon which to generalize. A better formulation must take up the spontaneous processes as a rightful subject of study and formulate a fundamental law. It would be a macroscopic theory of spontaneous processes to distinguish from the microscopic statistical mechanics. The reformulation is not merely an intellectual exercise to re-prove what is already known. Macroscopic theory, besides its logical necessity, eliminates all the detailed complexities of a microscopic theory and can neatly and simply lead to an exact solution. In reality, microscopic theories always involve approximations, and we already know approximations almost make perpetual motion machines possible.

With the benefit of hindsight, the macroscopic fundamental law of spontaneous processes must be the general principle of the increase of a certain quantity called entropy. The substantial mathematical task is then to identify the entropy change to dQ/T. At first the problem appears to be an attempt to derive something out of nothing, but the solution is possible by making use of the macroscopic conditions of equilibrium just as statistical mechanics makes use of the microscopic conditions of equilibrium. For example, the entropy change in a diffusion process can be established, by studying a reversible diffusion process, which is a process of macroscopic equilibrium. Likewise, by studying reversible themal and mechanical processes in macroscopic equilibrium, entropy changes in these processes can be established, eventually leading to the conclusion $dS = dQ/T$. Thus a macroscopic theory of equilibrium can be established, which is what thermodynamics is supposed to be. In such a formulation of thermodynamics, the application to the heat engine comes as a bonus, not as the starting point of a fundamental principle. Therefore, the difficult absolute proof for the impossibility of *all* perpetual motion machines is not necessary for the establishment of thermodynamics.

See also: BOLTZMANN DISTRIBUTION; CARNOT CYCLE; CLAUSIUS, RUDOLF JULIUS EMMANUEL; ENERGY; ENGINE, EFFICIENCY OF; ENTROPY; HEAT, CALORIC THEORY OF; HEAT ENGINE; KELVIN, LORD; LORENTZ FORCE; MAXWELL–BOLTZMANN STATISTICS; MAXWELL'S DEMON; NEWTONIAN MECHANICS; THERMODYNAMICS, HISTORY OF

Bibliography

FONG, P. *Foundations of Thermodynamics* (Oxford University Press, Oxford, Eng., 1963).

FONG, P. "Second Thoughts on the Second Law of Thermodynamics" in *A Critical Review of Thermodynamics* edited by E. B. Stuart, B. Gal-Or, and A. J. Brainerd (Mono Book, Baltimore, MD, 1970).

PETER FONG

THERMODYNAMICS, HISTORY OF

The scientific study of heat began in the eighteenth century when it was accepted that the unit of heat should be the amount that would raise the temperature of a unit weight of water by one degree. The discoveries of specific heat capacity and of latent heat followed from this. Consistent with these simple concepts, was the idea that heat was a kind of fluid, a tenuous gas that was strongly attracted to matter but, oddly, self-repellent. This was consistent with the fact that most substances expand when heated. The name given to this (material) cause of heat was "caloric." A rival theory was that heat is due to the rapid motion of the atomic particles thought to constitute all material bodies. At the end of the eighteenth century, Benjamin Thompson (Count Rumford) and, later, Humphry Davy published experiments on friction that, they claimed, showed that heat could not be material: The only thing associated with it was motion. But the theory was not accepted. Their experiments were not conclusive; the caloric theory was held to be more plausible. In any case, everyone agreed that heat is always conserved. It can be neither created nor destroyed. If it goes hidden or latent, as in the generation of steam or any other vapor, it can always be recovered in full. Indeed, the science of heat was thought to rest on the axiom of the conservation of heat.

The establishment of thermodynamics was the result of a union or cross-fertilization between two power technologies and the science of heat. Water power engineers had, by 1800, laid down the conditions under which the maximum possible power could be obtained from a given fall of water. The water wheel, or hydraulic engine, should harness the entire available fall, and the water should enter the machine without shock, or turbulence, and leave without appreciable velocity. A machine that met these practically impossible requirements would be perfect, for if reversed to act as a perfect pump, it could restore all the water to its source. Anything better than that would make a perpetual motion machine possible.

The steam engine, as improved by James Watt, worked by allowing steam under pressure to expand in a cylinder to drive a piston down. When the piston reached the end of the cylinder, the steam had expanded so much that its pressure had fallen substantially. Care was taken to prevent any waste of heat by unnecessary warming of the cylinder walls and so on. In this way the maximum amount of work (energy) was derived from the steam.

Paradoxically, thermodynamics was to be established on the basis of the caloric theory of heat. Sadi Carnot published his short book *Réflexions sur la*

Puissance Motrice du Feu in 1824; it marked the beginning of thermodynamics. Carnot wished to establish a general theory of *heat* power comparable to that for water power. To this end he postulated a basic heat engine (working on a closed cycle) with two distinctive features. First, the vapor, or working substance, in its passage from high to low temperature (and back) is never in contact with anything at a different temperature. And second, the engine is reversible; it can be driven backwards to pump heat up to the higher temperature.

The only results of this process, or cycle, are that net work has been done and heat has flowed—or fallen—from a hot body to a cold body. Since the working substance has never been in contact with a body at a different temperature, there has been no useless (turbulent) flow of heat. If that had happened, the cycle would not have been reversible. By accepting the caloric theory of heat, Carnot was able to postulate a perfect reversible engine on the exact analogy of a hydraulic engine. No engine can be more efficient than one working on a Carnot cycle. For if one could be made, then a Carnot engine driven in reverse could pump a net amount of heat, or caloric, up to the hot body, and this would make perpetual motion possible. From this Carnot concluded that no one working substance can be more economical than any other.

In 1847 William Thomson (Lord Kelvin) saw that a temperature scale that would be independent of the properties of any substance could be based on Carnot's theory. For whatever the working substance, the efficiency of a Carnot engine depends only on the temperature fall over which it works and not on the working substance. It could therefore be the basis for an absolute scale of temperature. It could therefore be the basis for an absolute scale of temperature. Thomson coined the word "thermodynamics" in 1849.

James Prescott Joule, studying of the heating effect of an electric current, could find no material source for the heat if the current was generated by a magneto (a primitive dynamo). With great experimental skill, Joule showed that the only possible source was the work, or mechanical energy, used to drive the magneto. He realized that heat and mechanical energy are interchangeable. Over four years (1843–1847), Joule showed that, no matter how much mechanical energy (work) was converted into heat, the exchange rate between them was always the same. Finally, he measured the rate as accurately as possible. In this way Joule established the true nature

of heat: It is more than motion; it is energy. This destroyed the axiom of the conservation of heat. Others, notably Julius Robert Mayer and Ludwig Colding, had independently reached the same conclusion, and in 1847 Hermann von Helmholtz published his influential paper, "On the Conservation of Force." But it was Joule who established the identity of heat and energy, the first law of thermodynamics, on a precise experimental foundation.

Rudolf Clausius reconciled Carnot and Joule (1851). He saw that in every cycle two processes take place: the flow of heat from hot to cold (Carnot) and the conversion of heat into mechanical energy (Joule). Clausius therefore retained the Carnot cycle. But he could not accept Carnot's argument about perpetual motion, for a heat engine was *not* strictly analogous to a hydraulic engine. Conceivably, an engine might be made that could use heat energy from a cold body, and this engine could be more efficient than a Carnot engine. A Carnot engine, driven in reverse by a more efficient engine, could make (net) heat flow from the cold body to a hot body. Clausius therefore proposed a second law of thermodynamics: Heat cannot flow from a cold body to a hot body without compensation. This may seem obvious in the everyday world, but it is by no means obvious in the varied and complex worlds of physical and chemical changes.

Thomson had shown that, where quantities of heat are absorbed or given out at different temperatures in a reversible cycle of change more complex (more general) than that of a simple heat engine, the sum total of each of the quantities of heat Q divided by the absolute temperatures T at which they are absorbed (positive) or given out (negative) is zero. If the sum is less than zero, then the second law is violated, for it would indicate a net flow of heat from cold to hot; if it is greater than zero, reversing the cycle would make it negative and so, again, contradict the law.

Realizing that heat engines merely transform one form of energy into another, Clausius introduced the idea of equivalent transformations. He showed, using Thomson's fraction, Q/T, that in a reversible cycle, the equivalent transformations—flow of heat and conversion of heat—exactly compensate each other, and their sum is zero. In irreversible cycles, the sum of the equivalent transformations always indicates a flow of heat from hot to cold, in accordance with the second law.

Clausius extended the notion of equivalent transformations to the energy changes in individual bodies. When a body gains heat it (usually) also expands, and internal work is done as its molecules are rearranged. Clausius argued that the sum of the equivalence values of these two transformations should be expressed by the same fraction, Q/T. It gives the energy state of the body. This, he says, deserves a distinctive name: the entropy. Taken around a closed reversible cycle, the entropy change of a vapor, liquid, or solid is zero.

A consequence of this is that entropy replaces heat as a defining factor of the state of a body, whether liquid, solid, or gaseous. Assuming the axiom of the conservation of heat, if a body changes from one state (of pressure, volume, and temperature) to another, it follows that a fixed amount of heat has entered or left the body. Under the new theory, this is no longer true as some heat will have been converted into (or from) work; how much will depend on the way the change took place, and there is an infinite number of ways in which this could have occurred. What, then, can take the place of heat content under the the new theory? The answer is the entropy, for if the change is made by a reversible path (part of a reversible cycle), then the entropy difference *is* fixed and independent of the path.

Although the entropy of a body can be reduced, this can only happen if the entropy of some other body (or bodies) is increased by a greater amount. The entropy of an isolated group of bodies can never decrease; it can only remain unchanged or increase. This led Clausius to lay down in 1865 his well-known principles: The energy of the universe is constant; the entropy tends always to a maximum. Entropy, then, is the measure of the unavailability of energy.

Joule (1851) and, independently, Clausius (1857) accepted that heat is the *vis viva,* or kinetic energy, of moving molecules and that the pressure of a gas depends on the mass of the atoms and their velocity squared. If we assume that all atoms have the same velocity and we know the weight and pressure of (say) hydrogen in a cubical vessel, we can calculate, by simple mechanics, that the velocity of hydrogen atoms at 15°C is about one mile a second. Clausius recognized that molecules probably travel with different velocities and that they spin as well as move like projectiles, so that the *vis viva* that causes heat will be greater than that causing pressure.

Among objections to this theory was that, if true, cigar smoke should not hang about in still air, as it does. Clausius answered such objections by an ex-

tension to the theory. This was the concept of the short mean free path that a molecule could travel before colliding with another one. To demonstrate this, he had to use statistics because he could only deal with the probability of a molecule traveling a certain distance before hitting another one. Lacking experimental data, he could only show that, among the host of molecules, the mean free path must be extremely short, which meant much longer journey times; this answered the objections.

Clausius's two papers were developed by James Clerk Maxwell. He could not, of course, specify the velocities of individual molecules and he realized that, at any given time, the velocities of the molecules ranged from (a few) very slow to (a few) very fast while the greater number were grouped around a most probable velocity. Maxwell found a mathematical formula that showed how the numbers of molecules varied with their velocities. He argued that the molecules would, undisturbed, settle down to the steady state indicated by the distribution. And he hoped that experimental evidence of the viscosity, diffusion, and thermal conductivity of gases would confirm his deductions. But, at the end of the first paper, Maxwell confessed that the one piece of experimental evidence seemed to refute his (surprising) conclusion that the viscosity of gases is independent of the pressure. Subsequent research has, however, confirmed his predictions. Statistics were used in physical and in social science, but in a subordinate, auxiliary capacity. What Maxwell, following Clausius, did was to frame a fundamental law as statistical; there was no getting beyond it to a more fundamental law, for no such law existed. Maxwell's fictional demon illustrates this point clearly.

The entropy of an isolated system cannot decrease, but Maxwell's demon suggests that, according to classical mechanics, the entropy of an isolated system *could* decrease *without compensation.* This led Josiah Willard Gibbs to suggest there was a relationship between entropy and probability. It was Ludwig Boltzmann who developed the ideas of Maxwell and Clausius along these lines. The conclusion Boltzmann presented in 1877 was

$$S \propto \log W,$$

where S is the entropy and W is the probability of the state.

While Maxwell and Boltzmann were establishing statistical mechanics, the principles of thermodynamics were being applied by François Massieu, Gibbs, Pierre Duhem, Helmholtz, and others to problems in other realms of physical science, particularly problems of equilibrium and chemical change. Carnot's original insights had proved fruitful in quite unexpected ways.

See also: CARNOT, NICOLAS-LÉONARD-SADI; CARNOT CYCLE; CLAUSIUS, RUDOLF JULIUS EMMANUEL; ENGINE, EFFICIENCY OF; ENTROPY; HEAT, CALORIC THEORY OF; HEAT, MECHANICAL EQUIVALENT OF; HEAT CAPACITY; HEAT ENGINE; HEAT PUMP; HEAT TRANSFER; KELVIN, LORD; MAXWELL, JAMES CLERK; MAXWELL'S DEMON; MEAN FREE PATH

Bibliography

CARNOT, S. *Réflexions sur la Puissance Motrice du Feu*, critical edition by R. Fox (J. Vrin, Paris, 1978); English edition (Manchester University Press, Manchester, Eng., 1986).

BRUSH, S. G. *Ludwig Boltzmann: Lectures on Gas Theory* (University of California Press, Berkeley, 1964).

BRUSH, S. G. *The Kind of Motion We Call Heat* (North-Holland, Amsterdam, 1976).

CARDWELL, D. S. L. *From Watt to Clausius: The Rise of Thermodynamics in the Early Industrial Age*, 2nd ed. (University of Iowa Press, Ames, 1989).

SMITH C. and WISE, N. *Energy and Empire: A Biographical Study of Lord Kelvin* (Cambridge University Press, Cambridge, Eng., 1989).

DONALD S. L. CARDWELL

THERMOELECTRIC EFFECT

As the name implies, thermoelectricity refers to effects that involve both thermal energy (heat) and electricity. Thermoelectricity is not an equilibrium process; instead, it is a steady state process like electrical conductivity and it requires the presence of mobile electrical charges. In the absence of a magnetic field there are three thermoelectric effects: the Seebeck effect, discovered by Thomas John Seebeck in 1822; the Peltier effect, discovered by Jean Charles Athanase Peltier in 1834; and the Thomson effect, predicted in 1854 and then experimentally confirmed a few years later by William Thomson. These three effects are not independent. Thomson (later honored with the title Lord Kelvin) used non-

rigorous thermodynamic arguments to make his prediction. Rigorous arguments using irreversible thermodynamics produce the same results, and the equations connecting the three effects are known as the Kelvin relations. The Joule heating that accompanies the flow of electrical charges through any nonsuperconductor is not a thermoelectric effect.

Let us consider the Seebeck effect first. If a material containing mobile electrons is subjected to a heat flow that causes a temperature difference (ΔT) to develop within the material, then an open-circuit voltage difference (ΔV) will occur. For a homogeneous material and a small ΔT, these two differences obey the relation

$$\Delta V = S_A(\overline{T}) \cdot \Delta T, \tag{1}$$

where $S_A(\overline{T})$ is the thermopower for material A at temperature $\overline{T}$, ΔT is $T_2 - T_1$, and $\overline{T}$ is $(T_2 + T_1)/2$. $S_A(T)$ is also called the thermoelectric power or the Seebeck coefficient; the latter name is commonly used for semiconductors. Equation (1) can be integrated to yield the more general equation

$$\Delta V = \int_{T_1}^{T_2} S_A(T)\, dT. \tag{2}$$

Contrary to a common misconception, the sign of the thermopower depends upon more than the sign of the charge carriers. The size of the thermopower

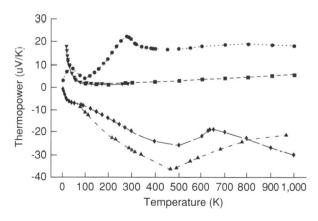

Figure 1 Thermopowers for a selection of materials. The materials are denoted by the following symbols: (●) pure Cr; (▼) intrinsic Ge values divided by 1,000; (■) pure Cu; (◆) pure Ni; and (▲) doped PbSe values divided by 10.

depends upon the statistics that describe the steady state relations between the charge carriers and the temperature. For metals, Fermi–Dirac statistics are generally valid and thermopowers are small; for semiconductors and semimetals, Boltzmann statistics are generally valid and larger thermopowers occur. Figure 1 gives some typical results. The most common application of the Seebeck effect is a thermocouple. Attempts to use natural or controlled temperature differences and the Seebeck effect to make voltage sources have had limited success.

The Peltier and Thomson effects differ in two essential respects from the Seebeck effect. First, an electrical current must flow: These effects do not occur in an electric open circuit. Second, reversible heat is involved. The Peltier effect is associated with an isothermal junction between two different materials. As current flows across this junction in one direction, heat is generated; reversing the current direction causes the same amount of heat to be absorbed rather than generated. This heat is directly proportional to the current density, and the current direction associated with heat generation is determined by the Seebeck coefficients of the two materials. The Thomson effect occurs in a single material when a temperature gradient is also present. Current in one direction generates heat while current in the reverse direction absorbs the same amount of heat. The Peltier effect can be used to make a device with no moving parts that cools or heats depending upon the current direction. Thermoelectric coolers based on this principle are used for a variety of optical detectors.

See also: CURRENT, DIRECT; ELECTRICAL CONDUCTIVITY; JOULE HEATING; KELVIN, LORD; SEMICONDUCTOR; TEMPERATURE; THERMODYNAMICS

Bibliography

BLATT, F. J.; SCHROEDER, P. A.; FOILES, C. L.; and GREIG, D. *Thermoelectric Power of Metals and Alloys* (Plenum, New York, 1976).

FOILES, C. L. "Thermopower of Pure Metals and Dilute Alloys" in *Metals: Electronic Transport Phenomena, Landolt–Bornstein New Series III/15b*, edited by K. H. Hellwege and J. L. Olson (Springer-Verlag, Berlin, 1985).

MACDONALD, D. K. C. *Thermoelectricity: An Introduction to the Principles* (Wiley, New York, 1962).

WILSON, A. H. *The Theory of Metals,* 2nd ed. (Cambridge University Press, Cambridge, Eng., 1953).

C. L. FOILES

THERMOLUMINESCENCE

Thermoluminescence (TL) means the emission of light when heated. It does not include light from incandescence. A few of the more common types of luminescence are fluorescence, phosphorescence, bioluminescence, chemiluminescence, and electroluminescence. TL is closely related to phosphorescence and can be thought of as "frozen-in" phosphorescence. That is, TL is phosphorescent light released by heating. Many insulating crystals exhibit TL. Ionizing radiation releases electrons into the conduction band and, in the process, some of these electrons are trapped at metastable states in the forbidden gap between the valence band and the conduction band. In commercial TL phosphors these traps are usually associated with added impurities. The trap depths are typically about 1 eV—much greater than the energy of molecules at room temperature. Thus the electrons may stay trapped for thousands of years at room temperature.

When the irradiated crystal is heated, the trapped charges are released into the electron band and subsequently combine with vacancies to release the stored energy as light—TL. During heating the TL gets brighter, goes through a maximum, and then fades away as all of the trapped electrons are released. A graph of TL versus time is called a glow curve. After heating it is possible to irradiate the crystal again to restore the TL.

Many natural minerals, such as calcium fluoride (fluorite), exhibit TL when heated since they have been exposed to ionizing radiation from nature for millions of years. Scientists have been aware of TL for more than 100 years. Scientists in Germany in 1894 produced the first artificial TL phosphor of $CaSO_4$:Mn (i.e., calcium sulfate doped with a little manganese). This phosphor produced TL after exposure to ultraviolet light. Marie Curie in 1902 found that the TL in this phosphor was restored when exposed to the radiation from radium. In the 1950s, Farrington Daniels at the University of Wisconsin noted several practical applications of TL. He showed that the quantity of TL was a measure of the radiation dose—he invented thermoluminescent dosimetry (TLD). He also proposed that the TL from a pottery shard from an archeological site could be used to determine how long ago it was fired. When pottery is fired it erases any stored TL that gradually accumulates over the years from exposure to natural radiation.

In the early 1960s the minor technical problems of TLD were solved, which permitted its widespread use for medical and radiation protection applications. Several commercial TLD phosphors and instruments to "read" the TL are now available. Each TLD phosphor is characterized by the temperature of its glow peak(s), its sensitivity to radiation, the color of its emitted TL, and its stability—how long the TL signal is retained with negligible fading. One of the most common TLD phosphors is lithium fluoride doped with trace amounts of magnesium and titanium—LiF:Mg,Ti. Millions of these TLDs are in use around the world for monitoring the radiation exposure of radiation workers in nuclear power plants and hospitals. Some TLD phosphors are sensitive to ambient light and some require care in their thermal treatment if they are to be reused. TLDs can measure the amount of background radiation in one day and yet can measure to much more than the lethal dose for humans (above 5 Gyr or 500 rad).

See also: FLOURESCENCE; LUMINESCENCE

Bibliography

CAMERON, J. R.; SUNTHARALINGAM, N.; and KENNEY, G. N. *Thermoluminescent Dosimetry* (University of Wisconsin Press, Madison, WI, 1968).

MCKINLAY, A. F. *Thermoluminescence Dosimetry* (IOP, Bristol, Eng., 1981).

JOHN R. CAMERON

THERMOMETER

A thermometer is an instrument for assigning a unique temperature to a system with which it is in thermal equilibrium. The thermometer must be calibrated to a specific temperature scale, such as Kelvins, degrees Celsius, or degrees Fahrenheit.

Any thermometer uniquely correlates some observable x to a temperature T. For instance, in the household mercury thermometer, x is the length of the mercury column in the glass tube, which is graduated in degrees Celsius or degrees Fahrenheit. Other thermometers correlate temperature to the pressure of a gas held at constant volume, or to the electrical resistance of a specific conductor.

Mercury Thermometer

The mercury thermometer exploits the expansion of liquid mercury with temperature. Placed in a thin tube of uniform cross section, as the temperature changes so does the length of the mercury column. Since the coefficient of thermal expansion of mercury is approximately constant for a modest range of temperatures, and since the coefficient of expansion of glass is very small compared to that of mercury, the change in length of the mercury column is to a good approximation directly proportional to the temperature change that produced it. Thus the thermometer scale is marked with equally spaced gradations. This linear approximation is valid for the temperature ranges expected in household use.

Gas Thermometer

The gas thermometer uses gas held in a container of constant volume. The pressure of the gas is correlated to temperature. Through a procedure described below, all constant-volume gas thermometers give the same answer for a system's temperature. This provides an empirical scale that is independent of any particular substance: the Kelvin scale, in terms of which all other temperature scales are rigorously defined.

For sufficiently high temperatures and sufficiently low pressures, the temperature of the gas varies linearly with pressure. Thus we may write

$$T = AP, \qquad (1)$$

where A is a constant. Suppose we choose helium gas for the thermometer. The helium thermometer is calibrated by placing it in thermal equilibrium with a standard state, the triple point of water, whose temperature T is defined to be 273.16 K. Equation (1) gives $A = (273.16 \text{ K})/(P_{tr})_1$ where $(P_{tr})_1$ is the pressure of the gas in the thermometer when it is in thermal equilibrium at the triple point, and when the mass of helium in the thermometer is m_1. Equation (1) now relates the provisional temperature T_1 of any state to the pressure reading P when the thermometer is calibrated with this mass m_1 of helium,

$$T_1 = (273.16 \text{ K}) \cdot \left[\frac{P}{(P_{tr})_1} \right]. \qquad (2)$$

Thus calibrated, we wish to measure the temperature of a system S by placing the thermometer in thermal equilibrium with S and reading P. However, the value T_1 we obtain depends on $(P_{tr})_1$, so it is not a property of S itself. To obtain a temperature for S that is independent of the amount of gas *in the thermometer*, some of the helium gas must be removed from the thermometer, reducing m_1 to $m_2 < m_1$, then the thermometer must once more be placed in thermal equilibrium with the triple point of water. The water's temperature is still 273.16 K by definition, but $(P_{tr})_2$ now has a different value than $(P_{tr})_1$. Placing the recalibrated thermometer once again in thermal equilibrium with S, the new provisional temperature T_2 is recorded. This process is repeated multiple times, using smaller and smaller masses of gas in the thermometer. When this has been done with helium, the entire procedure must be repeated using other gases, such as neon, argon, oxygen, and air. When the data for all gases has been collected, it must be plotted as in Fig. 1. Upon extrapolating the data to P_{tr} approaching zero, it is found that all gases give the same, unique value for the temperature of system S. This Kelvin scale, established empirically with the gas thermometer, is independent of the amount and chemical species of the gas.

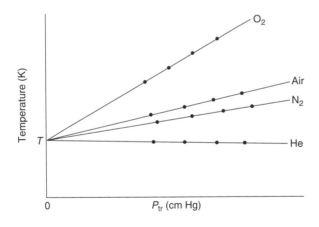

Figure 1 As the mass of gas in the constant-volume gas thermometer is reduced, the pressure of the gas at the calibration point (the triple point of water) is changed. Thus calibrated, the thermometer measures the temperature T for the system S. In the extrapolation to zero pressure at the triple-point calibration, all constant-volume gas thermometers give the same value for T, regardless of the chemical species of gas.

Electromagnetic Radiation Thermometer

Consider electromagnetic radiation in thermal equilibrium with matter at temperature T. Matter is made of charged particles, and the higher the temperature T the more vigorously the charged particles are vibrating. Since vibrating charged particles radiate waves in the electromagnetic field, the spectrum of intensity versus frequency for the emitted radiation is correlated to temperature. The human body, for example, radiates in the infrared, while the much hotter heating element in an electric oven radiates strongly in the visible and the infrared (the orange glow from the element is seen and the infrared heat is felt).

The intensity of each frequency ν emitted is a function of the temperature. It is shown in statistical mechanics that the energy density per frequency of the radiation spectrum is given by the Planck distribution,

Energy density per frequency =

$$\left(\frac{4\pi}{c^3}\right) \cdot (h\nu^3) \cdot \left[\exp\left(\frac{h\nu}{kT}\right) - 1\right]^{-1}, \tag{3}$$

where $h = 6.6 \times 10^{-34}$ J·s is Planck's constant, $c = 3.0 \times 10^8$ m/s is the speed of light in a vacuum, and $k = 1.4 \times 10^{-23}$ J/K is Boltzmann's constant. A sketch of this function for a "hot" and a "cold" temperature is shown in Fig. 2. It is essentially a plot of the "brightness" of each frequency's contribution to the radiation.

Notice that the location of the peak in the curve depends on the temperature. In terms of the radia-

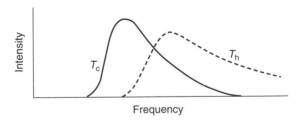

Figure 2 A sketch of the spectrum of intensity (or energy density per frequency) as a function of frequency, for electromagnetic radiation in thermal equilibrium with matter. Two curves, corresponding to two temperatures, T_h (for "hotter") and T_c (for "cooler") are shown.

tion's wavelength $\lambda = c/\nu$, the wavelength at the peak is correlated with the temperature according to Wien's law,

$$\lambda_{\text{peak}} = \frac{(2.90 \times 10^6 \, \text{nm·K})}{T}. \tag{4}$$

This is a "thermometer" that may be used to measure the temperature of matter and radiation when they are in thermal equilibrium. Given the necessary spectrometers, one could use this method to measure the temperature of the human body or an electric oven, although more convenient thermometers exist for taking their temperatures. But this "electromagnetic thermometer" is the only accessible technique for measuring the surface temperatures of stars, and the 2.7-K cosmic background radiation left over from the primordial fireball of the big bang.

See also: TEMPERATURE SCALE, CELSIUS; TEMPERATURE SCALE, FAHRENHEIT; TEMPERATURE SCALE, KELVIN; THERMOMETRY

Bibliography

FEYNMAN, R. P.; LEIGHTON, R. B.; and SANDS, M. *The Feynman Lectures on Physics* Vol. 1 (Addison-Wesley, Reading, MA, 1963).

HALLIDAY, D.; RESNICK, R.; and KRANE, K. S., eds. *Physics*, 4th ed. (Wiley, New York, 1992).

HUANG, K. *Statistical Mechanics* (Wiley, New York, 1963).

REIF, F. *Fundamentals of Statistical and Thermal Physics* (McGraw-Hill, New York, 1965).

SEARS, F. W. *An Introduction to Thermodynamics, the Kinetic Theory of Gases, and Statistical Mechanics,* 2nd ed. (Addison Wesley, Reading, MA, 1953).

SERWAY, R. A. *Physics for Scientists and Engineers with Modern Physics,* 3rd ed. (Saunders, Fort Worth, TX, 1990).

TIPLER, P. A. *Physics,* 2nd ed. (Worth, New York, 1982).

DWIGHT E. NEUENSCHWANDER

THERMOMETRY

Temperature is proportional to the average kinetic energy of microscopic particles. Measuring the kinetic energies of 10^{23} individual atoms is clearly out of the question. So a temperature scale is defined by correlating the temperature T to some other macroscopic observable x. This is "thermometry."

For instance, in the household mercury thermometer, x is the length of the mercury column in the glass tube, and T is defined in terms of some monotonic function of x. In other types of thermometers, x may be the pressure of a gas, or the electrical resistance of a specific conductor. In general, one constructs for the observable x some monotonic function $f(x)$, such that

$$T = f(x). \tag{1}$$

In the simplest case, $f(x)$ is linear in x,

$$T = Ax + B, \tag{2}$$

where A and B are constants determined by choosing two reproducible states of matter, such as the freezing and boiling points of water. To these states we assign, by definition, the numerical values T_1 and T_2 for their temperatures. For instance, if T_1 and T_2 are chosen to be 0 and 100 for water's freezing and boiling points, respectively, then we invent the Celsius scale; if the assigned temperatures are 32 and 212, respectively, we have the Fahrenheit scale. Once A and B are determined, then the temperature T for any state is determined by reading x whenever the thermometer is in thermal equilibrium with the system whose temperature is being measured.

It is not always possible to model the relation between T and x as linear. For example, if x is the length of a fluid column in a tube of uniform cross section, the change in x for the temperature change from 10 to 15 degrees may not be the same as the change in x for the temperature change from 110 to 115 degrees. Such variation is typical, because in general the coefficients of thermal expansion of materials are functions of temperature. This means the coefficients A and B are functions of T, and thus the relation between T and x is not truly linear. However, the linear approximation is usually adequate for modest temperature changes.

Another complexity is that the standard states whereby one assigns the reference temperatures T_1 and T_2 may depend on other variables besides x. For instance, the freezing and boiling points of water vary with atmospheric pressure. Thus, to establish a temperature scale based on these states in addition to values for T_1 and T_2, one must also specify the pressures under which the temperatures are assigned to the freezing and boiling points of water.

Once a scale is well-defined, any other scale may be defined in terms of it. The fundamental scale is the Kelvin scale, where $T = 0$ means the average kinetic energy of the microscopic particles is an absolute minimum. The triple point of water is assigned the temperature 273.16 K. The "size" of the Kelvin degree is the same as the Celsius degree. The Kelvin (T_K), the Celsius (T_C) and Fahrenheit (T_F) scales are related by $T_C = T_K - 273.16$, and $T_F = (9/5) T_C + 32$.

See also: TEMPERATURE SCALE, CELSIUS; TEMPERATURE SCALE, FAHRENHEIT; TEMPERATURE SCALE, KELVIN; THERMOMETER

Bibliography

HALLIDAY, D.; RESNICK, R.; and KRANE, K. S., eds. *Physics,* 4th ed. (Wiley, New York, 1992).

SEARS, F. W. *An Introduction to Thermodynamics, the Kinetic Theory of Gases, and Statistical Mechanics,* 2nd ed. (Addison-Wesley, Reading, MA, 1953).

SERWAY, R. A. *Physics for Scientists and Engineers with Modern Physics,* 3rd ed. (Saunders, Fort Worth, TX, 1990).

TIPLER, P. A. *Physics,* 2nd ed. (Worth, New York, 1982).

DWIGHT E. NEUENSCHWANDER

THIN FILM

Any substance that has a thickness of less than several micrometers for optical applications is referred to as a thin film. The thickness of such a film is on the order of the magnitude of the wavelength. Robert Hooke reported on the optical effects of thin films in 1671. He observed colored fringes from white light reflected from soap films and from a variable air wedge formed between the curved surface of a spherical lens and an underlying reflecting surface (Newton's rings). In 1672 Isaac Newton made more extended and detailed experimental studies of the same phenomena, and he was the first to relate the color of a film with thickness. However, he failed to correctly interpret the cause of the results.

Thomas Young conclusively demonstrated in 1809 that the fringes are a consequence of the wave nature of light. When light waves strike a thin film, constructive and destructive interference can occur for waves reflected from the front and back surfaces of the film. The waves reflected from the back surface travel an extra path equal to twice the film thickness (for normal incidence) before interfering with the top reflected wave, causing the two waves to get out of step. The interference depends not only on the thickness but also on the wavelength and the possibility of wave inversion upon reflection. Changing the angle of view for the reflected light requires the second reflected wave to travel a greater path in the film, thus changing the interference condition with the top reflected wave. The situation is illustrated in Fig. 1. The general condition for the destructive interference of reflected light of wavelength λ from a thin film of thickness d and refractive index n is given by

$$N\lambda = 2nd \cos \phi,$$

where $N = 1/2, 3/2, 5/2, \ldots$, if $n_1 > n > n_2$ or $n_1 < n < n_2$; and $N = 1, 2, 3, \ldots$, if $n < n_1, n_2$ or $n > n_1, n_2$, where n_1 and n_2 are the refractive indices of medium 1 and 2, respectively.

The most common method of producing thin films is thermal evaporation of a material onto a substrate in an evacuated environment. Other methods include ion beam deposition, chemical deposition from solutions or vapors, and chemical etching processes.

Thin film interference has many applications in optics. Materials such as MgF_2 ($n = 1.38$) are used as

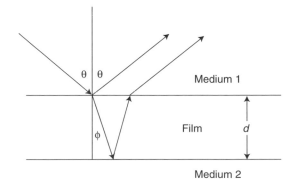

Figure 1 Illustration of destructive interference of reflected light from a thin film.

antireflective coatings on lenses and other optical components to cut down glare and improve image quality. A combination of thin film layers of appropriate refractive indices forms an interference filter, in which a desired color is transmitted as a result of the destructive interference that removes one or more wavelengths from incident polychromatic light. The flatness of a glass plate is tested by laying the plate on an optically flat glass plate such as to form an air wedge between the plates, and observing interference fringes in reflected monochromatic light due to the thickness variation of the air film. If the tested plate is flat, uniformly spaced fringes are seen. Applications of thin films abound in many other areas, such as electronics (e.g., integrated circuits), energy conversion (e.g., solar cells), corrosion and wear resistance (e.g., protected mirrors), superconductivity (e.g., Josephson junctions), magnetism (e.g., magnetic memories), and decorative designs.

See also: CIRCUIT, INTEGRATED; LIGHT, WAVE THEORY OF; NEWTON, ISAAC; OPTICS; REFLECTION; REFRACTION, INDEX OF; SUPERCONDUCTIVITY

Bibliography

ANDERS, H. *Thin Films in Optics* (Focal, London, 1967).

ECKERTORÁ, L. *Physics of Thin Films* (Plenum, New York, 1977).

HALLIDAY, D., and RESNICK, R. *Physics* (Wiley, New York, 1962).

HEWITT, P. G. *Conceptual Physics,* 5th ed. (Little, Brown, Boston, 1985).

KLABUND, K. J., ed. *Thin Films from Atoms and Particles* (Academic Press, New York, 1985).

SAM J. CIPOLLA

THOMSON, JOSEPH JOHN

b. Cheetham Hill near Manchester, England, December 18, 1856; *d.* Cambridge, England, August 30, 1940; *electron physics, atomic physics, electromagnetism, chemical physics.*

Joseph John Thomson is best remembered for his experimental discovery of the electron in 1897, for which he won the Nobel Prize in physics in 1906, but his influence was much wider. His lifelong interest was the relationship between the ether and matter, and his theoretical virtuosity was much admired by contemporaries. He was the first to suggest electromagnetic mass; his work on the structure of light, from 1907 onwards, paved the way for the acceptance of the quantum theory of radiation in Britain; and he laid the foundations for theories of ionic chemical bonding. Thomson was a leading spokesman for science to the government and guided the increasing professionalism of science in Britain. Finally, Thomson was a renowned research supervisor, and eight of his students won Nobel Prizes.

Thomson's father, Joseph James Thomson, was a Manchester bookseller. His mother was Emma Swindells. Thomson's younger brother, Frederick Vernon Thomson, went into business with a firm of calico merchants. Thomson's parents sympathized with his scientific interests, encouraged his lifelong interest in botany, and intended for him to become an engineer. At fourteen, Thomson entered Owens College, Manchester, to begin his training. His father died two years later, leaving the family poorly off and compelling Thomson to rely on scholarships, concentrating on subjects he excelled in—mathematics and physics, taught by Thomas Barker and Balfour Stewart, respectively.

In 1876 Thomson went to Cambridge to study mathematics. He received a thorough grounding in analytical dynamics (the use of Lagrange's equations and Hamilton's principle of least action) from his coach, Edward Routh. The emphasis on physical analogies and a mechanical world view is evident throughout the rest of his work. In 1880 he graduated as Second Wrangler (second place).

Thomson's early work was dominated by his commitment to analytical dynamics and Maxwell's electrodynamics, which he first encountered at Owens College and later learned from William Niven at Cambridge. In 1881 he showed, for the first time, that the mass of a charged particle increases as it moves. He thought the increase was due to the particle dragging some of the ether with it. In 1882 he won the Adams Prize with "A Treatise on Vortex Motion," investigating the stability of interlocked vortex rings and developing the then popular ether-vortex model of the atom to account for the periodic table.

Through this work, Thomson allied himself with the goals of the elite of Cambridge mathematical physicists, and he also identified himself with Cambridge values and social mores. In 1890 he married Rose Paget, daughter of a professor of medicine. He sent his son, George, and daughter, Joan, to private schools. He appeared religiously devout. He also joined the Athenaeum and Saville clubs. His conventionality and scientific accomplishments paid off, and in 1884 Thomson was elected Cavendish Professor of Experimental Physics at Cambridge, one of the top university positions in Britain, at the early age of twenty-eight.

Overnight, Thomson became a leader of science. He wrote review articles and held an increasing number of positions in scientific administration, as editor of journals, on education committees, and on the Board for Invention and Research during World War I. He was elected president of the Royal Society in 1915 and after the war became science's leading spokesman in Britain to the new Department for Scientific and Industrial Research. The esteem he gained was confirmed by a knighthood in 1908, the Order of Merit in 1912, and his election in 1918 as Master of Trinity College, a Crown appointment.

Under Thomson's leadership, the Cavendish Laboratory became a place of lively debate, at the forefront of modern experimental physics, but also one of great financial stringency. He instituted a colloquium, and the laboratory developed a social life of teas and an annual dinner.

As Cavendish Professor, Thomson had free choice of scientific direction, coinciding with a change in attitude away from analytical dynamics and toward a more experimental approach. He chose the academically unpopular subject of discharge of electricity through gases, and continued to experiment with it for the rest of his life. Around 1890 Thomson developed a concept of a discrete charge, modeled by the terminus of a vortex tube in the ether, which guided his subsequent experimental work.

The discovery of x rays in 1895 was the turning point of Thomson's work on discharge. X rays ionized the gas in a controllable manner and clearly distinguished the effects of ionization and secondary radiation. By the end of 1896 Thomson and Ernest Rutherford had convincing evidence for Thomson's theory of discharge by ionization of gas molecules.

The discovery of x rays revived interest in the nature of cathode rays. With new confidence in his apparatus and theories, derived from his success with x-ray ionization, Thomson in 1897 showed that all of the properties of cathode rays could be explained by assuming that they were subatomic charged particles, which were a universal constituent of matter. He called these corpuscles but they soon became known as electrons.

Over the next few years Thomson unified his ionization and corpuscle theories into a general theory of gaseous discharge that is still largely accepted today.

Thomson next investigated the role of corpuscles in matter. His "plum pudding" model of the atom, in which thousands of corpuscles orbited in a sphere of positive electrification, worked until 1906 when he calculated that the number of corpuscles in the atom was comparable with the atomic weight, raising problems with the origin of the atom's mass and of its stability. He began experimenting with the positive ions in a discharge tube to account for the mass of the atom. This work eventually led to the discovery of the first nonradioactive isotopes, those of neon, in 1913, and the invention by Thomson's collaborator Francis Aston of the mass spectrograph in 1919.

In 1919 Thomson resigned the Cavendish Professorship, a year after his appointment as Master of Trinity College, Cambridge. He now had a major social and administrative role. When he died twenty-one years later, his ashes were buried in Westminster Abbey.

See also: ATOMIC PHYSICS; CATHODE RAY; CHEMICAL PHYSICS; ELECTROMAGNETISM; ELECTRON; ELECTRON, DISCOVERY OF; LIGHT, ELECTROMAGNETIC THEORY OF; NOBEL PRIZE WINNERS; RUTHERFORD, ERNEST; WAVE–PARTICLE DUALITY, HISTORY OF; X RAY, DISCOVERY OF

Major Publications

RUTHERFORD, E., and THOMSON, J. J. "On the Passage of Electricity Through Gases Exposed to Roentgen Rays." *Philosophical Magazine* **V42,** 392–407 (1896)

THOMSON, J. J. "On the Electric and Magnetic Effects Produced by the Motion of Electrified Bodies." *Philosophical Magazine* **V11,** 229–249 (1881).

THOMSON, J. J. *Notes on Recent Researches in Electricity and Magnetism* (Clarendon, Oxford, Eng., 1893).

THOMSON, J. J. "Cathode Rays." *Philosophical Magazine* **V44,** 269–316 (1897).

THOMSON, J. J. "On the Masses of the Ions in Gases at Low Pressures." *Philosophical Magazine* **V48,** 547–567 (1899).

THOMSON, J. J. *Conduction of Electricity Through Gases* (Cambridge University Press, Cambridge, Eng., 1903).

THOMSON, J. J. "On the Number of Corpuscles in an Atom." *Philosophical Magazine* **V11,** 769–781 (1906).

THOMSON, J. J. *Rays of Positive Electricity and Their Application to Chemical Analysis* (Longmans Green, London, 1913).

THOMSON, J. J. *Recollections and Reflections* (Bell and Sons, London, 1936).

Bibliography

FALCONER, I. J. "Corpuscles, Electrons, and Cathode Rays: J. J. Thomson and the "Discovery of the Electron." *British Journal for the History of Science* **20**, 241–276 (1987).

FALCONER, I. J. "J. J. Thomson's Work on Positive Rays, 1906-1914." *Historical Studies in the Physical Sciences* **18**, 265–310 (1988).

FALCONER, I. J. "J. J. Thomson and 'Cavendish' Physics" in *The Development of the Laboratory*, edited by F. James (Macmillan, London, 1989).

McCORMMACH, R. "J. J. Thomson and the Structure of Light." *British Journal for the History of Science* **3**, 362–387 (1967).

RAYLEIGH, LORD. *The Life of Sir J. J. Thomson* (Cambridge University Press, Cambridge, Eng., 1942).

ROBOTTI, N. "J. J. Thomson at the Cavendish Laboratory: The History of an Electric Charge Measurement." *Annals of Science* 52, 265–284 (1995).

SALTZMAN, M. "J. J. Thomson and the Modern Revival of Dualism." *Journal of Chemical Education* **50**, 59 (1973).

THOMSON, G. P. *J. J. Thomson and the Cavendish Laboratory in His Day* (Doubleday, Garden City, New York, 1964).

WHEATON, B. *The Tiger and the Shark* (Cambridge University Press, Cambridge, Eng., 1983).

ISOBEL FALCONER

THOMSON, WILLIAM

See KELVIN, LORD

THUNDER

One of the features associated with lightning flashes is the superheating of air within the discharge channel to temperatures as high as 30,000 K. Such air has its pressure momentarily raised to a value greater than that of the air surrounding it. As a result, the cylindrical air column expands rapidly outward. The excess pressure initially propagates as a shock wave, having an overpressure of up to 10 atm at a distance of $\frac{1}{2}$ m from the source. However, by the time this wave has traveled some meters from its source, the air has cooled and the pressure front has been attenuated to become a sound wave. This is what we normally hear as thunder. Thunder contains frequencies ranging from 0.25 to 500 Hz, with most of its energy contained in the very low frequencies. The excess pressure at these lowest frequencies is, typically, about 0.001 atm at a distance of 1 km from the discharge.

There is a maximum distance at which thunder can be heard under normal conditions, with the value of this distance depending on the height, above ground, of the source. For a source located 4 km above ground, the maximum distance to which such thunder can normally be heard is about 25 km. This is because sound waves in air undergo refraction as they travel along a path whose temperature varies with altitude. Since the speed of sound in air varies as the square root of the air temperature, the sound waves continually refract away from the ground as they travel from the cloud toward the ground. Sound waves that would intercept the ground at greater distances, in the absence of refraction, are refracted such that they pass overhead and are not heard. However, under certain conditions, thunder can be heard at greater distances. Motion of the air itself can cause thunder to be heard at greater distances than otherwise possible in still air. It is also possible, under situations where an inversion layer (warmer air aloft) is present, for the sound waves to be refracted back down toward the ground and to intercept it at distances farther away than normally expected.

The intensity of thunder is influenced by a number of factors. Obviously the distance between listener and source and any motion of the intervening air play important roles in determining the loudness of the thunderclap arriving to the listener. Given the same distance and atmospheric conditions, it turns out that interference effects also can influence the intensity of sound heard by an observer. Sound waves starting out from different portions of the discharge path can interfere destructively, with the result that the thunderclap heard can be of reduced intensity. Because of this, jagged lightning extending over a given path length will generate thunder that is louder than that produced by a relatively straight line discharge of the same length.

See also: LIGHTNING; SHOCK WAVE; SOUND

Bibliography

BATTAN, L. J. *The Thunderstorm* (New American Library, New York, 1964).

UMAN, M. A. *Lightning* (Dover, New York, 1984).

DAVID JOHN GRIFFITHS

TIDES

The word "tides" refers to the relative displacements of the matter in a body, for example, a star or a planet, due to the gravitational action of external bodies. Such displacements occur in the solid body of Earth, in the oceans, and in the atmosphere due to the position dependence of the Sun's and the Moon's gravitational fields.

The gravitational field of a body weakens with increasing distance from the body. The acceleration of gravity in the Moon's gravitational field is greater at the point A (see Fig. 1) on Earth that is nearest the Moon than at the center O of Earth, and less at the most remote point B. Therefore, a particle at A will be acted upon by a greater lunar gravitational force toward the Moon than a similar particle at the center of Earth, while a particle at B will be acted upon by a lesser force. The difference of the lunar gravitational force at different positions of Earth is the lunar tide-generating force. It is the gravitational force at the point considered minus the force at the center of Earth. This tide-generating force field is depicted in Fig. 2.

The tide-generating force due to the Moon and the Sun can be expressed as the gradient of a tide-generating potential:

$$\psi = \frac{1}{2}\gamma R^2 \left\{ \left[\frac{M}{d^3}(1 - 3\cos^2\theta) \right]_{\text{Moon}} \right.$$

$$\left. + \left[\frac{M}{d^3}(1 - 3\cos^2\theta) \right]_{\text{Sun}} \right\}. \quad (1)$$

Here γ is Newton's gravitational constant, and R the radius of Earth, while M, d, and θ (with the subscripts "Moon" and "Sun") are the mass, the distance from the center of Earth, and the zenith distance of the Moon and the Sun, respectively. A useful reference is the so-called equilibrium tide. Its surface is determined by Earth's own gravitational field and the tide-generating field. The elevation of the surface due to the tidal forces is

$$h = H_{\text{Moon}}(\cos^2\theta_{\text{Moon}} - \tfrac{1}{3})$$

$$+ H_{\text{Sun}}(\cos^2\theta_{\text{Sun}} - \tfrac{1}{3}), \quad (2)$$

where

$$H_{\text{Moon}} = \frac{3\gamma R^2 M_{\text{Moon}}}{2gd_{\text{Moon}}^3},$$

$$H_{\text{Sun}} = \frac{3\gamma R^2 M_{\text{Sun}}}{2gd_{\text{Sun}}^3}. \quad (3)$$

Here g is the acceleration of gravity at the surface of Earth. Inserting numerical data gives $H_{\text{Moon}} = 54$ cm and $H_{\text{Sun}} = 24$ cm. When the Moon and the Sun are nearly at the same position on the sky (new moon) or nearly at opposite positions (full moon), the lunar and solar effects reinforce each other to produce high-range spring tides. When the directions of sight to the Moon and the Sun are normal to each

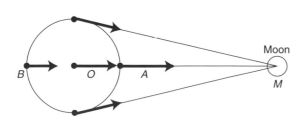

Figure 1 The lunar gravitational force at different points on Earth.

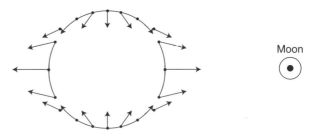

Figure 2 The tide-generating force on Earth due to the Moon.

other, the lunar and solar effects counteract each other to produce low-range neap tides.

The bodily tides are periodic deformations of the solid body of Earth. They manifest themselves by a slight variation of the direction of the plumb line with respect to a plane defined by Earth's crust, and by variations in the acceleration of gravity at fixed points on Earth. These local variations in the acceleration of gravity may be up to some tens of centimeters per square second.

The atmospheric tides manifest themselves as a small oscillatory variation in the atmospheric pressure at any place, with an amplitude of the order of 0.03 mbar.

The ocean tides deviate greatly from the equilibrium tide due especially to resonance effects induced by interactions between tidal currents and the coasts. The tides progress as waves around Earth due to the rotation of Earth. Meeting a coast, the height of the tidal wave may increase by several meters. The difference in level between successive high and low waters is called the range of the tide. For example, at London Bridge the greatest range for a two-week period has an average value of 7 m. The largest range is found at the Bay of Fundy in Canada and is about 15 m. The smallest range is found at some islands in the midst of the Pacific and over most of the Mediterranean, and is less than 30 cm. At most seaside places the water reaches its highest level twice a day, the average interval between two successive high waters varying around 12 h 23 min. However, at certain places in China, the interval is more than 24 h. Usually, the high water is about as much above the mean sea level as the succeeding low water is below it.

At a place in a straight or narrow sea the tidal current usually flows half the time in one direction and half the time in the opposite direction. At the reversal of such a current there is a state of rest, usually called slack water. In an estuary the current continues to flow upstream for some time after high water and to run downstream similarly after low water. When the current is directed toward land, or up an estuary, it is called the flood current. When it runs away from land, or down an estuary, it is called the ebb current. The speed of tidal currents vary greatly from place to place. For example, in the Seymour Narrows in British Columbia the maximum current reaches 10 kn, while in the North Sea it rarely exceeds 1 kn. At some distance up certain rivers—as, for example, where the Colorado River meets the tide—a wave more than 3 m high travels up the river almost like a wall of water. This phenomenon is called a bore. Near a headland separating two bays, there is sometimes a swift current called a race.

The tides on Earth tend to decrease the rate of Earth's rotation by about one second every 100,000 years and increase the distance to the Moon. Tides on the Moon caused by Earth have made the Moon keep the same face toward Earth at all times.

In Albert Einstein's theory of relativity, a tidal force field is represented by curvature of spacetime.

See also: GRAVITATIONAL ATTRACTION; GRAVITATIONAL FORCE LAW; MOON, PHASES OF; RELATIVITY, GENERAL THEORY OF

Bibliography

CLANSY, E. P. *The Tides: Pulse of the Earth* (Doubleday, New York, 1969).

CREAN, P. B. *Mathematical Modelling of Tides and Estuarine Circulation: The Coastal Seas of Southern British Columbia and Washington State* (Springer-Verlag, Berlin, 1988).

DEFANT, A. *Ebb and Flow* (University of Michigan Press, Ann Arbor, 1958).

DEFANT, A. *Physical Oceanography* (Pergamon, New York, 1961).

MELCHIOR, P. M. *The Tides of the Planet Earth*, 2nd ed. (Pergamon, Oxford, Eng., 1983).

OHANIAN, H. C. *Gravitation and Spacetime* (W. W. Norton, New York, 1976).

Ø. GRØN

TIME

The concept of time is connected to the idea of ongoing and repetitive change in the physical world. Change (and repetitive change) is obvious. Our bodies age, but at the same time new generations are born, and their bodies age. The sun comes up each morning; seasons change and repeat; our heartbeat occurs in a fairly steady pattern, and we have an internal psychological clock that lets us judge when our heartbeat is rapid or slow. Galileo observed that swinging pendula have a constant swing rate; he verified this by counting against his pulse. Pendulum clocks became at one time the most stable ways of telling time. Until very recently the rotation of Earth was the point of reference for timekeeping, and the most stable pendulum clocks are just about as stable timekeepers as is the rotation of Earth.

Prior to the invention of the portable clock (the watch) time designations were much looser, schedules revolved around terms like dawn, midmorning, noon, and so on. Each town kept its own time defined by when local noon occurred. Even with good municipal clocks, it was not until the introduction of rail transportation into the United States that clocks were synchronized over large areas into time zones.

As Earth rotates, each degree of longitude reaches noon at a different time. The difference is one hour per 15° of longitude, which means that 1°, about 50 miles in the midwest of the United States, leads to a four-minute difference in when noon occurs. This can cause havoc with train schedules. So the railway solution was to define four time zones (one hour apart) across the continental United States, and this system was soon implemented worldwide.

Timekeeping is today done by using the frequency of oscillation of atoms in specially constructed atomic clocks. The best of these, based on a hydrogen maser, can maintain high stability for extended periods of time, resulting in accuracy to within one-tenth of a microsecond over one year. The true accuracy of such a clock can be checked only by comparison with other hydrogen maser clocks.

The simple descriptions above used the common-sense notions of time, such as the idea that we can agree that noon occurs four minutes later at one location than at another. These common-sense ideas, which treat time like an evenly flowing stream that is the same for everyone, came into conflict in the late nineteenth century with measurements of the speed of light.

Light travels at a finite speed, often denoted c. The numerical value of c is about 300,000 km/s, about 186,000 miles/s. While this is extremely fast, it is still possible to measure such a speed. Even more interesting, one can attempt to measure any changes in the speed of light.

Common sense suggests that if we are moving toward the source of light, our speed v should be added to c to produce a higher measured speed of light; when we move away our speed v should subtract from c. But accurate experiments carried out by Albert Abraham Michelson and Edward W. Morley beginning in 1877 showed no such difference. The same value of c was always found for the speed of light. After a number of partly successful explanations, the situation was resolved by Albert Einstein's 1905 theory of special relativity. A fundamental concept is that space, and *time*, are affected by uniform motion in such a way that the speed of light is always the same constant c. (An inevitable conclusion of special relativity is that nothing can exceed the speed of light.) Consistency with observation requires that "moving clocks run slow" and this is correctly predicted by special relativity. For instance, a μ meson may be produced at the top of the atmosphere ~ 30 km up. A μ-meson is an unstable particle with a lifetime of approximately 2×10^{-6} (2 μs) when that lifetime is measured for nonmoving particles. Even traveling at the speed of light, a μ meson can go only 600 m in 2 μs. But μ mesons can be detected at the surface of Earth; they live to reach the surface because their "clocks run slow," so their decay is delayed. The formula from special relativity for this time delay is

$$(\text{elapsed indicated time})_{\text{moving object}} =$$
$$(\text{elapsed indicated time})_{\text{still object}} \sqrt{1 - v^2/c^2},$$

where v is the speed of the moving object. Similar results and conclusions apply in the more controlled circumstance of unstable particles generated in high-energy accelerator laboratories.

Phenomena even more distant from commonplace ideas of time occur in the vicinity of a black hole. As observed by a distant observer, the clock of a "diver" falling into the hole slows to a stop as she reaches the black hole surface. This clock rate difference arises because of the difference in gravitational potential. Even a difference in distance of 30 m or so in Earth's gravitational field can be detected in the rate at which clocks run. This was shown by R. V. Pound and G. A. Rebka in 1959 (using the frequency of gamma rays from radioactive decay). The global positioning system is a set of satellites each of which broadcasts its position and the time on its internal clock. By observing four satellites simultaneously, a ground receiver can determine four coordinates: x, y, z, and time at the receiver. The satellites are moving in orbit, at four earth radii from the center of Earth. Corrections for both the motion and the altitude (gravitational potential) effects are necessary (and are made) to keep the satellite clock rate consistent with that of ground clocks.

The Arrow of Time

We see things happening around us with a definite direction of order toward disorder. Dropped teacups shatter; we have never seen the broken pieces of teacups leap together to reassemble themselves and fly up into our hands. The basic one-directionality appears to be that induced by the expansion of the universe. The arrow of time is set by the initial low entropy state of the hot big bang. One feature of the big bang as we know it is that the universe begins containing about 75 percent hydrogen by mass. All this hydrogen is initially available for star formation. The stars that do form pour out their energy into the surrounding space, as the Sun does, and life on Earth makes use of this available energy to "make things happen." Because the direction of macroscopic reactions is toward the increase in entropy (increase in less-ordered energy), the flow of high-quality energy from the Sun to Earth defines a time direction based ultimately on the big bang.

Time Travel

Black holes suggest that connections can be made to other universes. For the simplest (Schwarzschild) black hole the throat is not open long enough for even a flash of light to get through, but there have been suggestions that "exotic matter" can make the throat stay open long enough for a signal (or a person) to get through. The other universe can in fact be a distant location in our own so this would lead to almost instantaneous travel. There could also be offsets in the time, so that passing through the black hole could take you back in time. The practical difficulties of building such a "worm hole" and carrying out such a procedure are of course immense.

The possibility of time travel raises all sorts of questions of logical paradox. Suppose you travel back in time to murder your mother before you are conceived. Then how would you have been born and grown to be the person who did the killing?

In fact, viewed from the four-dimensional description of general relativity, one has to have a four-dimensional consistency in any situation involving travel back in time. Stephen Hawking is so concerned by the logical paradoxes that he has posed the chronology protection conjecture, which achieves the protection by simply stating that time travel is never allowed. Alternately, if time travel is allowed, then since from the viewpoint of the universe there is only one overall four-dimensional structure, it must be a consistent picture: If you exist, you did not kill your mother before you were conceived, and there is no planning on your part that can accomplish that, your free will notwithstanding!

See also: ARROW OF TIME; ATOMIC CLOCK; BIG BANG THEORY; BLACK HOLE; MASER; MICHELSON, ALBERT ABRAHAM; RELATIVITY, SPECIAL THEORY OF; SPACE AND TIME

Bibliography

DAVIES, P. C. W. *The Physics of Time Assymmetry* (University of California Press, Berkeley, 1974).

THORNE, K. S. *Black Holes and Time Warps: Einstein's Outrageous Legacy* (W. W. Norton, New York, 1994).

WELCH, K. F. *Time Measurement: An Introductory History* (Newton Abbot, New York, 1972).

RICHARD A. MATZNER

TIME DILATION

Isaac Newton believed that time is absolute. Absolute time means that the interval of time between two events would be the same to all inertial observers in motion relative to each other. Since time is measured by a clock, absolute time also means that all clocks would keep time at the same rate. Such a view of time is certainly in accordance with our ordinary experience.

In 1905, however, long before there was any experimental evidence against absolute time, Albert Einstein discovered that absolute time was not consistent with the postulates of his new theory of special relativity. The postulates of special relativity are the principle of relativity and the principle of the constancy of the speed of light. The principle of relativity states that no physical experiment can distinguish rest from uniform motion. The principle of the constancy of the speed of light states that light has the same speed to all inertial (or unaccelerated) observers in relative uniform motion.

To see how these postulates lead to the relative nature of time, let us use a clock that is based on the constancy of the speed of light. Such a clock, which consists entirely of a cylinder with two parallel mirrors at its ends, is called a light-beam clock. A light pulse trapped in such a device would then be reflected back and forth between the mirrors at perfectly regular intervals; in fact, if each reflection off a mirror produced a tick, such a device would tick like a perfect clock.

Now let us see how the ticking rate of such a clock is affected by motion. First, note that if we start with two similar light-beam clocks—one on the ground and the other in a spaceship—they would, of course, tick at the same rate. Next, let the spaceship move at a constant velocity in the horizontal direction with respect to the ground. If we orient the light-beam clock in the spaceship to be at right angles to the direction of motion (see Fig. 1), our analysis will be simper.

We are now ready to have the ground- and spaceship-based observers compare their observations of the light-beam clock in the spaceship. To the ground-based observer, the pulse in the light-beam clock in the spaceship will trace a diagonal path between the mirrors. To the spaceship observer, by contrast, the same light pulse will simply bounce up and down vertically, as it did when the spaceship was at rest. Let us now ask, "Will the light-beam clock in the spaceship tick at the same rate to both observers?" Note to begin with that in a right triangle the hypotenuse (i.e., the diagonal path) is greater than the altitude (i.e., the vertical path) or the base. It then follows that the diagonal path will require a longer time for the light pulse to trace than the vertical up and down path, provided, of course, the speed of light is the same to both observers. But the speed of light is, indeed, the same to all observers according to Einstein's second postulate. So the pulse in the spaceship clock will take a longer time between the ticks (i.e., the mirrors) for the ground-based observer than for the spaceship observer. That is, the ground-based observer

will observe the spaceship clock to tick slower than the ground-based clock (see Fig. 2). But recall that these two clocks ticked at the same rate when they were at rest relative to each other. Hence, the radical result is that two clocks in relative motion do not tick at the same rate; the clock in motion keeps time at a slower rate. Motion thus slows down (dilates) time. This effect of motion on clock rates is called time dilation.

Einstein derived a quantitative formula for time dilation. If we denote the passage of time recorded on the clock at rest by t_0 and the passage of time recorded on the moving clock by t, then Einstein's time dilation equation would read

$$t = t_0 \sqrt{1 - v^2/c^2}$$

where v is the velocity of the moving clock and c is the speed of light.

Note further that time dilation is completely symmetrical between inertial observers; because the relative velocity is squared, the time dilation effect is independent of the direction of the velocity. Thus, if the ground-based observer observes the spaceship clock to tick slower, then the spaceship observer will observe the ground-based clock to tick slower also. Similarly, each one will observe the other's heart to pump slower. Otherwise, motion would be distinguishable from rest, and such would, of course, violate Einstein's first postulate, the principle of relativity. Time dilation, or the relative nature of time, is thus a natural and inescapable consequence of the postulates of special relativity.

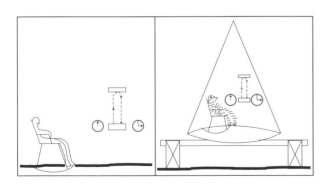

Figure 1 Two clocks: one on the ground and the other in a spaceship.

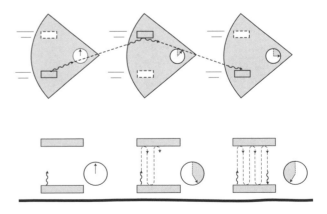

Figure 2 The clock in a moving spaceship advances at a slower rate than the ground-based clock.

See also: EVENT; RELATIVITY, SPECIAL THEORY OF; SPACE
AND TIME; SPACETIME; TIME; TIME REVERSAL INVARIANCE

Bibliography

MERMIN, N. D. *Space and Time in Special Relativity* (McGraw-
Hill, New York, 1968).
TAYLOR, E. F., and WHEELER, J. A. *Spacetime Physics*, 2nd ed.
(W. H. Freeman, New York, 1992).

SUNG KYU KIM

TIME REVERSAL INVARIANCE

Time reversal is an operation, something that transforms a physical process. In this case, the time coordinate is reversed, and this is effected symbolically
by an operator, denoted by T. It is illustrative to
compare and contrast this operation with the more
familiar one of space reversal; the corresponding
operator is denoted by P, for parity. There, one can
perform an experiment with a given system and see
if the result is the same when one or more of the
three spatial coordinates of every particle in the system is reflected through the origin of the coordinate system. Since quantum mechanically the results
of experiments are not identical with each trial, one
really studies a statistical ensemble of experiments
under the operation of space reversal.

When one performs space reversal twice, one gets
back the original configuration (state), and one has
$P^2 = 1$. Most systems studied by physicists respect
space reversal symmetry; in effect, one cannot tell by
the reported outcome of experiments whether the
experimenter performed the studies straight or
looking at the apparatus in a mirror. Quantum mechanically, one has states with eigenvalues of the P
operator of ± 1, and a system prepared in one eigenstate will remain with the same eigenvalue (i.e., parity is conserved). This is an example of how a
symmetry of a system leads to a corresponding conserved quantity.

The weak interactions, those responsible, for example, for the beta decay of nuclei, do *not* respect
parity. For example, radioactive nuclei with their
spin angular momentum pointing in the $+z$ direction emit negative beta rays more often in the $-z$ direction than in the $+z$ direction. When such a

configuration is observed in a coordinate system reflected through the z direction, one sees beta rays
being emitted with the opposite pattern. This is because while the momentum vector changes sign in
the reflected system, the spin vector does not, as can
be easily seen by construction. Formally, the spin
vector is given by $\mathbf{r} \times \mathbf{p}$ (where $\mathbf{r}$ is the spatial coordinate and $\mathbf{p}$ is the momentum), and each element of
the cross-product changes sign so that the product
itself does not.

The study of time reversal symmetry, then, would
involve the comparison of processes with time running normally or reversed. However, we are not at
liberty to physically reverse the direction of time, so
it is best to think of viewing a process first normally
and then in a movie of the process with the movie
running backwards. Quantum mechanically, one
checks whether transition amplitudes, or certain
static properties, depend upon the direction of the
movie. A very good example is the possible electric
dipole moment of an elementary particle, for example, the neutron. Such a moment is a vector (pointing from the negative to the positive side of the
dipole), and this vector must be collinear with the
spin vector of the particle in question. Time reversal
will not affect the charges and hence leaves the
dipole moment direction unchanged. However, the
spin direction *will* reverse when $t \rightarrow -t : \mathbf{r} \times \mathbf{p} =
\mathbf{r} \times m \ (d\mathbf{r}/dt)$. Hence, a finite electric dipole mo-
ment for the neutron, or for any elementary parti-
cle, would be a signature of the violation of time
reversal symmetry. Direct studies of reaction rates,
comparing the forward with the reversed direction
(detailed balance), are also made. In spite of many
very precise studies, there is as yet no evidence for a
nonzero electric dipole moment for any elementary
particle. Many reactions have been studied for possible time asymmetries with only null results.

Of course, for a *macroscopic* system with many degrees of freedom, there is from common experience
a non-reversible arrow of time (i.e., the direction in
which the randomness or entropy of the system increases). Examples are the breaking of an egg or the
shuffling of a new deck of cards. A movie shown
backwards of these events is clearly distinguishable
from the original events. This is, however, only a result of the setting up of the (low entropy) initial conditions that are relatively improbable to reach in
typical interactions.

A third operator we need to consider is one that
changes particles to antiparticles, denoted by C.
Again, systems can be characterized by their symme-

try properties under *C*. Can one differentiate between particle systems and antiparticle systems? Do the two behave differently? Again the weak interactions are found to violate this symmetry. However, the combined symmetry of *CP*, where one reverses spatial coordinates and simultaneously changes particles to antiparticles, is found to be a good symmetry for the vast majority of processes in particle physics.

Interestingly, there is an important relationship among these three operators, *P, C,* and *T*. The relationship stems from the fact that in the marriage of special relativity and quantum mechanics, it is required that every particle have an antiparticle. A positively charged particle traveling between spacetime points *A* and *B,* separated by a space-like interval, can be looked at as a negatively charged antiparticle traveling between points *B* and *A,* simply by a change of reference frame. This key relationship between spacetime symmetry (*PT*) and particle-antiparticle symmetry (*C*) is known as the *CPT* theorem. This theorem, provable under very general conditions, states that the combined symmetry *CPT* is a good symmetry for *all* the interactions in nature.

What is known about these symmetries? *CPT* symmetry has been found to be valid to high precision wherever it has been tested. On the other hand, *CP* symmetry—and hence time reversal—has been established to be clearly violated. This violation of *CP* symmetry was discovered by Jim Cronin and Val Fitch in 1964. The violation is manifest in the quantum mechanical representation of the neutral long-lived kaon: $K_L \approx (1 + \varepsilon) | K^0 > + (1 - \varepsilon) | \overline{K^0} >$. There are two things to note about this state vector. First, we have a quantum mechanical state that is a mixture of a particle and its antiparticle. This results from the $K^0 \leftrightarrow \overline{K^0}$ interchange that occurs to second order in the weak interaction. Second, the mixture is an unequal one, containing more particle than antiparticle. This is because the transition $K^0 \to \overline{K^0}$ evidently occurs at a slightly higher rate than $\overline{K^0} \to K^0$. The difference is characterized by the parameter ε, having a magnitude of order 10^{-3}.

The unequal mixture in the eigenstate is a sign of *CP* violation, while the transition rate asymmetry above is manifest *T* violation. Indeed such a violation is very important for a presumably symmetric universe (15 billion years ago) to evolve to one today that has a large matter-antimatter asymmetry. What is the origin of this violation in the kaon system? Is this violation related to the one operating in the early universe? Will further *CP* violating phenomena be seen in the neutral kaon system? Will the analogous system of *B* mesons prove fruitful for *CP* violation studies? The current standard model predicts positive answers to the last two questions, and experiments that will be underway in the near future should shed much light on this fundamental and important symmetry of nature.

See also: ARROW OF TIME; *CPT* THEOREM; DECAY, BETA; ELECTRIC MOMENT; INTERACTION, WEAK; KAON; PARITY; QUANTUM MECHANICS; SPIN; SYMMETRY; SYSTEMS

Bibliography

DAVIES, P. C. W. *The Physics of Time Asymmetry* (University of California Press, Berkeley, 1977).

SACHS, R. G. *The Physics of Time Reversal* (University of Chicago Press, Chicago, 1987).

WINSTEIN, B., and WOLFENSTEIN, L. "The Search for Direct CP Violation." *Rev. Mod. Phys.* **65,** 1113–1147 (1993).

BRUCE WINSTEIN

TOKAMAK

The tokamak is the best developed magnetic plasma confinement system used for fusion research. The word "tokamak" (toke-a-mack) is a Russian acronym for toroidal (i.e., donut-shaped) magnetic chamber, which aptly describes the geometry of these machines. Up to 10 million watts of fusion power has been obtained in a tokamak from the nuclear fusion between the heavy isotopes of hydrogen D (deuterium) and T (tritium) into a 14-MeV neutron and a 3.5-MeV alpha particle.

The key feature of a tokamak is its strong toroidal magnetic field of typically $B_T = 50$ kG, created by a set of about twenty magnetic field coils encircling the plasma chamber. This toroidal field creates small gyro-orbits for the charged ions and electrons in the direction transverse to B_T, and also helps to reduce plasma instabilities. However, in a purely toroidal magnetic field these gyro-orbits would drift vertically due to the spatial gradient in B_T, and so would be lost almost immediately. A tokamak is created by adding a smaller "poloidal" magnetic field to the toroidal field in order to form a helical magnetic field topology, which causes these drifts to be alternately inward and outward from the plasma center. This poloidal field is generated by a toroidal plasma current induced in the plasma as the secondary of an ohmic heating transformer, the primary of which is wound vertically through the center of the torus. The net result is a magnetic bottle that should perfectly confine charged particle orbits at fusion plasma temperatures, at least in the absence of collisions or plasma instabilities.

The first tokamaks, such as the T-3, were built in Russia in the early 1960s. The T-3 had a major radius of $R = 1$ m, a toroidal field of $B_T = 25$ kG, a plasma current of $I = 100$ kA, and an ion temperature of $T = 0.3$ keV (3,000,000°C) created by ohmic heating. By the mid-1990s about 100 tokamaks of various sizes had been built worldwide, with major radii of up to $R = 3$ m, toroidal fields of up to $B_T = 100$ kG, and plasma currents of up to $I = 7$ MA. The largest tokamaks, such as the Tokamak Fusion Test Reactor (TFTR) in the United States, the Joint European Torus (JET) in Europe, and the Japanese JT-60 Upgrade, have created ion temperatures up to $T = 40$ keV using auxiliary plasma heating systems such as high-energy neutral beam injection and ion cyclotron resonance heating. This temperature is sufficient for fusion energy production at the typical tokamak plasma density of $n = 10^{20}$ m^{-3}, that is, about a factor of 10^8 lower than solid density.

The plasma physics of a tokamak involves the equilibrium, stability, and transport of a fully ionized gas confined in a helical magnetic geometry. There has been a steady convergence of experiment and theory toward the optimum radial profiles of temperature, density, and current density consistent with the highest possible stability and lowest transport.

The plasma equilibrium in a tokamak is readily maintained by a vertical magnetic field which, when crossed with the toroidal plasma current, produces a radially inward force that balances the outward expansion forces due to the plasma and magnetic pressures. The plasma position and shape can be controlled with external equilibrium magnetic field coils to an accuracy considerably better than 1 percent of the major radius.

The magnetohydrodynamic (MHD) stability of the tokamak plasma is less easy to control, since strong helical kink motions can be driven by the gradients in the plasma pressure and/or plasma current. However, both theory and experiment have shown that adequate MHD stability can be obtained when the safety factor $q(a) = (B_T/B_p) R/a \geq 3$ at the plasma edge, where B_p is the poloidal magnetic field, and a is the minor radius. For example, an MHD-stable tokamak can be made with a plasma current of $I = 3$ MA at a toroidal field of $B_T = 50$ kG with $R = 2.6$ m and $a = 1$ m (the parameters of TFTR). The MHD stability of tokamak plasmas also deteriorates as the plasma pressure increases, but reactor-relevant plasma pressures can be obtained with a volume-averaged ratio of plasma to magnetic pressure of up to $\beta = 3nT/[(B_T)^2/8\pi] \approx 0.1$.

Plasma energy transport is the most challenging area of tokamak physics to understand. Under quasi-steady conditions, the plasma energy confinement time is defined by $\tau_E = (3/2) nTV/P_{in}$, where n and T are the average density and temperature over the plasma volume V, and P_{in} is the total power input from ohmic or auxiliary plasma heating systems. The measured energy confinement time in large tokamaks is typically $\tau_E \approx 0.1$-1 s, which is about 10–100 times less than expected from calculations of collisional transport rates. This anomalous transport is almost certainly due to plasma turbulence driven by the large radial gradients of density and/or temperature. Recently nonlinear computer simulations of this turbulence based on Maxwell's equations and Newton's laws have successfully predicted the size and frequency range of the measured turbulence, and in some cases have come to within about a factor of two in calculating the plasma energy confinement time from first principles. However, predictions of τ_E scaling to fusion power reactors are generally made from empirical scaling laws and not from basic theory, as is the case for most systems with highly turbulent flow.

The next major scientific milestone in tokamak fusion research will be ignition, at which point the plasma temperature will be self-sustained by the internal heating from the 3.5-MeV alpha particles created by the DT reactions. Ignition will occur when the alpha particle heating rate, which is proportional to $n^2 T^2$ in the temperature range of interest, balances the plasma energy loss rate due to transport, that is, $nT\tau_E \geq 3$-7×10^{21} m^{-3}·keV·s. This fusion triple product is about a factor of 5–10 higher than obtained in present tokamaks, which have just begun to detect the effects of alpha particle heating in DT plasmas.

A practical fusion reactor will need several other plasma control and engineering technologies to be developed around an ignited plasma. These include large superconducting magnets to create a steady-state toroidal field, continuous plasma current drive techniques using electromagnetic waves or particle beams, a magnetic divertor to control the plasma-wall interactions, and a 1-m-thick solid blanket to extract the 14-MeV neutron energy and breed tritium fuel from lithium. Each of these systems is under development in one or more tokamaks around the world, and an international design effort to integrate many of these features into an engineering test reactor called the International Thermonuclear Experimental Reactor (ITER) is underway.

See also: FUSION; ISOTOPES; MAGNETOHYDRODYNAMICS; MAXWELL'S EQUATIONS; PLASMA; TRANSPORT PROPERTIES; TURBULENCE; TURBULENT FLOW

Bibliography

CONN, R. W.; CHUYANOV, V. A.; INOUE, N.; and SWEETMAN, D. R. "The International Thermonuclear Experimental Reactor." *Sci. Am.* **266** (4), 102–110 (1992).

CORDEY, J. G.; GOLDSTON, R. J.; and PARKER, R. R. "Progress Toward a Tokamak Fusion Reactor." *Phys. Today* **45** (1), 22–30 (1992).

SHEFFIELD, J. "The Physics of Magnetic Fusion Reactors." *Rev. Mod. Phys.* **66** (3), 1015–1103 (1994).

WESSON, J. *Tokamaks* (Clarendon, Oxford, 1987).

STEWART J. ZWEBEN

RONALD C. DAVIDSON

TORNADO

A tornado is a column of swirling air (a columnar vortex), in contact with the ground, that is produced by a convective cloud, almost always a thunderstorm. Descriptive terms associated with various regions within a tornado are shown in Fig. 1.

It is the funnel cloud that gives a tornado its characteristic appearance. This consists of a tapered column of water droplets extending down from cloud base; this condensation funnel is frequently mixed with and surrounded by shrouds of dust and debris raised from surface. All other things being equal, the more moist the air and the more intense the tornado, the larger the funnel cloud; in very dry conditions there may be no condensation funnel. The funnel cloud outlines the central portion of a tornado; its diameter is typically one-tenth or less than that of the swirling column of air in which it is embedded.

Based on estimated wind speeds, a tornado is usually placed in one of three categories.

- Weak (winds 17.8 to 50.3 $m \cdot s^{-1}$) tornadoes typically have a single, nonturbulent funnel cloud, frequently in the form of a long, narrow, inverted cone with a smooth surface; the condensation funnel often does not reach to the ground. Vertical wind velocities appear to be greatest along the central axis.
- Strong (winds 50.4 to 91.9 $m \cdot s^{-1}$) tornadoes usually have a broad columnar funnel cloud. The flow is generally turbulent, so the surface of the funnel will usually have a rolling, boiling appearance. Vertical wind velocities tend to be highest in

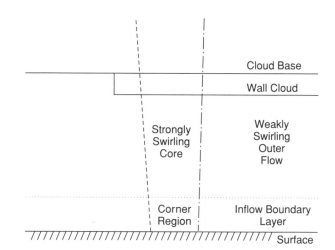

Figure 1 A schematic showing the major regions of a tornado. Just above the ground, air streams into a tornado's corner region from all directions through an inflow boundary layer a few tens of meters deep. In the corner region, this inflowing air turns to spiral upward within the strongly swirling core, a tall column usually no more than several hundred meters in diameter. The corner region is usually marked by a dust whirl or a debris fountain, where the erupting inflow carries aloft material ripped from the surface. Somewhere above cloud base, the core merges with the airflow in the generating thunderstorm. For most of its length, the core is surrounded by a weakly swirling outer flow which blends into the main updraft into the storm; this flow is in rough cyclostrophic balance so that radial motions are relatively small. Also depicted is the wall cloud, a local lowering of the cloud base that is often associated with a mesocyclone.

a cylindrical annulus around the central axis; along the axis they are reduced. Sometimes a suction vortex can be seen within the tornado core; this little-understood subsidiary feature appears to contain the highest wind speeds in the tornado.

- Violent (winds 92.0 to 142.5 $m \cdot s^{-1}$) tornadoes appear to have a central core containing a relatively calm, clear eye surrounded by an annulus of upward-spiraling air. In the eye, air motion is downward; nonswirling air from high in the thunderstorm descends in response to the low pressure present in the core near ground level. At the ground this inner flow turns outward and meets the primary inflow coming from outside the vortex core. The combined flow turns and swirls upward in a cylindrical sheath surrounding the central downflow. Two or more secondary vortices may form in this sheath. Air spirals upward, spinning rapidly about the helical axes of these vortices. Simultaneously, these secondary vortices are rotating about the center line of the tornado. When they are small, intense, and most apparent in the corner region, secondary vortices are also called suction vortices. It appears that winds greater than 135 $m \cdot s^{-1}$ can occur in the secondary vortices; these are the fastest known surface winds.

The current best estimates of wind speeds in tornadoes suggest that the maximum *possible* tangential speed occurs only 30 to 50 m above the ground and are in the range of 125 to 161 $m \cdot s^{-1}$, with some likelihood that the actual value is near the lower end of this range. Maximum vertical speeds in the core may be as high as 80 $m \cdot s^{-1}$, while maximum radial speeds in the inflow have been estimated to reach 50 $m \cdot s^{-1}$. These extreme values occur only rarely; in about 98 percent of tornadoes, speeds are considerably less than 90 $m \cdot s^{-1}$. When extreme speeds do occur, it is usually over a small portion of the tornado core and usually for only a short period of time. Also, since the nature of the airflow in tornadoes varies considerably with overall intensity, extremes in vertical speeds may not occur in conjunction with extremes in tangential speeds.

Some weak and almost all strong and violent tornadoes form near the interface between a storm's updraft and downdraft and so are perceived as being beneath the right-rear quadrant of the storm. Strong and violent tornadoes tend to be long lived and embedded within relatively large diameter circulations—mesocyclones—that extend to great heights within a parent thunderstorm.

Though exactly how it occurs is still being debated, it is through the interaction of a thunderstorm's updraft with the horizontal winds that rotation first appears in a storm and is then concentrated to form a strong or violent tornado. A strong, persistent updraft is necessary (to produce a concentration of vorticity and to prevent the tornado core from filling from above), but is not sufficient to insure the formation of a tornado. For this to occur, a proper vertical distribution of horizontal winds between surface and middle levels of the troposphere must be present. This distribution determines the amount of vorticity present in the air. Experience has shown that for the formation of tornadic thunderstorms, the wind's speed must increase and its direction must veer (usually from southeast to west in the Northern Hemisphere) with increasing height above surface.

A thunderstorm's updraft begins to rotate as it concentrates the vorticity contained in the quasihorizontal winds of the troposphere. Vorticity is present as the winds are almost always sheared vertically in both speed and direction. Vertical speed shear provides a source of rotation about a horizontal axis normal to the wind flow—crosswise vorticity. When air containing crosswise vorticity flows into an updraft, the vorticity is tilted into the vertical. For low-level winds coming from the south and increasing in speed with increasing height, the west flank of an updraft will develop clockwise rotation, the east flank will develop a counterclockwise rotation.

Vertical direction shear is another source of horizontal vorticity, now oriented in the same direction as the average wind flow—streamwise vorticity. When air with streamwise vorticity flows into an updraft, the vorticity is also tilted into the vertical. Low-level winds veering from southeast to southwest with increasing height produce counterclockwise rotation on the windward side of an updraft and clockwise rotation on the leeward side.

In reality, air drawn into an updraft contains both crosswise and streamwise vorticity. Observations of the evolution of tornado-producing storms have shown that both types of vorticity are important in the development of a rotating updraft. Updraft rotation—invariably counterclockwise in the Northern Hemisphere—appears to begin in the midtroposphere at altitudes of 4 to 8 km; tilting of crosswise vorticity appears to be the principal mechanism providing spin at the start. Later, as the updraft begins to rotate faster, tilting of streamwise vorticity becomes more important. Once the updraft rotation has begun, the spinning column of rising air, perhaps 10 to 20 km in diameter, is called a mesocyclone.

As spin-up proceeds, the local pressure field and the strongly curved wind field come into cyclostrophic balance; radial motions are suppressed. Cyclostrophic balance usually is established first at midlevels in the storm. There the mesocyclone begins to act as a dynamic pipe, with the airflow constrained by its own swirling motion. Whereas previously some air entered the updraft at midlevels, now almost all the air flowing along the mesocyclone's axis is drawn in through its lower end. Thus, by concentrating the inflow at its lower end, the dynamic pipe further intensifies the rotation there. This in turn extends the pipe downward as this now more rapidly rotating region itself comes into cyclostrophic balance. If the spin-up process continues, rotation builds down toward the ground through this mechanism.

As air parcels converge into the base of the pipe and are accelerated upward, they are stretched vertically. Stretching narrows the diameter of the mesocyclone to about 2 to 6 km, further increasing the speed of its winds as the angular momentum of the air is conserved. The result is a further intensification of the updraft and of the converging winds under the mesocyclone.

Tilting, convergence, vertical stretching and the dynamic-pipe effect can form a mesocyclone that extends from about one kilometer above the ground to near the top of the thunderstorm at about 15 km. Surface winds with speeds as high as 33 m·s^{-1} can blow over the region beneath the swirling column.

The generation of extreme surface winds comes in a second step: the formation of the swirling core. For reasons not yet understood, a region of enhanced convergence and stretching, probably no more than one kilometer in diameter, develops inside the mesocyclone, usually toward the side where the updraft interfaces with the thunderstorm's downdraft. Observations again suggest that intensification of spin begins aloft, at an altitude of several kilometers, then quickly builds down toward the ground. Over such a small area, rotational motion is strong enough for a smaller dynamic pipe to reach the ground.

Near the ground, friction prevents establishment of cyclostrophic balance. Responding to the steep pressure gradient between the core and the surrounding atmosphere, air streams rapidly inward through a thin layer near the ground. The inflow a few meters above the ground partially conserves its angular momentum and so picks up tangential speed as it approaches the center of the core before turning sharply to spiral upward. Because friction with the ground ultimately limits the rate of airflow into the base, it prevents the tornado's low-pressure core from filling from below.

In the Northern Hemisphere, winds in a tornado almost always swirl counterclockwise. This occurs because the parent thunderstorm is invariably embedded within a synoptic-scale weather system that establishes the speed and direction shear in the winds across the troposphere. The structure of the synoptic-scale weather system is in turn mostly determined by the direction of Earth's rotation; the resulting speed and direction shear strongly favors the formation of counterclockwise rotation in mesocyclones and tornadoes.

See also: HURRICANE; VORTEX

Bibliography

CHURCH, C. R.; BURGESS, D.; DOSWELL, C.; and DAVIES-JONES, R. P., eds. "The Tornado: Its Structure, Dynamics, Prediction, and Hazards." *Geophysical Monograph 79* (American Geophysical Union, Washington, DC, 1993).

JOHN T. SNOW

TORRICELLI'S THEOREM

Torricelli considered the outflow of water from a small hole in a container a depth h below the water surface. He argued that the speed of the water is given by

$$v = \sqrt{2gh},$$

where g is the acceleration of gravity. If the hole is made so that the outflow goes straight up, the water rises outside to the same level as the water in the container, except for a small difference ascribed to resistance from the air. Torricelli applied Galileo's results for the trajectories of solid objects to the water. This leads directly to the theorem. The facts that the pressure at the hole depends directly on the depth and that the expelling force is the same for any direction are needed in this argument. Torricelli established these earlier in establishing the basis for his invention of the barometer. The pressure-depth dependence has many applications. It limits the depth to which divers can go, since a diver must either be protected by a strong shell, like a submarine, or supplied air at a high pressure to compensate. The latter causes excess air to dissolve in the blood, with the potential for hazardous results.

With the same assumptions as Torricelli (that the fluid is incompressible and that frictional effects are negligible), the theorem can be shown to follow directly from the conservation of energy (established much later). If a small mass Δm passes through the hole, the increase in kinetic energy is $(1/2)\Delta m v^2$. The fluid in the container moves in such a way that the change is equivalent to removing a mass Δm from its top, and the resulting change in gravitational potential energy is $-\Delta mgh$. The total change in energy is the sum of these terms; conservation requires it to be zero, which produces Torricelli's result. The kinetic energy changes of the rest of the fluid can be neglected, since those speeds are small and the contributions from their squares are negligible.

It is easy to demonstrate the features of Torricelli's studies by punching holes in the side of a can and then filling it with water. Cans that contain stationary liquids and fail (for example from rust) burst at the bottom. This is another example of the effect of the pressure-depth relation.

See also: BERNOULLI'S PRINCIPLE; ENERGY, CONSERVATION OF; ENERGY, KINETIC; ENERGY, POTENTIAL; PRESSURE

Bibliography

OHANION, H. C. *Physics*, 2nd ed. (W. W. Norton, New York, 1989)

BRENTON F. STEARNS

TRAJECTORY

A trajectory is the path in space of a body, moving under the action of given forces, that has definite starting and ending points. If this path is closed and repetitive, it is called an orbit. More precisely, a trajectory is the solution to the following system of equations:

$$\dot{y}_1 = f_1(y_1, y_2, \ldots, y_n, t)$$
$$\dot{y}_2 = f_2(y_1, y_2, \ldots, y_n, t)$$
$$\vdots$$
$$\dot{y}_n = f_n(y_1, y_2, \ldots, y_n, t),$$

where time t is the independent variable, and the dependent variables $y_1, y_2, \ldots, y_n$ are position coordinates. The dots denote differentiation with respect to t. For a two-dimensional system, the trajectories are nonintersecting circles.

Historically, trajectory has pertained to trajection, which signifies passage or transmission through any medium or space; it evolved to its current meaning through studies of the motion of stars, comets, and planets. Johannes Kepler organized the existing data and determined the trajectories of planets to be ellipses, with the Sun at one focus. Isaac Newton, using calculus, formulated the universal law of gravitation, which acts equally on all objects and allowed him to determine the trajectories of comets and planets with greater accuracy.

Examples

When objects, such as basketballs and horseshoes, are thrown or when bullets are discharged from a gun with an initial velocity having a horizontal component, they continue their motion essentially under the influence of gravity and their trajectories are parabolic. Such objects are called projectiles.

Halley's comet, an example of a recurring comet, reappeared near the earth in 1986. Its trajectory, recomputed backward over twenty-two centuries, is an elongated ellipse with an eccentricity close to unity. Halley's comet has an irregular period of appearance varying between 74.4 and 79.6 years.

Objects in parabolic or hyperbolic trajectories, such as meteors and atomic-particle tracks in cloud chambers, occur once and never return. However, if a satellite at a given perigee has its velocity increased, its elliptical trajectory will become parabolic when the eccentricity reaches unity. The velocity required to place an object in a parabolic trajectory is called the escape velocity, which is approximately $\sqrt{2}$ times the circular velocity. Actual escape trajectories are hyperbolic curves, which are produced by any velocity greater than that for parabolic trajectories, and are generally complicated to compute.

Applications

Consider the travel of a spacecraft from Earth to Mars with the objective of using the least propellant possible. When the spacecraft is launched from Earth, it is already in orbit. The path of the spacecraft from Earth to Mars is called its trajectory. To land on the surface of Mars, the spacecraft must enter the interplanetary trajectory at such a time that it will intercept the orbit of Mars on arrival there.

Each constituent of the atom is characterized by its trajectory through matter. Silicon-microstrip detectors were invented to detect and study particles containing the charm quark. After its birth at the primary vertex in high-energy collision, a charmed particle will, depending on its energy and type, travel a few millimeters before decaying at the secondary vertex into several other particles. These vertices are determined by tracking the trajectories of the resultant particles from the collision using detectors whose recorded tracks are extrapolated back to the vicinity of the primary vertex. Trajectories are also important in accelerators such as synchrotrons, which maintain protons in a nearly circular trajectory using magnetic fields.

See also: APOGEE AND PERIGEE; GRAVITATIONAL ASSIST; GRAVITATIONAL FORCE LAW; KEPLER'S LAWS; NEWTON'S LAWS

Bibliography

BENDER, C. M., and ORSZAG, S. A. *Advanced Mathematical Methods for Scientists and Engineers* (McGraw-Hill, New York, 1978).

LITKE, A. M., and SCHWARZ, A. S. "The Silicon Microstrip Detector." *Sci. Am.* **272** (5), 76–81 (1995).

ALFRED Z. MSEZANE

JULIAN C. NILES

TRANSDUCER

Transducers are energy transformers. Transducing properties of materials are described thermodynamically by their equations of state as functions of stress T and strain S; electric E, displacement D, magnetic H, and induction B fields; temperature Θ; and entropy σ. Changes in these eight thermodynamic variables produced by mechanical, electric, magnetic, and thermal field effects cross couple to give rise to four types of transducing phenomena:

1. piezoelectric [PZE], piezomagnetic [PZM], and piezocaloric [PZC] coupling effects from variations in the applied mechanical field $(T \mid S)$;
2. electrostriction [ES], electro-magnetic [EM], and electrocaloric [EC] coupling effects from variations in the applied electric field $(E \mid D)$;
3. magnetostriction [MS], magnetoelectric [ME], and magnetocaloric [MC] coupling effects from variations in the applied magnetic field $(H \mid B)$; and
4. pyrostriction [PYS], pyroelectric [PYE], and pyromagnetic [PYM] coupling effects from variations in the applied thermal field $(\Theta \mid$ energy content$)$.

Brackets denote the effects or corresponding coefficients of response. The vertical bar indicates alternative choices. [ES] often, but not always, refers solely to that part of the converse [PZE] $\equiv$ [CPZE] that is proportional to the square of the electric field strength. Similar notation is also used for [MS] and [PYS]. Table 1 summarizes these transducing phenomena. The direct mechanical, electric, magnetic, and thermal responses are positioned along the main diagonal of this schematic 8 × 8 matrix representation of these equations of state with the transducing response coefficients displayed as the off-diagonal matrix elements. In terms of components, the matrix would be 13 × 13 because $(T \mid S)$ has six independent components while $(E \mid D)$ and $(H \mid B)$ are each three-component vectors.

Equations of state using Table 1 give the differential effect dX_i (first column) due to differential changes in the independent thermodynamic variables dW_j (first row) in terms of the response coefficients V_{ij} (remaining 4 × 4 matrix): $dX_i = \sum V_{ij} dW_j$. This leads to the following equations:

$$d(T \mid S) = [\text{Mechanical}]\, d(S \mid T) + [\text{ES}]\, d(D \mid E) \\ + [\text{MS}]\, d(B \mid H) + [\text{PYS}]\, d(\sigma \mid \Theta) \quad (1)$$

$$d(E \mid D) = [\text{PZE}]\, d(S \mid T) + [\text{Electric}]\, d(D \mid E) \\ + [\text{ME}]\, d(B \mid H) + [\text{PYE}]\, d(\sigma \mid \Theta) \quad (2)$$

Table 1 Transducing Phenomena

dX_i Effect ＼ dW_j Cause	Applied mechanical energy S T	Applied electric energy D E	Applied magnetic energy B H	Applied thermal energy σ Θ
T S	[Mechanical]	[CPZE] (ES)	[CPZM] (MS)	[CPZC] (PYS)
E D	[PZE]	[Electric]	[ME]	[PYE]
H B	[PZM]	[EM]	[Magnetic]	[PYM]
Θ σ	[PZC]	[EC]	[MC]	[Thermal]

$$d(H|B) = [\text{PZM}]\, d(S|T) + [\text{EM}]\, d(D|E)$$
$$+ [\text{Magnetic}]\, d(B|H)$$
$$+ [\text{PYM}]\, d(\sigma|\Theta) \tag{3}$$

$$d(\Theta|\sigma) = [\text{PZC}]\, d(S|T) + [\text{EC}]\, d(D|E)$$
$$+ [\text{MC}]\, d(B|H)$$
$$+ [\text{Thermal}]\, d(\sigma|\Theta). \tag{4}$$

Generally, one of each W_j pair is experimentally controlled. The differential of the appropriate thermodynamic-function (potential) density, whose second derivatives are V_{ij}, is given in terms of the imposed dW_j. For example, with T, D, B, and Θ as the independent (controllable) variables, the differential of the elastic Gibbs function, G_1, $[U - T_\alpha S_\alpha - \Theta_\sigma]$ is

$$dG_1 = -S_\alpha dT_\alpha + E_i dD_i + H_i dB_i - \sigma d\Theta. \tag{5}$$

The piezoelectric coefficient $g_{m\alpha}$ is given by the appropriate mixed second derivative of G_1:

$$\frac{\partial^2 G_1}{\partial T_\alpha \partial Dm} = \frac{\partial E_m}{\partial T_\alpha} = -g_{m\alpha}. \tag{6}$$

The derivative indicated is taken under isothermal conditions. As mixed second derivatives, the coefficients of transducing effects obey Maxwell relations. For the piezoelectric coefficient,

$$\frac{\partial E_m}{\partial T_\alpha} = -\frac{\partial S_\alpha}{\partial D_m}. \tag{7}$$

The relevant equations of state are not restricted to linear phenomena because the coefficients of response (e.g., piezoelectric tensor) are a function of the fields. Expanding these coefficients in powers of the appropriate dV_i easily leads to nonlinear expressions for the dW_j.

So-called smart materials, which are composites with large response coefficients, have been developed. Different schemes have been devised to enhance the transducing response by, for example, combining materials so that the resulting behavior is a function of the properties of different materials.

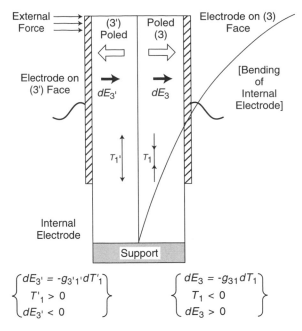

$$\left\{ \begin{array}{l} dE_{3'} = -g_{3'1'}dT'_1 \\ T'_1 > 0 \\ dE_{3'} < 0 \end{array} \right\} \qquad \left\{ \begin{array}{l} dE_3 = -g_{31}dT_1 \\ T_1 < 0 \\ dE_3 > 0 \end{array} \right\}$$

Figure 1 Accelerometer from piezoelectric lead-zirconate-titanate [$PbO - (Zr_xTi_{1-x})O_2$]. Bimorph bender beam picks up (dT, dT') at (3,3') faces. It should be noted that $dE_{3'}$ and dE_3 add in the (3) direction when bending in the (3) direction. Similarly, $dE_{3'}$ and dE_3 add in the (3') direction when bending in the (3') direction.

The design of the bimorph bender beam accelerometer in Fig. 1 is an example of the application of transducers. In this case, stress arises from the acceleration of the vehicle carrying the accelerometer, and, via the piezoelectric effect, is transduced to an electric field (voltage). If the material is a piezoceramic lead-zirconate-titanate (PZT), the polarization is along the ($z \equiv 3$) axis (by convention). A bimorph bender beam can be configured in such a way as to measure only the change in the stress component $T_1 \equiv T_{xx}$ by sensing the change in the electric field component E_3.

This example illustrates that transducing materials are selected to respond to a particular applied field. Smart materials and transducing devices are designed to reject all unwanted effects from other fields that might generate direct and/or transducing responses. The unwanted effects are reduced by such methods as chemical treatments, design geometry, signal processing, and system modeling.

See also: PIEZOELECTRIC EFFECT; MAGNETOSTRICTION

Bibliography

CADY, W. G. *Piezoelectricity,* rev. ed. (Dover, New York, 1964).

LANDAU, L. D., and LIFSCHITZ, E. M. *Electrodynamics of Continuous Media* (Pergamon, New York, 1960).

LINES, M. L., and GLASS, A. M. *Principles and Applications of Ferroelectrics and Related Materials* (Clarendon, Oxford, Eng., 1977).

MASON, W. P. *Piezoelectric Crystals and Their Applications to Ultrasonics* (Van Nostrand, Princeton, NJ, 1960).

ROSEN, C. Z.; HIREMATH, B. V.; and NEWNHAM, R., eds. *Piezoelectricity: Key Papers in Physics* (American Institute of Physics, New York, 1992).

CAROL ZWICK ROSEN

TRANSFORMER

Transformers are electrical control devices that increase or decrease voltage or current in alternating-current (ac) circuits. They are used to transfer energy between ac circuits operating at different voltages. Few electrical devices are without a transformer of some type.

The basic operating principle of the transformer is electromagnetic induction, which was first demonstrated by Michael Faraday in 1831. Faraday discovered that changing electric fields could generate changing magnetic fields that in turn induced electric fields and therefore current in any closed loop. Described in Faraday's time as the induction coil, the transformer stirred the imagination of the inventors and engineers of the time. The first book in the English language on transformers, *The Alternate Current Transformer in Theory and Practice* (1889), was written by John A. Fleming.

The simplest transformer (shown in Fig. 1) consists of at least one primary winding and one secondary winding of insulated wire on a common core. No electrical connection exists between these two circuits. The primary (or input) coil has N_1 turns of wire and is attached to a source of alternating voltage, V_1. The secondary (or output) coil has N_2 turns of wire and is connected, when the switch is closed, to an impedance, Z_2. The factor by which the voltage or current is changed between the coils depends on the ratio N_1/N_2.

Faraday's laws of electromagnetic induction suggest that the voltage induced in a coil depends on the total flux of magnetic field lines through the coil, which is a function of the number of turns of wire making up the coil. So $N_1/N_2 = V_1/V_2$. If N_2 is less than N_1, V_2 will be less than V_1 and the device is known as a step-down transformer. A step-up transformer has more turns of wire on the secondary coil.

In the ideal case, the coils have zero resistance and all the power supplied to the primary coil is transferred to the secondary coil. That is, the ideal transformer conserves energy perfectly. Real transformers have efficiencies that are generally in excess of 90 percent. Losses are due to ohmic resistance in the coils, eddy current induction, and hysteresis of the magnetic core material, caused by the changing polarity of the applied current. Since the ideal transformer transfers power perfectly, it is possible to predict the ideal current ratios of the two coils. Power (P) is the product of current (I) and voltage (V):

$$P_1 = P_2$$

$$V_1 \times I_1 = V_2 \times I_2.$$

Therefore, $V_1/V_2 = I_2/I_1$, and a step-down transformer increases current in the secondary coil.

Transformers used in electronics are classified by application. The most common examples are power transformers, audio transformers, and pulse transformers.

Power transformers change input voltage and current levels to meet the requirements of the circuit. Examples of these are generator transformers (a step-up transformer that transfers power supplied by an alternator to a higher voltage network), transmission transformers (step-down transformers that reduce voltage to levels more convenient to local usage), and distribution transformers (a final transformer that steps down voltage to the level required by the consumer).

Audio transformers, while similar to power transformers, are useful over a wider frequency range. These can act as impedance matching and coupling devices or perform filtering.

Pulse transformers are miniature transformers that are used for timing or triggering and are usually made for printed circuit boards. The core of a transformer is usually made of magnetically soft material, such as silicon steel, which is fabricated to minimize magnetic hysteresis. Transformers for high frequency-application sometimes do not use a ferro-

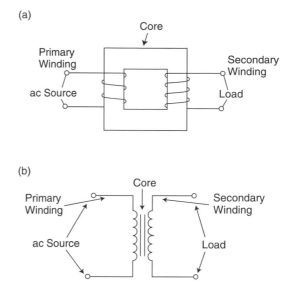

Figure 1 (a) Schematic diagram of an iron core transformer. (b) Circuit symbol of an iron core transformer.

magnetic core but an air core with concentric windings of the primary and secondary coils.

See also: CIRCUIT, AC; CURRENT, ALTERNATING; ELECTRICAL RESISTANCE; ELECTROMAGNETIC INDUCTION; ELECTROMAGNETIC INDUCTION, FARADAY'S LAW OF; FARADAY, MICHAEL; FARADAY EFFECT; FERROMAGNETISM; FIELD, MAGNETIC; HYSTERESIS; MAGNETIC FLUX; RESISTOR

Bibliography

FLANAGAN, W. M. *Handbook of Transformer Design and Applications,* 2nd ed. (McGraw-Hill, New York, 1993).

GROSSNER, N. R. *Transformers for Electric Circuits.* 2nd ed. (McGraw-Hill, New York, 1983).

PATRICK, D. R., and FARDO, S. N. *Electricity and Electronics: A Survey,* 2nd ed. (Prentice Hall, Englewood Cliffs, N.J., 1990).

GRACE A. BANKS

TRANSISTOR

Transistors were discovered by John Bardeen, Walter Brattain, and William Shockley in 1948 as a new device for amplifying electric signals. The name is derived from the phrase "transfer of signals through varistor." Transistors have all but replaced vacuum tubes for electric signal generation and processing (except in the domain of very high frequencies).

Transistors are three-terminal solid-state electronic devices fabricated from semiconducting material; they function essentially as controlled current sources in which the electrical current between two of the electrode terminals is determined, or controlled, by a current or voltage applied to the third electrode terminal. Transistors are active devices in that they exhibit power gain, and as such, can be used to amplify signals in amplifier circuits and can be operated as electrically controlled switches in digital logic circuits. Modern semiconductor fabrication technology allows transistors to be made extremely small and complete circuits containing thousands (and even millions) of transistors can be fashioned on a single piece of semiconductor material (usually silicon), producing an integrated circuit. Integrated circuits are widely used in most electronic systems: computers, stereo amplifiers, video recorders, and portable telephones, to name a few.

Transistors can be divided into two fundamental types: bipolar junction transistors (BJT), and field-effect transistors (FET). Field-effect transistors are further classified according to their structure: metal-oxide-semiconductor field-effect transistors (MOSFET) and junction field-effect transistors (JFET).

Bipolar Junction Transistors

A bipolar junction transistor is formed with two semiconductor pn junctions in close proximity. Currents in the device arise from both electrons (which carry a negative charge) and holes (which carry a positive charge), the term "bipolar" referring to current carriers of two polarities. Figure 1 depicts an NPN transistor structure in which the base region, consisting of a thin layer of p-type semiconductor material, is sandwiched between two n-type semiconductor regions, one the emitter and the other the collector; a complementary PNP structure also exists, consisting of an n-type base region sandwiched between two p-type regions. Electrical contact is made to the base, emitter and collector regions, and

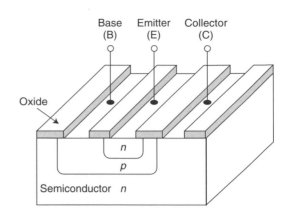

Figure 1 NPN bipolar junction transistor structure.

external voltages applied to these terminals controls the currents in the device.

Under normal operation the emitter-base junction is forward biased and the collector-base junction is reversed biased; for an NPN transistor (Fig. 2) the base-emitter voltage (V_{be}) is positive and the base-collector voltage (V_{bc}) is negative. For an NPN transistor with these bias voltages, electrons from the n-type emitter region are injected across the forward-biased emitter-base junction into the p-type base region; at the same time, holes are injected from the base region across the junction into the emitter region. The current resulting from both the injected electrons and holes that cross the emitter-base junction constitutes the emitter current (I_e) of the device and flows out of the emitter terminal. Normally, the concentration of impurity atoms used to form the emitter is made much higher than that used to form the base. This results in the injected hole current in the emitter being much smaller than the injected electron current. The emitter current is due mostly, then, to the injected electrons. Most of the electrons that are injected into the base from the emitter diffuse across the base to the collector-base junction, where, due to the reverse bias on this junction, are swept into the collector region, giving rise to a current in the collector (I_c) which flows into the collector terminal. This current, originating in the emitter, is thus controlled predominately by the emitter-base junction voltage and accounts for this structure being an active (transistor) device. The collector current as a function of base-emitter voltage is given by

$$I_c = I_s(e^{V_{be}/V_T} - 1),$$

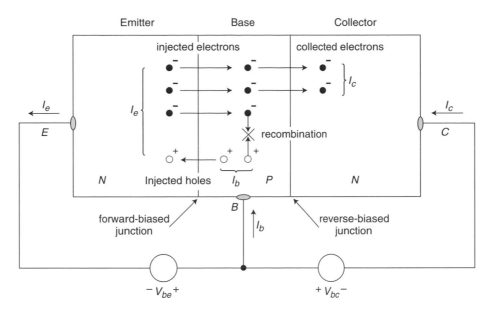

Figure 2 Components of current in an NPN BJT.

where I_S is the reverse saturation current (typically 10^{-12} to 10^{-17} A in value) and V_T is the thermal voltage (0.026 V at room temperature, 300 K). The collector current is seen to vary exponentially with base-emitter voltage.

Some of the injected electrons in transiting the base are lost to recombination with holes (of which there are many in this p-type region) and do not reach the collector, nor contribute to the collector current. The holes that support this recombination, as well as the holes that are injected into the emitter, are supplied by the base current (I_b), which flows into the base terminal. The base current is related to the collector current as

$$I_c = \beta I_b,$$

where β is the common-emitter current gain whose value is determined by the dimensions of the structure, the n- and p-type impurity doping concentrations, and properties of the semiconductor material; values for β typically range from about 50 to 200. Alternately, the collector current can be related to the emitter current as

$$I_c = \alpha I_e,$$

where α is the common-base current gain and is

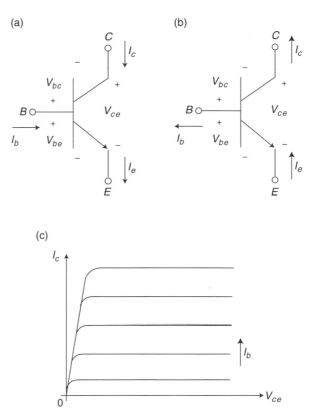

Figure 3 (a) Circuit symbol for NPN transistor. (b) Circuit symbol for PNP transistor. (c) Collector current characteristics.

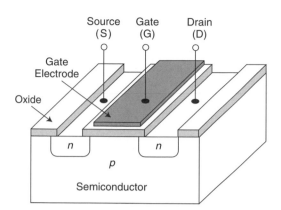

Figure 4 Structure of an *n*-channel MOSFET.

related to β as

$$\alpha = \frac{\beta}{\beta + 1}$$

and ranges in value from about 0.98 to 0.995.

The circuit symbols for NPN and PNP bipolar transistors are shown in Figs. 3a and 3b, respectively. For normal operation with the base-emitter junction forward biased and the base-collector junction reverse biased, V_{be} (which is approximately 0.7 V for a silicon transistor) is positive for an NPN and negative for a PNP, V_{bc} is negative for an NPN and positive for a PNP; with these biases, the currents flow in the directions depicted in the figure. Figure 3c depicts the output characteristics for the transistor.

Shown is the collector current I_c versus the collector-emitter voltage V_{ce} for various values of the input current (base current I_b); V_{ce} is positive for an NPN and negative for a PNP.

Field-Effect Transistors

Field-effect transistors represent a class of devices whose operation results from the modulation of a conducting channel by a voltage applied to a gate control electrode. Unlike the bipolar transistor where current transport involves carriers of both polarities, current transport in FET devices are by carriers of one polarity only, hence they are termed unipolar devices.

Metal-Oxide-Semiconductor Field-Effect Transistors

Figure 4 depicts an *n*-channel MOSFET structure in which the gate control electrode is physically separated from the rest of the structure by a thin insulating dielectric layer (normally SiO_2). A channel region in the *p*-type semiconductor is formed between two *n*-type regions that define the source and drain; a complementary *p*-channel structure also exists consisting of *p*-type source and drain regions surrounding an *n*-type channel region. Electrical contact is made to the source, drain, and gate regions and external voltages applied to these terminals controls the current in the channel region of the device.

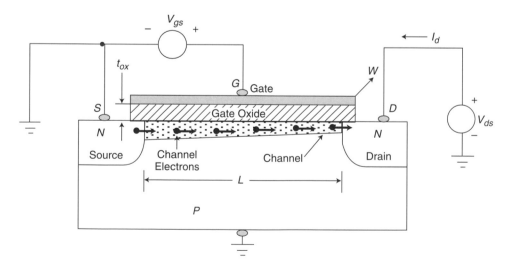

Figure 5 Current transport in the active region of an *n*-channel MOSFET

Figure 5 illustrates the active region of an n-channel MOSFET with normal biases applied: the gate-source voltage V_{gs} and the drain-source voltage V_{ds} are both positive (negative for a p-channel device). With a positive voltage applied to the gate, negative charge (electrons) is induced in the top surface of the p-type semiconductor beneath the gate by the capacitor structure comprising the gate, oxide, and semiconductor. This negative charge creates an n-type conducting channel between the source and drain (hence the term n-channel device). The gate voltage required to create the conducting channel is termed the threshold voltage V_{TH}; for V_{gs} less than V_{TH}, no conducting channel exists and the device is turned off. For V_{gs} greater than V_{TH} a complete n-type conducting path exists between the source and drain, and positive voltage applied to the drain produces an electron current from the source, through the channel, to the drain creating a positive drain current which enters the drain terminal. Since the gate electrode is insulated from the channel region there is no gate current. The drain current as a function of the gate-source and drain-source voltages is described as follows.

For $V_{ds} < V_{gs} - V_{TH}$ the transistor is operating in the triode region with

$$I_d = K \frac{W}{L}\left[(V_{gs} - V_{TH})V_{ds} - \tfrac{1}{2}V_{ds}^2\right].$$

For $V_{ds} \geq V_{gs} - V_{TH}$ the transistor is operating in the saturation region with

$$I_d = \frac{K}{2}\frac{W}{L}(V_{gs} - V_{TH})^2,$$

where K is a parameter dependent upon the gate oxide thickness (t_{ox}) and the mobility of the carriers in the channel. W is the width of the channel and L its length. These characteristics along with the circuit symbols for n-channel and p-channel MOSFETs are illustrated in Fig. 6. Shown is the drain current as a function of drain-source voltage for various values of gate-source voltage. The dashed curve denotes the boundary between the triode and saturation regions of operation. Notice that in the saturation region the drain current is independent of the drain voltage and depends only upon the gate voltage.

Junction Field-Effect Transistors

Figure 7 depicts an n-channel junction field-effect transistor structure in which a p-type semiconductor region forms the gate-control electrode. The gate forms a pn junction with the underlying n-type semiconductor. Under normal operation this junction is reverse biased, the value of which controls the con-

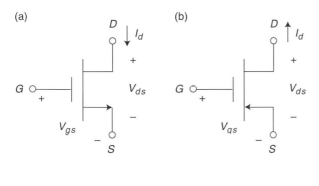

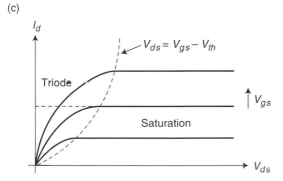

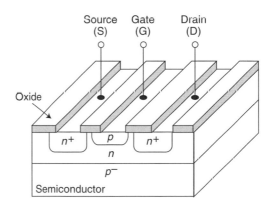

Figure 6   (a) Circuit symbol for an n-channel MOSFET. (b) Circuit symbol for a p-channel MOSFET. (c) Drain current characteristics.

Figure 7   Structure of an n-channel junction field-effect transistor.

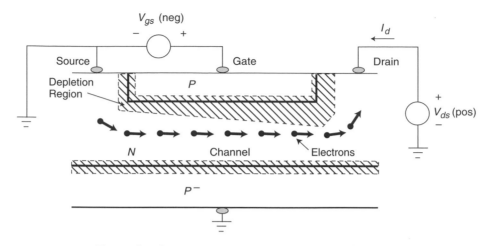

Figure 8 Current transport in an *n*-channel JFET.

duction in the *n*-type channel region beneath the gate. Heavily doped *n*-type semiconductor regions (n^+) form the source and drain of the device; a complementary *p*-channel structure also exists, consisting of an *n*-type semiconductor for the gate, *p*-type semiconductor for the source, drain and channel regions, and an underlying *n*-type semiconductor substrate.

Figure 8 illustrates the active region of the *n*-channel JFET with normal biases applied. The thickness of the depletion region surrounding the gate-channel *pn* junction is determined by the voltage across the junction, it being a function of the gate-source voltage (V_{gs}) and the drain-source voltage (V_{ds}). V_{gs} is normally negative and V_{ds} is positive, resulting in a reverse-biased gate junction. Increases in the reverse bias of the gate junction results in an increase in the thickness of the depletion region and a consequent decrease in the thickness of the undepleted portion of the conducting channel; this

results in an increase in the resistance of the channel between source and drain. The electron current in the channel is thereby reduced and is reflected as a decrease in the external drain current entering the drain terminal. In this mode of operation there is virtually no gate current owing to the reverse bias on the gate junction.

The drain current as a function of gate-source and drain-source voltages is described approximately as follows.

For $V_{ds} < V_{gs} - V_P$ the transistor is operating in the triode region with

$$I_d = I_{DSS}\left[2\left(1 - \frac{V_{gs}}{V_P}\right)\left(\frac{-V_{ds}}{V_P}\right) - \left(\frac{-V_{ds}}{V_P}\right)^2\right]$$

For $V_{ds} \geq V_{gs} - V_P$ the transistor is operating in the saturation region with

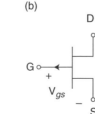

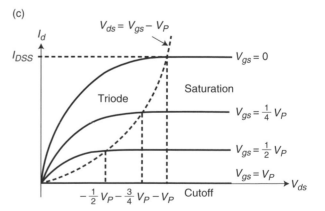

Figure 9 (a) Circuit symbol for an *n*-channel JFET. (b) Circuit symbol for a *p*-channel JFET. (c) Drain current characteristics.

$$I_d = I_{DSS}\left(1 - \frac{V_{gs}}{V_P}\right)^2,$$

where I_{DSS} is a parameter representing the maximum drain current that occurs for $V_{gs} = 0$. The pinch-off voltage parameter V_P, is the value of gate junction bias that completely depletes the channel region beneath the gate. V_P is negative for an n-channel device and positive for a p-channel device; for a reverse-bias gate-source voltage larger in magnitude than V_P no conducting channel exists and the device is cutoff with no current. These characteristics along with the circuit symbols for n-channel and p-channel JFETs are illustrated in Fig. 9. Shown is the drain current as a function of drain-source voltage for various values of gate-source voltage, illustrated as fractions of the pinch-off voltage. The boundary between the triode and saturation regions occurs at $V_{ds} = V_{gs} - V_P$. For normal operation with a p-channel JFET, V_{gs} is positive, V_{ds} is negative and drain current flows out of the drain terminal.

See also: CIRCUIT, INTEGRATED; SEMICONDUCTOR; TRANSISTOR, DISCOVERY OF

Bibliography

FERENDECI, A. M. *Physical Foundations of Solid-State and Electron Devices* (McGraw-Hill, New York, 1991).

MULLER, R. S., and KAMINS, T. I. *Device Electronics for Integrated Circuits*, 2nd ed. (Wiley, New York, 1986).

SZE, S. M. *Semiconductor Devices: Physics and Technology* (Wiley, New York, 1985).

ZAMBUTO, M. *Semiconductor Devices* (McGraw-Hill, New York, 1989).

EDWIN W. GREENEICH

TRANSISTOR, DISCOVERY OF

The transistor is a semiconductor device whose principal function is to amplify signals in electronic circuits. There have been several distinctly different types—the first being the point-contact transistor invented in December 1947 by John Bardeen and Walter Brattain at Bell Telephone Laboratories in Murray Hill, New Jersey. Soon thereafter, William Shockley developed the junction transistor, which began to be manufactured extensively in the 1950s and served as the amplifier in transistor radios. More recently, the field-effect transistor has become commonplace as one of the major components of microchips.

Before the transistor was developed, vacuum tubes were essentially the only devices used to amplify electrical signals. But they are bulky, fragile, and often burn out, while their red-hot filaments waste power generating heat that has to be removed if they are to continue functioning. Recognizing these severe limitations, Bell Labs scientists began seeking alternative solid-state amplifiers based on semiconductor materials in the 1930s. Shockley came to the Labs in 1936 expressly to work on solid-state research. He proposed two amplifier designs and—with Brattain's help—tried to fabricate a prototype in early 1940, but it failed miserably, for reasons he did not comprehend at the time.

The wartime development of radar and microwave equipment led to a vast improvement in the understanding of semiconductors—as well as much purer samples of silicon and germanium that could be carefully doped with tiny impurities to achieve carefully controlled electrical characteristics. Returning from his wartime work, Shockley headed a new solid-state physics group at Bell Labs. In April 1945 he worked up a design for a field-effect transistor, in which an electrical field applied to a semiconductor was intended to stimulate an increase in the density of negative charge carriers (i.e., quasi-free electrons) inside, thereby promoting the flow of greater electrical current through the device. But actual devices based on his design failed to have the desired amplification.

Later that year, Bardeen joined Bell Labs and began to examine why the field-effect device did not work as intended. In March 1946 he proposed his surface state theory, in which electrons drawn to the semiconductor surface by the electrical field became trapped there, shielding its interior from the field's influence. Thus began a research program into the nature of these states that would occupy Bardeen and Brattain for almost two years and ultimately lead to the invention of the transistor.

In November 1947 Brattain discovered he could neutralize the effects of the surface states by immersing the semiconductor in an electrolyte. Stimulated by this breakthrough, Bardeen proposed a design for a semiconductor amplifier in which one of two electrodes was a sharply pointed wire impinging on the surface of a silicon semiconductor. Working together over the next few weeks, the two men substituted germanium for silicon and employed two closely spaced point contacts instead of one. On December 16, 1947, they achieved significant power gains at a signal frequency of 1,000 Hz. The point-contact transistor had been born. A week later they demonstrated the revolutionary new device to Bell Labs executives, who listened with earphones to voices amplified by a circuit that incorporated the transistor as the only amplifying element.

With his deep physical intuition, Bardeen provided an explanation of what was happening inside the shiny germanium surface. Positively charged holes—quantum-mechanical entities that correspond to vacancies in a sea of electrons—were emitted into the surface layer at one of the two point contacts. A fair fraction of these holes reached the vicinity of the other contact, where the consequent increase in the density of charge carriers permitted much higher electrical currents to flow under the influence of an applied voltage. As power equals voltage times current, a substantial increase occurred in the power of the output signal. In May 1948 this semiconductor amplifier was dubbed the "transistor" at the suggestion of John Pierce of Bell Labs.

Spurred by Bardeen and Brattain's invention, and recognizing that it would probably be difficult to manufacture reliably on a large scale, Shockley quickly proposed an alternative solid-state amplifier. In January 1948 he designed a three-layer semiconductor sandwich with electrical leads attached to each layer. In this junction transistor, as it was soon called, the narrow central layer acts as a gate or valve regulating the flow of charge carriers (electrons or holes) through it from one end to the other—similar to the action of the grid in a vacuum-tube amplifier.

But fabricating a successful prototype based on Shockley's design proved to be no easy matter. It was finally achieved in April 1950 by his assistant Morgan Sparks, using crystal-growing and doping techniques recently developed by Bell Labs employees Gordon Teal and Ernest Buehler. By that time, the point-contact transistor had been put into limited production by Western Electric Company, the manufacturing arm of Bell's parent company AT&T; they were used for a time in switching devices on the Bell Telephone System.

Bell Labs made the new transistor technologies available on a royalty basis, and by the mid-1950s several other companies—such as Philco, RCA, SONY, and Texas Instruments—were manufacturing junction transistors. These solid-state devices began to replace vacuum tubes in commercial products such as hearing aids and portable radios, where a compact, energy-efficient amplifier was needed. In 1956 Bardeen, Brattain, and Shockley were awarded the Nobel Prize in physics for their invention and development of the transistor.

Further developments at Bell Labs and other companies finally permitted the large-scale manufacture in the 1960s of field-effect transistors, approximating Shockley's 1945 design. Carefully controlled diffusion of dopant impurities into specially prepared silicon surfaces inside a heated enclosure proved to be a key fabrication technique used in these advances. The millions of transistors found on a modern microchip are essentially all field-effect transistors.

The invention of the transistor and its offspring, the integrated circuit or microchip, has had a truly enormous impact on modern electronics, computers, and communications. What we are increasingly recognizing as the Information Age would be inconceivable without them. Computers that in the late 1940s weighted 30 tons, occupied several rooms, and required thousands of unreliable vacuum-tube amplifiers have been replaced by portable models that weigh less than 1 kg, fit easily in a suit pocket, and require only a few transistor-laden microchips for their operation. Cellular phones and satellite communications would be impossible without such compact, shock-resistant, lightweight, energy-efficient components. Microchips have led to completely new kinds of media and communications—such as telefaxes, global computer networks, electronic mail, and interactive multimedia programs. The transistor, which made all these advances possible, is arguably the most important technological artifact of the twentieth century.

See also: BARDEEN, JOHN; CIRCUIT, INTEGRATED; HOLES IN SOLIDS; SEMICONDUCTOR; TRANSISTOR

Bibliography

BRATTAIN, W. H. "Genesis of the Transistor." *Phys. Teach.* **6** (3), 109–114 (1968).

HODDESON, L. "The Discovery of the Point-Contact Transistor." *Historical Studies of the Physical Sciences* **12** (1), 41–76 (1981).

QUEISSER, H. *The Conquest of the Microchip* (Harvard University Press, Cambridge, MA, 1990).

MICHAEL RIORDAN

TRANSMISSION GRATING

See GRATING, TRANSMISSION

TRANSPORT PROPERTIES

Electrical transport properties involve the net motion of electrons or ions in the particular medium being considered. The motion is the result of some stimulus. For electrical conduction, the simplest example of an electron transport property, the stimulus is an electric field produced by applying a potential difference between two points on a conducting material. A flow of electrons, which constitutes an electric current, is produced. Another stimulus is a temperature gradient that leads to thermal conductivity and thermoelectric effects. A magnetic field is a third stimulus. By itself, it does not produce a flow of electrons; but, when electron flow is established by an electric field or by a temperature gradient, a magnetic field produces a wide variety of galvanomagnetic or thermomagnetic effects.

In thermal conductivity, energy is transported not only by electrons, but also by lattice vibrations (phonons). In insulating materials, all the heat is conducted by phonons. For electrically conducting materials the important concepts are the transfer of momentum from the applied electric field to the charge carriers, and the scattering of electrons by crystal imperfections such as impurities, atomic vacancies, dislocations, phonons, and so on. A steady state is reached when the rate of momentum transfer from the field equals the rate at which scattering tries to restore the initial equilibrium. Electrical resistance is a manifestation of the electron scattering.

Another steady state is set up on the application of a temperature gradient, but now thermal energy can be carried by electrons and phonons. In good electrical conductors, such as most pure metals, the electrons carry the major part of the energy, whereas in an electrical insulator the energy carriers are the phonons. When impurities are introduced into a metal, thereby forming an alloy, the electrons are scattered more than the phonons and the contributions of electrons and phonons to the thermal conductivity become comparable.

To expand on these concepts we consider a simple model—the free electron model of a metal. In this model the electrons are trapped in a potential box. Within that box quantum mechanics states that the electrons are quantized; that is, they exist in discrete energy states each of which can accept two electrons of opposite spin. In momentum (P), space—the volume occupied by electrons—is a sphere, called the Fermi surface, with a sharp cutoff radius, P_f, at absolute zero (0 K). This is illustrated by the circle in Fig. 1a. In the same figure we show $f(E)$ the probability that an electron state with energy E (where $E = P^2/2m$ and m is the mass of an electron) is occupied. The rectangular curve illustrates $f(E)$ at 0 K. At higher temperatures the probability curve spreads so that there are some states above the Fermi surface that are occupied (filled circles), and some below which are empty (empty circles). For zero applied field (Fig. 1a) equal numbers of electrons move in the $+x$ and $-x$ directions so that there is no net transfer of charge or energy. In subsequent figures the zero-field graphs of Fig. 1a are repeated in bold print. When an electric field ε is applied, the electrons are accelerated and the whole sphere is displaced in the opposite direction (Fig. 1b). Now more electrons flow in the $+x$ than in the $-x$ direction and a current J flows. The extent of the displacement is determined by the amount of electron scattering. In thermal conduction there is no net flow of electrons, but there is a flow of energy which is carried by the electrons! This is accomplished through the distribution illustrated in Fig. 1c. The number of electrons flowing in $+x$ and $-x$ directions are the same but now the electrons traveling in the $+x$ direction have a greater energy than those flowing in the reverse direction. The $+x$ electrons on average are "hotter" than $-x$ electrons. The result is that the electrons transmit energy along the conductor. Since the magnitude of an electric current depends both on the density and the velocity of the charge carriers, one might expect the "hot" electrons to give a larger current than the "cold" electrons flowing in the opposite direction. To offset this effect, and to ensure that no current flows, an electric field is set up in the conductor. This is the origin of the thermoelectric Seebeck effect.

These examples indicate that the type of transport depends on the form of the distribution function $f(E)$. Mathematically $f(E)$ is obtained by solving a complicated equation called the Boltzmann transport equation for the particular stimulus that is ap-

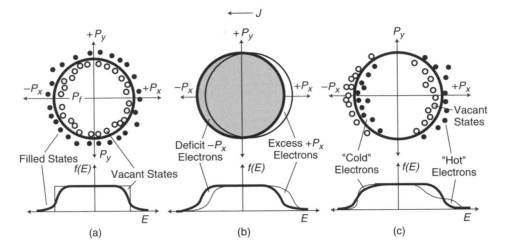

Figure 1 The sphere and $f(E)$ curve in bold print for each figure represent the Fermi surface and the distribution of energies, respectively, when no fields are applied. Filled and empty circles represent occupied and empty electron states, respectively. In (a) there is no applied field. In (b) an electric field pointing to the right is applied. In (c) a temperature gradient is applied. In (b) and (c) the fine $f(E)$ line represents the distribution function when the respective stimuli are applied.

plied. Figures 1b and 1c illustrate the solutions for an applied electric field and an applied temperature gradient, respectively.

A magnetic field is an important stimulus, and to describe its effect on transport properties, a term expressing the magnetic force on a moving charge must be inserted into the Boltzmann equation. In Fig. 1a the individual electrons do have velocities, but when the number of electrons moving in the $+x$ and $-x$ directions is equal, the resultant effect of the magnetic field on the electrons is zero. If, however, there is a preponderance of electrons moving in the $+x$ direction, magnetic forces perpendicular to the electron flow produce a curvature in the electron trajectory resulting in a potential difference transverse to the electron flow. This is the Hall effect. The curvatures in the trajectories may produce changes in resistance called magnetoresistance. Similarly in the presence of a temperature gradient the magnetic field will produce complex thermomagnetic effects.

In the free electron model, for zero scattering, the electrons' orbits in a magnetic field would be circles. In real metals the trajectories are more complex. For low fields only a small part of the electron orbit is traveled before the electron is scattered As the field increases more and more of the

electron orbit is covered before scattering, and the nature of the transport properties changes drastically. In the high field limit an electron would complete its orbit several times before being scattered. We then refer to high field galvanomagnetic properties. Another important effect occurs in high magnetic fields. A new set of quantized states replaces the zero field states, and if the thermal energy of the electrons is less than the separation of the new states, then the transport properties oscillate as the magnetic field is changed. The oscillations are generally referred to as quantum oscillations, but oscillations in the resistivity and magnetic susceptibility are specifically called de Haas–Schubnikov and de Haas–van Alphen oscillations, respectively.

Quantum oscillations are not the only situation where the semi-classical Boltzmann approach breaks down. For example, in superconductivity, conduction is by Cooper pairs—pairs of electrons that flow without resistance. Frequently the wave nature of the electrons has to be carefully considered. Interference between these waves produce complex weak localization effects and universal conductance fluctuations that are sensitive to the motion of individual atoms in the appropriate systems.

See also: CONDUCTION; COOPER PAIR; ELECTRICAL CONDUCTIVITY; HALL EFFECT; QUANTUM MECHANICS; SUPERCONDUCTIVITY; THERMAL CONDUCTIVITY; THERMOELECTRIC EFFECT

Bibliography

DUGDALE, J. S. *Electrical Properties of Metals and Alloys* (Edward Arnold, London, 1977).

GREIG, D. *Electrons in Metals and Semiconductors* (McGraw-Hill, New York, 1969).

ROSENBERG, H. M. *The Solid State: An Introduction to the Physics of Crystals for Students of Physics, Materials Science, and Engineering*, 3rd ed. (Oxford University Press, Oxford, Eng., 1988).

PETER A. SCHROEDER

TRIPLE POINT

The triple point refers to the unique temperature and pressure at which the three phases—solid, liquid, and gaseous—of a one-component (pure) system are coexistent. The triple point of water, at temperature $T_3 = 0.0100°C = 273.16$ K and pressure $P_3 = 4.58$ Torr $= 611$ Pa, is of great practical importance as it is used as the fixed point of the International temperature scale.

In order to understand the uniqueness of the triple point it is helpful to consider first a one-component system, say water, in one phase only and then in two, coexisting phases. When water is present in only one phase, that is as ice, or liquid water, or water vapor, both temperature and pressure of the system can be varied independently. The specific volume V, being another state variable of the system, is determined by the equation of state of the corresponding phase.

When two phases, say water and water vapor, are present in thermodynamic equilibrium, only one of the two variables, temperature or pressure, can be varied independently while the other variable follows dependently. The specific volume V of the combined system is determined by the mole fractions, x_l and x_g, and the specific volumes, V_l and V_g, of the liquid and gaseous phase at the temperature and pressure under consideration as $V = x_l v_l + x_g v_g$. The relation $P(T)$ is the vapor pressure curve of the system. When displayed in a PT diagram (phase diagram), $P(T)$ is represented by a curve separating regions of states in the liquid and gaseous phase, respectively. Similar $P(T)$ relations hold for the two other phase equilibria, that is between water and ice (freezing, melting) and between ice and vapor (evaporation, sublimation). In a PT diagram the three $P(T)$ curves meet at a common point, the triple point.

Represented in a phase diagram, the coordinates of the triple point are the unique triple-point pressure P_3 and triple-point temperature T_3 that necessarily must be present for the three phases to be coexistent. The specific volume V of the three-phase system is determined by the mole fractions and specific volumes of each of the three phases at P_3 and T_3.

The triple point can also be derived as a special case of the Gibbs' phase rule $(c + 2) - p = f$. According to this rule a system of c components, existing in p phases, has f thermodynamic degrees of freedom, that is the number of intensive state variables capable of independent variation. For example, pure water is a one-component system, $c = 1$. If water is present in only one phase (ice, or liquid water, or water vapor), $p = 1$, then $f = (1 + 2) - 1 = 2$ variables, namely P and T, are freely variable. At a phase equilibrium between two $(p = 2)$ phases, such as melting/freezing, or boiling/condensing, or evaporating/sublimating, only $f = (1 + 2) - 2 = 1$ degree of freedom, that is either P or T, exists as an independent variable. The other variable is determined by the vapor-pressure (or melt-pressure) relation $P(T)$. When three $(p = 3)$ phases are present, then the degree of freedom is $f = (1 + 2) - 3 = 0$. This means that the three-phase system can only exist at a unique pressure P_3 and temperature T_3, called the triple point.

The reason for calibrating the Celsius temperature scale with the triple point of water is because of its easy reproducibility. All that is necessary is purified water in a container connected to a vacuum pump capable of lowering pressure down about 1 Torr. Simultaneous presence of ice, water, and vapor occurs in the container (called the triple-point cell) when the pressure $P_3 = 4.58$ Torr is reached. The temperature of the system is then $T_3 = 0.0100°C$. The finding that the triple-point temperature of water is higher than the melting-point temperature of ice, $T_m = 0°C$ at $P = 1$ atm $= 760$ Torr, is a consequence of the anomalous properties of ice, particularly the lowering of the melting point with increasing pressure. Since the triple-point pressure

P_3 is less than 1 atm, the triple point must be higher than the melting point $T_3 > T_m$.

See also: ICE; PHASE RULE; PHASE TRANSITION; STATE, EQUATION OF; TEMPERATURE

Bibliography

SEARS, F. W., and SALINGER, G. L. *Thermodynamics*, 3rd ed. (Addison-Wesley, Reading, MA, 1975).

MANFRED BUCHER

TURBULENCE

Turbulence is a state of fluid motion characterized by unpredictable fluctuations in the flow variables (velocity, pressure, temperature, concentration), greatly enhanced mixing, three-dimensional vortical motions across a wide range of scales, and large energy dissipation. Typically, the velocity and pressure at any location may vary by 10 percent of the average values, although sudden large variations also occur at irregular intervals of time. Fluid moves in local swirls or vortices that become stretched, bent, and intensified by shearing action of the overall flow. Kinetic energy of the swirling motion is eventually converted to heat in domains within the flow where viscous friction is greatest. These domains are where vortices have been intensified and stretched to such small scales that nearby elements of fluid move past one another with much different velocities. Matter, momentum, and heat are rapidly mixed across turbulent flows by eddies of many different sizes that carry fluid from one point to another. Such mixing can be a hundred times faster than would occur in the absence of turbulence.

Turbulence is to be contrasted with the laminar state of fluid motion where, in the latter, the flow varies in a smooth and predictable way across the region of interest. Laminar flows occur only for small imposed forces on a fluid, and—as the externally imposed forces are increased—the motion undergoes a process of transition with an outcome of turbulent flow. Turbulence is by far the most common state of fluid motion.

Examples of turbulence are readily found, and observation of some turbulent flows is strongly recommended as a step toward understanding. For example, water flowing out of a faucet changes from laminar to turbulent motion as the valve is opened and the flow rate is increased. Flow in a river may be seen to contain irregular swirls and eddies made visible by the motion of objects floating in the water and by the mixing of silt carried away from river banks. Smoke rising from a smokestack or cigarette often emerges in a laminar stream that quickly develops a billowing structure associated with turbulence. Breezes are felt to be intermittent and unpredictable and are due to turbulence in the boundary layer formed as winds blow past the earth's surface. The wake of moving objects is usually turbulent, as is readily found in the buffeting that occurs while driving behind a large truck on the highway. Wake turbulence can be quite dangerous to small aircraft that follow too closely after large aircraft near airports. Atmospheric turbulence occurs in layers where fluids of different density flow past one another or when large amplitude wave-like disturbances of moving air masses break up; sometimes these processes result in the clear air turbulence that is so difficult for aircraft to detect ahead of time.

Turbulence can, however, be quite useful because it speeds up the process by which materials or heat may be mixed into a moving fluid. Transport by such mixing is orders of magnitude faster than can be achieved by molecular motion alone. This may be seen by carefully placing a drop of dye in the bottom of a glass of water and noticing that the dyed region remains quite confined until the water is stirred into turbulent motion. Turbulence is also useful to prevent the separation of flow streamlines from the surfaces of aircraft wings; such separation can otherwise cause a pressure jump that greatly increases the drag on the wing. On the other hand, turbulence generates much more friction and energy dissipation. Thus it takes more pumping power to move a turbulent fluid through pipes and ducts, and considerable research has gone into designing aircraft wings and boat hulls that maintain a laminar boundary layer over as much of the surface as possible. The unpredictability of turbulence generates unsteady forces that can cause structures to shake and aircraft to undergo sudden, dangerous accelerations. In all of these situations it is desirable to prevent or avoid turbulence.

The detailed understanding of turbulence is said to be the last unsolved problem of classical physics, and research in turbulence was increasingly active throughout the twentieth century. A vivid demonstration of the difference between laminar and turbulent flow through pipes was created by Osborne Reynolds in late-nineteenth-century England: A dye streak introduced into the center of fluid entering a transparent pipe remained quite thin and straight for low flow rates, but the dye rapidly spread through the pipe when the flow was increased and turbulence occurred. Reynolds found that the critical rate of flow causing transition to turbulence in pipes of different diameters could be compared, provided that the flow rate was expressed in a dimensionless combination of variables: $\text{Re} = U_c r / \nu$, where U_c is the velocity at the center of the pipe (a typical scale of the flow velocity), r is the radius of the pipe (a typical distance over which the velocity is varying), and ν is a fluid property called the kinematic viscosity (a measure of the fluid's internal frictional resistance to being deformed). This dimensionless combination is now called the Reynolds number, and it is the most important parameter distinguishing the type of flow that is expected in various conditions. Other important parameters include the geometric proportions of objects around which (or within which) fluid flows.

One of the most intriguing aspects of turbulence is the fact that the equations governing the motion of fluids are well known, and yet, solutions exist to these equations that are essentially unpredictable. Knowing the velocity, pressure, and temperature of a fluid at one point in space and time gives us very limited ability to predict these variables at other points in space and time when the fluid is in turbulent motion, even though we know the equations that describe how these quantities change. A deeper understanding of this apparent paradox has emerged in the study of chaos in much simpler systems. Even a mechanical system as simple as a pendulum driven by periodic motions of its pivot can exhibit behavior that becomes unpredictable after surprisingly short times. This is said to be due to sensitive dependence on initial conditions, meaning that the slightest uncertainty in the state of motion at a given time is magnified exponentially as time progresses. Thus, even if we obtained a snapshot that told us exactly how a turbulent fluid's velocity, pressure, and temperature varied across a region of space at one instant in time, we could never measure these variables to a precision sufficient to allow detailed prediction of the same variables after a time interval that turns out to be surprisingly short. This occurs even though the imposed forces (such as pumping rate) are quite steady and predictable, and

thus is to be contrasted with the sort of randomness that occurs when a large number of varying and unknown forces act on an object.

In view of such limitations in predicting the details of turbulent motion, one tries instead to predict average values of the flow variables. Much of the theoretical effort in turbulence research has been devoted to finding ways to supplement equations for the average quantities with information that allows the equations to be solved. The difficulty is that, in creating equations for averages, there are always more unknowns than equations—a situation called the closure problem. In particular, terms appear in the equations that involve averages of products of fluctuations in velocities. These act to distribute momentum across the flow, acting as though they were stresses imposed on a fictitious flow that varies only according to the average quantities. These are known as Reynolds stresses. One approach is to use empirical knowledge of how these stresses (or other averages) behave in experiments, but generalizations from one experimental condition to another are notoriously difficult. Progress has been aided in this regard by greatly improved experimental capabilities and by the expanding power of computers to model fluid flows numerically.

Experimentally, turbulence is studied both by qualitative visualization of the eddies and mixing in flows and by quantitative measurement of velocities and stresses at known locations within a turbulent flow. Flow patterns are made visible by the motion and alignment of particles carried by the flow, by following the paths of dye injected in the flow, or by observing tufts attached to surfaces affected by the flow. The motion of leaves caught by swirling breezes is an everyday example of visualization. Velocity measurements rely on two principal methods. One, the hot wire probe, measures the amount of cooling of a very thin wire placed in the flow; from this cooling rate, components of velocity perpendicular to the wire can be deduced. The laser doppler technique, on the other hand, does not require putting a probe into the flow but instead deduces velocities from the shift in frequency of laser light scattered by small particles moving with the flow. In either method, it is important to measure long time histories of the velocities so that statistical properties of the flow can be determined. Computers have become extremely important in collecting and analyzing the large amounts of data required.

In certain cases, dimensional reasoning can make surprisingly definite statements about turbulent flows. The most famous of these is the case of homogenous, isotropic turbulence, in which the statistical features of the turbulent motion do not vary with position or with direction. A good approximation to such a flow is obtained in the wake of a mesh of wires placed across a stream of fluid; it is called grid turbulence. For the idealization of homogenous, isotropic turbulence, the Russian physicist Andrei Nikolaevich Kolmogorov established an important statement about how energy was shared across various scales of motion in the flow. Imagine a turbulent flow to be made up of a superposition of velocity fluctuations of many different sizes. Kolmogorov showed that, over a considerable range of scales, the energy contained in the family of fluctuations of size λ would vary as $E(\lambda) \sim \lambda^{5/3}$. The larger eddies carry more of the energy. However, the eddies can grow no bigger than the domain of the turbulent flow, such as the diameter of the pipe transporting a fluid in turbulent motion.

Suppose for example that a stirrer of size L is putting energy into a fluid at rate epsilon units of energy per unit mass per unit time. Such energy is initially contained in an eddy of size L whose typical velocity U may be related to ϵ by dimensional analysis: $\epsilon \sim U^3/L$.

This energy cascades into smaller eddies until a size is reached where an eddy will lose all of its energy to viscous friction in the time it would take the eddy to turn over on itself. This leads, again by dimensional analysis, to a minimum scale called the Kolmogorov length: $\lambda_K = (\nu^3/\epsilon)^{1/4}$, where ν is the kinematic viscosity of the fluid. An important notion is the estimate of the number of degrees of freedom excited in a turbulent flow. We may estimate this as total volume L^3 of the turbulent region divided by the volume of the smallest eddy λ_K^3: degrees of freedom $\sim (L/\lambda_K)^3 \sim (UL/\nu)^{9/4} = \mathrm{Re}^{9/4}$. Thus, a moderately turbulent flow at Reynolds number $\mathrm{Re} = 10{,}000$ will contain on the order of 10^9 active degrees of freedom. On one hand, this is far smaller than the number of molecules in the fluid ($\sim 10^{24}$ in a cubic meter of air). However, it is a number that is just within the capacity of today's best computers, while many turbulent flows in nature and engineering have much higher Reynolds numbers (100,000–10,000,000). Turbulent flows are thus highly complex in two ways: They arise through dynamics that are inherently unpredictable because of sensitive dependence on initial conditions, and they develop into motions that contain a very large number of degrees of freedom.

One area of research seeks to obtain further understanding of strongly turbulent motion, aiming to derive further scaling relationships with a minimum of assumptions. In a sense, the details of highly complex motions cease to matter, and many important aspects of the behavior depends only on such global features as symmetry and spatial dimension. Another area of research aims to clarify the connection between chaotic dynamics and turbulence, focusing on the initial stages of turbulence formation as laminar flows become unstable. Understanding of intermediate regimes relies heavily on numerical computations, and these are often the only way to supplement experiments and obtain information about turbulent flows in useful but highly complex geometries such as automobile engines, turbines, and aircraft bodies. Turbulence remains an extremely active area of research, in which there is a crucial interplay between theory, numerical computation, and experiment.

See also: FLUID DYNAMICS; REYNOLDS NUMBER; TURBULENT FLOW; VISCOSITY; VORTEX

Bibliography

BAKER, G. L., and GOLLUB, J. P. *Chaotic Dynamics: An Introduction,* 2nd ed. (Cambridge University Press, Cambridge, Eng., 1995).

BRADSHAW, P. *An Introduction to Turbulence and Its Measurement* (Pergamon, Oxford, Eng., 1975).

FRISCH, U. *Turbulence* (Cambridge University Press, Cambridge, Eng., 1995).

LANDAHL, M. T., and MOLLO-CHRISTENSEN, E. *Turbulence and Random Processes in Fluid Mechanics* (Cambridge University Press, Cambridge, Eng., 1986).

TENNEKES, H., and LUMLEY, J. L. *A First Course in Turbulence* (MIT Press, Cambridge, MA, 1972).

RANDALL TAGG

TURBULENT FLOW

Most flows in nature and engineering are turbulent, and many details of these flows depend on the specific features of the systems in which they are created. However, there are certain prototypes from which scientists learn important, more generally useful features of turbulent flows.

Homogenous, isotropic turbulence is an idealization approximated after fluid flows through a grid or screen. Far enough downstream, statistical features of this type of flow depend only weakly on position or direction. However, in this region the turbulence is actually decaying because the average shear that is necessary to feed energy into fluctuations is no longer present. Nonetheless, the process of decay, mediated by exchange of energy between motions at different scales, is of considerable fundamental interest.

Turbulent flows of more direct practical interest arise in wakes, jets, and shear layers formed when one mass of fluid slides over another. Experiments often look at mean flows that are two-dimensional, such as the wake of a rod placed across a stream, the jet emerging from a slit, or the initially planar interface between two masses of fluid moving in the same direction but at different speeds. In all of these cases, instability quickly occurs as the fluid moves downstream. Initially regular structures appear in the flow and undergo a complex process of merging, bending, and further instability to generate turbulence. Even when the imposed conditions are two-dimensional (no variation in the third direction), the turbulence itself is strongly three-dimensional. Symmetries that were initially imposed on the flow are progressively and spontaneously broken.

Moving downstream from the source, the region of turbulence widens by causing surrounding fluid to become turbulent. This process is known as entrainment. Another significant feature is the appearance of large coherent structures within the turbulence, particularly near the boundary between turbulent and laminar regions of the flow. As these structures flow past probes in the flow, the measured signals vary unpredictably between quiet and strongly fluctuating—a phenomenon known as intermittency.

In the cases discussed so far, viscosity plays a relatively minor role in determining the structure of the turbulence. It sets the smallest scales reached by the turbulent fluctuations, it mediates the ultimate dissipation of turbulent kinetic energy into heat, and it completes the transmission of the vortical nature of turbulence to nearby patches of undisturbed fluid. Over most of the scales of the flow, however, inertia—subject to momentum conservation—dominates and many features are independent of viscosity. This is known as Reynolds number similarity.

By contrast, viscosity is much more important in turbulent flows that occur in the boundary layers formed when fluid moves past solid walls. A boundary layer is a relatively thin region near the wall where the fluid velocity rapidly changes from zero at the wall to a magnitude close to the velocity of the main stream. When the boundary layer is turbulent, sublayers form. There is a region across which the tangential stresses exchanged between the wall and the fluid and between layers of the fluid themselves are relatively constant. Closest to the wall, these stresses are transmitted primarily by viscosity, and this is known as the viscous sublayer. Farther out, the stresses are predominantly transmitted by the turbulent fluctuations. In between is a region where the two extremes must be joined, and dimensional reasoning leads to a characteristic logarithmic variation of mean flow with distance from the wall. This is known as the log law of the wall.

Other interesting features occur in flow near walls or within pipes, especially when the turbulence is just forming. In pipes, regions of turbulence appear surrounded by regions of laminar flow. These so-called turbulent slugs spread as they travel downstream, and ultimately the pipe becomes filled with turbulence. Similarly, in boundary layers or in flow between plane walls, turbulent spots appear adjoined by remarkable wave-like structures that penetrate into the laminar region. These spots spread and merge downstream until the flow is everywhere turbulent. Finally, in fully-developed turbulent boundary layers, small structures such as hairpin vortices erupt at irregular intervals from deep within the boundary layer.

There are several other important prototypes of turbulence. These include buoyancy-driven turbulence, which can produce mushroom-shaped thermal plumes as hot fluid suddenly rises into surrounding cool fluid. Flow between rotating cylinders (the Couette–Taylor system) produces a wide variety of turbulent patterns, including barber pole turbulence that spirals up or down the region filling the gap between the cylinders. Geophysical flows and flows in planetary atmospheres are usually turbulent. Such flows, at large scales, have a strongly two-dimensional character imposed by the effects of planetary rotation. It is intriguing to observe how vortices, randomly produced by shearing and jets in atmospheric flows, tend to merge into large long-lived structures. The most notable of these may be the Great Red Spot of Jupiter.

See also: FLUID DYNAMICS; REYNOLDS NUMBER; TURBULENCE; VISCOSITY; VORTEX

Bibliography

FABER, T. E. *Fluid Dynamics for Physicists* (Cambridge University Press, Cambridge, Eng., 1995).

TAGG, R. P. "Instabilities and the Origin of Complexity in Fluid Flows" in *1993 Lectures in Complex Systems,* edited by L. Nadel and D. L. Stein (Addison-Wesley, Reading, MA, 1995).

TRITTON, D. J. *Physical Fluid Dynamics,* 2nd ed. (Oxford University Press, Oxford, Eng., 1988).

RANDALL TAGG

TWIN PARADOX

The time interval between two events is not determined completely by the events themselves. It also depends on the reference frame from which these events are observed. For example, suppose an observer detects two events at the same place, separated in time by one year. Suppose also that these same two events are detected by a second observer, who moves with a speed of about 90 percent of the speed of light relative to the first observer. Then the second observer would measure the time interval between the two events to be about two years, twice as long as the measurement of the first observer for the same pair of events. Similarly, if the second observer detects two events at the same place separated in time by one year, the first observer would measure the time interval between them as two years. This phenomenon is usually referred to as time dilation. It implies that the time interval between two events is shortest when measured in the reference frame in which these events occur at the same place and will be larger by a factor of $1/\sqrt{1 - v^2/c^2}$ if measured in a reference frame moving with speed v relative to the frame in which the events occur at the same place.

Now imagine that two unpowered spaceships move with constant relative velocity $(\sqrt{3}/2)c$. Suppose that they pass very close to each other, and at that instant, Moe is born in the ship traveling west and Jo is born in the ship traveling east. A year later, as measured by her clock, Jo celebrates her first birthday. The two events (her birth and her first birthday party) occur at the same location relative to Jo's ship but at different locations relative to Moe's.

According to the introductory explanation, Moe will say that the time interval between these two events is two years, whereas Jo will say that the time interval is only one year.

Suppose further that, at her birthday celebration, Jo turns her spaceship around and heads west, back toward Moe. Just as it took one year (according to Jo's clock) for them to separate, it will take one year (according to Jo's clock) for them to come back together. Jo will say that she is two years old when they reunite. However, Moe says two years elapsed before she turned around and that it took her another two years to return, since the phenomenon of time dilation occurs regardless of the direction of relative velocity. Thus, Moe will say that four years have elapsed before their first reunion and that he is four years old. However, Jo will say that only two years have elapsed, and she will claim to be two years old. Thus, Jo will claim to be half the age of Moe, who was born at the same time and place as she was.

Now look at events from Jo's reference frame. She sees Moe travel away from her at a speed of $(\sqrt{3}/2)c$ then turn around and return. Since only relative motion is significant, she observes the same time dilation in Moe's clock that Moe observes in her clock. Thus, the symmetry of the situation implies that when they reunite, Jo will say that four years have elapsed so that she is four years old, whereas Moe will say he is only two years old. In this second scenario, Jo has aged at twice the rate of Moe, whereas previously, Moe aged at twice the rate of Jo. This is the so-called twin paradox. The symmetry of their relative motion implies that each is older than the other when they reunite, which is a logical contradiction.

In fact, there is no paradox. References in the preceding paragraph to symmetry are wrong. There is an essential difference between Moe's and Jo's experiences. Jo turned her ship around, whereas Moe did not. For the duration of the story, Moe was in an inertial reference frame, whereas Jo's reference frame was not inertial while she was reversing her direction. She could have observed this with the help of a simple apparatus, such as a pail half full of water. The level of the water would have tipped while she was reversing, whereas the level of water in Moe's pail would have remained the same the whole time. This noninertial episode would have a profound effect on Jo's perception of space and time and make it impossible for Jo to mimic the correct analysis given by her constantly inertial friend Moe. Moe's description, in which he is four years old

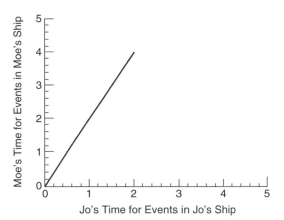

Figure 1 Events simultaneous for Moe.

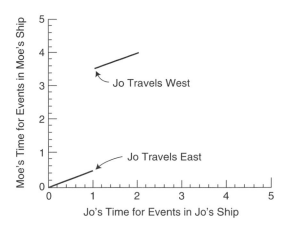

Figure 2 Events simultaneous for Jo.

when Jo returns, whereas she is only two, is correct. Experiments done by NASA, in which a very precise atomic clock was taken on a round-the-world trip, have verified this counterintuitive prediction of the theory of special relativity.

To understand the asymmetry of the two descriptions, consider a pair of simultaneous events, one in Moe's ship and the other in Jo's ship. According to special relativity, the question, "Simultaneous for whom?" must first be addressed. Suppose the events are simultaneous for Moe. For example, according to Moe, Jo's first birthday party (which occurred at one year on Jo's clock) is simultaneous with the appearance of two years on Moe's clock. Figure 1 shows a plot of Moe's time for the event in his ship versus Jo's time for the simultaneous event in her ship, the two events being simultaneous for Moe. The plot is a smooth line with a slope that reflects the time-dilation factor of 2 associated with a relative speed of the ships of $(\sqrt{3}/2)\,c$. Figure 2 shows a similar plot for events that are simultaneous for Jo. The striking feature of this plot is the discontinuity at Jo's time of one year. While she was moving east, her first birthday was simultaneous (according to her) with an event on Moe's ship that Moe said occurred at one-half a year. As soon as she was moving west, her first birthday was simultaneous (according to her) with

an event on Moe's ship that Moe said occurred at three and one-half years. This sudden change in the event on Moe's ship that is simultaneous (according to Jo) with Jo's first birthday party is a consequence of Jo's sudden change of velocity. Since Moe did not undergo a change of velocity, there is no corresponding discontinuity in the plot in Fig. 1. Notice that Figs. 1 and 2 both agree that the trip ends with an event that Moe says has a time of four years and Jo says has a time of two years. The stories that Moe and Jo tell are different as a result of their different motions, but they agree that when they meet again, she will be two years old and he will be four.

The lesson drawn from the twin paradox by the student of relativity is the need for extreme caution when the methods of special relativity are applied to situations in which accelerations occur, even when these accelerations are instantaneous.

See also: RELATIVITY, SPECIAL THEORY OF; TIME DILATION

Bibliography

TAYLOR, E. F., and WHEELER, J. A. *Spacetime Physics*, 2nd ed. (Freeman and Company, New York, 1992).

BENJAMIN F. BAYMAN

U

UHURU SATELLITE

The Uhuru satellite was the first earth-orbiting satellite devoted to the study of cosmic x-ray sources. The mission was launched by NASA as the first of its Small Astronomy Satellites (SAS-A) on December 12, 1970, from a launch platform in the Indian Ocean off the coast of Kenya. Upon successfully reaching orbit, its American designers and builders quickly renamed it Uhuru, which means "freedom" in Swahili, in honor of the launch day being Kenyan Independence Day.

Uhuru was an epochal milestone in the history of astronomy. It was launched to study and follow-up with a first all-sky survey of the small number (approximately forty) of cosmic x-ray sources that had been discovered in the preceding eight years of rocket and balloon flights of cosmic x-ray detectors above the earth's atmosphere. These had followed the pioneering 1962 rocket flight experiment of Riccardo Giacconi and his associates, which detected the first cosmic x-ray source, Sco X-1, as well as the diffuse x-ray background.

The Uhuru satellite carried two x-ray detectors, which were proportional counters (similar to Geiger counters, but actually ionization detectors that produced a charge pulse proportional to the total energy of the incoming x ray detected) mounted on opposite sides of the spacecraft, viewing the sky with $0.5° \times 5°$ and $5° \times 5°$ fields of view, respectively. Be-

cause the satellite was slowly spinning with a rotation period of about 720 s, the two detectors swept out a plane on the sky in which cosmic x-ray sources could be detected with 0.5° to 5° resolution. The finer resolution proved invaluable for detecting and locating (to better than 0.5°, by centroiding) point x-ray sources such as Sco X-1, while the broad field detectors allowed diffuse x-ray sources to be discovered and located. As the satellite orbited the earth (every 96 min), the scan path swept out a great circle on the sky. Because the satellite's solar power panels demanded an approximately fixed orientation with respect to the Sun, the scan path could cover virtually the entire sky over a six-month survey. In practice, three such sky survey scans were done over the nearly two-year life of the mission, and the first all-sky catalog of some 400 cosmic x-ray sources was produced.

Two major discoveries were made with Uhuru that have changed our view of the cosmos. First, the bright point x-ray sources discovered in our galaxy (e.g., Sco X-1) with the early rocket experiments were identified as x-ray binaries, whereby matter is transferred from a normal star onto a collapsed star (e.g., for the brightest systems, a neutron star or possibly a black hole), and x rays are produced with high luminosity by the process of accretion. Such high luminosity accretion sources are now recognized as playing a fundamental role in a wide range of cosmic settings, from x-ray binaries to quasars, and were by and large not anticipated theoretically.

Secondly, Uhuru enabled the discovery that galaxy clusters, which are the gigantic swarms of hundreds to even thousands of galaxies found as gravitationally bound entities in the universe, contain high masses of diffuse hot gas between the member galaxies. The gas is heated to temperatures of 10 million to 100 million degrees Kelvin by the characteristic velocity of the galaxies on their orbits in the cluster, and thus it naturally radiates x rays as originally discovered with Uhuru. This pervasive hot gas in clusters has altered our view of the origin and evolution of galaxy clusters and their constituent galaxies, and it has been studied in much greater detail with follow-up x-ray satellites such as the Einstein Observatory.

See also: ASTROPHYSICS, X-RAY; BLACK HOLE; COSMIC MICROWAVE BACKGROUND RADIATION; EINSTEIN OBSERVATORY; NEUTRON STAR; QUASAR; X-RAY BINARY

Bibliography

FORMAN, W., et al. "The Fourth Uhuru Catalogue of X-Ray Sources." *Astrophys. J. Suppl. Ser.* **38,** 357–412 (1978).

GIACCONI, R.; GURSKY, H.; PAOLINI, F.; and ROSSI, B. "Evidence for X Rays from Sources Outside the Solar System." *Phys. Rev. Lett.* **9,** 439–443 (1962).

JONATHAN E. GRINDLAY

ULTRASONICS

The range of frequencies that an average person can hear is from about 25 to 18,000 Hz. Frequencies higher than this are called "ultrasonic" or "supersonic" (supersonic usually is used to refer to audible sounds traveling faster than the speed of sound in air). The velocity of ultrasonic waves in air is the same as audible sound waves at the same temperature. It is given by the relation $331.7 + 0.61T$ m/s, where T is the temperature in degrees Celsius. Ultrasonic waves, like audible sounds, obey normal physical laws such as reflection, refraction, interference, and diffraction. The wavelengths of ultrasonic waves are all smaller than 2 cm.

The most common generator of ultrasonic waves is the piezoelectric crystal. When an alternating voltage of frequency f is applied to certain crystals such as quartz, the crystal changes its shape periodically with frequency f. A quartz crystal 1 cm long has a resonant wavelength of 2 cm and a resonant frequency of 275 kHz, since the velocity of longitudinal ultrasonic waves in quartz is 5,500 m/s. Other piezoelectric crystals are barium titanate, lithium sulfate, and lead zirconate. Magnetostriction is a similar effect—the change in shape of a body when placed in a magnetic field. This effect also is used in ultrasonic transducers with ferromagnetic materials. A thin steel rod, 10 cm long, clamped at its center and placed inside a coil carrying an alternating current, will resonate at a frequency of 25 kHz and produce 25-kHz ultrasonic sound waves.

In some situations, ultrasonic waves are preferred to audible sound waves for several reasons:

1. Audible sound of high intensity (above 130 dB) would be intolerable; ultrasonic waves are inaudible.
2. Greater accuracy of test measurements may be obtained with waves of shorter wavelength.
3. Ultrasonic waves of high frequency have better directional properties; they can be more easily focused into narrow, concentrated beams.

Ultrasonic sound waves are used in many practical applications. Low-intensity ultrasound is used for material analysis, nondestructive testing (NDT), nondestructive evaluation of foods (NDE), and in various areas of medical diagnosis. High-intensity ultrasound is used in drilling and cutting metals, and in cleaning by cavitation, in sonar, and in many areas of medical therapy. Materials interact with ultrasonic waves in a frequency-dependent manner so that measurements over a wide range of frequencies enable greater scope of measurement of their physical properties. This is called ultrasound spectroscopy. Ultrasound is used in NDT of nuclear reactors, forgings, welded materials, and concrete structures. The degree of ripening of foods, especially vegetables, is another use of low-intensity ultrasonic waves.

Diagnostic ultrasound is used in most areas of medicine. The advantages of using ultrasound as a medical diagnostic tool are that it is noninvasive and has no harmful effects. Areas of medicine that use ultrasound are echoencephalography (study of the brain), echocardiography (study of heart valves), pregnancy (fetal position, growth, monitoring of heart beats and blood flow, and sex determination), and abdominal and pelvic studies. In A-scanning devices, the piezoelectric transducer acts as both the transmitter and receiver. B-scanning involves multiple sweeps of the ultrasound beam, thus enabling a two-dimensional picture to be displayed on an oscilloscope screen. Sophisticated electronics is needed for computer control, analysis, and processing of the ultrasound data. The absorption coefficients of different parts of the human body, such as muscle, bone, and fat, vary considerably. The difference between healthy and malignant tissue may be detected with ultrasound for early diagnosis of cancer. The frequencies used vary from 1 to 20 MHz with power levels from 1/100 to 1 W. High intensity ultrasound is used in ultrasonic cleaners for sterilization and for the removal of tumors.

Echo ranging is based on sound reflection. In sonar (sound navigation and ranging) the ultrasonic transducer acts as both transmitter and receiver. It measures the time for the reflected echo and displays it as a distance on a screen. The typical sonar device uses frequencies of 20 to 40 kHz.

Bats use echoranging for navigation, mating, and individual recognition. The bat's brain is capable of interpreting the ultrasonic echoes that it receives into size, shape, and distance of objects. Echo location is also used by some birds, dolphins, sea lions, and whales. Many small animals, such as crickets, grasshoppers, and certain rodents, also communicate using ultrasound.

See also: CRYSTAL; INFRASONICS; MAGNETOSTRICTION; PIEZOELECTRIC EFFECT; SOUND

Bibliography

ENSMINGER, D. *Ulltrasonics: Fundamentals, Technology, Applications* (M. Decker, New York, 1988).

KUTTRUFF, H. *Ultrasonics Fundamentals and Applications* (Elsevier, New York, 1991).

SHUTILOV, V. A. *Fundamental Physics of Ultrasound* (Gordon and Breach, New York, 1988).

JOHN ASKILL

ULTRAVIOLET SPECTROSCOPY

See SPECTROSCOPY, ULTRAVIOLET

UNCERTAINTY PRINCIPLE

The uncertainty principle was formulated by Werner Heisenberg in the 1920s as part of the then new theory of quantum mechanics, which was developed in response to the inability of traditional "classical" physics to explain the properties of atoms and subatomic particles. In its simplest formulation the uncertainty principle states that it is impossible to exactly define both the position and the momentum of a particle at the same time, and that the product of the "uncertainties" in the position x and the component of momentum in the x direction (p_x) is always greater than a fundamental constant of nature known as Planck's constant (h), and is represented by the symbol h divided by 4π. In mathematical terms, if the uncertainties in position and momentum are represented by Δx and Δp_x, respectively, then

$$\Delta x \Delta p_x \geq \frac{h}{4\pi}.$$

In standard units h is extremely small, being about 6×10^{-34} J·s. This means that the effects of the principle on the behavior of everyday objects are completely undetectable. We can see this by considering a tiny grain of sand that might have a mass as small as a millionth of a gram. Remembering that momentum is the product of mass and velocity, such an object could have its position determined to an accuracy of a billionth of a millimeter at the same time as its speed was known to within a billionth of a meter per second before the limits of the uncertainty principle became relevant. Such accuracy is completely outside the limits of present-day technology; for heavier objects the detection of the effects of the uncertainty principle would be even more difficult. In the case of a subatomic particle such as an electron in an atom, however, it is quite a different story. Atoms are known to have a size of the order of 10^{-10} m, so if this is taken as a measure of the uncertainty in the electron's position, then, given the electron mass of about 9×10^{-31} kg, the uncertainty in its speed is about 10^7 m/s, which is large. This is why the uncertainty principle plays such an important role in the physics of objects of this scale.

The uncertainty principle should be understood as a consequence of the general theory of quan-

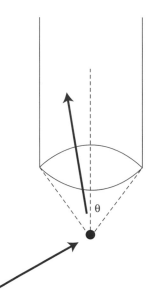

Figure 1 We imagine measuring the position of a particle, such as an electron, by illuminating it with light and observing it with a microscope. There is an uncertainty in the momentum of the electron because we do not know through which part of the lens the light photon passed.

tum physics and not as something added to it. In particular, it is closely connected to the idea of wave–particle duality, in which an object such as an electron has to be modeled as neither a particle nor a wave, but, in some sense we find very difficult to comprehend, as an object having both wave and particle properties simultaneously. In using this to understand the uncertainty principle further, it helps to consider specific situations, some of which are real practical experiments while others, known as thought experiments, are impossible to realize in practice for technical reasons. A famous example of this latter kind is what has become known as the Heisenberg microscope. We imagine an attempt to measure the position of a subatomic particle, such as an electron, by using a powerful microscope and illuminating it with radiation of wavelength λ (see Fig. 1). It is well known from the theory of optical diffraction that the wave properties of the radiation result in the image having some fuzziness that becomes greater as the wavelength becomes larger. This fuzziness introduces an uncertainty into our knowledge of the particle position, which therefore acquires an uncertainty Δx given by

$$\Delta x = \frac{\lambda}{\sin \theta}$$

where θ is the angle shown in Fig. 1. This results from the wave nature of the illuminating radiation, but the particle properties of this radiation also have consequences. These particles (known as photons) have a total momentum p that is related to the wavelength λ of the associated wave by an expression first derived by the French physicist Louis de Broglie:

$$p = \frac{h}{\lambda}.$$

From the particle point of view, the scattering of the light into the lens from the electron being studied means that a photon has had its momentum changed by a collision with the electron. Because momentum is always conserved, the electron has had its momentum changed by an amount equal and opposite to that acquired by the photon. Any uncertainty in our knowledge of the photon momentum must therefore be reflected in that of the electron. Although the total momentum of the photon always remains the same, there is an uncertainty in its component in the direction of the position measurement x. This arises because we have no knowledge of which part of the lens the photon passed through. Referring again to Fig. 1., the uncertainty in p_x, the x component of momentum, is therefore

$$\Delta p_x = p \sin \theta = \frac{h \sin \theta}{\lambda}.$$

If we combine this with the earlier expression for Δx, we get

$$\Delta x \, \Delta p_x = h,$$

which is consistent with the original statement of the uncertainty principle at the beginning of the article.

An example of the application of the uncertainty principle to an experiment that can actually be performed is the diffraction of light or other radiation by a single slit. The wave aspect of this situation is a standard example in physical optics. The waves passing through the slit interfere with each other and form a diffraction pattern that consists of a strong central band flanked by dark and weaker light where θ is the angle between the direction perpendicular to the plane of the slit and the ray joining the slit to the first zero of the diffraction pattern. From the standard diffraction theory,

$$\sin \theta = \frac{\lambda}{a}.$$

So, if we put all these results together, we get

$$\Delta x \Delta p_x \approx \frac{a}{2} \frac{h}{\lambda} \frac{\lambda}{a} = \frac{h}{2} > \frac{h}{4\pi},$$

again in agreement with the uncertainty principle.

This example provides a useful illustration of some of the more subtle aspects of the uncertainty principle. When the particle reaches the screen where the diffraction pattern is recorded, there is nothing to prevent us from measuring the position it arrives at much more accurately than the width of the diffraction pattern. We can therefore deduce the path apparently taken by the particle and hence its momentum to a much greater accuracy than we assumed above. It is tempting to believe that this has allowed us to beat the uncertainty principle! More careful thinking shows that this is not the case. The uncertainty principle refers to *simultaneous* knowledge of position and momentum—for example, while the particle is within the slit. Before we detect the particle at the screen, the momentum and position are uncertain by the amounts derived earlier, and the uncertainty principle applies in just the way we described. If we deduce a value from the momentum based on the position the particle has when it reaches the screen, it is the uncertainty in this latter position measurement that relates to that in the momentum. In fact a quite precise value for the momentum component can be deduced from quite a rough position measurement because the distance between the slit and the screen is quite large, and, in such a case, the momentum of the particle will be only slightly disturbed by this new position measurement. If, however, a very precise position measurement is made at this stage, the component of the particle's momentum will again be significantly affected and our ability to predict the result of a future measurement considerably reduced. In either case the uncertainty in this prediction will be related to that in the latest position measurement by the uncertainty principle.

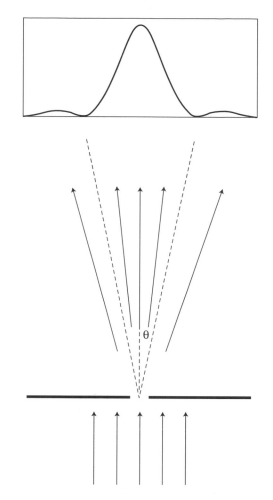

Figure 2 Light passing through a narrow slit forms a diffraction pattern. The width of the central minimum of this pattern implies an uncertainty in the momentum component, which is related to the width of the slit by the uncertainty principle.

bands, as shown in Fig. 2. The relevance to the uncertainty principle arises when we consider the particle properties of the system. When a particle passes through the slit, whose width we take to be a, its position is uncertain by an amount $\pm a/2$, because we do not know which part of the slit it has passed through. As it leaves the slit, all we know about its motion is that it will quite likely arrive somewhere within the central maximum of the diffraction pattern. Using the de Broglie relation again, we see that it follows that there is an uncertainty Δp_x in the component of momentum parallel to the slit, given by

$$\Delta p_x \approx \frac{h}{\lambda} \sin \theta$$

Attempts to find ways around the uncertainty principle features strongly in the famous debates between Albert Einstein and Niels Bohr in the 1920s and 1930s, soon after the quantum theory had been established. Usually by way of thought experiment, Einstein would suggest a way in which the principle could be circumvented, and Bohr would show by a more detailed analysis that it could not be done! For example, in a situation similar to the single-slit experiment described above, Einstein suggested that, in principle, the momentum of the photon leaving the slit could be deduced from a measurement of the recoil momentum of the screen carrying the slit. Bohr rejoined by pointing out that the uncertainty principle must be applied consistently and that a measurement of the screen momentum could only be performed at the cost of some uncertainty in our knowledge of its position. This in turn would mean that the effective width of the slit would be much larger and so, therefore, would be the uncertainty in the particle position. More detailed analysis showed that this means the standard form of the uncertainty principle still applies. Interest in this kind of argument faded as it was realized that the uncertainty principle is an inevitable consequence of the basic principles of quantum theory and as the experimental evidence supporting these principles continued to grow. Nowadays, although there is still considerable disagreement about its interpretation, it is almost universally accepted that the factual consequences of the uncertainty principle are completely established.

Although the most common form of the uncertainty principle relates position and momentum, the principle has been generalized much more widely. Another well-known example is the relation between the uncertainties in energy (E) and time (t) expressed as

$$\Delta E \Delta t \geq \frac{h}{4\pi}.$$

A common example of this relates to the emission of radiation by an atom. It is known that this radiation takes place by the emission of a photon as the atom undergoes a transition from one energy level to another, and that there is an intrinsic uncertainty in this energy. There is also an uncertainty in the time an atom will exist in its excited state before decaying, and these are found to be related by the energy-time uncertainty relation.

Similar reasoning leads to some interesting results in the field of fundamental particle physics. Many exotic particles are liable to decay, transforming into other more stable entities. Such a decay may take place at any time, but the time during which, on average, half of a sample of such particles will decay is well defined and known as the half-life. Since the actual time the particle exists can be from a time much shorter than its lifetime to one much larger, the half-life is also a measure of the uncertainty in the particle's lifetime. The energy of such a particle is mainly contained in its mass (m), according to Einstein's famous relation $E = mc^2$. When the mass of such a particle is measured, a spread of values is obtained and the width of this spread is related to the lifetime by the energy–time uncertainty principle.

Despite these successes, the energy-time uncertainty principle is considerably more controversial than that relating position and momentum, because time is quite different in nature from dynamic quantities such as position and momentum. The latter are properties particular to the object or system being considered, but time—in so far as we understand it at all—is a universal parameter, not clearly identified with any particular physical object. Its relation to energy is not at all obvious. The famous physicist Lev Landau asked, "Why should there be a relation between the fact that I measure the energy of an atom at the same time as I look at my watch?" Moreover, when position-momentum uncertainty was discussed earlier, the author emphasized the importance of the two measurements being simultaneous: if there is an uncertainty in the time, the whole concept of simultaneity appears to lose its meaning. There has been considerable controversy in this area, but it seems to be generally agreed that the energy-time uncertainty principle can be safely applied to cases of the type considered above, where a time such as the half-life is in some sense a property of the system—sometimes referred to as "internal" time. However, situations involving "external" time, such as the time when a measurement of the energy is made, may not be subject to this principle, although no experiment has ever been performed to demonstrate this.

It should be noted that all the discussion so far has been in the context of the conventional, or "Copenhagen," interpretation of quantum mechanics. Questions about the meaning of the uncertainty principle can lead to profound physical and philosophical problems that are still the subject of considerable controversy and debate.

See also: BROGLIE WAVELENGTH, DE; HEISENBERG, WERNER KARL; PLANCK CONSTANT; QUANTUM MECHANICS; QUANTUM MECHANICS, CREATION OF; QUANTUM THEORY, ORIGINS OF; QUANTUM THEORY OF MEASUREMENT

Bibliography

PEIERLS, R. *Surprises in Theoretical Physics* (Princeton University Press, Princeton, NJ, 1979).

RAE, A. I. M. *Quantum Mechanics,* 3rd ed. (IOPP, Philadelphia, 1992).

WHEELER, J. A., and ZUREK, W. H. Z. *Quantum Theory and Measurement* (Princeton University Press, Princeton, NJ, 1983).

ALASTAIR I. M. RAE

UNIT VECTOR

See VECTOR, UNIT

UNIVERSE

The *observable* universe extends out to approximately 10 billion light years. This is the approximate distance to the most remote objects, galaxies and quasars, that can be detected and identified on images taken with the largest telescopes on Earth. The universe contains approximately 1 billion galaxies comparable in luminosity to the Milky Way, and up to one hundred times more dwarf galaxies. According to the big bang cosmology, the observable universe spans the distance traversed by light since the epoch of the big bang, known as the *particle horizon,* hence it contained far less matter at early epochs. The beginning of classical cosmology is at the Planck instant, 10^{-43} s. At this point, the presently observable universe extended over about 0.01 cm, but the particle horizon then was only about 10^{-32} cm across. Hence cosmologists are confident that the actual universe today must be far larger than we can see at present. Otherwise, we would be living at a very special epoch in cosmic history when the universe was about to stop expanding.

According to the theory of *inflation,* the scale of the universe expanded exponentially with increasing time for a brief period, instead of its usual Friedmann–Lemaitre-like rate with a scale proportional to the square root of time. Although inflation only lasted from about 10^{-35} to 10^{-33} s, this sufficed for the size of the observable universe at this time to increase by e^{100} or more. Consequently, the universe today must be far larger than the horizon scale, perhaps by a factor of 10^{10}. That the cosmic microwave background is almost completely uniform to a level of about 1 part in 10^5 on the largest angular scales can be used as a fact to argue that the actual universe must be at least 10^5 larger than the present horizon, if inflation indeed occurred.

The contents of the observable universe show structure on an immense variety of scales, from subatomic to stellar, interstellar, and intergalactic. Subatomic structure, the theory of elementary particles, is believed to arise as a consequence of the breaking of symmetries between electromagnetic and weak nuclear forces, between electroweak and strong nuclear forces at the grand unified transition (GUT), and even between gravity and the grand unified forces. These occurred at epochs of 10^{-10} s (at an energy of 100 GeV), 10^{-35} s (at 10^{15} GeV), and 10^{-43} s (or 10^{19} GeV) after the big bang.

Large-scale structure is seeded by inflation, if indeed inflation occurred. One consequence of inflation is that fluctuations at the quantum scale are boosted to macroscopic scales during the inflationary period. In this way, density fluctuations are laid down on scales much larger than the horizon scale, and span the range from galaxies to galaxy clusters, and indeed to the scale of the observable universe. Equal strength fluctuations are predicted on all scales. Remarkably, the detection of infinitesimal temperature fluctuations in the cosmic microwave background by the COBE satellite in 1992 is in excellent accord with the inflationary prediction. The fluctuations grow by gravitational instability, once the radiation density has dropped below the matter density. This occurred when the universe was about 1/10,000 of its present size, about 10,000 years after the big bang. The equal-strength property of the fluctuations means that since the excess gravity exerts a similar role in terms of the local gravitational potential energy, the density is correspondingly larger for the smaller-scale fluctuations. Hence the smallest objects are the first to condense out of the expanding universe. Structure developed in a bottom-up sequence, from dwarf galaxies to the great clusters of galaxies that are still forming today.

Galactic mass clouds themselves fragment into stars. Elliptical galaxies, amounting to about 10 percent of the galaxies, underwent star formation in an initial burst of activity, whereas spirals undergo star formation at a steady rate. Spirals first collapse into a rotationally supported disk, in which the rate of star formation self-regulates as massive stars form and inject energy into the interstellar medium. Cold gas clouds are the raw material out of which stars form and are continuously accumulated as the galaxy rotates.

In the more distant universe, there is evidence for a higher fraction of star-forming galaxies than are seen in nearby samples. This is true both in random fields as well as in galaxy clusters. Approximately 1 percent of nearby galaxies are irregular, showing signs of a recent merger, whereas this fraction is considerably higher in the early universe. There is clear evidence of evolution in the population of galaxies.

Approximately 6 percent of galaxies are in clusters, containing 1,000 or more galaxies within a scale of approximately 3 Mpc. Clusters are gravitationally bound aggregates, and galaxy random motions are measured to be on the order of 1,000 km/s. As a consequence of this deep gravitational potential well, the intracluster gas, which amounts to about 10 percent or 20 percent of the cluster mass, is hot, at a temperature of several tens of millions of degrees Kelvin, and is detected via its diffuse x-ray emission. The gas is found to be enriched in iron and other elements, to a level of about 50 percent of the solar abundance, suggesting a past history that must have involved injection from galaxies. Indeed, most cluster galaxies, unlike those in lower density regions, are gas-poor ellipticals. Very distant clusters reveal a much higher fraction of star-forming, gas-rich galaxies as well as lower overall x-ray luminosities, consistent with the hypothesis of gas stripping or ejection as a source of at least some of the intracluster gas.

Some of the best candidates for the youngest galaxies are found by studying intervening systems of absorption lines that are detected in the spectra of distant quasars. The presence of primitive hydrogen clouds is inferred, with heavy element abundances only 1 percent or less than that of the Sun. Far more of these clouds are seen in the remote universe, when it was between one-third and one-quarter of its present size, than are seen nearby. The amount of gas in the largest clouds is close to what one needs to form the spiral galaxies; the cloud properties are tantalizingly similar, in terms of inferred column density of hydrogen, diameter, and rotation velocity, to the presumed galaxy precursors. There also are many more small absorbing clouds, the likely precursors of the numerous dwarf galaxies found in the nearby universe. Both these clouds and the faintest galaxies seen in the deepest images taken with very large telescopes are relatively unclustered in space, as compared with nearby galaxies. Clustering under the influence of gravitation is expected to grow and strengthen with time. The indications of evolution in the amplitude of clustering support the cosmological scheme, whereby gravitational instability is continuously operating as large-scale structure develops with time.

One of the greatest puzzles about the universe is common both to galaxies and galaxy clusters, although the solutions may differ. At least 90 percent of the mass of galaxies, and a comparable amount in galaxy clusters, is not detectable at any wavelengths. Evidence for the existence of the dark matter comes from galaxy rotation curves, which sample the total mass enclosed within the halos of galaxies, and from the dispersion in velocities of cluster galaxies. Halos extend to approximately 100,000 pc around galaxies similar to the Milky Way. Elliptical galaxies also are found to have dark halos: Here one infers the evidence for dark matter by measuring the random motions of orbiting planetary nebulae and globular star clusters. The dark matter in galaxy halos contributes about 6 percent toward the critical density for closure of the universe.

A convenient measure of dark matter is the ratio of mass-to-light, the latter referring to both stars and gas. For galaxies, this ratio is about one hundred solar masses per solar luminosity, whereas for the inner Milky Way, where one can account for almost all of the mass in terms of star and gas, the ratio is about three to one. For older stellar populations, in elliptical galaxies, the mass-to-light ratio is approximately ten to one. Anything larger is of unknown composition. By contrast, closure of the universe would require a mass-to-light ratio of 1,500. Galaxy clusters contain more dark matter per unit of luminous matter than do galaxies, a typical mass-to-luminosity ratio for a galaxy cluster being about 300. While clusters are the largest regions where mass is reliably measured, studies of the random motions of galaxies on scales of up to 20 million or even 50 million parsecs strongly suggest that the universe also is dominated to a similar level on these scales by dark matter. Astronomers infer that the dynamic mass content of the universe amounts to about 20 percent of the critical density.

The nature of the dark matter is an unsolved problem in cosmology. The successful prediction of light element nucleosynthesis in the first three minutes of the big bang requires an amount of baryonic dark matter that is coincidentally close to what is measured in halos. Because the most logical place for baryonic dark matter is in the vicinity of luminous baryonic matter in scenarios for structure formation, one suspects that on galaxy halo scales the dark matter may be baryonic. On larger scales, the dark matter is most likely nonbaryonic.

Baryonic dark matter should consist of compact objects, the leading candidate being brown dwarfs, objects too low in mass (below $0.08 M_\odot$) to be hydrogen-burning stars. However, white dwarfs, black holes, or even dense, cold molecular clouds cannot be excluded. Experiments are underway to detect these massive halo objects (MACHOs), utilizing the gravitational microlensing of stars to probe our dark halo in the direction of the Large Magellanic Cloud. A few MACHOs may have been detected in the first generation of these experiments, but one cannot yet tell if the detections suffice to account for the dark matter content of the Milky Way's dark halo.

Nonbaryonic dark matter consists of weakly interacting massive particles (WIMPs) that are plausible relics of supersymmetry (SUSY). SUSY, for which there is some experimental evidence, described the properties of matter at the high energies unique to the very early universe. This theory doubled the numbers of known particles by requiring a boson partner for every fermion, and vice versa. When the temperature of the universe dropped below the SUSY energy scale, almost all of the exotic particles decayed, except for the lightest supersymmetric particle (LSP). The LSP is the favored candidate for nonbaryonic dark matter, being weakly interacting (with roughly the cross section of a neutrino) and massive (with a predicted mass of between ten and a hundred proton masses). The large LSP mass guarantees that as the early universe expanded and cooled, the particles would lose any random motions and be equivalent to a gas of cold dark matter (CDM). In contrast, any stable light particles, such as neutrinos with small masses, could also contribute to the dark matter, but they would be relatively hot dark matter (HDM). In essence, CDM decouples early from the radiation content of the universe, whereas HDM decouples late.

There are important consequences for large-scale structure formation. HDM forms structure very late because gravitational instability is only effective once the dark matter has cooled by adiabatic expansion. The consequence is a top-down theory for structure formation: Large cluster-mass structures form at a late epoch, and consequently fragment into galaxies. Any primordial galaxy-scale fluctuations were erased by the large random motions of the hot dark matter particles. The top-down theory is now largely discredited, as it fails to form structure sufficiently early in the universe. In contrast, CDM results in a bottom-up structure formation sequence that does succeed in forming the first galaxies when the universe was about one-tenth of its present size.

Experiments are underway to search for the LSP, both in particle accelerators and as cosmological relics. The Sun and Earth continuously pass through a dilute sea of dark matter particles. The astrophysical experiments include direct detection of halo particles in the laboratory, utilizing cryogenic detectors. The LSP candidates are majorana particles, which means that the LSP is its own antiparticle. Consequently, when the weakly interacting particles aggregate together, occasional annihilations occur. Searches for signatures of LSP annihilations are being performed for the Sun, where dark matter particles are trapped as the Sun orbits the galaxy. The resulting annihilations produce high energy neutrinos that are quite distinct from the neutrinos produced by nuclear reactions in the solar core. Annihilations also occur in the halo, where signatures include gamma rays, cosmic ray antiprotons, and positrons.

Our knowledge of the universe is secure only insofar as we can observe its contents and infer its past evolution. The expansion of the universe is studied in detail over a look-back time of several billions of years, as far as we can securely identify rich galaxy clusters. It is the expansion that provided the first confirmation of the big bang theory. The most distant objects in the universe are a galaxy at redshift 4.25 and a quasar at redshift 4.9; one plus redshift is the measured factor by which the wavelength of light has increased between emission and observation, and also gives the factor by which the universe has since expanded. This takes us back to approximately 5 billion years after the big bang.

The microwave background probes even farther back in time. Photons traveled freely since they last scattered, at a redshift of 1,000, some 300,000 years after the big bang. We have detected temperature fluctuations created at the epoch of last scattering on angular scales from tens of arc minutes to tens of degrees. The blackbody spectrum of the microwave background testifies to an earlier epoch, about one year after the big bang, when the universe was last dense and hot enough to have acted like an ideal furnace and produced blackbody photons. No distortions are found from the blackbody spectrum to better than a fraction of 1 percent, and a cosmological origin provides the only successful explanation.

One can do even better, although the evidence is less direct: The light elements, helium, deuterium, and lithium, were synthesized in the first minutes of the big bang. The nuclear reaction sequence produced the abundances of each of these elements at a level similar to what is observed, provided that the baryon density is suitably adjusted. This may be considered to be the third experimental pedestal of the big bang explanation for the observed universe. Beyond that, the theory is increasingly less testable.

Baryon genesis at the electroweak scale, or earlier, accounts for the number of observed baryons per photon but with enormous theoretical uncertainty. Inflation, at the grand unification scale, accounts for the vast size of the observable, and unobservable, universe, for the origin of the density fluctuations that seeded large-scale structure, and for the proximity of the observed density to the critical value for closure. Indeed, inflation predicts that the density should be within less than $1/100,000$ of 1 percent of the closure value. This requires more dark matter than has yet been measured, and it poses an experimental challenge that still awaits resolution.

See also: BIG BANG THEORY; COSMIC MICROWAVE BACKGROUND RADIATION; COSMOLOGY; COSMOLOGY, INFLATIONARY; DARK MATTER; GALAXIES AND GALACTIC STRUCTURE; NEUTRINO; RADIATION, BLACKBODY; UNIVERSE, EXPANSION OF

Bibliography

BARROW, J., and SILK, J. *The Left Hand of Creation* (Oxford University Press, Oxford, Eng., 1994).

SILK, J. *The Big Bang* (W. H. Freeman, New York, 1989).

SILK, J. *A Short History of the Universe* (W. H. Freeman, New York, 1994).

JOSEPH SILK

UNIVERSE, EXPANSION OF

In 1929 Edwin Hubble demonstrated that the recession speed of a galaxy increased proportionately with its distance. This presented a turning point in the knowledge of the universe. The established viewpoint prior to Hubble's discovery was that the universe was static. This presented somewhat of a quandary to Albert Einstein, who had developed in 1916 the first cosmological model for the universe in the framework of his newly developed theory of gravitation—the theory of general relativity. Einstein realized that his cosmology, which was a model of a static universe, was unstable. The attractive force of gravity was unopposed by any countering force, and the static universe could not stay static: it would collapse. To avoid this disaster, Einstein hypothesized that there had to exist a repulsive force that only manifested itself on the very largest scale—that of the universe itself. Thus was the "cosmological constant" born, a term allowed by the general relativity theory, and one that has been subsequently reinterpreted in terms of the energy density of a vacuum.

However, the cosmological repulsion was destined first to die before any rebirth became possible. The attack came on two fronts: the observational evidence for expansion, developed by Hubble, and the theoretical argument for an expanding universe that was pioneered before the observational case was made for an expanding universe. In an expanding universe, the cosmological constant became redundant. The first indications that all was not necessarily in order with the proposed static universe were present in the work of Vesto Slipher, who, from 1912 onwards, working at the Lowell Observatory, systematically obtained the radial velocities of many spiral nebulae. These were believed to be, according to the conventional wisdom of the time, satellite companions of the Milky Way. Slipher found that almost all of the spiral nebulae had redshifted spectra, thus implying, according to the usual Doppler shift interpretation of spectral line shifts, that the nebulae were predominately receding from the Milky Way at velocities up to or exceeding 1,000 km/s.

The next milestone in the unfolding cosmological saga was set by Willem de Sitter, who immediately followed Einstein's static universe model with the discovery of a novel cosmological model that was empty, containing no matter whatsoever. However, the de Sitter universe did possess the bizarre property that space displayed a redshift, increasing systematically with distance. Cosmologists, theorists, and observers alike welcomed this development as a means of reconciling theory with Slipher's redshifts by now approaching the unprecedented level equivalent to velocities in excess of 1,000 km/s. The essence of the physics was lost in the debate between the relative merits of Einstein's and de Sitter's models of the universe.

Georges Lemaître was acutely aware that an empty universe was an absurdity. The Belgian cosmologist, ordained as a priest in 1923, spent time at the Mount Wilson and Harvard observatories and convinced himself of the need for a physical cosmological model. In 1927 Lemaître announced a new theory of the expanding universe: a universe containing matter, and expanding from a dense, singular origin in time. By a curious historical twist, the Russian mathematician Alexander Friedmann had already published an identical expanding universe model during the period from 1922 to 1924. Einstein was fully aware of Friedmann's work, critically attacking it for an alleged mathematical error. When Einstein conceded the error was his own, his subsequent reaction was to dismiss the expanding universe as devoid of physical content. The static nature of space remained a deeply embedded concept in the cosmological worldview until 1929.

Hubble's great achievement in that year was to have determined the distances to the nebulae for which Slipher had obtained radial velocities. The new distances enabled Hubble to demonstrate that redshift increases systematically with distance. Hubble derived a rate of recession that is now known to be too large by a factor between 5 and 10. This led to an expansion age of the universe that was only 2 billion years, or less than the age of the earth as inferred from the dating of the oldest rocks. For this reason, and also because, Lemaître apart, the cosmologists of the early 1930s tended to describe the cosmological models in the language of mathematical general relativity, the acceptance that space really was expanding proved to be a paradigm shift that was to take a decade or more before astronomers readily accepted the expanding universe.

A major breakthrough occurred in 1952 when Walter Baade revised Hubble's distance scale to derive what essentially is the modern value of the expansion rate of the universe. For every megaparsec of distance, the recession velocity increases, on the average, by about 100 km/s per megaparsec. This is within the currently accepted range, although some recent determinations result in values that are about 50 percent lower. The inferred duration of the expansion in the "big bang" cosmology, a term coined by Fred Hoyle to describe the Friedmann–Lemaître cosmological models, is now recognized as being between 7 billion and 20 billion years. This range comfortably exceeds the age of the solar system, about 4.6 billion years, and spans the ages of the oldest stars. Prior to Baade's distance scale revision, the expansion time had seemed to be less than the age of the earth, an uncomfortable situation that led to the birth of the steady-state theory of cosmology, in which continuous creation of matter assured that the universe had an infinite age. The distance scale revision removed much of the motivation for a steady-state universe. Subsequent cosmological discoveries—most notably those presenting evidence for an early dense and hot phase of the universe, inferred, respectively, from counts of distant radio galaxies and the cosmic microwave background radiation—contradicted the predictions of steady-state cosmology and supported the big bang origin of the universe.

The Hubble law has now been measured to a distance more than one hundred times further than Hubble originally probed, out to recession velocities that exceed one-third of the speed of light, or to about 100,000 km/s. No deviations from a linear expansion law have been confirmed. Deviations are predicted, because the fact that the universe contains matter means that gravity must cause some deceleration between our galaxy and the most distant galaxies. Detection of deceleration would provide a means of measuring the curvature of space, which is equivalent in Einstein's theory of gravity to a determination of the matter content of the universe. Such a measurement would help decide whether the density of the universe exceeds the critical density, at which the universe would barely continue to expand forever. This critical density constitutes the Einstein–de Sitter universe, in which gravitational and expansion energies are in exact balance, and space is consequently Euclidean. If the density is larger than the critical value, which is equal to $3H_0^2/8\pi G$, where H_0 is Hubble's constant and G is Newton's constant of gravity, space is positively curved, like the surface of a sphere, and the universe is eventually destined to decelerate, reach a point of maximum expansion approximately 10 billion years from now, and then recollapse.

On the other hand, if the density of the universe is below the critical density, space is negatively curved, like the surface of a saddle, and the universe will continue to expand forever. It has hitherto not been possible to decide between these alternative fates for the universe because the most distant galaxies are viewed at an epoch when they were much younger than nearby galaxies. We do not know if they are intrinsically more or less luminous than their local counterparts. Such youthful galaxies could dim or brighten as they age, depending on whether they mature in isolation or by merging with nearby systems. Hence it has not yet been possible to disentangle the effects of space curvature, which imply that in a positively curved universe, galaxies at a given redshift are closer than in a negatively curved universe.

The reality of the expansion of the universe was disputed in the 1930s and 1940s, but the supporting evidence has gradually become unchallengeable. For example, redshifts of distant galaxies are measured both at optical, radio, and most recently at x-ray wavelengths. There is no physical mechanism that could simulate the effects of redshift, such as a hypothesized loss of energy by light, over such a broad spectral range. Distances are measured directly in some cases by geometrical techniques, out to one-third or more of the scale of the observable universe. Counts of distant galaxies suggest that, when the universe was one-half of its present expansion age, it was correspondingly dense. An even more powerful probe of the expansion is provided by the cosmic microwave background, a relic of the early dense phase of the expanding universe, which has been measured at a distance corresponding to a look-back time of 90 percent of the age of the universe. The expanding universe model predicts the universe once was much denser, and the measured microwave background temperature at this early epoch is correspondingly higher than the value measured today. This is perhaps the most fundamental proof of the expansion of space.

In retrospect, one simple argument suggests that Hubble's law could have been predicted. The assumption of isotropy of space at all points in an expanding universe requires all galaxies to recede from one another. Indeed, this was the basis of the Newtonian cosmologies developed as physical counterparts of the relativistic Friedmann–Lemaître models in the 1930s by such cosmologists as Otto Heckman, William McCrea, and Edward Milne. One of the lessons from general relativity is that it is space that is expanding, and the galaxies are nonexpanding beacons that participate in the expansion of space. No deviations from isotropic expansion have been found, the uniformity in all directions of the microwave background radiation demonstrating that the expansion is isotropic to better than 1 part in 1,000,000.

The expansion of the universe implies that the universe originated in an extremely dense and hot phase. The extreme smoothness of the microwave background probes the universe when the radiation was last scattered by matter, some 300,000 years after the big bang. The blackbody spectrum, showing no spectral distortions to better than $1/100$ of 1 percent, must have been produced within 1 year of the big bang, when the universe was last dense and hot enough to create blackbody photons. The successful predictions of the abundance of the light elements helium, deuterium, and lithium require the expansion rate of the universe less than three minutes after the big bang to have been precisely that predicted by the Friedmann–Lemaître model. Indeed, the expanding universe model describes our cosmology back to within seconds of the big bang.

The theory of the expanding universe can be extrapolated back in time to the initial singularity itself, when the universe was infinitely dense. It is generally conceded that such an extrapolation is meaningless. The first instant of physical time occurred at the Planck instant, 10^{-43} s after the big bang singularity would have occurred. The Planck instant represents the scale where quantum theory and gravitation have comparable strengths, and we lack a unified theory that would describe smaller-scale earlier instants. The expanding universe theory describes the expansion from the Planck instant until the present time.

However, relics from the first second of the universe are elusive. The ordinary matter, or baryon, content of the universe is conjectured to have been created during a phase transition that occurred at most 10^{-10} s after the big bang. The density fluctuations that seeded galaxy formation and the development of large-scale structure are believed to be one of the consequences of an even earlier phase transition that occurred about 10^{-35} s after the big bang. Prior to this instant, the particle energies were so high that the fundamental forces of electromagnetism and the weak and strong nuclear forces were indistinguishable. As the universe expanded and the temperature dropped, the fundamental forces separated in strength, eventually attaining the distinct domains that are found in the present-day universe, where the nuclear forces that hold molecules together are far stronger than the electromagnetic forces that hold atoms together.

There are strong theoretical arguments for believing that force unification occurred, and there are even indications from relatively low-energy experiments in particle accelerators that unification would have occurred at the extremely high energies unique to the very early universe. The ensuing phase transition created not only density fluctuations, but the energy released—analogous to latent heat—is believed to have triggered a brief phase of exponential expansion, called inflation. The inflationary universe is responsible for the universe today being as large as it is, and for being as homogeneous and isotropic as it is measured to be. The large amount of rapid expansion acted to smooth out local deviations in space curvature that would have created unacceptably large inhomogeneities, and at the same time laid down the seeds for the future growth of structure. This extrapolation back in time of the expanding universe model is capable of accounting for many properties of the universe that are otherwise unexplainable in terms of physics and were previously attributed to the initial conditions of a unique universe. Inflation allows a wide variety of initial conditions to have evolved into the observed universe.

See also: BIG BANG THEORY; COSMIC MICROWAVE BACKGROUND RADIATION; COSMOLOGICAL CONSTANT; COSMOLOGY; COSMOLOGY, INFLATIONARY; EINSTEIN, ALBERT; HUBBLE, EDWIN POWELL; RADIATION, BLACKBODY; REDSHIFT; UNIVERSE

Bibliography

BARROW, J., and SILK, J. *The Left Hand of Creation* (Oxford University Press, Oxford, Eng., 1994).

SILK, J. *The Big Bang* (W. H. Freeman, New York, 1989).

SILK, J. *A Short History of the Universe* (W. H. Freeman, New York, 1994).

JOSEPH SILK

UNIVERSE, EXPANSION OF, DISCOVERY OF

A static universe has been assumed during much of human history. The idea of an expanding universe

seemed senseless and irritating even to Albert Einstein, and with the rise of relativity theory early in the twentieth century, astronomers initially sought only static solutions. The Dutch astronomer Willem de Sitter proposed a static model among whose observational consequences was an apparent but not real velocity of recession that was greater for objects at greater distances. Eventually other factors eliminated the model from consideration as a real representation of the universe, but not before the model stimulated searches for a velocity-distance relation. After the demise of de Sitter's theory, redshifts in the spectra of light from galaxies generally were interpreted as Doppler shifts indicative of real motion in an expanding universe.

The discovery of high radial velocities (the velocity component in the line of sight between object and observer—what is measured from the Doppler shift of spectral lines) actually occurred before de Sitter's theory, with Vesto M. Slipher's work at the Lowell Observatory in Arizona beginning in 1912. The first velocity he reported for a spiral nebula (only later was it determined to be a galaxy outside of our own) was so extraordinarily high that few other astronomers believed it. By 1920 Slipher had determined velocities for some twenty spiral nebulas, but their distances were unknown and de Sitter's prediction of an apparent velocity-distance relation resisted testing.

Distances, the other half of the predicted relation, only began to become available with the work of Edwin Hubble at the Mount Wilson Observatory during the 1920s. Using the new 100-in. telescope, he found Cepheid variable stars in several spiral nebulas. These stars are a useful indicator of distances because their brightness correlates with their period of variation. Using the period-luminosity relationship for Cepheids in our own galaxy (established by Harlow Shapley at Mount Wilson before he left for the Harvard College Observatory), Hubble determined distances for the Cepheids he had found and also for the galaxies in which they were embedded. Shapley's relation was between absolute luminosity (the apparent brightness measured at a standard distance) and period (the time over which the variable star's brightness changed from maximum to minimum and back to maximum). Hubble measured periods for Cepheids in spiral nebulas and then assumed they had the absolute luminosity corresponding to Cepheids of the same period in our galaxy. Finally, Hubble calculated how far away the Cepheids had to be for their absolute luminosity

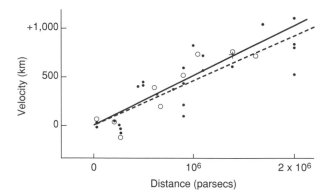

Figure 1 Hubble's graph of radial velocities of spiral nebulae (vertical axis) versus distances (horizontal axis). The solid circles and the solid line represent data for twenty-four nebulae for which individual distances were determined. The open circles and the dashed line represent data for the same twenty-four nebulae combined into nine groups according to proximity in direction and distance. The cross represents the mean velocity for twenty-two nebulae whose distances could not be estimated individually.

to be diminished to the apparent luminosity that he measured—luminosity being reduced in inverse proportion to the distance squared. To determine the distances of galaxies so far away (and thus so faint) that Cepheids were not detectable in them, Hubble first calculated an average absolute luminosity for galaxies at known distances. He then used this in conjunction with measured apparent luminosities to estimate distances from the difference between estimated absolute luminosity and measured apparent luminosity.

Hubble was aware of de Sitter's cosmological model and its predicted velocity-distance relation, and after a meeting in Holland in 1928 he returned to Mount Wilson determined to test the theory. Milton Humason, a meticulous and gifted observer, systematically measured velocities of fainter (and thus more distant) galaxies. In 1929 Hubble announced an empirical velocity-distance relation. Hubble's graph of radial velocities of spiral nebulas versus distances is shown in Fig. 1. Establishment of a velocity-distance relation was a great cosmological breakthrough, overthrowing entrenched belief in a static universe and establishing an expanding universe. Interpretation of the stunning result soon followed.

At a meeting of the Royal Astronomical Society in January 1930, de Sitter commented on the inability of existing relativistic models to represent adequately the observed universe. The observation by a fellow Dutch astronomer, Jan Oort, of considerable matter in the universe ruled out de Sitter's model, and Hubble's velocity-distance relation ruled out the only other static relativistic model, which had been proposed by Einstein himself. It was a time of crisis in astronomy. Rising after de Sitter to speak at the meeting was the English astronomer Arthur Eddington. "I suppose," he said, "the trouble is that people look for static solutions."

Eddington's comment, printed in a report of the meeting, stimulated the Belgian astronomer Georges Lemaître to send his nonstatic solution to his former teacher. Eddington immediately recognized in Lemaître's expanding model of the universe an explanation of the velocity-distance relation and resolution of the crisis. Much work remained to be done, and a few alternative possibilities to be eliminated, but Lemaître's solution, considerably developed and elaborated over the years, became the generally accepted big bang universe.

During the 1950s big bang cosmology was rivaled by steady-state cosmology, in which the creation of new matter was postulated at such a rate as to maintain a constant density in the universe despite its expansion. A constant density was attractive because it gave greater assurance that the laws of physics would remain unchanged over time. The battle between the two theories would be decided by the most important discovery in cosmology since Hubble's 1929 redshift-distance relation.

In 1948 George Gamow, a Russian-born physicist working in the United States, had predicted that Lemaître's big bang universe would change from radiation dominated to matter dominated. Two of his students, Ralph Alpher and Robert Herman, went on to predict the existence of a cosmic background radiation left over from the time when the universe had changed. But no one paid any attention to their result. In 1965 Arno Penzias and Robert Wilson at Bell Laboratories were unable to eliminate noise completely in a new radio antenna, even after removing a pair of roosting pigeons. The solution finally came when they saw a preprint of a paper by Robert Dicke and P. J. E. Peebles, physicists at nearby Princeton University, discussing a possible cosmic background radiation. The unwanted antenna noise was actually a measurement of the cosmic background radiation, and for its discovery Penzias and Wilson won a Nobel Prize.

Observations during the 1980s and into the 1990s have suggested the existence of large-scale inhomogeneities in the universe. If confirmed, such a discovery, violating the cosmological principle (that the universe is the same everywhere—homogeneous and isotropic), would raise serious difficulties for our current understanding of the expansion of the universe.

The inflationary universe theory, proposed in the early 1980s, features a tremendous expansion in the first tiny fraction of a second, after which the model reverts to the standard big bang cosmology. Future observational discoveries made to confirm or refute this theory also will be of considerable interest to particle physicists. Their theories have outgrown the energies attainable in particle accelerators and approach the tremendous energy level of the very early universe.

The expansion of the universe, hinted at in Slipher's early observations, established by Hubble, predicted from, incorporated within, and explained by relativity theory, and further confirmed by the discovery (and interpretation of the discovery) of the cosmic background radiation, now can safely be said to have been discovered, whatever actually constitutes the act of discovery. Interaction between theory and observation, especially fascinating in the history of cosmology, is not over, however, and discovery of the expansion of the universe continues.

See also: BIG BANG THEORY; COSMIC MICROWAVE BACKGROUND RADIATION; COSMOLOGICAL PRINCIPLE; COSMOLOGY; DOPPLER EFFECT; GALAXIES AND GALACTIC STRUCTURE; HUBBLE, EDWIN POWELL; REDSHIFT; UNIVERSE, EXPANSION OF

Bibliography

BERENDZEN, R.; HART, R.; and SEELEY, D. *Man Discovers the Galaxies* (Science History Publications, New York, 1976).

HETHERINGTON, N., ed. *Cosmology: Historical, Literary, Philosophical, Religious, and Scientific Perspectives* (Garland, New York, 1993).

HUBBLE, E. *The Realm of the Nebulae* (Yale University Press, New Haven, CT, 1936).

HUBBLE, E. "The Problem of the Expanding Universe." *Am. Sci.* **30,** 99–115 (1942).

SMITH, R. *The Expanding Universe: Astronomy's "Great Debate,"* *1900–1931* (Cambridge University Press, Cambridge, Eng., 1982).

NORRISS S. HETHERINGTON

V

VACUUM

Vacuum is defined as the condition of a gaseous environment in which the gas pressure is below atmospheric. Aristotle argued that, since light could not penetrate a vacuum, the fact that light from the stars could be seen on Earth demonstrated that a vacuum could not exist. Plutarch wrote that "nature abhors a vacuum." Aristotle's views were still upheld by the Church in the seventeenth century and the very name of "vacuum" was an anathema. René Descartes wrote, "it is contrary to reason to say that there is a vacuum or space in which there is absolutely nothing." Nevertheless, around 1640 Gasparo Berti constructed a water manometer and produced a vacuum in the space above the water column.

The famous experiment which finally convinced philosophers of the existence of vacuum was designed in 1643 by the Italian scientist Evangelista Torricelli and was performed in 1644 by Vincenzo Viviani. A glass tube about a meter long was sealed at one end and then filled with mercury. The experimenter closed the open end with his thumb and inverted the tube so that the open end was below the surface of mercury in a dish. He then removed his thumb and the mercury in the tube dropped to a level about 760 mm above the mercury surface, leaving an empty space above the mercury column. Torricelli's experiment was kept secret in Italy for fear of excommunication, but news of the creation of a vacuum soon reached other countries where the authority of the pope in Rome was not as strong. The Torricellian experiment was repeated in France (which had its own French pope at the time) and in Germany and England.

In 1654 the first piston-type vacuum pump was built in Germany by Otto von Guericke and an improved version was designed by Robert Boyle in England about 1660. By the end of the seventeenth century mechanical vacuum pumps and mercury manometers were in use for a variety of experiments. It was the invention of the incandescent lamp in the late nineteenth century, which had to be evacuated during manufacture, that first brought vacuum to manufacturing and created commercial vacuum technology.

Pressure in the vacuum range is measured in pascals (the SI unit), Torr, or millibar. Atmospheric pressure is 1.013×10^5 Pa, 760 Torr, or 1.013×10^3 mbar. The unit Torr is named after Torricelli and was originally known as the millimeter of mercury (mm Hg). The range of attainable pressures in vacuum is so enormous (from 760 to less than 10^{-20} Torr) that it is divided as shown in Table 1.

Pressure is related to the density of gas molecules by the equation $p = knT$ [k is Boltzmann's constant, n the number of molecules per milliliter, and T the temperature (K)], or $p = 1.036 \times 10^{-19}\, nT$ where p is in Torr. Several types of vacuum gauges (e.g., ionisation gauges) measure the molecular density (n) rather than pressure.

1657

Table 1 Range of Attainable Pressures in Vacuum

Vacuum	Torr	Pa	mbar
Low vacuum	760–1	10^5–10^2	10^3–1
Medium vacuum	1–10^{-3}	10^2–10^{-1}	1–10^{-3}
High vacuum	10^{-3}–10^{-8}	10^{-1}–10^{-6}	10^{-3}–10^{-8}
Ultrahigh vacuum (UHV)	10^{-8}–10^{-12}	10^{-6}–10^{-10}	10^{-8}–10^{-12}
Extreme high vacuum (XHV)	$< 10^{-12}$	$< 10^{-10}$	$< 10^{-12}$

Table 2 Conditions in Various Pressure Ranges

Pressure (Torr)	Molecular Density (mol·ml)	Molecular Flux (mol·cm^{-2}·s^{-1})	Mean Free Path	Monolayer Time
760	2.5×10^{19}	2.9×10^{23}	67 nm	2.9 ns
1	3.3×10^{16}	3.8×10^{20}	51 μm	2.2 μs
10^{-3}	3.3×10^{13}	3.8×10^{17}	5.1 cm	2.2 ms
10^{-8}	3.3×10^8	3.8×10^{12}	5.1 km	3.7 min
10^{-12}	3.3×10^4	3.8×10^8	5.1×10^4 km	25 days
10^{-16}	3.3	3.8×10^4	5.1×10^8 km (3.4 AU[a])	160 years

[a]Astronomical unit, the distance from Earth to the Sun.

The conditions in the various pressure ranges are very different as is indicated in Table 2. The second column shows the number of gas molecules per liter; at 10^{-16} Torr (the lowest pressure that can be both produced and measured) there are only about three molecules in a milliliter. The third column shows the number of gas molecules striking a square centimeter of surface per second. The fourth column indicates most clearly the enormous range of vacuum parameters, the mean free path (MFP) is the average distance between collisions of gas molecules; at atmospheric pressure the MFP is only 67 nm (about 200 times the spacing between atoms in a metal crystal), at 10^{-16} Torr the MFP is about three times the distance from Earth to the Sun. The last column shows the time taken to form a single layer of adsorbed gas molecules on a surface (assuming each gas molecule that strikes the surface sticks there) going from 2.9 ns at atmospheric pressure to 160 years at 10^{-16} Torr.

The pressure in interstellar space has been estimated as about 10^{-18} Torr. This may be compared with an earth-bound experiment where a one-liter sphere is pumped to 10^{-11} Torr and then immersed in liquid helium at 4.2 K; the estimated pressure is of the order of 10^{-30} Torr. The pressure at the surface of the Moon in the nighttime is about 10^{-13} Torr.

Vacuum is used widely in scientific research whenever it is necessary to (1) keep surfaces clean or in a well-characterized state (ultrahigh vacuum is used for studies in surface science), (2) create plasma and to keep plasma pure (plasma physics and tokamaks), (3) operate electron and ion beam apparatus, accelerators, colliders, and storage rings, and (4) simulate conditions in space.

In industrial applications vacuum is used for (1) lifting and transporting (low vacuum), (2) heat treatment, packaging, drying, degassing, and thermal or electrical insulation (high vacuum), and (3) the manufacture of lamps, vacuum tubes, and some solid state devices.

See also: PRESSURE, ATMOSPHERIC; VACUUM TECHNOLOGY

Bibliography

DUSHMAN, S., and LAFFERTY, J. M., eds. *Scientific Foundations of Vacuum Technique,* 2nd ed. (Wiley, New York, 1962).

REDHEAD, P. A.; HOBSON, J. P.; and KORNELSEN, E. V. *The Physical Basis of Ultrahigh Vacuum,* 2nd ed. (American Institute of Physics, Woodbury, NY, 1993).

SCHAFFER, S. *Leviathan and the Air-Pump* (Princeton University Press, Princeton, NJ, 1985).

P. A. REDHEAD

VACUUM STATE

In common usage, the word "vacuum" evokes the notion of emptiness, and one speaks of a region devoid of matter as the vacuum. This is also partly how technically the word is used in physics. Indeed, the study of how to achieve regions of very low pressure, or high vacuum, is of considerable technological importance. However, in physics the concept of the vacuum has also a deeper and broader meaning as a reference state for all measurements.

Perhaps the first instance of invoking the existence of a vacuum state as a reference state for measurements was the introduction in the nineteenth century of the notions of the ether. The need of having the ether as a reference state was precipitated by the appearance of the speed of light in James Clerk Maxwell's equations of electromagnetism. Classical thinking required that velocities, including the velocity of light, be measured relative to some frame. Thus presuming that the speed of light in Maxwell's equations was measured relative to the ether helped resolve an otherwise paradoxical situation. However, this construct was short lived, being dispelled by the Michelson–Morley experiment, which failed to find any motion of Earth relative to the ether! The right solution to this puzzle was found by Albert Einstein with the special theory of relativity. In special relativity the speed of light (c) is a universal constant independent of the frame it is measured in. So velocities are relative, but not the velocity of light and so there is no need to have an ether.

The notion of a vacuum state, however, re-emerged with the advent of quantum mechanics, and it brought along its own conundrums. In quantum mechanics, energy is quantized and physical systems have a well-defined state of minimum energy, known as the ground state. It is an intuitive requirement that the state describing a system with no particles, which one may properly call the vacuum state,

should carry no energy. Unfortunately, when one calculates in quantum mechanics the energy associated with such a vacuum state, one finds that its energy, rather than being zero, is infinite! Nevertheless, because only relative energies are measured, this is not really a major problem. It turns out that the same infinite energy also enters in describing states with particles, so that the energy difference between these states and the vacuum is well defined and finite.

The origin of the infinite energy of the quantum vacuum state can be understood as follows. In general, one can associate free particles of a given energy with harmonic oscillations of a given frequency of quantum fields defined at each point in space-time. In this description, the vacuum state corresponds to the state where all the quantum oscillators are in their ground state. In quantum mechanics, however, it turns out that a simple harmonic oscillator does not have zero energy in its ground state as it happens classically. Rather, the ground state energy of an oscillator is $E_0 = \frac{1}{2}h\nu$, where ν is the natural frequency of the oscillator and h is Planck's constant. This result is a consequence of Heisenberg's uncertainty principle, which does not allow the simultaneous setting to zero of both the position and the momentum of the oscillator.

Using this result, one sees that in the vacuum state each oscillator contributes a ground state energy $\frac{1}{2}h\nu$. Since one must sum over all possible oscillator frequencies ν, the resulting vacuum energy is infinite. This infinity is directly tied to having a nonvanishing ground state energy for the quantum oscillators. But there lies also the solution to the problem. This same infinite energy reappears when one considers, for example, the energy of a one-particle state. In this case, one of the oscillators is in the first excited state, with energy $E_1 = \frac{3}{2}h\nu'$, with ν' being related to the particle energy, while all the rest of the oscillators remain in the ground state. Although the energy of this one-particle state is also formally infinite, the difference in energy of this state to the vacuum state is simply $\frac{1}{2}h\nu'$—a perfectly finite and physically significant result.

Once the infinite zero-point energy is removed from the quantum vacuum state, this state is a zero-energy eigenstate. That is, the value of the quantum number associated with energy for the vacuum state is zero. This is, obviously, a property one wants for the vacuum state. Indeed, one expects, similarly, that the vacuum state should carry zero value for all other conserved quantum numbers: charge, momentum, angular momentum, and so on. Calling Q the operator associated with some conserved quantity and denoting the vacuum state by $|0>$, one expresses the fact that the vacuum does not carry this quantum number by the equation $Q|0> = 0$. Colloquially, one says that Q annihilates the vacuum.

Until the 1950s, the above equation embodied schematically all the features needed to characterize the quantum vacuum state. However, in 1956 our understanding of the nature of the quantum vacuum state was deepened as a result of the Bardeen–Cooper–Schrieffer (BCS) theory of superconductivity. In the BCS theory, the superconducting ground state plays the role of the vacuum state. Remarkably, one finds that in this state nonzero condensates of pairs of electrons with opposite spin form. That is, in the BCS vacuum the expectation value of the operator that describes two electrons with opposite spin does not vanish:

$$BCS < 0 | e^\uparrow e^\downarrow | 0 > BCS \neq 0.$$

The existence of these so-called Cooper pairs is an indication that the BCS vacuum state does not respect electron number. If electron number indeed had annihilated the state $|0> BCS$, then objects carrying two units of this quantum number could never have had an expectation value in this state. In the BCS theory, electron number, although a symmetry of the underlying dynamics, is not a symmetry of the solution. Such symmetries are known as spontaneously broken symmetries. The lesson of the BCS theory is that the vacuum state of a spontaneously broken theory, apparently, is able to carry some nonzero quantum number associated with the broken symmetry itself.

Because superconductivity is a property of materials and the formation of Cooper pairs is a result of the interaction of electrons with the underlying material lattice, the BCS vacuum is not quite the traditional vacuum state associated with the absence of any particle excitations. Thus it was not clear at first whether the notion of spontaneous symmetry breaking really could happen for the traditional vacuum. However, particularly through the work of Jeffrey Goldstone and Yoichiro Nambu, it was soon understood that spontaneous breakdown of a symmetry could occur, provided objects carrying nonzero quantum numbers of this symmetry (condensates) had a nonvanishing expectation value in the vacuum. Thus for spontaneously broken symmetries

the empty vacuum state really acts as if it is able to carry the quantum numbers associated with the broken symmetry. The term "degenerate vacuum state" is often used in this context because the symmetry operators acting on the vacuum state, apparently, do not annihilate the vacuum state but connect it to some other state of zero energy.

The vacuum state associated with theories where some symmetry is spontaneously broken is more complex, but also more interesting. It turns out that different physical phenomena occur depending on whether the symmetry in question is a global or a local symmetry. A global symmetry is one where there is an invariance of the underlying dynamics when one makes the same symmetry transformation for all points in spacetime. For local symmetries, on the other hand, one can make different symmetry transformations at each point in spacetime and still have an invariance of the dynamics. In the case of a spontaneously broken global symmetry, one can show that the action of a symmetry operator on the vacuum state rather than annihilating this state produces instead a particle of zero mass, called a Nambu–Goldstone boson. Unfortunately, no examples of truly massless Nambu–Goldstone bosons are known. However, there are examples of approximate global symmetries of nature that are spontaneously broken in which the associated Nambu–Goldstone bosons (which now have a small mass) have been identified.

More interesting, perhaps, is the case where a local symmetry is spontaneously broken. Local symmetries to occur physically need the presence of compensating gauge fields, one for each independent symmetry transformation. Again, if this local symmetry is spontaneously broken by the presence of some condensate, the action of each of the spontaneously broken symmetry operators on the vacuum will produce a Nambu–Goldstone boson. These excitations now, however, do not exist as independent massless particles. Rather, each Nambu–Goldstone boson combines with the two transverse polarizations of the spin-1 particles associated with each of the gauge fields to form a massive particle. This phenomena is known as the Higgs mechanism, and it is truly remarkable. The breakdown of a local symmetry, produced dynamically by having nonzero expectation values in the vacuum of objects carrying the symmetry, causes the massless gauge bosons associated with the symmetry to become massive. This transmutation transforms long-range forces, associated with the presence of zero mass particles, into short-range interactions, with the range being inversely proportional to the scale of the condensate that forms in the vacuum.

The combined theory of the weak and electromagnetic interactions, developed by Sheldon Glashow, Abdus Salam, and Steven Weinberg in the 1960s, is based on a spontaneously broken local symmetry. The vacuum state of this theory allows expectation values of nontrivial operators under this local symmetry that break it down just to the phase symmetry of electromagnetism. As a result, three of the four gauge bosons of the electroweak theory of Glashow, Salam, and Weinberg acquire a mass around 100 times the mass of the proton while the fourth, the photon, remains massless. The experimental observation of the $W^{\pm}$ and Z bosons in 1982, with precisely the properties expected of the carriers of the weak force, is direct proof of the correctness of the electroweak theory. It is also a confirmation of the existence in nature of the rich vacuum state associated with the spontaneous breakdown of the electroweak symmetry.

Although the spontaneous breakdown of the electroweak symmetry is established, this phenomenon has brought to the fore another conundrum. For the symmetry breakdown to occur one needs condensates carrying the symmetry to form in the vacuum. Such objects then necessarily also will contribute to the vacuum energy density. For the electroweak theory this contribution is of order

$$u_{\text{vacuum}} \sim \frac{(2\pi)^3 c^5 M_W^4}{h^5} \sim 10^{55} \text{ eV/cm}^3,$$

where MW is the mass of the W boson. This vacuum energy density, if taken at face value, would give an enormous and totally unacceptable contribution to the universe's cosmological constant. Whether there is such a cosmological constant is unclear, but one can at any rate put a bound on its magnitude. This bound, when translated in terms of a vacuum energy density, informs us that $u_{\text{vacuum}} < 10^4 \text{ eV/cm}^3$. It is an open question how to reconcile this stringent bound with the enormous energy density produced by the electroweak symmetry breakdown.

See also: BOSON, GAUGE; BOSON, HIGGS; BOSON, NAMBU–GOLDSTONE; COOPER PAIR; ELECTROMAGNETISM, DISCOVERY OF; GROUND STATE; INTERACTION, ELECTROWEAK; LIGHT, SPEED OF; PHOTON; QUANTUM FIELD THEORY; QUANTUM MECHANICS; RELATIVITY, SPECIAL THEORY OF; SPACETIME; SUPERCONDUCTIVITY; SYMMETRY BREAKING, SPONTANEOUS; UNCERTAINTY PRINCIPLE

Bibliography

ABBOTT, L. "The Mystery of the Cosmological Constant." *Sci. Am.* **258** (May), 106 (1988).
BOYER, T. "The Classical Vacuum." *Sci. Am.* **253** (Aug.), 70 (1985).

ROBERTO D. PECCEI

VACUUM TECHNOLOGY

Vacuum technology is concerned with the means to produce and measure vacuum. Vacuum is defined as the condition of a gaseous environment for which the gas pressure is below atmospheric.

Vacuum Pumps

The first vacuum pump was a piston pump constructed by Otto von Guericke in 1654. Many types of vacuum pumps have since been developed, each suitable to cover part of the range from atmospheric pressure (760 Torr) to less than 10^{-16} Torr. Vacuum pumps may be divided into two categories, those that remove the gas molecules from the system (removal pumps), and those that immobilize the gas molecules within the system by sorption on/in a solid (capture pumps) (see Fig. 1).

Removal pumps. Displacement pumps compress the gas and expel it from the system; they include piston pumps, mercury column pumps (now no longer used), rotary pumps, and Roots blowers. Kinetic pumps transfer momentum to gas molecules from a moving vane (molecular drag and turbopumps) or a stream of high velocity molecules (diffusion, vapor, and ejector pumps). Until 1905 the piston pumps and mercury column pumps were the only types available. Pressures of about 1 Torr were possible with the piston pumps and of about 10^{-5} Torr with mercury column pumps. In 1905 Wolfgang Gaede introduced both the rotary oil pump and the rotary mercury pump (capable of producing pressures of 10^{-2} and 10^{-6} Torr, respectively).

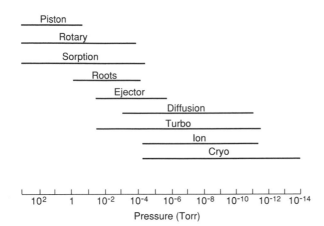

Figure 1 Operating pressure ranges of various types of vacuum pumps.

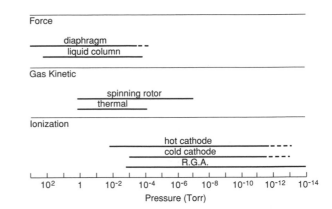

Figure 2 Operating pressure ranges of various types of pressure gauges.

This revolutionized vacuum technology since both pumps could be driven by electric motors. In 1915 Gaede and Irving Langmuir independently invented the diffusion pump, which can achieve pressures of less than 10^{-10} Torr by entraining the gas molecules in a stream of mercury or, in a later variant, oil molecules. The diffusion pump became the preferred pump for the production of high vacuum for four decades. The turbopump or sputter-ion pump have now replaced it for many applications.

Capture pumps. Ionization pumps, first developed in the 1950s, ionize the gas and drive the ions into a metal cathode. Sputter-ion pumps capture the rare gases by entrapping the ions in the cathode (usually of titanium); the chemically active gases are sorbed on metal films sputtered from the cathode; in getter-ion pumps they are sorbed on evaporated films. Pumps that immobilize gas molecules by adsorption or absorption include getter pumps, sorption pumps, and cryopumps. Getter-pumps (both evaporable and nonevaporable) sorb chemically active gases usually near room temperature. Sorption pumps physisorb gases on high area solids (e.g., molecular sieves in liquid nitrogen). Cryopumps operate at low temperatures to adsorb or condense gases. These pumps are widely used from high vacuum to extreme high vacuum.

Pressure Measurement

The range of pressure to be measured is so vast (from 760 Torr to less than 10^{-16} Torr) that several different types of gauges are required to cover the full range. They may be arranged into three groups measuring respectively force, gas kinetic effects, and ionization (see Fig. 2).

Force gauges. The first gauge for vacuum was developed in about 1660 by Robert Boyle, who placed a mercury manometer in an evacuated bell-jar. The mercury manometer can measure from atmospheric pressure to about 10^{-1} Torr. In 1874 H. G. McLeod showed that gas could be compressed by a known ratio, using a mercury column, to a readily measurable higher pressure, the original pressure being calculated from Boyle's law. The McLeod gauge can cover the range from 10^{-2} to 10^{-6} Torr and was used for many years to calibrate other gauges. Various forms of diaphragm gauges have been developed that measure the deflection of a metal diaphragm or tube coupled through a mechanical linkage to a pointer on a scale. They operate in the range from 760 to 10^{-2} Torr. The capacitance manometer (1929) measures the displacement of a metal diaphragm by the change in capacitance and, in most cases, the diaphragm is restored to its undeflected position by an electrical force. These gauges are now widely used from 760 to 10^{-5} Torr. All the force gauges measure true pressure independent of the nature of the gas, with some limitations for mercury manometers that require cold-traps. All other gauges require calibration against a standard gauge.

Gas kinetic gauges. These gauges depend on either the thermal conductivity of the gas or the viscosity or drag of the gas. Thermal conductivity gauges measure the heat loss through the gas from a heated filament by sensing the filament temperature either by its change in resistance (Pirani gauge, 1906), or by a thermocouple (thermocouple gauge, 1906). These gauges are now the preferred types in the range from 1 to 10^{-4} Torr.

Spinning rotor gauges are the only type of viscosity gauges still in wide use. A magnetically levitated steel ball is spun up to about 10^6 rev/s and allowed to coast. The decrement in rotational frequency is a measure of pressure. This gauge is now used to calibrate other gauges from 10^{-2} to 10^{-7} Torr.

Ionization gauges. Ionization gauges measure the positive ion current produced by electrons from a hot cathode (hot-cathode gauge, 1916) or a cold-cathode discharge in a magnetic field (cold-cathode gauge, 1937). These gauges measure molecular density and their sensitivity is dependent on the nature of the gas. Hot-cathode gauges are limited in their lowest operating pressure by the x-ray effect. The Bayard–Alpert gauge (1950) was the first to lower this limit into the ultrahigh vacuum range. Several other designs have reduced the limit still further to about 10^{-13} Torr. Cold-cathode gauges (magnetron and inverted-magnetron gauges, 1959) will operate from 10^{-4} to 10^{-12} Torr.

All the above gauges measure total pressure. Residual gas analyzers, which are suitably modified mass-spectrometers (usually quadrupoles) are used to measure partial pressures in the range from 10^{-3} to 10^{-16} Torr.

Vacuum Systems

A wide variety of vacuum components are available (valves, flanges, feedthroughs, motions, etc.) constructed of selected materials to minimize leakage and outgassing. The completed system requires baking or other cleaning procedures to reduce outgassing. Vacuum systems vary in size from table-top versions to accelerators of several kilometers in length.

See also: PRESSURE, ATMOSPHERIC; VACUUM

Bibliography

BERMAN, A. *Total Pressure Measurements in Vacuum Technology* (Academic, London, 1985).
KOHL, W. H. *Handbook of Materials and Techniques for Vacuum Devices,* 2nd ed. (American Institute of Physics, Woodbury, NY, 1995).
LECK, J. H. *Total and Partial Pressure Measurement in Vacuum Systems* (Blackie, London, 1989).
O'HANLON, J. *A Users Guide to Vacuum Technology,* 2nd ed. (Wiley, New York, 1989).
ROTH, A. *Vacuum Technology* (North-Holland, Amsterdam, 1985).
WELCH, K. M. *Capture Pumping Technology* (Pergamon, Oxford, Eng. 1991).
WESTON, G. F. *Ultrahigh Vacuum Practice* (Butterworth, London, 1985).
WUTZ, M.; ADAM, H.; and WALCHER, W. *Theory and Practice of Vacuum Technology* (Vieweg, Braunschweig, 1989).

P. A. REDHEAD

VAN ALLEN BELTS

One of the first major discoveries from experiments flown on orbiting spacecraft in the late 1950s was a zone of intense radiation, composed of high-energy charged particles, beyond Earth's atmosphere. Although there had been some theoretical predictions prior to the space age of charged particles trapped by Earth's geomagnetic field, the discovery of this radiation by James A. Van Allen, using data from Explorers I and III, was unanticipated. Electrons and protons dominate the Van Allen radiation belt; they are distributed from 1.2 to about 8 earth radii from the center of the earth at the magnetic equator and are concentrated in the equatorial plane, where the geomagnetic field is weakest. Energies of the protons up to a few hundred mega-electron-volts have been observed, while electron energies range up to several mega-electron-volts. Although early experiments suggested at least two distinct zones, or belts, of radiation, the distribution of particles is fairly uniform; the energy distribution of particles does vary with altitude, however, with the average energy per particle decreasing with increasing altitude; this gave the impression of distinct belts.

The major source of the particles in the belts is the solar wind, a supersonic particle flux resulting from the expansion of the solar corona into interstellar space. For a planet with an intrinsic magnetic field, the field deflects the charged particles and obstructs this flow of the solar wind. The pressure of the solar wind compresses the geomagnetic field until equilibrium is reached at the magnetopause (the boundary between the interplanetary medium and the magnetosphere, which is the cavity surrounding a planet into which the planetary magnetic field is confined by the solar plasma), where it is balanced by the magnetic pressure. Because Earth's dipole field deflects positive ions and electrons in opposite directions, an effective current sheet tangent to the magnetopause and orthogonal to the magnetic field in the magnetosphere is created. The field created by this current opposes further compression of the magnetosphere and is responsible for isolating the solar wind and the magnetosphere in the ideal case.

The idealized magnetopause provides an impermeable boundary between the solar wind and the magnetosphere. However, a fraction of the solar wind flux does penetrate the magnetopause and, together with ionospheric particles, is the major source of the plasma in the radiation belts. Instabilities in the current sheet at the magnetopause allow solar wind plasma to leak through the barrier via reconnection of some solar and planetary field lines, which are otherwise isolated.

Trapping of charged particles in the geomagnetic field is a good exercise in classical physics. The particles spiral around the magnetic field lines with cyclotron frequencies that range from microseconds for the lowest energy particles to milliseconds for the most energetic. If the magnetic field strength does not significantly vary spatially within the orbit of a particle or over a single orbital period of the particle, the flux linked by the orbit of the particle (essentially $\mathbf{B} \cdot \mathbf{ds}$) is an adiabatic invariant, that is, it can be taken to be constant for the motion. This condition is equivalent to the relation

$$P_t^2/B = \text{constant},$$

where P_t is the transverse component of the particle's momentum. Also, if the magnetic field is constant in time it does no work on the particles, and their kinetic energies are therefore conserved. These results are combined in the following constant of the motion for the particles:

$$\sin^2\alpha/B = \text{constant},$$

where α is the angle between the particle's velocity vector and $\mathbf{B}$, called the pitch angle.

For a dipole field, which Earth's field approximates closely in this region, the field strength (proportional to the number of field lines per unit area) increases as one proceeds from the equator toward the magnetic poles. Therefore, α must increase as the particle spirals toward the poles until the velocity vector is orthogonal to $\mathbf{B}$, that is, the component parallel to $\mathbf{B}$ vanishes. Inasmuch as $\sin \alpha$ cannot exceed 1, the particle then reverses its direction. In this way the particles bounce back and forth between the "mirrors" at the two magnetic poles and are thereby trapped in the geomagnetic field. A complete trip from one pole to the other and back takes on the order of 1 s for most of the particles in the radiation belt. The relatively small radial gradient of $\mathbf{B}$ causes longitudinal drift of ions and electrons in opposite directions with a period on the order of 1 h. Once trapped, particles may be retained in the magnetosphere for times on the order of months before being lost due to collisions with atoms and nuclei in the atmosphere at low altitudes and perturbations of the magnetosphere closer to the magnetopause. Particles are lost preferentially in the South Atlantic anomaly, a region of weak geomagnetic field where the belt dips into the upper atmosphere; this is a region of especial hazard to low orbiting spacecraft, such as the Hubble Space Telescope, because of the increased density of radiation at low altitudes.

Radiation belts also exist in the magnetospheres of other planets that have internally generated magnetic fields. Jupiter has a huge magnetosphere, both because its dipole moment is larger than that of Earth and because the pressure from the solar wind is much smaller there, which actually encompasses the orbits of three of the major, Galilean satellites. Interactions of these satellites, especially Io, with Jupiter's magnetic environment are important in controlling the number of particles trapped in the Jovian Van Allen belt. Even so, the intensity of radiation in the Jovian belt exceeds that in the terrestrial belt by orders of magnitude. The average energy of trapped particles is also an order of magnitude greater than in Earth's belt, and the spiraling electrons in the Jovian magnetosphere are a source of synchrotron radiation from the planet. This intense Jovian radiation belt must be considered in designing Jovian space missions because of the deleterious effects of high-energy particles on solid-state components.

See also: MAGNETOSPHERE; RADIATION BELT; SOLAR WIND

Bibliography

HAYMES, R. C. *Introduction to Space Science* (Wiley, New York, 1971).

HILL, T. W., and DESSLER, A. J. "Plasma Motions in Planetary Magnetospheres." *Science* **252**, 410–415 (1991).

JACKSON, J. D. *Classical Electrodynamics* (Wiley, New York, 1975).

PHILIP B. JAMES

VAN DE GRAAFF ACCELERATOR

An accelerator is a machine used to produce a beam of swiftly moving charged particles, either electrons or positively charged ions. Originally designed for nuclear and high-energy physics research, accelerators have found uses in studies of atomic structure, in materials science, and in medicine. One type of accelerator derives the energy to accelerate charged particles from an electrostatic generator that was developed by Robert J. Van de Graaff at Princeton University in 1929.

A schematic diagram of a Van de Graaff accelerator is shown in Fig. 1. The essential components are a high-voltage terminal (A), a moving belt (B) made of insulating material such as rubber, and an insulated column and evacuated tube (C) through which the charged particles are accelerated. In some designs, a chain with alternating links of conducting and insulating materials is used instead of a belt. Inside the terminal is a source (D) of the particles to be acceler-

ated. Charge is deposited on the belt through a row of corona points (E_1) at ground potential by corona discharge. The belt carries the charge up to the high-voltage terminal and deposits it onto the terminal by corona discharge through a row of points (E_2) inside the terminal. Since the terminal is made of conducting material, the charge moves to the outside surface, leaving the region inside the terminal free of an electric field. In this way, terminal potentials up to about 10 MV, either positive or negative, can be generated. The terminal potential is regulated by drawing charge off the terminal at a controlled rate through a third set of corona points (E_3) located outside the terminal. The pulley over which the belt moves inside the terminal is used to run a generator to produce electric power to operate the charged particle source.

Van de Graaff accelerators are most commonly used to accelerate positive ions. The terminal is positively charged, and ions are produced in a radio-frequency discharge tube inside the terminal. In this kind of ion source, gas at low pressure is introduced into the tube, and electrons driven by an electric field oscillating at radio-frequencies collide with gas molecules to produce positively ionized atoms. A small bias voltage focuses the ions into a beam and repels them out of the field-free region inside the terminal and into the evacuated accelerating tube. Inside the accelerating tube, the positive ions feel a repulsive force due to the positively charged terminal and are accelerated down the accelerating tube toward the electrically grounded end. In electron machines the terminal is negatively charged, and electrons are produced by thermionic emission in a heated wire.

The accelerating tube is made in sections, with insulating sections made of glass or ceramic separated by metal disk electrodes called "equipotential planes" (F). The electrodes are connected electrically, each to the next, through a chain of resistors (G). This establishes a uniform voltage gradient from the terminal to ground, which helps to keep the beam focused.

The tandem accelerator is a variation of the positive ion accelerator, which uses the terminal potential to accelerate ions twice. In this variation the terminal is positively charged, but it has two accelerating tubes. Negative atomic ions are produced at ground potential instead of inside the terminal. The ions are injected into an accelerating tube and are attracted toward the terminal. As their momentum carries them through the field-free region inside the terminal, the negative ions are stripped of

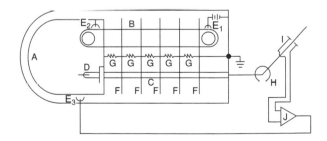

Figure 1 Schematic diagram of a Van de Graaff accelerator: A, terminal; B, belt; C, column and accelerating tube; D, ion source; E, corona points; F, equipotential planes; G, resistor; H, magnet; I, control slit; J, differential amplifier.

some of their electrons during collisions with atoms in a thin metal foil or with gas molecules in a capillary tube. After they drift out of the terminal, the stripped ions, now positively charged, are accelerated again by the repulsive force they feel inside a second accelerating tube. Since the negative ions are singly charged, the final kinetic energy of the positive ions is $(q + 1)V$, where q is the charge of the positive ions and V is the terminal potential. Hence, for example, a tandem accelerator running at a terminal potential of 1 MV can produce helium nuclei (α particles) with a kinetic energy of 3 MeV.

In general, such ion accelerators produce ion beams composed of several different charge states and therefore of several different energies. A monoenergetic beam of charge state q can be separated from the primary beam by passing the beam through a magnetic field **B** perpendicular to the beam. (The magnet is labeled H in Fig. 1.) Since the magnetic force on an ion moving with velocity **v** is $q(\mathbf{v} \times \mathbf{B})$, the magnetic field does no work on the ions, and it produces only a sideways deflection that depends on the charge, with no change in the energy of the ions. By adjusting the magnetic field, an ion beam of a desired charge state and energy can be directed through an evacuated beamline to its intended target. The deflection of the beam also allows for a feedback mechanism that can be used to stabilize the terminal potential, and, therefore, the beam energy. The beam is passed through a slit (I) whose sides are connected to a differential amplifier (J). If the terminal potential increases or decreases, the deflection of the beam by the magnetic field decreases or increases, respectively. This sweeps the beam over onto one side of the slit, increasing the beam current detected by the slit, causing an imbalance in the differential amplifier. The output of the differential amplifier can be used to control the charge being drawn off the terminal by the corona points (E_3), thus stabilizing the terminal potential.

See also: ACCELERATOR; ACCELERATOR, HISTORY OF

Bibliography

BROMLEY, D. A. "The Development of Electrostatic Accelerators." *Nucl. Instrum. Methods* **122**, 1 (1974).

LIVINGSTON, M. S., and BLEWETT, J. P. *Particle Accelerators* (McGraw-Hill, New York, 1962).

VAN DE GRAAFF, R. J.; COMPTON, K. T.; and VAN ATTA, L. C. "The Electrostatic Production of High Voltage for Nuclear Investigations." *Phys. Rev.* **43**, 149 (1933).

WILSON, R. R., and LITTAUER, R. *Accelerators* (Doubleday, Garden City, New York, 1960).

JAMES R. HUDDLE

VAN DER WAALS FORCE

Much effort in the first part of the twentieth century was directed toward developing a theory of molecular bonding which could be used to explain chemical reactions. Gilbert Newton Lewis observed that many molecules comprised of main group elements (those in the same columns of the periodic table as hydrogen, beryllium, boron, carbon, nitrogen, oxygen, fluorine, and helium) would form molecules with predictable compositions. Lewis observed that many of these elements formed molecules such that each atom of the molecule would be surrounded by eight valence electrons. For example, nitrogen atoms, which have five valence electrons, form a molecule composed of two nitrogen atoms. Lewis noted that if three of the five electrons were shared by each nitrogen atom, then each atom would be surrounded by six shared electrons and two unshared electrons, giving a total of eight valence electrons around each atom. Lewis called this rule governing molecular compositions the "octet rule" and used it to explain the elemental compositions of many molecules.

The octet rule accurately accounted for the fact that rare gases such as helium, neon, argon, and krypton were nonreactive, as each of these elements is surrounded by eight valence electrons and does not need to share electrons in order to complete an octet. However, at low temperatures and sometimes high pressure, each of the rare gases forms a solid. Because each atom already has a complete octet, it was necessary to develop some theory for why these atoms formed solids and the nature of the bond that held these solids together. A weak force attracting the atom was necessary.

Because negatively charged electrons were known to move about a positively charged nucleus, at any given instant there could be more electrons on one side of a nucleus than another. This would lead to an instantaneous dipole, or separation of charge. Nearby atoms would also experience instantaneous dipoles. When the dipoles on near atoms are of opposite phase, there would be an attractive force between the atoms. Thus it was reasoned, at very low temperatures an instantaneous dipole on one atom might induce an instantaneous dipole of opposite phase on near atoms, resulting in an attractive force between the atoms that would hold the rare gas solids together. This force was called an induced dipole, London, or van der Waals force. As this force is caused by dipole-dipole interactions, the attractive interaction between two atoms bound by van der Waals forces varies as the minus sixth power of the separation between the atoms.

With the development of quantum mechanical methods, it became possible to test the theory that rare gas solids are bound by van der Waals forces. Sam Trickey and others used a method to calculate the cohesive energy of solid argon, which did not include induced dipole interactions. If van der Waals forces were responsible for the cohesion in rare gas solids, these calculations should give wrong answers. To his surprise, Trickey found that the cohesive energies he computed agreed well with the experimentally determined numbers. This suggested that the formation of rare gas solids was not due to van der Waals forces but was the result of electron sharing, giving rise to very weak covalent bonds. However, because the term had been used to explain bonding in atoms and molecules where there was already a complete octet, the term survives to this day, referring to weak chemical bonding in molecules and atoms with complete octets.

See also: ATOM; DIPOLE MOMENT; ELEMENTS; MOLECULE

Bibliography

LEWIS, G. N. "The Atom and the Molecule." *J. Am. Chem. Soc.* **38,** 762–782 (1916).

TRICKEY, S. B.; AVRILL, F. W.; and GREEN, F. R., JR. "Self-Consistent Electron Calculation of the Zero-Temperature Cohesive Properties of Solid Argon." *Phys. Rev. Lett. A* **41,** 385 (1972).

M. E. EBERHART

VAPOR PRESSURE

See PRESSURE, VAPOR

VECTOR

We live in a world with three space dimensions (length, width, and height), and these three dimensions have fundamentally the same properties. In everyday experience, the gravitational attraction of the earth gives the vertical dimension a special significance, but if this is allowed for, or if one thinks more universally as an astronaut might, general statements made about one dimension are also true of the others. Consider, for example, a projectile subjected to gravity near the earth and to air resistance proportional to the velocity. This problem, which only needs two dimensions, may be handled using separate equations for the horizontal x and vertical y motions, but the equations describing the motions are essentially the same, except that the equation for the horizontal motion has the gravitational acceleration set to zero ($ma_x = -bv_x$ and $ma_y = -mg - bv_y$; with m the mass, a the acceleration, g the acceleration due to gravity, b the resistive strength, and v the velocity). Once the solution for the vertical motion is obtained, it can easily be converted to yield the solution for the horizontal motion. This applies whether the solution is an analytic expression or a computational technique.

To take advantage of this spatial isotropy (the equivalence between space dimensions), we define quantities that incorporate all three dimensions: vectors. These are quantities that have both magnitude and direction. They may be represented by arrows (the length of the arrow represents the magnitude of the vector) and they are given a descriptive notation such as **r** for the position, **v** for the velocity, and **a** for the acceleration. The projectile equations above would then be combined into one equation: $m\mathbf{a} = m\mathbf{g} - b\mathbf{v}$, where **g** is a vector with magnitude g and direction "down."

Vectors may be polar or axial. Polar vectors change sign on reflection, axial vectors do not. Examples of polar vectors in physics are position, velocity, acceleration, force, momentum, electric field, and Poynting's vector (energy flux of electromagnetic fields). Examples of axial vectors are angular velocity, angular momentum, torque, and magnetic field.

Since using boldface characters is not always convenient, the vector **v** may also be denoted by $\vec{v}$. The magnitude of a vector **v** is denoted by $|\mathbf{v}|$ or by v. A unit vector in the direction of **v** is often denoted by $\hat{\mathbf{v}}$ or $\hat{v}$. Note that $\hat{\mathbf{v}} = \mathbf{v}/|\mathbf{v}|$.

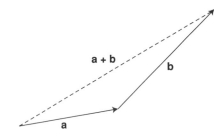

Figure 1 Illustration of vector addition.

If referred to a coordinate system (e.g., x north, y up, and z east), then a vector may be specified in terms of its components. These are the projections of the vector along the three axes and, for the velocity, these would be v_x, v_y, and v_z. A further extension of the notation is achieved by introducing unit vectors $\hat{\mathbf{x}}$, $\hat{\mathbf{y}}$, and $\hat{\mathbf{z}}$, (or $\mathbf{i}$, $\mathbf{j}$, and $\mathbf{k}$) in the x, y, and z directions, respectively. Then, using the property of vector addition (see below),

$$\mathbf{v} = v_x\hat{\mathbf{x}}, + v_y\hat{\mathbf{y}}, + v_z\hat{\mathbf{z}}.$$

If vectors are represented by arrows, then vector addition consists of placing the start of the second arrow at the end of the first, and the resultant vector is an arrow from the start of the first vector to the end of the second. Figure 1 shows an example in two dimensions.

Using a geometric analysis based on the combination of arrows, one finds that if the vectors are represented by components, then the vector sum is obtained by adding the respective components. Thus if a vector $\mathbf{p}$ has components p_x, p_y, and p_z, and a vector $\mathbf{q}$ has components q_x, q_y, and q_z, then $\mathbf{s} = \mathbf{p} + \mathbf{q}$ has components $s_x = p_x + q_x$, $s_y = p_y + q_y$, and $s_z = p_z + q_z$. An alternative way of writing this is

$$\mathbf{p} + \mathbf{q} = (p_x + q_x)\hat{\mathbf{x}} + (p_y + q_y)\hat{\mathbf{y}} + (p_z + q_z)\hat{\mathbf{z}}.$$

The negative of a vector has the arrow reversed and its components have their signs changed. Subtraction, of course, is the same as adding a vector and a negated vector.

Multiplication of a vector by a factor (number) changes the length of the arrow by the factor and leaves the direction unchanged. Equivalently, each of the components is multiplied by the factor.

There are three multiplicative style operations involving two vectors: the scalar product, the vector product, and the direct product.

The scalar product of two vectors is the magnitude of the first times the projected length of the second on the first. This may be calculated as the product of the magnitudes of the two vectors times the cosine of the angle between them. The scalar product of $\mathbf{p}$ and $\mathbf{q}$ is denoted by $\mathbf{p} \cdot \mathbf{q}$ and is a number, not a vector. In terms of the components of $\mathbf{p}$ and $\mathbf{q}$,

$$\mathbf{p} \cdot \mathbf{q} = p_x q_x + p_y q_y + p_z q_z;$$

note that all three directions are treated equally. The scalar product of a vector with itself is the square of its magnitude, and the angle θ between the vectors $\mathbf{p}$ and $\mathbf{q}$ is given by

$$\cos \theta = \frac{\mathbf{p} \cdot \mathbf{q}}{|\mathbf{p}| |\mathbf{q}|}.$$

Scalar products appear in such physical quantities as work and flux.

The vector product of two vectors is a vector that is perpendicular to both the given vectors and has a magnitude that is the product of the magnitudes of the two vectors times the sine of the angle between them. The sense of the perpendicular vector is given by the right-hand rule so the vector product of $\hat{\mathbf{x}}$ and $\hat{\mathbf{y}}$ is $\hat{\mathbf{z}}$. The vector product of vectors $\mathbf{p}$ and $\mathbf{q}$ is denoted by $\mathbf{p} \times \mathbf{q}$. Its evaluation in terms of the components of $\mathbf{p}$ and $\mathbf{q}$ is as follows:

$$\mathbf{p} \times \mathbf{q} = (p_y q_z - p_z q_y)\,\hat{\mathbf{x}} + (p_z q_x - p_x q_z)\,\hat{\mathbf{y}} + (p_x q_y - p_y q_x)\,\hat{\mathbf{z}},$$

a complicated but powerful result. Note that $\mathbf{p} \times \mathbf{p} = 0$, and $\mathbf{q} \times \mathbf{p} = -\mathbf{p} \times \mathbf{q}$. Vector products appear in such physical quantities as angular momentum and torque.

The direct product of two vectors is not a vector, but a second-rank tensor (also referred to as a dyadic). This is an example of an operation with one concept (vectors) requiring the introduction of a new concept (tensors). The direct product of $\mathbf{p}$ and $\mathbf{q}$ has nine components, each being the product of a component of $\mathbf{p}$ with a component of $\mathbf{q}$ and the corresponding pair of unit vectors (order dependent).

Equations involving division of one vector by another are usually replaced by equations using scalar products of tensors and vectors. The theory of quaternions, developed in the mid-nineteenth century, includes division of vectors, and in 1845 William R. Hamilton solved the planetary orbit problem by this method.

If the coordinate system is changed by a rotation, the components of a vector change correspondingly. Using two dimensions, consider a coordinate rotation through 30° from $\hat{\mathbf{x}}$, $\hat{\mathbf{y}}$ to $\hat{\mathbf{x}}'$, $\hat{\mathbf{y}}'$. Then, for a vector $\mathbf{v}$,

$$v_x' = \cos(30°)\, v_x + \sin(30°)\, v_y$$

$$= \frac{\sqrt{3}\, v_x}{2} + \frac{v_y}{2}$$

and

$$v_y' = -\sin(30°)\, v_x + \cos(30°)\, v_y$$

$$= \frac{-v_x}{2} + \frac{\sqrt{3}\, v_y}{2}$$

(see Fig. 2). Under a rotation, the scalar product is unchanged:

$$\mathbf{v} \cdot \mathbf{v} = v_x^2 + v_y^2 = v_x'^2 + v_y'^2.$$

Note that if $\mathbf{v} = v_x\hat{\mathbf{x}} + v_y\hat{\mathbf{y}}$ is a vector, then $v_x^2\hat{\mathbf{x}} + v_y^2\hat{\mathbf{y}}$ is *not* a vector, since

$$(v_x^2)' = \frac{\sqrt{3}(v_x^2)}{2} + \frac{(v_y^2)}{2}$$

and

$$(v_x')^2 = \frac{3v_x^2}{4} + \frac{\sqrt{3}\,v_x v_y}{2} + \frac{v_y^2}{4}$$

are not the same. This rather esoteric result has important physical consequences. In the case of a projectile with a resistive force proportional to the square of the velocity, the expression $-b(v_x^2\hat{\mathbf{x}} + v_y^2\hat{\mathbf{y}})$ cannot describe the resistive force. Rather it is

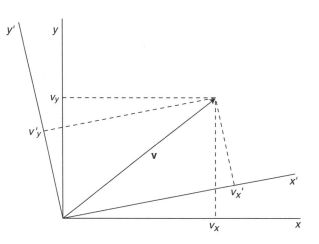

Figure 2 Illustration of changing vector components due to rotation of the coordinate system.

$$\mathbf{F}_r = -b|\mathbf{v}|\mathbf{v} = -b\sqrt{v_x^2 + v_y^2}\,(v_x\hat{\mathbf{x}} + v_y\hat{\mathbf{y}}).$$

The latter expression does behave properly when the coordinate system is rotated and exemplifies the power of using vector equations.

Quantities that are unchanged when the coordinate system is rotated are called scalars. The scalar product, defined above, has exactly this property. Scalars, such as the kinetic energy and the potential energy, have the same value regardless of any rotation of the coordinate system. This is a valuable feature in the study of rigid body motion in three dimensions, where principal axes, oriented with the body, materially simplify the analysis.

When first encountered, vectors seem rather sophisticated. This is quite natural. Vectors cannot be measured directly—only scalars. The response of a measuring device is typically the scalar product of the vector in question and a vector associated with the orientation of the measuring device. Three measurements are needed to determine a vector (or, equivalently, a measuring device with three mutually perpendicular parts). But the concept of a vector (significantly aided by the notation) provides more compact, and hence more understandable, equations and a better guide to developing physical laws.

However, not all vectors in physics are three-dimensional. In relativity theory the Lorentz transformation connecting inertial frames supersedes the rotation transformation and leads to space–time combinations. As a result, vectors become four-dimensional, the most noteworthy being $(ct, \mathbf{r})$ and

$(E/c, \mathbf{p})$, where $\mathbf{r}$ is position (as before), c is the speed of light, t is time, $\mathbf{p}$ is momentum, and E is energy. The energy–momentum four-vector is a powerful concept in the analysis of relativistic collisions where the conservation of energy and momentum is combined with the relativistic extension of the scalar product: $(E/c)^2 - |\mathbf{p}|^2$, which is an invariant (i.e., has the same value in all inertial frames).

The concept of a vector in mathematics and in computational applications is not as restrictive as in physics. There is not necessarily any equivalent to a rotation so the components are not required to transform into each other. Indeed, the components of the vector need not have the same dimensions and there may be any number of them. Rather, the vector is a set of quantities that are processed in the same way. While this wider definition expands the usefulness of vectors, there is a loss of physical significance.

Statistical physics and quantum physics use state vectors that are of the mathematical form. In statistical physics the positions of n particles can be represented by a vector that is $3n$ long, and n can be of order 10^{23}. Probabilities based on the amount of space occupied by such vectors involve hyperspheres and hypervolumes. In quantum mechanics the possible basis states are often discrete and a general (mixed) state is designated by a vector in which the components specify the amount of each basis state. The behavior of the general state is then described by a matrix operation on the vector where each component of the matrix describes the behavior of a basis state or its connection to other basis states (matrix mechanics).

A computational technique that uses mixed component vectors is the numerical solution of second-order differential equations using the Runge–Kutta–Fehlberg method (designed for first-order equations). In the case of Newton's second law (a second-order equation) the position and velocity are combined into one vector that is updated in time using the time step size and a vector that is a combination of the average velocity and the average acceleration over the time step.

See also: Coordinate System, Cartesian; Momentum; Relativity, General Theory of; Right-Hand Rule; Scalar; Tensor; Vector, Unit; Velocity

Bibliography

DeVries, P. L. *First Course in Computational Physics* (Wiley, New York, 1994).

Gatland, I. R. "Numerical Integration of Newton's Equations Including Velocity-Dependent Forces." *Am. J. Phys.* **62** (March), 259–265 (1994).

Halliday, D., and Resnick, R. *Fundamentals of Physics,* 3rd ed. (Wiley, New York, 1988).

Marion, J. B. *Classical Dynamics,* 2nd ed. (Academic Press, New York, 1970).

Rindler, W. *Introduction to Special Relativity,* 2nd ed. (Clarendon Press, Oxford, 1991).

Ian R. Gatland

VECTOR, UNIT

A unit vector is a vector whose magnitude is one. As such, it conveniently extracts the directional content of a vector. Unit vectors are typically denoted by a lower case letter in bold (i.e., $\mathbf{a}$), or by a lower case letter with a caret above it (i.e., $\hat{\mathbf{a}}$). Unit vectors are used together with coordinate systems to represent any vector and to provide a concise notation for vector manipulation and visualization. Unit vectors are often used in situations where certain directions are inherent. For example, navigation of a ship on the

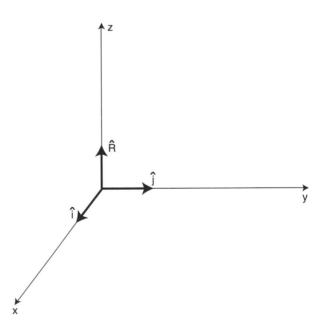

Figure 1 Unit vectors, $\mathbf{i}$, $\mathbf{j}$, $\mathbf{k}$ in a Cartesian coordinate system.

ocean involves motion in the north/south and east/west directions, while navigation of an aircraft also includes motion in the vertical direction (i.e., up/down). These directions can be indicated on a navigational chart by unit vectors. Unit vectors are also useful in depicting the flow of fluids. At each point in space a unit vector is drawn to indicate the direction of fluid flow at that point. Such flow fields can be used to illustrate the flow of water in a stream or the flow of air around an airfoil (i.e., aircraft or automobile model) in a wind tunnel.

Any vector having the same direction as a unit vector may be expressed as a scalar multiple of that unit vector. For example, a velocity vector $\mathbf{V} = 25$ cm/s in the north direction may be represented by $\mathbf{V} = 25$ cm/s $\hat{\mathbf{n}}$, where $\hat{\mathbf{n}}$ represents a unit vector in the north direction. In general any vector in the northward direction may be written as b times $\hat{\mathbf{n}}$ ($b\hat{\mathbf{n}}$), where b is any real number and $\hat{\mathbf{n}}$ is the northward unit vector. A vector in the southward direction would be represented by multiplying $\hat{\mathbf{n}}$ by a negative number. Conversely, a unit vector in the direction of vector $\mathbf{A}$ can be written as $\hat{\mathbf{a}} = \mathbf{A}/A$, where A is the magnitude of the vector $\mathbf{A}$.

Unit vectors are particularly useful as a basis set from which any vector may be constructed. In three-dimensional space three independent unit vectors (north/south, east/west, up/down) are needed to completely specify an arbitrary vector. In a Cartesian coordinate system, these unit vectors would point along the positive x, y, and z axes and are typically denoted $\mathbf{i}$, $\mathbf{j}$, and $\mathbf{k}$, respectively (see Fig. 1). The unit vectors ($\hat{\mathbf{r}}, \hat{\theta}, \hat{\phi}$) in spherical coordinates and ($\hat{\mathbf{r}}, \hat{\phi}, \hat{\mathbf{z}}$) in cylindrical coordinates are shown in Figs. 2 and 3. Note that the spherical and cylindrical unit vectors are not space-fixed. At the point ($x = 0, y = 1, z = 0$) the cylindrical unit vector $\hat{\phi}$ points in the direction of the negative x axis, whereas at the point (1,0,0) $\hat{\phi}$ points in the direction of the positive y axis.

An arbitrary vector $\mathbf{A}$ may be written as a linear combination of any basis set of unit vectors. Such sets of basis vectors are said to span the space of three-dimensional vectors. For example, $\mathbf{A} = A_x\mathbf{i} + A_y\mathbf{j} + A_z\mathbf{k}$ where A_x is the projection of $\mathbf{A}$ onto the x axis, A_y is the projection of $\mathbf{A}$ onto the y axis, and A_z is the projection of $\mathbf{A}$ onto the z axis. A_x, A_y, and A_z are called the Cartesian components of $\mathbf{A}$. This leads to a simple representation of $\mathbf{A}$ as an ordered triple (A_x, A_y, A_z). Similarly, $\mathbf{A}$ could be written in terms of spherical or cylindrical unit vectors $\mathbf{A} = A_r\hat{\mathbf{r}} + A_\theta\hat{\theta} + A_\phi\hat{\phi} = A_r\hat{\mathbf{r}} + A_\phi\hat{\phi} + A_z\hat{\mathbf{z}}$, where each component is the projection of $\mathbf{A}$ onto the associated unit vector.

The unit vectors associated with each of the coordinate systems discussed above are orthogonal and right-handed. Orthogonality indicates that the three unit vectors are mutually perpendicular. Right-handedness defines the relative orientation of the three unit vectors.

The ordered triple $\mathbf{i}, \mathbf{j}, \mathbf{k}$ is oriented such that if a (right-handed) screw pointed in the $\mathbf{k}$ direction is turned clockwise (from $\mathbf{i}$ toward $\mathbf{j}$) then the screw will move inward in the $\mathbf{k}$ direction. Nonorthogonal basis vectors are used in describing physical phenomena such as crystalline structure wherein a "natural" set of nonorthogonal directions is found.

Basis sets of unit vectors which span the same space are interrelated. For example, the unit vector $\mathbf{i}$ may be written in spherical coordinates and unit vectors as:

$$\mathbf{i} = \hat{\mathbf{r}} \sin \theta \cos \phi + \hat{\theta} \cos \theta \cos \phi - \hat{\phi} \sin \phi,$$

where $\hat{\theta}$ and $\hat{\phi}$ are as shown in Fig. 2, and in cylindrical coordinates and unit vectors as

$$\mathbf{i} = \hat{\mathbf{r}} \cos \phi - \hat{\phi} \sin \phi,$$

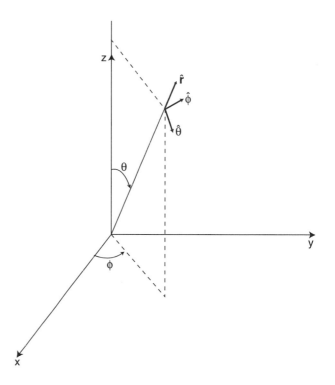

Figure 2   Unit vectors $\hat{\mathbf{r}}, \hat{\theta}, \hat{\phi}$ in a spherical coordinate system.

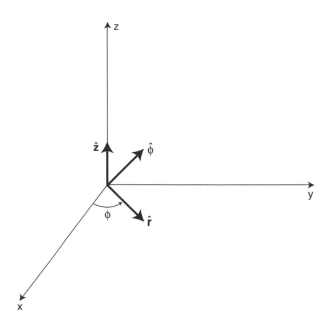

Figure 3 Unit vectors $\hat{\mathbf{r}}, \hat{\phi}, \hat{\mathbf{z}}$ in a cylindrical coordinate system.

where $\hat{\phi}$ is as shown in Fig. 3. Similar conversions between other unit vectors can be determined by projecting a unit vector from one basis set onto all three unit vectors from a different basis set.

For any orthogonal, right-handed basis set of vectors $(\mathbf{a}, \mathbf{b}, \mathbf{c})$, scalar (dot) and vector (cross) products have the following form: $\mathbf{a} \cdot \mathbf{b} = \mathbf{a} \cdot \mathbf{c} = \mathbf{b} \cdot \mathbf{c} = 0$, $\mathbf{a} \cdot \mathbf{a} = \mathbf{b} \cdot \mathbf{b} = \mathbf{c} \cdot \mathbf{c} = 1$ and $\mathbf{a} \times \mathbf{b} = \mathbf{c}, \mathbf{b} \times \mathbf{c} = \mathbf{a}$, $\mathbf{c} \times \mathbf{a} = \mathbf{b}, \mathbf{b} \times \mathbf{a} = -\mathbf{c}, \mathbf{c} \times \mathbf{b} = -\mathbf{a}, \mathbf{a} \times \mathbf{c} = -\mathbf{b}, \mathbf{a} \times \mathbf{a} = \mathbf{b} \times \mathbf{b} = \mathbf{c} \times \mathbf{c} = 0$. These results and the distributive law can be used to determine dot and cross products between vectors written in terms of the unit vectors $\mathbf{a}, \mathbf{b}$, and $\mathbf{c}$.

See also: COORDINATE SYSTEM, CARTESIAN; COORDINATE SYSTEM, CYLINDRICAL; COORDINATE SYSTEM, POLAR; COORDINATE SYSTEM, SPHERICAL; SCALAR; VECTOR

Bibliography

ARYA, A. P. *Introduction to Classical Mechanics* (Allyn & Bacon, Boston, 1990).

CRUMMETT, W., and WESTERN, A. *University Physics* (Wm. C. Brown, Dubuque, IA, 1994).

GRIFFITHS, D. J. *Introduction to Electrodynamics,* 2nd ed. (Prentice Hall, Englewood Cliffs, NJ, 1989).

HALLIDAY, D.; RESNICK, R.; KRANE, K. *Physics,* 4th ed. (Wiley, New York, 1992).

MARION, J. B., and THORNTON, S. T. *Classical Dynamics of Particles and Systems,* 3rd ed. (Harcourt Brace Jovanovich, New York, 1988).

PAUL R. SIMONY

VELOCITY

Velocity is the rate that the position of a body, relative to some frame of reference, changes with time. Velocity is a vector quantity, and it possesses both a direction and a magnitude called "speed." For example, an automobile may be traveling at a speed of 88 kilometers per hour (kph). If it is driving toward the northwest, then its velocity is 88 kph northwest. Another automobile may have the same speed as the first, but it will have a different velocity if it travels in a different direction (88 kph south, for example).

If a body travels in a straight line, and its initial position is x_0 at time t_0, and its position is x_1 at some later time t_1, then the magnitude of the average velocity $\overline{v}$ is

$$\overline{v} = \frac{x_1 - x_0}{t_1 - t_0} = \frac{\Delta x}{\Delta t}. \tag{1}$$

However, the object may have been moving faster or slower than the average velocity at some instant during the time Δt. To know the velocity at a particular instant in time, it is necessary to use the instantaneous velocity. The magnitude of the instantaneous velocity is found by taking smaller and smaller Δt in Eq. (1). In the notation of calculus, the instantaneous velocity is the derivative of the position

$$v = \frac{dx}{dt}. \tag{2}$$

If the object travels on a curved path, then Eqs. (1) and (2) must be written as vector equations. The average velocity is

$$\overline{\mathbf{v}} = \frac{\mathbf{x}_1 - \mathbf{x}_0}{t_1 - t_0} = \frac{\Delta \mathbf{x}}{\Delta t}, \tag{3}$$

and the instantaneous velocity is

$$\mathbf{v} = \frac{d\mathbf{x}}{dt}. \qquad (4)$$

Velocity, or rather speed, may be measured in several ways. One simple method of measuring the average speed of an object is by a direct application of Eq. (1); that is, to divide the displacement of the object by the time required for the observed displacement. Perhaps the most commonly used device for measuring the magnitude of velocity (speed) is the speedometer used in vehicles such as cars and bicycles. The speedometer computes the speed of the vehicle from the angular velocity of the wheels.

The actual velocity of an object, that is, both its speed and direction, can be directly measured by using the Doppler effect. The Doppler effect causes the frequency of sound or light emitted from an object to shift to higher frequencies when the object is moving toward the observer, or to shift to lower frequencies when the object is moving away from the observer. By measuring this change in frequency of sound or light as it reflects from a moving object, we can calculate the speed of the object. By knowing whether the frequency shifted up or down, we can know whether the traveling object is approaching or receding from us. Radar "guns" use this technique to measure the velocity of automobiles on highways. Doppler radar also is used to measure the velocity of air currents from storms. The velocity of distant stars and galaxies can be measured by observing the Doppler shift of the light that they emit.

See also: DOPPLER EFFECT; ESCAPE VELOCITY; FRAME OF REFERENCE; GROUP VELOCITY; VECTOR; VELOCITY, ANGULAR; VELOCITY, TERMINAL

Bibliography

HALLIDAY, D.; RESNICK, R.; and WALKER, J. *Fundamentals of Physics, Extended,* 4th ed. (Wiley, New York, 1993).

MARION, J. B., and THORNTON, S. T. *Classical Dynamics of Particles and Systems,* 4th ed. (Saunders, Philadelphia, 1995).

SERWAY, R. A. *Physics for Scientists and Engineers,* 4th ed. (Saunders, Philadelphia, 1996).

JUSTIN M. SANDERS

VELOCITY, ANGULAR

Angular velocity (symbolized by ω or Ω) is a vector quantity used to describe rotational motion. The magnitude of the instantaneous angular velocity vector is the rate of change of the angular displacement θ with time ($d\theta/dt$), and the direction of the vector is the direction in which an observer would look along the axis of rotation so that the rotation appears to be clockwise. The direction of ω can also be described using a right-hand rule: if the fingers of the right hand are curled in the direction of rotation, the extended thumb points in the direction of ω.

For an illustration of the vector's definition, consider the spinning top shown in Fig. 1. In Fig. 1a, the direction of ω is upward, because an observer looking upward from below at the top would see it spinning clockwise. In Fig. 1b, a view of the top from below shows the angular displacement θ. The hand positions for using the right-hand rule are also shown.

Angular displacement, defined as the angle separating the present position of a point on a rotating object and the point's position at some arbitrary starting time, is usually given in radians (2π rad = 360°), so its rate of change (i.e., angular velocity) is usually given in radians per second. For example, if the top is turning in the direction shown at 10 revolutions per second, then its angular velocity is $10 \times 2\pi = 20\pi$ rad/s, with direction vertically upward. Many other units can be used for angular velocity, including revolutions per second and revolutions per minute (familiar to auto enthusiasts and phonograph record collectors).

(a)   (b)

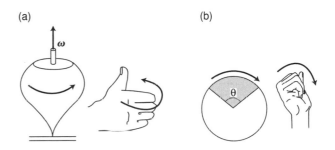

Figure 1 Spinning top shown (a) from the side and (b) from below (ω points into page).

Relationship to Linear Velocity

Angular velocity is related to linear velocity through a vector cross-product. If a point P is moving with respect to an axis in space, $\mathbf{r}$ represents the position vector drawn from the origin (any point on the axis) to P, $\mathbf{v}$ is P's instantaneous linear velocity, and $\boldsymbol{\omega}$ is P's angular velocity with respect to the axis, then the relationship among these quantities is $\mathbf{v} = \boldsymbol{\omega} \times \mathbf{r}$. This relationship holds for all motion, not only for circular rotation.

Multiple Rotational Motions

Angular velocities for the same body about different axes add vectorially to give the body's resultant angular velocity. For example, when Earth rotates on its axis while revolving around the Sun, the resultant angular velocity of these two motions is the sum of the angular velocity vectors for rotation and revolution.

Application of Angular Velocity

Geostationary satellites, which orbit Earth while remaining in position over a single point on the equator, must have angular velocities identical to that of Earth in order to maintain their positions. This angular velocity can be expressed as one revolution per day or about 7.3×10^{-5} rad/s, and its direction is north along Earth's axis of rotation. Note that the linear velocities are not the same: a person standing at the equator has a linear velocity of 4.6×10^2 m/s, but a geostationary satellite has a linear velocity of 3.1×10^3 m/s.

See also: MOTION, CIRCULAR; MOTION, ROTATIONAL; VECTOR; VELOCITY

Bibliography

HALLIDAY, D., and RESNICK, R. *Fundamentals of Physics*, 2nd ed. (Wiley, New York, 1988).

MARION, J. B., and THORNTON, S. T. *Classical Dynamics of Particles and Systems*, 4th ed. (Saunders, Philadelphia, 1995).

ALFRED S. SCHLACHTER
DEBORAH J. DIXON

VELOCITY, TERMINAL

Terminal velocity (v_t) is the maximum velocity attained by an object falling from rest through a fluid less dense than the object. The force of gravity (mg for an object of mass m) accelerates the falling object downward, and three forces act upward to retard its acceleration. Two retarding forces, viscous drag and aerodynamic drag, are frictional forces that increase with the object's velocity. The third, buoyant force, is constant in a fluid of constant density. As the object accelerates, the drag forces increase, and the object asymptotically approaches its terminal velocity, for which the sum of the three retarding forces equals the gravitational force. The net force on the object is then zero, so it stops accelerating and travels at its terminal velocity.

Figure 1 shows the relationships existing between gravity, the retarding forces, velocity, and time. The characteristic time t_c is the time required for the object's velocity to come within $1/e$ of the terminal velocity.

Calculating Terminal Velocity

An object reaches its terminal velocity for a given fluid when the force of gravity on the object is exactly balanced by the sum of the viscous drag, the aerodynamic drag, and the buoyant force:

$$mg = F_v + F_D + F_b. \tag{1}$$

Viscous drag, which arises from attractive forces among the molecules of the fluid, is $F_v = 6\pi\eta kv$. The constant k depends on the shape and size of the falling object (for a sphere, it is the radius r), η is the viscosity of the fluid (Pa·s in SI units), and v is the object's velocity. The aerodynamic drag, which results from the transfer of momentum from the falling object to the fluid, is $F_D = \frac{1}{2}C_D\rho_f Av^2$, where C_D is a dimensionless drag coefficient of order 1 determined by direct measurement, A is the cross-sectional area of the falling object (in a plane perpendicular to the direction of motion), and ρ_f is the density of the fluid. The buoyant force is $F_b = \rho_f gV$, or the weight of fluid displaced by an object of volume V. Substituting these definitions into Eq. (1) gives

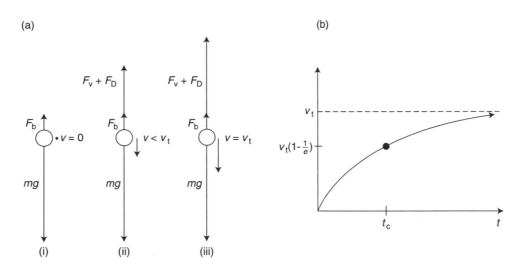

Figure 1 Free body diagrams (a) and a qualitative velocity plot (b) for an object falling from rest in a fluid less dense than the object.

$$mg = 6\pi\eta k v_t + \tfrac{1}{2}C_D\rho_f A v_t^2 + \rho_f gV. \qquad (2)$$

Solving this equation for v_t using the quadratic formula gives the terminal velocity:

$$v_t = \frac{-6\pi\eta k \pm \sqrt{36\pi^2\eta^2 k^2 - 2C_D\rho_f Ag(\rho_f V - m)}}{C_D\rho_f A}.$$

It is seldom necessary to include all three retarding forces to find a reasonable estimate for terminal velocity; for example, the buoyant force is often negligible for heavy objects falling in air because of the low density of air compared with such objects (skydivers, metal projectiles, and so on).

Simplifying Calculations

Often one of the drag forces is negligible compared with the other and can be omitted in a calculation of terminal velocity. A useful tool for deciding which drag force will dominate is the Reynolds number, which for an object of cross-sectional diameter d is defined as

$$R = \frac{\rho_f v d}{\eta}.$$

If R is small (of order one or less), then viscous drag dominates. One such case is that of small sediment particles settling out of liquid suspension. In such situations the buoyant force is often significant, so the terminal velocity is given by dropping the aerodynamic drag term from Eq. (2) and solving for v_t:

$$v_t = \frac{(m - V\rho_f)g}{6\pi\eta k}.$$

For a spherical object, $k = r$ and $V = \tfrac{4}{3}\pi r^3$, so

$$v_t = \frac{mg - \tfrac{4}{3}\pi r^3 \rho_f g}{6\pi\eta r}.$$

If the object's density is ρ_{obj}, this simplifies to

$$v_t = \frac{2r^2 g}{9\eta}(\rho_{obj} - \rho_f).$$

If, on the other hand, R is large, then aerodynamic drag dominates. This is true for skydivers and other large objects falling through fluids of low viscosity, and it is typically accompanied by a turbulent fluid flow in the object's wake. If the fluid has a low density, buoyant force also is negligible, so the terminal velocity is given by dropping the buoyant force and viscous drag terms from Eq. (2):

$$v_t = \sqrt{\frac{2mg}{C_D \rho_F A}}.$$

Sample Calculation

Why are parachutes standard equipment for sky-divers? Terminal velocity plays a central role in answering this question. To estimate a skydiver's terminal velocity (without an open parachute), first you need an estimate of the Reynolds number R; if you assume the skydiver will fall at least several meters (rather than millimeters) per second, R is quite large (on the order of 10^6), indicating that viscous drag is insignificant. Since the density of air (1.3 kg/m³) is so much smaller than the density of a human (approximately that of water, 1,000 kg/m³), you can also neglect the buoyant force. Therefore, assuming a mass of 70 kg, a drag coefficient of 0.35, and a cross-sectional area of of 1 m² for a human in spread-eagle position in air,

$$v_t = \sqrt{\frac{2mg}{C_D \rho_F A}}$$

$$= \sqrt{\frac{2(70 \text{ kg})(9.8 \text{ m/s}^2)}{(0.35)(1.3 \text{ kg/m}^3)(1 \text{m}^2)}} \approx 55 \text{ m/s}.$$

This is nearly 200 km/h, certainly not a safe landing speed for a human. The purpose of a parachute is to increase both the cross-sectional area A and the drag coefficient C_D, thereby lowering the terminal velocity to a safe value (about 3.5 m/s for round military parachutes, and far less for square stunt parachutes, which by virtue of their shape generate lift as well as decreasing terminal velocity).

See also: AERODYNAMICS; BUOYANT FORCE; DENSITY; FREE BODY DIAGRAM; FREE FALL; FRICTION; REYNOLDS NUMBER; VISCOSITY

Bibliography

BAIERLEIN, R. *Newtonian Dynamics.* (McGraw-Hill, New York, 1983).

HALLIDAY, D., and RESNICK, R. *Fundamentals of Physics,* 2nd ed. (Wiley, New York, 1988).

JONES, E. R., and CHILDERS, R. L. *Contemporary College Physics* (Addison-Wesley, Reading, MA, 1992).

ALFRED S. SCHLACHTER
DEBORAH J. DIXON

VIRTUAL IMAGE

See IMAGE, VIRTUAL

VISCOSITY

Fluids have adjacent layers that exhibit resistance to moving relative to one another. This resistance may be thought of as the internal friction of a fluid and is called viscosity. In order to cause one layer of a viscous fluid to slide past its adjacent layer, a tangential force must be applied. Thus, viscosity characterizes a fluid's resistance to shear when the fluid is in motion. All fluids exhibit viscosity, with liquids being much more viscous than gases.

Imagine two parallel plates separated by a fluid (see Fig. 1). The bottom plate is stationary and the top plate moves with velocity v. Since fluids stick to the surface of solids, the fluid next to the top plate moves with velocity v and the layer next to the sta-

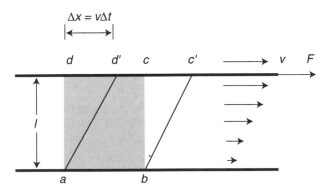

Figure 1 Laminar flow of a layer of viscous fluid between two solid surfaces. The upper surface moves with velocity v while the lower surface is fixed, $v = 0$.

tionary bottom plate has no velocity. Note that the velocity of each adjacent fluid layer in Fig. 1 increases linearly from zero to v as one moves from the bottom plate to the top plate. Because of this motion, a portion of the fluid is distorted from its original shape abcd to the shape abc′d′ after a short time interval Δt. Thus, the liquid has undergone a shear strain defined by the ratio $\Delta x/l$.

Shear stress is defined as the ratio of the tangential force to the area over which it is applied, or F/A. In the time Δt during which the deformation takes place, the fluid next to the upper plate has moved a distance $\Delta x = v\,\Delta t$. This gives us a rate of change of shearing strain as

$$\frac{\text{shear strain}}{\Delta t} = \frac{\Delta x/1}{\Delta t} = \frac{v}{l}.$$

For the case where the velocity increases linearly with increasing distance from the stationary lower plate, the coefficient of viscosity η is defined as the ratio of the shearing stress to the rate of change of the shear strain:

$$\eta = \frac{F/A}{v/l} = \frac{Fl}{Av}.$$

From the equation above, the SI unit for the coefficient of viscosity η is N·s/m². The most commonly used unit for η is the poise, which is 10^{-1} N·s/m².

In those cases where the velocity of the fluid does not increase linearly with increasing distance from a stationary plate, the coefficient of viscosity must be expressed in the general form

$$\eta = \frac{F/A}{dv/dy},$$

where dv/dy is the change in velocity with position measured perpendicular to the direction of fluid flow (i.e., velocity gradient). A viscous fluid flowing through a tube exhibits a velocity distribution as shown in Fig. 2.

Figures 1 and 2 illustrate fluids with their adjacent layers flowing smoothly over one another, thereby exhibiting laminar flow. Laminar flow is encountered only at low velocity or with the more viscous fluids, such as heavy oil. As the velocity of a fluid increases, a critical point is reached where the flow becomes turbulent, or highly irregular. The velocity where turbulence begins is determined by the

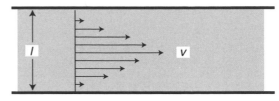

Figure 2 Velocity distribution for laminar flow of viscous fluid in a tube. The layer of fluid next to the tube has zero velocity.

viscosity of the moving fluid and the shape of its surroundings. A dimensionless parameter, called the Reynolds number R, defines the flow pattern as laminar ($R < 2,000$), unstable ($2,000 < R < 3,000$), or turbulent ($R > 3,000$).

Additionally, viscosity varies with temperature. Think about warming up cold molasses or motor oil and you will be reminded that the viscosity of liquids decreases as the temperature increases. Gases increase their viscosity with an increase in temperature. Pressure also affects the viscosity of fluids, but its influence is usually minor compared to the temperature variation in most cases where fluid dynamics play a role. Table 1 illustrates coefficients of viscosity for a few gases and liquids over a wide temperature range.

A common example of the effect of the viscosity of air occurs when a topspin is put on a tennis ball. Topspin causes the ball to drop. Why? During a tennis match, the ball moves at high speeds, causing some turbulence to occur behind it as it moves. If

Table 1 Typical Values of Viscosity

Fluid	Temperature (^{0}C)	Viscosity ($N \cdot s/m^2 \times 10^{-3}$)
Hydrogen	0	0.0083
	100	0.010
	300	0.014
Air	0	0.017
	20	0.018
	100	0.022
Water	0	1.79
	20	1.00
	100	0.28
Glycerin	20	830.00
	40	0.16
	60	0.044

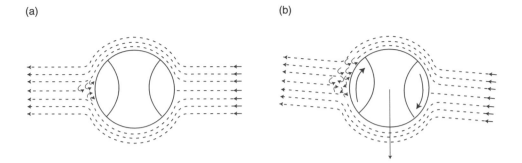

Figure 3 (a) Air flow past a nonrotating ball. Turbulence behind the ball is symmetric. (b) Deflected air flow past a rotating ball. The region of turbulence is asymmetric, and the net force *F* on the ball is downward.

the ball is not spinning, the turbulence behind the ball is symmetric as shown in Fig. 3a. However, when a topspin is applied, the ball spins in the forward direction. The viscosity of air causes layers of air closest to the ball to be dragged around in the direction of spin (see Fig. 3b). This results in the net velocity of air with respect to the ball at the top to be less than that at the bottom, causing the turbulence to become asymmetric as shown. Thus, there is more pressure on the top than the bottom, and the ball experiences a net downward force resulting in its deflection downward.

Oil and gas pipelines need to maintain a constant flow of the fluid. As these pipelines traverse thousands of miles, temperatures along the way may vary considerably. As the viscosity changes with temperature, the power required to pump these fluids at a constant rate also changes. It is cost efficient to design these systems to respond automatically to changes in viscosity to keep the flow rate constant, and to have the available power to do so.

See also: FLUID DYNAMICS; LIQUID; REYNOLDS NUMBER; STRAIN; STRESS; TURBULENT FLOW; VELOCITY

Bibliography

ARFKEN, G. B.; GRIFFING, D. F.; KELLY, D. C.; and PRIEST, J. *University Physics* (Academic Press, Orlando, FL, 1984).

BENSON, H. *University Physics* (Wiley, New York, 1991).

MIRONER, A. *Engineering Fluid Mechanics* (McGraw-Hill, New York, 1979).

TRITTON, D. J. *Physical Fluid Dynamics* (Van Nostrand Reinhold, New York, 1977).

ELIZABETH S. IVEY

VISIBLE SPECTROSCOPY

See SPECTROSCOPY, VISIBLE

VISION

How individuals see, and how they recognize and interpret what they see, are mysteries that have challenged scientists for decades and intrigued philosophers for centuries.

Philosophy of Vision

Early Greek philosophers suggested that the human senses are affected by tiny, particle-like effluences that are emitted by objects. The effluences were termed "atoms" and were thought to be microscopic replicas of the objects. As the effluences strike the body, they lodge in one set of pores or another depending on their size and configuration. Each set of pores was believed to be responsible for a particular sensation. For a stone to be seen as a round, gray object, its effluences would have to be captured by the pores in the eyes that characterize gray, round objects. In this materialistic theory, no mental imagery or information processing occurs, and visual detection, recognition, and interpretation are all one and the same process.

Aristotle altered the theory of vision by suggesting that effluences are a subtle, nonmaterialistic influence of the object on the observer. He proposed that the viewer emits visual spirits or "pneuma" that originate in the brain, pass through the hollow optic nerve into the eye, and then emanate into space as a cone of linear rays. These pneuma reflect off external objects and return to the eye. By this mechanism, the observer perceives the form of an object by receiving "sense-data" such as color and shape without any exchange of matter between the object and the viewer. The observer integrates the sense-data information into a unified perception of the object through exercise of the faculty of "common sense" located in the heart. This perception, termed a phantasm, remains after the object is removed from view and contributes to imagination, memory, and thinking.

René Descartes proposed a philosophy of dualism in which the mind and body are distinctly separate entities, with a subtle connection related to the "secretion" of mental events by the brain. Benedict de Spinoza countered with the theory of "substance monism" in which the mind and body are one and the same manifestation of the only reality—God. According to Spinoza, physical stimulation of the retina by light rays (a modified form of effluences) from an object yields a misleading image because it is simply the body's reaction to light and has nothing to do with the object itself. Hence, the true nature of an object, and therefore the external world, is essentially unknowable.

In the English philosopher John Locke's "causal theory" of perception, the appearance of an object is an "idea" that is distinct from, but causally related to, the object itself. Locke proposed two categories of properties, one of which consists of properties of objects such as hardness, mass, and spatial and temporal extension that exist in external reality. The second category consists of properties such as color, texture, and shape that exist in the mind but not in external reality. A causal relationship exists between the two categories of properties as a result of experiences of the observer with objects in the external world. Locke's approach was adopted by many of his colleagues, including Isaac Newton, who argued that properties such as color were entirely a manifestation of sensation in the observer and had only a tenuous connection at best with any real property of the object. This approach became known as the empiricist school of philosophy.

In *An Essay Towards a New Theory of Vision* (1709), the Anglican bishop George Berkeley argued that the only connection of an observer with the physical universe is through ideas generated by the senses. The existence of any physical object, including the physical universe, can never be proved or disproved. In Berkeley's interpretation, the world is just as it appears because it is the appearance that constitutes the world.

Immanuel Kant suggested that the imagination correlates a sensory impression of an object with past impressions, leading to recognition of the object through its resemblance to similar impressions stored in the mind's memory. Kant postulated that reason is a higher mental faculty whose use permits complete understanding of the external world. David Hume countered Kant's theory by suggesting that ideas about objects evolve from a set of beliefs that are not direct products of experience. He suggested that generalizations of sensory experiences require ideas which in turn require a system of beliefs because no single object necessarily implies the existence of another. Hume was skeptical of the observer's ability to achieve rational knowledge about external reality, and he and his followers became known as the school of skeptical philosophy.

The German physicist and physiologist Hermann L. F. von Helmholtz exerted a major influence on theories of vision. He believed that the observer is isolated from the external world and experiences it only by neural signals. Visual images are interpreted by imposing stored knowledge on sensory signals according to a "top down" model of perception. Among the many challenges to the perceptual hypothesis theory has been J. J. Gibson's theory of "ecological optics" in which perception occurs independent of mental processing or analysis by the mind. Gibson's work has been particularly influential in the field of computer vision.

In contrast to the ideas of Helmholtz and other experimentalists, proponents of the gestalt theory of vision suggest that visual signals are interpreted by use of mental fields that are organized to yield shapes out of which "form" is subconsciously induced in the observer. Objects and events are perceived not because the observer learns how to interpret sensations, but rather because the nervous system yields perceptual forms for superimposition onto sensory stimuli. The physiological origin of these mentally derived forms is unclear.

Of the modern approaches to the study of vision, the work of physicist David Marr has been particularly influential. He has suggested that the shapes of objects are perceived by a three-stage process to

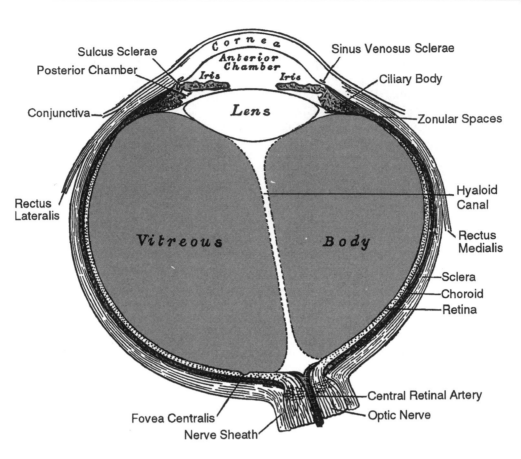

Figure 1 Horizontal section through the human eye.

yield an image termed a two-and-one-half-dimensional sketch because it is more than a two-dimensional image but does not convey the full range of depth information. The first stage is the formation of a primal sketch consisting of major features and intensity variations. The next stage involves the registration of more subtle features such as surface discontinuities and depth referenced to a coordinate frame centered in the viewer. Finally, the third stage permits a mental construction of the object referenced to a coordinate frame centered in the object. The product of this three-stage process is a mental model of the object suspended in object-oriented space to yield the impression that the object is somewhere "out there."

Current theories of visual perception suggest that the detection and recognition of objects involves a constant interplay between sensation and cognition rather than a single step in which neural signals are integrated into a visual image somewhere in the brain. It is no longer possible to sepa-

rate the mechanisms of detection, recognition, and interpretation of visual images. Instead, these processes must be considered as a single interactive process in which the acquisition of visual information is integrated with recognition and interpretation, and even consciousness.

Anatomy of Vision

The eye contains several transparent elements (cornea, aqueous and vitreous humors, and lens) that collectively are termed the ocular refractive media (Fig. 1). Light entering the eye is refracted at the anterior surface of the cornea, passes through the pupil, and is refracted by the lens to form a focused image on the retina. The iris of the lens opens and closes to adjust the amount of light reaching the retina, a process known as accommodation. The lens is an elastic structure that is rounded or flattened by the ciliary muscles to bring near and far objects into focus on the retina.

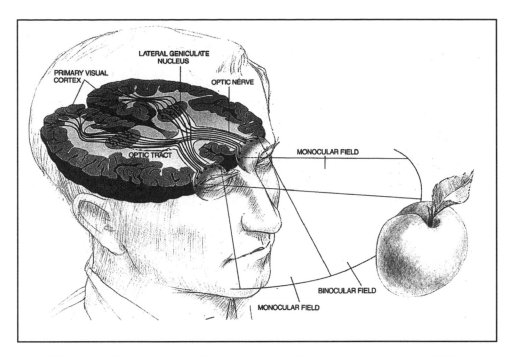

Figure 2   Visual pathway in the human (with permission, Schatz 1992).

The visual system responds to visible light—electromagnetic radiation of wavelengths between 400 and 700 nm. The retina is protected from radiation of shorter wavelength (ultraviolet radiation) by filtration of this radiation in the cornea and lens. Longer wavelength radiation (infrared radiation) reaches the retina but is too low in energy to affect the retinal molecules.

Light striking the retina is absorbed by the visual pigment in photoreceptors called rods and cones because of their shapes. The retina contains about 120 million rods, all located outside the fovea, and approximately 6 million cones, mostly situated in the foveal and parafoveal regions of the retina. The visual pigment in the rods is rhodopsin with a spectral sensitivity peak at 500 nm. Rhodopsin consists of a light-absorbing substance (chromophore), called 11-*cis*-retinal, complexed with the lipoprotein opsin. The cones contain one of three visual pigments with the same chromophore as rhodopsin but with different concentrations of opsin to provide different spectral sensitivities [450 nm (blue cones), 525 nm (green cones), and 555 nm (red cones)]. When illuminated, the chromophore is altered from the *cis* to the *trans* form, accompanied by hyperpolarization of the photoreceptor membrane to produce a neural impulse. The chromophore is returned to its *cis* form by enzymatic action for repetition of the visual cycle.

The retina contains four other groups of cells, termed horizontal, bipolar, amacrine, and ganglion, that preprocess visual information by converging signals from the 120 million rod photoreceptors into approximately 1 million ganglion cells, whose axons form the optic nerve. The large ratio of rod photoreceptors to ganglion cells enhances the sensitivity of rod vision and facilitates its use under low levels of illumination. In contrast, each cone in the fovea is associated with a single ganglion cell, which explains the high spatial resolution of the visual system under bright illumination where the cones are the principle receptors employed in producing a visual image. Cone vision is not possible under low levels of illumination because the neural signals are too small to be distinguishable from noise. The intermediate cells also refine the signals from specific ganglion cells to add information about motion, direction, and configuration.

The axons of the ganglion cells leave the eye as the optic nerve. The optic nerves from the two eyes meet at the optic chiasm and ultimately terminate in the lateral geniculate nucleus located in the thalamus (Fig. 2). From the lateral geniculate nucleus, the visual pathway consists of optic radiations that

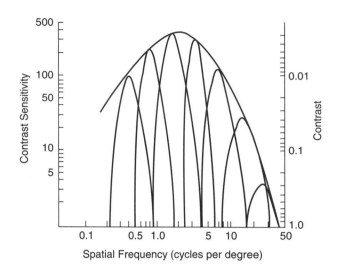

Figure 3 Contrast sensitivity curve (with permission, Ginsburg and Hendee, 1993)

pass through the parietal and temporal lobes of the brain and terminate in the primary visual cortex. Output from this region is fed to the prestriate visual cortex containing several areas, some of which serve as a "post office" to parcel out signals to appropriate areas, while others further discriminate visual signals in terms of variables such as motion, color, orientation, and form.

The specialized areas in the prestriate visual cortex are connected to sites of recognition in the visual association cortex located in the parieto-occipital and temporo-occipital areas of the cerebral cortex of the brain. The actual function of the prestriate visual cortex and its connections to the visual association cortex are more complex than the simple model presented here, because many interconnections exist between areas in the visual prestriate cortex and between the prestriate cortex and the visual association cortex. These interconnections provide many feedback loops and interchange pathways that make it very difficult to unravel the process by which visual stimuli are recognized and interpreted.

Visual System Performance

The resolving ability of the visual system is usually measured with a sine wave test pattern of varying contrast levels under conditions of bright illumination so that cone vision is employed. A typ-

ical response curve is shown in Fig. 3, where maximum sensitivity occurs at two cycles per degree, and the cutoff frequency is approximately fifty cycles per degree. The resolving ability is determined by the size of the photoreceptors in the retina. At high spatial frequencies the summation of signals from the rods degrades resolution, while the decreased response at low frequencies is primarily a result of lateral inhibition that filters out these frequencies.

The ability of the visual system to respond to rapid changes in illumination is described in terms of the flicker fusion frequency. The maximum flicker rate detectable by the eye is about sixty cycles per second. In the display of discrete film or video images for human viewing, images are presented at a temporal frequency that exceeds the flicker fusion frequency so that the action appears continuous.

The eye has a very wide dynamic range (about 10^{13}), enhanced by the ability of the lens iris to limit the amount of light reaching the retina. In addition, the use of cones under conditions of bright illumination and rods when the illumination is low provides the ability to respond to a wide range of brightnesses. Also, the summation of output from many rods to a single ganglion cell improves performance at low light levels, as does the ability of the eye to dark-adapt to provide a chemical method of gain control. The eye is remarkably sensitive to low levels of illumination. The detection threshold for light has been described as the ability to see a candle flame at a distance of thirty miles on a clear dark night. The response of the visual system remains relatively constant over a dynamic range of about 10^4 and degrades gradually beyond that range.

The degree of change in a visual stimulus required to produce a "just noticeable difference" (JND) in the sensory response of an observer is described by Weber's law, which is

$$\frac{dI}{I} = k,$$

where the change in light intensity dI divided by the intensity I is a constant k, termed the Weber fraction. This expression reveals that the observer's response depends on the relative rather than the absolute magnitude of change in a visual stimulus. Fechner's law provides a scale that relates the intensity (I) of a physical stimulus to the magnitude (R) of the psychological reaction. Fechner's law is

$$R = w \log I,$$

where w is a constant. An alternative expression is the Stevens power law, which is

$$R = aI^n$$

where a and n are constants for a particular stimulus over a selected range of intensities.

The eye is capable of furnishing visual information at a much higher rate than can be transmitted by the optic nerve. Hence, considerable data compression must be employed if important information is to be preserved. One major method of data compression is to emphasize the transmission of data that signify changes in the information present in the visual scene. This method is accomplished by "on center-off surround" photoreceptors in the retina that act as a bandpass filter to remove dc and low-spatial-frequency information from the image so that only information about changes in the scene is transmitted. This process by itself would cause a stationary scene to fade rapidly from view. However, the rapid, low amplitude (saccadic) motion of the eye causes the retinal image to change even when the visual scene is stationary, so that the image is preserved. Also, the retina contains cells that respond to specific features, such as lines and orientation, that lead to a reduction in the total information to be transmitted.

Early investigators of vision assumed that the eye served as a type of camera to project an image of a visual scene onto the retina where it could be transmitted intact by neural signals onto the visual cortex. Today it is understood that the eye is a complex structure that involves considerable data compression and processing. This complexity permits the capture of a much wider range of visual information than would be possible by a simple camera mechanism, and it also facilitates the transfer of this information to the brain for interpretation. In this manner the eye itself is part of the interpretative process for visual information and cannot be considered separately from the visual cortex as a process for detecting, recognizing, and interpreting visual information.

The eye is extremely sensitive to detecting motion in a visual scene, as can be attested to by any big-game hunter or video-game player. The visual system is also able to detect internal inconsistencies or inappropriate configurations in a visual scene almost instantaneously. Proofreaders and image analysts employ this capability to identify misspellings in a text rapidly or focus in quickly on abnormalities in an image. This ability of the visual system to recognize certain features of an image almost immediately is termed the "early warning," "distributed preattentive," or "global" phase of the visual response. The early warning system provides a very rapid (less than 150 msec) detection of clues that suggest something different or anomalous in the visual environment.

Identification and interpretation of the difference detected by the preattentive phase of vision requires a slower and more thoughtful analysis of the visual scene. This process involves the attentive or "local" phase of viewing during which the eye scans the visual scene and attention is focused on specific features that have been identified as being different during the preattentive phase. During attentive vision, information is processed from an area of the retina that includes the fovea but which also extends beyond the fovea. This area is termed the "useful field of view," "visual lobe," or "functional visual field." The viewer uses this two-phase process to detect unusual features in an image, and then to identify and interpret them by directing visual attention to the features.

Some images contain features that are not distinguishable by preattentive viewing but which are nevertheless quickly discernible by the viewer. The distinction appears to result from rapid processing of visual data during the attentive phase. This process represents an intermediate phase of visual recognition that permits rapid extraction of local information from a visual scene by concentrating on the presence of conspicuous features called "textons" in the image. According to Bela Julesz, only three classes of textons exist: color, elongated blobs, and termination number. It is the presence of textons in images that permits an analysis of image texture, an important feature of many types of images. An example of an image with texture is shown in Fig. 4.

The concept of "fractal dimension" has also been introduced to explain the interpretation of texture patterns. As defined by Benoit B. Mandelbrot, fractals are sets of numbers with the properties of similarity and randomness extended over a range of dimensional scales, defined as the fractal dimension. Interest is growing in applying fractal analysis to many different areas of imaging science.

Figure 4 Dalmatian (with permission, Thurston and Carraher, 1986).

Digital Imaging

The introduction of digital techniques into image processing and display presents a new order of complexity in the analysis of vision. The ability to transform digital images into an almost unlimited array of altered appearances through processing algorithms to sharpen edges, enhance contrast, and suppress noise, and through windowing techniques to limit the range of displayed image brightness and contrast greatly expands the range of information available from images. Management of this expanded scale of information permits selection of displayed images that are optimally suited for interpretation by the observer. This flexibility demands a firm understanding of the characteristics of human vision so that images can be matched to the characteristics to facilitate optimum image interpretation.

See also: BIOPHYSICS; FRACTAL; HELMHOLTZ, HERMANN L. F. VON; IMAGE, OPTICAL; LENS; NEWTON, ISAAC; OPTICS

Bibliography

BERKELEY, G. *An Essay Towards a New Theory of Vision* (Dutton, New York, [1709] 1910).

GIBSON, J. J. *The Perception of the Visual World* (Houghton Mifflin, Boston, 1950).

GINSBURG, A. P., and HENDEE, W. R. "Quantification of Visual Capability" in *Perception of Visual Information,* edited by W. R. Hendee and P. N. T. Wells (Springer-Verlag, New York, 1993).

GREGORY, R. L. *Concepts and Mechanisms of Perception* (Scribner, New York, 1974).

HELMHOLTZ, H. VON. *A Treatise on Physiological Optics* (American Institute for Psychological Research, Albuquerque, NM, [1856, 1860, 1866] 1987).

HENDEE, W. R. "The Perception of Visual Information." *RadioGraphics* **7,** 1213–1219 (1987).

HENDEE, W. R., and WELLS, P. N. T., eds. *Perception of Visual Information* (Springer-Verlag, New York, 1993).

JULESZ, B. "Textons: The Elements of Texture Perception and Their Interactions." *Nature* (London) **290,** 91–97 (1981).

KANT, I. *Critique of Pure Reason,* trans. by N. Kemp Smith (St. Martin's Press, New York, [1929] 1969).

LOCKE, J. *An Essay Concerning Human Understanding,* edited by P. H. Nidditch (Oxford University Press, New York, [1690] 1975).

MANDELBROT, B. B. *The Fractal Geometry of Nature* (W. H. Freeman, New York, 1982).

MARR, D. *Vision* (W. H. Freeman, New York, 1982).

NEWTON, I. *Opticks* (Dover, New York, [1704] 1952).

PRICE, H. *Hume's Theory of the External World* (Clarendon, Oxford, 1940).

SCHATZ, C. J. "The Developing Brain." *Sci. Am.* **267,** 61–67 (1992).

SCRUTON, R. *Spinoza* (Oxford University Press, New York, 1986).

THURSTON, J. B., and CARRAHER, R. G. *Optical Illustration and the Visual Arts* (Van Nostrand Reinhold, New York, 1986).

WILLIAM R. HENDEE

VOLCANO

With more than 80 percent of Earth's surface being of volcanic origin, it is no wonder that volcanoes are intertwined with human history, mythology, and folklore. Early peoples sometimes worshipped volcanoes as gods and goddess and, in some cultures such as that of native Hawaiians, volcanoes are still looked upon as deities. Vulcan, the Roman god of fire, gives his name to what modern-day people call volcano. Science has done much to dispel the mysteries of volcanoes, yet much is still unknown about them.

Volcanoes are expressions of Earth's warm interior and mobile lithosphere. Heat from within the earth stirs the interior into large convection currents. Where a convection cell rises toward the surface the lithosphere bulges, breaks, and moves away from the warm area, rafting the lithosphere on the slowly moving top portion of the cell. This process breaks Earth's surface into a series of rigid plates that are in slow but constant motion. At their edges—where the plates bump and grind into or past each other—much of the world's active volcanism and earthquake activity takes place.

One large plate makes up much of the Pacific Ocean floor. The plate's boundary is defined by the "ring of fire" volcanoes that periodically erupt with explosive force. Located along the western coast of South and North America, the eastern coast of Asia, the islands of Japan, and on south to New Zealand are some of the world's better-know volcanoes. Stretching from regal Popocatepetl in Mexico, to stately Mount Shasta in California and explosive Mount St. Helens in Washington, to respectful Mount Fugiyama in Japan, volcanoes are powerful reminders of Earth's tectonic forces.

The chemical composition, amount of dissolved gases, and temperature of the molten material that erupts determines whether the volcano will be explosive, like Mount St. Helens, or effusive, like the Hawaiian volcanoes. Magma, molten rock beneath the earth's surface, is a complex mixture of melted minerals and dissolved gases. The three factors of mineral composition, amount of dissolved gas, and temperature affects the magma's mobility or viscosity.

The higher the silica (SiO_2) content, the more viscous the magma. As the magma cools, silica tetrahedrons join in lengthy chains and linked structures, increasing the viscosity of the magma. Magma that contains higher amounts of silica   more than 70 percent—melt at lower temperatures (around 650°C) and form rocks of a granitic composition. If this magma cools slowly underground, it will form rocks in the granitic family. If it is erupted to the surface and rapidly cools, it forms rocks in the rhyolitic family. Magma that contains 50 to 60 percent silica melts at higher temperatures (>1,000°C) and forms rocks in the basaltic family.

Water makes up around 70 percent by volume of the gases released by volcanoes. The other gases include carbon dioxide (15%), nitrogen and hydrogen compounds (4%), and other compounds (1%). Dissolved gases decrease viscosity, making the magma more fluid. At depth, confining pressure

from overlying rocks keeps the gases dissolved in the magma. As magma migrates upward through the crust, confining pressure becomes less and dissolved gases come out of solution, much the same as when a carbonated beverage is opened. In a high-silica magma the gases cannot escape easily and the volcano may erupt explosively. In lower-silica magmas the gases will force the fluid magma out of the vent in spectacular fire fountains of molten rock that may be several hundred meters high. A 1959 eruption of Kilauea Iki created a fire fountain that was measured at 575 m (1,900 ft) high.

Granitic magmas, cooler and low in gas content, tend to create an explosive type of volcano with periodic ash eruptions and viscous lava flows. These volcanoes make up one of the general groups of volcanoes, stratovolcanoes, or as they are also known, composite volcanoes. The lava flows from these types of volcanoes tend to be viscous and do not flow far from the vent. Characterized by steep, cone-shaped mountains, stratovolcanoes such as Mount St. Helens, Mount Pelee, and Mount Vesuvius pose the greatest threat to human life. Mount Pelee, located on the island of Martinique, erupted in 1902, destroying the town of St. Pierre and killing more than 30,000 people with fiery clouds of incandescent ash and gas.

Basaltic magma, hotter and with relatively low silica, allows the gases to escape more easily and are therefore less explosive. The higher temperature keeps the lava mobile and this builds volcanoes with broad, fluid lava flows that cover large areas. Volcanic mountains that form around a single vent or localized vents build low mounds composed of numerous overlapping lava flows. These types of volcanoes are called Hawaiian, or shield, volcanoes because when viewed in cross section they have the appearance of a warrior's shield. Typically, shield volcanoes have slopes between 6 and 8 degrees, rarely exceeding 15 degrees in slope. The summits of shield volcanoes often have wide, steep, walled calderas that form when the surface collapses into the empty magma chamber under it.

In some basaltic eruptions a very fluid lava erupts along long fissures. Called "flood basalts" after the type of rock this lava forms, the flows cover large areas, erupting over a period of time to build plateaus that may be 2 to 3 km thick. The 200,000 km² (80,000 mi²) Columbia River Plateau, its smaller neighbor the 50,000 km² (20,000 miles²) Snake River Plain, and the 500,000 km² (200,000 miles²) Deccan Traps of India are examples of this type of volcanism. A single fissure eruption in Iceland in 1783 covered 565 km^2 (200 miles^2), creating a famine by destroying farm land and killing farm animals.

Volcanic eruptions are often looked upon as dangerous and destructive events. While this is true for those who live in the shadow of volcanoes, it should be remembered that volcanoes are part of the natural processes that have built Earth's crust and contributed to the early atmosphere and oceans. Rich, volcanic-derived soils support a wide variety of crops. New land area is added to Earth's land surface.

While science has done much to dispel the mysteries of volcanoes they remain potentially dangerous. However, volcanology can mitigate the hazards posed by volcanic eruptions by giving timely warnings of impending eruptions.

See also: EARTHQUAKE; GEOPHYSICS

Bibliography

EASTERBROOK, D. J. *Surface Processes and Landforms* (Macmillan, New York, 1993).

LINK, P. K.; KUNTZ, M. A.; and PLATT, L. B., eds. *Regional Geology of Eastern Idaho and Western Wyoming* (Geological Society of America, Boulder, CO, 1992).

TARBUCK, E. J., and LUTKINS, F. K. *The Earth: An Introduction to Physical Geology,* 4th ed. (Macmillan, New York, 1992).

THORNBURY, W. D. *Principles of Geomorphology* (Wiley, New York, 1969).

TILLINGS, R. I., ed. *How Volcanoes Work* (American Geophysical Union, Washington, DC, 1988).

M. FRANK WATT IRETON

VOLTMETER

The voltmeter is an instrument used to measure the electrical potential difference (voltage difference) between two points, A and B, in an electrical circuit, or the electromotive force (emf) of a source of electrical potential difference (for example, an electrical cell or battery). The reading given by a voltmeter is in volts (joules per coulomb). If the potential difference (voltage) between two points in the circuit is to be found, the two measuring connections (leads)

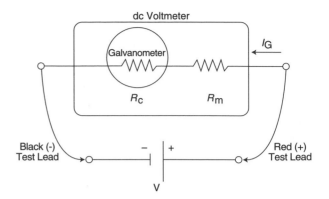

Figure 1 A dc voltmeter constructed from a D'Arsonval meter. The voltmeter is shown connected to a battery to measure its emf or voltage (V).

of the voltmeter are connected to the two points, and the voltmeter reads $V_B - V_A$, where B is the point to which the red or (+) lead is connected, and A is the point to which the black or (−) lead is connected.

Suppose the voltage drop across a resistor in a circuit is to be measured; then the voltmeter is connected across the resistor, or in parallel. But an ideal voltmeter should not alter the current that is flowing in the resistor or the rest of the circuit. Therefore, the resistance of an ideal voltmeter is infinite. Practical voltmeters have a finite resistance, as noted below.

The common analog (or moving needle) voltmeter is based on a D'Arsonval galvanometer. The galvanometer is in fact a sensitive dc ammeter. To adapt it for use as a dc voltmeter, a multiplier resistor R_m is connected in series with the galvanometer; the coil of the galvanometer also has some resistance R_c (see Fig. 1). Let the galvanometer have a sensitivity (current for full-scale reading) of I_G. Consider the design of a voltmeter with a full-scale voltage reading of V. When this voltmeter is connected to an emf (e.g., a battery) of V volts, the needle points full scale due to current I_G that flows through the series resistance $R_c + R_m$. By Ohm's law we have $V = I_G(R_c + R_m)$. Note that the resistance between the test leads of the voltmeter is given by $R_c + R_m = (1/I_G)V$.

The quantity $(1/I_G)$ has units of ohms per volt and is called the "sensitivity of the voltmeter." Then multiplying the ohms/volt sensitivity of the voltmeter by the full-scale voltage of the range gives the

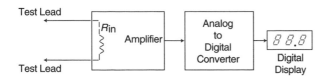

Figure 2 Block diagram of a digital voltmeter (DVM).

Bibliography

GREGORY, B. *An Introduction to Electrical Instrumentation* (Macmillan, New York, 1973).
JONES, L. *Electrical and Electronic Measuring Instruments* (Wiley, New York, 1983).
STOUT, M. B. *Basic Electrical Measurements*, 2nd ed. (Prentice Hall, Englewood Cliffs, NJ, 1960).

DENNIS BARNAAL

resistance of the voltmeter. For example, a common sensitivity is 20,000 Ω/V (corresponding to a galvanometer sensitivity of 50 μA). If a 10-V full-scale voltmeter is built from this galvanometer, the resistance between the test leads will then be 200,000 Ω.

A versatile multirange voltmeter is built by arranging a switch that can connect in one of several different multiplier resistors R_m, each giving a particular full-scale voltage capability for the meter. For even more versatility, the switch can be arranged to select ammeter ranges (by connecting in various shunt resistors) or to select ohmmeter capability. Then the meter is termed a multimeter or a VOM (volt-ohmmeter). Common analog VOMs have accuracies of 1 to 3 percent and can read from 0.5 V full scale to 1,000 V.

An ac voltmeter is generally obtained by semiconductor diodes in the meter that are arranged in a rectification connection to produce a dc voltage from the input ac voltage. This dc voltage is input to a dc voltmeter, but the scale is marked to give the root-mean-square voltage corresponding to a sinusoidal ac voltage.

To approach the ideal very high voltmeter resistance, an electronic amplifying circuit is used, based on vacuum tubes, field-effect transistors (FETs), or bipolar transistors. Then the resistance (between its test leads) of the voltmeter is the input resistance (R_{in}) of the amplifier. A typical vacuum-tube voltmeter (VTVM) or FET voltmeter (FTVM) has a resistance of 10 MΩ. A modern digital voltmeter (DVM) uses amplifier circuitry connected to an analog-to-digital converter or ADC, which is in turn connected to a digital display (see Fig. 2). The amplifier and ADC circuitry can be designed to high precision so that voltage accuracies of 0.1 to 0.001 percent are obtained (with better accuracy commanding a corresponding higher price).

See also: AMMETER; ELECTRICAL CONDUCTIVITY; ELECTRICAL RESISTANCE; GALVANOMETER; OHMMETER

VORTEX

A vortex is commonly associated with the rotating motion of fluid around a common centerline. It is defined by the vorticity in the fluid. The vorticity measures the rate with which a small fluid volume spins about itself. Mathematically, it is given by

$$\boldsymbol{\omega} = \nabla \times \mathbf{u},$$

where $\mathbf{u} = (u, v, w)$ is the fluid velocity. A vortex is a region of large vorticity. Typically, the fluid circulates around the vortex, the speed increases as the vortex (or vortex core) is approached and the pressure decreases. Vortices come in a large range of sizes; some examples are given in Table 1. The simplest model for a vortex is a straight line vortex, where the vorticity is zero except on a line. In a cross section through this flow, the streamlines are circles about the line vortex and the fluid speed increases without bound as the distance to the vortex decreases (Fig. 1).

Table 1 Examples of Vortices

Vortex	Core Diameter
Quantized vortices in superfluid helium	10^{-8} cm (= 1 Å)
Smoke rings / Bathtub vortex	0.1–10 cm
Dust devils	1–10 m
Tornadoes	10–500 m
Hurricanes	100–2,000 km
Spiral galaxies	Thousands of light-years

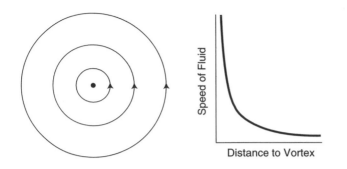

Figure 1 Cross section of a straight line vortex, along with a graph of the relationship between speed of the fluid and distance to the vortex.

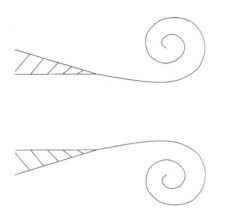

Figure 2 Vortex ring.

Figure 3 Trailing vortices.

Figure 4 Kármán vortex street.

Vortex Formation

Vortices are formed in various ways. They can be created by gravity, as when a bathtub drain vortex is formed. They can be created by differences in density and temperature. For example, warm-air vortices are formed when a layer of hot air is trapped underneath cooler air. Vortices also can be formed by frictional or viscous effects in a fluid near solid surfaces. Viscosity generates vorticity at the fluid walls, and this vorticity convects and diffuses into the flow. If fluid (air or water, for instance) is ejected from a tube, boundary vorticity separates at the opening, rolls up and forms a vortex ring (Fig. 2). Boundary vorticity around the wings of an airplane separates and rolls up into a pair of trailing vortices. These trailing vortices can be dangerous to small planes that fly into the wake of large planes (Fig. 3). The vorticity shed by a moving cylinder is often observed to form a staggered row of vortices called the Kármán vortex street (Fig. 4).

Vortex Evolution

Curved vortices, such as vortex rings or a twisting tornado, induce velocity on themselves. The thinner the vortex core, the larger is the induced speed. Thus a thin smoke ring travels faster than a thick ring. As vorticity diffuses, the core spreads and the velocities decrease. In some situations flow instabilities cause phenomena like vortex breakdown or the development of turbulence.

Vortices in Superfluids and Superconductors

At temperatures below 2.2 K, liquid helium is a superfluid. This means that it acts essentially like a fluid with zero viscosity. By quantum mechanical processes, extremely thin vortex lines are formed. These quantum vortices have discrete values of circulation (nh/m, where h is Planck's constant, m is mass of helium atom, and n is an integer), core sizes of about 1 Å (roughly the diameter of a single hydrogen atom) and move without viscosity. Vortices of magnetic flux with somewhat analogous properties are formed in superconductors. Here, these vortices can have the unwanted effect of increasing the resistance of the superconducting material.

Vortices in the Atmosphere and the Ocean

Whirlpools, tornadoes, and hurricanes are examples of large-scale vortices with enough force to cause great damage. Whirlpools are a hazard to fishing boats and swimmers. They are formed by tidal currents, most often in straits where ocean velocities are large. Tornadoes often occur in conjunction with hurricanes. They are columnar vortices, with destructive, high wind velocities of up to 200 m/s. Hurricanes are much larger disklike vortices, with the well-known eye of relatively clear weather in the center. The high wind speeds, heavy rainfall, and tidal surges associated with hurricanes can cause great material damage and loss of life. With the advent of supercomputers, large-scale computations are able to predict the path of hurricanes better and to give advance warnings of their landing. Aided by high-tech, on-site measurements and satellite measurements, predictions of hurricane landings have improved and the human toll has been reduced dramatically. The material damage, however, has increased, mostly because of the increasing population density in hurricane-prone areas.

See also: FLUID DYNAMICS; HURRICANE; TORNADO

Bibliography

BISHOP, D. J.; GAMMEL, P. L.; and HUSE, D. A. "Resistance in High-Temperature Superconductors." *Sci. Am.* **268** (2), 48 (1993).

DONNELLY, R. J. "Superfluid Turbulence." *Sci. Am.* **259** (5), 100 (1988).

FISHBANE, P. M.; GASIOROWICZ, S.; and THORNTON, S. T. *Physics for Scientists and Engineers* (Prentice Hall, Englewood Cliffs, NJ, 1993)

LUGT, H. J. *Vortex Flow in Nature and Technology* (Wiley, New York, 1983).

SAFFMAN, P. *Vortex Dynamics* (Cambridge University Press, New York, 1992).

TRITTON, D. J. *Physical Fluid Dynamics*, 2nd ed. (Clarendon Press, Oxford, Eng., 1988).

VAN DYKE, M. *An Album of Fluid Motion* (Parabolic Press, Stanford, CA, 1982).

MONIKA NITSCHE

W

WATER

Water (or hydrogen oxide, H_2O) has many special properties that have made it uniquely important in biology, chemistry, and physics. Approximately 71 percent of the surface of the earth is covered with water, which is critical to all known forms of life. Water is a solvent for an unusually large number of chemicals and the natural motions of water are among the most important factors in shaping the surface of the land, redistributing materials, and concentrating resources.

The O–H bond length is 0.0958 nm and the H–O–H bond angle is 104° 27′, only slightly less than the natural tetrahedral angle 109° 28′. The three independent vibrational modes occur in the vapor at wave number ($1/\lambda = \nu/c$) values of 1,595 cm^{-1} (bending mode) and 3652 cm^{-1} and 3,756 cm^{-1} (symmetric and antisymmetric stretches).

The four valence electrons of oxygen not involved in O–H bonding are described as lone-pair electrons, occupying approximately the locations in which additional bonds would occur in tetrahedral bonding. The polar character of water (hydrogen atoms relatively positive, oxygen negative) is a major cause of the solvent power of water for polar and ionic compounds.

The properties of water are strongly influenced by hydrogen bonding, between adjacent molecules, with the hydrogen of one molecule attracted by the lone-pair electrons of the oxygen of another molecule, forming an approximately linear O–H $\cdots$ O bond. The bond energy of such hydrogen bonds is about 3.4 kcal/mol or 14 kJ/mol, much lower than normal chemical bonds but much higher than typical van der Waals bonding energies between chemically nonbonded atoms.

Effects of hydrogen bonding include an unusually high triple point (0.1°C), melting point (0°C), and boiling point (100°C), in comparison with other molecules of comparable size (e.g., ammonia, NH_3; hydrogen fluoride, HF; and hydrogen sulfide, H_2S) which are gases at room temperature. Hydrogen bonding gives ice a relatively open structure that is less dense than the liquid. The expansion of water upon freezing in small cracks and pores of rock is a major contributor to cleavage and erosion of the rocks.

The persistence of some of the ice structure into the cold liquid causes a contraction as the liquid is warmed from 0 to 3.98°C, where it has maximum density. This produces convection currents in bodies of water as they cool, until the lowest layers approximate 4°C and the surface freezes first, with the ice remaining on top. Because ice is less dense than liquid, increasing pressure lowers the freezing point of water slightly (about 8×10^{-8}°C/Pa or 0.008°C/atm).

As water is warmed, the average thermal energy in each degree of freedom approaches the energy of a hydrogen bond, causing dissociation of these bonds.

This internal energy conversion gives liquid water an exceptionally high specific heat of 1 cal/g·K = 4.2 J/g·K, approximately constant with temperature. Residual hydrogen bonding gives a heat of vaporization, at 100°C, larger than expected (Trouton constant = ΔS_{vap} = 109 J/mol·K, compared with approximately 92 J/mol·K for "normal" liquids).

Hydrogen bonding also causes water to have surprisingly high viscosity (1,006 μPa·s at 20°C) and surface tension (0.07275 N/m) in comparison with comparable nonhydrogen bonded liquids. (Although much larger, ethyl ether, $C_2H_5OC_2H_5$, has a viscosity of 234 μPa·s and surface tension of 0.0170 N/m, a melting point of approximately −120°C, and a boiling point of 34.6°C.)

Hydrogen bonding and dipole–dipole attractions provide important cohesive forces that hold biological molecules together in helical coils and other conformations. Loss of water from such structures produces irreversible changes and loss of function.

Dissociation of water into hydrogen and oxygen may be accomplished with electrical currents. Thermal dissociation occurs only at temperatures of thousands of kelvin. At room temperature, molecules in the liquid phase show a slight tendency to dissociate ionically:

$$H_2O \rightarrow H^+ + OH^-,$$

where the ions are closely tied to undissociated water molecule clusters (e.g., $[H_2O]_xH^+$, with $x \gg 1$). The dissociation constant at room temperature is $10^{-14} = C_{H^+} \cdot C_{OH^-}$ for concentrations in mol/l. (More precisely, concentrations should be replaced with activities.) The collective "strength" of hydrogen ions is given by the pH = $-\log C_{H^+}$. The pH is low for acidic solutions; high for basic solutions. At room temperature, the pH of neutral water is 7. This value decreases as the water is warmed and dissociation increases. It is 6.5 for neutral water at 60°C.

Humidity is measured as the partial pressure of water vapor. At equilibrium this value (the vapor pressure) increases from 4.579 Torr (610.5 Pa) at 0°C to 23.756 Torr (3,167 Pa) at 25°C to 760 Torr (1.01×10^5 Pa) at 100°C. Relative humidity is the ratio of the actual partial pressure of water vapor to the equilibrium value. Relative humidity, usually quoted as a percent, strongly influences human comfort because it affects energy loss by evaporation of moisture from the skin.

Water has traditionally provided a reference value for physical quantities of other materials. The ratio of the physical quantity to the value for water is typically called the specific value (e.g., specific heat, specific gravity). The original definition of the kilogram was the mass of 1 liter (1,000 cm^3) of water, and the calorie is the thermal energy added to raise the temperature of 1 g of water 1°C, so specific values are often also values per gram of the substance.

The familiar solid form of water, known as ice I (or simply ice), includes snow, which consists of hexagonal ice crystals in a variety of geometric arrangements. At high pressures, ten other crystalline forms of water are stable, designated ice II, ice III, and so on. These other ices are denser than water.

Deuterium, $D \equiv {}^2_1H$, is an isotopic form of hydrogen of approximately twice the mass of normal hydrogen. Water containing deuterium (D_2O, or HDO) is called heavy water. (H_2O is then called light water.) The physical properties of D_2O differ slightly from H_2O. For example, the melting point is 3.8°C, boiling point 101.42°C, and density about 10 percent greater. Because of the greater mass, the average molecular speeds are about 5 percent less, so D_2O is concentrated in the residual liquid in electrolysis of water.

Heavy water has been important as a moderator in nuclear reactors, to slow fast neutrons emitted in radioactive decay and thus increase the probability of neutron capture by other nuclei. Because the chemistry of deuterium is nearly identical to that of ordinary hydrogen, heavy water provides a source of tracer molecules that permit chemical processes to be followed in the laboratory and in living organisms.

Seawater varies from about 0.3 percent (in the Baltic Sea) to about 6 percent (Red Sea) dissolved solids. A typical concentration (about 4 percent by weight) would be 0.55 M (mole per liter), of which about 90 percent is NaCl and 10 percent is $MgCl_2$, with sulfates and other halides also present. A reported polymeric form of water, called anomalous water or polywater, was later found to be ordinary water with a high level of impurities.

See also: CONVECTION; HYDROGEN BOND; ICE; PRESSURE, VAPOR; SPECIFIC HEAT; SURFACE TENSION; VAN DER WAALS FORCE; VISCOSITY

Bibliography

DORSEY, N. E. *Properties of Ordinary Water-Substance* (Van Nostrand Reinhold, New York, 1940).

EISENBERG, D. S., and KAUZMANN, W. *The Structure and Properties of Water* (Clarendon, Oxford, 1969).

PIMENTEL, G. C., and MCCLELLAN, A. L. *The Hydrogen Bond* (W. H. Freeman, San Francisco, 1960).

ROBERT P. BAUMAN

WAVE

See ALFVEN WAVE; ELECTROMAGNETIC WAVE; GRAVITATIONAL WAVE; LIGHT, WAVE THEORY OF; RADIO WAVE; SEISMIC WAVE; SHOCK WAVE; STANDING WAVE; WAVE MOTION

WAVE FUNCTION

An isolated particle is characterized according to quantum mechanics, not by its position at a given time, but rather by its wave function, $\psi(t, \mathbf{r})$. This is a mathematical function of time and of space. The variable t catalogs time; the position vector variable $\mathbf{r}$ (representing x, y, and z) catalogs space. This function obeys the laws of quantum mechanics as embodied in the Schrödinger equation. Any solution of this equation is a wave function.

The wave function is generally complex, but its absolute value squared, $|\psi|^2$, is real. This measures the probability of finding the particle at any particular time and place specified. This probability is the only information predicted by quantum mechanics, and it represents the maximum knowable information in a quantum problem.

For a closed or isolated system of two or more particles, the wave function depends on time and position for all of the particles involved:

$$\psi = \psi(t, \mathbf{r}_1, \mathbf{r}_2, \ldots \mathbf{r}n),$$

if there are n particles. Again, the absolute square, evaluated at any particular time and set of positions, $|\psi(t, \mathbf{r}_1, \mathbf{r}_2, \ldots \mathbf{r}n)|^2$, measures the probability of finding the first particle at $\mathbf{r}_1$, the second particle at

$\mathbf{r}_2$, the third particle at $\mathbf{r}_3$, and so on. Hence the probability of finding particle 3 at $\mathbf{r}_3$ depends on the $\mathbf{r}_1$ and $\mathbf{r}_2$ chosen in asking about particles 1 and 2.

See also: EIGENFUNCTION AND EIGENVALUE; QUANTUM MECHANICS; QUANTUM STATISTICS; SCHRÖDINGER EQUATION; WAVE MECHANICS

Bibliography

CHESTER, M. *Primer of Quantum Mechanics* (Krieger, Malabar, FL, 1992).

LÉVY-LEBLOND, J. M., and BALIBAR, F. *Quantics*, trans. by S. T. Ali (North-Holland, New York, 1990).

MARVIN CHESTER

WAVEGUIDE

If a person yells into the air, the acoustic energy, originating at the mouth, spreads out over a spherical wave. A listener, sitting in the bleachers a little distance away, receives only a small fraction of the acoustic energy. But if the person yells into a megaphone, the acoustic energy is concentrated in the forward direction and the same bleacher fan hears the person loud and clear. A waveguide does for electromagnetic waves what a megaphone does for sound waves. A waveguide guides electromagnetic waves, and, as such, it can efficiently channel electromagnetic energy.

A waveguide is a hollow metallic pipe (typically copper) with a rectangular cross section, where the rectangular dimensions determine the wavelengths of the electromagnetic waves that can be propagated. Waveguides are most commonly used for electromagnetic waves that occur between the infrared and the radio regions of the electromagnetic spectrum; that is, the microwave region that embraces wavelengths from approximately 0.1 cm (3×10^{11} Hz) to 30 cm (10^9 Hz).

There is a basic difference between electromagnetic power transmission with microwaves and the power transmission that occurs in a house. Houses are powered by an alternating voltage source (ac) with a frequency of 60 Hz (50 Hz in Europe). Electric power is transmitted from a source to a house by means of a conducting wire. A flow of electrical

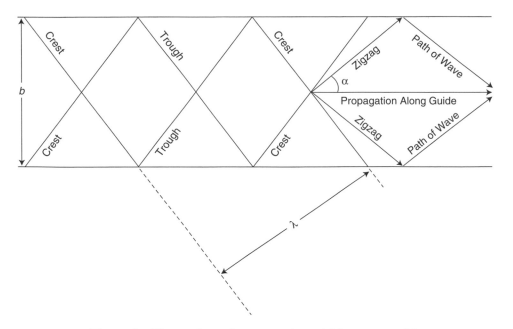

Figure 1   Illustration of wave motion within a waveguide.

charge, in the form of drifting electrons, occurs between the voltage source and the appliance, say, a light bulb. Electric energy is transmitted from the source (the wall plug and the power company) to an appliance (the lightbulb), and the electric energy is transformed into light and heat.

Transmission is different for microwaves. A waveguide replaces the conducting wire, and electromagnetic power is delivered not by electric-charge flow but by electric and magnetic fields traveling through the waveguide as electromagnetic waves. The configuration of the electromagnetic waves, as well as that of the electric and magnetic fields propagating within the waveguide, is determined by the dimensions of the waveguide, the wavelength of the electromagnetic wave, and the conductance of the metallic walls of the waveguide. Just as a stretched string can vibrate with different wavelengths, called "modes," a waveguide can accommodate electromagnetic waves in different modes. At the metallic conducting surfaces, the electric field must be essentially perpendicular or zero. The magnetic field must be tangential. The absence of electric fields tangential to the conducting surfaces means that no current will be stimulated by them. However, the magnetic fields do give rise to surface currents that lead to losses of electromagnetic energy as the electromagnetic wave propagates through the waveguide.

Recall that in free space, the electric and magnetic fields are perpendicular to each other and to the direction of propagation. It is essentially the same in the confines of a waveguide; however, in order for the electric field vector to be either normal or zero at the sides, it is most common for two electromagnetic waves to propagate simultaneously through the waveguide. Specifically, two waves zigzag between the walls of the waveguide, as shown in Fig. 1. In this illustration, three parameters are shown: the width of the waveguide, b; the wavelength of the two zigzagging waves, λ; and the angle between the normal to each wavefront and the direction of propagation, α. The two parameters b and λ determine the angle α and the maximum wavelength that the waveguide can propagate. If $\lambda = 2b$, $\alpha = 90°$; thus the wave bounces back and forth between the two sides and ceases to propagate along the guide. This particular wavelength, $\lambda = 2b = \lambda_c$, is called the "cut-off wavelength" λ_c. A waveguide with inside dimensions of $a = 1.27$ cm and $b = 2.54$ cm is called an "X-band waveguide" and commonly is used for wavelengths between 3.0 and 3.5 cm.

Note from the above that the wavelengths typically used in X-band are considerably below the cut-off wavelength of 5.08 cm. Why is this? The answer brings us back to the issue of energy losses and the mode of the propagating electromagnetic wave. As acknowledged earlier, there are currents stimulated in the walls of the waveguide and this leads to an attenuation of energy propagating through the guide. These losses approach infinity as the wavelength approaches the cut-off wavelength. The attenuation is a minimum for wavelengths equal to approximately 0.4 times the cut-off wavelength. In practice, however, the wavelengths employed are somewhat larger than λ_c to discourage electromagnetic wave patterns of unwanted modes.

See also: ELECTROMAGNETIC WAVE; FIELD, ELECTRIC; FIELD, MAGNETIC; WAVELENGTH; WAVE MOTION

Bibliography

SUGDEN, T. M., and KENNEY, C. N. *Microwave Spectroscopy of Gases* (Van Nostrand, London, 1965).

TOWNES, C. H., and SCHAWLOW, A. L. *Microwave Spectroscopy* (McGraw-Hill, New York, 1955).

JOHN S. RIGDEN

WAVELENGTH

A traveling wave can be generated by a periodic disturbance in some medium. Waves can be transverse or longitudinal. Sound waves in air are longitudinal, which means that the wave travels in the same direction as the disturbance in the air. In contrast, waves in a stretched string or wire are transverse, vibrating at right angles to the length of the string or wire. Electromagnetic waves, of which visible light is a special case, are transverse.

One way to generate a sound wave of a particular frequency is to force the diaphragm of a loudspeaker to oscillate at a given frequency. As the diaphragm periodically vibrates forward and backward, it periodically compresses and rarefies the air. The periodic compressions (high-pressure regions) and rarefactions (low-pressure regions) set up a longitudinal wave traveling in the air.

The wavelength (λ) is the distance a wave travels forward before its oscillations or vibrations are repeated. The time between the periodic disturbances is called the period (T) of the wave. The number of disturbances per second is the frequency (f) of the wave. If the period is known in seconds, then $f = 1/T$ will define the number of cycles per second (in hertz, Hz) for the wave. If ν is the speed of the wave, the wavelength is given by $\lambda = \nu T$ or $\lambda = \nu/f$, because $T = 1/f$.

The speed of a wave depends on the properties of the medium. For example, the speed of a wave on a wire depends on how tightly the wire is stretched. In air, the speed of a sound wave depends on the temperature and density of the air. The speed of sound in air at room temperature is about 340 m/s. A good human ear can hear frequencies between 20 and 20,000 Hz, corresponding to wavelengths from 17 m to 1.6 cm.

The speed of electromagnetic waves also depends on the medium. Electromagnetic waves travel fastest in a vacuum, at a speed designated as c, the "speed of light," which is 3×10^8 m/s. The speed of electromagnetic waves in air is essentially the same as the speed in a vacuum. A good human eye can see electromagnetic waves with wavelengths between about 400 and 700 nm, corresponding to colors from violet to red. This part of the electromagnetic spectrum is known as visible light.

It is very convenient to think of a traveling wave as a sinusoidal wave (as shown in Fig. 1), which means that the wave can be represented mathematically as a sine (or cosine) function. A sinusoidal wave looks like a sine function varying perpendicular to its direction of travel. The wavelength is the distance the wave travels before it repeats a cycle on the sine function.

See also: ELECTROMAGNETIC WAVE; OSCILLATION; WAVE MOTION; WAVE SPEED

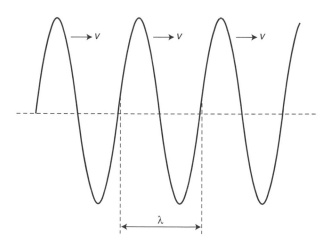

Figure 1   Illustration of a sinusoidal wave.

Bibliography

FEYNMAN, R. P.; LEIGHTON, R. B.; and SANDS, R. L., eds. *The Feynman Lectures on Physics,* Vol. 1 (Addison-Wesley, Reading, MA, 1965).

M. KIMURA

J. L. PEACHER

WAVE MECHANICS

In the days of classical physics it was thought that there were two distinct kinds of physical entities, that is, particles and waves. The motion of a particle is described by specifying the position of the particle at different instants of time. As the motion continues, the position of the particle changes continuously, forming a trajectory. Newton's laws provide a set of equations, the solutions of which give the position as a function of time so that one can predict the trajectory once the particle is initially set into motion. If we are dealing with an object of finite size rather than a particle, the former can be regarded as a system of many particles. Each particle obeys Newton's laws so that the motion of the object is entirely prescribed. In contrast, waves, which include light and sound, do not lend themselves to division into microscopic units. Unlike a particle, a wave is not localized at a particular point but is spread over a spatial domain. One manifestation of this delocalized nature is the phenonena of the interference of waves. When two waves come together, they may annihilate each other at some locations (which is called destructive interference) and enhance each other at other locations (which is called constructive interference). Interference is a signature of waves and does not arise in our particle description. In the language of physics a wave is a traveling disturbance. The disturbance may be an electric field (e.g., light) or mechanical displacement (e.g., sound). The intensity or the energy of a wave is proportional to the square of the amplitude of the disturbance, and it is always a positive quantity. When two waves intersect, the total disturbance is simply the superposition of the two individual disturbances. If at a certain point the disturbances of the two waves are opposite to each other, the net disturbance and, hence, the intensity at that point becomes small, resulting in destructive interference. As a wave propagates, the disturbance at each point changes continually and a full description of the wave requires knowing the disturbance as a function of time and position.

The division of physical entities into particles and waves was made obscure by a number of experiments that laid the foundation of modern physics. One of these experiments is the photoelectric effect, the emission of electrons from a metal surface when illuminated by light. The observed energies of the emitted electrons were found to be very different from the predictions based on the wave theory of light. Albert Einstein, however, pointed out that the results of the photoelectric effect can be explained if one adopts a corpuscular description of light. Here the light is regarded as a stream of minute corpuscles that behave like particles and are referred to as photons. The interference phenomena told us that light is a wave (as opposed to particles) whereas the photoelectric effect points toward the particle nature of light, not explicable by the wave theory. To reconcile these two opposing views it was proposed that light has a dual nature of both wave and particle-like characters. Which character appears depends on the type of experiments that one performs. The interference experiment reveals the wave nature of light whereas the photoelectric experiment brings out the corpuscular character. An analogy is that a casual observer may find a coin to be either a "head" or a "tail" depending on which side is looked at, even though the coin has both a "head" and a "tail."

After learning that a wave may appear like particles, one naturally wonders if a particle may exhibit the properties of a wave. That an electron may behave like both a wave and a particle was first proposed in 1924 by Louis de Broglie and subsequently confirmed in 1927 by the famous electron diffraction experiments, in which a beam of electrons is found to exhibit constructive and destructive interference. Thus to study the behaviors of electrons one can no longer use Newton's laws, which are based on the particle description. A new form of the fundamental equations of motion that allows for the wavelike delocalization of particles is needed.

Related to the wave–particle duality is the quantum theory of atoms, pioneered in 1913 by Niels Bohr. Bohr postulated that electrons in an atom can move only in a set of discrete orbits. An electron in a particular orbit has a fixed energy so that the electrons in an atom are allowed to have only certain discrete values of energy, named the quantized energy levels. The Bohr theory met with great success; however, the concept of discrete orbits and quantized energy levels cannot be explained by classical physics. Based on Newton's laws it is possible to vary the energy of a particle by any desired increment, and no quantized discrete energies are predicted from classical mechanics. It appears that the new theory (the new physical law of motion) not only must accommodate the wave–particle duality but also predict quantized energy levels.

In a series of papers published in 1926, Erwin Schrödinger originated a new form of mechanics which is now called wave mechanics. (Wave mechanics is one branch of a more general subject of quantum mechanics.) Let us begin with a discussion of some conceptual points. Imagine that we initially set a particle into motion at a starting point with an initial velocity and observed it at a later time, say, two minutes. We measured its position and found it 20 cm away from the starting point. Suppose we repeat this experiment; that is, we set the particle into motion in the same way and check it two minutes later. We would again expect to find the particle 20 cm away, at least according to classical mechanics. In wave mechanics the particle is no longer completely localized. A more precise statement of this delocalization is that if we repeat this exercise over and over, we do not always find the particle at the distance 20 cm, sometimes slightly more and sometimes slightly less. Upon collecting the results of repeated measurement of the particle's position, we see a statistical distribution corresponding to the probability of finding the particle two minutes later at a distance x for different values of x. For example, the probability may be comparatively large at $x = 20$ cm but much smaller as x differs substantially from 20 cm. This probabilistic description signifies a profound change of our physical concept. We no longer assign a definite position to a particle (at each instant of time) but speak only of the probability of finding the particle at various points. What the new theory does is to predict the results of measurement. So long as this is accomplished, the philosophical issue of the position of the particle is of less concern.

For a more quantitative exposition we assign to the particle a "wave function" that depends on both the position and time and may have real, including positive and negative, or complex, values. The absolute square of the wave function gives the probability of finding the particle at the particular position and time. Interference occurs if the wave function contains two terms such that they have opposite signs of comparable magnitude in one region and the same sign in another region. In the first region the wave function is small or there is little chance of seeing the particle there (destructive interference), whereas the particle is likely to be found in the second region (constructive interference). The resemblance of the wave function to the disturbance of a wave mentioned earlier is worth noting. Indeed, the wave function is a quantitative means to amalgamate the particle and wave behaviors, allowing for particle interference that is absent in classical mechanics. While the wave function may have negative or complex values, the probability obtained from the absolute square of the wave function is always real and positive, as it must be.

To illustrate how the wave function is determined, consider a particle moving under a conservative force which is represented by a potential function. We use the Cartesian coordinates (x, y, z) to describe a point in space so that the wave function of the particle is a function of x, y, z and the time t. We denote the (time-dependent) wave function as $\Psi(x, y, z, t)$ and the particle's potential energy as $V(x, y, z)$. For a conservative system (no energy loss) it can be shown that $\Psi(x, y, z, t)$ is expressible as a product of a function of x, y, z (but not t) times a factor that contains t only, in the form

$$\Psi(x,y,z,t) = \psi(x,y,z)\, e^{-\frac{2\pi i}{h}Et},$$

where E is the total energy of the particle, i is $\sqrt{-1}$, h is Planck's constant (6.62×10^{-34} J·s), and $\psi(x, y, z)$, the (time-independent) wave function, is the solution of the differential equation

$$-\frac{h^2}{8\pi^2 m}\left(\frac{\partial^2 \psi}{\partial x^2} + \frac{\partial^2 \psi}{\partial y^2} + \frac{\partial^2 \psi}{\partial z^2}\right) + V(x,y,z)\psi = E\psi,$$

along with some auxiliary conditions. This equation is now known as the Schrödinger equation and is regarded as the new fundamental equation of motion. For the case of an electron in a hydrogen atom it can be shown that acceptable solutions of ψ to the Schrödinger equation exist only if the energy (E in that equation) assumes certain discrete values. If its energy is not equal to one of those discrete values, the electron wave function simply does not exist. In other words, the discrete (quantized) energy levels previously postulated by Bohr are the direct consequence of the Schrödinger equation. That some differential equations admit no solution unless a constant therein (like E) takes on some special values, as we see here, is well known in mathematics. Those special values are called eigenvalues (or characteristic values), and the resulting solutions to the differential equations are called eigenfunctions (or characteristic functions). Much of the mystery of the quantized energy levels now disappears as they are just the eigenvalues of the new equation of motion. This is an illustration of an ideal matching of a mathematical tool to a physical problem.

Wave mechanics was an immediate success. After the initial work on the hydrogen atom, wave mechanics was applied to determine the energy levels and wave functions of electrons in atoms (other than hydrogen), molecules, and crystalline solids. For systems containing many atoms, the Schrödinger equation becomes very complicated so that only approximate solutions could be obtained. The advent of high speed computers, however, has made it feasible to obtain solutions for such systems with good accuracy. Studies of the electronic wave functions for diatomic molecules led to the modern theory of chemical valence and the idea of molecular orbitals. The chemical bond between two atoms is understood as an interference-like enhancement of the probability of the electrons being concentrated in the region between the nuclei of the two atoms. Consideration of the molecular orbitals allows one to make predictions of chemical reactions. For crystalline solids, wave mechanics shows that the electronic energy levels are grouped together as energy bands, now a fundamental concept in solid-state physics. Energy levels are not limited to electrons. For example, one can determine the wave functions and energy levels associated with the motion of the nuclei of the constituent atoms in a molecule (molecular vibration and rotation) in addition to the wave functions and energy levels associated with the motion of the electrons in the molecule.

The energy levels and wave functions of an atomic system are the major factors that determine its electric, magnetic, and optical properties. Absorption and emission of radiation result from transitions between energy levels, thus it is not surprising that a detailed knowledge of the energy levels is needed to understand many phenomena related to light emission, radiation, and lasers. Another example is the transistor, in which the existence of a group of energy levels associated with some impurity atoms in the crystal gives rise to special electrical properties of the transistor. Much of the modern technology is based on devices of novel properties. Wave mechanics is the key to understanding these properties and to advancing the frontier of increasingly novel materials.

See also: BROGLIE, LOUIS-VICTOR-PIERRE-RAYMOND DE; ENERGY LEVELS; INTERFERENCE; PHOTOELECTRIC EFFECT; QUANTUM THEORY, ORIGINS OF; SCHRÖDINGER, ERWIN; SCHRÖDINGER EQUATION; WAVE FUNCTION; WAVE MOTION; WAVE–PARTICLE DUALITY, HISTORY OF

Bibliography

GAMOW, G. *Thirty Years That Shook Physics* (Doubleday, New York, 1966).

LIGHTMAN, A. *Great Ideas in Physics* (McGraw-Hill, New York, 1992).

CHUN C. LIN

WAVE MOTION

A wave is a repetitive oscillation in which nearest neighbors' changes influence one another. For example, the displacement of a small piece of rope from its equilibrium position depends on the displacement of the adjacent sections. Since the displacement changes, a wave must move.

Waves transfer momentum and energy from one location to another. We can think of three stages of wave motion: waves are generated, waves move through the medium in which they exist, and waves are received at a detector. There are many sorts of waves: sound waves, electromagnetic waves, and water waves, to name just a few. A sound wave may be generated at a mouth or speaker, travel through air, and be detected by someone's ear or a microphone. An electromagnetic wave may be generated by an oscillating electron in a transmitter, travel through any transparent medium (including empty space, since the electromagnetic wave is its own medium), and detected in an antenna. A water wave may be generated by wind, travel through water, and be detected on a ship, at a beach, or on a headland.

For all waves, the characteristic parameters (see Figs. 1 and 2) are amplitude (A, maximum displacement from equilibrium), period (T, repetition time), and wavelength (λ, repetition distance). Often the number of cycles in a given time, the frequency $f = 1/T$, is used instead of the period to characterize a wave. The wave may be represented by the relation

$$\Psi(x, t) = A \cos \phi(x, t)$$
$$= A \cos\left(2\pi\frac{t}{T} \pm 2\pi\frac{x}{\lambda} + \eta\right),$$

where x is the position coordinate (the direction in which the wave moves), t is the time coordinate, $\Psi(x, t)$ is the displacement, and $\phi(x, t) = 2\pi\,(t/T) \pm 2\pi(x/\lambda) + \eta$ is the phase function. The constant phase η represents information about the initial conditions (conditions when the clock began to tick). If the displacement is 0 at the origin when t is 0, the cosine function must be zero; this means that the phase function must be $\eta = \pi/2$ or $3\pi/2$. The velocity of the elements of the medium is needed to determine which of these two phases is appropriate to the problem.

When a wave is moving, it has a characteristic speed. This wave speed may be found by considering what happens to a point of constant phase, that is, for which $\phi(x, t) = $ constant. In this case, $d\phi(x, t)/dt = 0$, and so $0 = (2\pi/T) \pm (2\pi/\lambda)(dx/dt)$. Hence,

$$\frac{dx}{dt} = \mp\frac{\lambda}{2\pi}\frac{2\pi}{T} = \mp\frac{\lambda}{T} = \mp\lambda f = \mp c.$$

Here, c represents the wave speed. For a sound wave in air at room temperature, $c = 345$ m/s. For an electromagnetic wave in vacuum, $c = 3 \times 10^8$ m/s. Note that a negative velocity means that the wave propagates in a direction opposite to the positive x coordinate, and a positive velocity means that the wave moves in a direction along the positive x coordinate. This means a wave propagating in the $+x$ direction has a phase function

$$\phi_+(x, t) = 2\pi\frac{t}{T} - 2\pi\frac{x}{\lambda} + \eta$$

and a wave propagating in the $-x$ direction has a phase function

$$\phi_-(x, t) = 2\pi\frac{t}{T} + 2\pi\frac{x}{\lambda} + \eta.$$

Two factors, one related to the elasticity of the medium, the other related to the mass, determine the propagation speed of mechanical waves in the medium. Roughly speaking, the elasticity reflects the effects of intermolecular forces; the stronger they are, the greater the speed at which a disturbance is transmitted. For example, a loose spring connecting two masses takes longer to transmit an impulse than a stronger spring. Conversely, the greater the inertia of an object, the smaller effect an applied force has; as the inertial factor increases, the speed should decrease. In all cases of mechanical waves, the wave speed may be given as

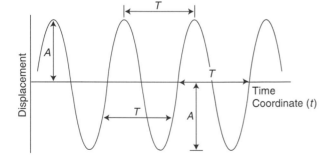

Figure 1 The displacement at a fixed point in space (the discrepancy compared to the equilibrium condition) in a wave changes regularly as the clock ticks. The time interval between adjacent points of the same displacement is the period, T.

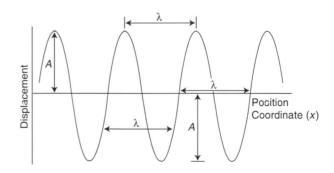

Figure 2 The displacement at a fixed time (the discrepancy compared to the equilibrium condition) in a wave changes regularly as one moves from one place to another. The distance between adjacent points of the same displacement is the wavelength, λ.

c = some constant × (elastic term/density)$^{1/2}$.

This implies, for example, that the speed of sound in a solid (where elastic intermolecular forces are large) will be much greater than the 345 m/s speed of sound in air. Speeds of several kilometers per second are common for solids.

In some waves, the motion of the particles of the medium is perpendicular to the direction of motion of the wave. These sorts of waves are called transverse. Electromagnetic waves are transverse undulations of electric and magnetic fields. Electromagnetic waves arise because changing magnetic fields give rise to currents (meaning that there must be electric fields to cause the charge to flow) and changing electric fields give rise to magnetic fields (as James Clerk Maxwell's invention of the displacement current term in Faraday's law showed). Thus, the changes in electric fields cause magnetic fields that change, giving rise to changing electric fields ad infinitum. Heinrich Hertz's 1888 experiments showed that electromagnetic waves were real. Knowing that all mechanical waves required a medium, physicists postulated the ether as the medium in which the waves traveled. If there were an ether, it would drag light waves along in it, depending on the relative directions of motion. However, Albert Michelson and Edward Morley proved in their experiment that no measurable ether drag existed, a finding that has been amply verified many

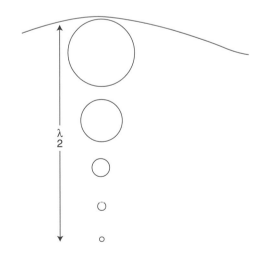

Figure 3 Trajectories of water molecules in a water wave in deep water are circles. The radius of these circles decreases as the water is deeper below the resting water level.

times since. The motion of the particles making up a string are at right angles to the direction of motion, so a wave in a string is transverse. In transverse waves in media, the forces of particles in the medium on one another are sidewise to the direction of motion.

In other waves, the motion of the particles of the medium is forward and backward along the direction of propogation of the wave. These sorts of waves are called longitudinal. The motion of the molecules in the air is back and forth in a sound wave, so a sound wave is longitudinal. Air cannot support sidewise forces, so for this reason it cannot be transverse. Seismic waves are produced in both transverse and longitudinal varieties by earthquakes and avalanches and travel through the earth, radiating in all directions from the center of the event. Many observing stations see both varieties of wave, but some stations are in the shadow of the core, which (being liquid) does not transmit transverse waves. Thus the difference between transverse and longitudinal waves' ability to move through a fluid is the basis of geophysical knowledge that Earth's core is liquid.

Water waves are the most commonly observed waves. Water, a fluid, cannot support sidewise forces, so it should transmit longitudinal waves. However, water waves are neither longitudinal nor transverse, but rather they constitute a special case. Water waves are surface waves, waves traveling on the surface of the water. A boat in water bobs up and down in a wave. It also moves back and forth somewhat as it moves up and down—a circular pattern. How does the water itself move? The water molecules on the surface must move in the same manner as the boat in the water, that is, in generally circular patterns that get smaller and smaller in diameter as the distance from the surface increases (see Fig. 3).

It is observed for water waves that the water underneath the surface moves in a circular pattern as well, but with a radius of motion smaller than on the surface. The motion of the water molecules decreases with depth until, at a distance of half the wavelength below the surface, the circular motion vanishes altogether. When the bottom is closer than half a wavelength, the water molecules can no longer move circularly. The circles become flattened, and the motion back and forth can move sand and silt in a direction along or opposite the wave's motion. Such particulate motion can build up a sandbar or destroy a beach.

The speed of a wave in water is

$$c = \left(\frac{g\lambda}{2\pi} \tanh \frac{2\pi d}{\lambda} \right)^{\frac{1}{2}},$$

where g is 9.8 N/kg (the gravitational acceleration at Earth's surface), λ is the wavelength, and d the water depth. In the case that $d \ll \lambda$, the wave is called a shallow water wave; the argument of the hyperbolic tangent is very small, and the expression can be approximated by

$$c \approx \left(\frac{g\lambda}{2\pi} \times \frac{2\pi d}{\lambda} \right)^{\frac{1}{2}} = \left(gd \right)^{\frac{1}{2}},$$

which is independent of the wavelength. In the case that $d \gg \lambda$, the wave is called a deep water wave; the hyperbolic tangent approaches 1, and

$$c \approx \left(\frac{g\lambda}{2\pi} \right)^{\frac{1}{2}},$$

independent of the depth. Because the speed of deep-water waves depends on the wavelength, water waves exhibit the phenomenon of dispersion; waves of different wavelengths travel at different speeds. The longest-wavelength waves generated by a storm at sea arrive far away first, followed by waves of decreasing wavelength.

Water waves exhibit an interesting behavior called breaking. The foaming waves dissipating on beaches are called breakers or breaking waves. Only some waves break, since the water moving in circles near the surface moves at a certain speed, and the wave itself could be moving slower or faster than the water molecules. If the molecules' speed is slower than c, there is no breaking. However, if the molecules' speed is faster than c, the molecules overshoot the wave itself and the wave breaks. Clearly, the circular motion of the water molecules has a greater speed with a greater amplitude (that is, the greater the radius of the circle). Fluid dynamicists and oceanographers have found that when the wave amplitude exceeds $\frac{1}{14}\lambda$, the wave will break. Breaking waves give up the energy and momentum they carried and cease to exist.

Breaking waves will occur when waves come ashore and "feel bottom." Recall that for shallow-water waves, the speed depends on the depth. Eventually, the speed of the incoming wave is too slow relative to the speed of the water molecules and the wave breaks. The energy released in this case can cause erosion of a beach or even destroy a headland over a long period of time. The decrease in wave speed with depth is also responsible for the observation that all waves come in parallel to the beach. The wave coming in at an angle is slowed most where the depth is least, so the slowed parts of the waves wait for the faster parts to catch up. Eventually the waves are moving toward the beach parallel to the shoreline.

Shallow water waves include waves near beaches and waves from underwater earthquakes (called tsunamis). Waves from underwater earthquakes or avalanches are shallow water waves because their wavelength is so long. A tsunami is dangerous because the amplitude may not be large while the wave is in deeper water. However, because the wave is hundreds of kilometers in length, the volume of water in a wave crest or trough can be great. When the wave is slowed down by a beach, where the depth becomes very small indeed, this piled-up water can cause the breaking tsunami to race far inland at a crest and will cause the water to pull back a great distance from the beach exposing large areas of what is usually ocean bottom at a trough.

The mean speed of water waves generated by the winds depends on the windspeed and on the distance across which the winds blow (the fetch). The greater the wind speed, the greater the speed of the waves generated. The longer the fetch, the greater the speed of the water waves generated. For small amplitude waves in deep water, the speed at which breaking occurs is low. Winds blowing across water make waves of all wavelengths, but the smaller wavelength waves break as the wind continues blowing. These breaking waves give up their energy to the longer-wavelength waves. Soon, only longer-wavelength waves are found in the wave spectrum. The longest waves also have the greatest amplitude, so the stormiest seas send waves out that are graded in speed and height. Because of the dispersion, the highest waves from a storm arrive the fastest.

See also: CURRENT, DISPLACEMENT; DISPERSION; ELECTROMAGNETIC WAVE; FIELD, ELECTRIC; FIELD, MAGNETIC; FLUID DYNAMICS; GEOPHYSICS; SEISMIC WAVE; SEISMOLOGY; WATER; WAVELENGTH; WAVE MECHANICS

Bibliography

BASCOM, W. *Waves and Beaches* (Anchor, New York, 1980).

GEORGI, H. *The Physcis of Waves* (Prentice Hall, Englewood Cliffs, NJ, 1993).

PAIN, H. J. *The Physics of Vibrations and Waves* (Wiley, New York, 1993).

GORDON J. AUBRECHT II

WAVE PACKET

A traveling wave is a periodic disturbance that moves through some medium with a speed of propagation that depends on the medium. The distance the wave travels before it repeats itself is known as the wavelength λ. Likewise, the elapsed time before the wave repeats its motion is known as the period T. The frequency f is defined as $f = 1/T$. A wave pulse can be generated by some abrupt change in a medium. For example, hitting a drum will generate a sound pulse in air, flipping the end of a horizontal taut string will set up a wave pulse in the string,

and turning a laser on and off quickly will create a light pulse. A wave pulse can be thought of as a "bump" that travels at the speed of propagation in the medium. The speed of the wave pulse is called the group velocity, because the wave pulse can be represented as many superimposed sinusoidal waves traveling together as a group. Each component wave has a different wavelength λ and frequency f, but the waves travel at the same speed u, such that $u = \lambda f$ for each wave. As Fig. 1a shows, the center of the wave pulse travels a distance ut in time t without changing its shape.

The description of particles in terms of their wave properties is called wave (or quantum) mechanics. The motion of a free particle is represented by that of a wave packet, which is a wave pulse composed of superimposed sinusoidal matter waves that are solutions of the Schrödinger equation. A sinusoidal matter wave $y = A \sin(2\pi x/\lambda)$ has a wavelength of $\lambda = h/p$, where h is Planck's constant, and p is the particle momentum of the wave (which equals mu for a nonrelativistic particle of mass m and speed u). This wavelength is known as the de Broglie wavelength. The frequency of a matter wave is given by $f = E/h$, where E is the particle energy of the wave (which equals $p^2/2m$ for a nonrelativistic particle). The speed of propagation of the matter wave is then determined as $u = \lambda f = h/2m\lambda$. This speed, called the phase velocity of the matter wave, is different for each wavelength. Thus, a wave packet is a superposition of many different matter waves, each having a different wavelength λ and traveling at a different speed u. The wave packet travels at a speed that is equal to the speed v of the free particle represented by the wave packet. However, as the wave packet travels, it also spreads; that is, the "bump" becomes wider. The wave packet spreads because each matter wave component of the wave packet travels at a different speed. As Fig. 1b shows, the center of the wave travels a distance vt in time t as its peak decreases and its width increases.

See also: WAVELENGTH; WAVE MECHANICS; WAVE SPEED

Bibliography

FEYNMAN, R. P.; LEIGHTON, R. B.; and SANDS, M. L. *The Feynman Lectures on Physics,* Vol. 1 (Addison-Wesley, Reading, MA, 1963).

M. KIMURA

J. L. PEACHER

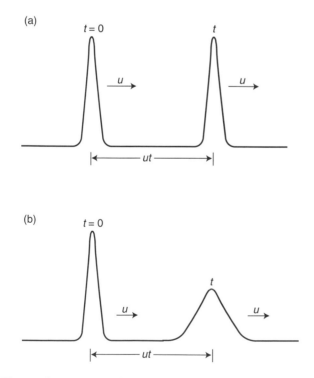

Figure 1 (a) Traveling wave pulse and (b) traveling wave packet.

WAVE–PARTICLE DUALITY

Before the advent of quantum mechanics early in the twentieth century, the treatment and the description of continuous and discrete physical systems was characteristically and strikingly different. In a discrete system—such as a system of interacting particles—the system was described by the locations and velocities of the individual particles. A given particle at a definite time had a well-defined position, hence, a definite potential energy. Together with the kinetic energy of that particle, this conferred a definite energy to a particular particle. In the course of time, the particles would generally move in complicated trajectories. The discreteness of the system was expressed by the fact that in some locations, there are no particles, the energy is localized on the particles, and exchanges of energy could take place only via the interaction of particles, either with each other or with outside agencies. These features are very different in a continuous medium or a field. Of special importance are the localization features of a discrete system. A particle at a definite time is "here" or "not there."

In a continuous medium such as a fluid, physical quantities are defined and, in principle, observable at any point of the medium. In a classical fluid such physical quantities could be density or temperature. They would indeed be "everywhere" in the fluid. In the motion of such a continuous medium, all points participate and each point has its own velocity. The medium, as a whole, is involved in the dynamic processes. For example, the total kinetic energy of the medium is the sum (the integral) of all local kinetic energies. Exactly the same concepts can be used in describing a field. In an electric field, an electric field strength is defined (and observable) at any point. The energy of an electric (or magnetic, or gravitational) field is again not localized; it is spread out over the field.

A wave phenomenon is a special kind of motion of a continuous medium. Its distinguishing features are two kinds of periodicity. A wave phenomenon is periodic in space, the physical state at time t at location x is identical to the physical state at time t at location $x + n\lambda$, for all n. There also is a periodicity in time. The physical situation at x, t is identical with that at $x, t + nT$ for all x, n, t. λ is the wavelength of the wave, T is the period, and $1/T = \nu$ is the frequency. The energy of a wave is not localized at any, or a few, points, but is spread out over the whole medium.

One of the signal successes of nineteenth-century physics was the demonstration that light was an electromagnetic wave. A monochromatic light wave propagating in the z direction is a sequence of oscillating electric and magnetic fields (oscillating with the same frequency) in the plane perpendicular to z. The characteristic wave phenomena of light, such as interference and diffraction, found a natural explanation as the combined effect of several waves with appropriate phase differences. Many of the most accurate instruments, such as diffraction gratings and the Michelson interferometer, were based on the wave description of light. The electromagnetic waves themselves emerged as a mathematical consequence of the Maxwell equations, with the current value for the speed of light, making for a convincing and compelling scheme.

With the discovery of the electron in 1897, new problems appeared. How does light (an electromagnetic wave) interact with an electron (a simple charged particle)? This should be a straightforward question easily handled by electrodynamics.

Experiments showed that when monochromatic light (a light wave with a single definite frequency ν) falls on a thin metal screen, electrons are liberated from the screen and emerge with a definite maximum velocity (or maximum kinetic energy), which depends solely on the frequency of the light and *not* on the intensity. The light is absorbed, and its energy presumably imparted to individual electrons. This photoelectric effect is classically impossible. On the wave theory, the electromagnetic energy is distributed all over the screen. The amount of energy in a volume of atomic size is much too small to knock an electron out of an atom, let alone give it additional kinetic energy.

These considerations, and an incisive calculation, suggested to Albert Einstein that in certain instances (as in the interaction between light and matter), light of frequency ν behaves as if it consists of independent particle-like objects of energy $h\nu$, where h is Planck's constant. Einstein called these objects light quanta; nowadays they are called photons. The interaction between light and matter is then just a collision between an electron and a photon in which the photon gives up its energy (and existence!) to the electron. If it takes the electron an energy P to straggle and struggle out of the metal, the conservation of energy gives the equation $\in_{electron} = h\nu - P$ (P is a property of the metal called the work function). Robert A. Millikan tried for more than ten years to show this formula to be wrong, but he did not succeed. He intensely disliked the photon idea, as did practically all leading physicists (Max Planck, Max von Laue, and, especially, Niels Bohr). But his own experiments, more and more refined, left no doubt that Einstein's equation was precisely correct.

All the opponents of the photon idea did not and could not come to terms with the notion that light could behave as a stream of identical particles with energy $h\nu$, momentum $h\nu/c$, and the ability to exchange energy and momentum with material objects at a definite location, maintaining the exact local conservation laws in such collisions. Such ideas were uncomfortable and strange. The photon in such processes acted exactly like a localizable material object, and that precisely was the trouble. The overriding reason for the unease and skepticism with the photon character of light is that all the quintessential wave features depend crucially on the notion of the phase of a wave. The combined effect of two (or more) waves depends on the relative phases of the waves. Whether the result is an amplification or a cancellation, whether the interference is constructive or destructive, is determined exclusively by the phase difference. The interference fringes and the diffraction peaks are direct consequences of the phase differences of the waves. The central difficulty of describing light in terms of particle-like photons is that in the classical description of particles there is no phase notion at all. That is why the critics of Einstein were so puzzled and concerned about an explanation of interference on a photon basis. Without a phase notion, which requires a wave, it is difficult to see how interference can be described or explained.

Furthermore, ν, the frequency (which also determines the energy of a photon), has an immediate and intuitive meaning in a wave picture, but it was unclear (especially to Bohr) what meaning could be ascribed to "the" frequency ν (or a characteristic time) of a particle. It thus appeared that light needed contradictory and mutually exclusive features to explain all its experimental characteristics. As a wave, its energy could not be localized, but via a stream of photons, energy could be transferred to localized electrons. As a wave, the phase notion was essential, and in photon terms, no phase was to be seen. This "multiple personality aspect" of light is usually referred to as the wave–particle duality.

Puzzling and frustrating as this was, it was shown by Louis de Broglie that the wave–particle duality was not just restricted to light. There is no doubt that an electron is the quintessential particle. But through a remarkable series of arguments, de Broglie conjectured during 1923 and 1924 that with every free particle (of constant momentum p), there is associated a plane wave of wavelength $\lambda = h/p$. De Broglie's motivation came in part from relativity, in part from a strong belief in the essential unity of nature—if light (at times) can behave like a particle, why should a particle (at times) not behave like a wave?—and in part from brilliance. Although initially received with considerable skepticism, two years later, Clinton J. Davisson and Lester H. Germer (who did not know of de Broglie's ideas) observed curious peaks in the scattering of slow electrons from a nickel sample. (They did not know that the sample had fused to a crystal, either). It was noted that these peaks agreed precisely with the diffraction peaks of a wave. It was then a simple matter to determine the wavelength from the diffraction data. Since both λ and the momentum p could be directly measured, de Broglie's relation could be quantitatively verified. All later experiments confirmed the existence of the de Broglie waves and verified the de Broglie relation with great precision. Further studies showed that all material objects (in addition to electrons), such as protons, neutrons, hydrogen molecules, and the earth, possess a de Broglie wavelength. Since $\lambda = h/mv$ (for low velocities v), slow neutrons have a larger wavelength than do high-energy neutrons. The earth has a wavelength that is so small as to preclude any physical consequences because it is much smaller than the size of the earth. The wavelength of a 10^4 eV electron is about 10^{-9} cm.

There is a touch of irony in the circumstance that the only truly universal particle attribute is the wavelength. There are particles without mass (neutrinos and photons), particles without spin (π mesons), and particles without charge (neutrons), but all possess an associated wave field and corresponding wavelength. It also is possible to associate a phase with the wave and, hence, with the particle. Even though it was generally presupposed and almost automatically accepted that particle and wave aspects were exclusive categories, neutrons, electrons, and photons, in fact, all objects, possess features of both. This duality imposes a number of limitations on the simultaneous measurability of certain quantities. For example, to establish a phenomenon as a wave, measurements must be made that test distances of at least the size of several wavelengths. Otherwise, the required spatial periodicity could not be observed. So the experiment must examine lengths ℓ, where $\ell \gg \lambda$.

To make measurements on a system to check its wave character and measure its wavelength, the spatial domain examined cannot be too small. It has a definite lower limit. But if it is desired to measure the position of a particle as accurately as possible, the system (the particle) must be confined to as small a spatial domain as possible. To obtain the best position measurement, the apparatus must localize the object (the particle) in a small region. For an object that possesses or can exhibit both particle and wave features, these requirements conflict. If, in the inequality expressing the possibility of a wave measurement, the de Broglie formula for the wavelength is substituted, the resulting inequality is $\ell p > h$. This shows that it is impossible to have a totally accurate position measurement (ℓ would be very small) and still measure the momentum.

These rather heuristic comments can be made precise, leading to a rigorous inequality in the precision of momentum and position measurements. If Δp and Δx are the uncertainties in these measurements, the inequalities are $\Delta p \cdot \Delta x \geq h/2\pi$. (This is more rigorous, but of the same type as the relation $\ell p > h$ that was suggested earlier.) There is a similar relation, $\Delta \in \cdot \Delta t \geq h/2\pi$, where $\Delta \in$ and Δt are the uncertainties in energy and time. This last relation is the result of the conflicting requirements of the accurate measurement of an instant of time and the finite time it takes to establish the temporal periodicity of a wave phenomenon. These relations are the celebrated Heisenberg uncertainty relations. But it must be emphasized that the incompatibility of exact measurements is an inevitable consequence of the dual and classically conflicting attributes.

The qualitative considerations presented so far are largely independent of the particular interpretation of the wave field (almost always denoted by $\psi(x,t)$. The most common interpretation, first suggested by Max Born and P. A. M. Dirac, is that $|\psi|^2$ defines the probability of finding the object (usually a particle) at the position x at time t. With that interpretation, the uncertainty relations follow as a mathematical consequence from the equation that ψ satisfies. As a consequence, it follows that individual measurements (say of the position) carried out on the same system under identical circumstances will not always give the same answer.

Quantum theory allows, via the ψ function, the calculation of various averages. These calculated averages can be compared with the averages obtained by observations. As in all statistical analysis, one can calculate the root-mean-square variation values for either momentum or position. These are the quantities that actually enter the uncertainty relations. In this manner, Δp and Δx are precisely defined and can be calculated from ψ, but they always satisfy the uncertainty relations, which, in turn, always express inherent limitations of the measuring process.

The origin of the limitation is the property that the act of observation will influence and change the state of the system observed. There is an inevitable interaction between the measuring instrument and the observed object. In many (most) experiments, there is an exchange of energy between the two. But since energy is quantized, this interaction between observer and object cannot continuously be extrapolated to zero, nor can it be neglected. It was especially Bohr who emphasized repeatedly that a statement such as "measure the momentum" (or any physical quantity for that matter) is much too sketchy and vague to be of use in a precise discussion. He would insist that to analyze the result of a measurement—or the compatibility and accuracy of several measurements—the detailed experimental procedure, including the instrumental set-up, has to be specified in detail. Thus, the experimental procedure and the interaction between the system and the measuring device (according to Bohr) have to be analyzed jointly. This was suggested by Bohr's principle of complementarity, which asserted that in the interpretation of the experimental behavior of systems (in any science) there will be complementarity features. These are mutually exclusive, incompatible characteristics that are nevertheless all necessary and, in fact, indispensable for the complete description of the empirical results. This incompatibility is intrinsic; it is not a consequence of an incomplete or poorly designed experiment. It is the recognition that the response of a system to different "experimental inquiries" (as expressed by different instrumental arrangements) may have to be described in terms of distinctly different notions, which notions when considered by themselves might well be incompatible. It is the specific experimental arrangement that determines what features of the system will enter into the response, so that it is the experimental arrangement that actually determines what aspect of the system is examined. As an example, consider the arrangement where an electron is directed toward a screen with two holes in it. In a classical picture, where the electron possesses just particle characteristics, the electron will pass through one hole or the other, independent of how far apart or how near the holes are to each other.

Classically, this is a statement that can be made without specifying how the passage through one hole or the other is to be measured. In a quantum description, both the wave and particle attributes are always present. If no effort is made (no equipment supplied) to measure through which hole the electron passes, the wave attributes of the electron come into play, and the result will be a typical two-slit diffraction pattern if the distance between the holes is comparable to the wavelength of the wave. If, however, even in this favorable case, an instrument (a bell, a light) is inserted in one of the holes, so that the arrangement does determine through which hole the electron passes, then the diffraction pattern disappears.

This example illustrates that different experimental arrangements elicit different features. Stated more colloquially: "What something is, or appears to be, depends on how it is observed." It is really not possible in the quantum domain to totally disengage the object and its properties from the manner in which it is measured. To Bohr and the Copenhagen school, the wave–particle duality and the inevitable existence of complementary descriptions were the most profound results of quantum theory. As John Wheeler often stresses, "No phenomenon is real unless it is observed." Bohr might add (much to Einstein's consternation) "reality is not external, but instrumentally determined." On that view, the existence of incompatible features, as expressed by the principle of complementarity, is not all that surprising nor paradoxical. In fact, more examples of incompatible features should be anticipated.

Although incredibly successful, it is a good idea to stress that what is successful is the quantum mechanical formalism, on which is grafted a congenial probability interpretation. It is logically not excluded that other interpretations with a very comparable formalism, but with different concepts, language, philosophy, and ideology, would exist. To many beginners, and indeed to many professionals, the rules that govern quantum mechanics are so strange and uncomfortable that many attempts have been made (and are being made) to obtain the quantum mechanical result on a more classical, causal basis. Such schemes have been known and analyzed for years. Within these schemes, the uncertainty relations and the complementarity principle acquire a quite different status. Unfortunately, these schemes are extremely contrived and mathematically almost unmanageable. They are also physically strange and involved. Perhaps most important, these schemes have not led to phenomena, effects, or observations that are beyond (the now traditional) quantum mechanical ideas.

See also: BROGLIE WAVELENGTH, DE; COMPLEMENTARITY PRINCIPLE; DAVISSON–GERMER EXPERIMENT; DOUBLE-SLIT EXPERIMENT; ELECTROMAGNETIC WAVE; INTERFERENCE; MAXWELL'S EQUATIONS; PHOTON; QUANTUM MECHANICS; UNCERTAINTY PRINCIPLE; WAVE–PARTICLE DUALITY, HISTORY OF

Bibliography

PAGELS, H. R. *The Cosmic Code* (Simon & Schuster, New York, 1982).

WILCZEK, F., and DE VINE, B. *Longing for the Harmonies* (W. W. Norton, New York, 1988).

ZEE, A. *Fearful Symmetry* (Macmillan, New York, 1986).

MAX DRESDEN

WAVE–PARTICLE DUALITY, HISTORY OF

During the second decade of the twentieth century it was recognized that light waves and matter particles do not always behave simply as waves and particles, respectively, but possess a dual nature: light and other electromagnetic waves may exhibit corpuscular properties, and particles may act like waves. Although this wave–particle duality appears as a unified feature in quantum mechanics, historically the two types of duality developed differently.

In a famous paper of 1905, Albert Einstein challenged the universally held view that light is a wave phenomenon. He suggested that, at least under certain circumstances, light of frequency ν should be described as a flow of localized energy quanta $h\nu$ and thus be assigned a corpuscular nature. Einstein's daring light quantum hypothesis was rejected by almost all physicists, one of the few exceptions being the German Johannes Stark, later one of Einstein's main antagonists. Stark suggested in 1909 that the light quanta did not only possess an energy $h\lambda$, but also a momentum h/λ (where $\lambda = c/\nu$ is the wavelength). Einstein, who sought for a theoretical justification, was more cautious. He admitted the incongruence between light quanta and the experimentally verified wave theory, and he emphasized that his light quantum hypothesis was provisional. Yet he was convinced that the corpuscular aspect of light was unavoidable. In 1909 he studied the energy fluctuations of blackbody radiation and found by means of Planck's distribution law an expression consisting of two terms: The one term corresponded to the fluctuations that would arise if the radiation consisted of light quanta, and the other corresponded to a radiation consisting of waves. This corresponded again to considering Planck's law a compromise between the Rayleigh–Jeans law (which embodied the wave aspects) and the Wien law (which embodied the particle aspects). The fact that particle and wave aspects appeared side by side indicated to Einstein a deep-lying duality in the nature of light and similar radiation: "The next phase in the development of theoretical physics," Einstein conjectured in 1909, "will bring us a theory of light that can be interpreted as a kind of fusion of the wave and the emission [particle] theory." Although few physicists followed Einstein, he was not alone in his advocacy of wave–particle duality. In 1914, for example, James Jeans argued for "some kind of reconciliation . . . between the demands of the quantum theory and those of the undulatory theory of light." But neither Einstein nor Jeans had any idea of how to effect the reconciliation sought for.

Wave–particle duality also was discussed in a very different area of physics; namely, with regard to the nature of x rays. About 1910 there was evidence for x rays being both corpuscular and wavelike, and, according to some physicists, they consisted of localized ether-pulses with both wave and particle properties. According to William Bragg, x rays and gamma rays were best described as being corpuscular in nature, but after the discovery of x-ray diffraction in crystals in 1912 it became generally accepted that the wave theory is correct. However, a few physicists continued to emphasize the corpuscular properties and felt that a future theory would have to include both aspects. Thus to Bragg the problem was "not to decide between two theories of x rays, but to find . . . one theory which possesses the capacity of both." Such a theory was not found until after quantum mechanics had changed the whole situation.

Einstein felt frustrated over the problems of quantum theory and between 1911 and 1915 he concentrated on his theory of general relativity. Then, in 1916 and 1917, he returned to the quantum theory of radiation with an important theory that not only was to form the basis of the later laser technology (through the concept of stimulated emission), but also constituted a completion of his corpuscular picture of light. From statistical-mechanical considerations he deduced that the light quanta had to have a momentum of $p = h/\lambda$ (as earlier conjectured by Stark), and with this insight he became fully convinced of the reality of light quanta. However, he also realized, as he wrote in 1918, that "I stand quite alone in this conviction." Although Einstein's 1905 prediction of a linear relationship between the frequency of light and the (maximum) energy of photoelectrons had by then been confirmed by Robert Millikan, the confirmation was not interpreted in favor of the light quantum hypothesis. (When Einstein received the Nobel Prize in 1921, the Nobel Committee was careful to distinguish between the light quantum hypothesis and Einstein's theory of the photoelectric effect.) Other experimental evidence was missing, and it was only in 1922 and 1923 that strong evidence in favor of Einstein's view appeared.

Arthur Compton's celebrated experiments with scattering of x rays on matter showed a change in wavelength (Compton's scattering formula) that could be nicely explained on the assumption of radiation quanta carrying with them energies $h\nu$ and momenta h/λ. As was shown at the same time, other optical phenomena, including the Doppler effect and reflection of x rays, could be accounted for in terms of the quantum theory of light. The Compton effect was instrumental in changing the attitude of physicists toward Einstein's light quantum hypothesis, which changed its status from a "mere hypothesis" to a "fact." Still, it was not universally accepted. Niels Bohr, for one, was not convinced. Together with John Slater and Hendrik Kramers, he formulated in 1924 a statistical theory of physical-optical phenomena that did not rely on the concept of light quanta. However, this alternative (known as the BKS theory) was soon refuted by experiments and with it the last resistance against light quanta disappeared. In spite of the vindication of the light quantum, Einstein was not entirely satisfied with the situation. In 1924, he concluded that there were two theories of light, "both indispensable, and—as one must admit today despite twenty years of tremendous effort on the part of theoretical physics—without any logical connection." The problem was that despite the successes of the quantum-corpuscular point of view in optical processes involving interaction between radiation and matter, the classical wave theory seemed indispensable when it came to phenomena such as interference and diffraction.

There was a widespread feeling that the two pictures would have to be connected, to be parts of a new synthetic theory, but no one could tell what the theory would look like. The connection eventually came with quantum mechanics, but then in a version that did not satisfy Einstein. Before quantum mechanics—still unborn in 1924—could provide the final synthesis, the other horn of the wave–particle dilemma had to be resolved: the question of how particles could exhibit wave properties.

Attempts to reconcile the wave and particle picture, and to conceive particles as consisting of or being associated with waves, go back to the nineteenth century when such speculations were cultivated by a few physicists. But it was only with Louis de Broglie's search for a dualistic theory of matter and radiation that progress was made. In de Broglie's theory, dating from 1922 to 1924, the wave–particle duality for light was extended to electrons; that is, particles were provided with wave properties. This extension relied on de Broglie's initial conception of light quanta as having a nonzero mass and in this respect being similar to ordinary particles. De Broglie suggested a particle of rest mass m to be associated with a wave phenomenon of frequency ν in the simple way that $E = h\nu = mc^2$. Basing his arguments on the special theory of relativity and the statistical theory of ideal gases, he was led to an association between the momentum of a particle p and its wavelength: $\lambda = h/p$. The symmetry between particles and waves now appeared in a striking manner: The expressions $E = h\nu$ and $p = h/\lambda$, valid for light quanta, also were valid for particles, although in this case more appropriately written $\nu = E/c$ and $\lambda = h/p$. But what was the physical significance, if any, of the matter waves thus introduced formally?

De Broglie believed that his matter waves were real and hence should be physically detectable. After the essence of the theory had been incorporated into Erwin Schrödinger's new wave mechanics, experiments performed by Clinton J. Davisson and Lester H. Germer in the United States showed that electrons striking a metallic surface produce a diffraction pattern, a typical wave phenomenon. Moreover, by varying the speed of the electrons, Davisson and Germer (and also, slightly later, George P. Thomson in England) showed quantitative agreement with de Broglie's formula $\lambda = h/p = h/mv$. The wave nature of electrons was now confirmed and the wave–particle duality a reality for both waves and particles. However, although de Broglie's formula was vindicated, his theory survived only partially, in the form of wave mechanics. Einstein was one of the very few physicists who had paid attention to de Broglie's work, and it was through Einstein that Schrödinger came to study it and then was led to his theory of wave mechanics in 1926. In this theory the behavior of particles are determined by a new kind of wave, Schrödinger's famous ψ function. Whereas Einstein and de Broglie stressed the dualistic aspects of the theory, at first Schrödinger interpreted the new theory as a pure wave theory of matter where particles were made up of localized packets of ψ waves.

The last chapter in the history of wave–particle duality coincides with the conceptual completion of quantum mechanics. It was soon realized that Schrödinger's wave mechanics was mathematically equivalent with the earlier quantum mechanics of Werner Heisenberg and others (from 1925), but also that its physical interpretation was widely different. According to Max Born's interpretation of quantum mechanics, the electron is a particle, not a wave; the wave function is an expression of the probability that the particle attains certain values for its position and momentum. A full understanding of the duality came with the final formulation of quantum mechanics in 1927, primarily due to the work of Heisenberg and Bohr. Heisenberg's indeterminacy (or uncertainty) principle states that the simultaneous determination of certain pairs of physical variables, such as position and momentum, cannot be made with an arbitrarily high degree of accuracy. If one of the variables, which may correspond to wave properties, is measured more accurately, the measurement of the other variable, which may give information about particle properties, will be less accurate. By means of thought experiments based on the indeterminacy relations, Heisenberg and Bohr concluded that the wave–particle duality is an inherent and completely general trait in our knowledge about nature.

The wider, more philosophical expression of this view was offered by Bohr in his complementarity principle, first proposed in 1927. Two modes of description of a physical system are said to be complementary if they are mutually exclusive (in a certain sense), but nonetheless both necessary for a complete understanding of the system. According to Bohr, wave and particle theories are just examples of complementary modes of description. "The two views of the nature of light [or particles]," he said in 1927, "are rather to be considered as different attempts at an interpretation of experimental evidence in which the limitation of the classical concepts is expressed in complementary ways." By itself, independent of being observed, the electron is neither a wave nor a particle. "Wave" and "particle" are words we use to describe experiments, not an underlying reality, and the complementarity principle, and quantum mechanics in general, tell us how wave and particle aspects will turn up in experiments.

The discussion about wave–particle duality did not, of course, stop in 1927. Bohr's view was generally, but not universally, accepted. Among the nonbelievers were Max von Laue, Einstein, de Broglie, and Schrödinger. As an important element of the interpretation of quantum mechanics, wave–particle duality continues to be discussed, and a minority of physicists still feel that it has not been satisfactorily explained. They feel that the situation has not really improved since the late 1920s, when Bragg joked that physicists used a wave description on Mondays, Wednesdays, and Fridays, and a particle description on Tuesdays, Thursdays, and Saturdays.

See also: BOHR, NIELS HENRIK DAVID; BROGLIE, LOUIS-VICTOR-PIERRE-RAYMOND DE; COMPLEMENTARITY PRINCIPLE; COMPTON EFFECT; DAVISSON–GERMER EXPERIMENT; EINSTEIN, ALBERT; HEISENBERG, WERNER KARL; LIGHT, ELECTROMAGNETIC THEORY OF; LIGHT, WAVE THEORY OF; QUANTUM MECHANICS, CREATION OF; QUANTUM THEORY, ORIGINS OF; SCHRÖDINGER, ERWIN; UNCERTAINTY PRINCIPLE; WAVE–PARTICLE DUALITY

Bibliography

HENDRY, J. "The Development of Attitudes to the Wave–Particle Duality of Light and Quantum Theory, 1900–1920." *Ann. Sci.* **37**, 59–79 (1980).

JAMMER, M. *The Conceptual Development of Quantum Mechanics* (McGraw-Hill, New York, 1966).

KLEIN, M. J. "Einstein and the Wave–Particle Duality." *Natural Philosopher* **3**, 1–49 (1964).

PAIS, A. *'Subtle is the Lord . . .' The Science and the Life of Albert Einstein* (Clarendon Press, Oxford, Eng., 1982).

STUEWER, R. H. *The Compton Effect: Turning Point in Physics* (Science History Publications, New York, 1975).

WHEATON, B. *The Tiger and the Shark: Empirical Roots of Wave–Particle Dualism* (Cambridge University Press, Cambridge, Eng., 1983).

HELGE KRAGH

WAVE SPEED

If you shake one end of a long stretched string up and down in continuous simple harmonic motion, a (nearly) sinusoidal disturbance or wave travels along the string from particle to particle. Although individual particles anywhere along the string simply move up and down with a frequency v (Hz) determined by the shaking rate, the wave is characterized by regularly spaced crests and troughs traveling at constant velocity, known as the wave or phase velocity. Any stationary observer along the string sees v crests pass per second, and each crest is a distance λ (m) apart. This distance is known as the wavelength. From these, it is possible to determine the wave speed or magnitude of velocity, which is $v = \lambda v$ (m/s). This is in fact a universal relation that characterizes any sinusoidal wave motion, for example, water waves, light or electromagnetic waves, and de Broglie or matter waves. For waves on a string, v can be shown to be proportional to the square root of the tension in the string. Similarly, for sound waves in a gas, v is proportional to the square root of the gas pressure, whereas for water waves, v is proportional to the square root of the water depth. The wave speed of light in a refractive medium defines the index of refraction of the medium n according to $n = c/v$, where c is the speed of light in vacuum. The wave speed of say a free electron is given by $h/2m\lambda$, where h is Planck's constant, m is the electron mass, and λ is the electron's de Broglie wavelength.

If instead you simply give one end of the string a single sharp jerk up and down, a disturbance in the form of a single pulse travels down the string with a constant velocity known as the group velocity. The pulse can be shown to be a (Fourier) superposition or sum of a group of sinusoidal component waves of various frequencies. (Note, even though very long nearly sinusoidal waves can be generated under certain circumstances, only finite pulses really ever exist in practice.) For waves on a string, the group velocity equals the wave velocity of each component, although in general in a dispersive medium the index of refraction and hence the wave velocity varies with frequency and differs from the group velocity. Thus, a prism bends blue light more strongly than red and produces a rainbow of colors from white light. This also has the consequence that a pulse in a dispersive medium broadens as the phases of the components, and hence the coherence of the original pulse, is lost.

Table 1 Miscellaneous Wave Speeds

Wave Type	Medium	Speed (m/s)
Sound	Air (dry)	331.5[a]
	Helium	965[a]
	Pure Water	1,402[a]
	Seawater	1,449[a]
	Aluminum	6,420
	Gold	3,240
	Pyrex Glass	5,640
Light	Vacuum	2.99792458×10^8[b]
Longitudinal Seismic Wave	Earth's Mantle	8,500
Transverse Seismic Wave	Earth's Mantle	4,500

[a]At normal atmospheric pressure and 0°C.
[b]SI defined exact value.

For normal dispersion, the transport of energy occurs with the group velocity. In regions of anomalous dispersion, however, the index of refraction can vary strongly with frequency and the group velocity differs greatly from the wave velocity, often becoming larger than c, or superluminal. In such situations the behavior of the pulse is usually much more involved and group velocity not a useful concept.

The question arises as to how a pulse carries information or transmits a signal and whether or not special relativity might be violated, and hence whether or not effect might precede cause, that is, if causality might be violated. To send a message or cause a real effect, a shutter must be opened or something else happen to create a detectable break in the pulse. A pulse can never overtake this boundary or front. Likewise, it can be shown under quite general assumptions that the front of any electromagnetic signal travels at c regardless of the medium. (This initial signal is usually very weak, however, and hence difficult to detect.) Thus, a stone tossed into water creates a pulse that spreads outward in a circle moving on the whole with the group velocity. The ripples that make it up can be seen to move with the phase velocity, which in the case of deep water is twice as fast as the group velocity. They first appear inside the circular peak of the pulse, growing as they move out towards the peak, then shrinking again and fading away beyond the peak.

In recent years, investigators have turned their attention to various pulse-reshaping phenomena that exhibit superluminal effects. For example, while traversing or tunneling a slab of dispersive material, the later parts of a light pulse can be attenuated under the right conditions to a greater extent than the earlier parts, so that the peak of the pulse appears on the far side of the slab before the peak of a control pulse propagated the same distance through air. Despite a fascinating effect, the front velocity of the pulse never exceeds c, and there is no violation of causality.

See also: BARRIER PENETRATION; BROGLIE WAVELENGTH, DE; DISPERSION; ELECTROMAGNETIC WAVE; FOURIER SERIES AND FOURIER TRANSFORM; GROUP VELOCITY; LIGHT, SPEED OF; VELOCITY; WAVE MOTION; WAVE PACKET

Bibliography

FRENCH, A. P. *Vibrations and Waves* (Van Nostrand Reinhold, New York, 1982).

HALIDAY, D.; RESNICK, R.; and WALKER, J. *Fundamentals of Physics*, 4th ed. (Wiley, New York, 1993).

JACKSON, J. D. *Classical Electrodynamics* (Wiley, New York, 1975).

JAMES M. FEAGIN

WAVE THEORY

See LIGHT, WAVE THEORY OF

WEAK INTERACTION

See INTERACTION, WEAK

WEIGHT

Weight is the force exerted on an object by a massive body such as a planet, moon, or asteroid. It is, for example, the pull that holds things down to Earth and keeps them from flying off into space. The weight of an object is proportional to its mass and depends upon the location of the object; weight is therefore an extrinsic property of any object. The term "weight" has a very different meaning for the scientist and the nonscientist. For the scientist the precise definition is that weight is a vector quantity that is defined by $\mathbf{W} = m\mathbf{g}$, where $\mathbf{W}$ is the weight of the object, m is its mass, and $\mathbf{g}$ is the acceleration that the object would have when allowed to fall freely. While the surface of Earth is not an inertial reference frame, the vector $\mathbf{g}$ can still be approximated by the gravitational force law and has a magnitude of about $9.80 \ \text{m/s}^2$ at the surface of Earth and a direction downward toward the center of Earth.

The weight of an object is determined typically by the use of calibrated spring scales. However, because of the relationship between mass and weight, spring scales can be calibrated in either mass units or weight units. A spring scale for determining weight can be as simple as a bathroom scale. The weight of an object can also be determined by first finding the mass using a sensitive balance that compares the mass of the object to known masses and then calculating the weight from the equation above. The SI unit for weight is the newton (N), which is derived from the fundamental units for mass (kg), length (m), and time (s). One newton is the force required to accelerate a 1 kg object at $1 \ \text{m/s}^2$. A common unit of weight in the United States is the pound (lb) which is equal to 4.448 N.

Although weight for the scientist has a very precise definition it has a very different everyday meaning. The term "weight" has been applied to an important quantity of measure throughout recorded history. The ancient Greeks used weights as a common measure of goods in trade and commerce. Money, precious gems, and metals such as gold and silver were traded according to standard weights. Similar standards were spread throughout Europe by the Romans. The common method of measurement, however, was to compare the goods to be traded with a known mass. The benefit of this was that there was no need to adjust the scales of commerce for differences in altitude or latitude. Today, much of the world has adopted the metric system of units and the SI unit of mass, the kilogram, has replaced the pound as the measure of goods.

Consider an astronaut whose weight is 170 lb with a necessary life support backpack that has a weight of 80 lb while both are on Earth. The mass of the astronaut is the same whether on Earth or the Moon or in a weightless environment. On the Moon, however, an object's weight is only about one-sixth its weight on Earth. Thus, on the Moon, the weight of the backpack is just over 13 lb while the weight of the astronaut is only 28 lb. An astronaut's muscles that are capable of carrying (with some difficulty) the astronaut and the backpack on Earth have no difficulty carrying what feels like a mere 41 lb total on the Moon. This is very much in evidence in film footage of the Moon walks from NASA's Apollo space program as the astronauts bounded across the surface of the Moon as they collected samples and performed experiments. In fact, the astronauts had to be careful not to go too fast or too high in order to avoid a fall that could result in a potentially lethal tear in the space suit.

Weightlessness is a condition in which the weight, or the apparent weight, of an object is nearly zero. Because there is almost always some residual gravitational force or acceleration some scientists use the term micro gravity instead of the term weightlessness. This condition can be achieved in two ways. One is to move the object far enough away from all gravitational forces and to maintain an inertial reference frame such that the weight of the object is reduced to nearly zero. The other way is to allow the object and its environment to fall freely under the influence of gravity. An example of the second case might be that of a cosmonaut in a space station in orbit around the earth. If the cosmonaut tries to stand on a scale in the space station there will be no net force between the cosmonaut and the scale, giving an apparent weight of zero. This would be equivalent to dropping an object and a bathroom scale out of an airplane and then trying to find the weight of the object by placing it on the scale as both the object and the scale plummet toward Earth.

See also: GRAVITATIONAL CONSTANT; MASS; SI UNITS; WEIGHTLESSNESS

Bibliography

HEWITT, P. G. *Conceptual Physics* (HarperCollins, New York, 1993).

ROGERS, E. M. *Physics for the Enquiring Mind* (Princeton University Press, Princeton, NJ, 1966).

MARK W. PLANO CLARK

WEIGHTLESSNESS

Weight is the force of gravity on an object. It is the downward force that causes something to fall—unless there is a counterbalancing upward force. "A shotput weighs 16 lb on Earth" means that the earth pulls on the shotput with a force of 16 lb. The mass of an object and its weight are often confused. Mass is, roughly speaking, how much "stuff" an object is made of. More precisely, it is the resistance of an object to acceleration. Mass is an inherent property of an object, which does not depend on where the object is. The weight of an object is proportional to its mass, but it does depend on where the object is, since gravity has different strengths in different locations. At a height of 4,000 miles above Earth, the shotput would weigh only about 4 lb. In deep space, very far from the earth and all other large sources of gravity, the weight of either the shotput, subatomic particles, mountains, or people would be zero; they would be weightless.

When we think about being weightless we think first about being freed from Earth's surface, where we are confined by gravity. But this is only one aspect of weightlessness. A soaring bird has escaped the confines of Earth's surface but is not weightless. Earth still pulls down on the bird; the bird still has the same weight as when it sat on a tree branch. In the air or on the branch, the bird has upward support forces that balance the downward weight force, thus keeping the bird from falling. On the branch the bird gets those forces from the upward pressure of the branch on her feet; in the air the forces are the less obvious forces of moving air pushing upward on the wings. The wings support the body of the bird, the body supports the head, and so forth. Each part of the bird has a weight and must have an upward force to counterbalance that weight.

In a gravity-free environment every part of the bird would be weightless. One part of the bird would not be "holding up" any other part. If we were weightless, say in outer space, each part of our body would be weightless, and we would feel strange due to the absence of the usual interactions of the parts. Our spine would not be compressed by the weight of our upper body on our lower body; the location of the fluid in our middle ear would be different, as would the distribution of blood in our body.

Much more than our bodily sensations would be changed. We are familiar with processes on the surface of Earth, and the role of gravity, since it is inescapable, is often not realized. In a weightless environment plants would not grow upward (there would be no meaning to "upward"); liquids would not stay on the bottom of a container (there would be no meaning to "bottom"). The smoke from a candle flame would not drift upward; in fact, robbed of gravity, the convected currents of air that feed the flame would have a very different nature, and the vertical shape of the flame could not exist (there would be no meaning to "vertical").

It turns out that you do not have to go into deep space to achieve weightlessness. If you jump off a diving board, from the time you leave the board until the time you hit the water you are in "free fall." Every part of your body is in free fall and is accelerating downward at 9.81 m/s^2. No part is falling faster or slower than any other part, and therefore there is no force needed between any one part and any other. It is precisely the same set of interactions as if you were in outer space, and it does not only apply to your body. If you were holding a container of liquid, the liquid would have no preference for the bottom of the container. Both the liquid and the container would be in free fall. In fact, there is no phenomenon that could distinguish between free fall and weightlessness. In Isaac Newton's classical theory of gravity, this is a consequence of the remarkable fact that all objects happen to fall the same, independent of their mass and composition (the equivalence principle). In the modern theory of gravity proposed by Albert Einstein, the relationship is much more profound. In Einstein's description of gravity, weight disappears in a freely falling system of reference the way that centrifugal force disappears in a reference system that is not rotating. Both centrifugal and weight forces on an object are proportional to its mass, and both are now considered not to be true forces. Because of this, it is justified to speak of weightlessness in a freely falling system interchangeably with the weightlessness of gravity-free deep space.

One of the consequences of the equivalence of free-fall reference systems and weightlessness is that astronauts, and scientific experiments, can be exposed to the effects of weightlessness by putting them in a plane that goes into extended free-fall dives from high altitudes. The astronauts float inside the plane, just as if they were in deep space. Such a dive, of course, can last only a relatively short time. Astronauts and scientific experiments are put into protracted periods of weightlessness in orbital flights. When satellites are in orbit they are freely falling around Earth, and they are equivalent to weightless environments. This is true not because of the somewhat reduced gravity at the orbital altitude, but because they are part of a freely falling system.

In a space station it would be useful if an Earth-like environment could be created by providing gravity. Actual gravity of significant strength can only be generated by the mass of astronomically large bodies, but a useful substitute is based on the similarity of weight and centrifugal forces (in particular, the fact that both are proportional to mass). The space station could be constructed, in principle, with a living space in the shape of a thin doughnut. If the doughnut were rotating at the correct rate, the outward centrifugal force could be made equal to the downward weight force that would be experienced on Earth's surface. To the space station's inhabitants, a doughnut with a 1,000-m radius, turning about once per minute, would be just like home.

See also: ACCELERATION; EINSTEIN, ALBERT; EQUIVALENCE PRINCIPLE; NEWTON, ISAAC; WEIGHT

Bibliography

GANNON, R. "The Unbearable Lightness of Space Travel." *Popular Science* **242** (3), 74–79 (1993).
WOOD-KACZMAR, B. "Making the Most of Weightlessness." *New Scientist* **135** (1829), 38–41 (1992).

RICHARD H. PRICE

WHISKERS

Whiskers are very small diameter single crystal fibers. They are noted for having tensile strengths close to the theoretical limit, well in excess of 10^6 psi for some materials. Whiskers have been observed for hundreds of years, but serious study on how to eliminate them was begun when metal whiskers were found to be the cause of electrical shorts in miniature electronics components. Besides metals, many other elements and compounds can be made to form whiskers. The reason for their great strength is their near-perfect crystal structure.

Whiskers can be grown from a supersaturated vapor of the desired element or compound. Crystal growth at reasonable rates requires a surface with sites where new atoms can stick. The original model for whisker growth is shown in Fig. 1. At the center is a screw dislocation, so that there is a spiral staircase arrangement of atoms. New atoms come in and stick at the step causing growth in the direction of the dislocation. While some whiskers may grow this way, many others form without dislocations. In addition to growth directly from the vapor to the solid

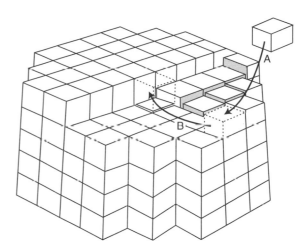

Figure 1 Each cube represents an atom of the crystal. The screw dislocation is the vertical line about which the planes of atoms spiral. Note that the crystal structure is normal in all regions a few atoms away from the dislocation core. A new atom reaching the top surface from the vapor (or melt) is shown contacting the surface and then diffusing on the surface until it reaches the step where it becomes tightly bound. As more atoms are added in this manner, the crystal grows upward.

whisker, a vapor-liquid-solid method (in which the presence of impurities plays a key role) and "pulling" from the melt have also been successful. Whiskers have diameters from 10^{-6} to 10^{-9} m and lengths of several cm or more depending on the method of growth. Carefully chosen temperatures, pressures, and concentrations are required to maintain the very small diameters and thus great perfection and strength.

The absolute strength of a single whisker is of course quite small. Thus, to make practical use of their strength, large numbers of whiskers are added to other materials. Research on materials that bond to the whisker and have suitable properties has resulted in composites that are very lightweight and yet very strong (but, of course, not nearly as strong as the whiskers).

See also: CRYSTAL; CRYSTAL STRUCTURE

Bibliography

FIGUEIREDO, J. L.; BERNARDS, C. A.; BAKER, R. T. K.; and HÜTTINGER, K. J. *Carbon Fibers Filaments and Composites, NATO ASI Series E: Applied Sciences* 177 (Kluwer, Boston, 1989).

LEVITT, A. P. *Whisker Technology* (Wiley, New York, 1970).

WANG, H., and FISCHMAN, G. S. "Role of Liquid Drop Surface Diffusion in the Vapor-Liquid-Solid Whisker Growth Mechanism." *J. Appl. Phys.* **76**, 1557 (1994).

ROY M. EMRICK

WORK

See ENERGY AND WORK

WORK FUNCTION

The work function W is the minimum energy required to remove an electron from within the surface of a metal or semiconductor to a point immediately outside the surface. For metals, the work

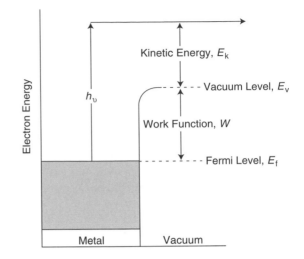

Figure 1 Model of electrons in a metal showing photon-stimulated electron emission.

function is identical to the threshold energy for photoelectron emission and to electron affinity. Figure 1 shows a simplified model of the surface of a metal, with electronic states in the metal occupied up to the Fermi level, the point at which one-half of the quantum states are occupied. The work function is

$$W = E_v - E_f,$$

where E_v is the energy of an electron at rest outside the solid, and E_f is the energy of an electron at the Fermi level inside the solid.

The work function is determined experimentally by measuring the minimum amount of excitation energy required to emit an electron from the solid. There is a high density of filled electronic states near the Fermi level of a metal, and clear-cut theoretical relationships exist that relate photoemission and thermionic emission of electrons from these states to the work function. For example, in Fig. 1, if an electron is excited from the Fermi level by a photon of energy $h\nu$, and the electron is emitted from the solid into vacuum without energy loss, then

$$W = h\nu - E_k,$$

where E_k is the kinetic energy of the electron outside the solid.

Since the Fermi level of a semiconductor or insulator generally lies in the bandgap, the work func-

Table 1 Experimental Work Function Values

Metals	W (in eV)
Cs	2.14
Na	2.75
Al	4.28
W (tungsten)	4.55
Ni	5.15
Pt	5.65

tion of a nonmetal sample is usually measured by first determining the work function of a metal surface and then measuring the difference between the work functions of the metal and the sample. The difference is equal to the contact potential difference, which can be measured directly in a Kelvin probe or retarding potential experiment.

Table 1 lists the experimental values for the work function W of some polycrystalline metals.

See also: ELECTRON; METAL; PHOTOELECTRIC EFFECT

Bibliography

APKER, L.; TAFT, E.; and DICKEY, J. "Photoelectric Emission and Contact Potentials of Semiconductors." *Phys. Rev.* **74,** 1462–1474 (1948).

BERGLUND, C., and SPICER, W. "Photoemission Studies of Copper and Silver: Theory and Experiment." *Phys. Rev.* **136,** A1030, A1044 (1964).

DEKKER, A. L. *Solid-State Physics* (Prentice Hall, Englewood Cliffs, NJ, 1957).

FOWLER, R. H. "The Analysis of Photoelectric Sensitivity Curves for Clean Metals at Various Temperatures." *Phys. Rev.* **38,** 45 (1931).

T. M. DONOVAN

A. D. BAER

X

X RAY

X rays, a form of electromagnetic radiation with wavelengths hundreds of times shorter than visible light, were discovered in 1895 by Wilhelm Conrad Röntgen, the first recipient of the Nobel Prize in physics. Working on cathode rays, Röntgen observed that if an electric current passed through a discharge tube, a nearby fluorescent screen lit up even though the tube was wrapped; he also noticed a mysterious darkening of photographic plates. It seemed to him that a highly penetrating and invisible radiation was emerging from the tube. Since he had no idea of the nature of the radiation, he called it x rays.

X rays, like any form of electromagnetic radiation, have a dual nature, behaving both as electromagnetic waves and as a stream of massless particles, called "photons." The wavelength range of the x rays is $\lambda \approx 0.01$–10 nm, corresponding to photon energies $E \approx 0.12$–120 keV. Among the many properties of x rays discovered by Röntgen were the various ways in which they are absorbed by different substances; that gases become ionized by the passage of x rays; that they do not respond to electric and magnetic fields; that they can cause many substances to fluoresce. Early attempts to observe wavelike characteristics of x rays such as interference, diffraction, and polarization were unsuccessful. In 1906 Charles G. Barkla observed their polarization. In 1912 Max von Laue suggested that the regular array of atoms in crystals could be used as a diffraction grating, since the average distance of the atoms is of the same order of magnitude of the x-ray wavelength. His results were excellent and offered a method to measure the wavelength of the x rays; furthermore, using x rays of known wavelength made it possible to study the atomic structure of crystals. Later, William L. Bragg described the diffraction pattern for x rays striking a crystal at grazing angle θ (equal to the complement of the angle of incidence), wavelength λ, and distance d between crystal planes. He found that $n\lambda = 2d \sin \theta$, which is known as Bragg's law.

The particle nature of x rays is exhibited through the photoelectric effect and the Compton effect. The photoelectric effect occurs when electromagnetic radiation shines on a clean metal surface and electrons are released. Using Max Planck's postulate of energy quantization, Albert Einstein explained the photoelectric effect for photons of visible light, but it also holds for x rays. The Compton effect occurs when x rays are scattered by "free electrons." Arthur H. Compton observed an increase in the wavelength of the scattered x rays, depending only on the scattering angle. In order to explain this effect, he proposed that x ray photons have corpuscular properties in the same sense as billiard balls. He derived the shift in wavelength as $\Delta\lambda = \lambda_c (1 - \cos \theta)$, where $\lambda_c = 0.024$ Å is the Compton wavelength.

There are several sources of x rays. The x-ray sources developed by Röntgen were of the Crook's type of gas discharge tube. When a voltage was applied between the cathode and anode, the dilute gas inside the tube was ionized, the ions bombarded the cathode, which ejected electrons, and the electrons hit the walls of the tube, thereby producing low-energy x rays. In 1913 William Coolidge opened the era of modern x-ray tubes, consisting of cathode and anode enclosed in a shielded high-vacuum chamber. The cathode is a heated filament that controls the electron emission current, and the anode is normally a metal mounted onto a cooled copper block. X rays are emitted through windows made from beryllium or aluminum. In solid-target sources the x rays are produced by bremsstrahlung ("braking radiation" in German), which occurs when fast electrons come close to the positively charged nucleus of an atom of the target and are deflected and accelerated. The bremsstrahlung spectrum is continuous and similar for different target elements. Sharp peaks appear superimposed to it, the characteristic line spectra, due to the x rays produced when a vacancy formed by impact ionization of an inner electron of the target is filled by an outer electron. The x ray resulting from this x-ray fluorescence has an energy equal to the difference between the electron state energies involved. This spectrum strongly depends on the target material.

X rays generated by bending the path of relativistic electrons are called synchrotron radiation. It was first observed in 1947. The first storage ring, dedicated to x-ray production was built in 1966. In 1979 the insertion devices (undulators and wigglers) were introduced and dramatically improved x-ray production. In the 1990s advances in technology are leading to the development of a third generation of synchrotron radiation sources that produce x rays of unprecedented brightness with an unlimited number of applications.

Plasma x-ray sources, currently in the research stage, are produced in plasmas by transitions of bound electrons in ions or by electron-electron collisions.

Virtually all classes of astronomical objects, from planets to stars to galaxies, have been found to be natural emitters of x rays, produced under cosmic conditions by astrophysical plasmas or synchrotron radiation. A new window on the study of celestial objects and cosmic phenomena has been opened by interpreting the x rays they emit or absorb.

X-ray detectors are based on the properties of x rays. The most widely used detectors are photographic films, channel electron multipliers, gas-filled detectors, and semiconductor detectors.

Few discoveries have had such an immediate and enormous impact as Röntgen's discovery. Within three weeks of their discovery, x rays were used to photograph broken bones. Since then, x rays offered a new tool for medical and dental diagnosis. A modern medical application is angiography using synchrotron radiation. Through x-ray diffraction the determination of the crystal structure of proteins and synthetic polymers is possible. X-ray microscopy is used to obtain images of biological specimens in their natural environment. In industry, x rays are used for nanofabrication, integrated circuits, development of new plastics or magnetic materials, and quality control.

See also: BRAGG'S LAW; BREMSSTRAHLUNG; COMPTON EFFECT; RADIATION, SYNCHROTRON; RÖNTGEN, WILHELM CONRAD; X RAY, DISCOVERY OF

Bibliography

COMPTON, A. H., and ALLISON, S. K. *X-Rays in Theory and Experiment*, 2nd ed. (Van Nostrand, Princeton, NJ, 1935).
MICHETTE, A. G., and BUCKLEY, C. J., eds. *X-Ray Science and Technology* (IOP Publishing, Bristol, Eng., 1993).

CARMEN CISNEROS

X RAY, DISCOVERY OF

X rays were discovered late in 1895 by Wilhelm Conrad Röntgen, professor of physics at the University of Würzburg in Germany. It was an astonishing discovery, and the news spread rapidly because of the disturbing power of x rays to photograph the bones inside a living hand. It was astonishing also because these strangely penetrating rays were completely new. There seemed no place for them in the standard theories of physics; they set a riddle that had to be solved. As it happened, that riddle led to others, and from their solutions an unexpected physics of atoms developed.

We do not know what Röntgen's plans had been, except that he was working with cathode rays when he was diverted. Cathode rays appeared when an electric current was sent at high voltage between widely separated metal electrodes in a moderately deep vacuum. They formed blue streamers that sprang directly from the cathode or negative electrode; they could be concentrated into a beam by giving the cathode a proper shape; and wherever they touched the glass wall of the tube they excited it to a fluorescent glow. They might be electricity, they might be light, or, since they could pass through a thin aluminum foil, as Philipp Lenard had recently shown, they might be neither.

What diverted Röntgen was a paper screen coated with barium platinocyanide, which lit in its own fluorescence whenever his cathode-ray tube was running. He knew it responded to ultraviolet light, but what came from the tube was not the ordinary ultraviolet. This radiation was far more penetrating. It passed freely through paper and wood, metals only dimmed the glow, and when Röntgen held his hand above the screen he could see the shadow of his bones inside the fainter outline of the flesh.

Since the new radiation cast shadows, Röntgen realized that it traveled in straight lines like light. Tracing back from the shadows, he found its source in the fluorescent spot on the wall of the tube. Yet it was not light; its rays did not bend in either reflection or refraction. Neither were they shifted by a magnet as an electric current or the cathode rays would be. For their straight-line paths, Röntgen was willing to call them rays but to mark their utter strangeness he added an algebraic x for unknown.

If he could not tell what they were, Röntgen could still describe how they behaved, and he invented experiment after experiment to extend and confirm what he had seen. He found that x rays were produced not only at the glass wall, but at any obstacle on which the cathode rays fell. Like light, they exposed photographic plates, and so could give permanent records of the curious shadows he had seen.

There is a bargain among scientists to give credit for discoveries only to those who share them. You earn credit by telling the world what you have seen and done, and what you think it means. When everyone is free to repeat your work, to question it, confirm it, or refute it, then the credit is yours—but (and this also is part of the bargain) only for what stands up under that examination. It is a good bargain for the discoverer, as well as for the world of science. The discovery is opened up to other people (with different backgrounds, different skills, and different imaginations) who will not just repeat what has been done, but push it farther or even branch off in unexpected directions.

When Röntgen was ready, he made his announcement in a common German style. On December 28,

he took his report to the secretary of the local scientific society, who accepted it for immediate printing. Three days later, on January 1, 1896, he mailed out these "separates" to a long list of prominent scientists, and since he knew that his x rays were too outlandish to be believed, he enclosed nine of his shadow pictures with each of them. These pictures included a set of brass weights nested in their wooden box, metal wire twined around a wooden spool, a steel compass needle seen through its aluminum case, and, finally and amazingly, the bones of a living hand.

One packet went to Franz Exner in Vienna, who shared it with colleagues on the evening of January 4. One of them, Ernst Lecher, took the story home, and his father, Z. K. Lecher, editor of the Vienna *Presse,* put it in print the next morning. From Vienna, it went out by telegraph to appear in London on the 6th, Berlin and Frankfurt on the 7th, New York on the 8th, and in Würzburg not until the 9th.

The sensation was enormous. The newspapers were hard to believe, but their stories were promptly confirmed. Röntgen had honorably kept the bargain. Anyone who read his paper and had a decent cathode-ray tube could generate x rays, and a great many people did. Hands were photographed all over Europe and America. By the end of the year, nearly fifty books and a thousand papers on x rays had appeared.

Much of this was repetition, some was aimless, some was leveled at the immediate needs of medicine. The skeletal hands had been exciting, but surgeons needed sharper, more detailed shadows and rays with the power to penetrate thicker parts of the body. This called for improved tubes and for technicians who could manage their high-voltage supplies and keep them running. It also called for doctors who could learn how to aim the tubes and interpret what were still only shadow pictures.

For the scientists, x rays remained perplexing. The earliest progress and the greatest excitement lay in the new lines of investigation they opened. From the discovery that x rays turned air into a temporary conductor of electricity, J. J. Thomson of Cambridge University worked out a theory of the ionization of gases. He then went on to demonstrate that the cathode rays were streams of tiny, negatively charged fragments of atoms, leading to the 1899 discovery of the electron.

In Paris, Henri Becquerel explored the link between x rays and fluorescence that Röntgen's tubes seemed to indicate. He did find penetrating, ionizing rays from some uranium-containing fluorescent crystals, but in the end, his experiments could link those rays only with the presence of uranium. In 1898, acting on that clue, Marie Curie hunted out and found three other ray-giving elements: thorium, which was already known, and an unknown pair that she and her husband, Pierre, managed to separate from the ores of uranium and named polonium and radium. This began the science of radioactivity, which the Curies also named.

It was also in 1898, at McGill University in Montreal, that Ernest Rutherford started to work on the ionizing rays from thorium and so discovered the group of temporary radioactivities from which he and Frederick Soddy developed their disintegration theory in 1902. This was the radical proposal that radioactivity was a sign of transmutation, that radioactive atoms were changing their chemical natures by emitting one or the other of the rays that Rutherford had called "alpha" and "beta." Becquerel had already shown that the beta rays were high-speed electrons, and as Rutherford would presently show, the alpha rays were atom-sized positive ions, probably of helium, although it would be 1909 before he could prove that to his own satisfaction.

By then Rutherford was in England, at the University of Manchester, to which he had moved in 1907. There he began a new investigation, setting Hans Geiger to study how alpha particles were scattered when they passed through thin metal foils. Although Geiger found this scattering to be very small for the overwhelming majority, the scattering was very large for an uncomfortably big minority in a student project for an undergraduate named Ernest Marsden. These findings created a puzzle, which Rutherford solved in 1911 with the invention of his nuclear atom and the development of a scattering theory that Geiger and Marsden could check experimentally.

In 1904 Charles G. Barkla at the University of Liverpool began a broad study of the scattering of x rays. With carbon, as he found, the scattered beam was polarized (much as light was polarized by reflection) and preserved the mixture of "hard" and "soft" (or penetrating and non-penetrating) rays that his tube had generated. With heavier materials, in contrast, the scattered beam acquired a single well-defined hardness and was not polarized. This hardness, as he found, was characteristic of the scattering material and increased as its atomic weight increased. At high atomic weights, a second, softer ray appeared, and Barkla distinguished the two in 1911 as K (the harder) and L (the softer.)

In 1912 Max von Laue at the University of Munich (to which Röntgen had been called in 1900) began to see that if x rays were electromagnetic waves and if the atoms in crystals stood in the evenly-spaced lattices that their natural shapes suggested, then a beam of x rays aimed through a crystal might form a diffraction pattern. Both assumptions were controversial, but when Walter Friedrich and Paul Knipping offered to try the experiment, their photographic plate showed the pattern he expected. X rays were definitely and unmistakably waves.

It was also in 1912 that Niels Bohr visited Cambridge and Manchester (where Geiger and Marsden had just finished their scattering experiments) and went back to Copenhagen to imagine how atoms might be built using Rutherford's nucleus, Thomson's electrons, and Planck's quanta. By July of 1913 he had contrived a one-electron atom that gave the spectrum of hydrogen. In September he was proposing that the chemical behavior of an atom was set by the number of its electrons and that this and the matching charge on the nucleus were simply equal to its place number as an element in the periodic table. That separated the chemistry of matter from its gravity and radioactivity, which Bohr took as nuclear properties, and established the independence of atomic weight and atomic number.

Laue's paper interested William Lawrence Bragg, then an undergraduate at Cambridge, who saw a way to simplify its analysis. Through 1913, he and his father, William Henry Bragg at the University of Leeds, worked vigorously to measure the wavelengths of x rays and to examine their spectra. Using different metals for the targets in their tubes, they managed to excite Barkla's K and L lines directly, checking them by their penetrating power against those Barkla had excited by scattering, and measured their wavelengths.

In Manchester, H. G. J. Moseley and C. G. Darwin were close behind the Braggs, and in the fall of 1913 Moseley saw an opportunity. If x rays were produced by an inner electron, as Bohr suggested, and if Bohr's hydrogen theory also held for that electron, then he could calculate back from the x-ray wavelength to find the charge on the nucleus around which it circled. Using a tube whose target he could change without breaking the vacuum, he measured the wavelengths of the K lines from ten of the eleven elements that ran from calcium to zinc along the third row of the periodic table. Bohr found that their nuclear charges neatly matched to their place numbers, as he had proposed.

The route from Röntgen to Bohr formed an interlacing network. The direct strand through Thomson's ionization theory branched out to Rutherford, the Curies, Barkla, and the Braggs, all of whom used ionization as a measuring tool, and branched again in Thomson's hands with his discovery of the electron. The direct strand through Becquerel to the Curies also crossed to Rutherford and branched again in his laboratory through the scattering experiments to the nuclear atom and then to Bohr's extraordinarily competent development of it. Strands through Barkla, Laue, and the Braggs interwove to solve the riddle of the x ray's nature and branched through Moseley to validate Bohr's fruitful hypothesis of the atomic number. Through the power of the bargain of scientific discovery, Röntgen's barium platinocyanide screen had engendered a remarkable amount of science.

See also: ATOM, RUTHERFORD–BOHR; ATOMIC NUMBER; BRAGG'S LAW; CATHODE RAY; CURIE, MARIE SKLODOWSKA; DIFFRACTION; NUCLEAR PHYSICS; POLARIZATION; RADIOACTIVITY, DISCOVERY OF; RÖNTGEN, WILHELM CONRAD; RUTHERFORD, ERNEST; SCATTERING, RUTHERFORD; THOMSON, JOSEPH JOHN; X RAY

Bibliography

ANDRADE, E. N. DA C. *Rutherford and the Nature of the Atom* (Doubleday, Garden City, NY, 1964).

GLASSER, O. *Wilhelm Conrad Röntgen and the Early History of the Roentgen Rays* (Charles C Thomas, Springfield, IL, 1934).

NITSKE, W. R. *The Life of Wilhelm Conrad Röntgen, Discoverer of the X Ray* (University of Arizona Press, Tucson, AZ, 1971).

ROMER, A. *The Restless Atom: The Awakening of Nuclear Physics* (Doubleday, Garden City, NY, 1960).

SEGRÈ, E. *From X Rays to Quarks: Modern Physicists and Their Discoveries* (W. H. Freeman, San Francisco, 1980).

WATSON, E. C. "The Discovery of X Rays." *Am. J. Phys.* **13**, 281–291 (1945).

ALFRED ROMER

X-RAY ASTROPHYSICS

See ASTROPHYSICS, X-RAY

X-RAY BINARY

X-ray binaries are binary star systems in which one member is typically a neutron star and accretes, or gravitationally collects, matter from its binary companion, which is close enough that its outer atmosphere can overflow onto the compact neutron star. The first x-ray binaries were discovered as the bright cosmic x-ray sources found in the early rocket-borne x-ray snapshots of limited regions of the sky that followed the discovery of the brightest such source, Sco X-1, in 1962. The realization that these sources were in fact binary systems containing a compact object came with the 1972 discovery of the binary x-ray pulsar Cen X-3 with the Uhuru satellite; the variable time delay experienced by the x-ray pulses as the pulsar moved in its orbit about its companion star revealed unequivocally that the systems were in fact binaries.

As the matter rushes down the potential well of the compact object, its free-fall velocity approaches half the speed of light, $c/2$, and the corresponding kinetic energy per proton reaches 100 MeV at the ~ 10-km radius of the neutron star surface. This kinetic energy is thermalized at the neutron star surface since the opacities in the incoming accretion flow are high. The resulting accretion luminosity is $L_{acc} = GM\dot{m}/R$, where G is the gravitational constant, M is the neutron star mass, R is its radius, and $\dot{m}$ is the accretion rate. L_{acc} is thus emitted as thermal radiation with an approximately blackbody form. Setting $L_{acc} = 4\pi R^2 \sigma T^4$ in accordance with the Stefan–Boltzmann law (with σ being the Stefan–Boltzmann constant) for blackbody emitters of temperature T, the radiation temperature is found to be $T \approx 10^7$ K for a typical x-ray binary luminosity of $L_{acc} \approx 10^{37}$ erg/s. Thus the radiation is emitted primarily in the soft x-ray band, since the peak of the blackbody (from Wien's law) is then at photon energies of about 1 keV. Not all the x-ray emission is from the surface of the neutron star. Separate spectral components, both softer and harder in energy, reveal the presence of emitting regions in an extended, optically thick accretion disk and diffuse corona, respectively.

X-ray binaries containing a black hole rather than a neutron star have been discovered both in our galaxy and in our companion satellite galaxies, the Magellanic Clouds. Approximately ten black hole candidates have now been found in our galaxy, although their usually transient x-ray emission implies that many more are present. It now appears that black hole x-ray binaries in which the companion star (to the black hole) is a star of much lower mass (typically only 0.5 $M_\odot$, versus about 10 $M_\odot$ for the black hole) are the most common type of x-ray binaries in the galaxy. The total number of these systems, which are usually detected as x-ray transient sources that display novalike outbursts lasting about a month and recurring every ten to fifty years, may be in excess of a thousand. The total number of x-ray binaries containing neutron stars actually detected is, in contrast, about 150. The transient outbursts may be caused by instabilities in the accretion flow through the accretion disk onto the black hole or neutron star.

Although some x-ray binaries containing neutron stars are indeed transients, these systems are usually more stable and persistent x-ray emitters. However, the neutron star x-ray binaries exhibit another type of remarkable x-ray variability: x-ray bursts. These are dramatic increases of x-ray intensity by (typically) factors of 10 to 100 in time scales of only a few seconds, followed by exponential decays back to the quiescent x-ray emission over time scales of typically 10 to 100 s. The x-ray bursts are due to thermonuclear burning of accreted material (H and He) on the surface of the neutron star when the density of accreted material reaches the critical value for nuclear ignition. The total energy in a typical burst is 10^{39} ergs, or equivalent to the accretion energy released over about 10^3 s for a typical burster. Since nuclear burning efficiencies are only about 0.7 per-cent or the rest mass energy, whereas the accretion process releases about 15 percent of the rest mass energy (making accretion the most efficient energy source known in the universe), the time between bursts is expected—and observed—to be about $10^3 \times (15/0.7) \approx 20{,}000$ s.

See also: ASTROPHYSICS, X-RAY; BLACK HOLE; COSMIC MICROWAVE BACKGROUND RADIATION; NEUTRON STAR; RADIATION, BLACKBODY; STEFAN–BOLTZMANN LAW; UHURU SATELLITE

Bibliography

BRADT, H., and McCLINTOCK, J. "The Optical Counterparts of Compact Galactic X-Ray Sources." *Ann. Rev. of Astron. and Astrophys.* **21,** 13–66 (1983).

GIACCONI, R.; GURSKY, H.; PAOLINI, F., and ROSSI, B. "Evidence for X Rays from Sources Outside the Solar System." *Phys. Rev. Lett.* **9,** 439–443 (1962).

VAN DEN HEUVEL, E. P. J., and VAN PARADIJS, J. "X-Ray Binaries." *Sci. Am.* **269** (5), 66–71 (1993).

JONATHAN E. GRINDLAY

X-RAY SPECTROSCOPY

See SPECTROSCOPY, X-RAY

Y

YOUNG, THOMAS

b. Milverton, Somerset, England, June 13, 1773;
d. London, England, May 10, 1829; *optics.*

The eldest of ten children, Young was born into a Quaker family, his father being a cloth merchant with banking interests. Although Young attended Compton School in Dorsetshire and later had a private tutor, he was partly self-taught. He is often referred to as a child prodigy since he is reputed to have mastered several languages at an early age. He commenced his medical education in London at the age of nineteen, and a few days after his twenty-first birthday he was elected to the prestigious Royal Society of London—one of the Society's youngest Fellows. Over the next five years his medical studies took him to Edinburgh, Göttingen, and Cambridge, during which time he was disunited from the Quakers. In 1799 Young settled in London as a medical practitioner. Although medicine remained his principal occupation and a major source of income, he also held for two crucial years (1801–1803) the post of Professor of Natural Philosophy at the recently founded Royal Institution of Great Britain.

Although Young's lectures were dry and failed to capture his audience's interest, the published version of his lectures demonstrates his intellectual command of science and his innovations in several areas, especially optics. While still a medical student he had written on vision and later on sound, including an account of the phenomenon of beats explained by the interference of two sound waves. In a paper published in the *Philosophical Transactions of the Royal Society* for 1800, Young first pursued the analogy between sound and light, arguing that a wave theory is more acceptable than the prevalent corpuscular theory. Over the next three years Young published three more papers on the subject in which he demonstrated the explanatory power of his wave theory. The first (published in 1802) opened with his proposal that light is an undulation of the ubiquitous ether and that the frequency of these undulations is responsible for the sensation of color.

Young's most significant innovation was the application of a simple principle of interference to optics—constructive or destructive interference being produced when two similar waves are either in or (180°) out of phase. In contrast to the principle of interference later formulated by August Fresnel, Young was concerned with the interference between two rays of light. Proclaiming interference to be a general law, he employed it to account for such phenomena as Newton's rings, the colors of thin plates, the internal diffraction fringes produced in the shadow of a fiber, and (in 1807) the well-known Young's double-slit experiment. In the late 1810s he extended his theory to explain polarization by suggesting that light is a transverse vibratory motion.

Several other innovations are connected with Young's name, including the modulus of elasticity and an eriometer for optically measuring the size of fibers or particles. He wrote extensively on medical subjects and on ancient languages, including the deciphering of Egyptian hieroglyphics on the Rosetta Stone. An active member of the London scientific community, he served as Foreign Secretary of the Royal Society from 1804 until his death and as Secretary to the Board of Longitude from 1818 to 1828. He was a Tory, and in 1804 he married into the minor aristocracy.

See also: BEATS; DOUBLE-SLIT EXPERIMENT; INTERFERENCE; LIGHT, WAVE THEORY OF

Bibliography

BUCHWALD, J. Z. *The Rise of the Wave Theory of Light* (University of Chicago Press, Chicago, 1989).

CANTOR, G. N. *Optics After Newton: Theories of Light in Britain and Ireland, 1704–1840* (Manchester University Press, Manchester, Eng., 1983).

YOUNG, T. *A Course of Lectures on Natural Philosophy and the Mechanical Arts* (J. Johnson, London, 1807).

GEOFFREY CANTOR

YUKAWA, HIDEKI

b. Tokyo, Japan, January 23, 1907; *d.* Kyoto, Japan, September 8, 1981; *nuclear physics, particle physics, quantum field theory.*

Yukawa, the originator of the meson theory of nuclear forces, was the first Japanese Nobel Laureate. He was born in Tokyo but spent most of his life in Kyoto, Japan's ancient capital and cultural center. He was the fifth of seven children of Koyuki and Takuji Ogawa, both of his parents stemming from scholarly families of the Samurai tradition. The family moved to Kyoto in 1908 when Yukawa's father was appointed Professor of Geography at Kyoto Imperial University. Besides Hideki (who changed his name to Yukawa when he married Sumi Yukawa and was adopted by her family in 1932), three other Ogawa sons became university professors and renowned scholars in their respective fields.

Yukawa grew up in a traditional extended Japanese family, which included three grandparents. As a youth, his interests were mainly literary, not scientific, and he was widely read in world literature and philosophy. He enjoyed mathematics and had an excellent liberal education through high school. One of his classmates, Sin-itiro Tomonaga, won a Nobel Prize in physics in 1965 for his contributions to quantum electrodynamics (QED).

Yukawa and Tomonaga enrolled in physics at Kyoto Imperial University, graduating in 1929 and staying on as unpaid assistants at the university. Yukawa tried to solve the so-called divergence problems of QED: The theory predicted infinite electron charge and mass, both predictions being absurd. Because he failed in this attempt (in which Tomonaga succeeded in the 1940s), Yukawa turned to the "easier" problem of nuclear forces.

In the latter field, he tried in 1933 to make a fundamental version of a theory that was proposed in 1932 by Werner Heisenberg, in which the main nuclear forces arise through the exchange of an electron between a neutron and a proton. Yukawa took as his model the electromagnetic force that arises from the exchange of light quanta (photons). Discovering in 1934 an important relation between the mass of the exchanged quanta and the range of the force in question, Yukawa inferred that the quanta of the nuclear force field must be about one hundred times as massive as the electron.

Yukawa's theory of heavy charged quanta (now called mesons) was published (in English) at the beginning of 1935 but was noticed only in 1937 after particles that appeared to fit Yukawa's requirements were found in cosmic rays. In 1947 it was demonstrated that those particles (muons) are not Yukawa mesons, but rather decay products of the mesons (now called pions). The latter are produced by collisions of cosmic rays with air molecules, which take place high in the atmosphere. In the 1930s many theorists, including Yukawa and his students, worked out versions of the meson theory that accounted for phenomena occurring in nuclear physics as well as in the cosmic rays.

In 1933 Yukawa taught at Osaka Imperial University, and in 1939 he returned to Kyoto as a full professor. During 1948 and 1949 he was a member of the Institute for Advanced Study in Princeton, New Jersey. Yukawa then became a visiting professor at Columbia University in New York City until 1951, when he was made a full professor, having been awarded the Nobel Prize in 1949. In 1953 he returned to Kyoto to become the director of a new interuniversity research institute founded (and later named) in his honor. He wrote many essays on cultural and scientific subjects and participated in international movements for world federation and peace.

See also: NUCLEAR PHYSICS; PARTICLE PHYSICS; QUANTUM FIELD THEORY

Bibliography

BROWN, L. M. "Yukawa's Prediction of the Meson." *Centaurus* **25,** 71–132 (1981).

HAYAKAWA, S. "The Development of Meson Physics in Japan" in *Birth of Particle Physics,* edited by L. M. Brown and L. Hoddeson (Cambridge University Press, Cambridge, Eng., 1983).

KEMMER, N. "Hideki Yukawa." *Biographical Memoirs of Fellows of the Royal Society* **29,** 661–676 (1983).

MUKHERJI, V. "History of the Meson Theory of Nuclear Forces from 1935 to 1952." *Archive for the History of Exact Sciences* **13,** 27–102 (1974).

TANIKAWA, Y. *Hideki Yukawa, Scientific Works* (Iwanami Shoten, Tokyo, Japan, 1979).

YUKAWA, H. *Creativity and Intuition,* trans. by J. Bester (Kodansha, New York and Tokyo, 1973).

YUKAWA, H. *Tabibito (The Traveler),* trans. by L. M. Brown and R. Yoshida (World Scientific, Singapore, 1982).

LAURIE M. BROWN

Z

ZEEMAN EFFECT

The effect of a magnetic field on energy levels of atoms (and molecules) and thereby on the frequencies of the emitted electromagnetic radiation was first observed by the Dutch spectroscopist, Pieter Zeeman, in 1896. He shared the 1902 Nobel Prize in physics with Hendrik Lorentz, who gave an early and partial explanation of the phenomenon.

This early explanation, which predates the quantum-mechanical description of atomic structure, regarded electrons in matter as bound quasi-elastically and oscillating harmonically with characteristic frequencies ν_0. These are also the frequencies of the electromagnetic radiation emitted or absorbed by them. An applied magnetic field, of strength B, exerts forces perpendicular to the direction of motion of the electrons, thereby impressing an additional frequency $\nu_L = eB/4\pi m \simeq 1.4$ MHz/G for this transverse motion. Their superposition leads to sum and difference frequencies $\nu_0 \pm \nu_L$ for oscillations perpendicular to the field direction, together with the unshifted ν_0 for the motion parallel to the field. This picture of Lorentz's, along with an equivalent one by Joseph Larmor of electrons rotating with frequency ν_0 and, in addition, precessing with ν_L about the magnetic field, led to the expectation of a splitting of each spectral line into a Lorentz triplet. For laboratory magnetic fields, which usually range up to a few 10,000 G, ν_L is very small compared to $\nu_0 (\simeq 10^9$ MHz).

While some atoms exhibit this "normal" Zeeman triplet, most do not, including sodium, in which Zeeman first observed the effect. A much more complex splitting, historically dubbed "anomalous," is generally seen, and the correct explanation had to await the quantum theory of atomic structure. An electron in an atom can only be in specific energy levels that are determined in the main by a principal quantum number n, which takes integer values. To a much smaller extent, the energy depends on the orbital angular momentum of the electron, taking integer values (in units of $h/2\pi$ where h is Planck's constant) denoted by a quantum number l ($= 0, 1, 2, ..., n-1$). Orbital motion of a charge constitutes a current and, thereby, a magnetic moment, which can couple to an external magnetic field. Guided strongly by the data on the Zeeman effect, a third quantum number was introduced to specify the orientation of the magnetic moment with respect to the field direction. Denoted by m, it takes integer values between $-l$ and $+l$ in steps of unity. So long as there is no external magnetic field, states differing only in m have the same energy. But the magnetic field splits the level into $(2l + 1)$ distinct, equally separated ones, with a spacing of $h\nu_L$. Since transitions of the electron between energy levels leads to radiation, this splitting of levels translates into the Zeeman splitting of the corresponding spectral lines.

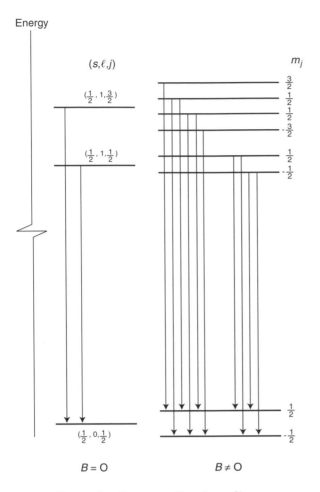

Figure 1   Zeeman effect in sodium.

one, which applies to atomic states with very weak spin-orbit coupling or when B is large, is dubbed the "Paschen–Back effect" after two contemporaries of Zeeman.

The spin and orbital angular momenta together provide a total angular momentum denoted by j. Energy levels, which depend only on j when $B = 0$, split into $(2j + 1)$ levels in a magnetic field with additional energies $gh\nu_L mj$, where $mj = -j, -j + 1, ..., j - 1, j$. The so-called Landé parameter g is a simple algebraic expression in terms of s, l, and j. Figure 1 shows as an example the levels and transitions that give the famous two yellow lines in the sodium spectrum with wavelengths of 589.0 and 589.6 nm. The transitions originate from an upper spin-orbit split pair and end in the ground state. A magnetic field splits the doublet into ten lines as shown. Zeeman's original observations were precisely on this system although he only observed a broadening of the doublet and not a full splitting because of insufficient spectral resolution.

The Zeeman effect is very useful for measuring magnetic field strengths or determining the quantum labels (s, l, j) for atomic and molecular states. Broadening and splitting of spectral lines, both in the laboratory and from distant stars, have been extensively studied for these reasons ever since the work of Zeeman and his contemporaries. The mathematical apparatus of quantum-mechanical perturbation theory for calculating energy levels and wave functions (necessary for computing intensities of transitions) was developed in the late 1920s with the Zeeman effect and its counterpart, the Stark effect with electric fields, as primary instances where a weak additional force disturbs the motion due to a dominant one.

At very high values of B, such as on certain magnetic white-dwarf or neutron stars, or, with laboratory fields applied to highly excited states of atoms, an additional coupling beside the one linear in B due to the magnetic moment becomes important. This coupling is quadratic in B and depends also on n, so that it becomes dominant for large principal quantum numbers. Rich and interesting phenomena due to this so-called quadratic Zeeman effect (also called a diamagnetic effect because this B^2 term is the same one that leads to diamagnetism in matter) are of active research interest in atomic physics.

While accounting for some of the more complex Zeeman multiplets than the simple triplet (which could now be associated with the transition between $l = 1$, $m = 0, \pm 1$ and $l = m = 0$), this picture still failed for others. In particular, multiplets with an even number of lines led to the introduction of an additional half-integer angular momentum, later recognized as an intrinsic spin of the electron with magnitude $\frac{1}{2}(h/2\pi)$. The spin s and its projection m_s on the field direction constitute additional quantum labels for the states of an atomic electron. This additional magnetic moment can couple to the external magnetic field. Also, the magnetic moments due to spin and orbital angular momentum can themselves interact to provide small changes in the energy levels. This latter effect, called spin-orbit coupling, is often stronger than the couplings to the external B; therefore, a distinction is made with the term "Zeeman effect" reserved for this situation. The opposite

See also: ATOMIC PHYSICS; ENERGY LEVELS; FIELD, MAGNETIC; LORENTZ, HENDRIK ANTOON; QUANTUM MECHANICS; SPECTROSCOPY

Bibliography

BETHE, H. A., and SALPETER, E. E. *Quantum Mechanics of One- and Two-Electron Atoms* (Plenum, New York, 1977).

FANO, U., and RAU, A. R. P. *Atomic Collisions and Spectra* (Academic Press, Orlando, FL, 1986).

LANDAU, L. D., and LIFSHITZ, E. M. *Quantum Mechanics: Non-Relativistic Theory, 3rd ed.* (Pergamon, Oxford, 1977).

A. R. P. RAU

GLOSSARY

All cross-references refer to main encyclopedia entries unless followed by (G),
in which case the reference is to another glossary term.

Acceleration Due to Gravity. The acceleration due to gravity (i.e., the initial acceleration of freely falling bodies) near Earth's surface varies with location because of the distribution of Earth's mass and the centripetal acceleration, which is not measurable. Since acceleration due to gravity enters in the definition of some units of measure, a value measured at 45° latitude and corrected for sea level has been adopted as the standard value: $g_s = 9.80665$ m/s^2. *See also:* POUND (G).

Ampere. The ampere (A), a unit of electric current, is an SI base unit. The definition is based on the equation for the force F on a length L of two very long, thin, parallel wires with steady currents I_1 and I_2 a distance d apart: $F = \mu_0 \cdot I_1 \cdot I_2 \cdot L / 2\pi \cdot d$. The currents are 1 A each if the force is 2×10^{-7} N on 1-m length of the wire when the separation is 1 m. This equation also defines the constant μ_0, the magnetic permeability of space, as $\mu_0 = 4\pi \times 10^{-7}$ N·A^{-2}. Although the ampere is defined in terms of currents in wires, currents also may be due to positive charges moving in one direction and negative charges moving in the opposite direction. *See also:* AMPÈRE, ANDRÉ-MARIE; SI UNITS.

Amplitude. The term "amplitude" is well defined in physics only for harmonic (sinusoidal) oscillations and is given by the A in the equation $x = A \sin \theta$, where it is the maximum deflection, positive and negative, from the average. In these cases it is also called the peak-value or height of a wave crest. In alternating-current (ac) applications, the amplitude is often called peak-value. It is sometimes misleadingly used to describe the peak-value of irregular pulses. *See also:* FOURIER SERIES AND FOURIER TRANSFORM; OSCILLATION; WAVE MOTION.

Angstrom. The angstrom (A or Å; 1 Å = 10^{-10} m) is a unit historically used by spectroscopists for measuring the wavelength of radiation in and near the visible range. It is named after the Swedish physicist Anders Jonas Ångström and is temporarily accepted for use with the SI. *See also:* SI UNITS.

Atmosphere. The standard atmosphere (atm) is an obsolete unit of pressure. It is approximately the average pressure of the atmosphere at sea level. It is defined as 1 (st.) atm = 101.325 kPa, which is also given as 760 mmHg or 760 Torr. It is the reference value used in the "standard temperature and pressure." *See also:* STANDARD TEMPERATURE AND PRESSURE.

Bar. The bar (1 bar = 100 kPa) is a pressure unit only temporarily accepted for use with the SI. It is close to the standard atmosphere, but it is more convenient for conversion to SI. The millibar can be directly replaced by the hectopascal. *See also:* ATMOSPHERE (G); SI UNITS.

British Thermal Unit. The British thermal unit (Btu or BTU) is a unit for measuring thermal energy. It is defined as the heat required to raise the temperature of 1 lbm of water by 1°F. Since this value changes with the temperature and other conditions, several slightly different values for the Btu are in use. Modern definitions are usually given in terms of calories. The rounded, defined value of the International Tables is 1 Btu$_{int.tab.}$ = 1,055.056 J. *See also:* CALORIE (G); POUND (G).

Calorie. The calorie (cal) is an obsolete unit of thermal energy. It is defined as the amount of heat required to raise the temperature of 1 g of water by 1°C. The calorie was used with outdated metric systems, but it was not part of any of those systems. Because the value depends on the temperature and other conditions of the water, many different calories have been defined, yet all are near the defined value of the International Tables, 1 cal$_{int.tab.}$ ≡ 4.1868 J. In nutrition, a "large calorie" (sometimes abbreviated Cal.), equal to 1 kcal, is used, but often it is also called calorie and abbreviated cal. *See also:* JOULE (G); SI UNITS.

Coulomb. The coulomb (C) is the SI unit of electric charge. It is the net amount of charge passing through a cross section of a circuit during 1 s when there is a steady current of 1 A: 1 C = 1 A·s. The coulomb is approximately equal to the charge on 6.24151×10^{18} protons. *See also:* COULOMB, CHARLES AUGUSTIN; SI UNITS.

Curie. The curie (Ci, formerly c) is an obsolete unit of activity of a radioactive material. Activity is the product of the number of radioactive nuclei present and the decay constant. Originally the unit was defined as the number of disintegrations per second of 1 g of radium. It was later redefined as 1 Ci = 3.7×10^{10} s^{-1}. In SI notation, 1 Ci = 3.7×10^{10} Bq. *See also:* CURIE, MARIE SKLODOWSKA; HALF-LIFE (G); RADIOACTIVITY; SI UNITS.

Debye. The debye (1 D ≡ 10^{-18} statcoulomb·cm = 3.335641×10^{-30} C·m) is a unit of electric dipole moment named after the Dutch-U.S. physicist Peter J. W. Debye. The debye, which is not part of the SI, was used in the description of molecular charge distributions. *See also:* DIPOLE MOMENT; METRIC SYSTEMS (G); SI UNITS.

Decibel. The decibel (dB) is a unit used to measure or compare power amplification and levels. The bel (1 bel = 10 dB) is based on logarithms to the base 10. The bel is rarely used, and the defining equations usually carry a factor of 10 to give results in decibels. Neither the bel nor the decibel are part of any unit system. The units are named after the Scottish-U.S. scientist Alexander Graham Bell.

If the power is amplified, for example, by a factor 10 (where P_f is the final power and P_i is the initial power), one deals with an amplification of 1 bel or 10 dB ($P_f/P_i = 10$; $\log_{10} 10 = 1$). A 1,000-fold increase would be an amplification of 3 bel or 30 dB. Power and intensities typically depend on the square of some quantity (e.g., electrical power is proportional to the square of the voltage), which is more easily measured and may be used for the description of the power level difference. For example, an increase of power by a factor of 50 ($P_f/P_i = 50$; $\log_{10} 50 = 1.7$), which is an amplification of 17 dB, will result from a voltage increase by a factor of $\sqrt{50}$ (i.e., $V_f/V_i = \sqrt{50}$). Note that the logarithmic increase of the voltage is only half the logarithmic increase of the power ($\log_{10} \sqrt{50} = \frac{1}{2}\log_{10} 50 = 0.85$). However, the amplification is expressed, or the meter reading is given, as 2 $\log_{10} V_f/V_i$ bel. This power level increase may be described as a voltage level increase to indicate that it has been obtained by voltage measurements. In general it is necessary that the conditions for the measurements, such as frequency, wave form, and load, at the two levels are the same, especially if a variable other than power is used. Likewise, the conditions of measurement have to be established when a power level is stated with respect to a reference level that has been generally adopted. For example, 10^{-12} W/m^2 is often the 0-dB level of sounds at 1,000 kHz, and decibel measurements with voltmeters are often with respect to 1 mW dissipated in a 600-Ω load.

Diopter. The diopter (D) is primarily used for describing the "power" of a lens. In this application it is the reciprocal of the focal length measured in meters. The unit is not part of the SI. *See also:* FOCAL LENGTH (G).

Dyne. The dyne (1 dyn ≡ 1 cm·g·s^{-2} ≡ 10^{-5} N) is the unit for force in the now obsolete CGS systems. *See also:* METRIC SYSTEMS (G); SI UNITS.

Electron Volt. The electron volt (1 eV ≈ 1.602×10^{-19} J) is an energy unit used in atomic physics. The electron volt is the kinetic energy acquired by an electron in passing through a potential difference of 1 V in a vacuum. *See also:* SI UNITS.

Erg. The erg (1 erg ≡ 1 cm^2·g·s^{-2} ≡ 1 dyn·cm ≡ 10^{-7} J) is the unit for energy in the now obsolete CGS systems. *See also:* METRIC SYSTEMS (G); SI UNITS.

Farad. The farad (F) is the SI unit of capacitance. A capacitor has a capacitance of 1 F if the potential difference between its plates is 1 V when it is charged with 1 C: 1 F = (1 C)/(1 V). *See also:* CAPACITANCE; FARADAY, MICHAEL; SI UNITS.

Focal Length. The focal length of a curved mirror or thin lens is the distance from the vertex of the mirror or the center of the lens to the (principal) focal point. The focal point is the point at which parallel incident light forms an image. For converging mirrors and lenses, the focal point is on the side on which the light is emerging, and the focal length is considered positive. For diverging mirrors or lenses, the focal point is on the side opposite the one from which the light is emerging, and the focal length is considered negative. *See also:* DIOPTER (G).

Foot-Pound. The foot-pound is the unit of work in the system using the pound-force (lbf) as the force unit. Since all the contributing factors are defined in terms of SI units, the conversion factor to seven digits is 1 ft lbf = 1.355818 J. *See also:* POUND (G); SI UNITS; WORK (G).

Force Constant. The force constant, also called the spring constant, describes the stiffness of a spring. It is the force per unit length in extension or compression and is obtained by dividing the force applied on a spring by the resulting change in length. The SI unit is newtons per meter (N/m). *See also:* HOOKE'S LAW.

Frequency. The term "frequency" describes how many cycles of a regularly repeating event, such as oscillations, occur during a second. In the SI, the unit $1/s$ has, for this application, the special name hertz (Hz) so that $1/s = 1$ Hz.

The term is also used in applications like frequency distribution to indicate the number of times a certain event occurs in comparison to slightly different events (e.g., the number of times measurement values fall into a given interval in comparison to the number of measurements with values falling into other intervals).

See also: HERTZ (G); OSCILLATION; PERIOD (G); SPEED, ANGULAR (G); WAVE MOTION.

Frequency, Angular. There are two related meanings of the term "angular frequency" (ω). One meaning is related to angular speed; it is used in describing the time rate at which the rotation angle increases in terms of the time it takes for one revolution (period T): $\omega = 2\pi/T = 2\pi \cdot n$, where n is the frequency of turning (the number of revolutions per second). The second meaning is as a mathematical concept. In order to relate a periodic or oscillatory motion (or periodic process in general) to a mathematical function with periodicity (e.g., the sine function), one has to relate the time of the progressing physical phenomenon to the angle that defines the sine function (sin θ). This is done by a simple proportion. The time t at which the process is described is related to the period at which it repeats, in the same way that the angle θ of the sine function is related to the angle of one revolution (2π): $t/T = \theta/2\pi$. The angle in the sine function is, therefore, $\theta = (2\pi/T) \cdot t = \omega t$. *See also:* AMPLITUDE (G); FREQUENCY (G); PERIOD (G); SPEED, ANGULAR (G); VELOCITY, ANGULAR.

Gram. *see* KILOGRAM (G).

Half-Life. Half-life is the popular way to describe the activity of a radioactive isotope. It specifies the time $T_{1/2}$ in which half the material will decay. The dependence of radioactivity A on time t is described by the equation $A = A_0 e^{-\lambda t} = A_0 e^{-t/\tau}$, where A_0 is the initial activity, λ is the decay constant, and $\tau = 1/\lambda$ is the average or mean lifetime of the radioactive nuclei. $T_{1/2}$ can be obtained by solving $A_{1/2} = \frac{1}{2}A_0 = A_0 e^{-T_{1/2}/\tau}$ for $T_{1/2} = \tau \ln 2 = (\ln 2)/\lambda$. The term "half-life" is also used in relation to radioactive materials introduced into human or animal bodies to describe approximately the rate at which the material is eliminated by biological processes. Assuming exponential decrease due to these processes, the biological and radioactive decay constants can be added. *See also:* CURIE (G); RADIOACTIVITY.

Henry. The henry (H) is the SI unit of inductance. The unit is named for the U.S. physicist Joseph Henry. The unit is defined in relation to the equation $\mathcal{E} = -L \, dI/dt$ as the self-inductance L of a circuit in which a voltage difference ($\mathcal{E}$) of 1 V is induced when the current I changes at a rate of 1 A/s. *See also:* INDUCTANCE; INDUCTANCE, MUTUAL; SELF-INDUCTANCE; SI UNITS.

Hertz. The hertz (1 Hz = s^{-1}) is the SI unit for the frequency of regular periodic processes. The unit is named after the German physicist Heinrich Rudolph Hertz. *See also:* FREQUENCY (G); SI UNITS.

Horsepower. Horsepower (hp) is a unit of power used in several obsolete unit systems. Most measures of horsepower are close to that of the "electrical" horsepower, which is defined as 1 hp$_{el.}$ = 746 W. *See also:* POWER (G); SI UNITS; WATT (W).

Hyperon. Hyperons are baryons, which are more massive than protons and neutrons. Hyperons are unstable and decay directly, or in a chain of decays, to protons or neutrons and other products. Hyperons require a quantum number called strangeness for a more complete description of their properties. They are produced in high-energy collisions where there is enough energy to produce such massive particles. An example of a hyperon is the lambda particle. *See also:* BARYON NUMBER; LAMBDA PARTICLE (G); QUARK, STRANGE.

Joule. The joule (J) is the SI unit of energy applicable to all its forms (e.g., heat and electric energy). The joule is defined as the work done by a force of 1 N when the point of application of the force moves 1 m in the direction of the force: 1 J = 1 N·m. The use of the term "joule" allows one to distinguish clearly between a quantity measured in joules and a torque (moment of a force), which has the same dimensions. *See also:* CALORIE (G); KILOWATTHOUR (G); SI UNITS; WORK (G).

J/Psi Particle. The J/psi particle (J/Ψ) is a neutral meson composed of a charm quark and its antiparticle. The double name is used because in 1974 the particle was apparently discovered and named simultaneously by two different groups of scientists. The particle, which is also called charmonium, was predicted before its experimental observation, and its discovery was used at the time as strong evidence of the existence of a fourth quark (later identified as the charm quark). *See also:* QUARK, CHARM.

Kelvin. The definition of kelvin (K), the SI base unit for temperature, is based on heat transfers calculated for an ideal heat engine operating between the temperature to be described and the temperature of the triple point of water (which is defined as being at 273.16 K or 0.01°C). Both kelvins and degrees Celsius are used for designating temperature (K = °C + 273.15) and temperature intervals (1 K = 1°C). *See also:* CARNOT CYCLE; HEAT ENGINE; KELVIN, LORD; SI UNITS.

Kilogram. The kilogram (kg), which is the SI base unit of mass, was historically defined as the mass of a cubic decimeter of water. Refinements were made in the definition, and soon it was represented as the mass of a standard block of noncorrosive alloy. The final prototype was made in 1889, and copies were distributed to many of the nations who had signed the *Convention du Mètre* (Meter Convention). *See also:* SI UNITS.

Kilowatthour. The kilowatthour [kW h or kW·h; 1 kW h = (1,000 J/s)·(3,600 s) = 3.6 × 10^6 J = 3.6 MJ] is an energy unit outside the SI. It is frequently used to measure electric energy. *See also:* SI UNITS.

Lambda Particle. The lambda particle (Λ or Λ^0) was named after the shape of some tracks in cloud chamber pictures of cosmic ray events. The events showed two charged particles moving from the same point nearly in the same direction. This was interpreted as the decay of the (neutral) Λ particle into a proton (p) and a negative pi meson (π^-). The name was kept although it was found that these particles can also decay into two neutral particles, a neutron (n) and a pi zero (π^0). The production occurred in high-energy collisions in which enough energy was available to produce such massive particles. The lambda particle is also found as a decay product of still more massive hadrons. Its composition in terms of quarks is *uds*. *See also:* HYPERON (G); QUARK.

Length. Determining a length (e.g., the separation between two points) usually refers to a process represented by using the size of an object (measuring stick) as a "unit of length" and determining how often it can be laid end to end in going between the two points. This process is usually performed along a straight line unless it is specified that the length along a certain path is sought. In the case of a curved path, one has to use a sufficiently small unit (short measuring stick) so that laying it end to end does not significantly deviate from the path. If the path is limited to a surface, one might lay a non-stretchable string along the path and then straighten it out for a measurement of its length. *See also:* LIGHT-YEAR (G); PROPER LENGTH.

Light-Year. The light-year (ly or l.y.; 1 ly = 9.46073 × 10^{15} m) is a unit for measuring astronomical distances. This unit is the distance light travels in a vacuum during a year of 365.25 days. *See also:* METER (G); SI UNITS.

Liter. The liter (l or L) is a unit of volume. It was redefined in 1964 as being a name for the cubic decimeter. Althought it is not part of the SI, it is permitted for use with SI units. Since it was defined for a while as the volume occupied by 1 kg of water at the temperature when its density is greatest (at 4°C), it was a little larger than 1 dm^3. To avoid confusion, it is recommended not to use it for precision specification. It is primarily used for measuring the volume of liquids and gases. In using the liter in calculation with SI units, one must exercise special care in establishing the power of ten or the prefix of the result. *See also:* METER (G); SI UNITS.

Meter. The meter (m) is the base unit for length measurement in the SI. It was originally defined as 1/10,000,000 of the length of the meridian through Paris from the North Pole to the equator. This value was soon replaced by the length of a specific platinum bar, which was replaced in 1889 by the distance between lines on a platinum-iridium bar. In 1983 the meter was redefined as the distance light travels in a vacuum during a time interval of 1/299,792,458 s. *See also:* METRIC SYSTEMS (G); SI UNITS.

Metric Systems. The name "metric system" is used for a variety of systems of units (all of which are decimal systems) based in some way on the meter. The first metric system was adopted in France in 1795 after the French Revolution, but with the introduction of the SI in 1960, all other metric systems became obsolete.

In all of the metric systems, efforts were made to obtain coherence over a broader field, that is, to have the same relation between units as between the physical quantities.

The CGS systems were based on the centimeter, gram, and second. Using Newton's law without any special constants, where the force applied to a mass equals the product of the mass and the resulting acceleration, leads to a force unit, the dyne (1 dyn $\equiv$ 1 cm·g·s^{-2}), and an energy unit, the erg (1 erg $\equiv$ 1 dyn·cm).

To accommodate electrical units, Coulomb's law, which states that the force between two point charges is proportional to the product of the charges and inversely proportional to the square of their separation, was used to define a charge unit by setting the constant of proportionality equal to 1 dyn·cm^2·statcoulomb^{-2}. Units of electrical quantities in the CGS system are called electrostatic units (esu) and use the "stat-" prefix (e.g., statcoulomb and statampere).

Another approach to incorporate electric and magnetic units into a CGS system was to define a theoretical, fictitious magnetic pole and the magnetic field of such a pole (in analogy to the electric charge and field in the electrostatic unit system described above) and then to define an electric current unit as that current that produces such a magnetic field, for example, at the center of a current loop with a radius of 1 cm. The units were called electromagnetic units (emu) and used the "ab-" prefix (e.g., abampere and abvolt).

A combination of the electrostatic and electromagnetic CGS units, known as Gaussian units, is still sometimes used in theoretical electromagnetic calculations because of the symmetry of electrical and magnetic units. Since these units come from two different systems, the equations of electromagnetism will have various factors of c, the speed of light.

In making conversions between the various CGS electrical units and the SI units, one must consider the different magnitudes, as well as the fact that sometimes the units have different dimensions in different systems.

The electromagnetic units were considered to be of inconvenient size, and "practical" units were defined with the unit for current, the ampere, equal to 0.1 abampere.

The MKS system of mechanical units, based on the meter, kilogram, and second, became popular when it was found that the practical electrical units could be incorporated easily, as is seen, for example, by the fact that the product (1 V) $\times$ (1 A) = 1 W.

In the various electrical systems there are so-called rationalized versions in which the defining equations have a factor of 4π in the expression where it might not appear in the simplest form of the equation, but where it seems acceptable because of the geometrical configuration (e.g., in Coulomb's law, which deals with point charges with basically spherical symmetry). This results in simpler equations in many applications where the appearance of π would appear strange, as for example, in the expression for the capacitance of a parallel plate capacitor. This has little effect on the units because the change of the equations is compensated for by modifying the two constants that enter the same equations (i.e., the electrical permittivity of space and the magnetic permeability of space).

The SI was developed from a rationalized MKS system by including the practical electrical units, by using the ampere as a base unit, and by adding three base units (the kelvin, the mole, and the candela) to expand the system. The units discussed so far are sometimes called absolute, to distinguish them from units that depend on local conditions, such as the early forms of the so-called gravitational units that depended on the local acceleration due to gravity. Although there is now a standard value of the acceleration due to gravity being used, the name still persists.

A metric system based on the gravity force on a mass of 1 kg was used by engineers. This force was called kilogram force, but the qualifier was often omitted. The use of the kilogram as force unit introduced a factor of the acceleration due to gravity into Newton's law. To avoid that, a new mass unit, $|g_s|$ times larger than the kilogram, was introduced. Various names such as metric slug and technical mass unit were used. These units should not be used with the SI.

See also: ACCELERATION DUE TO GRAVITY (G); KILOGRAM (G); METER (G); POUND (G); SECOND (G); SI UNITS.

Microwaves. The term "microwaves" has been used to characterize electromagnetic waves having wavelengths that are longer than those of infrared radiation and shorter than those of short-wave radio, but with some overlap. The range of wavelengths stretches from about 10^{-3} to 10^{-1} m. This range includes most radar applications, the shortest wavelengths that can be produced with common electronic devices, and the longest wavelengths observed to have been emitted by atoms and molecules. *See also:* ELECTROMAGNETIC SPECTRUM; ELECTROMAGNETIC WAVE.

Mole. The mole (mol), which is the SI base unit for amount of substance, measures the substance in units having a given number of particles. The unit is the number of particles in 0.012 kg of carbon-12, the isotope of carbon with mass number 12. Carbon-12 was chosen because its relative atomic mass (formerly called atomic weight), using the scale that was originally based on the relative atomic mass of the natural mixture of oxygen isotopes, is very close to 12, so that the old tables of atomic masses did not have to be changed. Determining such a number (the Avogadro number) of particles of a substance can be accomplished by using an amount in grams equal to the relative atomic (or molecular) mass of the substance. The unit can also be applied to particles other than atoms and molecules, such as electrons. *See also:* ATOMIC WEIGHT; AVOGADRO NUMBER; SI UNITS.

Muonic Atom. A muonic atom is an atom where a negative muon (μ^-) has been captured by an atom into a state described by quantum numbers, such as the states of the various electrons in an atom. However, since the mass of the muon is approximately 200 times larger than the electron mass, the distribution in space is on a much smaller scale and the energy of the states is 200 times greater than for corresponding electron states. Most radiation due to muon transitions will therefore be in the x-ray range and may give some information about the nucleus because of the close proximity. *See also:* ATOM, RUTHERFORD–BOHR; MUON.

Muonium. Muonium has a structure similar to the hydrogen atom, with the proton replaced by a positive muon (μ^+). Muonium can sometimes re-place hydrogen for a short time in some molecules. *See also:* ATOM, RUTHERFORD–BOHR; MUON.

Newton. The newton (N), the SI unit of force, is defined as the force necessary to give an acceleration of 1 m/s^2 to a mass of 1 kg. *See also:* SI UNITS.

Ohm. The ohm (Ω) is the SI unit of electric resistance. The definition of the ohm is based on the definition of resistance R, which is the ratio of a constant potential difference V applied between two points on a conductor divided by the resulting current I: $R = V/I$, so $1\ \Omega = (1\ V)/(1\ A)$. The ohm is also used as a unit for reactance, the ratio of potential difference and current in alternating-current (ac) circuits. The unit is named after the German physicist Georg Simon Ohm. *See also:* CURRENT, ALTERNATING; REACTANCE; SI UNITS.

Pascal. The pascal (Pa), the SI unit of pressure, may be expressed in base units or in a form that shows its relation to force more clearly: $1\ Pa = 1\ m^{-1}\cdot kg\cdot s^{-2} = 1\ N\cdot m^{-2}$. The unit, which is also used for other forms of stress, is named after the French physicist Blaise Pascal. *See also:* SI UNITS.

Period. The period, in the context of a time interval, means the time between (fairly) regularly repeating processes, such as an oscillation, orbital motion of a planet, or rotation of an object. The period T of an oscillation is the reciprocal of the frequency f: $T = 1/f$. In wave motion, the period is the time in which the wave moves a distance of one wavelength. It is sometimes confusing that the adjective "periodic" has, in everyday language, almost the opposite meaning, namely that a process, such as an inspection, is repeated occasionally (i.e., at irregular intervals). *See also:* FREQUENCY (G); OSCILLATION; WAVE MOTION.

Pound. The name "pound" (lb) is used for both the unit of mass and the unit of force. Since physical standards were used and no location was specified, and since the unit was used in trade, one can assume that the term was historically introduced as a unit of mass. To avoid misunderstanding, the unit should be called pound-mass [lbm or lb-(avoirdupois)]. In the United States, the pound was redefined in 1893 in terms of the kilogram. The current value is 1 lbm $\equiv$ 0.45359237 kg. In common language, the term is often used as a unit of force (i.e., the force required to support an object of 1 lbm on Earth). For greater clarity the unit should be called pound-force (lbf) when used in that sense. The modifiers are often omitted, making the distinction between mass and force and weight difficult. Since the force to support an object depends on the magnitude of the local acceleration due to gravity, unit systems that use this force unit as a base were called gravitational. A unit changing with location became unacceptable, so the standard value of the acceleration due to gravity ($g_s = 9.80665$ m/s^2) has been used to obtain a fixed value of the force unit: 1 lbf $\equiv$ 4.4482216152605 N. *See also:* FORCE; MASS; SLUG (G); WEIGHT.

Power. Power is the time rate at which (1) work is done, (2) energy is transferred, or (3) energy is converted from one form to another. *See also:* HORSEPOWER (G); SI UNITS; WATT (G); WORK (G).

Radian. The radian (rad) is the SI unit for plane angle. Angles can be described by the ratio of the arc subtended when they are drawn from the center of a circle to the radius of the circle: angle = arc/radius. Since the length units cancel, the angular measure is a pure number without units. The angle where the two lengths are equal is 1 rad. Expressed in base units, 1 rad = 1 m/m = 1. A full circle has an angle of 2π rad. The unit "rad" may generally be either written or omitted, but it should be included when it adds to clarity, such as in stating how large an angle is or in describing angular speed (rad/s). Other examples are angular acceleration (rad/s^2) and the torsion constant (N/rad). In calculations it will often enter with the radian designation, since it helps in clarifying what quantity is substituted, but the "rad" should be dropped in later steps of the calculations when it does not serve any clarifying purpose. *See also:* SI UNITS.

Reluctance. Reluctance ($R = L/A \cdot \mu$) is the combination of the factors (i.e., cross section A, length L, and permeability μ) that enter in the description of the magnetic flux ϕ in configurations of iron cores (possibly with air gaps), as in transformers or electromagnets that relate the material and geometric quantities to the electric current i and the number of turns n, producing the flux $\phi = n \cdot i / R$. This relation is similar to the relations of the electric current in a network of resistive wires to the applied voltage, so reluctance may be considered as the analog of resistance in electric circuits. The fact that the electric current is strictly confined to the wires, while magnetic flux is only concentrated in iron, limits the usefulness of the analogy in more complicated situations. The unit of measurement for reluctance is the reciprocal henry (H^{-1}). *See also:* ELECTRICAL RESIS-TANCE; MAGNETIC FLUX; MAGNETIC PERMEABILITY; MAGNETIZATION.

Roentgen. The roentgen (1 R $\equiv$ 2.58 $\times$ 10^{-4} C/kg) is an obsolete unit for the measurement of the radiation dose of x rays measured by the ionization produced in air. It is temporarily in use with the SI, but it is superseded by the gray: 1 R $\approx$ 8.69 $\times$ 10^{-3} Gy, using an average energy used to ionize an atom. *See also:* RADIATION PHYSICS; RÖNTGEN, WILHELM CONRAD; SI UNITS.

Second. The second (s in SI, with sec frequently used in other systems) is the unit of time in all scientific measuring systems. The second is the duration of 9,192,631,770 periods of the radiation corresponding to the transition between the two hyperfine levels of the ground state of the cesium-133 atom. *See also:* METRIC SYSTEMS (G); SI UNITS.

Slug. The slug is the unit of mass in the "gravitational" (or engineering, or U.S. Customary) system of units. It was introduced to avoid the need for special constants in equations (e.g., Newton's law, $F = ma$). Since the pound-force gives the pound-mass an acceleration of about $g = 32$ ft/s^2, a mass unit had to be chosen that was g times larger than the pound-mass, so that the acceleration is 1 ft/s^2 when a force of 1 lbf is applied. Therefore, 1 slug $\approx$ 32 lbm. Using the standard value of g and the definition of the pound-mass, 1 slug = 14.59390 kg. *See also:* POUND (G); SI UNITS.

Speed. The speed of a moving point is the time rate of the change of length along a path. The average speed can be determined by dividing the length of the path covered during a time interval by the duration of the time interval. If the speed is changing, the instantaneous speed at any point is obtained by determining the limit of the ratio of distance over time as the time interval approaches zero. Speed at any point is the magnitude of the (instantaneous) velocity. However, in general, speed is not the magnitude of any average velocity. *See also:* ACCELERATION; LENGTH (G); VELOCITY.

Speed, Angular. Angular speed of a rotating body is the time rate of change of the angle of rotation. It is measured in radians per second (rad/s). In applications to machinery, angular speed is frequently measured in revolutions per minute (1 rpm = $2\pi/60$ rad/s). *See also:* FREQUENCY (G); FREQUENCY, ANGULAR (G); RADIAN (G); SI UNITS; SPEED (G); VELOCITY, ANGULAR.

Steradian. The steradian (sr) is the SI unit for solid angle. A solid angle can be described by the ratio of the area subtended on the surface of a sphere (when the angle is located at the center of the sphere) to the area described as the square of the radius: (Solid Angle) = (area on sphere)/(radius squared). The solid angle where these two areas are equal is 1 sr. Expressed in base units, $1 \text{ sr} = 1 \text{ m}^2/\text{m}^2 = 1$. For example, a complete sphere has a solid angle of 4π sr. The unit "steradian" should be written when it adds clarity, but it should be omitted otherwise. For example, it is useful in distinguishing the two SI units candela (cd) for luminous intensity and lumen (lm) for luminous flux: $1 \text{ lm} = 1 \text{ cd} \cdot \text{sr}$. A light source will have a certain luminous intensity, but it may radiate only in some directions. The flux is then the product of the intensity and the solid angle into which it radiates. *See also:* SI UNITS.

Tesla. The tesla ($1 \text{ T} = 1 \text{ Wb/m}^2$) is the SI unit of magnetic flux density, sometimes called magnetic field intensity or magnetic induction. The tesla is used in relations describing the magnetic field produced by currents and takes the magnetic permeability of the medium into account. It also determines the force experienced by moving charges (currents) in a magnetic field. The unit is named after the Austrian-U.S. engineer Nicola Tesla. *See also:* MAGNETIC FLUX; MAGNETIC PERMEABILITY; SI UNITS; WEBER (G).

Torque. The torque (τ), or moment of a force, with respect to an axis of rotation (i.e., when only two-dimensional motion is considered), is defined as the product of the force arm and the applied force **F**. The force arm, also called lever arm, is the distance of the line of action of the force from the axis. If the vector from the axis to the point of application of the force is **r**, the moment arm is $\mathbf{r} \sin \theta$, where θ is the angle between **r** and the line of action of the force, and the magnitude of the torque is $\tau = r \cdot F \sin \theta$. These relations can be expressed as a vector cross product, $\tau = \mathbf{r} \times \mathbf{F}$, which describes the torque as a vector along the axis. *See also:* VECTOR.

Torr. The torr ($1 \text{ Torr} = 133.3224 \text{ Pa}$) is an obsolete unit of pressure, named after the Italian physicist Evangelista Torricelli. It is the name given to the millimeter mercury (mmHg) at standard temperature ($0°C$) or $1/760$ of the standard atmosphere. *See also:* SI UNITS.

Volt. The volt (V) is the SI unit of electric potential or "voltage." Operationally one says that point Y has a potential 1 V higher than point X when the work done in moving a unit of charge (1 C) against electrical forces from X to Y is 1 J: $1 \text{ V} = 1 \text{ J/C}$. In the context of circuits, the volt is usually defined by stating that there is a potential difference of 1 V between two points of a wire carrying a constant current of 1 A if the power dissipated between these points is 1 W: $1 \text{ V} = 1 \text{ W/A}$. To assign a potential value to each point in a given situation requires the specification of a reference value. In electrostatics, zero potential at infinity is often chosen. In circuits, a point connected to ground and/or the chassis is usually chosen as being at zero potential. The unit is named after the Italian physicist Alessandro Volta. *See also:* SI UNITS.

Watt. The watt ($1 \text{ W} = 1 \text{ J/s}$) is the SI unit of power. In electrical terms for direct-current (dc) circuits, the watt is the product of potential difference (in V) and current (in A): $1 \text{ W} = 1 \text{ V} \cdot \text{A}$. In alternating-current (ac) circuits, the power dissipated is less than the product of the effective voltage and effective current by a factor of $\cos \theta$ known as the power factor. This factor is due to the phase difference (by an angle θ) between current and voltage. The unit is named after the Scottish engineer James Watt. *See also:* POWER (G); SI UNITS.

Weber. The Weber (Wb) is the SI unit of magnetic flux. The definition of the weber is based on Faraday's law of induction, which states that a voltage (called an electromotive force, $\mathcal{E}$) will be induced in a circuit of a single turn equal to the time rate of change of the magnetic flux (ϕ) through the circuit: $\mathcal{E} = d\phi/dt$. The weber is defined as the initial net flux through the area of a closed circuit of one turn in which a voltage of 1 V would be induced if the current decreases at a constant rate to zero in 1 s. The unit is named after the German physicist Wilhelm Eduard Weber. *See also:* ELECTROMAGNETIC INDUCTION, FARADAY'S LAW OF; MAGNETIC FLUX; SI UNITS; TESLA (G).

Work. Work (W) is defined as the product of the magnitude of a force F applied on a system and the distance the point of application moves in the direction of the force, s_F: $W = F \cdot s_F$. The component of the force at right angles to the displacement does not contribute to the work. Work can also be considered as the product of the (rectangular) component of the force in the direction of the displacement: $W = F_s \cdot s$. In general, $W = F \cdot s \cos \theta$, where θ is the angle between the force and displacement directions. In vector notation, work can be described as the dot product of the force and displacement vectors: $W = \mathbf{F} \cdot \mathbf{s}$. If the angle is obtuse, the work done by the force is negative. Doing work in mechanical systems is sometimes described as the process of converting one form of energy to another. The SI unit for work is the joule (J). *See also:* SI UNITS.

MARIO IONA

STEVEN IONA

INDEX

Page numbers in **boldface** refer to the main entry on the subject.
Page numbers in *italics* refer to illustrations.

A

AAPM. *See* American Association of Physicists in Medicine

Abbreviations, table of common scientific, 1417

Abelson, Philip H., 469

Aberration, **1–2**
  adaptive optical removal of, 1113–1115
  Huygens's studies, 729
  lens, 843, 844–845, 1116, 1350, 1573
  principle forms of, 1111, 1116
  refraction, 1348, 1350
  telescopic, 1573, 1574

Aberration, chromatic, 1, **2–3**, 1039
  defined, 1117
  lens, 843, 844, 845, 1576
  refraction, 1348, 1350
  telescopic, 1573, 1575, 1576

Aberration, monochromatic, 1, 844–845, 1573

Aberration, spherical, 1, **3–4**, 1573
  defined, 1116
  Hubble Space Telescope, 724–725
  lens, 843, 844–845

ABF models, 298

Abraham, Max, 1366, 1367

Abrikosov lattice, 255

Absolute simultaneity, 881, 883, 1368; *see also* Relativity, special theory of

Absolute space and time, 1244, 1365

Absolute temperature scale, 1582, 1583

Absolute zero, **4–6**
  cryogenics at, 299
  ideal gas law, 1443, 1583
  liquid helium nonsolidification, 880
  negative absolute temperature, 4–5, 1024, 1025, 1027
  semiconduction at, 1178
  standardization, 1581
  temperature scale, international, 1581
  temperature scale, Kelvin, 1443, 1582, 1583
  thermodynamics laws, 4, 165, 1296

Absorption. *See* Sound absorption

AC (alternating current). *See* Circuit, AC; Current, alternating

Academy of Sciences. *See* French Academy of Sciences

Acceleration, **6–9**
  absolute meaning of, 893
  centrifugal force, 178
  Coriolis force, 269
  of cosmic rays, 279, 281
  equivalence principle, 1351–1352, 1355

force, 604
Galilean concept, 1011, 1044, 1046
gravitational, 729, 1731
historical background, 7–8
inertial vs. gravitational mass, 931, 932, 1352, 1378
initial (due to gravity), 1731
Mach's principle, 893
motion and, 6–7, 892, 1010–1012
Newton's law, 1011, 1046, 1246
in particle mass definition, 1145
propulsion and, 1246, 1247
ratio for average, 6
relativity theories of, 932, 1351–1356, 1357, 1358, 1571
speed and, 1737
terminal velocity and, 1674
units, 6

Acceleration, angular, **9–11**, 1003
  average, 9
  example of, 1019
  graphical representations, 10
  and nonconsistent atomic model, 61
  servomechanism, 1430–1433
  see also Motion, rotational; Velocity, angular

Aerodynamics, **33–34**, 597
  atmospheric pressure effects,
    1237
  hydrodynamics and, 729–733
  lift and drag, 32–33, 34
  Mach's work, 891
  Maxwell's work as foundation
    of, 956
  propulsion, 1246–1247
  Reynolds number,
    1380–1381
  shock wave, 1433–1434
  terminal velocity, 1674–1676
  turbulence effects, 1634
Aerosol particles, 58
Aether. *See* Ether hypothesis
AFM. *See* Atomic force
  microscopy
AGB. *See* Asymptotic giant
  branch
Age of materials. *See* Radioactive
  dating
Age of universe. *See* Universe,
  age of
AGN. *See* Active galactic
  nucleus
Agricola, Georgius, 977
AGS. *See* Alternating Gradient
  Synchrotron
Air. *See* Atmosphere;
  Atmospheric physics;
  Pressure, atmospheric
Air bags, 8
Aircraft lift. *See* Aerodynamic
  lift
Airflow. *See* Aerodynamic lift
Airplane. *See* Aerodynamic lift;
  Aerodynamics
Air pressure. *See* Pressure;
  Pressure, atmospheric
Air resistance. *See* Aerodynamic
  drag
Airy disk, 357
ALARA principle, 699
Albrecht, Andreas, 288
Alchemy, 977, 1040, 1386
Alembert, Jean Le Rond d', 38,
  1172–1173
Alfven, Hannes, Nobel Prize,
  919, 1060
Alfven wave, **34–35**, 919, 920,
  1207, 1211

Algebra. *See* Clifford algebra;
  Computational physics;
  Mathematical constants;
  Mathematics; *SU*(3) color
  charge
Algebraic numbers, 949
Alhazen (Al Hazen ibn
  Al-Haytham), 842, 1111
Alkali halide crystals, 227–228
Alkenes, 1222
Alloy, **35–37**, 975
  Archimedes' principle, 49
  iron-carbon system, *36*
  magnetization, 894, 904, 905,
    910
  properties and uses, 35,
    36–37, 904, 905
  superconductivity, 1547, 1550
Almagest (Ptolemy), 265,
  266–267, 1010
Alnico (alloy), 894, 905
Alpha particles. *See* Decay, alpha
Alpha rays. *See* Helium, nucleus
Alpher, Ralph, 108, 278, 1093,
  1654
*Alternate Current Transformer in
  Theory and Practice, The*
  (Fleming), 1622
Alternating current. *See* Circuit,
  AC; Current, alternating
Alternating gradient focusing,
  18–20, 916, 1567
Alternating Gradient
  Synchrotron (Brookhaven),
  19, 1567–1568
Altman, Sidney, Nobel Prize,
  1056
Aluminum, 1482, 1483
Alvarez, Luis W., Nobel Prize,
  839, 1060
Alzheimer's disease, 14
Ambiguity. *See* Complementarity
  principle
Ambler, Evans, 336, 561, 1141
American Association for the
  Advancement of Science,
  990, 1452
American Association of
  Physicists in Medicine, 120,
  974
American Board of Health
  Physics, 698

American Board of Medical
  Physics, 974, 1324
American Board of Radiology,
  1324
American College of Medical
  Physics, 974
American Geophysical Union,
  665
American Institute of Physics,
  Center for History of
  Physics, 1188
American Physical Society
  Condensed Matter Physics
    division, 243
  congressional science
    fellowship funding, 1451
  Physical Review journal, 1586
  Physics Today magazine, 98–99
  presidents, 92–93
  "science court," 1452
American Society of Rheology,
  1382
Americium, 471
Amidie, Adolfo, 546
Ammeter, **37–38**, 313, 650; *see
  also* Ohmmeter; Voltmeter
Ammonia
  atomic weight, 77
  maser dynamics, 929, 1232
  schematic structure, *929*
Amontons, Guillaume, 632
Ampere (unit of electric current), 38, 313, 1443, 1731
  as SI base unit, 979, 1439,
    1731
Ampère, André-Marie, **38–39**
  action-at-a-distance force
    concept, 26
  Coulomb's influence on,
    290
  electromagnetic field concept,
    427, 442, 542, 886, 907
  monopole debunking by, 907,
    908
  particle concept, 1142
  unit named for, 1731
Ampère's law, **39–41**
  application, 40–41, 579, 660
  displacement current,
    315–316
  electromagnetic spectrum,
    433

Astrophysics (cont'd)
  telescope, 1572–1578
  see also Celestial mechanics;
    Cosmology; Optics; Space
    travel; Universe; Universe,
    expansion of
Astrophysics, x-ray, **55–57**
  active galactic nucleus, 28,
    54
  space observatory, 30–31, 56,
    397–398
  Uhuru satellite studies,
    1641–1642
  x-ray binaries, 1721–1722
  x-ray emission, 1718
Asymptotic freedom, 1261–1262,
  1264
Asymptotic giant branch, 1534
AT&T. *See* Bell Telephone
  Laboratories
Atmosphere, 1731
  ionosphere, 785–787
  movement of objects through.
    See Aerodynamics
  specific gravity of, 1482
  viscosity, 1677–1678
  window, 508
  see also Pressure, atmospheric;
    Space
Atmospheric physics, **57–60**
  acoustical studies, 25
  adaptive optics, 1113–1115
  aurora, 85–86
  Boyle's law, 144
  chaos theory, 184, 1125
  convection, 252–253, 710
  cosmic microwave
    background radiation,
    274–275
  fallout, 537–539
  hurricane formation,
    726–728, 1688–1689
  ionosphere, 785–787
  lightning, 872
  meteor shower, 978–979
  photosphere, 1187
  planetary formation,
    1205–1206
  plasmas, 1208
  pressure, 1236–1237
  radioactive dating, 1325
  resonance, 1376

scattering, 1401–1402, 1406
study of, 665
thermal radiation, 1321
thunder, 1607–1608
tornado formation,
  1616–1618, 1688–1689
turbulence, 1634
vortices, 1688–1689
see also Aerodynamics;
  Celestial mechanics; Sun
Atmospheric pressure. *See*
  Pressure, atmospheric
Atmospheric window, 58
Atom, **60–62**
  alloy arrangement of, 35
  anti-entropic behavior, 52
  Auger effect, 84–85
  baryon number of, 95
  big bang and, 285
  Boscovitch concept of, 541
  conservation of mass in,
    934
  core electron, 999
  covalent bond, 293
  crystal arrangements of,
    301–302, 303, 306,
    1713–1714
  degeneracy, 340–341
  Dirac theory of, 368
  disintegration, artificial,
    369–371
  doping, 377
  Einstein-Podolsky-Rosen
    experiment, 399
  electron. *See* Electron
  electronegative, 421
  electron sharing, 293
  elementary particles. *See*
    Elementary particles
  energy levels and, 496
  exchange interaction, 928
  excited state, 530
  fermions and bosons. *See*
    Fermions and bosons
  fine and hyperfine states,
    76
  first (Thomson) model, 60,
    62, 70, 293, 1098, 1208,
    1387, 1606
  first splitting of, 1402; *see also*
    Accelerator, history of;
    Fission

historical background, 60–61,
  62, 70, 72–73, 76–79,
  123, 1678; *see also* Atomic
  theory, origins of; Atom,
  Rutherford–Bohr; Bohr's
  atomic theory
hydrogen bond, 733
hyperfine structure, 736
inner constituents of, 62–65
interaction, 759
interaction, electromagnetic,
  761
ion, 781
ionic bond, 782
ionization, 783
ionization potential, 785
ionization source, 942–943
Jahn-Teller effect, 799–800
K capture, 808–809
kinetic energy limits, 4
Lamb shift, 825–826
laser cooling, 836–838
low temperature effects on,
  299–300
magnetic moment, 906
magnetic properties, 74
magnum quantum of
  excitation, 928
mass number, 940–941
mass spectrometer, 941–946
Millikan "building" theory,
  990
modern structural theory, 61,
  63–66, 73–74, 75, 293, 860,
  941, 990, 1098, 1143, 1407,
  1409
mole unit, 1736
momentum, 1019–1020
motion in liquid vs. solid,
  1460
Newtonian view of, 541
nucleic emissions. *See* Cosmic
  ray
nucleus. *See* Nucleus
number. *See* Atomic number
number of types, 1142
old quantum theory, 1283
Pauli's exclusion principle,
  1155–1157
perturbation theory,
  1162–1164, 1285
phonon, 1176–1177

Atomic weight (cont'd)
  interaction, weak, 770
  international standard, 80
  mass number, 941
  mole unit, 1736
  periodic table, 461–463
  and radioactive properties,
    1098
  relative system, 78
Atomist philosophy. *See* Atomic
    theory, origins of
Atoms for Peace Award, first
    (1957), 124
"Atom smasher." *See* Accelerator
Atom trap, **81–84**, 838, 1497
Attraction. *See* Electrostatic
    attraction and repulsion;
    Gravitational attraction
Attractor, Lorenz, 184–185, 186
AU. *See* Astronomical units
Audibility threshold, 1237, 1464;
    see also Ultrasonics
Audio tape, 895, 904, 1112
Audio transformers, 1623
Auditory sensation. *See* Sound
Auger, Pierre, 84
Auger effect, **84–85**
  K capture process, 808, 809
Auger electron. *See* Electron,
    Auger
Aurora, **85–87**, 1208
  luminescence, 889
  as magnetospheric
    phenomena, 1322
Aurora australis, 86, 1322
Aurora borealis, 86, 889, 1322
Austin, William, 77
Austria
  Boltzmann, Ludwig, 132
  Mach, Ernst, 891–892
  Meitner, Lise, 974–975
  Nobel Prize winners, 1053,
    1058
  Pauli, Wolfgang, 1153–1155
  Schrödinger, Erwin,
    1408–1409
Automobile
  aerodynamic applications, 33
  battery function, 100
  Bernoulli's principle
    applications, 105
  centrifugal force, 178

eddy current tachometer,
    317
engine efficiency, 165
propulsion, 1246, 1247
speed measurement, 1673
tire pressure, 1236
Avalanche, **87–88**
Aviation. *See* Aerodynamic lift;
    Aerodynamics
Avogadro, Amadeo, 72, 78, 88,
    1142
Avogadro constant. *See* Avogadro
    number
Avogadro number, 78, **88–89**,
    1142
  atomic weight determination,
    80, 88
  Boltzmann constant, 133, 654,
    655
  determination of, 89, 1443
  ideal gas law, 741, 1583
  mole unit, 1736
  Planck's constant, 1197
Avogadro's hypothesis, 38, 78,
    88
AXAF. *See* Advanced X-Ray
    Astrophysics Facility
Axial chromatic aberrations, 2
Axial symmetry, 257, 258
Axial vector, 1667
Axion (particle), dark matter
    hypothesis, 287, 325,
    326–327
Axis. *See* Coordinate system
    headings; Motion, rotational;
    Parallel axis theorem;
    Pendulum
Azetrope, 1167–1168

B

B. See Baryon number
Baade, Walter
  neutron stars postulate, 54,
    1037
  redshift distance, 1345, 1346,
    1651
BAAS. *See* British Association
    for the Advancement of
    Science
Babbage, Charles, 523, 524
Babcock, Horrace (H. D.), 80,
    1113

Background radiation. *See*
    Cosmic microwave
    background radiation
Bacon, Francis, 1191
Bacon, Roger, 842
Baeyer, Johann Friedrich
    Wilhelm Adolf von, Nobel
    Prize, 1052
Baksan (Russia), solar neutrino
    telescope, 1031
Balance wheel,
    hairspring-driven, 1126
Ballistic pendulum. *See*
    Pendulum, ballistic
Ballistics, shock waves, 1434
Ball lightning, 872
Balloon
  Charles's law application, 195
  first hydrogen gas, 194
  propulsion of punctured, 1247
Ballot, Buys, 379
Balmer, Johann, 61, 126,
    1388–1389, 1489
Balmer formula of hydrogen
    spectrum
  Bohr's atomic theory and, 64,
    126, 129–130, 131, 1389
  as experimental check, 1415
  red emission line, 1469
  for star classification, 1187
  Stark effect and, 1519–1520
  statement of, 1388–1389
  wavelengths, 1489, 1493
Band theory (electrical conduc-
    tivity), 405, 714–715, 1178
Bar (unit of pressure), 1731
Bardeen, John, **91–93**
  on superconductivity, 1548
  transistor discovery, 91, 92,
    450, 749, 750, 1051,
    1529–1630, 1623–1624,
    1629–1630
  two Nobel Prizes, 91, 105, 749,
    1050, 1059, 1060, 1630
Bardeen-Cooper-Schrieffer
    (BCS) theory, 91, 92, 254,
    801, 828
  examples of pairing, 255
  and integration of
    superconductivity into
    solid-state physics,
    1550–1551

Dark matter, hot, **327**, 1649
Dark matter, nonbaryonic, 325,
   327, 346, 779, 1649
Dark of the moon, 1007
D'Arsonval galvanometer, 37,
   650, 1686
Darwin, Charles Galton, 63, 809,
   810, 1720
Data analysis, **328–331**
   statistical error, 509–511, 519
   systematic error, 514–516
Data storage
   holography, 718
   laser uses, 1112–1113
   magnetic materials, 895, 904,
      905
Dating, radioactive. *See*
   Radioactive dating
Davidson, George, 1577
Davies, Roger, 686
Davis, Raymond, Jr., 773, 1029,
   1542
Davisson, Clinton Joseph
   electron diffraction
      observation, 776
   Nobel Prize, 333
   see also Davisson-Germer
      experiment
Davisson-Germer experiment,
   153, 154, **331–333**, 358, 359,
   1257, 1259, 1281, 1402,
   1410, 1704, 1708
Davy, Humphry, 421, 540, 1596
DC (direct current). *See* Circuit,
   DC; Current, direct
Deafness, 25
Dearborn Observatory
   (Chicago), 1576
Debierne, André, 310, 1333
Debris flows, 87; *see also* Dust;
   Meteoroid
De Broglie, Louis-Victor-Pierre-
   Raymond. *See* Broglie,
   Louis-Victor-Pierre-
   Raymond de
Debye (unit), 1732
Debye, Peter
   chemical physics, 196
   crystallography, 1402
   extension of Einstein's
      specific heat theory, 1485,
      1487, 342, 506, 705

large particle scattering, 1403,
   1404
magnetic cooling process, 898
Nobel Prize, 1053
quantum theory, 1535
unit named for, 1732
Debye equation, 355, 417
Debye length, plasma, 1206,
   1207, 1210
Debye sphere, plasma, 1209,
   1210
Debye temperature, 1485–1486,
   1487
Decay. *See* Exponential growth
   and decay; *headings below*
Decay, alpha, **334–335**, 340,
   1035
   barrier penetration, 93–95
   defined, 1327
   energy diagram, 1231
   first theory of, 1328
   Joliot-Curies' radiation
      experiments, 1330
   nuclear binding energy and,
      1072–1073
   nuclear size and, 1090
   parity experiment, 1413
   radioactive dating, 1324, 1325,
      1326, 1327
   radioactivity, 1327, 1328,
      1387
Decay, beta, 278, **335–337**, 339,
   1093
   boson, Higgs, 139, 140
   boson, *W*, 142
   boson, *Z*, 142, 143
   defined, 1327
   down quark, 1304
   Fermi theory, 546, 1029, 1036,
      1329, 1414–1415
   isomeric nucleus, 1100, 1101
   K capture as, 808
   KU theory, 1414–1415
   Meitner's work, 975
   neutrino role, 848, 1027,
      1028, 1029, 1033, 1143,
      1155
   parity nonconservation,
      1140–1141, 1413, 1613
   P symmetry and, 1564
   radioactivity, 1327, 1328–1329,
      1387

role in nuclear reaction cycles,
   1029
slowness of process, 1329
from weak interaction, 336,
   762, 769, 770, 772, 776; *see
   also* Interaction, weak
Decay, gamma, **337–338**
   defined, 1327
   half-life, 1733
   isomeric nucleus, 1100–1101
   Mössbauer effect, 1009
   radioactivity, 1327, 1328, 1329
Decay, nuclear, **339–340**
   exponential, 532–535
   hadron, 694–695
   interaction and, 759
   lepton, Tau, 849
   Mössbauer effect, 1009–1010
   muon, 1022
   neutron, 1031, 1071–1072,
      1248
   neutron plus proton
      conservation, 935
   phosphorescence vs.
      fluorescence timing,
      1177–1178
   positronium, 1227–1228
   and positron production,
      1226
   proton lifetime, 1248
   radioactive dating use, 1324,
      1325, 1326
   Rutherford-Soddy
      transformation theory, 1386
   spontaneous, 1071; *See also*
      Radioactivity
   subatomic particle, 937–938,
      940, 1300, 1301, 1302, 1303,
      1306
   supernova, 1555–1556
Decibel (unit), 24, 1237, 1464,
   1732
Decomposition, electrochemi-
   cal, 543
Defect, crystal. *See* Crystal defect
Defect, mass. *See* Mass, defect
Defect, optical. *See* Aberration
Defects. *See* Strain; Stress
DeForest, Lee, 331–332, 1126
Deformation. *See* Strain; Stress
Degeneracy, **340–341**
Degenerate vacuum state, 1660

Gaede, Wolfgang, 1661, 1662
Galactic halo. *See* Halo, galactic
Galaxies and galactic structure,
    643–645
    active galactic nucleus, 27–28,
        54
    age estimates, 283
    astrophysical studies, 53, 54
    black hole, 115–117
    celestial mechanics, 173
    clusters and superclusters,
        1468, 1470, 1642, 1648
    cosmic microwave
        background radiation, 274,
        275
    cosmic rays, 279, 280
    cosmic x-ray studies, 56, 57
    cosmological studies, 287
    cosmology, inflationary, 288
    dark matter, 322–326, 327,
        988, 1648–1649
    development of, 1648
    Einstein Observatory, 398
    ellipses, 644
    extragalactic distance scale,
        107, 108
    first map of, 1468
    gamma ray bursters, 651
    Great Attractor effects on,
        686–688
    halos, 919
    Hubble's discoveries, 285,
        722, 986, 1650
    Hubble Space Telescope,
        724–726
    intergalactic hot gas, 1470,
        1642
    interstellar and intergalactic
        medium, 779–780, 1469
    irregular, 645, 1648
    linear relationship between
        speeds and distances. *See*
        Hubble constant
    magnetic fields, 919, 920
    magnetosphere, 923–926
    matter vs. antimatter, 44
    Milky Way, 984–988
    nucleosynthesis, 1093–1097
    numbers in universe, 1647
    properties, 643–644
    pulsars, 1249–1251
    quasars, 1310–1311

    redshift, 107, 1310, 1344–1346
    rotational movement, 1012,
        1019
    space and, 1468
    spiral, 644–645
    supernovas and supernova
        remnants, 1554
    telescopic viewing, 1577
    uniform distribution of, 285
    x-ray binary, 1721–1722
    see also Interstellar and
        intergalactic medium; Stars
        and stellar structure
Galilean reference frame. *See*
    Frame of reference, inertial;
    Galilean transformation
Galilean telescope, 172, 262,
    648, 1111, *1572*, 1573, 1575
Galilean transformation,
    645–647
    acceleration, 7, 1011, 1044,
        1046
    and Einstein's special relativity
        theory, 1368
    ether hypothesis and, 521, 522
    frame of reference, 614, 1046,
        1047–1048, 1365, 1471
    Newtonian synthesis, 1044,
        1046–1048, 1365, 1420,
        1471
    on Sun's rotation, 1543
Galilci, Galileo, **647–649**
    astronomical observations,
        262, 266, 1011, 1044, 1111
    and beginning of real physics,
        172
    and Copernican Revolution,
        262, 1192
    equivalence principle, 882
    first thermometer, 1582
    galaxy study begun by, 643,
        677
    gravitation theory, 395, 506,
        573, 627, 678, 755; *see also*
        Galilean transformation
    identicality of gravitational
        mass and inertial mass
        experiment, 931, 1044, 1357
    inertia, law of, 7, 506, 615,
        1041, 1044, 1365, 1419,
        1471, 1519, 1543; *see also*
        Galilean transformation

    inertia, moment of, 754, 755
    mathematics, 1045
    Milky Way viewing, 985, 1468
    pendulum experiments, 1126,
        1157, 1158
    projectile studies, 729
    telescope, 172, 262, 648, 1111,
        1572, 1573, 1575
Galileo spacecraft, 1008
Galle, Johann G., 1586
GALLEX (Gallium Experiment),
    1542
Galvani, Luigi, 420, 424, 447
Galvanometer, 37–38, **649–650**,
    1686
Gamba, Marina, 647
Gamma decay. *See* Decay,
    gamma
Gamma ray
    applications, 471
    applications and Compton
        effect, 236
    beryllium nuclei emission,
        1035
    discovery of, 1333
    Meitner's studies, 975
    Nobel Prize winner, 1059
    as nuclear photons, 1092,
        1143
    photoelectric detectors,
        1181
    pulsar emission, 1250
    radiant energy, 489
    radiation dosimetry, 1323
    spectroscopy, 1492
Gamma ray bursters, **651**
Gamma Ray Observatory, 55,
    236, **651–652**
Gamma ray telescope, 329
Gamow, George, 826
    alpha decay theory, 334–335,
        1231, 1328
    barrier penetration, 94
    big bang theory, 108, 276,
        278, 1093, 1654
    complementarity principle,
        231
    disintegration, artificial, 370,
        371
    gamma rays, 1035
    tunneling, 1259
Ganymede (moon), 1456

Gas, **652–654**

absorption spectra to identify specific, 1428

astrophysical studies, 53

black hole ingestion of, 27, 28, 54

Boyle's law, 143–144

Charles's law, 194–195

critical points for phase transition, 298–299

dark matter in, 323

degree of freedom, 341

density determination, 342, 343

as diatomic molecules, 88

diffusion coefficient, 245

discharge theory, 1606

displacement, 372–373, 376

distribution function, 375

elasticity, 400

electrical conductivity, 405

equation of state, 1251, 1524–1525, 1529–1530

equipartition theorem, 504–505

fluid dynamics, 597

friction, 631–633

in giant planets' interiors, 1455–1456

glow from, 447

heat transfer, 710

ideal law. See Ideal gas law

as infrared absorber, 58

intergalactic, 1470, 1642, 1648

ionic bond, 782

ionization chamber, 784

ionization potential, 785

ionized. See Plasma

ion production, 782

isochoric process, 791

Joule-Thomson effect, 805, 806

kinetic theory of, 195, 213, 653–654, 956, 971

magnetic and electric fields, 898

Maxwell speed distribution, 967–970, 998, 999

Maxwell's statistical description of, 51

Milky Way, 988

molecular correlations in, 51–52

nonlinear optics, 1119–1120

paramagnetism, 1136–1137

photosphere, 1186–1187

planetary, 1202–1203, 1204–1205, 1206

plasma differences, 1206, *1207*, 1209, 1211

pressure, 1235–1236; *see also* Vacuum

quantum fluid, 1273–1275

scattering, 1404

solubility, 1166

in space, 1469, 1470

specific gravity, 1482

specific heat, 1482–1483

spectral series, 1488–1490

state of, 1524

temperature measurement, 1583; *see also* Gas constant; Ideal gas law

triple point, 1633–1634

vacuum pressure measurement, 1662–1663

van der Waals force, 28–29, 1666–1667

vapor pressure, 1238–1239

viscosity, 88–89, 1677

volcanic release of, 1685

Gas, natural

helium isotopes in, 879

pipeline viscosity, 1678

Gas chromatographic, 941

Gas clouds, 1097

Gas constant, **654–655**

absolute temperature use, 1582, 1583

Boltzmann's constant and, 133

defined, 1524

Gas constant per molecule. See Boltzmann constant

Gases. See Gas

Gases, rare. See Rare gases

Gas giants (planets). See Planetary systems, giant planets

Gas laser, 832, 834; *see also* Laser, ion

Gassegranian telescope, 1573

Gassendi, Pierre, 263, 1039, 1044

Gas thermometer, 1601–1602

Gauge boson. *See* Boson, gauge

Gauge field, 575, 658, 882–883

Gauge invariance, **655–657**

conservation laws and, 251

Gauge pressure, 1236, 1239, 1662–1663

Gauge symmetry, 138, 1564–1565

spontaneous breaking, 1566, 1660

Gauge theories, **657–659**

boson, gauge, 137–138

described, 138

electromagnetism and, 882–883

electroweak interactions and, 252

gauge invariance, 655–657

interaction, weak, 770

quantum chromodynamics, 1261–1264

quantum electrodynamics, 1261

renormalization and, 828, 1272–1273

Gauge transformation, 657

Gauss, Karl Friedrich, 363

action-at-a-distance, 26

computation of orbits, 172–173

curved surfaces theory, 1357

electric field theory. *See* Gauss's law

geometrical optics treatise, 1111, 1116

image formation theory, 1, 1111

resonance, 1376

Gaussian distribution

described, 374–375

for error, 512–513, 519

for probability, 1240–1241, 1242, 1243

Gaussian integral, 949–950

Gaussian units, 1735

Gauss's law, **659–661**

for charge conservation, 189–190, 191

for electric field, 40, 41, 571, 579, 659, 760

electric flux, 408

Luminosity. *See* Luminescence
Luminous flux, 1184, 1738
Lummer, Otto, 1070, 1294, 1317
Lunar calendar, 1008, 1017
Lunar month. *See* Moon, phases of
Lux (unit of illuminance), 1441
LWRs (light-water reactor), 1343
Lyapunov exponent, 184, 186, 187, 188
Lyman series, 1489, 1493
Lynden-Bell, Donald, 686
Lyotropic liquid crystal, 877

M

Mach, Ernst, 62, **891–892**, 1122
  concept of absolute space, 1471
  and logical positivism, 892, 1192
  misgiving about reality of atoms and molecules, 1142
  Pauli relationship, 1154
  philosophically oriented history of physics, 1188
  see also Mach's principle
Mach bands, 892
Mach collar, 1434
Mach cones, 891, 1433
Mach number, 1433, 1434
MACHOs (massive compact halo objects), 324, 325, 1649
Mach's principle, **892–893**
  and general relativity theory, 891, 1357, 1471
  shock wave, 1433, 1434
Mach-Zehnder interferometer, 778
Macromolecule. *See* Polymer
Madison, James, 1449
Maglev (magnetically levitated trains), 852, 855
Magma, 1685
Magnesium, 79, 941
Magnet, **893–895**
  accelerator, 14, 18, 19, 1567
  electromagnet, 425–426
  magnetic moment, 905–906, 916

materials, 904–905, 916, 1514–1516
  mental visualization of, 911
  paramagnet susceptibility, 914–915
  polarity, 1214
  poles, 894, 910
  properties of solids, 1461
  workings of external phenomena, 908
  see also Field, magnetic; *headings below*
Magnetically levitated trains (maglev), 852, 855
Magnetic analyzers, 943–944
Magnetic atom trap, 81–82, 241
Magnetic behavior, **895–898**
  Alfven wave, 34–35
  antiferromagnetism, 41–42
  antimatter, 43
  bipolar attraction, 909
  bremsstrahlung, 147
  categories, 896
  confinement of charge, 909
  cooling effects on, 300, 898–900
  Coulomb experiments, 290, 291–292, 908
  critical phenomena, 297–298
  Curie temperature effects, 311–312
  electromagnet, 425–426
  electromagnetism, 426–428, 438–441
  electron discovery, 448
  energy conversion into heat, 919–920
  Faraday discoveries, 540–545
  in grand unified theory, 671
  induced, 908
  inverse square law, 290
  levitation, 850–852, 852–855
  magnetic poles, 910–911
  of materials. *See* Magnetic material
  permeability, 909–910
  phase transition, second-order, 1170
  polarity, 1213–1214
  susceptibility, 914–916

see also Electromagnetism; Field, magnetic; Magnetization; Paramagnetism; Planetary magnetism
Magnetic bending and focusing, 12–13
Magnetic circular birefringence, 920, 922
Magnetic circular dichroism, 920, 921, 922
Magnetic cooling, 4–5, **898–900**
Magnetic domain, **900–902**, 923
Magnetic field. *See* Field, magnetic
Magnetic flux, 408–409, 428, **902–903**, 907
  Cooper pairs and, 254
  density, 577
  gauge theories, 658–659
  inductance, 746
  interaction, electromagnetic, 760
  reluctance, 1737
  superconductivity and, 1549, 1550
  tesla unit, 1738
  weber unit, 1441, 1738
  see also Electric flux
Magnetic force microscope, 1394, *1395*
Magnetic levitation. *See* Levitation, magnetic
Magnetic linear birefringence, 922
Magnetic linear dichroism, 922
Magnetic material, **903–905**
  characteristics, 1514
  hard (permanent), 893–895, 904–905, 911
  magnetization, 916–917
  magneto-optical effects, 920–923
  magnetostriction, 926–927
  materials science and, 948
  paramagnetism, 1136–1137
  permeabilities of typical, table of, 910
  permeability calculation, 910
  polarity, 1213–1214
  soft, 904, 910
  spin glass, 1514–1516

symmetry and, 1563
and theoretical framework, 992
wave function, 94, 152, 271,
    333, 1000, 1155, 1286–1287,
    1298, 1299, 1410–1412,
    1693, 1702
wave packet, 1702
Schumacher, Elisabeth, 711
Schuster, Arthur, 448
Schwartz, Melvin, 595, 848,
    1022, 1029
    Nobel Prize, 1061
Schwarz, John H., 1556
Schwarzschild, Karl
    action-at-a-distance, 26
    atomic spectrum splitting,
        1519
    black hole prediction, 53, 116,
        117, 118–120, 574, 992, 993,
        1200
    radius, 1200
    solution of Einstein's
        spacetime equations,
        1354–1355
Schwinger, Julian
    electron magnetic moment
        anomaly, 192, 1267
    Nobel Prize, 1059
    quantum electrodynamics
        creation, 560, 561, 679,
        1264, 1495
    relativistic theory of protons,
        1186
Science, history of (as academic
    field), 1188
Science Advisory Committee,
    1314
Scientific method, 1147,
    1412–1416
    accuracy and precision, 21–22
    Scientific Revolution and,
        1420
    and scientific specialization,
        1585–1586
    systems, 1569–1570
Scientific notation, **1416–1418**
    significant figures, 1437, 1438
    see also SI units
Scientific Revolution, **1418–1421**
    Copernican Revolution as
        component of, 261, 262,
        268, 1418

emphasis on experimentation,
    1420
as historiography of physics
    subject, 1189, 1190
Kepler's laws importance to,
    1418
mathematics importance in,
    1045
Newtonian synthesis as
    culmination of, 1043–1045,
    1420
Scintillation counter, **1421**
Scotopic vision, 1183
Scott-Russell, J., 1462
Sco X-1 (cosmic ray source), 56,
    1641, 1721
SCR (silicon controlled rectifier),
    211
SCRAM (supersonic ram jet),
    1479
Seaborg, Glenn T.
    element named for, 471
    Nobel Prize, 839, 1054
    transuranium elements,
        discoveries of, 72, 469, 470,
        1074
Seaborgium, 471
Seasons, **1421–1423**
    oscillation, 1126
    periodic motion, 1017
    precession, 1233–1234,
        1421–1423
    see also Moon, phases of
Seat-of-the pants friction, 178,
    180
Seawater, 1692
Second
    definition, 67, 1443, 1472,
        1737
    as SI base unit, 979, 1439,
        1442, 1472, 1737
Second harmonic generation,
    1111
Second law of thermodynamics.
    See Thermodynamics,
    second law of
Second-order phase transition.
    See Critical phenomena
Second sound (liquid helium),
    880
Secular perturbations, 1163
Sedimentation, 179

Sedov, L., 1434
Seebeck, Thomas John, 1599
Seebeck effect, 410, 1599, 1600,
    1631
Segrè, Emilio, 1059, 1248
    Nobel Prize, 839
Seiberg, Nathan, 909
Seidel, Ludwig, 1, 2, 845
Seidel aberrations, 1–2, 843, 845
Seismic wave, **1423–1424**
    acoustical studies, 25
    earthquake, 385–387
    infrasonics and, 757
    magnitudes, 1425
    seismological studies, 1424–
        1425
    speed of, 1710
Seismograms, 1424
Seismology, 663, **1424–1425**
    earthquake, 385–387
Seismometers, 1424, 1425
Seitz, Frederick, 242
Selection rule, **1426**
Selenium, 1180
Self-inductance, 746, **1426–1427**,
    1733
SEM. *See* Scanning electron
    microscopy
Semenov, Nikolay Nikolaevich,
    Nobel Prize, 1054
Semiconductor, 415, **1427–1430**
    acceptor, 20–21
    basic physics of, 1427–1429
    Bohr model application to,
        131
    circuit, integrated, 208–210
    condensed matter physics
        work in, 242–244
    conduction properties, 247,
        1178
    covalent bond, 1460
    diode, 366
    donor, 376–377
    doping, 377, 715, 1429–1430
    electrical conductivity, 246,
        405, 415, 1427
    electrical resistance, 406, 1427
    electrical resistivity, 409
    electroluminescence, 423
    electron, drift speed of, 449
    holes in solids, 715
    infrared, 756